Integrated Mathematics

COURSE I

Isidore Dressler

Former Chairman
Department of Mathematics
Bayside High School, New York City

AND

Edward P. Keenan

District Supervisor of Mathematics
Sewanhaka Central High School District
Floral Park, New York

Dedicated to serving

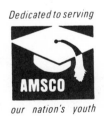

AMSCO

our nation's youth

When ordering this book please specify: *either* **R 230 H** *or*
INTEGRATED MATHEMATICS: COURSE I, HARDBOUND

AMSCO SCHOOL PUBLICATIONS, INC.
315 Hudson Street   **New York, N.Y. 10013**

ISBN 0-87720-249-4

PRINTED IN THE UNITED STATES OF AMERICA

Today, groups of professional mathematicians and mathematics educators are suggesting that major revisions be made in the secondary school mathematics curricula. The following two suggestions have been proposed by state bureaus of mathematics, among them the New York State Bureau of Education:

1. A contemporary course in high school mathematics should achieve the integration and unification of topics that have traditionally been segregated in a three-year sequence consisting of algebra, geometry, and intermediate algebra and trigonometry.

2. Students will benefit from the early introduction of practical modern aspects of mathematics, particularly logic, probability, and statistics.

Integrated Mathematics: Course I is written to provide effective teaching materials for a unified program appropriate for 9th-year mathematics students. The book includes topics not previously contained in a traditional elementary algebra course. Students are introduced to basic concepts of logic, probability, statistics, and high school geometry up to but not including formal proof. At the same time some topics, such as postulates and properties of operations, polynomial fractions, and the ratios of trigonometry, have been de-emphasized.

To make the book of greatest service to average students, the authors have avoided an extremely rigorous treatment of the subject matter. Concepts are carefully developed in simple language and with the use of only necessary symbolism. General principles and procedures are stated clearly and concisely. The numerous model problems are solved through detailed step-by-step explanations. Varied and carefully graded exercises, in abundance, test student understanding of manipulative and arithmetic skills.

Integrated Mathematics: Course I develops a genuinely integrated sequence of topics. No longer are algebra and geometry treated as separate entities. Students are shown how topics that may seem totally unrelated are actually based on the same mathematical principles. For example, the study of circle graphs shows how aspects of statistics and of geometry are interrelated. Throughout the book, various topics are presented in a spiral development and are so intertwined that there is a constant review and linking of old and new.

The authors hope that *Integrated Mathematics: Course I* will prove to be an effective tool with which teachers can help students to comprehend, master, and enjoy mathematics from an integrated point of view.

The authors dedicate this book to their wives, Hilda and Joan, whose sacrifice, patience, and understanding were towers of strength during its creation.

Isidore Dressler

Edward P. Keenan

contents

■ chapter two   ALGEBRAIC EXPRESSIONS AND OPEN SENTENCES

■ chapter three   PROPERTIES OF OPERATIONS

■ chapter six   SIGNED NUMBERS

■ **chapter nine** FIRST-DEGREE
EQUATIONS AND
INEQUALITIES IN
ONE VARIABLE

■ chapter ten   RATIO AND PROPORTION

■ chapter eleven   GEOMETRY

■ chapter twelve   SIMILARITY, CONGRUENCE, AND CONSTRUCTIONS

■ chapter fifteen FRACTIONS AND FIRST-DEGREE EQUATIONS AND INEQUALITIES INVOLVING FRACTIONS

■ chapter sixteen PROBABILITY

■ chapter seventeen STATISTICS

■ chapter twenty   THE REAL NUMBERS

■ chapter twenty-one THE GEOMETRY OF THE CIRCLE

■ chapter twenty-two QUADRATIC EQUATIONS

chapter one

Mathematical Operations

1 THE BASIC OPERATIONS

In arithmetic we study numbers and perform computations involving operations on numbers. It is important to review certain ideas from arithmetic because these ideas will be used to aid us in the study of many other branches of mathematics this year. Arithmetic helps us to understand concepts in algebra. The numbers in arithmetic are used in measuring geometric objects. Also, arithmetic plays a key role in the study of probability and statistics. Although arithmetic is only one small part of mathematics, it is an important thread that binds together the many different branches of mathematics.

Symbols for Numbers

A *number* is really an idea; it is something that we can talk about and think about. When we try to represent a number in writing, we use a symbol. "1," "2," "3," "4," and so on, are *not* numbers; they are symbols we use to represent numbers. These symbols are called *numerals* or *numerical expressions*.

Counting Numbers or Natural Numbers

The *counting numbers*, which are also called *natural numbers*, are represented by the symbols:

$$1, 2, 3, 4, 5, 6, 7, 8, 9, 10, 11, 12, \ldots$$

The three dots after the 12 indicate that the numbers continue in the same pattern without end. The smallest counting number is called "1."

Every counting number has a *successor* that is one more than the number. The successor of 1 is named 2; the successor of 2 is called 3. Since this process of counting is endless, there is no last counting number.

Whole Numbers

Zero is not a counting number. By combining zero with all the counting numbers, we form the set of *whole numbers*. The whole numbers are represented by the symbols:

$$0, 1, 2, 3, 4, 5, 6, 7, 8, 9, 10, 11, 12, \ldots$$

The smallest whole number is shown by the symbol "0." The three dots after the 12 indicate that the pattern continues so that there is no largest whole number.

Subsets of the Whole Numbers

In earlier years we learned that a *set* is a collection of distinct objects or elements, such as the set of whole numbers. Sometimes it becomes necessary to limit the numbers we are using in a problem.

For example, the whole numbers from 0 through 100 would name the set or collection of possible scores earned on a test. Instead of listing all these numbers, we can establish a pattern and make use of the three dots before writing the ending number:

$$0, 1, 2, 3, \ldots, 100$$

When all of the elements of a set are whole numbers only, no matter how many or how few, we can call this set a *subset* of the set of whole numbers. Patterns can often be seen by listing only a few of the earliest elements of a set.

Some subsets of the whole numbers are endless. For example:

1. The odd whole numbers: 1, 3, 5, 7, . . .

2. The even whole numbers: 0, 2, 4, 6, . . .

3. Whole-number multiples of "5":   0, 5, 10, 15, 20, . . .

Other subsets of the whole numbers have a definite last number, which must be shown. For example:

1. One-digit whole numbers: 0, 1, 2, 3, . . . , 9

2. Odd whole numbers less than "100":   1, 3, 5, . . . , 99

3. The whole numbers on a clock: 1, 2, 3, . . . , 12

Symbols for Operations

The basic operations in arithmetic are called addition, subtraction, multiplication, and division. An *operation* is a process or a rule that tells us how to handle elements in a set. When an operation is performed on two elements, it is called a binary operation.

In a *binary operation* two elements are taken from one set and replaced by "exactly one" element of the set in question.

For example, in the addition of the whole numbers 8 and 7, we say that 8 and 7 are replaced by "exactly one" element called 15. Here the set in question is the whole numbers, and the operation is addition. Notice that there must be "one and only one" answer. In a binary operation there cannot be more than one answer to a problem, and there can be no problem that lacks an answer. We can use the word *unique* to mean "one and only one" response.

There are different ways to say in words what we have just done:

8 in addition with 7 equals 15

8   added to   7 equals 15

8   plus   7 equals 15

However, just as we express numbers by the use of symbols, we can show operations by the use of symbols. Using the symbol "+" we write:

$$8 + 7 = 15$$

In subtraction of the whole numbers 8 and 7, we say that 8 and 7 are replaced by a unique element called 1. Using the symbol "−" we write:

$$8 - 7 = 1$$

But we must be careful. If the order of the elements 8 and 7 were reversed and we wrote "7 − 8," the result or replacement would *not* be found in the set of whole numbers. Because of problems like this where no solution can be found within the set in question, we say that subtraction is *not* a binary operation for whole numbers. In the future we will study a set of numbers for which subtraction is a binary operation.

This example has shown us that the *order* of the elements is important when we work with a binary operation. Since two elements form a "pair" and since "order" counts, we are really working with an *ordered pair*. An ordered pair is sometimes written in symbols as (a, b) to show that a is the first element and that b is the second element. While we will use this notation later in this book, it is easier to show a binary operation in symbols as:

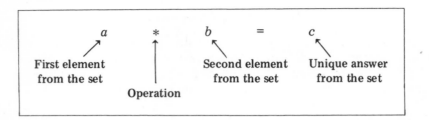

■ **DEFINITION.** A *binary operation* (called ∗) in a set is a way of assigning to every ordered pair of elements (called *a* and *b*) from the set a unique answer (called *c*) where the answer is from the set in question.

Knowing this general definition of a binary operation, we will be able to see many different binary operations in mathematics. For now, let us consider the basic operations in arithmetic.

Symbols for Arithmetic Operations

We will use the symbols for arithmetic operations when we study other branches of mathematics such as algebra, geometry, and probability. It is important to know all of the symbols listed here as well as the words used to describe the results of these operations.

The symbol "+" is used to indicate the operation of *addition*. When we write "6 + 2," we think of starting with 6, the first element of the ordered pair, and adding 2, the second element of the pair. The result, 8, is called the *sum*.

The symbol "−" is used to indicate the operation of *subtraction*. When we write "6 − 2," we think of starting with 6, the first element of the ordered pair, and subtracting 2, the second element of the pair. The result, 4, is called the *difference*.

The symbol "×" is used to indicate the operation of *multiplication*. When we write "6 × 2," we think of starting with 6, the first element of the ordered pair, and multiplying that number by 2, the second element of the pair. The result, 12, is called the *product*.

A particular operation can sometimes be shown by the use of different symbols. For example, to indicate multiplication, a centered dot "·" or parentheses "( )" can be used. We can write:

$$6 \times 2 = 12 \quad or \quad 6 \cdot 2 = 12 \quad or \quad (6)(2) = 12 \quad or \quad 6(2) = 12$$

The symbol "÷" is used to indicate the operation of *division*. When we write "6 ÷ 2," we think of starting with 6, the first element of the ordered pair, and dividing that number by 2, the second element of the pair. The result, 3, is called the *quotient*.

Division can also be represented symbolically by using a fraction where the numerator, or first element of the ordered pair, is divided by the denominator, or second element of the pair. We can write:

$$6 \div 2 = 3 \quad or \quad \frac{6}{2} = 3$$

Numerical Expression

We can think of "6 + 2" as a binary operation whose result is shown by the numeral "8." However, "6 + 2" and "8" can also be thought of as numerical expressions for the same number value. A *numerical expression* is a way of writing a number in symbols. The expression can be a single numeral or it can be a collection of numerals under one or more operations. For example:

6 + 2	18 − 10	4 × 2	640 ÷ 80
2 × 2 × 2	2 + 2 + 2 + 2	1 × 7 + 1	8

Each of these numerical expressions results in the number that we call "8." In general, every numerical expression is a way of naming a number.

| **MODEL PROBLEMS** |

In 1 and 2, each row contains four numerical expressions. Three of the four represent the same whole number. Which expression does *not* represent that number?

1. 8 + 4   3 × 4   12 ÷ 1   5 + 6

    Solution: In order, the expressions represent 12, 12, 12, and 11. Therefore, 5 + 6 does not represent the same number that the other expressions represent.   *Answer:* 5 + 6

2. 0 + 8   8 − 0   8 × 0   8 + 0

    Solution: In order, the expressions represent 8, 8, 0, and 8. Therefore, 8 × 0 does not represent the same number that the other expressions represent.   *Answer:* 8 × 0

3. From the quotient of 10 and 2, subtract 1.

    Solution:

    First divide 10 by 2.   10 ÷ 2 = 5

    Then, from the result 5, subtract 1.   5 − 1 = 4   *Answer:* 4

4. Add 6 to the product of 3 and 9.

Solution:

First multiply 3 by 9. $3 \times 9 = 27$

Then add 6 to the product 27. $27 + 6 = 33$ *Answer:* 33

| EXERCISES |

In 1-20, use the set of whole numbers, symbolized by {0, 1, 2, 3, . . .}, and the indicated binary operations to find whole-number answers. If no whole-number answer is possible, write the word *None*.

1. $12 + 4$ 2. $12 - 4$ 3. 12×4 4. $12 \div 4$
5. $4 + 8$ 6. $4 - 8$ 7. 4×8 8. $4 \div 8$
9. $20 + 20$ 10. $20 - 20$ 11. 20×20 12. $20 \div 20$
13. $6 + 0$ 14. $6 - 0$ 15. 6×0 16. $6 \div 0$
17. $78 + 97$ 18. $93 - 19$ 19. 27×38 20. $594 \div 11$

In 21–30, use the set of whole numbers to answer the question or to perform the operations.

21. What is the product of 2 and 8?
22. What is the difference of 12 and 3?
23. What is the sum of 18 and 6?
24. What is the quotient of 10 and 2?
25. From the quotient of 20 and 4, subtract 2.
26. From the difference of 20 and 4, subtract 4.
27. To the product of 20 and 4, add 8.
28. To the sum of 20 and 4, add 8.
29. Subtract 3 from the product of 4 and 8.
30. Add 7 to the quotient of 6 and 3.

In 31–39, each row contains four numerical expressions. Three of the four expressions result in the same numerical value. Which expression has a numerical value different from the other three?

31. $3 + 7$ 2×5 $10 + 0$ $12 - 3$
32. $3 + 6$ $12 - 3$ $3 \cdot 3$ $3 - 12$
33. $2 + 3$ $(2)(3)$ $6 \div 1$ $10 - 4$
34. $10 + 0$ $10 - 0$ 10×0 $0 + 10$
35. $14 + 37$ 17×3 $63 - 9$ $51 \div 1$
36. $14 - 14$ 14×0 $0 \div 14$ $14 \div 14$
37. $10 \cdot 3$ $4 \cdot 8$ 2×16 $32 \div 1$
38. 75×80 25×200 40×125 8×625
39. $522 \div 29$ $697 \div 41$ $\frac{476}{28}$ $\frac{612}{36}$

In 40–49, write the numeral that answers each of the following. If no answer is possible, explain why.

40. Name the first counting number.
41. Name the first whole number.
42. Name the successor of the whole number 75.
43. Name the successor of the counting number 999.
44. Name the successor of the natural number 1909.
45. Name a whole number that is *not* a counting number.
46. Name a counting number that is *not* a whole number.
47. Name the largest whole number.
48. Name the product of the smallest whole number and the largest one-digit counting number.
49. Name the product of the smallest counting number and the largest one-digit whole number.

50. In Column I, sets of numbers are described in words. In Column II, the sets are listed using patterns and dots. Match the lists from Column II with their correct sets in Column I.

Column I	*Column II*
1. Counting numbers	a. 0, 1, 2, . . . , 9
2. Whole numbers	b. 0, 1, 2, . . .
3. Even whole numbers	c. 0, 2, 4, 6, . . .
4. Odd whole numbers	d. 0, 2, 4, 6, 8
5. Even counting numbers	e. 1, 2, 3, 4, . . .
6. One-digit whole numbers	f. 1, 2, 3, . . . , 9
7. One-digit counting numbers	g. 1, 3, 5, 7, . . .
8. Odd whole numbers less than 10	h. 1, 3, 5, 7, 9
9. Even whole numbers less than 10	i. 2, 4, 6, 8, . . .

2 OPERATIONS WITH FRACTIONS AND DECIMALS

Fractions

In arithmetic we learned several meanings of a fraction. We shall say that a *fraction* is a symbol that indicates the quotient of two numbers. Since division by zero is meaningless, however, zero cannot be used as a denominator. We are familiar with fractions such as $\frac{1}{2}$, $\frac{3}{4}$, $\frac{12}{5}$, $\frac{8}{8}$, and $\frac{20}{10}$.

There are many different fractions that name the same number. For example, each of the different symbols $\frac{6}{2}$, $\frac{9}{3}$, $\frac{12}{4}$, and $\frac{36}{12}$ is a fraction that names the number 3.

The basic operations of addition, subtraction, multiplication, and division can be performed with fractions.

In addition and subtraction the fractions are easily combined if they have like denominators, as follows:

$$\frac{3}{7} + \frac{2}{7} = \frac{3+2}{7} = \frac{5}{7} \quad \text{and} \quad \frac{9}{10} - \frac{6}{10} = \frac{9-6}{10} = \frac{3}{10}$$

If the fractions do not have the same denominators, we first change them to equivalent fractions all of which have the same denominator and then combine the resulting fractions. For example, to do the addition $\frac{1}{3} + \frac{1}{2}$, we first change $\frac{1}{3}$ and $\frac{1}{2}$ to equivalent fractions each of which has 6 as its denominator. Then we combine the resulting fractions as follows:

$$\frac{1}{3} + \frac{1}{2} = \frac{1}{3} \times \left(\frac{2}{2}\right) + \frac{1}{2} \times \left(\frac{3}{3}\right) = \frac{2}{6} + \frac{3}{6} = \frac{2+3}{6} = \frac{5}{6}$$

To do the subtraction $\frac{4}{5} - \frac{3}{10}$, we proceed in a similar manner. In this case the common denominator is 10.

$$\frac{4}{5} - \frac{3}{10} = \frac{4}{5} \times \left(\frac{2}{2}\right) - \frac{3}{10} = \frac{8}{10} - \frac{3}{10} = \frac{8-3}{10} = \frac{5}{10} = \frac{1}{2}$$

Note that the fraction $\frac{5}{10}$ was reduced to its lowest terms by dividing the numerator and the denominator by the same number 5.

$$\frac{5}{10} = \frac{5 \div 5}{10 \div 5} = \frac{1}{2}$$

In multiplication and division of fractions it is not necessary for the fractions to have like denominators. The answers should be expressed in lowest terms. We can multiply $\frac{3}{5} \times \frac{5}{6}$ in two ways:

Method 1	*Method 2*
$\frac{3}{5} \times \frac{5}{6} = \frac{3 \times 5}{5 \times 6} = \frac{15}{30} = \frac{15 \div 15}{30 \div 15} = \frac{1}{2}$	$\frac{3}{5} \times \frac{5}{6} = \frac{\overset{1}{\cancel{3}} \times \overset{1}{\cancel{5}}}{\cancel{5} \times \cancel{6}} = \frac{1 \times 1}{1 \times 2} = \frac{1}{2}$

We can perform the division $\frac{2}{5} \div \frac{1}{10}$ as follows:

$$\frac{2}{5} \div \frac{1}{10} = \frac{2}{5} \times \frac{10}{1} = \frac{2 \times \overset{2}{\cancel{10}}}{\underset{1}{\cancel{5}} \times 1} = \frac{2 \times 2}{1 \times 1} = \frac{4}{1} = 4$$

Mixed Numbers

Mixed numbers are numbers that are named by symbols such as $1\frac{1}{4}$, $4\frac{2}{3}$, and $5\frac{3}{8}$. Note that a mixed number is the sum of a whole number and a proper fraction. A mixed number may be named by many different fractions. For example, the number named by $1\frac{1}{4}$ can be represented by the fractions $\frac{5}{4}, \frac{10}{8}, \frac{15}{12}$, etc.

Every mixed number can be changed to an equivalent fraction. For example:

$$3\frac{2}{5} = 3 + \frac{2}{5} = \frac{3}{1} \times (\frac{5}{5}) + \frac{2}{5} = \frac{15}{5} + \frac{2}{5} = \frac{17}{5}$$

See how this fact is used in multiplication and division involving mixed numbers:

$$3\frac{2}{5} \times 2\frac{1}{2} = \frac{17}{\cancel{5}} \times \frac{\cancel{5}^{1}}{2} = \frac{17}{2} = 8\frac{1}{2}$$

$$5\frac{1}{4} \div 3\frac{1}{2} = \frac{21}{4} \div \frac{7}{2} = \frac{\cancel{21}^{3}}{\cancel{4}_{2}} \times \frac{\cancel{2}^{1}}{\cancel{7}_{1}} = \frac{3}{2} = 1\frac{1}{2}$$

In addition and subtraction it is not necessary to change mixed numbers to fractions. For example:

$$
\begin{array}{l}
5\frac{3}{8} = \quad 5\frac{3}{8} \\
+ 2\frac{1}{4} = + 2\frac{2}{8} \\
\hline
\quad\quad\quad 7\frac{5}{8}
\end{array}
\qquad
\begin{array}{l}
2\frac{1}{3} = 2\frac{3}{9} = 1 + 1\frac{3}{9} = 1 + \frac{12}{9} \\
- \frac{7}{9} = - \frac{7}{9} = \quad\quad - \frac{7}{9} = \quad - \frac{7}{9} \\
\hline
\quad\quad\quad\quad\quad\quad\quad = 1 + \frac{5}{9} = 1\frac{5}{9}
\end{array}
$$

Final answers should be put into proper mixed-number form. For example:

$$2\frac{3}{5} + 1\frac{4}{5} = 3\frac{7}{5} = 3 + \frac{7}{5} = 3 + 1\frac{2}{5} = 4\frac{2}{5}$$

Decimals

Decimal fractions are numbers that are named by symbols such as .4, .23, .035, 2.5. They can also be represented by quotients. For example, the number named by .4 can be represented by $\frac{4}{10}, \frac{2}{5}, \frac{8}{20}$, etc.

Since decimals can be represented by quotients that are fractions, we can perform the basic operations with decimals. Most people make use of place value to perform operations directly with decimals, rather than change the decimals to a quotient form.

The computation .4 + .28 = .68 could be done by changing the decimals to fractions as shown at the right. But it is simpler to make use of place value by "lining up the decimal points":

$$\begin{array}{r} .4 \\ +.28 \\ \hline .68 \end{array}$$

$$.4 = .40 = \frac{40}{100}$$

$$.28 = \frac{28}{100}$$

$$\frac{68}{100} = .68$$

Subtraction can be done as shown at the right. But we prefer to make use of place value:

$$\begin{array}{r} .60 \\ -.15 \\ \hline .45 \end{array}$$

$$.6 = .60 = \frac{60}{100}$$

$$.15 = \frac{15}{100}$$

$$\frac{45}{100} = .45$$

Similarly, multiplication and division are simpler using decimals:

$$.6 \times .15 = \begin{array}{r} .60 \\ \times .15 \\ \hline 300 \\ 60 \\ \hline .0900 = .09 \end{array}$$

$$.6 = \frac{6}{10}; \quad .15 = \frac{15}{100}$$

$$\frac{6}{10} \times \frac{15}{100} = \frac{90}{1000} = \frac{9}{100} = .09$$

$$.6 \div .15 = \frac{.60}{.15} = \frac{60}{15} = 4$$

$$\frac{6}{10} \div \frac{15}{100} = \frac{6}{\underset{1}{\cancel{10}}} \times \frac{\overset{10}{\cancel{100}}}{15} = \frac{60}{15} = 4$$

Percent Equivalents

We have learned that *percent* means *per hundred* or *hundredths*. For example, 17% can be expressed as a fraction $\frac{17}{100}$ or as a decimal .17. Likewise, 8% can be expressed as $\frac{8}{100}$ or .08, 100% = $\frac{100}{100}$ or 1, and 125% = $\frac{125}{100}$ or 1.25. Notice that, to represent the "whole" of anything, we can write 100% or 1. The following are examples of some fractions represented as equivalent decimals and equivalent percents:

$$\tfrac{1}{4} = .25 = 25\% \qquad \tfrac{1}{10} = .10 = 10\%$$

$$\tfrac{1}{2} = .50 = 50\% \qquad \tfrac{4}{10} \text{ (or } \tfrac{2}{5}) = .4 \text{ (or } .40) = 40\%$$

$$\tfrac{3}{4} = .75 = 75\% \qquad \tfrac{8}{10} \text{ (or } \tfrac{4}{5}) = .8 \text{ (or } .80) = 80\%$$

Other Operations in Arithmetic

There are many operations in arithmetic other than addition, subtraction, multiplication, and division. Remember that a binary operation is simply a way of assigning, to some ordered pair of numbers in a set, a unique answer that is a number from that set.

Students are often very concerned about their average in a subject. To find an *average* of two numbers, we add the numbers and divide the sum by 2.

For example, the average of 75 and 87 $= \dfrac{75 + 87}{2} = \dfrac{162}{2} = 81.$

This is a binary operation. We could rewrite this problem in the form of the binary operation, $a * b = c$. By replacing $*$, the symbol for the operation, with "avg," we would obtain the result 75 avg 87 = 81. To find averages of two decimals or two fractions or two percents, we use the same procedure as was used for averaging two whole numbers. Add the two numbers and divide by 2.

MODEL PROBLEMS

1. Compute 98 avg 84.

   Solution: (1) Add the numbers given.　98 + 84 = 182

   　　　　　(2) Divide the sum by 2.　　182 ÷ 2 = 91　*Ans.*

2. The high temperature of the day was 33.5° Celsius and the low temperature was 19°C. What was the recorded average temperature for the day?

   Solution: 33.5 avg 19 $= \dfrac{33.5 + 19.0}{2} = \dfrac{52.5}{2} = \dfrac{52.50}{2} = 26.25$

   Answer: The records should show 26.25° Celsius.

There are times when we have to discover which of two numbers is the larger. Finding the larger of two numbers can be thought of as a binary operation called *maximum*. For example, the maximum of 13 and 17 is 17. Recall that the general form of a binary operation is $a * b = c$. By replacing $*$, the symbol for the operation, with "max," we would obtain the result 13 max 17 = 17.

To compare fractions, we first express them as equivalent fractions that have the same denominators. Then we can say that the fraction with the larger numerator is greater than the fraction with the smaller numerator.

MODEL PROBLEM

Is there more gasoline in the tank of a car when the tank is $\frac{2}{3}$ full or when the tank is $\frac{3}{5}$ full?

Solution: We can answer this problem by evaluating $\frac{2}{3}$ max $\frac{3}{5}$.

Step 1. Change the fractions to equivalent forms with common denominators.	$\frac{2}{3}$ max $\frac{3}{5}$ = $\frac{2}{3} \times \frac{5}{5}$ max $\frac{3}{5} \times \frac{3}{3}$ = $\frac{10}{15}$ max $\frac{9}{15}$
Step 2. Of the two fractions that have the same denominator, select the fraction that has the larger numerator.	= $\frac{10}{15}$
Step 3. Rewrite this number in its original form.	= $\frac{2}{3}$ *Ans.*

EXERCISES

In 1-5, write three fractions that are different names for the given number.

1. 4   2. 0   3. .5   4. $\frac{1}{3}$ 5. $1\frac{1}{4}$

6. Answer the questions using the symbols 0, 1, $\frac{0}{1}$, $\frac{1}{0}$.
   a. Which represent counting numbers?
   b. Which represent whole numbers?
   c. Which represent numbers that can be written as fractions?
   d. Which are meaningless?

In 7-22, write the number that each numerical expression represents.

7. $\frac{3}{5} + \frac{7}{5}$ 8. .75 + 1.25   9. $\frac{3}{8} + \frac{5}{8}$ 10. $\frac{3}{2} + \frac{7}{4}$

11. $\frac{12}{7} - \frac{5}{7}$ 12. 4.65 - 2.25   13. $\frac{7}{8} - \frac{2}{8}$ 14. $\frac{15}{3} - \frac{1}{2}$

15. $12 \times \frac{1}{3}$ **16.** $\frac{21}{2} \times \frac{1}{7}$ **17.** $\frac{1}{4} \times 4$ **18.** $2.5 \times .64$

19. $6.5 - .35$ **20.** 1.25×4 **21.** $6.28 \div 4$ **22.** $60 \div 1.25$

In 23-54, perform the indicated operations within the set of all *numbers of arithmetic* (all those numbers that we studied in arithmetic).

23. $\frac{3}{5} + \frac{1}{2}$ **24.** $1\frac{2}{5} + \frac{3}{10}$ **25.** $\frac{5}{9} + 3\frac{1}{2}$ **26.** $\frac{7}{8} + \frac{3}{4}$

27. $3\frac{1}{3} - \frac{1}{5}$ **28.** $7\frac{1}{3} - \frac{1}{2}$ **29.** $5\frac{4}{5} - 2\frac{1}{2}$ **30.** $6\frac{1}{4} - 3\frac{7}{8}$

31. $2\frac{1}{4} \times \frac{2}{3}$ **32.** $3\frac{1}{5} \times \frac{1}{4}$ **33.** $2\frac{2}{5} \times 2\frac{1}{2}$ **34.** $6\frac{2}{3} \times 2\frac{2}{5}$

35. $2\frac{1}{2} \div 3\frac{3}{4}$ **36.** $3\frac{1}{8} \div 1\frac{1}{4}$ **37.** $2\frac{1}{3} \div 7$ **38.** $7 \div 2\frac{1}{3}$

39. $3.7 + .37$ **40.** $1.9 + .09$ **41.** $1.9 - .09$ **42.** $3.2 - .31$

43. $.8 \times .5$ **44.** $.375 \times .8$ **45.** $.125 \div 5$ **46.** $.008 \div .4$

47. $3 - 1\frac{1}{5}$ **48.** $3 - 1.2$ **49.** $12\frac{3}{4} - 8$ **50.** $12.75 - 8$

51. $1\frac{1}{2} \times .6$ **52.** $\frac{2}{3} \div 1.5$ **53.** $\frac{4}{5} - .45$ **54.** $1.8 + \frac{1}{4}$

In 55-66, find the unique answer using the numbers of arithmetic.

55. $1\frac{1}{2}$ avg $4\frac{1}{2}$ **56.** 3.4 avg 6.6 **57.** $1\frac{1}{4}$ avg $\frac{3}{4}$

58. 8 avg 3 **59.** 80 avg 85 **60.** 2.9 avg 4.1

61. $\frac{3}{8}$ avg $\frac{7}{8}$ **62.** $\frac{5}{6}$ avg $\frac{3}{6}$ **63.** $\frac{6}{8}$ avg $\frac{1}{2}$

64. $.5$ avg $.2$ **65.** 1.8 avg $.9$ **66.** $.24$ avg 2.4

In 67-72, each row contains five numerals. Four of the five are equivalent. Which numeral is *not* equivalent to the other four?

67. $.5$	50%	$.50$	$.05$	$\frac{5}{10}$
68. $\frac{3}{4}$	$.75$	$\frac{3}{4}\%$	75%	$\frac{6}{8}$
69. 1	100%	$.1$	1.0	$\frac{1}{1}$
70. $.2$	2%	$\frac{1}{5}$	20%	$.20$
71. 90%	$.90$	$\frac{9}{10}$	$.9$	$.09$
72. $1\frac{1}{4}\%$	125%	$\frac{5}{4}$	1.25	$1\frac{1}{4}$

In 73-84, find the unique answer using the numbers of arithmetic. (We will define a max $a = a$, as in 3 max 3 = 3.)

73. 8 max 3 **74.** 8 max 11 **75.** 8 max 8

76. 1.2 max $.12$ **77.** $.2$ max $.15$ **78.** $.8$ max $.30$

79. $.4$ max $.40$ **80.** $\frac{1}{5}$ max $\frac{2}{5}$ **81.** $\frac{1}{5}$ max $\frac{1}{10}$

82. $\frac{8}{5}$ max 1.3 **83.** $\frac{8}{5}$ max 1.6 **84.** $\frac{3}{5}$ max $\frac{5}{8}$

3 BASE, EXPONENT, AND POWER

Factors

We know that when multiplication is the operation being used, the result is called the *product*. In 2 × 8 = 16, we call 16 the product.

When two or more numbers are multiplied to give us a certain product, each of these numbers is called a *factor* of the product. Thus, 2 and 8 are factors of 16. There are other factors of 16.

Since 1 × 16 = 16, then 1 and 16 are factors of 16.
Since 2 × 8 = 16, then 2 and 8 are factors of 16.
Since 4 × 4 = 16, then 4 is a factor of 16.

Observe that the numbers 1, 2, 4, 8, and 16 are all factors of 16.

Base, Exponent, Power

Notice that in the statement 4 × 4 = 16, the number 4 is used as a factor two times. We can rewrite 4 × 4 = 16 as 4^2 = 16. We can read 4^2 as "four squared," "four raised to the second power," or "the second power of four." In 4^2, the small ^{2} above and to the right of 4 tells us that 4 is to be used as a factor two times. In 4^2 = 16, 4 is called the *base*, 2 is called the *exponent*, and 4^2 or 16 is called the *power*. The exponent is always written in smaller size, to the upper right of the base.

The *base* is a number that is used two or more times as a factor in the product.

The *exponent* is a number that tells how many times the base is to be used as a factor.

The *power* is a number that can be expressed as a product in which all the factors are the same.

In the same way the product 4 × 4 × 4 may be written 4^3, which is read as "four cubed," "four raised to the third power," or "the third power of four." Since 4 × 4 × 4 = 64, then 4^3 = 64. Here, 4 is the base, 3 is the exponent, and 4^3 or 64 is the power. The exponent 3 tells us that the base 4 is to be used as a factor 3 times.

The product 3 × 3 × 3 × 3 may be written 3^4, which is read "three to the fourth power." Since 3 × 3 × 3 × 3 = 81, 3^4 names the same number as 81. We say that the value of 3^4 is 81. We can also say that 81 is the fourth power of 3.

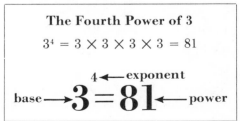

The Fourth Power of 3

$$3^4 = 3 \times 3 \times 3 \times 3 = 81$$

base → $3 = 81$ ← power, 4 ← exponent

We will agree that a number "raised to the first power" is the number itself, as in 5^1 = 5 and 4^1 = 4.

Raising a number to a power is an arithmetic operation, just as addition and multiplication are operations. Although raising to a power is defined as repeated multiplication of a base, it can be thought of as a binary operation. The base is the first element of the ordered pair; the exponent is the second element of the ordered pair; the power is the result.

In the general form of a binary operation, $a * b = c$, the base would be a, the exponent would be b, and the power would be c. Some hand calculators and computers use a symbol to show raising to a power: $3 \uparrow 4 = 81$ or $3 ** 4 = 81$. However, it is more convenient to write the expression without an operation symbol simply by raising the exponent to the upper right of the base: $3^4 = 81$. Examples like $3^4 = 81$ and $4^3 = 64$ point out the importance of order in binary operations.

MODEL PROBLEMS

Compute the value of the given expression.

1. 5^4 2. $(.4)^3$ 3. $(\frac{2}{3})^2$ 4. $(1\frac{1}{2})^2$

Solution:

1. $5^4 = 5 \times 5 \times 5 \times 5 = 625$ *Ans.*
2. $(.4)^3 = .4 \times .4 \times .4 = .064$ *Ans.*
3. $(\frac{2}{3})^2 = \frac{2}{3} \times \frac{2}{3} = \frac{4}{9}$ *Ans.*
4. $(1\frac{1}{2})^2 = 1\frac{1}{2} \times 1\frac{1}{2} = \frac{3}{2} \times \frac{3}{2} = \frac{9}{4} = 2\frac{1}{4}$ *Ans.*

EXERCISES

In 1–24, compute the value of the given expression.

1. 9^2 2. 10^3 3. 5^3 4. 15^2
5. 10^5 6. 4^5 7. $(\frac{1}{3})^2$ 8. $(\frac{1}{2})^2$
9. $(\frac{1}{10})^3$ 10. $(\frac{3}{4})^2$ 11. $(\frac{1}{10})^4$ 12. $(\frac{8}{9})^1$
13. $(.8)^2$ 14. $(.5)^3$ 15. $(.3)^2$ 16. $(.2)^4$
17. $(.1)^5$ 18. $(.25)^2$ 19. $(1.1)^3$ 20. $(3.1)^2$
21. $(2.5)^2$ 22. $(2\frac{1}{2})^2$ 23. $(3\frac{1}{10})^2$ 24. $(1\frac{1}{3})^3$

In 25–32: **a.** Find the value of each of the three given expressions. **b.** Name the expression that has the greatest value.

25. $(5)^2$ $(5)^3$ $(5)^4$ 26. $(.5)^2$ $(.6)^2$ $(.7)^2$
27. $(1.1)^2$ $(1.1)^3$ $(1.1)^4$ 28. $(1.0)^2$ $(1.2)^2$ $(1.4)^2$
29. $(\frac{1}{5})^2$ $(\frac{1}{6})^2$ $(\frac{1}{7})^2$ 30. $(.1)^3$ $(.2)^2$ $(.3)^1$
31. $(.5)^3$ $(.4)^2$ $(.2)^4$ 32. $(1.5)^3$ $(1.4)^2$ $(1.2)^4$

4 ORDER OF OPERATIONS

We saw the importance of order in working with simple binary operations. $12 \div 3$ and $3 \div 12$ do not name the same number. When we work with numerical expressions involving two or more operations, we need to agree upon the order of operations. For example, to evaluate:

$$\text{"}5 + 3 \times 2\text{"}$$

One person may wish to multiply first. Then:	Another person may wish to add first. Then:
$5 + 3 \times 2 = 5 + 6$ $= 11$	$5 + 3 \times 2 = 8 \times 2$ $= 16$

Who is right?

In order to give a single meaning to the expression "$5 + 3 \times 2$" and others like it, mathematicians have agreed on a procedure that gives an exact order to follow in dealing with the basic operations in any numerical expression.

■ **PROCEDURE.** In numerical expressions involving numerals along with signs of operation:

1. Do all multiplications and divisions first, performing them in order from left to right.

2. Then do all additions and subtractions, performing them in order from left to right.

By following the above procedure, the expression "$5 + 3 \times 2$" means $5 + 6$ or 11.

MODEL PROBLEMS

1. Give the meaning of the numerical expression $15 - 12 \div 2$.

   Solution: $15 - 12 \div 2$ means the quotient of 12 and 2 is to be subtracted from 15.

2. Find the simplest name for the numerical expression $28 - 4 \times 2$.

How to Proceed	*Solution*
(1) Write the numerical expression.	$28 - 4 \times 2$
(2) Do the multiplication first.	$= 28 - 8$
(3) Then do the subtraction.	$= 20$ *Ans.*

| EXERCISES |

In 1–9: **a.** Give the meaning of the numerical expression.   **b.** Find the simplest name for the numerical expression.

1. $5 + 3 \times 7$ 2. $6 + 8 \times 2$ 3. $15 - 6 \times 2$
4. $14 - 2 \times 5$ 5. $10 + 8 \div 2$ 6. $16 \div 4 + 4$
7. $26 - 14 \div 2$ 8. $72 \div 8 - 2$ 9. $9 \times 2 + 3 \times 4$

In 10–15, simplify the numerical expression.

10. $6 \times 5 - 8 \times 2$ 11. $20 + 20 \div 5 + 5$
12. $36 - 12 \div 4 - 1$ 13. $36 + \frac{1}{2} \times 10$
14. $24 - 4 \div \frac{1}{2}$ 15. $28 + 0 \div 4 - 10 \times .2$

5 USING GROUPING SYMBOLS IN THE ORDER OF OPERATIONS

In mathematics, *parentheses* are used to indicate the meaning of an expression. For example, $(4 \times 6) + 7$ and $4 \times (6 + 7)$ have two completely different meanings.

If we wish to show that 7 is to be added to the product 4×6, we would enclose the product 4×6 in parentheses, as follows: $(4 \times 6) + 7$.

Here it is necessary to find the product before doing the addition.

$$(4 \times 6) + 7 = 24 + 7$$
$$= 31$$

Note that the normal order of operations tells us to multiply before adding. For this reason, "$(4 \times 6) + 7$" has the same meaning as "$4 \times 6 + 7$."

If we wish to show that the sum of 6 and 7 is to be multiplied 4 times, we would enclose the sum $6 + 7$ in parentheses, as follows: $4 \times (6 + 7)$.

Here it is necessary to find the sum before doing the multiplication.

$$4 \times (6 + 7) = 4 \times 13$$
$$= 52$$

Note that this is *not* the normal order of operations without parentheses. "$4 \times 6 + 7$" does *not* name the same number as "$4 \times (6 + 7)$." We can write "$4 \times (6 + 7)$" as "$4(6 + 7)$" since $4(13)$ is an acceptable way to show multiplication.

In brief, parentheses act as a grouping symbol. In simplifying any numerical expression, our first step is to perform the operations indicated on the numbers within the parentheses. For example:

$$30 - (6 + 5) \text{ means } 30 - 11, \text{ or } 19$$

$$6(4 + 1) \text{ becomes } 6(5), \text{ or } 30$$

$$(4 + 5 \times 2) \div 2 = (4 + 10) \div 2 = (14) \div 2 = 7$$

Besides parentheses ( ), there are other symbols to indicate grouping. Grouping can be shown by the use of *brackets*, which are written [ ]. The expressions $2(5 + 9)$ and $2[5 + 9]$ have the same meaning, where 2 is multiplied by the sum of 5 and 9. A *bar*, or *fraction line*, tells us to perform operations in the numerator and denominator first. Since $\dfrac{20 - 8}{3}$ has the same meaning as $(20 - 8) \div 3$, we can write $\dfrac{20 - 8}{3} = \dfrac{12}{3} = 4$.

When there are *two or more* grouping symbols in an expression, we perform the operations on the numbers in the *innermost symbol first*. For example:

$$
\begin{aligned}
& 5 + 2[6 + (3 - 1) \times 4] \\
={}& 5 + 2[6 + 2 \times 4] \\
={}& 5 + 2[6 + 8] \\
={}& 5 + 2 \times 14 \\
={}& 5 + 28 \\
={}& 33
\end{aligned}
$$

■ **PROCEDURE.** To simplify a numerical expression that involves parentheses (or any grouping symbols):

1. First perform the operations within the parentheses (or any grouping symbols), starting with the innermost group.

2. Then do all multiplications and divisions, performing them in order from left to right.

3. Finally do all additions and subtractions, performing them in order from left to right.

MODEL PROBLEM

Simplify the numerical expression $80 - 4(6 - 4)$.

How to Proceed	*Solution*
(1) Write the expression.	$80 - 4(6 - 4)$
(2) Simplify the expression within the parentheses.	$= 80 - 4(2)$
(3) Do the multiplication.	$= 80 - 8$
(4) Do the subtraction.	$= 72$ *Ans.*

EXERCISES

In 1–8, state the meaning of the expression in part **a** and the meaning of the expression in part **b** and give the most common (simplest) name for each expression.

1. a. $20 + (6 + 1)$ b. $20 + 6 + 1$
2. a. $18 - (4 + 3)$ b. $18 - 4 + 3$
3. a. $17 + (6 - 4)$ b. $17 + 6 - 4$
4. a. $12 - (3 - \frac{1}{2})$ b. $12 - 3 - \frac{1}{2}$
5. a. $15 \times (2 + 1)$ b. $15 \times 2 + 1$
6. a. $.4 \times (8 + 2)$ b. $.4 \times 8 + 2$
7. a. $(12 + 8) \div 4$ b. $12 + 8 \div 4$
8. a. $48 \div (8 - 4)$ b. $48 \div 8 - 4$

In 9–14, use parentheses to express the sentence in symbols.

9. The sum of 10 and 8 is to be found, and then 5 is to be subtracted from this sum.
10. 15 is to be subtracted from 25, and 7 is to be added to the difference.
11. 8 is to be multiplied by the difference of 6 and 2.
12. 12 is to be subtracted from the product of 10 and 5.
13. The difference of 12 and 2 is to be multiplied by the sum of 3 and 4.
14. The quotient of 20 and 5 is to be subtracted from the product of 16 and 3.

In 15–35, simplify the number expression.

15. $10 + (1 + 4)$ 16. $13 - (9 + 1)$ 17. $36 - (10 - 8)$
18. $7(5 + 2)$ 19. $(6 - 1)10$ 20. $20 \div (7 + 3)$
21. $48 \div (15 - 3)$ 22. $(24 - 8) \div 2$ 23. $(17 + 13) \div 10$
24. $15 - (15 \div 5)$ 25. $3(6 + 3) - 4$ 26. $25 + 3(10 - 4)$
27. $26 - 4(7 - 5)$ 28. $25 \div (6 - 1) + 3$ 29. $3(6 + 4)(6 - 4)$

30. $\dfrac{12 - 5 + 14}{3}$ 31. $\dfrac{39}{8 + 7 - 2}$ 32. $\dfrac{10 + 14}{10 - 2}$

33. $\dfrac{7(6 + 14)}{2}$ 34. $\dfrac{3}{2}(6 + 9)$ 35. $\dfrac{1}{2}(8)(12 + 14)$

6 SIMPLIFYING NUMERICAL EXPRESSIONS CONTAINING POWERS

Just as there is a precise order to use when we work with parentheses and the basic operations, mathematicians have agreed upon a procedure to use when working with powers.

To find the value of the expression $40 - 3^2$, we must remember that 3^2 means 3×3. Hence, $40 - 3^2 = 40 - 3 \times 3$. Since multiplication is performed before subtraction, we see that $40 - 3^2 = 40 - 3 \times 3 = 40 - 9 = 31$. We can think of 31 as the simplest name for the numerical expression $40 - 3^2$, or as the answer to a series of binary operations taken one step at a time.

Since $2(3)^2$ means $2(3 \times 3)$, then $2(3)^2 = 2(9) = 18$.

Since $40 - 2(3)^2$ means $40 - 2(3 \times 3)$, then $40 - 2(3)^2 = 40 - 2(9) = 40 - 18 = 22$.

The preceding examples illustrate the fact that in simplifying numerical expressions that contain powers, we first evaluate the powers and then follow the usual order for the other operations.

To evaluate $40 - 2(2 + 1)^2$, we first represent the numeral within the parentheses, "$2 + 1$," as "3." Then we simplify $40 - 2(3)^2$ as we did before, and get 22.

■ **PROCEDURE.** To simplify a numerical expression:

1. Simplify any numerical expressions that are within parentheses or within other symbols of grouping, working from the innermost, first.

2. Simplify any powers and roots. (Roots will be studied later.)

3. Do all multiplications and divisions, performing them in order from left to right.

4. Do all additions and subtractions, performing them in order from left to right.

MODEL PROBLEM

Evaluate $5(6 - 4)^3 - 5$.

How to Proceed	*Solution*
(1) Write the expression.	$5(6 - 4)^3 - 5$
(2) Simplify the expression within the parentheses.	$= 5(2)^3 - 5$
(3) Evaluate the power.	$= 5(8) - 5 \quad [2^3 = 2 \times 2 \times 2 = 8]$
(4) Do the multiplication.	$= 40 - 5$
(5) Do the subtraction.	$= 35 \quad Ans.$

EXERCISES

In 1–24, simplify the numerical expression.

1. 2×3^2
2. 4×5^2
3. $81 \times (\frac{1}{3})^3$
4. $64 \times (.5)^2$
5. $2^3 \times 1^2$
6. $10^2 \times 3^3$
7. $1^4 \times 9^2$
8. $(2^5)(\frac{1}{2})^3$
9. $5^2 + 12^2$
10. $16^2 + 9^2$
11. $13^2 - 5^2$
12. $20^2 - 12$
13. $6 + 4(5)^2$
14. $3(2)^2 + 6$
15. $120 - 6(2)^4$
16. $100(6)^2 - 75$
17. $(4 + 6)^2$
18. $(5 + 12)^2$
19. $(20 - 15)^2$
20. $(7 - 2 \times 3)^3$
21. $2(4 + 6)^2 - 10$
22. $200 - 3(5 - 1)^3$
23. $12(5^2 - 4^2)$
24. $(7^2 - 6^2)(1^2 + 2^2)$

7 COMPARING NUMBERS

In our daily lives we are often asked to compare quantities. Which is cheaper? Which weighs more? Who is taller? Which will last longer? Are they the same size? The answers to these questions are given by comparing quantities that are stated in numerical terms.

Symbol of Equality

To indicate that two numerical expressions represent the same number, we use an equals sign, =, which is read as "equals" or "is equal to." To indicate that 7 + 2 and 5 + 4 both represent the same number 9, we write "7 + 2 = 5 + 4," which is read "seven plus two equals five plus four."

A statement that two numerical expressions represent the same number is called an *equality*.

Symbols of Inequality

To show that two quantities do not name the same number, we can use the symbol of inequality, $\neq$, which is read "is not equal to." Since 7 + 2 represents the number 9 while 5 + 1 represents the number 6, we can write "7 + 2 $\neq$ 5 + 1," which is read as "seven plus two is not equal to five plus one." We know that this is true because the numbers 9 and 6 are not equal: $9 \neq 6$.

A statement that one number is not equal to another number is called an *inequality*.

For any two numbers of arithmetic, we can say that one must be greater than the other, equal to the other, or less than the other. To compare unequal numbers, we use the following symbols:

$>$ is read "is greater than." Thus, $8 > 7$ is read "8 is greater than 7."

$<$ is read "is less than." Thus, $3 < 8$ is read "3 is less than 8."

When we say 8 max 7 = 8, we are comparing the numbers 8 and 7, and saying that the first element 8 is greater than the second element 7. Thus:

$$8 \text{ max } 7 = 8 \quad \text{and} \quad 8 > 7$$

are different ways of stating the relationship between 8 and 7.

In the case of 3 max 8 = 8, the first element 3 is less than the second element 8. Thus:

$$3 \text{ max } 8 = 8 \quad \text{and} \quad 3 < 8$$

are different ways of stating the relationship between 3 and 8. Notice that the symbols $>$ and $<$ point to the smaller number when the inequality is true.

We used a slash mark to change "=" (is equal to) to "$\neq$" (is not equal to). In the same way we can draw a slash mark through the inequality symbols $>$ (is greater than) and $<$ (is less than) to create the following two new symbols.

$\not>$ is read "is not greater than." Thus, $2 \not> 7$ is read "2 is not greater than 7."

$\not<$ is read "is not less than." Thus, $5 \not< 4$ is read "5 is not less than 4."

With these six symbols for comparison of numbers, it is possible to write six statements to show the relationships of any two numbers. Three of these statements will be true and three will be false. For example, we can compare 6 and 9 using the order in which they are given:

$6 < 9$ is true	$6 \not< 9$ is false
$6 \neq 9$ is true	$6 = 9$ is false
$6 \not> 9$ is true	$6 > 9$ is false

| MODEL PROBLEMS |

In 1–6, tell whether the statement is true or false.

1. $6 + 7 \neq 15$ True *Ans.*   2. $0 \neq 8 - 8$ False *Ans.*
3. $8 + 6 > 10$ True *Ans.*   4. $3 \times 6 \not> 10$ False *Ans.*
5. $20 \div 5 < 8$ True *Ans.*   6. $15 - 13 \not< 7$ False *Ans.*

In 7 and 8, write three true statements to compare the numbers in the order given.

7. 8 and 2   *Answer:* $8 > 2; 8 \neq 2; 8 \not< 2$
8. 12 and 12   *Answer:* $12 = 12; 12 \not> 12; 12 \not< 12$

| EXERCISES |

In 1–12, state whether the statement is true or false. Give a reason for your answer.

1. $5 + 4 = 4 + 5$ 2. $12 \times 4 = 4 \times 12$ 3. $5 - 3 = 3 - 5$
4. $12 \div 4 = 4 \div 12$ 5. $6 + 0 = 6$ 6. $6 \times 0 = 6$
7. $6 - 0 = 6$ 8. $0 \div 6 = 0$ 9. $6 \div 0 = 6$
10. $.5 + .4 = .09$ 11. $5 \times .4 = 10 \times .2$ 12. $5 \times \frac{1}{5} = 2 \div 2$

In 13–20, replace the question mark with a numeral that will make the resulting statement true.

13. $8 + ? = 4 + 6$ 14. $8 - ? = 5 \times 1$ 15. $7 - ? = 7 \times 1$
16. $\frac{1}{4} + ? = 1 - \frac{1}{4}$ 17. $.8 + .2 = 4 \times ?$ 18. $4 \times .5 = 12 \div ?$
19. 3 max $? = 7$ max 5 20. 3 avg $? = 7$ avg 5

In 21–25, state whether the inequality is true or false.

21. $8 + 5 \neq 6 + 4$ 22. $9 + 2 \neq 2 + 9$ 23. $6 \times 0 \neq 4 \times 0$
24. The sum of 8 and 12 is not equal to the product of 24 and 4.
25. The product of 5 and 4 is not equal to 5 divided by 4.

In 26–31, write the inequality using the symbol $>$ or the symbol $<$.

26. 25 is greater than 20.   27. $12 + 3$ is less than 20.
28. $6 - 3$ is less than $5 + 4$.   29. $80 \div 4$ is greater than $6 + 3$.
30. The sum of 9 and 4 is less than the product of 10 and 5.
31. The sum of 8 and 7 is greater than the quotient 20 divided by 5.

In 32–34, express each inequality in words.

32. $9 + 8 > 16$ **33.** $12 - 2 < 4 \times 7$ **34.** $5 + 24 \not< 90 \div 3$

In 35–43, state whether the inequality is true or false.

35. $20 - 4 < 5 + 8$ **36.** $6 \times 0 > 3 + 5$ **37.** $18 + 0 > 4 + 0$

38. $2.05 < 20.5$ **39.** $\frac{1}{2} + \frac{1}{8} < .8$ **40.** $3 - .25 > 2\frac{1}{2}$

41. $4.6 - 2.1 > 1.5 + .9$ **42.** $8 \times .5 \not< 6 \div \frac{1}{2}$ **43.** $\frac{1}{2} + \frac{1}{3} \not> 1 - \frac{1}{4}$

In 44–49, replace the question mark with a numeral that will make the resulting statement true.

44. $5 + ? \neq 11$ **45.** $? - 7 > 3$ **46.** $15 \div 5 < ? \div 2$

47. $8 \times \frac{1}{2} \neq 6 - ?$ **48.** $10 \div ? \not> 10$ **49.** $4 - .7 \not< 1 \times ?$

In 50–58, write three true statements to show the comparison of the numerals, using the order in which they are given.

50. 8 and 14   **51.** 9 and 3   **52.** 15 and 15

53. .11 and .6   **54.** .3 and .21   **55.** .8 and .80

56. .8 and .08   **57.** $\frac{2}{3}$ and $\frac{3}{4}$ **58.** $\frac{1}{5}$ and $\frac{1}{8}$

8   THE NUMBER LINE

Geometry is a branch of mathematics that deals with points, lines, planes, and solid figures. Arithmetic is a branch of mathematics that deals with numbers and computation. By bringing together ideas from geometry and arithmetic, we can build powerful tools. One of the most important tools we use in our daily lives is a *ruler*. We use a ruler to measure objects in our physical world.

If we think of a straight line as a collection or set of points, we can assign all the numbers of arithmetic to points on the line. This line, sometimes thought of as a ruler, is called a *number line*.

To build a number line, we begin with two points. We label the first point "0" and the second point "1." We use the length of the segment from 0 to 1 as a *unit measure* and, going in the direction of 1, we continue along a straight line, marking equally spaced segments. Every segment is equal in measure to the unit segment, so that we can assign the numbers 2, 3, 4, and so on, to these points. An arrowhead indicates that the number line extends without end, just as the whole numbers are endless.

A number line can go in any direction, but once we assign "0" and "1," we cannot change its direction. A number line can have any size

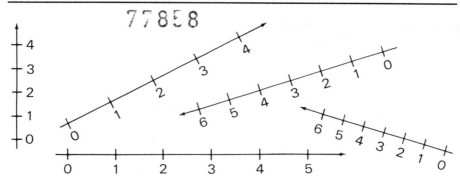

for its unit measure, but once we assign "0" and "1," we cannot change the unit for the remainder of the line.

Of all the possible directions that can be used for number lines, we have come to use two directions most often in our daily lives. A *vertical* number line is used in thermometers to show us temperatures or in rulers to measure heights. In the vertical line, we think of the numbers increasing as we move up the line.

A *horizontal* line, like a ruler used in school, is drawn so that the numbers increase as we move to the right. In the two horizontal lines drawn below, the first uses a unit measure of one inch and the second uses a unit measure of one centimeter.

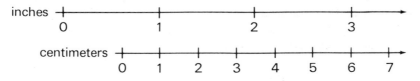

No matter what scale is used, once we have assigned "0" and "1," it is possible to assign every whole number to a point on the line.

Consider a number line on which points have been associated with whole numbers. If we divide the intervals between whole numbers into halves, thirds, quarters, etc., we can label additional points as shown.

In this manner we can assign fractions, decimals, mixed numbers, and, in fact, all of the numbers of arithmetic to specific points on the number line. The number that is associated with a point on the number line is called the *coordinate* of that point. The point on the number line that is associated with a number is called the *graph* of that number.

No matter how close two points may be on a number line, there is always an endless number of points between them. These points can be graphed (determined) by dividing the interval between the points that are associated with the whole numbers into more and more equal parts. For example, the interval between the points that are associated with the numbers 0 and 1 can be divided first into halves, then into thirds, then into fourths, etc., thus obtaining an infinite number of points.

Since there are infinitely many points between any two points, there are infinitely many numbers that can be named between any two given numbers.

While it is true that every number of arithmetic can be associated with a point on a number line, there are some points that are not associated with the numbers of arithmetic. We will study these points and numbers later on in this course.

Ordering Numbers on a Number Line

Consider the binary operation 4 max 2. When the two numbers involved are graphed on a standard horizontal number line, the larger of the two numbers appears to the right of the smaller; the smaller of the two numbers appears to the left of the larger.

Thus, the true statement $2 < 4$ tells us that on a number line the graph of 2 is to the left of the graph of 4. Also, the true statement $4 > 2$ tells us that the graph of 4 is to the right of the graph of 2. We say that the phrases "less than" and "greater than" express an *order relation* as is illustrated by the order in which the numbers appear on a number line.

We know that the statement "4 is *between* 2 and 6" means that 4 is greater than 2 $(4 > 2)$ and also 4 is less than 6 $(4 < 6)$. On a number line, 2 is to the left of 4 and also 4 is to the left of 6. Hence, we can combine the symbols $4 > 2$ and $4 < 6$ into a single symbol "$2 < 4 < 6$." This symbol is read "2 is less than 4 and 4 is less than 6" or "4 is between 2 and 6." We may also express the statement "4 is between 2 and 6" as follows: "$6 > 4 > 2$." This symbol is read "6 is greater than 4 and 4 is greater than 2."

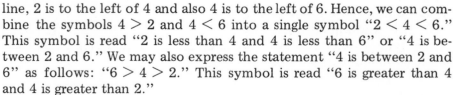

| MODEL PROBLEMS |

Use the number line in the figure to answer questions 1–4.

N   U   M   B   E   R   S

$0 \quad \frac{1}{2} \quad 1 \quad \frac{3}{2} \quad 2 \quad \frac{5}{2} \quad 3$

1. Name the number assigned to point S.   3   *Ans.*

2. Name the coordinate of point M.   1   *Ans.*

3. Name the point that is the graph of $\frac{1}{2}$. U *Ans.*

4. Name the point that is the graph of $1\frac{1}{2}$. B *Ans.*

5. On the number line shown at the right, locate the points that can be associated with the numbers:

M   A   T

$0 \qquad 1 \qquad 2$

    a. $\frac{1}{3}$ b. .5   c. $\frac{20}{20}$ d. $1\frac{2}{3}$ e. 1.8

Answer:

   a. Point G, which is $\frac{1}{3}$ of the way from M to A.

M   G R   A   PH T

$0 \qquad 1 \qquad 2$

   b. Point R, which is $\frac{1}{2}$ of the way from M to A. (Remember that .5 names the same number as $\frac{1}{2}$.)

   c. Point A. (Remember that $\frac{20}{20}$ names the same number as 1.)

   d. Point P, which is $\frac{2}{3}$ of the way from A to T. (Remember that $1\frac{2}{3}$ names the same number as $\frac{5}{3}$.)

   e. Point H, which is $\frac{4}{5}$ of the way from A to T. (Remember that 1.8 names the same number as $\frac{18}{10}$ or $\frac{9}{5}$.)

6. a. How many whole numbers are there between 3 and 6?   Two   *Ans.*
   b. List these numbers.   4, 5   *Ans.*

7. a. How many numbers are there between 3 and 6?   Infinitely many   *Ans.*
   b. List four numbers between 3 and 6.   3.5, $\frac{13}{3}$, 5, $5\frac{1}{2}$ *Ans.*
                                          (There are many other possible answers.)

| EXERCISES |

In 1-4, name the number that can be associated with each of the labeled points on the number line.

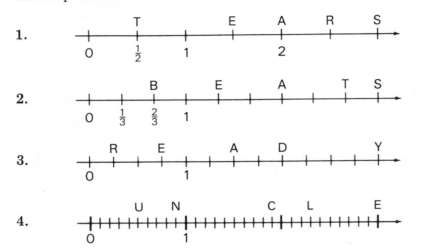

1.

2.

3.

4.

5. Draw a number line and on it locate the points whose coordinates are:

a. $\frac{1}{2}, \frac{3}{2}, \frac{6}{2}, \frac{9}{2}, \frac{11}{2}$

b. $\frac{1}{3}, \frac{2}{3}, \frac{5}{3}, \frac{6}{3}, \frac{13}{3}, \frac{15}{3}$

c. $\frac{1}{4}, \frac{3}{4}, \frac{6}{4}, \frac{8}{4}, \frac{13}{4}, \frac{16}{4}$

d. $\frac{1}{10}, \frac{5}{10}, \frac{9}{10}, \frac{13}{10}, \frac{25}{10}, \frac{30}{10}$

e. $\frac{1}{5}, \frac{3}{5}, \frac{9}{5}, \frac{10}{5}, 2\frac{1}{5}, 3\frac{2}{5}$

f. .1, .3, .7, 1.0, 2.7, 3.4

g. $\frac{1}{4}, \frac{1}{2}, \frac{3}{8}, 1\frac{1}{4}, 2.25, \frac{25}{8}$

h. $\frac{1}{4}, \frac{1}{3}, \frac{5}{12}, \frac{9}{6}, 2\frac{1}{2}, 3.75$

i. numbers represented by fractions whose denominators are 3, beginning with $\frac{1}{3}$ and ending with $\frac{15}{3}$

In 6, use the following number line:

6. Name the point that is the graph of the number:

a. 1   b. $\frac{8}{4}$ c. $1\frac{3}{4}$ d. $2\frac{1}{2}$ e. .5   f. 1.25   g. 2.75

In 7-18: a. State whether on a standard number line the graph of the first number lies to the left or to the right of the graph of the second number. b. State whether the first number is smaller or greater than the second number by inserting the symbol $>$ or $<$ between the numbers given.

7. 12, 18   8. 29, 23   9. $\frac{9}{2}, \frac{4}{2}$ 10. $\frac{1}{4}, \frac{1}{8}$

11. $3\frac{2}{3}, 5\frac{1}{3}$ 12. 3.9, 1.3   13. 3.1, 9.3   14. .5, .05

15. 11, 110   16. .47, 4.7   17. 6.4, 6.45   18. .95, .905

In 19-28, arrange the numbers in proper order so that they will appear from left to right on a number line.

19. 5, 8   20. 16, 4   21. $\frac{1}{2}, \frac{1}{4}$

22. 2.5, 3.2   23. $2\frac{3}{5}$, 2.8   24. 2, 3, 9

25. 9, 6, 11   26. $\frac{1}{4}, \frac{7}{8}, \frac{2}{3}$ 27. 3.2, 2.6, 4.3

28. $3\frac{1}{3}$, 3.75, $3\frac{1}{4}$

In 29-37, select the number that is between the other two numbers. Then rearrange the numbers to show the proper ordering: (a) using the symbol $<$ (as in $2 < 3 < 5$); (b) using the symbol $>$ (as in $5 > 3 > 2$).

29. 13, 17, 9   30. $5\frac{1}{3}, 4\frac{1}{2}, 6\frac{1}{4}$ 31. 4.7, 6.6, 5.3

32. $4\frac{7}{8}$, 4.5, $5\frac{1}{4}$ 33. 0, .1, .12   34. .5, .05, .55

35. $\frac{1}{4}, \frac{1}{5}, \frac{1}{3}$ 36. $\frac{1}{3}$, .3, .13   37. .909, .9, .91

9   THE METRIC SYSTEM OF MEASUREMENT

A ruler can have any unit length ("unit length" is the distance from 0 to 1), but the most convenient rulers are those that use standard units of length. A standard unit is the same no matter who uses it or where it is used.

People in the United States have been using English units of measure, but we are currently changing over to the metric system for general use. Scientists, the medical profession, and many industries worldwide use the metric system. The metric system, developed around 1790 in France, is called a *decimal system* because it is based on the number ten and powers of ten. The metric system is easy to use because we multiply and divide by 10, by 100, and by 1000.

In some problems in this book we will use the metric system. In other problems we will use English units of measure. Because of the increasing use of the metric system in our country, we will concentrate on developing the standard units for the metric system.

Metric Units of Length

In the metric system the basic unit of length is the *meter* (abbreviated m). A meter is slightly larger than a yard, or a few inches more than three feet.

To measure short lengths, we use the *centimeter* (cm), which is about as wide as a person's fingernail. There are 100 centimeters in 1 meter, or we can say 1 centimeter = $\frac{1}{100}$ of a meter. The centimeter is the standard unit of length used in the ruler shown below. We measure our heights in centimeters. For example, Mary is 163 cm tall.

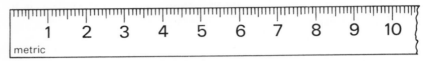

To measure shorter, more precise lengths, we use the *millimeter* (mm). In the ruler a centimeter is divided into ten equal parts; each small length is a millimeter. There are 1000 millimeters in 1 meter, or we can say 1 millimeter = $\frac{1}{1000}$ of a meter. Film, such as 35 mm, uses this measure.

To measure long distances, such as the distance between two cities, we use the *kilometer* (km). One kilometer equals 1000 meters. We can also say that 1 meter = $\frac{1}{1000}$ of a kilometer, or 1 meter = .001 kilometer.

Although there are other lengths in the metric system, the commonly used units of length are the kilometer, meter, centimeter, and millimeter. (The English system uses the mile, yard, foot, and inch.)

Metric Lengths	
1 km = 1000 m	1 m = .001 km
1 m = 100 cm	1 cm = .01 m
1 m = 1000 mm	1 mm = .001 m

Metric Units of Weight or Mass

When we weigh ourselves, we use an instrument called a scale. The basic unit of metric weight or mass is the *gram* (abbreviated g). A gram is very light, about the weight of a ping-pong ball or a paper clip. The net weight of packaged food is often listed in grams. For example, a box of cereal may weigh 210 grams.

To measure heavier weights, we use the *kilogram* (kg), which is slightly more than 2 pounds. There are 1000 grams in 1 kilogram. We can say that 1 gram = $\frac{1}{1000}$ of a kilogram, or 1 g = .001 kg. We measure our own weights in kilograms. For example, Mike weighs 63 kilograms.

Pharmacists use a very light weight called the *milligram* (mg) to measure prescription drugs. There are 1000 milligrams in 1 gram, which means that 1 mg = $\frac{1}{1000}$ g.

Although there are other weights in the metric system, the commonly used units of weight are the kilogram, gram, and milligram. (The English system uses the ton, pound, and ounce.)

Metric Weights	
1 kg = 1000 g	1 g = .001 kg
1 g = 1000 mg	1 mg = .001 g

Metric Units of Liquid Measure

The basic unit of metric liquid measure is the *liter* (abbreviated l), which is slightly more than a quart. Milk and gasoline are measured in liters.

We use the *milliliter* (ml) for smaller liquid measures, such as those used in cooking. There are 1000 milliliters in 1 liter, or we can say 1 milliliter = .001 liter. A teaspoon in metric recipes holds 5 milliliters.

Only industry will use the *kiloliter* (kl) to measure very large liquid measures, where 1 kiloliter = 1000 liters.

Although there are other liquid measures in the metric system, the commonly used units are the liter and milliliter. (The English system uses the gallon, quart, pint, cup, ounce, tablespoon, and teaspoon.)

Liquid Metric Measures	
1 l = 1000 ml	1 ml = .001 l

Metric Area

Area is based on square units. In the metric system one *square centimeter* (abbreviated as 1 cm^2) is a square that measures one centimeter on every side. Notice that the metric system uses an exponent of 2 to abbreviate square units of measure. The common metric area measures are the square meter (m^2), the square centimeter (cm^2) and the square millimeter (mm^2).

Metric Volume

Volume is based on cubic units. In the metric system one *cubic centimeter* (abbreviated as 1 cm^3) is a cube that measures one centimeter on every edge. Notice that the metric system uses an exponent of 3 to abbreviate cubic units of measure. The common metric volume

LENGTH	AREA	VOLUME
H————H 1 cm	1 cm 1 cm ☐ 1 cm 1 cm	1 cm 1 cm 1 cm
one centimeter (1 cm)	one square centimeter (1 cm²)	one cubic centimeter (1 cm³)

measures are the cubic meter (m^3), the cubic centimeter (cm^3), and the cubic millimeter (mm^3).

Prefixes

In the metric system, six prefixes are used to name larger and smaller units of measure. A prefix is a syllable that is placed in front of a word to change its meaning.

Prefix	*Meaning*		
kilo (k)	thousand	or	1000
hecto (h)	hundred	or	100
deka (da)	ten	or	10
deci (d)	tenths	or	$\frac{1}{10}$ or .1
centi (c)	hundredths	or	$\frac{1}{100}$ or .01
milli (m)	thousandths	or	$\frac{1}{1000}$ or .001

For example:

a kilogram   is 1000 grams

a hectoliter is   100 liters

a dekameter is   10 meters

a deciliter   is $\frac{1}{10}$ of a liter, or .1 liter

a centimeter is $\frac{1}{100}$ of a meter, or .01 meter

a milligram   is $\frac{1}{1000}$ of a gram, or .001 gram

We are often faced with the problem of changing one unit in a system of measures to another unit. In the metric system, this can easily be done by multiplying a given value by one of the numbers 10, 100, 1000, .1, .01, .001. The number used is determined by the prefixes of the metric measures involved in the problem.

| MODEL PROBLEMS |

To change from a larger metric unit to a smaller metric unit, we multiply by 10, 100, or 1000.

1. a. Change 6 centimeters to millimeters.

   Solution:
   Since 1 cm = 10 mm
   and 6 cm = 6 × 1 cm,
   then 6 cm = 6 × 10 mm,
   or 6 cm = 60 mm   *Ans.*

   b. What numeral, when written in the blank, will make the statement true?

   4.5 km = _____ m

Solution:
Since 1 km   = 1000 m
and 4.5 km = 4.5 × 1 km,
then 4.5 km = 4.5 × 1000 m,
or 4.5 km = 4500 m   *Ans.*

To change from a smaller metric unit to a larger metric unit, we multiply by .1, .01, or .001.

2. a. Change 40 millimeters to centimeters.

   Solution:
   Since   1 mm = .1 cm
   and 40 mm = 40 × 1 mm,
   then 40 mm = 40 × .1 cm,
   or 40 mm = 4 cm   *Ans.*

   b. What numeral, when written in the blank, will make the statement true?

   3750 g = _____ kg

Solution:
Since 1 g   = .001 kg
and 3750 g = 3750 × 1 g,
then 3750 g = 3750 × .001 kg,
or 3750 g = 3.75 kg   *Ans.*

| EXERCISES |

In 1–14, write the abbreviation for the given metric unit.

1. millimeter   2. centimeter   3. meter   4. kilometer
5. milliliter   6. liter   7. kilogram   8. gram
9. square meter   10. square centimeter   11. square millimeter
12. cubic meter   13. cubic millimeter   14. cubic kilometer

In 15–26, write the metric unit represented by each symbol or abbreviation.

15. m   16. mg   17. g   18. cm   19. mm   20. kl
21. ml   22. km   23. mm^2 24. cm^3 25. km^2 26. m^3

In 27–35, tell which is the larger of the two given measures.

27. gram, kilogram   28. liter, milliliter
29. meter, centimeter   30. meter, millimeter
31. meter, kilometer   32. centimeter, millimeter

33. kiloliter, liter   34. gram, milligram
35. kilometer, millimeter

In 36-41, for every two measures given, write an equation to show how many units of the smaller unit of measure are needed to equal one unit of the larger unit of measure.

For example: centimeter, meter.   *Answer:* 100 cm = 1 m

36. meter, kilometer   37. gram, milligram
38. liter, centiliter   39. centimeter, millimeter
40. millimeter, meter   41. gram, kilogram

In 42-54, fill in a metric unit of measure that is the most correct unit to use in the sentence.

42. The school hall is 75 ____ long.
43. My math teacher is 178 ____ tall.
44. This box of cereal weighs 510 ____.
45. Nancy Anderson weighs 51 ____.
46. I bought 0.3 ____ of milk in the lunchroom.
47. A football player weighs 110 ____.
48. My thermos holds 750 ____ of liquid.
49. A bicycle weighs about 10 ____.
50. A bicycle can obtain speeds of 40 ____ per hour.
51. This postage stamp has an area of 10 ____.
52. The volume of a classroom is about 200 ____.
53. The nurse took 12 ____ of blood for a sample.
54. A soda machine has a slot to take in coins. The slot is about 4 ____ by 20 ____.

In 55-64, of the three given measures, select the one that is most appropriate for the problem.

55.	the weight of a dime	20 g	2 g	0.2 g
56.	the height of a doorway	195 km	195 cm	195 m
57.	the contents of a glass of juice	0.4 l	4 l	4 ml
58.	the thickness of a human hair	0.1 mm	0.1 m	0.1 km
59.	the thickness of a textbook	3.1 mm	3.1 cm	3.1 km
60.	a dose of medicine	6 ml	6 l	60 l
61.	the weight of an apple	0.2 g	0.2 kg	2 kg
62.	the length of a piece of chalk	95 mm	95 cm	95 m
63.	the distance traveled in a bus	45 cm	45 m	45 km
64.	the measure of a person's waist	20 cm	70 cm	80 mm

In 65–92, write the numeral that, when written in the blank, will make the resulting statement true.

65. 1 centimeter = ___ meter
66. 1 meter = ___ millimeters
67. 1 kilometer = ___ meters
68. 1 meter = ___ centimeters
69. 1 milligram = ___ gram
70. 1 kiloliter = ___ liters
71. 1 liter = ___ milliliters
72. 1 gram = ___ kilogram
73. 4000 m = ___ km
74. 18,000 m = ___ km
75. 3000 g = ___ kg
76. 280 g = ___ kg
77. 500 cm = ___ m
78. 375 cm = ___ m
79. 6500 mg = ___ g
80. 750 mg = ___ g
81. 8000 ml = ___ l
82. 4500 ml = ___ l
83. 3000 l = ___ kl
84. 6000 ml = ___ l
85. 70 mm = ___ cm
86. 1.5 km = ___ m
87. 90 cm = ___ mm
88. 0.2 km = ___ m
89. 70 cm = ___ mm
90. 0.7 kl = ___ l
91. 2.5 cm = ___ mm
92. 1.6 kg = ___ g

93. If the length of a steel rod is 3 meters, find its length in centimeters.
94. The distance between two towns is 8.5 kilometers. Express this distance in meters.
95. A plane is flying at an altitude of 10,000 meters. Express its altitude in kilometers.
96. The length of a picture is 25 centimeters. Express its length in meters.
97. A box of candy weighs 800 grams. Express its weight in kilograms.
98. A package weighs 2.75 kilograms. Express its weight in grams.
99. A pill contains 500 milligrams of vitamin C. Express this weight in grams.
100. An oil tank contains 2 kiloliters of oil. Express its contents in liters.
101. A bottle contains 1.2 liters of milk. Express its contents in milliliters.

10 OPERATIONS IN GEOMETRY

Just as there are operations in arithmetic, there are operations in other branches of mathematics. Many of the binary operations in geometry depend on arithmetic. In this section we will discuss only a few examples of operations in geometry. Many more will be found in later work.

Distance

When we studied the number line, we spoke of a ruler to measure objects in our world. We find the length of an object by finding the distance between two points, usually called endpoints. To find the distance between two points, say A and B, we place a ruler (or number line) so that it touches both points. We read the numbers from the ruler that are associated with points A and B. These numbers are called coordinates. If we let the "0" coordinate (or the end of the ruler) be associated with point A, then the number that is associated with point B is the distance. In the figure shown, when we place the given ruler so that 0 lines up with point A, then the coordinate 3 will line up with point B. We say the distance between points A and B is 3 units, usually written as $AB = 3$.

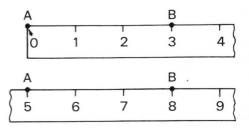

If we use the same ruler but let a different number, say 5, be associated with point A, we see that point B is now associated with the number 8. Observe that the distance between A and B is still 3.

We can find the distance 3 by using either pair of numbers, 0 and 3 or 5 and 8, as follows:

$$3 - 0 = 3 \qquad \text{and} \qquad 8 - 5 = 3$$

Notice that in each case we subtracted the smaller number from the larger number. It does not matter which two numbers or coordinates are associated with points A and B. The distance will always be 3 if we use this ruler.

At present we will define the distance between two points on a number line as follows:

■ **DEFINITION.** The *distance* between any two points on a number line is the difference between the coordinates of the two points, always subtracting the smaller coordinate from the larger.

Note that the distance from A to B is exactly the same as the distance from B to A, that is $AB = BA$.

We can think of finding the distance between two points as a binary operation that behaves exactly like subtraction with one variation. Before we perform the subtraction, we may have to arrange the coordinates placing the larger coordinate first and the smaller second when we write them as an ordered pair of numbers.

| MODEL PROBLEMS |

In 1–4, use the number line and the associated points to find the distances named.

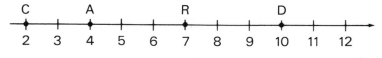

Solutions

1. *CD*   Since 2 is at point *C* and 10 is at point *D*, the distance *CD* = 10 – 2 = 8.

2. *DC*   Again, 2 is at *C* and 10 is at *D*. Subtract the smaller number from the larger: *DC* = 10 – 2 = 8

3. *CR*   *CR* = 7 – 2 = 5

4. *DA*   *DA* = 10 – 4 = 6

5. *X* is a point on the number line such that the distance *RX* equals 2 units. The coordinate of *R* is 7. What are the possible coordinates for point *X*?

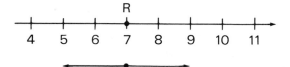

Solution: Since *RX* = 2, and 7 is the coordinate at *R*, count two units from 7 on the number line to find the coordinate of point *X*. Counting to the right, we find *X* is at 9. Counting to the left, we find *X* is at 5. There are two possible coordinates for *X* since 9 – 7 = 2 and 7 – 5 = 2.   *X* = 9 or *X* = 5   *Ans.*

Line Segments

A line segment can be thought of as a part of a line. It is determined by two points. In the same way that we discussed a distance between two points, we could have discussed the length of a line segment determined by those two points.

■ **DEFINITION.** A *line segment* is a set of points consisting of two points on the line (called endpoints) and all the points on the line between these endpoints.

A line segment whose endpoints are *A* and *B* can be named "segment *AB*" or "segment *BA*," symbolized as $\overline{AB}$ or $\overline{BA}$. Notice that a bar is placed over the capital letters to distinguish "segment AB" ($\overline{AB}$) from "distance AB" (AB). $\overline{AB}$ is a line segment; AB is a number.

A ●————————————● B

The figure shows a line segment, written as $\overline{AB}$ or $\overline{BA}$.

Perimeter of Rectangles

In earlier years we learned that the *perimeter* of a simple polygon is found by adding the lengths of all the sides. In a rectangle, which is a four-sided polygon, each side is a segment, which has a length. The length of each segment (or side) is the distance between its endpoints. Once we know the lengths of the four sides, we can find the perimeter by adding the four numbers (or lengths). This is a geometric operation based on "addition."

For example, consider the rectangle named by points $ABCD$. In the figure the lengths of the sides are indicated by $AB = 5$, $BC = 3$, $CD = 5$, $DA = 3$. We say that the perimeter is the sum of these lengths. Perimeter = AB + $BC + CD + DA = 5 + 3 + 5 + 3 = 16$ units.

Recall that the perimeter of a rectangle was also found by a formula, $P = 2l + 2w$. This formula or rule tells us that we are really dealing with two quantities called l and w, where l represents the length of the rectangle and w represents the width. We can use this rule because opposite sides of a rectangle are always equal in length. In the example just stated, l and w are given as 5 and 3. Using the order of operations, we can write:

$$P = 2l + 2w = 2(5) + 2(3) = 10 + 6 = 16 \text{ units}$$

Because the formula $P = 2l + 2w$ depends on two elements, we can think of finding the perimeter of a rectangle as a binary operation. Using the general binary form, $l * w = P$, we find the answer P by multiplying each element of the ordered pair (l, w) by 2 and then adding these products.

Area of Rectangles

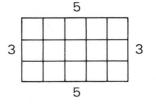

The area of a plane figure, such as a rectangle, is determined by a different formula or rule. Area tells us how many "square units" of measure are enclosed within the plane figure. Once again, using the same rectangle in which $l = 5$ and $w = 3$, we can describe the area as "15 square units." Recall that one square unit is a square that measures 1 unit on every side.

We can describe the area of any rectangle by a general rule: $A = l \cdot w$. Since area of a rectangle is based on two quantities, called l and w, we again have a binary operation in geometry. Using the general binary form $l * w = A$, we find the answer A by multiplying the elements of the ordered pair (l, w).

$$A = 5 \cdot 3 = 15 \text{ square units}$$

Midpoint of a Line Segment

Every line segment is a set of points. In this set there is a unique point (one and only one) called the midpoint.

■ **DEFINITION.** The *midpoint* of a line segment is a point that divides the segment into two smaller segments that are equal in length.

In the figure below, if M is the midpoint of $\overline{AB}$, then $AM = MB$.

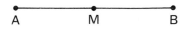

We can use a number line to see that this operation in geometry relates directly to a binary operation in arithmetic. For example, place a number line so that coordinate 0 is at A, coordinate 6 is at B, and $AB = 6$.

If we wish to find the midpoint M of $\overline{AB}$, we must find the point M such that $AM = MB$. Since the length of segment AB is 6 – 0, or 6, point M must be 3 units from A and 3 units from B. Hence, the coordinate of M must be 3.

Notice that the binary operation "average" takes the ordered pair 0 and 6 and assigns the number 3 as the result, "0 avg 6 = 3."

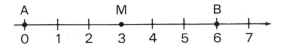

Using the same number line, let us place $\overline{AB}$ so that the coordinate of A is 5 and the coordinate of B is 11. AB is still 6 because 11 – 5 = 6. Once again, point M must be 3 units from A and 3 units from B. Hence, the coordinate of M must be 8.

Here, too, we see that the binary operation "average" will take the ordered pair 5 and 11 and assign the number 8 as the result, "5 avg 11 = 8."

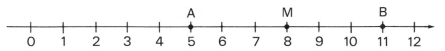

MODEL PROBLEMS

In problem 1 the coordinates of A and B, the endpoints of $\overline{AB}$, are given. Name the coordinate assigned to midpoint M of $\overline{AB}$.

1. A is at coordinate 12, B is at coordinate 15.

    Solution: The coordinate of M is the average of 12 and 15.

    $$12 \text{ avg } 15 = \frac{12 + 15}{2} = \frac{27}{2} = 13\frac{1}{2} \quad Ans.$$

2. $\overline{RS}$ is a segment with midpoint K. The coordinates assigned to R and K are 5 and 12, respectively. Name the coordinate at point S.

    Solution: Since K is the midpoint, $RK = KS$. $RK = 12 - 5 = 7$. Then KS must equal 7. Add this distance 7 to the coordinate 12 to obtain the coordinate 19 at point S.

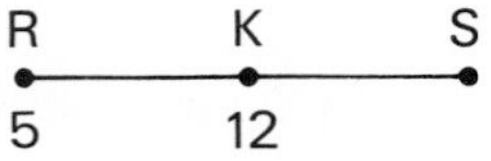

    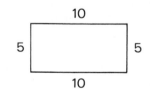

    Answer: 19

3. The length of a rectangle is given as 5 and the perimeter of the rectangle is given as 30. Find **(a)** the width of the rectangle and **(b)** the area of the rectangle.

    Solution

    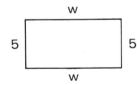

    a. Since $P = 2l + 2w$, find a value for w where $30 = 2(5) + 2w$ or $30 = 10 + 2w$. Here, $2w$ must equal 20. So $w = 10$ *Ans.*

    b. Since $A = l \cdot w$, substitute and multiply: $A = 5 \cdot 10$ $A = 50$ *Ans.*

EXERCISES

In 1–6, use the number line and the associated points shown.

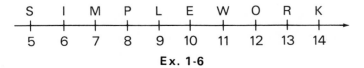

Ex. 1-6

1. Find the distances named:
   a. *SL* b. *MR* c. *MS* d. *OK* e. *KS* f. *PI*
2. Name the midpoint of the segments given:
   a. $\overline{SL}$ b. $\overline{MR}$ c. $\overline{MS}$ d. $\overline{OP}$ e. $\overline{RS}$ f. $\overline{PI}$
3. Name four segments on the line whose midpoint is *L*.
4. If *X* is a point such that *E* is the midpoint of $\overline{PX}$, what coordinate is assigned to point *X*?
5. If *Y* is a point such that *R* is the midpoint of $\overline{PY}$, what coordinate if assigned to point *Y*?
6. If *Z* is a point such that *K* is the midpoint of $\overline{SZ}$, what coordinate is assigned to point *Z*?

In 7 and 8, the number line is shown so that the points named are spaced at equal intervals: *TO* = *OU* = *UG*, and so on. The coordinate 15 is assigned to point *G* in every problem.

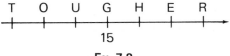

Ex. 7-8

7. If the coordinate 12 is assigned to point *U*, find the distances named.
   a. *UG* b. *GH* c. *UH* d. *TE* e. *RO* f. *GO*
8. If the coordinate 13.5 is assigned to point *U*, find the distances named.
   a. *UG* b. *GH* c. *UH* d. *TE* e. *RO* f. *GO*

In 9–16, the coordinates of *A* and *B*, the endpoints of $\overline{AB}$, are given. Find the coordinate assigned to *X*, the midpoint of $\overline{AB}$.

9. 3 and 5 10. 8 and 2 11. 7 and 26 12. 40 and 17
13. 8 and 12.8 14. 8 and 2.8 15. $\frac{2}{3}$ and $\frac{1}{3}$ 16. $1\frac{1}{4}$ and 5

In 17–20, a segment $\overline{AB}$ has a midpoint *X*. The coordinate of *X* is 15. Find the coordinate of endpoint *B* when the coordinate of endpoint *A* is the given number.

17. 14 18. 10 19. 20 20. $10\frac{1}{3}$

In 21–28, the segment $\overline{AB}$ has the coordinate 12 assigned to endpoint *A*. Find the possible coordinate(s) assigned to endpoint *B* for the given length of $\overline{AB}$.

21. *AB* = 1 22. *AB* = 3 23. *AB* = 10 24. *AB* = 12
25. *AB* = $\frac{1}{2}$ 26. *AB* = 1.5 27. *AB* = .8 28. *AB* = $\frac{2}{3}$

29. What must be true about the endpoints of $\overline{AB}$ in order that the distance AB on a number line be equal to zero?

In 30–37, for the given length and width of a rectangle: a. Find the perimeter of the rectangle in units. b. Find the area of the rectangle in square units.

30. $l = 18$, $w = 2$ **31.** $l = 4$, $w = 13$

32. $l = 20$, $w = 1$ **33.** $l = 9$ cm, $w = 7$ cm

34. $l = 10$ mm, $w = 3$ mm   **35.** $l = 8$ m, $w = 1.5$ m

36. $l = .2$ cm, $w = .3$ cm   **37.** $l = \frac{2}{3}$ ft., $w = \frac{1}{3}$ ft.

In 38–42, find the area of the rectangle whose perimeter and length are given.

38. perimeter = 20, length = 8   **39.** perimeter = 20, length = 6

40. perimeter = 20, length = $9\frac{1}{2}$ **41.** perimeter = 20, length = 2.5

42. perimeter = 14 cm, length = 6 cm

In 43–47, find the perimeter of the rectangle whose area and length are given.

43. area = 30, length = 5   **44.** area = 54, length = 9

45. area = 12, length = 1.5   **46.** area = 14, length = $3\frac{1}{2}$

47. area = 30 sq. ft., length = 30 ft.

11 SETS

We speak of sets of numbers in arithmetic and sets of points in geometry. Sets will play an important role in the algebra and probability we will be studying this year. It is important to recall some definitions about sets before beginning algebra.

The Elements of a Set

When a collection of distinct objects is so clearly described that we can always tell whether or not an object belongs to it, we call the collection a *well-defined collection*, or more simply a *set*. For example, the odd counting numbers less than 10 form a well-defined collection, or set. The numbers 1, 3, 5, 7, and 9 belong to this set. These numbers are called the ***members***, or ***elements***, of the set. The number 2 does not belong to this set and is therefore not an element of this set.

One way of indicating a set is to list the names of its elements within braces, { }. For example, to indicate the set whose elements are 1, 3, 5,

7, 9 we can write {1, 3, 5, 7, 9}. It does not matter in which order the elements are listed.

By using a capital letter such as A to represent the set, we can write A = {1, 3, 5, 7, 9}. This is read "A is the set whose elements are 1, 3, 5, 7, and 9." To indicate that the number 3 is an element of set A, or is contained in set A, we use the symbol $\in$ and write $3 \in A$. To indicate that the number 2 is not an element of set A, or is not contained in set A, we use the symbol $\notin$ and write $2 \notin A$.

Another way of describing a set is to state a rule for selecting the elements of the set.

For example, A = {all odd counting numbers less than ten} is read "A is the set of all odd counting numbers less than ten." Observe that this is another way of describing the set A = {1, 3, 5, 7, 9}.

To represent a set without writing a list of all its members, we can make use of patterns and three dots. For example, {1, 2, 3, 4, ...} names the set of counting numbers while {1, 2, 3, 4, ..., 200} names the set of the first two hundred counting numbers.

There is still another way of describing a set, by using a method called the **set-builder notation**, as shown in the following example:

$$\{n \mid n \text{ is a counting number between 1 and 200}\}$$

This is read:
  "the set of ————↑↑↑
  all elements n ————┘││   ↑
  such that ————————┘│   │
  n is a counting number between 1 and 200"——┘

In the sentence "n is a counting number between 1 and 200," the letter n does not name a specific number as do 1 and 200. The letter n is a **placeholder** for any element of a given set of numbers. When a symbol such as n, x, or y is used in this way, it is called a **variable**. We shall discuss variables in greater detail in a later chapter.

Some examples of sets described by the set-builder notation are:

1. {$x \mid x$ is a natural number}
2. {$n \mid n$ is an odd number}

To indicate that the number 5 belongs to {$n \mid n$ is an odd number}, we use the symbol $\in$ and we write:

$$5 \in \{n \mid n \text{ is an odd number}\}$$

To indicate that the number 2 does not belong to {$n \mid n$ is an odd number}, we use the symbol $\notin$ and we write:

$$2 \notin \{n \mid n \text{ is an odd number}\}$$

Kinds of Sets

A *finite set* is a set whose elements can be counted, and in which the counting process comes to an end. Some examples of finite sets are:

1. the set of all pupils in your mathematics class
2. {2, 4, 6, 8, . . . , 9200}
3. {a, b, c, d, e, f, g, h, i, j}
4. {x | x is a whole number less than 20}

An *infinite set* is a set whose elements cannot be counted, and in which the counting process does not come to an end. Some examples of infinite sets are:

1. the set of counting numbers
2. the set of points that are on a straight line
3. {2, 4, 6, 8, . . .}
4. {n | n is a whole number}

The *empty set*, or *null set*, is the set that has no elements. Since the empty set does not have an infinite number of elements, it is a finite set. Some descriptions of the empty set are:

1. the set of months that begin with the letter Q
2. the set of odd numbers exactly divisible by 2
3. {x | x is an even number between 2 and 3}

The empty set may be represented by the symbol $\emptyset$ or by a pair of empty braces, { }. By drawing a slash mark through the symbol normally used for zero, we might think of $\emptyset$ as "*not* even zero" is a member of this set.

Note that the set which has as its only element the number 0, represented by {0}, is *not* the empty set, because it does contain an element.

Relationships Between Sets

Set A is *equal* to set B if every element of A is an element of B and every element of B is an element of A. In other words, set A and set B contain exactly the same elements.

For example, if A = {1, 3, 5, 7, 9} and B = {all odd counting numbers less than ten}, then set A is equal to set B, denoted by $A = B$, because both A and B contain exactly the same elements, namely, 1, 3, 5, 7, and 9.

To indicate that set C is not equal to set D, we write $C \neq D$.
For example, if C = {1, 2} and D = {2, 3}, then $C \neq D$.

Set A and set B are *matching sets*, or *equivalent sets*, denoted by $A \sim B$, if each element of set A can be matched with (or corresponded with) exactly one element of set B, and each element of set B can be matched with exactly one element of set A. When two sets can be matched in this way, we say that there is a *one-to-one correspondence* between the two sets.

For example, the two sets A = {1, 3, 5} and B = {2, 4, 6} are equivalent sets because the elements of set A can be matched with the elements of set B. The figure shows one possible matching, called a one-to-one correspondence. The double-headed arrows show that the matching works in both directions.

$$A = \{1, 3, 5\}$$

$$B = \{2, 4, 6\}$$

If every student in a class were assigned to a seat and there were no empty seats left over, there would be a match of students to seats and a match of seats to students.

If there were unassigned seats, however, or if there were students left standing, then there would not be a match of students to seats.

Notice that if two sets are equal sets, they are also equivalent sets. However, if two sets are equivalent sets, they are not necessarily equal sets.

The *universal set*, or the *universe*, is the entire set of elements under consideration in a given situation and is usually denoted by the letter U.

For example:

1. In arithmetic, the universal set in a given situation may be the set of all numbers that can be written as fractions.
2. In geometry, the universal set in a given situation may be the set of all points in a line.
3. In measurements the universal set may be the set of all distances, or the set of all numbers associated with points on the number line we have studied.
4. In given situations, like scores on a classroom test, the universal set may be whole numbers from 0 to 100. We can write that the universe = {0, 1, 2, 3, . . . , 100}.

Subsets

Set A is a *subset* of set B, denoted by $A \subset B$, if every element of set A is an element of set B. For example:

1. The set A = {Harry, Paul} is a subset of the set B = {Sue, Harry, Mary, Paul}.
2. The set A = {1, 2} is a subset of the set B = {1, 2, 3, 4, 5}.
3. The set of odd whole numbers {1, 3, 5, 7, . . .} is a subset of the set of whole numbers, {0, 1, 2, 3, . . .}.

4. $\overline{AB}$ is a segment containing a set of points. If M is the midpoint of $\overline{AB}$, then set M contains one point. Set M is a subset of the set of points found on the segment $\overline{AB}$.

Since a subset of a set may contain all the elements of the set itself, a subset can have the very same elements as the set itself. When this is true, the two sets are equal. We see, therefore, that every set is a subset of itself.

Mathematicians can show that the empty set $\emptyset$ is a subset of every set.

Consider the set $A = \{1, 2, 3\}$. To list all the subsets of set A, we can follow a simple pattern:

(1) List all subsets of three elements. $\{1, 2, 3\}$
(2) List all subsets of two elements. $\{1, 2\}$ $\{1, 3\}$ $\{2, 3\}$
(3) List all subsets of one element. $\{1\}$ $\{2\}$ $\{3\}$
(4) List all subsets of no elements. $\{\ \}$

There are eight subsets that can be formed from the set $\{1, 2, 3\}$. Notice that $\{1, 2\}$ and $\{2, 1\}$ are not both listed, because they are simply two ways to name the same set.

EXERCISES

In 1–3, list the elements of the set that is described.

1. {days of the week that begin with the letter T}
2. {even integers greater than 3 and less than 12}
3. {natural numbers less than 100 that are the squares of natural numbers}

In 4 and 5, tabulate the elements of the set that is described. Use three dots when convenient or necessary.

4. the set of all even counting numbers
5. the set of all whole numbers greater than 10 and less than 1000

In 6–18, state whether the set is a finite non-empty set, an infinite set, or the empty set.

6. the set of all the people who live in the United States today
7. the set of all women who are 120 cm tall
8. the set of all women who are 120 feet tall
9. the set of points on a line segment, $\overline{AB}$
10. the set of endpoints on a line segment, $\overline{AB}$
11. the set of midpoints on a line segment, $\overline{AB}$
12. the set of segments that contain the same midpoint M

13. the set of natural numbers less than 1 billion
14. the set of natural numbers greater than 1 billion
15. the set of natural numbers between 0 and 1
16. the set of rectangles
17. the set of rectangles with area = 15 cm^2
18. the set of rectangles with perimeter = 15 cm and length = 10 cm

In 19–21, give a description of the given set.

19. {January, June, July}
20. {2, 4, 6, 8, 10, . . .}
21. {3, 6, 9, 12, . . . , 999}

In 22–24, use the symbol = or $\neq$ to write a true sentence about the two sets.

22. A = {5, 10, 15, 20} and B = {20, 15, 10, 5}
23. C = {1, 3, 5} and D = {1, 3, 5, 7}
24. K = {0} and L = $\emptyset$

In 25–27, **(a)** tell whether or not there is a one-to-one correspondence between the two sets and **(b)** state whether the two sets are equivalent.

25. {6, 7, 8, 9} and {1, 2, 3, 4}
26. {a, b, c, d} and {x, y, z}
27. {Tom, Dick, Harry} and {Sally, Mary, Sue}

In 28 and 29, show two ways in which the elements of set A can be matched in one-to-one correspondence with the elements of set B.

28. A = {Tom, Dick, Harry} and B = {Sally, Mary, Sue}
29. A = {R, S, T} and B = {D, E, F}

30. **a.** If set A has three elements and set B has four elements, can set A and set B be put into one-to-one correspondence?
    b. Explain the answer given in part **a**.

In 31–42, tell whether the sentence is true or false. Justify the answer.

31. {Sam, Bill} is a subset of {Joan, Bill, Sam}
32. {6, 7, 8, 9} is a subset of {6, 7, 8}
33. $\emptyset$ is a subset of {10, 11, 12}
34. {2, 4, 6} $\subset$ {1, 2, 3, 4, 5, 6}
35. {odd natural numbers} $\subset$ {odd natural numbers}
36. {rectangles} $\subset$ {polygons}
37. {squares} $\subset$ {rectangles}
38. {Y, E, A, S} $\subset$ {E, A, S, Y}
39. $4 \in \{n \mid n$ is a counting number}
40. $4 \in \{x \mid x$ is an odd number}

41. $5 \notin \{y \mid y \text{ is an even number}\}$
42. $5 \in \{y \mid y \text{ is an odd number greater than } 10\}$

In 43–46, $A = \{13, 14, 15\}$. Write all the subsets of A that meet the indicated condition.

43. contain one element
44. contain two elements
45. contain three elements
46. contain no elements

In 47–54, list all the subsets of B.

47. $B = \{5\}$
48. $B = \{3, 7\}$
49. $B = \{m, l, g\}$
50. $B = \{ \}$
51. $B = \{0\}$
52. $B = \{\text{true, false}\}$
53. $B = \{1, 2, 3, 4\}$
54. $B = \{5, 10, 15, 20\}$

In 55–58, represent the set by listing its members.

55. $\{x \mid x \text{ is a whole number less than } 6\}$
56. $\{n \mid n \text{ is an even whole number between } 1 \text{ and } 9\}$
57. $\{y \mid y \text{ is an odd whole number less than } 10\}$
58. $\{n \mid n \text{ is a natural number greater than } 4 \text{ and less than } 12\}$

12 OPERATIONS WITH SETS

Just as we have seen operations in arithmetic and in geometry, there are operations with sets.

Intersection of Sets

Set A and set B are said to *intersect* if there is at least one element common to both A and B.

For example, if $A = \{1, 2, 3, 4, 5\}$ and $B = \{2, 4, 6, 8, 10\}$, then set A and set B intersect because they have the elements 2 and 4 in common.

The *intersection of two sets*, A and B, denoted by $A \cap B$, is the set of all elements that belong to both sets, A and B. For example:

1. When $A = \{1, 2, 3, 4, 5\}$ and $B = \{2, 4, 6, 8, 10\}$, then the intersection of A and B, written $A \cap B$, is $\{2, 4\}$.

2. In the figure, two line segments called $\overline{AB}$ and $\overline{CD}$ intersect. The intersection is a set that has one element, point E. We write the intersection of the segments in the example shown as $\overline{AB} \cap \overline{CD} = E$.

Line segments are sets of points. In fact, any geometric figure can be considered as a set of points. The intersection of any two geometric figures will be a set of points common to both.

Two sets, C and D, are *disjoint sets* if set C and set D do not intersect.

For example, the sets {1, 3, 5, 7} and {2, 4, 6, 8} are disjoint sets because they do not have a common element. When sets C and D are disjoint, then their intersection set, which has no elements, is the empty set. We can, therefore, write $C \cap D = \emptyset$.

For example, when C = {1, 3, 5, 7} and D = {2, 4, 6, 8}, then $C \cap D = \emptyset$.

Remember that a *binary operation* was shown symbolically as $a * b = c$, where two elements called "a" and "b," under some operation called "$*$," were replaced by a unique element called "c." When we write {1, 2, 3} $\cap$ {1, 3, 5} = {1, 3}, the elements called a, b, and c are sets themselves and the operation is intersection, shown by the symbol $\cap$. We can think of {1, 2, 3}, {1, 3, 5}, and {1, 3} as elements of a larger set, perhaps {1, 2, 3, 5}. These elements are some of the subsets of {1, 2, 3, 5}. In this way we are taking two elements (or subsets) from a universal set and we are performing an operation that results in assigning a unique element (or subset) from that universal set. Intersection is a binary operation for a universal set.

Union of Sets

The **union** of two sets, A and B, denoted by $A \cup B$, is the set of all elements that belong to set A or to set B, or to both set A and set B. For example:

1. If A = {1, 2, 3, 4, 5} and B = {2, 4, 6, 8}, then the union of A and B, written $A \cup B$, is {1, 2, 3, 4, 5, 6, 8}.

Note that an element is not repeated in the union of two sets if it is an element of each set.

2. In the figure, both region R (vertical shading) and region S (horizontal shading) represent sets of points. The shaded parts of both regions represent $R \cup S$, and the cross-hatched part where both regions overlap represents $R \cap S$.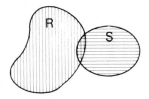

3. If A = {1, 2} and B = {1, 2, 3, 4, 5}, then the union of A and B is {1, 2, 3, 4, 5}. We can write $A \cup B$ = {1, 2, 3, 4, 5}, or $A \cup B = B$. Once again we have an example of a *binary operation*, where the elements (or subsets) are taken from a universal set and where the operation is "union," written symbolically as $\cup$.

Complement of a Set

To discuss the complement of a set A, it is necessary to know the universal set U. The *complement* of a set A, denoted by $\overline{A}$, is the set of all elements that belong to the universe U but do not belong to set A.

For example:

1. If $A = \{3, 4, 5\}$ and the universe $U = \{1, 2, 3, 4, 5\}$, then the complement of A, written $\overline{A}$, is $\{1, 2\}$ because 1 and 2 belong to the universal set U but do not belong to set A.

2. If the universe is {whole numbers} and $A = $ {even whole numbers}, then $\overline{A} = $ {odd whole numbers} because the odd whole numbers belong to the universal set but do not belong to set A.

3. In the figure shown, the rectangular plate, before it is stamped out by a machine, represents the universe. The keyhole punched out represents set A. The shaded region represents the complement of A, written $\overline{A}$. The complement of A corresponds to the metal plate found on the door after the keyhole has been stamped out.

Although it seems at first that only one set is being considered in writing the complement of A as $\overline{A}$, there are two sets. This suggests a binary operation, where the universe U and set A are the "a" and "b" elements, where "complement" is the operation "∗," and where the unique result is $\overline{A}$, the "c" element.

Just as we used an easier form to write exponents and powers, we use an easier symbolism here called $\overline{A}$.

The complement of any universe is the null set or empty set, written $\overline{U} = \{\ \}$.

| MODEL PROBLEM |

If $U = \{1, 2, 3, 4, 5, 6, 7\}$, $A = \{6, 7\}$, and $B = \{3, 5, 7\}$, determine $\overline{A} \cap \overline{B}$.

Solution

$U = \{1, 2, 3, 4, 5, 6, 7\}$

Since $A = \{6, 7\}$, then $\overline{A} = \{1, 2, 3, 4, 5\}$.

Since $B = \{3, 5, 7\}$, then $\overline{B} = \{1, 2, 4, 6\}$.

Since 1, 2, and 4 are elements in both $\overline{A}$ and $\overline{B}$, we can write:

$$\overline{A} \cap \overline{B} = \{1, 2, 4\} \quad Ans.$$

| EXERCISES |

In 1-8, $A = \{1, 2, 3\}$, $B = \{3, 4, 5, 6\}$, $C = \{1, 3, 4, 6\}$. List the elements of the given sets.

1. $A \cap B$
5. $B \cap C$
2. $A \cap C$
6. $B \cap \emptyset$
3. $A \cup B$
7. $B \cup C$
4. $A \cup C$
8. $B \cup \emptyset$

9. For the sets A, B, and C given in problems 1 to 8, list the elements of the smallest possible universal set of which A, B, and C are all subsets.

In 10-17, let the universe $= \{1, 2, 3, 4, 5\}$ and subsets $A = \{1, 5\}$, $B = \{2, 5\}$, $C = \{2\}$. List the elements of the given sets.

10. $\overline{A}$
14. $A \cap B$
11. $\overline{B}$
15. $A \cup \overline{B}$
12. $\overline{C}$
16. $\overline{A} \cap \overline{B}$
13. $A \cup B$
17. $\overline{A} \cup \overline{B}$

In 18-33, the universe $U = \{2, 4, 6, 8\}$. Subsets include $A = \{2, 4\}$, $B = \{2, 4, 8\}$, $C = \{8\}$, $D = \{6, 8\}$. Indicate the answer to each set operation by writing the capital letter that names the resulting set. (Example: $A \cap B = A$.) If the result is the null set, write $\emptyset$.

18. $A \cup C$
22. $A \cap C$
26. $B \cap D$
30. $A \cup D$
19. $B \cup C$
23. $B \cap C$
27. $\overline{A}$
31. $B \cup D$
20. $C \cup D$
24. $C \cap D$
28. $\overline{A} \cap D$
32. $B \cap U$
21. $A \cup A$
25. $A \cap A$
29. $\overline{D} \cup B$
33. $B \cup U$

34. Suppose set A has two elements and set B has three elements.
    a. What is the greatest number of elements that $A \cup B$ can have?
    b. What is the least number of elements that $A \cup B$ can have?
    c. What is the greatest number of elements that $A \cap B$ can have?
    d. What is the least number of elements that $A \cap B$ can have?

chapter two

Algebraic Expressions and Open Sentences

1 TRANSLATING VERBAL PHRASES INTO ALGEBRAIC LANGUAGE

A machine can produce 25 articles in one day. The number of articles the machine can produce would be:

in one day:	25 × 1
in two days:	25 × 2
in three days:	25 × 3
in four days:	25 × 4
in five days:	25 × 5

Observe that each of these expressions is of the form $25 \times n$, where n may represent a member of the set $\{1, 2, 3, 4, 5\}$. We call "n" a *variable*. A variable is called a placeholder because it represents any member of a given set. The set whose members the variable may represent is called the *domain* or the *replacement set* of the variable. In the previous discussion the domain is the set $\{1, 2, 3, 4, 5\}$.

An expression or mathematical phrase that contains one or more variables is called an *open expression* or *open phrase*. For example, $25 \times n$ is an open phrase because we do not know what number $25 \times n$ represents until we know what number n represents, that is, the value of n. An open phrase such as $25 \times n$ is also called an *algebraic expression*.

In Chapter 1 we saw how number relationships could be expressed with mathematical symbols. Now we will see how verbal phrases can be translated into the language of algebra. In algebra we use letters to represent variables and we use symbols to represent operations on numbers.

Verbal Phrases Involving Addition

5 + 4 means that 5 and 4 are to be added.

$a + b$ means that a and b are to be added.

The algebraic expression $a + b$ may be used to represent several different verbal phrases, such as:

a plus b	a and b are added	a is increased by b
the sum of a and b	b is added to a	b more than a

When we say "7 exceeds 5 by 2," we mean that 7 is 2 more than 5, or $7 = 5 + 2$. If we wish to write a number that exceeds 10 by 4, we write a number that is 4 more than 10, namely, $(10 + 4)$, or 14. To write a number that exceeds a by b, we write a number that is b more than a, or $a + b$.

Verbal Phrases Involving Subtraction

5 – 4 means from 5 subtract 4.

$a - b$ means from a subtract b.

The algebraic expression $a - b$ may be used to represent several different verbal phrases, such as:

a minus b	the difference between a and b	b subtracted from a
a decreased by b	a diminished by b b less than a	a reduced by b

Verbal Phrases Involving Multiplication

5 × 4 and 5 · 4 mean that 5 and 4 are to be multiplied.

$a \times b$ and $a \cdot b$ mean that a and b are to be multiplied.

The algebraic expression $a \times b$, or $a \cdot b$, may be used to represent several different verbal phrases, such as:

a times b	the product of a and b	b multiplied by a

Caution: Do not confuse "×," the symbol for multiplication, with the letter "x."

In algebra multiplication may be indicated in several ways. For example, to write in symbols that 7 and t are to be multiplied, we can use the following methods:

1. $7 \times t$, using the symbol × between 7 and t.
2. $7 \cdot t$, using a raised center dot between 7 and t. (Be careful not to confuse the dot with a decimal point.)
3. $7t$, omitting the multiplication symbol and placing 7 and t next to each other. Note that this cannot be done with numbers of arithmetic. If we wish to multiply 5 and 4, we *may not* place the 5 next

to the 4 and write 54. We know that 54 means the number fifty-four, whereas 5 × 4 is a numeral that names the same number as twenty.
4. $7(t)$, $(7)t$, $(7)(t)$, placing the 7 and t next to each other and enclosing one or both in parentheses.

Similarly there are many ways in which we may write in symbols that a and b are to be multiplied: $a \cdot b$, ab, $(a)(b)$, $a(b)$. Although we may write $a \times b$ to represent the multiplication, it is best to avoid this form since "×" can be confused with the letter "x."

Verbal Phrases Involving Division

$5 \div 4$ and $\dfrac{5}{4}$ mean that 5 is to be divided by 4.

$a \div b$ and $\dfrac{a}{b}$ mean that a is to be divided by b.

The symbols $a \div 4$ and $\dfrac{a}{4}$ may mean one-fourth of a as well as a divided by 4.

In some verbal phrases we can use a comma to prevent misreading. For example, in "the product of x and y, decreased by 2," the comma after y tells us that the phrase means $(xy) - 2$ and not $x(y - 2)$.

| MODEL PROBLEMS |

1. Use mathematical symbols to translate each of the following verbal phrases into algebraic language:

Answers

a. w more than 3 — $3 + w$
b. r decreased by 2 — $r - 2$
c. the product of $5r$ and s — $5rs$
d. 4 divided by x — $4 \div x$
e. twice x decreased by 10 — $2x - 10$
f. 25, diminished by 4 times n — $25 - 4n$
g. the sum of t and u, divided by 6 — $\dfrac{t + u}{6}$
h. 100 decreased by twice $(x + 5)$ — $100 - 2(x + 5)$

2. Represent in algebraic language:

a. a number that exceeds 5 by m — $5 + m$
b. a number that x exceeds by 5 — $x - 5$
c. twice the sum of x and y — $2(x + y)$

| EXERCISES |

In 1–28, use mathematical symbols to translate the verbal phrase into algebraic language.

1. y plus 8
2. 8 plus y
3. r minus 4
4. 4 minus r
5. 7 times x
6. x times 7
7. x divided by 10
8. 10 divided by x
9. product of 6 and d
10. c decreased by 6
11. 15 added to b
12. one-tenth of w
13. the sum of b and 8
14. x diminished by y
15. the product of x and y
16. the quotient of s and t
17. 12 increased by a
18. 5 less than d
19. 8 divided by y
20. y multiplied by 10
21. the product of $2c$ and $3d$
22. t more than w
23. one-third of z
24. twice the difference of p and q
25. a number that exceeds m by 4
26. one half of the sum of L and W
27. 5 times x, increased by 2
28. 10 decreased by twice a

In 29–39, using the letter n to represent the variable "a number," write the verbal phrase in algebraic language.

29. a number increased by 2
30. 20 more than a number
31. 8 increased by a number
32. a number decreased by 6
33. 2 less than a number
34. 3 times a number
35. three-fourths of a number
36. 4 times a number, increased by 3
37. 10 times a number, decreased by 2
38. 3 less than twice a number
39. the product of 5 more than a number, and 4

In 40–45, translate the verbal phrase into algebraic language, representing the two numbers by L and W, with L being the larger.

40. the sum of the two numbers
41. the product of the two numbers
42. the larger number decreased by the smaller number
43. the smaller number divided by the larger number
44. the sum of twice the larger number and twice the smaller number
45. 10 times the smaller number, decreased by 6 times the larger number

2 PROBLEMS INVOLVING VARIABLES REPRESENTED BY LETTERS

A knowledge of arithmetic is important in algebra. Since the variables represent numbers that are familiar to us, it will be helpful to relate algebraic problems to similar arithmetic problems. If we can handle the problem involving numbers, then we can use the same method to solve the related problem involving letters.

■ **PROCEDURE.** To solve problems in which letters represent variables:

1. Write a similar problem involving numbers of arithmetic.

2. Solve this arithmetic problem.

3. Use the same method to solve the problem involving the letters.

| MODEL PROBLEMS |

In 1-3, represent in algebraic language:

1. a weight that is 40 lb. heavier than p lb. $p + 40$ lb.   *Ans.*

2. a distance that is 20 meters shorter than x meters. $x - 20$ m   *Ans.*

3. a sum of money that is twice d dollars. $2d$ dollars   *Ans.*

4. Represent the value of n hats, each worth d dollars.

Solution: First write a similar problem. Represent the value of 5 hats, each worth 10 dollars. We can solve this problem by multiplying the number of hats, 5, by the value of each hat, 10 dollars, giving 5×10, or 50 dollars. Similarly, in the original problem, the value of all the hats will be the number of hats, n, times the value of each hat, d, which is $n \cdot d$, or nd dollars.   *Ans.*

| EXERCISES |

In 1-18, represent the answer in algebraic language, using the variable mentioned in the problem.

1. The number of kilometers traveled by a bus is represented by x. If a train traveled 200 kilometers farther than the bus, represent the number of kilometers traveled by the train.

2. Mr. Gold invested $1000 in stocks. If he lost d dollars when he sold them, represent the amount he received for them.

3. The cost of a fur coat is 5 times the cost of a cloth coat. If the cloth coat costs x dollars, represent the cost of the fur coat.

4. The length of a rectangle is represented by L. If the width of the rectangle is one-half of its length, represent its width.

5. After 12 centimeters had been cut from a piece of lumber, there were c centimeters left. Represent the length of the original piece of lumber.

6. Paul and Martha saved 100 dollars. If the amount saved by Paul is represented by x, represent the amount saved by Martha.

7. The sum of two numbers is s. If one number is represented by x, represent the other number in terms of s and x.

8. A suit costs $150. Represent the cost of n suits.

9. A ballpoint pen sells for 39 cents. Represent the cost of x pens.

10. Represent the cost of t feet of lumber that sells for g cents a foot.

11. If Hilda weighed 45 kilograms, represent her weight after she had lost x kilograms.

12. Ronald, who weighs c pounds, is d pounds overweight. Represent the number of pounds Ronald should weigh.

13. A man spent $250 for a suit and a coat. If he spent y dollars for the coat, represent the amount he spent for the suit.

14. A man bought an article for c dollars and sold it at a profit of $25. Represent the amount for which he sold it.

15. The width of a rectangle is represented by W meters. Represent the length of the rectangle if it exceeds the width by 8 meters.

16. The width of a rectangle is x centimeters. Represent the length of the rectangle if it exceeds twice the width by 3 centimeters.

17. If a plane travels 550 kilometers per hour, represent the distance it will travel in h hours.

18. If an auto traveled for 5 hours at an average rate of r kilometers per hour, represent the distance it has traveled.

19. Represent algebraically the number of:
    a. centimeters in m meters
    b. meters in i centimeters
    c. days in w weeks
    d. weeks in d days
    e. hours in d days
    f. days in h hours
    g. feet in c inches
    h. grams in k kilograms

20. Represent the total number of days in w weeks and d days.

21. Represent the number of baseballs you can buy with c dollars if each baseball costs m dollars.

22. Represent the total number of calories in x peanuts and y potato chips if each peanut contains 15 calories and each potato chip contains 18 calories.

23. Represent the total cost of r liters of oil and s liters of gasoline if a liter of oil costs $1.65 and a liter of gasoline costs $.30.

24. The charges for a long-distance telephone call are $.45 for the first 3 minutes and $.09 for each additional minute. Represent the cost of a telephone call that lasts m minutes when m is greater than 3.

25. The charges for a taxi ride are $.75 for the first $\frac{1}{7}$ of a mile and $.10 for each additional $\frac{1}{7}$ of a mile. Represent the cost of a taxi ride of m miles.

3 UNDERSTANDING THE MEANING OF SOME VOCABULARY USED IN ALGEBRA

Term

A *term* is a numeral, a variable, or both numerals and variables that are connected by multiplication signs. For example, 5, x, $4y$, and $8ab$ are terms. In an algebraic expression such as $4a + 2b - 5c$, which has more than one term, the terms $4a$, $2b$, and $5c$ are separated by + and – signs.

Factors of a Product

If an indicated product involves two or more numbers, each of the numbers, as well as the product of any of them, is a *factor* of the product. For example, in the product $3xy$, the factors are $1, 3, x, y, 3x, 3y, xy$, and $3xy$. Note that when we factor whole numbers, we usually concern ourselves only with factors that are whole numbers.

Coefficient

In a product any factor is the *coefficient* of the remaining factor or factors.

For example, in the product $4ab$:

> 4 is the coefficient of ab
> $4a$ is the coefficient of b
> $4b$ is the coefficient of a
> ab is the coefficient of 4

When a numeral and variables are factors of a product, the numeral is called the *numerical coefficient* of the product. For example, in $8y$ the numerical coefficient is 8; in $4ab$ the numerical coefficient is 4.

When the word "coefficient" is used alone, it usually means the numerical coefficient. For example, in the term $7rs$ the coefficient is 7.

Since x names the same number as $1 \cdot x$, we sometimes say that the coefficient of x is understood to be 1. Likewise, we may say that the coefficient of ab is understood to be 1.

Base, Exponent, Power

We know that 4×4 may be written 4^2, which is read "four squared," or "4 to the second power." The product $s \cdot s$ may be written s^2, which is read "s square," "s squared," or "s to the second power." In s^2, the small ^{2} above and to the right of s tells us that s is to be used as a factor 2 times.

The product $c \cdot c \cdot c$ may be written c^3, which is read "c cube," "c cubed," or "c to the third power."

In a^4, which is read "a to the fourth power," "a" is called the *base*, 4 is called the *exponent*, and "a^4" is called the *power*. Remember that the *base* is the number that is used as a factor two or more times; the *exponent* is the number that tells how many times the base is to be used as a factor. We will agree that $a^1 = a$.

Note that an exponent refers only to the base that is directly to the left of it. Thus:

$c^3 d^4$ means $cccdddd$ cd^4 means $cdddd$ $5d^2$ means $5dd$

If we wish to use $5d$ as a factor 2 times, that is, $(5d)(5d)$, we write $(5d)^2$. Notice how the meanings of $5d^2$ and $(5d)^2$ differ: $5d^2$ means $5dd$, whereas $(5d)^2$ means $(5d)(5d)$, which we will learn is equal to $25d^2$.

MODEL PROBLEM

Name the numerical coefficient, base, and exponent in the term $4x^5$.

Answer: The numerical coefficient is 4, the base is x, and the exponent is 5.

EXERCISES

In 1–6, name the factors (other than 1) of each product.

1. xy 2. $3a$ 3. $5n$ 4. $7mn$ 5. $13xy$ 6. $11st$

In 7–12, name the numerical coefficient of x.

7. $8x$ 8. $(5 + 2)x$ 9. $\frac{1}{2}x$ 10. x 11. $1.4x$ ·   12. $2 + 7x$

In 13–18, name the base and exponent in the term.

13. m^2 14. s^3 15. t 16. 10^6 17. $(5y)^4$ 18. $(x + y)^5$

In 19–31, write each expression, using exponents.

19. $m \cdot m \cdot m$
20. $b \cdot b \cdot b \cdot b \cdot b$
21. $e \cdot e \cdot e \cdot e$
22. $4 \cdot x \cdot x \cdot x \cdot x$
23. $\pi \cdot r \cdot r$
24. $a \cdot a \cdot a \cdot a \cdot b \cdot b$
25. $7 \cdot r \cdot r \cdot r \cdot s \cdot s$
26. $9 \cdot c \cdot c \cdot c \cdot d$
27. $(6a)(6a)(6a)$
28. $(x + y)(x + y)$
29. $(a - b)(a - b)(a - b)$
30. the square of $(b - 5)$
31. the fourth power of $(m + 2n)$

In 32–37, write the term as a product without using exponents.

32. r^6 33. $5x^4$ 34. $x^3 y^5$ 35. $4a^4 b^2$ 36. $3c^2 d^3 e$ 37. $(3y)^5$

4   EVALUATING ALGEBRAIC EXPRESSIONS

The algebraic expression $3n + 1$ represents an unspecified number. It is only when we replace the variable n by a specific number that $3n + 1$ represents a specific number. For example, suppose that the domain of n is $\{1, 2, 3\}$. The specific numbers that $3n + 1$ represents (the values of $3n + 1$) can be found as follows:

$$\text{If } n = 1, \ 3n + 1 = 3(1) + 1 = 3 + 1 = 4.$$

$$\text{If } n = 2, \ 3n + 1 = 3(2) + 1 = 6 + 1 = 7.$$

$$\text{If } n = 3, \ 3n + 1 = 3(3) + 1 = 9 + 1 = 10.$$

When we determine the number that an algebraic expression represents for specified values of its variables, we are *evaluating the algebraic expression*; that is, we are finding its value or values.

■ **PROCEDURE.**   To evalute an algebraic expression:

1. Replace the variables by their specific values.
2. Simplify any number expressions that may be included within symbols of grouping such as parentheses. Remember to simplify the number expression in the innermost symbols of grouping first.
3. Simplify any powers and roots. (Roots will be studied later.)
4. Do all multiplications and divisions, performing them in order from left to right.
5. Do all additions and subtractions, performing them in order from left to right.

5 EVALUATING ALGEBRAIC EXPRESSIONS INVOLVING ADDITION, SUBTRACTION, MULTIPLICATION, AND DIVISION

1. Evaluate $50 - 3x$ when $x = 7$.

How to Proceed	*Solution*
(1) Write the expression.	$50 - 3x$
(2) Replace the variable by its given value.	$= 50 - 3(7)$
(3) Do the multiplication.	$= 50 - 21$
(4) Do the subtraction.	$= 29$ *Ans.*

2. Evaluate $\dfrac{5r}{3} + \dfrac{7s}{2} - \dfrac{t}{5}$ when $r = 6$, $s = 4$, and $t = 15$.

How to Proceed	*Solution*
(1) Write the expression.	$\dfrac{5r}{3} + \dfrac{7s}{2} - \dfrac{t}{5}$
(2) Replace the variables by the given values.	$= \dfrac{5(6)}{3} + \dfrac{7(4)}{2} - \dfrac{15}{5}$
(3) Do the multiplications.	$= \dfrac{30}{3} + \dfrac{28}{2} - \dfrac{15}{5}$
(4) Do the divisions.	$= 10 + 14 - 3$
(5) Do the addition and subtraction.	$= 21$ *Ans.*

EXERCISES

In 1–24, find the numerical value of the expression. Use $a = 8$, $b = 6$, $d = 3$, $x = 4$, $y = 5$, and $z = 1$.

1. $5a$
2. $9b$
3. $\dfrac{1}{2}x$
4. $.3y$
5. $a + 3$
6. $7 + y$

7. $a - 2$
8. $5 - y$
9. $a - b$
10. ax
11. $3xy$
12. $\dfrac{2b}{3}$

13. $\dfrac{3bd}{9}$
14. $2x + 9$
15. $3y - b$

16. $20 - 4z$
17. $5x + 2y$
18. $ab - dx$

19. $a + 5d + 3x$
20. $9y + 6b - d$
21. $ab - d - xy$

22. $\dfrac{7y}{5} + \dfrac{b}{2}$ **23.** $\dfrac{dy}{3z} - \dfrac{z}{d}$ **24.** $\dfrac{xy}{z} - \dfrac{y}{x} - \dfrac{dy}{xz}$

25. Evaluate $\dfrac{9}{5}C + 32$ when:

    a. $C = 25$ **b.** $C = 40$ **c.** $C = 55$ **d.** $C = 0$ **e.** $C = 100$

6   EVALUATING ALGEBRAIC EXPRESSIONS INVOLVING POWERS

1.   If $a = 5$, find the value of $3a^2$.

How to Proceed	*Solution*
(1) Write the expression.	$3a^2$
(2) Replace the variable by its given value.	$= 3(5)^2$
(3) Evaluate the power.	$= 3(5 \times 5) = 3(25)$
(4) Do the multiplication.	$= 75$ *Ans.*

2.   Evaluate $4x^3y^2$ when $x = 2$ and $y = 3$.

How to Proceed	*Solution*
(1) Write the expression.	$4x^3y^2$
(2) Replace the variables by their given values.	$= 4(2)^3(3)^2$
(3) Evaluate the powers.	$= 4(2 \times 2 \times 2)(3 \times 3) = 4(8)(9)$
(4) Do the multiplication.	$= 288$ *Ans.*

3.   Evaluate $x^2 - 5x + 4$ when $x = 7$.

How to Proceed	*Solution*
(1) Write the expression.	$x^2 - 5x + 4$
(2) Replace the variable by its given value.	$= (7)^2 - 5(7) + 4$
(3) Evaluate the power.	$= 49 - 5(7) + 4$
(4) Do the multiplication.	$= 49 - 35 + 4$
(5) Do the addition and subtraction.	$= 18$ *Ans.*

EXERCISES

In 1–30, find the numerical value of the expression. Use $a = 8$, $b = 6$, $d = 3$, $x = 4$, $y = 5$, and $z = 1$.

   1. a^2 **2.** x^2 **3.** b^3 **4.** y^3 **5.** d^4 **6.** z^5

7. $2x^2$ 8. $3b^2$ 9. $4d^3$ 10. $6z^5$ 11. $\dfrac{b^2}{9}$ 12. $\dfrac{1}{2}x^3$

13. $\dfrac{3}{4}x^3$ 14. a^2d 15. xy^2

16. $3z^2a$ 17. $2a^2b^3$ 18. $\dfrac{1}{4}x^2y^2$

19. $(2d)^2$ 20. $a^2 + b^2$ 21. $b^2 - y^2$
22. $a^2 + b^2 - d^2$ 23. $x^2 + x$ 24. $b^2 + 2b$
25. $y^2 - 4y$ 26. $2b^2 + b$ 27. $9a - a^2$
28. $x^2 + 3x + 5$ 29. $y^2 + 2y - 7$ 30. $2a^2 - 4a + 6$

31. Find the value of $x^2 - 8y$ when $x = 5$ and $y = \frac{1}{2}$.
32. Find the value of $r^2 + 4s$ when $r = 3$ and $s = .5$.

7 EVALUATING EXPRESSIONS CONTAINING PARENTHESES OR OTHER SYMBOLS OF GROUPING

1. Evaluate $a + (n - 1)d$ when $a = 40$, $n = 10$, and $d = 3$.

How to Proceed	*Solution*
(1) Write the expression.	$a + (n - 1)d$
(2) Replace the variables by their given values.	$= 40 + (10 - 1)(3)$
(3) Simplify the expression within the parentheses.	$= 40 + (9)(3)$
(4) Do the multiplication.	$= 40 + 27$
(5) Do the addition.	$= 67$ *Ans.*

2. Evaluate $(2x)^2 - 2x^2$ when $x = 4$.

How to Proceed	*Solution*
(1) Write the expression.	$(2x)^2 - 2x^2$
(2) Replace the variable by its given value.	$= (2 \times 4)^2 - 2(4)^2$
(3) Simplify the expression within the parentheses.	$= (8)^2 - 2(4)^2$
(4) Evaluate the powers.	$= 64 - 2(16)$
(5) Do the multiplication.	$= 64 - 32$
(6) Do the subtraction.	$= 32$ *Ans.*

| EXERCISES |

In 1–21, find the value of the expression. Use $w = 10$, $x = 8$, $y = 5$, and $z = 2$.

1. $2(x + 5)$ 2. $x(y - 2)$ 3. $3(2x + z)$

4. $4(2x - 3y)$ 5. $\frac{x}{2}(y + z)$ 6. $\frac{1}{2}x(y + z)$

7. $3y - (x - z)$ 8. $2x + 5(y - 1)$ 9. $2(x + z) - 5$

10. $3x^2$ 11. $(3x)^2$ 12. $y^2 + z^2$

13. $(y + z)^2$ 14. $w^3 - x^3$ 15. $(w - x)^3$

16. $3w^2 - 2x^2$ 17. $(3w - 2x)^2$ 18. $(3w)^2 - (2x)^2$

19. $(xy)^2$ 20. $(yw)^2$ 21. $(w^2)(x^2)$

22. Evaluate $\frac{5}{9}(F - 32)$ when:
    a. $F = 50$ b. $F = 77$ c. $F = 86$ d. $F = 32$ e. $F = 212$

8 TRANSLATING VERBAL SENTENCES INTO FORMULAS

A formula uses mathematical language to express the relationship between two or more variables. For example, a relationship that you have previously studied, "the area of a rectangle is equal to its length multiplied by its width," can be expressed by the formula $A = l \cdot w$. Here, l, w, and A are variables that represent the length, width, and area of the rectangle, respectively.

A *formula* is an algebraic expression that contains variables and states a rule for operating with these variables. Let us learn how to translate verbal sentences into formulas.

| MODEL PROBLEMS |

1. Write a formula for each of the following relationships:

   a. The perimeter P of a square is equal to 4 times the length of each side s.

   Answer: $P = 4s$

   b. The cost C of a number of articles is the product of the number of articles n and the price p of each article.

   Answer: $C = np$

c. The area A of a circle is equal to π times the square of the radius r.

Answer: $A = \pi r^2$

2. Write a formula that expresses the number of months m that there are in y years, in terms of y.

Solution: First discover the rule that states the relation between the variables m and y. Then write this rule as a formula.

Since there are 12 months in a year, the number of months m that there are in y years is equal to 12 times the number of years y.

Answer: $m = 12y$

| EXERCISES |

In 1–15, write a formula that expresses the relationship.

1. The total length l of 10 pieces of lumber, each m meters in length, is 10 times the length of each piece of lumber.
2. The selling price of an article, s, equals its cost c plus the margin m.
3. The perimeter p of a rectangle is equal to the sum of twice its length l and twice its width w.
4. The average M of three numbers, a, b, c, is their sum divided by 3.
5. The area A of a triangle is equal to one-half the length of the base b multiplied by the length of the altitude h.
6. The area A of a square is equal to the square of the length of a side s.
7. The volume V of a cube is equal to the cube of the length of an edge e.
8. The surface S of a cube is equal to 6 times the square of the length of an edge e.
9. The surface S of a sphere is equal to the product of 4π and the square of the radius r.
10. The average rate of speed, R, is equal to the distance that is traveled, D, divided by the time spent on the trip, T.
11. The Fahrenheit temperature F is 32° more than nine-fifths of the Celsius temperature C.
12. The Celsius temperature C is equal to five-ninths of the difference between the Fahrenheit temperature F and 32.
13. The dividend D equals the product of the divisor d and the quotient Q plus the remainder R.

14. A sales tax T that must be paid when an article is purchased is equal to 8% of the value of the article, V.

15. A salesman's weekly earnings E is equal to his weekly salary S increased by 2% of his total volume of sales, V.

In 16–23, each required formula will express one of the variables in terms of the others.

16. Write a formula for finding the number of trees, n, in an orchard containing r rows of t trees each.

17. Write the formula for the total number of seats, n, in the school auditorium, if it has two sections, each with r rows having s seats in each row.

18. Write a formula for the number of centimeters C in m meters.

19. Write a formula for the number of feet f in i inches.

20. Write a formula for the number of milliliters M in L liters.

21. A group of n persons in an automobile crosses the Hudson River on a ferry. Write a formula for the total ferry charge c in cents, if the charge is \$2.00 for the car and driver and t cents for each additional person.

22. Write a formula for the cost in cents c of a telephone conversation lasting 9 minutes if the charge for the first 3 minutes is x cents and the charge for each additional minute is y cents.

23. Write a formula for the cost in cents c of sending a telegram of 18 words if the cost of sending the first 10 words is a cents and each additional word costs b cents.

24. A gasoline dealer is allowed a profit of 12 cents a gallon for each gallon he sells. If he sells more than 25,000 gallons in a month, he is given an additional profit of 3 cents for every gallon over that number. Assuming that he always sells more than 25,000 gallons a month, express as a formula the number of dollars D in his monthly income in terms of the number N of gallons sold.

9 EVALUATING THE SUBJECT OF A FORMULA

The variable for which a formula is solved is called the *subject of the formula*. For example, P is the subject of $P = 4s$, the formula for the perimeter P of a square each of whose sides has a length represented by s.

If the values of all the variables of a formula except the subject are known, we can compute its value; that is, we can evaluate the subject of the formula.

■ **PROCEDURE.** To evaluate the subject of a formula:

1. Replace the other variables in the formula by their values.
2. Perform the indicated operations.

Let us recall the meanings of some geometric terms that you have met in your previous study of mathematics.

Evaluating Perimeter Formulas

Recall that the *perimeter* of a geometric figure is the sum of the lengths of its sides.

1. If $P = 3s$, find P when $s = 5$ ft.

Solution

$P = 3s$
$P = 3(5)$ $[s = 5]$
$P = 15$

Answer: 15 ft.

2. If $P = 2b + 2h$, find P when $b = 3$ cm and $h = 7$ cm.

Solution

$P = 2b + 2h$
$P = 2(3) + 2(7)$ $[b = 3, h = 7]$
$P = 6 + 14 = 20$

Answer: 20 cm

KEEP IN MIND

Examples of units that are used to measure lengths are the inch (in.), the foot (ft.), the yard (yd.), the mile (mi.), the millimeter (mm), the centimeter (cm), the meter (m), and the kilometer (km).

| **EXERCISES** |

1. The formula for the perimeter of a triangle is $P = a + b + c$. Find P when:
   a. $a = 12$ cm, $b = 8$ cm, $c = 6$ cm
   b. $a = 15$ in., $b = 10$ in., $c = 7$ in.
   c. $a = 4.5$ m, $b = 1.7$ m, $c = 3.8$ m
   d. $a = 7\frac{1}{2}$ ft., $b = 5\frac{3}{4}$ ft., $c = 6\frac{1}{2}$ ft.
   e. $a = 9$ ft., $b = 8$ ft., $c = 18$ in.

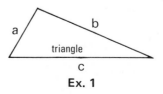

triangle

Ex. 1

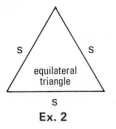

Ex. 2

2. The formula for the perimeter of an equilateral triangle is $P = 3s$. Find P when s equals: **a.** 6 ft.   **b.** 12 cm   **c.** 4.8 m
   d. $9\frac{1}{3}$ ft.   **e.** $8\frac{1}{2}$ in.

3. The formula for the perimeter of an isosceles triangle is $P = 2a + b$. Find P when:
   a. $a = 6$ m, $b = 4$ m
   b. $a = 8$ cm, $b = 7$ cm
   c. $a = 3\frac{1}{2}$ ft., $b = 5$ ft.
   d. $a = 7.5$ m, $b = 5.4$ m

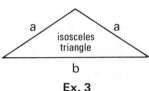

Ex. 3

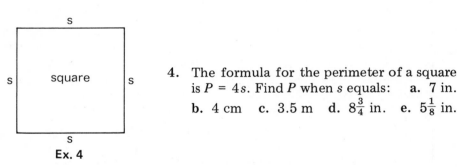

Ex. 4

4. The formula for the perimeter of a square is $P = 4s$. Find P when s equals: **a.** 7 in.
   b. 4 cm   **c.** 3.5 m   **d.** $8\frac{3}{4}$ in.   **e.** $5\frac{1}{8}$ in.

5. The formula for the perimeter of a rectangle is $P = 2b + 2h$. Find P when:
   a. $b = 20$ cm, $h = 9$ cm
   b. $b = 7.3$ m, $h = 6.9$ m
   c. $b = 5\frac{1}{2}$ in., $h = 5\frac{1}{4}$ in.
   d. $b = 5\frac{1}{3}$ ft., $h = 6\frac{1}{2}$ ft.

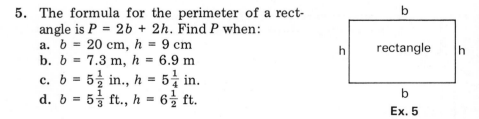

Ex. 5

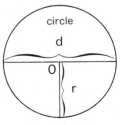

Ex. 6 and 7

6. The formula for the circumference of a circle is $C = \pi d$. Find C when $\pi = \frac{22}{7}$ and d equals:
   a. 14 ft.   **b.** 7 m   **c.** 21 cm
   d. 3 ft.   **e.** 10 in.

7. The formula for the circumference of a circle is $C = 2\pi r$. Find C when $\pi = 3.14$ and r equals:
   a. 10 ft.   **b.** 5 m   **c.** 40 cm
   d. 13 ft.   **e.** 5.6 in.

Evaluating Area Formulas

Recall that the *area* of a region is the number of unit squares it contains.

1. If $A = s^2$, find A when $s = 7$ yd.

2. If $A = \frac{1}{2}h(b + c)$, find A when $h = 3$ m, $b = 4$ m, and $c = 5$ m.

Solution

$A = s^2$

$A = (7)^2$ $[s = 7]$

$A = (7)(7) = 49$

Answer: $A = 49$ sq. yd.

Solution

$A = \frac{1}{2}h(b + c)$

$A = \frac{1}{2}(3)(4 + 5)$

     $[h = 3, b = 4, c = 5]$

$A = \frac{1}{2}(3)(9) = \frac{1}{2}(27) = 13.5$

Answer: $A = 13.5$ m^2

KEEP IN MIND

Examples of units that are used to measure areas are the square inch (sq. in.), the square foot (sq. ft.), the square yard (sq. yd.), the square mile (sq. mi.), the square millimeter (mm^2), the square centimeter (cm^2), the square meter (m^2), and the square kilometer (km^2).

EXERCISES

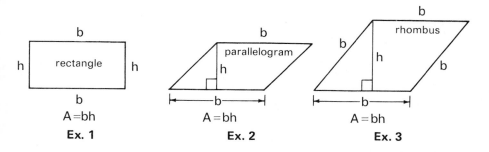

rectangle	parallelogram	rhombus
$A = bh$	$A = bh$	$A = bh$
Ex. 1	**Ex. 2**	**Ex. 3**

1. The formula for the area of a rectangle is $A = bh$. Find A when:

   a. $b = 10$ cm, $h = 8$ cm   **b.** $b = 15$ ft., $h = 13$ ft.

   c. $b = 7.5$ m, $h = 3.4$ m   **d.** $b = 8\frac{1}{2}$ ft., $h = 6$ ft.

   e. $b = 1$ m, $h = 40$ cm   **f.** $b = 4\frac{1}{3}$ yd., $h = 8$ ft.

2. The formula for the area of a parallelogram is $A = bh$. Find A when:

   a. $b = 8$ ft., $h = 12$ ft.

   b. $b = 11$ m, $h = 9$ m

   c. $b = 3.5$ m, $h = 6.4$ m

   d. $b = 7\frac{1}{2}$ in., $h = 8$ in.

   e. $b = 1$ m, $h = 10$ cm

   f. $b = 5\frac{1}{2}$ in., $h = 8\frac{1}{4}$ in.

3. The formula for the area of a rhombus (a parallelogram all of whose sides have the same length) is $A = bh$. Find A when:

   a. $b = 5$ m, $h = 3$ m

   b. $b = 7$ in., $h = 4.5$ in.

   c. $b = 10$ ft., $h = 8\frac{1}{2}$ ft.

   d. $b = 14.5$ cm, $h = 11.4$ cm

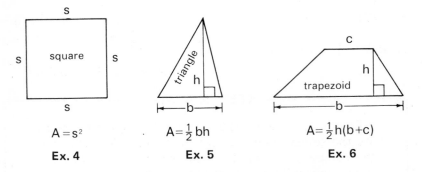

$A = s^2$	$A = \frac{1}{2}bh$	$A = \frac{1}{2}h(b+c)$
Ex. 4	Ex. 5	Ex. 6

4. The formula for the area of a square is $A = s^2$. Find A when s equals:

   a. 25 in.   b. 32 ft.   c. 9 cm   d. $2\frac{1}{2}$ ft.   e. 6.1 m

5. The formula for the area of a triangle is $A = \frac{1}{2}bh$. Find A when:

   a. $b = 10$ cm, $h = 6$ cm

   b. $b = 7$ ft., $h = 14$ ft.

   c. $b = 3$ yd., $h = 5$ yd.

   d. $b = 10.5$ m, $h = 7.6$ m

   e. $b = 3\frac{1}{2}$ in., $h = 8$ in.

   f. $b = 1$ ft., $h = 5\frac{1}{2}$ in.

6. The formula for the area of a trapezoid is $A = \frac{1}{2}h(b + c)$. Find A when:

   a. $h = 10$ cm, $b = 8$ cm, $c = 6$ cm

   b. $h = 9$ ft., $b = 14$ ft., $c = 8$ ft.

   c. $h = 5$ in., $b = 3\frac{1}{4}$ in., $c = \frac{3}{4}$ in.

   d. $h = 2$ m, $b = 1.8$ m, $c = 1.1$ m

Evaluating Formulas for Volumes of Solids

Recall that the *volume* of a solid is the number of unit cubes it contains.

Examples of unit cubes that are used to measure volumes are the cubic inch (cu. in.), the cubic foot (cu. ft.), the cubic centimeter (cm^3), and the cubic meter (m^3).

EXERCISES

1. The formula for the volume of a rectangular solid is $V = LWH$. Find V when:

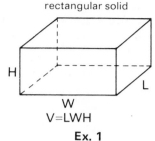
rectangular solid

   a. L = 5 ft., W = 4 ft., H = 7 ft.
   b. L = 8 cm, W = 7 cm, H = 5 cm
   c. L = 8.5 m, W = 4.2 m, H = 6.0 m
   d. L = $2\frac{1}{2}$ in., W = 8 in., H = $5\frac{1}{4}$ in.

V=LWH

Ex. 1

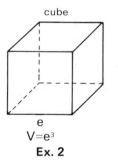
cube

e
V=e³

Ex. 2

2. The formula for the volume of a cube is $V = e^3$. Find V when e equals: a. 2 in.   b. 3 m   c. 8 cm   d. $\frac{1}{3}$ ft.   e. 1.5 in.

Finding Perimeters and Areas of Geometric Figures

The base of a rectangle measures 6 cm and its height measures 4 cm.
a. Find its perimeter.   b. Find its area.

a.   *How to Proceed*   *Solution*

(1) Write the proper perimeter formula. $P = 2b + 2h$ [b = 6, h = 4]
(2) Substitute the given values of the variables. $P = 2(6) + 2(4)$
(3) Perform the computation. $P = 12 + 8 = 20$

Answer: Perimeter = 20 cm

b.   *How to Proceed*   *Solution*

(1) Write the proper area formula. $A = bh$ [b = 6, h = 4]
(2) Substitute the given values of the variables. $A = (6)(4)$
(3) Perform the computation. $A = 24$

Answer: Area = 24 cm^2

| EXERCISES |

In 1–8: For each figure find (a) its perimeter and (b) its area. Recall that: (1) For figures such as the parallelogram and the rectangle, the opposite sides are equal in length. (2) For the square and the rhombus, all sides are equal in length.

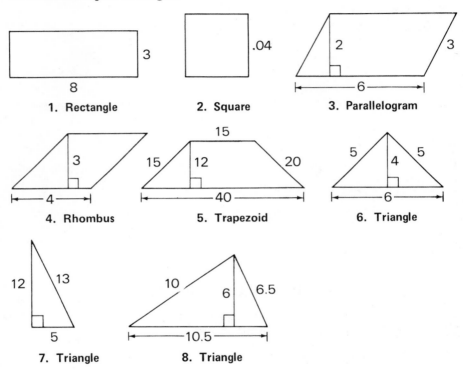

1. Rectangle   2. Square   3. Parallelogram

4. Rhombus   5. Trapezoid   6. Triangle

7. Triangle   8. Triangle

9. Find the area of a rectangle in which the base measures 20 cm and the height is half the length of the base.
10. Find the area of a parallelogram in which the height measures 14 inches and the base measures 6 inches more than the height.
11. Find the area of a triangle in which the base measures 8.5 cm and the height measures 3 cm less than the base.

In 12–16, the given measure represents the perimeter of a square. Find: (a) the length of a side of the square; (b) the area of the square.

12. 20 cm   **13.** 100 mm   **14.** 4 ft.   **15.** 2 in.   **16.** 2.8 m

In 17–29: a. Find the numerical measure of each length whose algebraic representation is given, when $x = 5$ and $y = 4$. b. Using the results found in part a, find the area of the geometric figure.

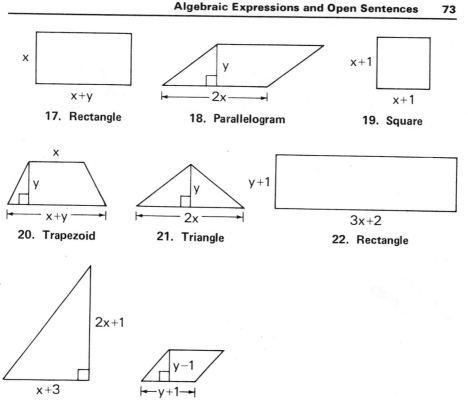

17. Rectangle

18. Parallelogram

19. Square

20. Trapezoid

21. Triangle

22. Rectangle

23. Triangle

24. Parallelogram

25. a triangle in which base = $3x + 1$; height = $2x$
26. a rectangle in which length = $2x$; width = $y + 2$
27. a square in which side = $2x$

28. a parallelogram in which base = $\dfrac{y}{2}$; height = $x + 7$

29. a trapezoid in which height = $x + 3$; bases are $y + 3$ and $x + y$

In 30–34: When $x = 3$, evaluate the volume of a cube each of whose edges is represented by the given expression.

30. x **31.** $x + 2$ **32.** $2x - 5$ **33.** $2(x - 1)$ **34.** $\dfrac{x}{2}$

In 35 and 36: When $x = 4$, evaluate the volume of a rectangular solid whose measures are represented.

35. length = $x + 2$, width = $x - 1$, height = $2x$
36. length = $2x + 1$, width = $\frac{1}{2}x$, height = $\frac{3}{4}x + 1$

10 OPEN SENTENCES AND SOLUTION SETS

Consider the following sentence: "A number + 3 = 7." If we use a letter such as n to represent "A number," this sentence can be written "$n + 3 = 7$." We cannot tell whether this sentence is true or false until more information, the number that "n" represents, is known. Such a sentence is called an *open sentence*. Let us assume that "n" can be replaced by an element of the set $\{1, 2, 3, 4, 5\}$. If "n" is replaced by 4, the resulting sentence "$4 + 3 = 7$" is a *true* sentence. Suppose "n" is replaced by any other element of the given set of numbers, for example, 1. Now, the resulting sentence "$1 + 3 = 7$" is a *false* sentence.

In the sentence "$n + 3 = 7$," n does not refer to a definite number, but to any one of a set of numbers. Since "n" is a symbol which holds a place for, or represents, any one of a given set of numbers, "n" is called a *variable*. The set $\{1, 2, 3, 4, 5\}$ is the *replacement set* or *domain* of the variable. It may also be called the *universe* or the *universal set*.

The subset of the domain of the variable consisting of those elements of the domain that make the open sentence true is called the *solution set*, or the *truth set*, of the open sentence.

See how we can discover the solution set of the open sentence $n + 3 = 7$ when the domain is $\{1, 2, 3, 4, 5\}$.

$$n + 3 = 7$$
If $n = 1$, then $1 + 3 = 7$ is a false sentence.
If $n = 2$, then $2 + 3 = 7$ is a false sentence.
If $n = 3$, then $3 + 3 = 7$ is a false sentence.
If $n = 4$, then $4 + 3 = 7$ is a *true* sentence.
If $n = 5$, then $5 + 3 = 7$ is a false sentence.

Observe that 4 is the only element of the domain that makes the open sentence a true sentence. Therefore, the solution set of the open sentence $n + 3 = 7$ is $\{4\}$.

This is sometimes written as $\{n \mid n + 3 = 7\} = \{4\}$, and is read "the set of all numbers n such that $n + 3 = 7$ is the set consisting of the number 4." We must remember that $n \in \{1, 2, 3, 4, 5\}$.

The elements of the domain of a variable are called the *values* of the variable. Thus, in the previous problem the values of the variable n were 1, 2, 3, 4, and 5. If a variable has only one value, it is called a *constant*.

If no member of a replacement set will make a sentence a true sentence, we say that the solution set is the *empty set*, or *null set*, represented by the symbol $\emptyset$.

MODEL PROBLEMS

1. Using the replacement set {0, 1, 2, 3}, find the solution set for the open sentence $2n > 3$.

   Solution: Replace the variable n in the open sentence $2n > 3$ by each member of the replacement set.

$$2n > 3$$
   If $n = 0$, then $2(0) > 3$, or $0 > 3$, is a false sentence.
   If $n = 1$, then $2(1) > 3$, or $2 > 3$, is a false sentence.
   If $n = 2$, then $2(2) > 3$, or $4 > 3$, is a *true* sentence.
   If $n = 3$, then $2(3) > 3$, or $6 > 3$, is a *true* sentence.

   Answer: Since $n = 2$ and $n = 3$ are replacements that make $2n > 3$ a true sentence, the solution set is {2, 3}.

   The answer may also be written as follows:

$$\{n \mid 2n > 3\} = \{2, 3\} \text{ when } n \in \{0, 1, 2, 3\}$$

2. Using the replacement set {1, 2, 3}, find the solution set for the open sentence $y + 5 = 9$.

   Solution: Replace the variable y in the open sentence $y + 5 = 9$ by each member of the replacement set.

$$y + 5 = 9$$
   If $y = 1$, then $1 + 5 = 9$ is a false sentence.
   If $y = 2$, then $2 + 5 = 9$ is a false sentence.
   If $y = 3$, then $3 + 5 = 9$ is a false sentence.

   Answer: Since no member of the replacement set changes the open sentence $y + 5 = 9$ into a true statement, we say that the solution set has no members. In other words, the solution set is the empty set, or null set, symbolized $\emptyset$.

   This answer may also be written as follows:

$$\{y \mid y + 5 = 9\} = \emptyset \text{ when } y \in \{1, 2, 3\}$$

EXERCISES

In 1–6, tell whether or not the sentences are open sentences.

1. $2 + 3 = 5 + 0$
2. $x + 10 = 14$
3. $y - 4 = 12$
4. $3 + 2 < 10 \times 0$
5. $n > 7$
6. $r < 5 + 2$

In 7–9, name the variable.

7. $x + 5 = 9$ **8.** $4y = 20$ **9.** $r - 6 = 12$

In 10–21, use the domain $\{0, 1, 2, 3, 4, 5\}$ to find all the replacements that will change the open sentence to a true sentence. If no replacement will make a true sentence, write *None*.

10. $n + 3 = 7$ **11.** $5 - n = 2$ **12.** $5z = 0$

13. $2m = 7$ **14.** $x - x = 0$ **15.** $n > 2$

16. $n + 3 > 9$ **17.** $2n + 1 < 8$ **18.** $\dfrac{n + 1}{2} = 2$

19. $\dfrac{2n + 1}{3} = 4$ **20.** $\dfrac{n}{4} > 1$ **21.** $\dfrac{3x}{2} < x$

In 22–29, using the replacement set $\{1, 2, 3, 4, 5, 6, 7, 8, 9, 10\}$, find the solution set.

22. $x + 6 = 9$ **23.** $8 - x = 5$ **24.** $2x + 1 = 24$ **25.** $16 = 18 - x$

26. $y > 9$ **27.** $4 < m$ **28.** $2m > 17$ **29.** $2x - 1 > 50$

In 30–37, using the domain $\{2, 2\frac{1}{2}, 3, 3\frac{1}{2}, 4, 4\frac{1}{2}\}$, find the solution set.

30. $x + 2 = 4\frac{1}{2}$ **31.** $2x = 7$ **32.** $5 - r = \frac{1}{2}$ **33.** $\dfrac{x}{2} = 2.25$

34. $y > 4$ **35.** $m < 3$ **36.** $2x > 8$ **37.** $3a < 4.5$

In 38–41, using the domain $\{2.1, 2.2, 2.3, 2.4, 2.5\}$, find the solution set.

38. $x + .1 = 2.4$ **39.** $3x - 4 = 2.3$ **40.** $\dfrac{y}{2} = 3.6$ **41.** $2x + 3 < 6.5$

In 42–47, determine the elements of the set if the domain of the variable is the one indicated.

42. $\{n \mid n + 2 = 5\}$, $n \in \{0, 1, 2, 3, 4, 5\}$
43. $\{x \mid x - 4 = 6\}$, $x \in \{7, 8, 9, 10\}$
44. $\{y \mid y - 1 < 8\}$, $y \in \{7, 8, 9, 10\}$
45. $\{r \mid 2r - 1 > 4\}$, $r \in \{1, 2, 3, 4\}$
46. $\{d \mid 9 - d = 5\}$, $d \in \{0, 1, 2, 3, 4, 5\}$
47. $\{x \mid 3x + 1 < 12\}$, $x \in \{0, 1, 2, 3, 4, 5\}$

11 GRAPHING THE SOLUTION SET OF AN OPEN SENTENCE CONTAINING ONE VARIABLE

Sometimes a picture of the solution set of an open sentence can help us to see the solution quickly. We can graph the solution set of an equation or an inequality by using the procedure we have already learned for graphing sets on a number line.

| MODEL PROBLEMS |

1. Find and graph the solution set of $n + 1 > 2$ when the domain is $\{0, 1, 2, 3, 4\}$.

    Solution:

    Step 1. Replace the variable n in the open sentence $n + 1 > 2$ by each element of the domain.

    $$n + 1 > 2$$
    If $n = 0$, then $0 + 1 > 2$ is a false sentence.
    If $n = 1$, then $1 + 1 > 2$ is a false sentence.
    If $n = 2$, then $2 + 1 > 2$ is a *true* sentence.
    If $n = 3$, then $3 + 1 > 2$ is a *true* sentence.
    If $n = 4$, then $4 + 1 > 2$ is a *true* sentence.

    Step 2. Since the values 2, 3, and 4 are the elements of the domain that change the open sentence to a true sentence, the solution set is $\{2, 3, 4\}$.

    Step 3. Graph the solution set $\{2, 3, 4\}$.

2. Using the replacement set $\{0, 1, 2, 3, 4\}$, find and graph the solution set for $2x + 1 = 5$.

    Solution:

    Step 1. If we replace the variable x in the open sentence $2x + 1 = 5$ by each element of the replacement set, we find that 2 is the only element that changes the open sentence to a true sentence. Hence, the solution set is $\{2\}$.

    Step 2. Graph the solution set $\{2\}$.

3. If the domain is {numbers of arithmetic}, graph the solution set of $x > 2$ or $x = 2$ (meaning x is greater than 2 or x is equal to 2; $x > 2$ or $x = 2$ may be written more compactly $x \geq 2$).

Solution:

Step 1. We see that 2 or any number greater than 2 are elements of the domain that change the open sentence to a true sentence. Therefore, the solution set is {2 and the numbers greater than 2}.

Step 2. Graph the solution set {2 and the numbers greater than 2}.

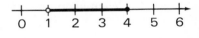

4.   Graph the solution set of $1 < x \leq 4; x \in$ {numbers of arithmetic}.

Solution:

Step 1. We see that 4 and any number that is greater than 1 and also less than 4 are elements of the domain that change the open sentence to a true sentence. Therefore, the solution set is {4 and the numbers between 1 and 4}.

Step 2. Graph the solution set {4 and the numbers between 1 and 4}. Note that the nondarkened circle at 1 indicates that 1 is not an element of the solution set.

EXERCISES

In 1–8, find and graph the solution set when the replacement set is {0, 1, 2, 3, 4, 5}.

1. $2n = 4$ 2. $n + 3 = 6$ 3. $2x - 1 = 7$ 4. $5x = 0$
5. $y > 4$ 6. $t \leq 1$ 7. $t - 3 > 1$ 8. $3t + 1 \leq 7$

In 9–16, find and graph the solution set when the domain is {0, 1, 2, 3, 4, 5, 6, 7, 8, 9, 10}.

9. $4x = 12$ 10. $y - 6 = 4$ 11. $2z + 8 = 8$ 12. $3a - 1 = 26$
13. $t \geq 5$ 14. $s + 2 < 11$ 15. $19 < 3x + 2$ 16. $14 > 5x + 1$

In 17–31, if $x \in$ {coordinates of points on the number line}, graph the solution set.

17. $x = 5$ 18. $x + 7 = 10$ 19. $x - 3 = 5$
20. $2x = 14$ 21. $2x + 1 = 13$ 22. $x > 4$
23. $x < 6$ 24. $2x > 6$ 25. $x \geq 5$
26. $x \leq 8$ 27. $1 < x < 5$ 28. $2 \leq x < 6$
29. $4 < x \leq 8$ 30. $0 \leq x \leq 7$ 31. $x + 3 = x + 3$

In 32–35, choose the inequality that is represented by the accompanying graph.

32. (1) $x < 3$
    (2) $x \leq 3$
    (3) $x \geq 3$
    (4) $x > 3$

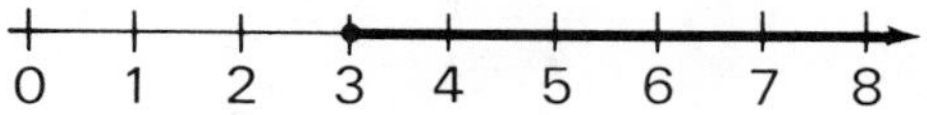

33. (1) $2 \leq x < 6$
    (2) $2 < x \leq 6$
    (3) $2 \leq x \leq 6$
    (4) $2 < x < 6$

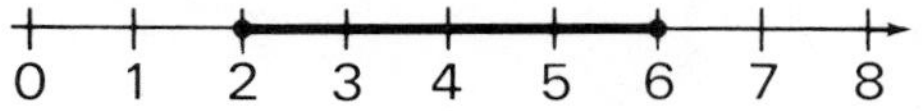

34. (1) $1 \leq x \leq 7$
    (2) $1 \leq x < 7$
    (3) $1 < x < 7$
    (4) $1 < x \leq 7$

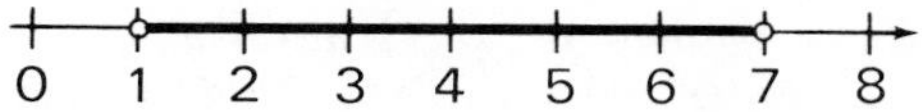

35. (1) $2 < x < 8$
    (2) $2 \leq x \leq 8$
    (3) $2 < x \leq 8$
    (4) $2 \leq x < 8$

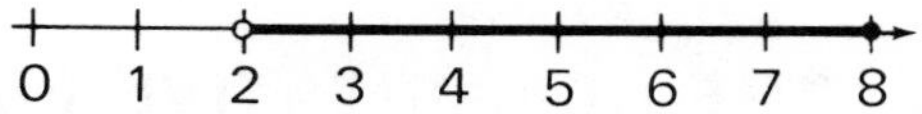

chapter three

Properties of Operations

In this chapter we will examine different properties of operations. When numbers behave in a certain way for an operation, we can describe this behavior as a property. The most important of these properties involve *addition* and *multiplication* because they will help us in every branch of mathematics that we will study this year.

1 THE COMMUTATIVE PROPERTY

To get to work, a commuter first takes a bus and then a train. If the bus ride is 4 miles and the train ride is 19 miles, we can add $4 + 19 = 23$ and say that the ride from home to work is 23 miles. To travel home, using the same route, the commuter must first take a train and then a bus. How far is the ride from work to home? You will probably answer 23 miles without performing the operation of $19 + 4$.

If you answered 23 without adding $19 + 4$, then you were using the truth of a principle that *the order in which two numbers are added does not affect the sum*. Actually you do not know that this is always true. Perhaps there are two numbers that will give different sums when their order of addition is changed. Mathematicians can prove that this will never happen and that this property of addition is always true. We will not study the proof at this time; we will simply assume that this property is true.

Commutative Property of Addition

When we add numbers of arithmetic, we assume that we may change the order in which two numbers are added without changing the sum. For example, $4 + 5 = 5 + 4$, and $\frac{1}{2} + \frac{1}{4} = \frac{1}{4} + \frac{1}{2}$. These examples illustrate the *commutative property of addition*.

In general, we assume that for every number a and every number b:

$$a + b = b + a$$

The name of this property is very much like the word "commuter."

When we check addition of two numbers by adding in the opposite direction, we are using the commutative property of addition.

Adding	Checking
3489 ↓	3489 ↑
1546	1546
5035	5035

Commutative Property of Multiplication

In the same way, when we multiply numbers of arithmetic, we assume that we may change the order of the factors without changing the product. For example, $5 \times 4 = 4 \times 5$, and $\frac{1}{2} \times \frac{1}{4} = \frac{1}{4} \times \frac{1}{2}$. These examples illustrate the *commutative property of multiplication*.

In general, we assume that for every number a and every number b:

$$a \cdot b = b \cdot a$$

We may also write:

$$ab = ba$$

When we check multiplication of two numbers by changing the order of the factors, we are using the commutative property of multiplication.

Multiplying	Checking
57	23
× 23	× 57
171	161
114	115
1311	1311

The General Commutative Property

Recall that $a * b = c$ was the general form used for a binary operation where a, b, and c were numbers in a set and where $*$ was the symbol used for the operation. If we can change the order of every pair of numbers, a and b, in the set without changing the answer obtained, c, then the *commutative property holds for the operation* $*$.

In general, when $a * b = c$ and $b * a = c$ for every number a and every number b, we may state:

$$a * b = b * a$$

However, if we can find one or more cases where $a * b$ and $b * a$ produce different answers, then we say that the operation $*$ does not have the commutative property. For example:

The operation *subtraction* does not have the commutative property because $5 - 4 \neq 4 - 5$.

The operation *division* does not have the commutative property because $8 \div 4 \neq 4 \div 8$.

It is easy to demonstrate that the commutative property *for a particular operation* does not hold. To do this, we merely find one example where the property does not work. However, at this time, we are not ready to show that the commutative property for a particular operation always holds. For now we will simply say "it appears" that an operation is commutative. For example:

3 avg 11 = 7   and 11 avg 3 = 7,   so 3 avg 11 = 11 avg 3.

2 avg 9 = $5\frac{1}{2}$ and 9 avg 2 = $5\frac{1}{2}$, so 2 avg 9 = 9 avg 2.

"It appears" that the commutative property holds for the operation of "averaging" two numbers. Or, for every a and b:

$$a \text{ avg } b = b \text{ avg } a$$

Many other operations can be tested for commutativity.

EXERCISES

In 1-8: a. Give a replacement for the question mark that makes the sentence true. b. Name the property illustrated in the sentence that is formed when the replacement is made.

1. 8 + 6 = 6 + ?
2. 17 × 5 = ? × 17
3. $\frac{1}{2}$ × 10 = 10 × ?
4. 4 avg ? = 12 avg 4
5. 2 + (5 + 7) = 2 + (? + 5)
6. (3 × 7) + 5 = (? × 3) + 5
7. 2 + (5 + 7) = (5 + 7) + ?
8. (3 × 7) + 5 = ? + (3 × 7)

In 9-14, replace the question mark with = or ≠ to make the sentence true.

9. 357 + 19 ? 19 + 357
10. 2 ÷ 1   ?   1 ÷ 2
11. 25 - 7   ?   7 - 25
12. (18)($2\frac{1}{2}$) ? ($2\frac{1}{2}$)(18)
13. $\frac{2}{5} + \frac{3}{10}$? $\frac{3}{10} + \frac{2}{5}$
14. 5 - 0   ?   0 - 5

15. a. Find the unique solution of 7 max 12.
    b. Find the unique solution of 12 max 7.
    c. Are the solutions in a and b the same or different?
    d. Find the unique solution of $1\frac{1}{2}$ max $1\frac{2}{3}$.
    e. Find the unique solution of $1\frac{2}{3}$ max $1\frac{1}{2}$.
    f. Does $1\frac{1}{2}$ max $1\frac{2}{3}$ = $1\frac{2}{3}$ max $1\frac{1}{2}$?
    g. Does it appear that the operation max is commutative?

2 THE ASSOCIATIVE PROPERTY

Associative Property of Addition

When adding three numbers, we assume that we may group the numbers in different ways without changing the sum. For example, $2 + 5 + 8$ can be found by first adding 2 and 5, getting 7, and then adding 7 to 8, getting 15. In the symbols of mathematics, this is written $(2 + 5) + 8 = 15$. Or, we may add 5 and 8, getting 13, and then add 13 to 2, getting 15. This is written $2 + (5 + 8) = 15$.

Therefore, we see that $(2 + 5) + 8 = 2 + (5 + 8)$. This example illustrates the *associative property of addition*.

In general, we assume that for every number a, every number b, and every number c:

$$(a + b) + c = a + (b + c)$$

Associative Property of Multiplication

In a similar way, to find a product that involves three factors, we first multiply any two factors and then multiply this result by the third factor. We assume that we do not change the product when we group the numbers differently. For example, to find the product $5 \times 4 \times 2$, we can multiply as follows:

$$5 \times 4 \times 2 = (5 \times 4) \times 2 = 20 \times 2 = 40$$

We can also multiply in a different way as follows:

$$5 \times 4 \times 2 = 5 \times (4 \times 2) = 5 \times 8 = 40$$

Therefore, $(5 \times 4) \times 2 = 5 \times (4 \times 2)$.

This example illustrates the *associative property of multiplication*.

In general, we assume that for every number a, every number b, and every number c:

$$(a \cdot b) \cdot c = a \cdot (b \cdot c)$$

We may also write: $(ab)c = a(bc)$

The General Associative Property

In a binary operation, symbolized by $*$, we work with two numbers at a time. In the order of operations we must simplify operations within parentheses first.

In general, for every number a, for every number b, and for every number c:

$$(a * b) * c = a * (b * c)$$

Remember, we need to find only one case where $(a * b) * c$ and $a * (b * c)$ produce different answers to say that the operation $*$ does not have the associative property. For example: The operation *subtraction* is not associative because $(10 - 8) - 2 \neq 10 - (8 - 2)$.

Also, the operation *division* is not associative.
$(8 \div 4) \div 2 = 2 \div 2 = 1$, but $8 \div (4 \div 2) = 8 \div 2 = 4$.
Therefore, $(8 \div 4) \div 2 \neq 8 \div (4 \div 2)$.

At present we are not ready to show that the associative property is true for a particular operation. At present we will simply say "it appears" that the operation is associative.

| EXERCISES |

In 1–8:   **a.** Give a replacement for the question mark that makes the sentence true.   **b.** Name the property illustrated in the sentence that is formed when the replacement is made.

1. $(3 \times 9) \times 15 = 3 \times (9 \times ?)$ 2. $(5 + ?) + 2 = 5 + (6 + 2)$
3. $(\frac{1}{3} + \frac{1}{6}) + \frac{1}{2} = ? + (\frac{1}{6} + \frac{1}{2})$
4. $(7 \max 9) \max 4 = 7 \max (? \max 4)$
5. $(19 \times 2) \times 50 = ? \times (2 \times 50)$ 6. $(xy)z = x(? z)$
7. $(19 \times 2) \times 50 = ? \times (19 \times 2)$
8. $(19 + 2) + 50 = (? + 19) + 50$

In 9–14, replace the question mark with = or ≠ to make the sentence true.

9. $(73 \times 68) \times 92 \ ? \ 73 \times (68 \times 92)$
10. $(24 \div 6) \div 2 \ ? \ 24 \div (6 \div 2)$ 11. $(19 - 8) - 5 \ ? \ 19 - (8 - 5)$
12. $(9 + .3) + .7 \ ? \ 9 + (.3 + .7)$ 13. $(8 \div 4) \div 2 \ ? \ 8 \div (4 \div 2)$
14. $(40 - 20) - 10 \ ? \ 40 - (20 - 10)$

15. Which is an illustration of the commutative property of addition?
    (1) $a + 0 = a$ (2) $a(b + c) = ab + ac$
    (3) $a + b = b + a$ (4) $(a + b) + c = a + (b + c)$
16. Which statement illustrates the associative property of multiplication?
    (1) $2(\frac{1}{2}) = 1$ (2) $2(3 + 4) = 2(3) + 2(4)$
    (3) $2(1) = 2$ (4) $2(3 \cdot 4) = (2 \cdot 3)4$
17. **a.** Find the unique solution of (10 avg 14) avg 2.
    b. Find the unique solution of 10 avg (14 avg 2).
    c. Are the solutions in parts a and b the same or different?
    d. Does it appear that the operation of "averaging" two numbers at a time is associative?
    e. What is the average of the numbers 10, 14, and 2?
    f. Give a reason why the solution in part e does not equal the solutions found in parts a and b.

3 THE DISTRIBUTIVE PROPERTY

We know that 4(3 + 2) = 4(5) = 20 and that 4(3) + 4(2) = 12 + 8 = 20. Therefore, we see that 4(3 + 2) = 4(3) + 4(2).

This result can be illustrated geometrically. Remember that the area of a rectangle is equal to the product of its length and its width.

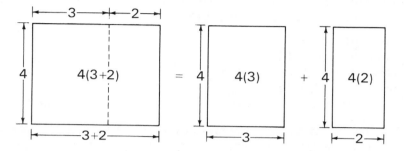

This example illustrates the *distributive property of multiplication over addition*, also called the *distributive property*. This means that the product of one number times the sum of a second and a third number equals the product of the first and second numbers plus the product of the first and third numbers.

Thus, 4(3 + 2) = 4(3) + 4(2).

In general, we assume that for every number a, every number b, and every number c:

$$a(b + c) = ab + ac \quad \text{and} \quad ab + ac = a(b + c)$$

Since multiplication is commutative, the distributive property can be written in other forms:

$$(b + c)a = ba + ca \quad \text{and} \quad (b + c)a = ab + ac$$

The distributive property is also assumed to be true for more than three numbers:

$$a(b + c + d + \ldots + x) = ab + ac + ad + \ldots + ax$$

The distributive property is also assumed to be true for subtraction:

$$a(b - c) = ab - ac \quad \text{and} \quad ab - ac = a(b - c)$$

Using the Distributive Property

Observe how the distributive property may be used to find the following indicated products:

1. $6 \times 23 = 6(20 + 3) = 6 \times 20 + 6 \times 3 = 120 + 18 = 138$
2. $20(\frac{1}{4} + \frac{1}{5}) = 20 \times \frac{1}{4} + 20 \times \frac{1}{5} = 5 + 4 = 9$

3. $9 \times 3\frac{1}{3} = 9(3 + \frac{1}{3}) = 9 \times 3 + 9 \times \frac{1}{3} = 27 + 3 = 30$

4. $6.5 \times 8 = (6 + .5)8 = 6 \times 8 + .5 \times 8 = 48 + 4 = 52$

The distributive property can be used to *transform*, or change, the form of an algebraic expression. When a given expression is an indicated product, note how it may be transformed to an equivalent expression, which is in the form of a sum or a difference.

1. $5(a + b) = 5a + 5b$
2. $9(a - b) = 9a - 9b$
3. $r(m + n + t) = rm + rn + rt$
4. $6(3x + 5) = 6 \cdot 3x + 6 \cdot 5 = 18x + 30$
5. $(x + y)(m + n) = (x + y)m + (x + y)n = xm + ym + xn + yn$

In 5 notice that in the first transformation $(x + y)$ is considered as one number, whereas $(m + n)$ is considered as the sum of two numbers. If we wish, we may consider $(m + n)$ to be one number and $(x + y)$ to be the sum of two numbers. The result will be the same.

The use of the distributive property also makes it possible to transform an algebraic expression that is an indicated sum or an indicated difference to an equivalent expression that is an indicated product.
Study the following examples:

1. $3c + 3d = 3(c + d)$
3. $5L + 3L = (5 + 3)L = 8L$

2. $xa + xb + xc = x(a + b + c)$
4. $9y - 4y = (9 - 4)y = 5y$

Note that the *substitution principle* allows us to replace one numerical expression for another as long as we do not change the value of the number being represented. Thus, $(9 - 4)y = 5y$ by the substitution principle. Similarly, $(3 \cdot 4)x = 12x$ by substitution.

EXERCISES

In 1–14, state whether the sentence is a correct application of the distributive property. If you believe that it is not, state your reason.

1. $6(5 + 8) = 6 \times 5 + 6 \times 8$

2. $10(\frac{1}{2} + \frac{1}{5}) = 10 \times \frac{1}{2} + \frac{1}{5}$

3. $(7 + 9)5 = 7 + 9 \times 5$

4. $3(x + 5) = 3x + 3 \times 5$

5. $2(y + 6) = 2y + 6$

6. $(b + 2)a = ba + 2a$

7. $4a(b + c) = 4ab + 4ac$

8. $4b(c - 2) = 4bc - 2$

9. $8m + 6m = (8 + 6)m$

10. $14x - 4x = (14 - 4)x$

11. $2.7a + 5.3a = 8a$

12. $7\frac{1}{2}r - 2\frac{1}{2}r = 5r$

13. $7r + 7s = 7(r + s)$

14. $2(L + W) = 2L + 2W$

In 15-20, complete the sentence so that it is an application of the distributive property.

15. $9(7 + 3) = $ _____

16. _____ $= 12 \times \frac{1}{2} + 12 \times \frac{1}{3}$

17. $4(p + q) = $ _____

18. _____ $= 2x - 2y$

19. $8t + 13t = $ _____

20. _____ $= (15 - 7)m$

In 21-28, find the value of the numerical phrase by using the distributive property to simplify the computation.

21. $15 \times 36 + 15 \times 64$

22. $3 \times 89 + 5 \times 89 + 2 \times 89$

23. $128 \times 615 - 28 \times 615$

24. $1\frac{3}{4} \times 576 + 8\frac{1}{4} \times 576$

25. $937 \times .8 + 937 \times .2$

26. $36(\frac{1}{3} + \frac{1}{4})$

27. $50 \times 8\frac{3}{5}$

28. $73 \times 632 + 47 \times 632 - 20 \times 632$

In 29-34, use the distributive property to transform the expression to an equivalent expression without parentheses.

29. $4(m + n)$

30. $(x - y)8$

31. $12(\frac{2}{3}x + 2)$

32. $(\frac{1}{3}m - \frac{3}{5}n)30$

33. $3a(7 - b)$

34. $(a + b)(s + t)$

In 35-40, use the distributive property to express each indicated sum as a product.

35. $2p + 2q$

36. $8p - 8m$

37. $12y - 4y$

38. $4a + 5a + 3a$

39. $2bc + 4b$

40. $9r + 6d$

41. Recall that the perimeter of a rectangle is found by the formula $P = 2l + 2w$. Use the distributive law to write another representation of the formula for the perimeter of the rectangle.

In 42-45, name the property that justifies each step in the set of related equations. Use the substitution principle if necessary.

42. a. $(5x + 8x) + 4 = (5 + 8)x + 4$

    b. $ = 13x + 4$

43. a. $(9x - 3x) + 7 = (9 - 3)x + 7$

    b. $ = 6x + 7$

44. a. $5x + 6x + 9x = (5 + 6 + 9)x$

    b. $ = 20x$

45. a. $5x + (3x + 4) = (5x + 3x) + 4$

    b. $ = (5 + 3)x + 4$

    c. $ = 8x + 4$

4 PROPERTIES OF ZERO AND ONE

Addition Property of Zero

The true sentences $5 + 0 = 5$ and $0 + 8 = 8$ illustrate that the sum of any number and zero is that number itself. These examples illustrate the *addition property of zero*.

In general, we assume that for every number a:

$$a + 0 = a \quad \text{and} \quad 0 + a = a$$

We call 0 the *identity element of addition*, or the *additive identity element*, for the numbers of arithmetic. We will also agree that if $a + x = a$ for any number a, then $x = 0$.

Multiplication Property of Zero

The true sentences $4 \times 0 = 0$ and $0 \times 3 = 0$ illustrate that the product of any number and zero is zero. These examples illustrate the *multiplication property of zero*.

In general, we assume that for every number a:

$$a \cdot 0 = 0 \quad \text{and} \quad 0 \cdot a = 0$$

Multiplication Property of One

The true sentences $5 \times 1 = 5$ and $1 \times 9 = 9$ illustrate that the product of any number and one is that number itself. These examples illustrate the *multiplication property of one*.

In general, we assume that for every number a:

$$a \cdot 1 = a \quad \text{and} \quad 1 \cdot a = a$$

We call 1 the *identity element of multiplication*, or the *multiplicative identity element*, for the numbers of arithmetic.

| MODEL PROBLEMS |

1. Evaluate the number expression $3 \times 1 + (8 + 0)$ and give the reason for each step of the procedure.

    Solution:

Step		Reason
(1) $3 \times 1 + (8 + 0) = 3 \times 1 + 8$		(1) Addition property of 0.
(2) $= 3 + 8$		(2) Multiplication property of 1.
(3) $= 11$		(3) Substitution principle.

    Answer: 11

88

2. Express $6t + t$ as a product and give the reason for each step of the procedure.

Solution:

<table>
<tr><td align="center">*Step*</td><td align="center">*Reason*</td></tr>
<tr><td>(1) $6t + t = 6t + 1t$</td><td>(1) Multiplication property of 1.</td></tr>
<tr><td>(2) $= (6 + 1)t$</td><td>(2) Distributive property.</td></tr>
<tr><td>(3) $= 7t$</td><td>(3) Substitution principle.</td></tr>
</table>

Answer: $7t$

EXERCISES

1. Name the number that is the additive identity element for the numbers of arithmetic.
2. Name the identity element of multiplication for the numbers of arithmetic.
3. Give the value of each number expression.
    a. $9 + 0$ **b.** 9×0 **c.** 9×1 **d.** $\frac{2}{3} \times 0$ **e.** $0 + \frac{2}{3}$ **f.** $1 \times \frac{2}{3}$

In 4–9, evaluate the number expression and give the reason for each step in the procedure.

4. $10 \times 0 + 6 \times 1$ 5. $(7 + 0) + 7 \times 0$ 6. $(0 + 6) + 1 \times 8$
7. $6(\frac{1}{2} + 0) - 5 \times 0$ 8. $4 \times 1 - (0 + 2)$ 9. $12(8 - 7) + (\frac{3}{4} \times 0)$

In 10–14, write the algebraic expression as a product and give the reason for each step in the procedure.

10. $10x + x$ 11. $3b + b$ 12. $8y - y$ 13. $7ab + ab$ 14. $8x^2 - x^2$

15. Give the simplest expression possible for each algebraic expression.
     a. $y + 0$ **b.** $y \cdot 0$ **c.** $y \cdot 1$ **d.** $0 \cdot y$ **e.** $1 \cdot y$ **f.** $0 + y$
16. If $r + s = r$: **a.** What is the numerical value of s?   **b.** What is the numerical value of rs?
17. If $x + y = x$, what is the numerical value of xy?
18. If $xy = 0$ and $x \neq 0$, what is the numerical value of y?
19. If $xy = x$: **a.** What is the numerical value of y?   **b.** What is the numerical value of y^2?   **c.** What is the numerical value of $2y$?

5   SIMPLIFYING CALCULATIONS BY COMBINING LIKE TERMS

The properties that we have just studied help us to perform operations with algebraic terms. We have seen that an algebraic term is found by the multiplication of numbers and variables, for example, $3x^2y$.

Two or more terms containing the same variables, with corresponding variables having the same exponents, are called *like terms*. For example, pairs of like terms include:

$3L$ and $5L$ $\qquad$ $5x^2$ and $7x^2$ $\qquad$ $9ab$ and $2ab$

$6k$ and k $\qquad$ $7c^2d^3$ and $2c^2d^3$ $\qquad$ $4(x + y)$ and $5(x + y)$

Two or more terms are called *unlike terms* when they are not like terms. For example, pairs of unlike terms include:

$3x$ and $4y$ $\qquad$ $5x^2$ and $5x^3$ $\qquad$ $9ab$ and $2a$

$6ax$ and $5bx$ $\qquad$ $3x^2y$ and $3xy^2$ $\qquad$ $14x$ and 14

We have learned that the distributive property enables us to transform an indicated sum or difference to an indicated product:

$$9x + 2x = (9 + 2)x = 11x \qquad 16cd + 3cd = (16 + 3)cd = 19cd$$

$$18y - y = 18y - 1y = (18 - 1)y = 17y$$

When we express the indicated sum or the indicated difference of like terms as a single term, we *combine like terms*. Combining two like terms is an example of a binary operation in algebra.

Note in the above examples that when two like terms are combined:
1. The result has the same variable factors as the original terms.
2. The numerical coefficient of the result is:
   (a) the sum of the numerical coefficients of the terms when the terms are to be added

   or

   (b) the difference of the numerical coefficients of the terms when the terms are to be subtracted.

The indicated sum or difference of two unlike terms cannot be expressed as a single term. For example, $2x + 3y$ and $4ac - 5bd$ cannot be simplified.

| MODEL PROBLEMS |

1. Show that $4x + 5x = 9x$ is a true sentence when $x = 10$.

How to Proceed	*Solution*
(1) Write the sentence.	$4x + 5x = 9x$
(2) Replace the variable by its value.	$4 \times 10 + 5 \times 10 \overset{?}{=} 9 \times 10$
(3) Do the multiplication.	$40 + 50 \overset{?}{=} 90$
(4) Do the addition. The result is a true sentence.	$90 = 90$ (True)

In 2–5, simplify the expression by combining like terms.

2. $8a + 3a$

    Solution: $8a + 3a = (8 + 3)a = 11a$ *Ans.*

3. $3.9xy - 3.9xy$

    Solution: $3.9xy - 3.9xy = (3.9 - 3.9)xy = 0 \cdot xy = 0$ *Ans.*

4. $9t + 4t - t$

    Solution: $9t + 4t - t = 9t + 4t - 1t$
    $$= (9 + 4 - 1)t = 12t \quad Ans.$$

5. $7a + 6b + 5a - 2b$

    Solution:

$7a + 6b + 5a - 2b = 7a + 5a + 6b - 2b$	Commutative property
$= (7a + 5a) + (6b - 2b)$	Associative property
$= 12a + 4b$	Distributive property

    Answer: $12a + 4b$

EXERCISES

1. Show that $3x + 5x = 8x$ is a true sentence when x equals:
    a. 7   b. 10   c. .4   d. $\frac{1}{2}$ e. 0

2. Show that $5y^2 - 2y^2 = 3y^2$ is a true sentence when y equals:
    a. 3   b. 12   c. .2   d. $\frac{1}{3}$ e. 0

3. Show that $6c + 9d + c + 2d = 7c + 11d$ is a true sentence when:
    a. $c = 10, d = 7$ b. $c = 1.2, d = .1$ c. $c = \frac{3}{4}, d = \frac{2}{3}$

In 4–18, simplify the expression by combining like terms.

4. $7x + 3x$ 5. $9t - 5t$ 6. $10c + c$
7. $2\frac{1}{2}d + 1\frac{1}{2}d$ 8. $13n - 6\frac{2}{3}n$ 9. $3.4y + 1.3y$
10. $6.2r - r$ 11. $9ab + 2ab$ 12. $8z^2 + z^2$
13. $8m + 5m + m$ 14. $9w + 8w - 3w$
15. $8s + 5\frac{1}{2}s + 6\frac{3}{4}s$ 16. $8.2b + 3.8b - 12b$
17. $2\frac{3}{4}xy - 2xy + \frac{1}{2}xy$ 18. $9d^2 - 6d^2 - d^2$

In 19 and 20, simplify the sentence by combining like terms.

19. $P = 5x + 5x + 5x$ 20. $P = x + \frac{3}{2}x + x + \frac{3}{2}x$

21. Express the perimeter of each of the following figures and simplify the result by combining like terms. (Remember that the perimeter P of a geometric figure, which is the distance around the figure, can be found by adding the lengths of its sides.)

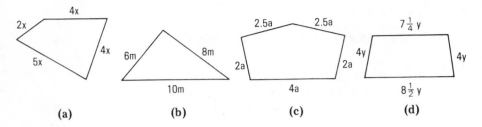

| (a) | (b) | (c) | (d) |

In 22–31, simplify the expression by combining like terms.

22. $8m + 5m + 7n + 6n$

23. $5c + 9c + 12d + d$

24. $a + 5m + 2a - 4m$

25. $1.5a + 7.2b + 5.1a + 8.6b$

26. $5a + 3m + a + m$

27. $5a + b + 3c + 1\frac{1}{3}a + b + \frac{3}{4}c$

28. $8x + 10 + 4x + 5$

29. $2x + 9 + 3x + 1 + 5x - 8$

30. $5y^2 + 25 + 2y^2 - 10$

31. $5ac + 6ab + 3ac - ab$

In 32 and 33, simplify the sentence by combining like terms.

32. $P = 4r + 5s + 4r + s$

33. $S = 6a + 2\frac{1}{2}b + 3\frac{1}{4}a + \frac{3}{4}b$

34. Express the perimeter P of each of the following figures and simplify the result by combining like terms:

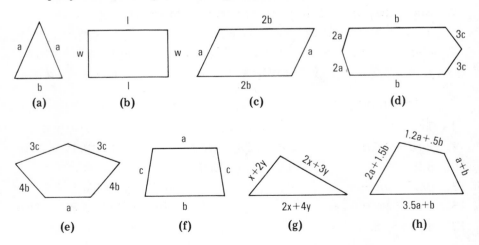

| (a) | (b) | (c) | (d) |

| (e) | (f) | (g) | (h) |

chapter four

Simple Equations and Problems

1 UNDERSTANDING THE MEANING OF SOLVING AN EQUATION

An *equation* is a sentence that uses the symbol = to state that two algebraic expressions are equal. For example, $x + 3 = 9$ is an equation in which $x + 3$ is called the *left side*, or *left member*, and 9 is called the *right side*, or *right member*.

An equation may be a true sentence such as $5 + 2 = 7$ or a false sentence such as $6 - 3 = 4$. When the equation contains a variable such as x in $x + 3 = 9$, then we call this equation an open sentence. We cannot determine whether an open sentence is true or false until the value of the variable is known.

Consider the equation $x + 3 = 9$. When x is replaced by an element of {numbers of arithmetic}, the sentence may become either a true sentence or a false sentence. Only when x is replaced by 6 does $x + 3 = 9$ become a true sentence: $6 + 3 = 9$. The number 6, which satisfies the equation $x + 3 = 9$, is called a *root*, or a *solution*, of the equation. The set consisting of all the solutions of an equation is called its *solution set*, or *truth set*.

The solution set of an equation is a subset of the replacement set (the domain) of the variable. This subset consists of the elements of the replacement set that make the open sentence true. Therefore, if the replacement set of x is {numbers of arithmetic}, then the solution set of $x + 3 = 9$ is {6}. Observe that {6} is a subset of {numbers of arithmetic}.

To *solve an equation* means to find its solution set.

If only some elements of the domain satisfy an equation, the equation is called a *conditional equation*, or simply an "equation." Therefore, $x + 3 = 9$ is a conditional equation.

If every element of the domain satisfies an equation, the equation is called an *identity*. Thus, $5 + x = x + 5$ is an identity when the domain of x is {numbers of arithmetic} because every element of the domain makes the sentence true.

■ **PROCEDURE.** To verify, or check, whether a number is a root of an equation:

1. Replace the variable in the equation by the number.
2. Perform the indicated operations to determine whether the resulting statement is true.

MODEL PROBLEMS

1. Is 7 a root of the equation $5x - 10 = 25$?

How to Proceed	*Solution*
(1) Write the equation.	$5x - 10 = 25$
(2) Replace the variable x by 7.	$5(7) - 10 \overset{?}{=} 25$
(3) Do the multiplication.	$35 - 10 \overset{?}{=} 25$
(4) Do the subtraction. A true statement results.	$25 = 25$ (True)

Answer: Yes

2. Is 4 a root of the equation $3x + 9 = 27$?

How to Proceed	*Solution*
(1) Write the equation.	$3x + 9 = 27$
(2) Replace the variable x by 4.	$3(4) + 9 \overset{?}{=} 27$
(3) Do the multiplication.	$12 + 9 \overset{?}{=} 27$
(4) Do the addition. A false statement results.	$21 = 27$ (False)

Answer: No

EXERCISES

In 1–12, find the number of arithmetic that can replace the question mark and make the resulting equation a true statement.

1. $10 - 3 = ?$
2. $? - 5 = 3\frac{1}{2}$
3. $10 + ? = 18$
4. $7 + ? = 9\frac{2}{3}$
5. $12(4) = ?$
6. $4(?) = 10$
7. $16 \div 8 = ?$
8. $? \div 2 = 3.5$
9. $3(8) + 4 = ?$
10. $2(?) + 6 = 14$
11. $5(?) - 1 = 34$
12. $\frac{1}{3}(?) - 1 = 2$

In 13–21, tell whether the number in the parentheses is a root of the given equation.

13. $5x = 50$ (10)   14. $\frac{1}{2}x = 18$ (36)   15. $\frac{1}{3}y = 12$ (4)

16. $x + 5 = 11$ (6)   17. $y + 8 = 14$ (22)   18. $x - 5 = 13$ (8)

19. $m - 4\frac{1}{2} = 9$ $(4\frac{1}{2})$ 20. $2x + 7 = 21$ (14)   21. $19 = 4x - 1$ (.5)

In 22–30, using the domain $\{1, 2, 3, 4, 5, 6, 7, 8, 9, 10\}$, find the solution set of the equation. If the equation has no roots, indicate the solution set as the null set, $\emptyset$.

22. $x + 5 = 7$ 23. $y - 3 = 4$ 24. $2x + 1 = 9$

25. $6 = 3x - 1.8$ 26. $\frac{1}{2}x + 4 = 50$ 27. $14 - 2x = 2$

28. $\dfrac{x + 8}{4} = 3$ 29. $3x + .2 = 2.8$ 30. $\dfrac{5x}{4} - 1 = 49$

In 31–36, using the domain $\{5, 6, 7, 8, 9, 10\}$, tell whether the equation is a conditional equation or an identity.

31. $x + 3 = 3 + x$ 32. $x + 3 = 10$ 33. $y + 3 + 4 = 7 + y$

34. $5a = a \cdot 5$ 35. $5a = 40$ 36. $5 \cdot 2 \cdot a = a \cdot 2 \cdot 5$

2 POSTULATES OF EQUALITY

In mathematics any statement that we accept as being true without proof is called an *assumption*, a *postulate*, or an *axiom*.

At this point we will study several postulates of equality. These postulates will be used to solve equations in a systematic manner.

Postulate 1: Reflexive Property of Equality

The *reflexive property of equality* states that for every number a:

$$a = a$$

Postulate 2: Symmetric Property of Equality

The *symmetric property of equality* states that for every number a and every number b:

$$\text{If } a = b, \text{ then } b = a.$$

Postulate 3: Transitive Property of Equality

The *transitive property of equality* states that for every number a, every number b, and every number c:

$$\text{If } a = b, \text{ and } b = c, \text{ then } a = c.$$

The transitive property of equality is useful in the following ways:

If (1) $a = b$ and (2) $b = c$, the transitive property of equality makes it possible for us to replace b in (2) by a and to obtain $a = c$.

Also, we may replace b in (1) by c and obtain $a = c$. We call this replacement process *substitution*, or the *substitution principle*.

Finally, the transitive property of equality allows us to state that two numbers are equal if each of them is equal to a third number.

EXERCISES

In 1-6, name the property of equality that the sentence illustrates.

1. $5 + 2 = 5 + 2$
2. If $6 + 2 = 5 + 3$, and $5 + 3 = 7 + 1$, then $6 + 2 = 7 + 1$.
3. If $4 + 3 = 6 + 1$, then $6 + 1 = 4 + 3$.
4. $x + y = x + y$
5. If $x = y$, then $y = x$.
6. If $m + n = r + s$, and $r + s = x + y$, then $m + n = x + y$.

3 PREPARING TO SOLVE EQUATIONS BY USING INVERSE OPERATIONS

Consider the expression $8 - 2$. Since 2 has been subtracted from 8, it can be seen that if we add 2 to the indicated difference, we will get a result of 8. Thus, $8 - 2 + 2 = 8$. Similarly, if x and a represent numbers, then $x - a + a = x$.

Consider the expression $8 + 2$. Since 2 has been added to 8, it can be seen that if we subtract 2 from the indicated sum, we will get a result of 8. Thus, $8 + 2 - 2 = 8$. Similarly, if x and a represent numbers, then $x + a - a = x$.

Since subtracting a number undoes the effect of having added that number, and adding a number undoes the effect of having subtracted that number, *addition and subtraction are called inverse operations*.

Consider the expression 8×2. Since 8 has been multiplied by 2, it can be seen that if we divide the indicated product by 2, we will get a result of 8. Thus, $\dfrac{8 \times 2}{2} = 8$. Similarly, if x and a represent numbers $(a \neq 0)$, then $\dfrac{ax}{a} = x$.

Consider the expression $8 \div 2$, or $\frac{8}{2}$. Since 8 has been divided by 2, it can be seen that if we multiply the indicated quotient by 2, we will get a result of 8. Thus, $2 \times \frac{8}{2} = 8$. Similarly, if x and a represent numbers $(a \neq 0)$, then $a \cdot \dfrac{x}{a} = x$.

Since dividing by a number undoes the effect of having multiplied by that number, and multiplying by a number undoes the effect of having divided by that number, *multiplication and division are called inverse operations*, where the numbers $\neq 0$.

Whenever a variable and a number of arithmetic are related by the operation of addition, subtraction, multiplication, or division, we can use the inverse operation to obtain the variable itself.

MODEL PROBLEMS

In each of the following: **a.** State the operation that involves the variable and the number of arithmetic. **b.** State the operation you will use to obtain the variable itself. **c.** Give the number you will use when adding, subtracting, multiplying, or dividing to obtain the variable itself. **d.** Perform the operation.

1. $5x$	**2.** $\dfrac{d}{6}$	**3.** $t + 4$	**4.** $y - 8$
Solution	*Solution*	*Solution*	*Solution*
a. multiplication	**a.** division	**a.** addition	**a.** subtraction
b. division	**b.** multiplication	**b.** subtraction	**b.** addition
c. 5	**c.** 6	**c.** 4	**c.** 8
d. $\dfrac{5x}{5} = x$	**d.** $6 \cdot \dfrac{d}{6} = d$	**d.** $t + 4 - 4 = t$	**d.** $y - 8 + 8 = y$

EXERCISES

In 1–25: **a.** State the operation that involves the variable and the number of arithmetic. **b.** State the operation you will use to obtain the variable itself. **c.** Give the number you will use when adding, subtracting, multiplying, or dividing to obtain the variable itself. **d.** Perform the operation.

1. $7x$ 2. $\dfrac{w}{5}$ 3. $x + 1$ 4. $x - 4$ 5. $20z$

6. $8y$ 7. $\dfrac{m}{4}$ 8. $d + 3$ 9. $x - 6$ 10. $\dfrac{m}{5}$

11. $\frac{1}{5}w$ 12. $\frac{1}{3}y$ 13. $c + 7$ 14. $t - 1$ 15. $d + 14$

16. $1\frac{1}{4}m$ 17. $\dfrac{m}{10}$ 18. $d + 1\frac{1}{2}$ 19. $r - \frac{2}{3}$ 20. $c + 2\frac{1}{2}$

21. $.5c$ 22. $\dfrac{r}{100}$ 23. $n + .7$ 24. $s - .8$ 25. $x - 1.5$

4 SOLVING SIMPLE EQUATIONS BY USING ADDITION OR SUBTRACTION POSTULATES

Postulate 4: Addition Property of Equality

The *addition property of equality* states that for all numbers a, b, and c:

$$\text{If } a = b, \text{ then } a + c = b + c.$$

Therefore, we can say: **If the same number is added to both members of an equality, the equality is retained.** Study the following examples:

In Arithmetic	*In Algebra*	
If $8 = 8$	If $x - 2 = 8$	
Then $8 + 2 = 8 + 2$	Then $x - 2 + 2 = 8 + 2$ A_2	(Add 2 to both members of the previous equation.)
And $10 = 10$	And $x = 10$	

In the preceding algebraic example, let us use the substitution principle and replace x with 10 in the first equation.

$$x - 2 = 8$$
$$10 - 2 \overset{?}{=} 8$$
$$8 = 8$$

We see that replacing x with 10 results in a true sentence. This serves as a check of our work.

If we replace x with 10 in the second equation, $x - 2 + 2 = 8 + 2$, we likewise obtain a true sentence. In fact, the number 10 is the only number that can replace x in each of the equations and make the resulting sentence true. Therefore, 10 is the root and $\{10\}$ is the solution set of each of these equations. Equations that have the same solution set are called *equivalent equations*. Notice that when the addition property is applied in an equation, we obtain an equivalent equation.

When we solve an equation, we transform it into a simpler equivalent equation that reveals the value that can replace the variable and make the resulting sentence true (the truth value of the variable). Now we will use the addition property of equality in solving equations.

In this chapter when the domain of the variable is not stated, we will assume that it is the set of the numbers of arithmetic.

MODEL PROBLEMS

1. Solve and check: $x - 5 = 4$

    Solution

    $$x - 5 = 4$$
    $$x - 5 + 5 = 4 + 5 \quad A_5$$
    $$x = 9$$

    Check

    $$x - 5 = 4$$
    $$9 - 5 \overset{?}{=} 4$$
    $$4 = 4$$

    (Notice that when the variable x is replaced by 9, the resulting sentence is true.)

    Answer: $x = 9$, or solution set is $\{9\}$.

2. Solve and check: $5 = y - 3\frac{1}{2}$

    Solution

    $$5 = y - 3\frac{1}{2}$$
    $$5 + 3\frac{1}{2} = y - 3\frac{1}{2} + 3\frac{1}{2} \quad A_{3\frac{1}{2}}$$
    $$8\frac{1}{2} = y$$

    Check

    $$5 = y - 3\frac{1}{2}$$
    $$5 \overset{?}{=} 8\frac{1}{2} - 3\frac{1}{2}$$
    $$5 = 5 \quad \text{(True)}$$

    Answer: $y = 8\frac{1}{2}$, or solution set is $\{8\frac{1}{2}\}$.

Postulate 5: Subtraction Property of Equality

The *subtraction property of equality* states that for all numbers a, b, and c:

$$\text{If } a = b, \text{ then } a - c = b - c.$$

Therefore, we can say: **If the same number is subtracted from both members of an equality, the equality is retained.**

Study the following examples:

In Arithmetic	*In Algebra*	
If $8 = 8$	If $x + 3 = 8$	
Then $8 - 3 = 8 - 3$	Then $x + 3 - 3 = 8 - 3$ S_3	(Subtract 3 from both members of the previous equation.)
And $5 = 5$	And $x = 5$	

Notice that the application of the subtraction property in the equation $x + 3 = 8$ resulted in the equivalent equations $x + 3 - 3 = 8 - 3$ and $x = 5$. All three equations have the same solution set $\{5\}$.

Now we will use the subtraction property of equality in solving equations.

MODEL PROBLEMS

1. Solve and check: $n + 7 = 9$

    Solution

    $n + 7 = 9$
    $n + 7 - 7 = 9 - 7$ S_7
    $n = 2$

    Check

    $n + 7 = 9$
    $2 + 7 \stackrel{?}{=} 9$
    $9 = 9$ (True)

    Answer: $n = 2$, or solution set is $\{2\}$.

2. Solve and check: $.8 = .3 + t$

    Solution

    $.8 = .3 + t$
    $.8 = t + .3$ (Commutative property)
    $.8 - .3 = t + .3 - .3$ $S_{.3}$
    $.5 = t$

    Check

    $.8 = .3 + t$
    $.8 \stackrel{?}{=} .3 + .5$
    $.8 = .8$ (True)

    Answer: $t = .5$, or solution set is $\{.5\}$.

■ **PROCEDURE.** To solve an equation in which a variable and a constant are related by the operation of addition or subtraction:

1. Use the inverse operation, subtracting the constant from or adding the constant to both members of the equation. Perform the indicated operation(s) to obtain an equivalent equation in which only the variable itself is one member of the equation.

2. Check by determining that when the value obtained for the variable replaces it in the given equation, the resulting statement is true.

EXERCISES

In 1–60, solve and check the equation.

1. $x - 1 = 7$
2. $m - 3 = 0$
3. $x - 13 = 25$
4. $y - 64 = 77$
5. $9 = x - 3$
6. $15 = w - 15$
7. $17 = x - 21$
8. $89 = b - 73$
9. $x - .3 = .4$
10. $r - .07 = .32$
11. $.9 = c - .3$
12. $7 = d - .7$
13. $y - \frac{1}{2} = \frac{1}{2}$
14. $t - 1\frac{1}{3} = 4$
15. $4\frac{2}{3} = m - \frac{1}{3}$
16. $12\frac{1}{2} = y - 7\frac{3}{4}$
17. $y + 1 = 8$
18. $t + 8 = 8$
19. $y + 18 = 29$
20. $d + 53 = 81$
21. $9 = x + 3$
22. $17 = t + 17$
23. $39 = e + 21$
24. $98 = f + 39$
25. $x + .7 = .8$
26. $s + .02 = .08$
27. $.9 = m + .3$
28. $12.9 = k + .6$
29. $x + \frac{3}{8} = \frac{7}{8}$
30. $r + \frac{1}{2} = \frac{3}{4}$
31. $3\frac{2}{3} = n + \frac{1}{6}$
32. $18\frac{3}{10} = k + 5\frac{7}{10}$
33. $a - 4 = 9$
34. $a + 5 = 17$
35. $b + 4 = 13$
36. $d + 1 = 12$
37. $18 = a - 3$
38. $16 = r + 2$
39. $25 = s + 11$
40. $54 = t + 39$
41. $y - 13 = 14$
42. $m + 15 = 15$
43. $n - 7 = 3\frac{1}{3}$
44. $y + 5 = 8\frac{1}{4}$
45. $x + \frac{1}{2} = 14\frac{1}{2}$
46. $3\frac{2}{3} = m - \frac{1}{3}$
47. $b - 2\frac{3}{4} = 9$
48. $\frac{7}{8} = y + \frac{3}{4}$
49. $c - 1\frac{1}{4} = 6\frac{1}{2}$
50. $9\frac{1}{4} = d + 3\frac{1}{2}$
51. $d - 5 = 2.3$
52. $m + .7 = 2.9$
53. $8.6 = c - .2$
54. $12 = p + 1.8$
55. $15 = x + 1.5$
56. $3.1 = z - .8$
57. $4 + x = 50$
58. $19 = 7 + y$
59. $1 + x = 7\frac{1}{2}$
60. $.15 + y = 2.25$

61. If $g + 9 = 11$, find the value of $7g$.
62. If $t - .5 = 2.5$, find the value of $t + 7$.
63. If $22 = y + 8$, find the value of $\frac{1}{2}y$.
64. If $c - 1\frac{1}{4} = 2\frac{1}{2}$, find the value of $8c - 2$.
65. If $1.8 + b = 2.7$, find the value of $\frac{1}{3}b - .3$.

5 WRITING VERBAL SENTENCES AS EQUATIONS

In algebra many verbal problems involving number relations are solved by using equations. Therefore, we must be able to express verbal sentences as equations. Study the following examples to see how verbal sentences may be expressed as equations:

Verbal Sentence: Four times a number s equals   20.

Equation: $4s$ $=$ 20

Verbal Sentence: A number y increased by   6   equals   8.

Equation: y $+$ 6 $=$ 8

Verbal Sentence: A number x decreased by   3   equals   5.

Equation: x $-$ 3 $=$ 5

Verbal Sentence: A number n divided by   2   equals   4.

Equation: n $\div$ 2 $=$ 4

■ **PROCEDURE.**   To write a verbal sentence as an equation, choose a letter to represent the variable. Then use this letter, with the symbols for arithmetic operations, to express the verbal sentence as an equation.

| MODEL PROBLEM |

Write the following sentence as an equation: "5 times a number decreased by 7 equals 13."

Solution: Let x represent the number.

5 times a number   decreased by   7   equals   13.

              $5x$ $-$ 7 $=$ 13

Answer: $5x - 7 = 13$

| EXERCISES |

In 1-9, select the equation that represents, in terms of the given variable, the numerical relationship expressed in the sentence.

1. Three times Harold's height is 108 inches. Let h = Harold's height.
    (1) $h + 3 = 108$ (2) $3h = 108$ (3) $h - 3 = 108$ (4) $\frac{1}{3}h = 108$

2. One-half of Mary's weight is 20 kilograms. Let w = Mary's weight.

   (1) $\frac{1}{2}w = 20$ (2) $2w = 20$ (3) $w - 2 = 20$ (4) $w + 2 = 20$

3. A number increased by 7 equals 28. Let n = the number.

   (1) $7n = 28$ (2) $n + 7 = 28$ (3) $n - 7 = 28$ (4) $\frac{1}{7}n = 28$

4. A number decreased by 5 equals 15. Let x = the number.

   (1) $x + 5 = 15$ (2) $5x = 15$ (3) $\frac{1}{5}x = 15$ (4) $x - 5 = 15$

5. If 7 is subtracted from a number, the result is 8. Let x = the number.

   (1) $7 - x = 8$ (2) $x - 7 = 8$ (3) $8 - x = 7$ (4) $x + 8 = 7$

6. A movie star bought 15 suits and now has 75 suits. Let s = the number of suits he had originally.

   (1) $s + 15 = 75$ (2) $s - 15 = 75$ (3) $15s = 75$ (4) $\frac{s}{15} = 75$

7. In a rectangle four times the width is 100 cm. Let w = width of the rectangle.

   (1) $w + 4 = 100$ (2) $4w = 100$ (3) $w - 4 = 100$ (4) $\frac{1}{4}w = 100$

8. In a parallelogram whose area measures 24 cm^2 the base measures 6 cm. Let h = height of the parallelogram.

   (1) $h + 6 = 24$ (2) $6h = 24$ (3) $h \div 6 = 24$ (4) $24h = 6$

9. In a triangle whose area measures 32 m^2 the base measures 4 m. Let h = height of the triangle.

   (1) $4h = 32$ (2) $2(4h) = 32$ (3) $\frac{1}{2}(h + 4) = 32$ (4) $\frac{1}{2}(4h) = 32$

In 10–26, write the sentence as an equation. Use n to represent the number.

10. Eight more than a number is 15.
11. Four less than a number is 24.
12. Twelve added to a number is 26.
13. A number decreased by 5 equals 25.
14. A number multiplied by 3 equals 39.
15. A number divided by 4 equals 16.
16. The product of 7 and a number equals 70.
17. One-half of a number decreased by 7 equals 11.
18. Twice a number, increased by 7, equals 27.
19. Twice a number, decreased by 5, equals 25.
20. The sum of three times a number and 7 is 22.
21. When 9 is subtracted from 5 times a number, the result is 31.
22. The sum of 100 and a number is equal to three times that number.

23. If 3 times a number is increased by 12, the result is the same as when twice the number is increased by 24.
24. If 8 times a number is decreased by 20, the result is the same as when 3 times the number is increased by 80.
25. The sum of a number and twice that number equals 45.
26. Three times a number decreased by half of that number equals 40.

6 SOLVING PROBLEMS BY USING VARIABLES AND EQUATIONS

Now we are ready to solve verbal problems algebraically.

■ **PROCEDURE.** To solve a verbal problem by using an equation involving one variable:

1. Read the problem carefully until you understand it.

2. Determine what is given in the problem and what is to be found.

3. Select a variable that can be used in representing every number that the problem requires you to find.

4. Write an equation that symbolizes the information and relationships stated in the problem.

5. Find the root, or solution set, of the equation.

6. Check the answer by testing it in the word statement of the original problem to see that it satisfies all the required conditions.

| MODEL PROBLEMS |

1. When a number is decreased by 7, the result is 9. Find the number.

How to Proceed	*Solution*
(1) Represent the number by a variable.	Let x = the number.
(2) Write the word statement as an equation.	$x - 7 = 9$
(3) Solve the equation. A_7 (mentally)	$x = 16$
(4) Check in the original problem.	Is 16 decreased by 7 equal to 9? Yes.

Answer: The number is 16.

2. The length of a sheet of paper is 9.5 cm more than its width. If the length of the sheet is 32 cm, find its width.

How to Proceed	*Solution*
(1) Represent the width of the sheet by a variable.	Let w = the width of the sheet.
(2) Represent the length of the sheet, using the same variable.	Then $w + 9.5$ = the length of the sheet.
(3) Write the word statement as an equation.	$w + 9.5 = 32$ (the length is 32 cm).
(4) Solve the equation. $S_{9.5}$ (mentally)	$w = 22.5$
(5) Check in the original problem.	The width is 22.5 cm; the length is 32 cm. Is the length 9.5 cm more than the width? Yes.

Answer: The width is 22.5 cm.

EXERCISES

In 1–21, solve the problem using a variable and an equation.

1. A number decreased by 20 equals 36. Find the number.
2. If 7 is subtracted from a number, the result is 46. Find the number.
3. What number increased by 25 equals 40?
4. If 18 is added to a number, the result is 32. Find the number.
5. Ten less than a number is 42. Find the number.
6. The sum of 42 and a number is 96. Find the number.
7. After Helen had spent \$.25, she had \$.85 left. How much money did she have originally?
8. After he had lost 13 kg, Ben weighed 90 kg. Find Ben's original weight.
9. After $2\frac{1}{2}$ feet had been cut from a piece of lumber, there were $9\frac{1}{2}$ feet left. What was the original length of the piece of lumber?
10. After a car had increased its rate of speed by 24 kilometers per hour, it was traveling 76 kilometers per hour. What was its original rate of speed?
11. During a charity drive the boys in a class contributed \$3.75 more than the girls. If the boys contributed \$8.25, how much did the girls contribute?

12. The width of a rectangle is 8 feet less than its length. If the width is 9.5 feet, find the length of the rectangle.

13. A high school admitted 1125 sophomores, which was 78 fewer than the number admitted last year. How many sophomores were admitted last year?

14. A dealer sold an electric broiler for $39.98. This sum was $12.50 more than the broiler had cost him. How much did the broiler cost the dealer?

15. After using his baseball glove for some time, Charles sold it for $12.25 less than he paid for it. If Charles sold the glove for $3.50, how much did he pay for it originally?

16. Sue wishes to buy a radio that costs $38. If she has already saved $26 for this purpose, how much must she still save to buy the radio?

17. A merchant bought 8 dozen shirts. If he has sold all but 18 of them, how many shirts has he sold?

18. Mr. Alvarez withdrew from his savings account $25 per week for each of 8 weeks. He then had $1623 in his account. How much did he have in his account before he made these withdrawals?

19. In a basketball game the Knicks scored 12 points more than the Celtics. If the Knicks scored 108 points, how many points did the Celtics score?

20. One year Mr. Rico and his wife earned $28,632.35. If Mrs. Rico earned $9,757.80, how much did Mr. Rico earn?

21. Rita is taking a vacation on which she plans to spend $375. If she has already spent $193, how much does she have left to spend?

7   SOLVING SIMPLE EQUATIONS BY USING DIVISION OR MULTIPLICATION POSTULATES

Postulate 6: Division Property of Equality

The *division property of equality* states that for all numbers a, b, and c ($c \neq 0$):

$$\text{If } a = b, \text{ then } \frac{a}{c} = \frac{b}{c}.$$

Therefore, we can say: If both members of an equality are divided by the same nonzero number, the equality is retained.

Study the following examples:

In Arithmetic	*In Algebra*
If $8 = 8$	If $4w = 8$
Then $\dfrac{8}{4} = \dfrac{8}{4}$	Then $\dfrac{4w}{4} = \dfrac{8}{4}$ D_4 (Divide both members of the previous equation by 4.)
And $2 = 2$	And $w = 2$

Notice that the application of the division property in the equation $4w = 8$ resulted in the equivalent equations $\dfrac{4w}{4} = \dfrac{8}{4}$ and $w = 2$. All three equations have the same solution set $\{2\}$.

It is important to remember that when we apply the division property of equality, we divide both members of an equation by the same *non-zero* number. Division by zero is impossible.

Now we will use the division property of equality in solving equations.

MODEL PROBLEMS

Solve and check:

1. $8y = 56$	2. $22 = 4x$	3. $.3x = 9$
Solution	*Solution*	*Solution*
$8y = 56$	$22 = 4x$	$.3x = 9$
$\dfrac{8y}{8} = \dfrac{56}{8}$ D_8	$\dfrac{22}{4} = \dfrac{4x}{4}$ D_4	$\dfrac{.3x}{.3} = \dfrac{9}{.3}$ $D_{.3}$
		$\left[{\scriptstyle .3\overline{)9.0}}^{\,30.} \right]$
$y = 7$	$5\tfrac{1}{2} = x$	$x = 30$
Check	*Check*	*Check*
$8y = 56$	$22 = 4x$	$.3x = 9$
$8(7) \stackrel{?}{=} 56$	$22 \stackrel{?}{=} 4(5\tfrac{1}{2})$	$.3(30) \stackrel{?}{=} 9$
$56 = 56$ (True)	$22 = 22$ (True)	$9 = 9$ (True)
Answer: $y = 7$, or solution set is $\{7\}$.	*Answer:* $x = 5\tfrac{1}{2}$, or solution set is $\{5\tfrac{1}{2}\}$.	*Answer:* $x = 30$, or solution set is $\{30\}$.

4. The cost of putting up aluminum siding on a house is 5 times as much as the cost of painting it. If the aluminum siding costs $4000, find the cost of painting the house.

How to Proceed	*Solution*
(1) Represent the cost of painting the house by a variable.	Let y = cost of painting.
(2) Using the same variable, represent the cost of the aluminum siding.	Then $5y$ = cost of aluminum siding.
(3) Write the word statement as an equation.	$5y = 4000$ (Aluminum siding costs $4000.)
(4) Solve the equation. D_5 (mentally)	$y = 800$
(5) Check the original problem.	Painting costs $800; aluminum siding costs $4000. Does the siding cost 5 times as much as painting? Yes.

Answer: The cost of painting is $800.

Postulate 7: Multiplication Property of Equality

The *multiplication property of equality* states that for all numbers a, b, and c:

$$\text{If } a = b, \text{ then } ac = bc.$$

Therefore, we can say: **If both members of an equality are multiplied by the same number, the equality is retained.**

Study the following examples:

In Arithmetic	*In Algebra*	
If $8 = 8$	If $\dfrac{x}{4} = 8$	
Then $4 \cdot 8 = 4 \cdot 8$	Then $4 \cdot \dfrac{x}{4} = 4 \cdot 8$ M_4	(Multiply both members of the previous equation by 4.)
And $32 = 32$	And $x = 32$	

Notice that the application of the multiplication property in the equation $\dfrac{x}{4} = 8$ resulted in the equivalent equations $4 \cdot \dfrac{x}{4} = 4 \cdot 8$ and $x = 32$. All three equations have the same solution set $\{32\}$.

One might now expect that the application of the multiplication property of equality to an equation always gives an equivalent equation.

This is true, *with one important exception*. We may not multiply both members of an equation by zero to obtain an equivalent equation. The solution set of the equation $x = 2$ is $\{2\}$. If we multiply both members of this equation by zero, we obtain the equation $0 \cdot x = 0 \cdot 2$ or $0 \cdot x = 0$. The new equation $0 \cdot x = 0$ is not equivalent to the original equation $x = 2$, because the two equations do not have the same solution set. The number 1 is a member of the solution set of $0 \cdot x = 0$, but not a member of the solution set of $x = 2$. If we multiply both members of an equation by the same nonzero number, then we always obtain an equivalent equation. For example, if we multiply both members of $x = 2$ by 3, we obtain the equivalent equations $3x = 3 \cdot 2$ and $3x = 6$.

Now we will use the multiplication property of equality in solving equations.

MODEL PROBLEMS

In 1–3, solve and check.

1. $\dfrac{n}{3} = 12$

Solution

$$\dfrac{n}{3} = 12$$

$$3 \cdot \dfrac{n}{3} = 3 \cdot 12 \quad \text{M}_3$$

$$n = 36$$

Check

$$\dfrac{n}{3} = 12$$

$$\dfrac{36}{3} \overset{?}{=} 12$$

$$12 = 12 \quad \text{(True)}$$

Answer: $n = 36$, or solution set is $\{36\}$.

2. $8 = \dfrac{1}{2} x$

Solution

$$8 = \dfrac{1}{2} x$$

$$\left(\dfrac{1}{2} x \text{ is the same as } \dfrac{x}{2}. \right)$$

$$2 \cdot 8 = 2 \cdot \dfrac{x}{2} \quad \text{M}_2$$

$$16 = x$$

Check

$$8 = \dfrac{1}{2} x$$

$$8 \overset{?}{=} \dfrac{1}{2} (16)$$

$$8 = 8 \quad \text{(True)}$$

Answer: $x = 16$, or solution set is $\{16\}$.

3. $\dfrac{x}{9} = \dfrac{4}{3}$

Solution

$$\dfrac{x}{9} = \dfrac{4}{3}$$

$$9 \cdot \dfrac{x}{9} = 9 \cdot \dfrac{4}{3} \quad \text{M}_9$$

$$x = 12$$

Check

$$\dfrac{x}{9} = \dfrac{4}{3}$$

$$\dfrac{12}{9} \overset{?}{=} \dfrac{4}{3}$$

$$\dfrac{4}{3} = \dfrac{4}{3} \quad \text{(True)}$$

Answer: $x = 12$, or solution set is $\{12\}$.

4. Ned traveled $\frac{1}{4}$ of the distance that Ben traveled. If Ned traveled 12 kilometers, how far did Ben travel?

How to Proceed	*Solution*
(1) Represent the distance Ben traveled by a variable.	Let d = distance Ben traveled.
(2) Using the same variable, represent the distance Ned traveled.	Then $\frac{1}{4}d$ = distance Ned traveled.
(3) Write the word statement as an equation.	$\frac{1}{4}d = 12$ (Ned traveled 12 kilometers.)
(4) Solve the equation. M_4 (mentally)	$d = 48$
(5) Check in the original problem.	Ben traveled 48 kilometers and Ned traveled 12 kilometers. Did Ned travel $\frac{1}{4}$ of the distance that Ben traveled? Yes.

Answer: Ben traveled 48 kilometers.

■ **PROCEDURE.** To solve an equation in which a variable and a constant are related by the operation of multiplication or division:

1. Use the inverse operation, multiplying or dividing (as the case may be) both members of the equation by the constant. Perform the indicated operation(s) to obtain an equivalent equation in which only the variable itself is one member of the equation.

2. Check by determining that when the value obtained for the variable replaces it in the given equation, the resulting statement is true.

| EXERCISES |

In 1–40, solve and check the equation.

1. $3x = 15$	2. $10c = 90$	3. $20 = 5d$	4. $84 = 7y$
5. $5c = 5$	6. $6s = 0$	7. $5p = 9$	8. $16 = 4y$
9. $8m = 1$	10. $1 = 6b$	11. $4x = .8$	12. $.36 = 6m$
13. $\frac{1}{2}d = 18$	14. $20 = \frac{1}{10}r$	15. $\frac{2}{3}x = 18$	16. $\frac{a}{2} = 3$
17. $3y = 3$	18. $2b = 0$	19. $81 = 27q$	20. $15 = 2y$

21. $6c = 44$ **22.** $6w = 3$ **23.** $\frac{1}{10}x = 0$ **24.** $2a = .6$

25. $.4x = 3.2$ **26.** $1.4x = 5.6$ **27.** $.3c = 1.2$ **28.** $.02x = 25$

29. $.06x = 54$ **30.** $32 = .04z$ **31.** $.06y = 12$ **32.** $.15c = 300$

33. $\frac{1}{8}x = \frac{1}{4}$ **34.** $\frac{1}{3} = \frac{m}{4}$ **35.** $\frac{2}{3}b = 8$ **36.** $3\frac{1}{2}x = 7$

37. $7x = 12\frac{1}{4}$ **38.** $\frac{1}{3}y = \frac{5}{9}$ **39.** $\frac{x}{.5} = 4$ **40.** $\frac{t}{1.4} = 1$

41. If $9x = 36$, find the value of $2x$.

42. If $2x = 64$, find the value of $\frac{1}{4}x$.

43. If $\frac{t}{2} = 12$, find the value of $5t$.

44. If $\frac{2}{3}y = 16$, find the value of $3y + 7$.

45. If $.08y = .96$, find the value of $\frac{1}{2}y - 3$.

In 46–74, solve the problem using a variable and an equation.

46. Seven times a number is 63. Find the number.

47. Five times a number is 50. Find the number.

48. When a number is doubled, the result is 36. Find the number.

49. A number divided by 5 equals 17. Find the number.

50. A number divided by 4 is $3\frac{1}{2}$. Find the number.

51. One-half of a number is 12. Find the number.

52. Three-fifths of a number is 30. Find the number.

53. A number multiplied by .3 is 6. Find the number.

54. Four-hundredths of a number is 16. Find the number.

55. 4% of a number is 8. Find the number.

56. 15% of a number is 4.5. Find the number.

57. One-eighth of a number is $4\frac{1}{2}$. Find the number.

58. $33\frac{1}{3}$% of a number is $3\frac{2}{3}$. Find the number.

59. How many hours do you have to work to earn $132 if you are paid $5.50 per hour?

60. A man earned $1000 in 4 weeks. What was his weekly salary?

61. Marvin saved 25% of his allowance. If he saved $2.50, how much was his allowance?

62. John gained 12 pounds during the last year. If this represents one-tenth of his present weight, find his present weight.

63. Baseballs cost $3.50 each. How many baseballs can be bought for $28.00?

64. The width of a rectangle is $\frac{1}{5}$ of its length. If the width of the rectangle is 6 meters, what is its length?

65. The Giants won 24 games, which was 60% of all the games they played. How many games did they play?

66. Pearl bought a coat at a "40% off" sale. If she saved $48, what was the original price of the coat?

67. William deposited $90 in the bank last month. This was $2\frac{1}{2}$ times as much as Robert deposited. How much did Robert deposit last month?

68. Sandra cut a piece of lumber into 6 pieces of equal length. If each piece was $1\frac{1}{2}$ meters long, what was the length of the original piece of lumber?

69. Six months after Mr. Doyle had bought a car, he sold it, taking a loss of $\frac{1}{5}$ of the original price of the car. If he lost $850, what was the original price of the car?

70. At a sale a radio sold for $20. This amount was 80% of the original price. What was the original price?

71. A dealer sold a suit for 150% of the amount he paid for it. If the dealer sold the suit for $120, how much did it cost him?

72. The selling price of an article is 175% of the dealer's cost price. If the dealer sold the article for $28, how much did he pay for it?

73. When Irene bought a dress, she had to pay an 8% sales tax. If the sales tax was $2.40, what was the original price of the dress?

74. The Surevalve Company tested 5% of the valves it had produced. If 350 valves were tested, how many valves had the company produced?

8 SOLVING EQUATIONS BY COMBINING LIKE TERMS

■ **PROCEDURE.** To solve an equation in which like terms appear in either member of the equation:

1. Use the distributive property of multiplication to combine the like terms.

2. Solve the resulting equation by using inverse operations.

| MODEL PROBLEMS |

1. Solve and check: $6x + 3x = 36$

How to Proceed	*Solution*	*Check*
(1) Write the equation.	$6x + 3x = 36$	$6x + 3x = 36$ $6 \times 4 + 3 \times 4 \stackrel{?}{=} 36$
(2) Use the distributive property to combine like terms.	$(6 + 3)x = 36$ $9x = 36$	$24 + 12 \stackrel{?}{=} 36$ $36 = 36$ (True)
(3) Use the division property, D_9.	$x = 4$	

Answer: $x = 4$, or solution set is $\{4\}$.

2. The larger of two numbers is 4 times the smaller. If the sum of the two numbers is 55, find the numbers.

How to Proceed	*Solution*
(1) Represent the smaller number by a letter.	Let x = the smaller number.
(2) Represent "the larger of two numbers is 4 times the smaller."	Then $4x$ = the larger number.
(3) Write as an equation "the sum of the two numbers is 55."	$x + 4x = 55$ or $1x + 4x = 55$
(4) Solve the equation. First, combine like terms. Then, D_5.	$5x = 55$ $x = 11$
(5) Find the larger number.	$4x = 44$

Check: Is the larger number 4 times the smaller? $44 \stackrel{?}{=} 4 \times 11$. Yes.
Is the sum of the two numbers 55? $11 + 44 \stackrel{?}{=} 55$. Yes.

Answer: The smaller number is 11 and the larger number is 44.

| EXERCISES |

In 1–21, solve and check the equation.

1. $2a + 2a = 60$ 2. $8x + x = 72$ 3. $144 = 9b + 3b$
4. $12x - 4x = 108$ 5. $5x - 3x = 22$ 6. $18 = 7x - x$

7. $3\frac{1}{2}c + 2\frac{1}{2}c = 54$ 8. $3.6d - 2.4d = 24$ 9. $8x + 3x + 4x = 60$

10. $7y + 4y - y = 70$ 11. $3e - e + 4e = 90$ 12. $39 = 8c + 6c - c$

13. $3.6x + 1.4x = 30$ 14. $8.7x - 3.7x = 24$ 15. $18 = 1.4a + 4.6a$

16. $\frac{2}{3}x + \frac{5}{3}x = 21$ 17. $\frac{3}{4}y - \frac{1}{4}y = 17$ 18. $\frac{1}{4}a + \frac{1}{2}a = 18$

19. $\frac{3}{8}r - \frac{1}{4}r = 5$ 20. $40 = 1\frac{1}{2}b - \frac{1}{4}b$ 21. $38 = 1\frac{1}{5}s + 2\frac{3}{5}s$

In 22–30, use an algebraic equation to solve the problem.

22. The larger of two numbers is twice the smaller. If the sum of the two numbers is 96, find the numbers.

23. One number is 5 times another. If their difference is 96, find the numbers.

24. A number is one-half of another number. Find the numbers if their difference is 28.

25. A number is $\frac{2}{3}$ of another number. The sum of the two numbers is 50. Find the numbers.

26. Bob and Dan earned a total of $24 shoveling snow. If Bob earned 3 times as much as Dan, how much did each boy earn?

27. Lily spent 4 times as much as her sister Sue. If the girls spent $24, how much did each girl spend?

28. Herb bought a sandwich and a soft drink for $2.50. What was the price of each if the sandwich cost four times as much as the drink?

29. A house and a lot are worth $60,000. If the house is worth 6.5 times as much as the lot, find how much each is worth.

30. An electrician's hourly wage is 5 times that of his helper's. They were paid a total of $135 for a job on which the electrician worked 8 hours and the helper worked 5 hours. Find the hourly wage of the helper.

9 SOLVING EQUATIONS BY USING SEVERAL OPERATIONS

In the equation $2x + 3 = 15$, there are two operations indicated in the left member: *multiplication and addition.* To solve the equation we use the inverse operations: *division and subtraction.* In method 1 we first perform subtraction to undo the addition and then perform division to undo the multiplication. In method 2 we first perform division to undo the multiplication and then perform subtraction to undo the addition. Notice that both methods result in the same root.

Method 1	*Method* 2
$2x + 3 = 15$	$2x + 3 = 15$
$2x + 3 - 3 = 15 - 3$ S_3	$\dfrac{2x + 3}{2} = \dfrac{15}{2}$ D_2
$2x = 12$	
$x = 6$ D_2	$\dfrac{2x}{2} + \dfrac{3}{2} = \dfrac{15}{2}$ $\left(\dfrac{2x}{2} = x\right)$
Check	$x = \dfrac{12}{2}$ $S_{\frac{3}{2}}$
$2x + 3 = 15$	$x = 6$
$2(6) + 3 \overset{?}{=} 15$	
$12 + 3 \overset{?}{=} 15$	*Check* is shown at the left.
$15 = 15$ (True)	

Answer: $x = 6$, or solution set is $\{6\}$.

While both method 1 and method 2 yield the correct answer, method 1 usually avoids awkward fractions. In general it is preferable to perform addition or subtraction first and then to perform multiplication or division.

■ **PROCEDURE.** To solve an equation in which several operations are indicated, perform their inverse operations.

MODEL PROBLEMS

1. a. Solve and check: $5x + 15 + 2x = 71$
    b. Graph the solution set of the equation.

a. *How to Proceed*	*Solution*	*Check*
(1) Write the equation.	$5x + 15 + 2x = 71$	$5x + 15 + 2x = 71$
(2) Use the commutative property.	$5x + 2x + 15 = 71$	$5(8) + 15 + 2(8) \overset{?}{=} 71$
		$40 + 15 + 16 \overset{?}{=} 71$
		$71 = 71$
(3) Use the distributive property to combine like terms.	$(5 + 2)x + 15 = 71$	(True)
	$7x + 15 = 71$	
(4) Use the subtraction property, S_{15}.	$7x + 15 - 15 = 71 - 15$	
	$7x = 56$	
(5) Use the division property, D_7.	$x = 8$	

Answer: $x = 8$, or solution set is $\{8\}$.

b. Graph the solu-
   tion set $\{8\}$.

```
+--+--+--+--+--+--+--+--+--+--+->
0  1  2  3  4  5  6  7  8  9  10
```

2. Solve and check: $\frac{3}{5}x - 6 = 12$

Solution

$\frac{3x}{5} - 6 = 12$

$\frac{3x}{5} = 18$ A_6 (Mentally)

$5\left(\frac{3x}{5}\right) = 5(18)$ M_5

$3x = 90$

$x = 30$ D_3

Check

$\frac{3}{5}x - 6 = 12$

$\frac{3(30)}{5} - 6 \overset{?}{=} 12$

$\frac{90}{5} - 6 \overset{?}{=} 12$

$18 - 6 \overset{?}{=} 12$

$12 = 12$ (True)

Answer: $x = 30$, or solution set is $\{30\}$.

3. If 4 times a number is increased by 7, the result is 43. Find the number.

How to Proceed

(1) Represent the number by a letter.
(2) Write the word statement as an equation.
(3) Solve the equation.

Solution

Let x = the number.

$4x + 7 = 43$

$4x = 36$ S_7 (Mentally)

$x = 9$ D_4

Check: Does 4×9, increased by 7, give a result of 43?
        Yes, $36 + 7 = 43$.

Answer: The number is 9.

EXERCISES

In 1–18: a. Solve and check the equation. b. Graph the solution set of the equation.

1. $3x + 5 = 35$	2. $5a + 17 = 47$	3. $4x - 1 = 15$
4. $3y - 5 = 16$	5. $55 = 6a + 7$	6. $17 = 8c - 4$
7. $15x + 14 = 19$	8. $75 = 11 + 16x$	9. $14 = 12b + 8$
10. $8 = 18c - 1$	11. $11 = 15t + 1$	12. $11 = 16d - 1$

13. $6y + 2y - 3 = 21$ 14. $5y + 7 + y = 37$ 15. $26 = 3y + 2y - 9$
16. $8y - 3y + 7 = 87$ 17. $6x - x + 12 = 52$ 18. $95 = 8c - 3c + 65$

In 19–39, solve and check the equation.

19. $\dfrac{3a}{8} = 12$ 20. $\dfrac{4c}{9} = 20$ 21. $42 = \dfrac{7d}{8}$

22. $\frac{2}{3}x = 18$ 23. $12 = \frac{3}{4}y$ 24. $\frac{3}{5}m = 30$

25. $\dfrac{5t}{4} = \dfrac{45}{2}$ 26. $\dfrac{7t}{3} = \dfrac{14}{3}$ 27. $1.2 = \dfrac{4m}{5}$

28. $\dfrac{x}{3} + 4 = 13$ 29. $\dfrac{a}{4} - 9 = 51$ 30. $15 = \dfrac{b}{7} - 8$

31. $12 = \dfrac{y}{5} + 3$ 32. $.6m + \frac{1}{3} = 18\frac{1}{3}$ 33. $9d - \frac{1}{2} = 17\frac{1}{2}$

34. $4a + .2 = 5$ 35. $4 = 3t - .2$ 36. $\frac{1}{4}x - 5 = 11$
37. $\frac{1}{9}x + 4 = 13$ 38. $13 = \frac{1}{3}y - 5$ 39. $47 = \frac{4}{5}t + 7$

In 40–55, use an algebraic equation to solve the problem.

40. Ten times a number, increased by 9, is 59. Find the number.
41. The sum of 8 times a number and 5 is 37. Find the number.
42. If six times a number is decreased by 4, the result is 68. Find the number.
43. The difference between 4 times a number and 3 is 25. Find the number.
44. If a number is multiplied by 7, and the product is increased by 2, the result is 100. Find the number.
45. When 12 is subtracted from 3 times a number, the result is 24. Find the number.
46. Five-ninths of a number is 45. Find the number.
47. If 9 is added to one-half of a number, the result is 29. Find the number.
48. If two-thirds of a number is decreased by 4, the result is 56. Find the number.
49. If 38 is added to $\frac{5}{9}$ of a number, the result is 128. Find the number.
50. The sum of $\frac{3}{5}$ of a number and 2.3 is 14.6. Find the number.
51. The larger of two numbers is 12 more than the smaller. The sum of the numbers is 36. Find the numbers.
52. The larger of two numbers exceeds the smaller by 10. If the sum of the numbers is 76, find the numbers.
53. Dr. Cortes spent one hour driving from his home to Seaview Hospital and back. The trip to the hospital took 6 minutes less than the trip back. How long did it take him each way?

54. The Knicks beat the Nets by 12 points in a basketball game. The total number of points scored in the game was 208. How many points did each team score?

55. The total number of hours that George and Juan worked on a job was 89. If George worked 7 hours more than 3 times the number of hours Juan worked, find the number of hours each man worked.

10 MORE PRACTICE IN SOLVING EQUATIONS

In 1–42, solve and check the equation.

1. $9x = 108$
2. $9b + 8 = 8$
3. $4y + 2y = 39$
4. $.15x = .06$
5. $79 = 5x - 6$
6. $5y + 19 = 27$
7. $18 = 4a + 10$
8. $14 = n - 5.6$
9. $\frac{5}{7}b = 35$
10. $39 = x + 5x$
11. $7x - 3x = 68$
12. $48 = 7m - 1$
13. $48 = 5.7b - 4.5b$
14. $\frac{2x}{5} + 15 = 37$
15. $3x - \frac{1}{3} = 5\frac{2}{3}$
16. $87 = 2x - 13$
17. $.11a = 44$
18. $x - 3\frac{1}{8} = 7\frac{1}{4}$
19. $3y + 19 = 94$
20. $\frac{3t}{4} = 84$
21. $6x + 3x - x = 60$
22. $10r = 2$
23. $\frac{s}{4} - 5 = 7$
24. $.8c - 4 = 3.2$
25. $.01x = 5$
26. $.9b = .18$
27. $5n + 2n - 5 = 30$
28. $8m + 3 = 91$
29. $.3x + .2x = 8$
30. $\frac{n}{6} + 5\frac{2}{3} = 12\frac{1}{3}$
31. $\frac{4e}{5} - 32 = 28$
32. $29 = \frac{1}{3}a + 12$
33. $9x - 3x - x = 95$
34. $\frac{15}{4} = \frac{r}{8}$
35. $\frac{7}{10}x = 35$
36. $\frac{1}{2}t + \frac{1}{4}t = 12$
37. $\frac{x}{14} = \frac{5}{7}$
38. $x + \frac{1}{8} = \frac{7}{8}$
39. $\frac{1}{3}c - 1 = 14$
40. $3m - 6\frac{1}{2} = 8\frac{1}{2}$
41. $\frac{y}{8} = \frac{9}{2}$
42. $18 = 8c - 2c + 3$

chapter five

Logic

1 SENTENCES, STATEMENTS, AND TRUTH VALUES

To help us improve the way we reason, we will examine a branch of mathematics called logic. *Logic* is the study of reasoning. All *reasoning*, whether it is in mathematics or in everyday living, is based on the ways in which we put sentences together.

Sentences That Are True or False

In mathematics we are concerned with only one type of sentence. A *mathematical sentence* must state a fact or contain a complete idea. A mathematical sentence is like a simple declarative sentence in English. It contains a subject and a predicate. Because every mathematical sentence states a fact, we can sometimes judge such a sentence to be true or false. For example:

1. "Every triangle has three sides."   True mathematical sentence
2. "5 + 7 = 12"   True mathematical sentence
3. "Chicago is a city."   True mathematical sentence
4. "3 + 5 = 7"   False mathematical sentence
5. "Chicago is the capital of New York State."   False mathematical sentence

Non-Mathematical Sentences and Phrases

Sentences that ask questions or give commands are not mathematical sentences. We never use these sentences in reasoning because we cannot judge if they are true or false. Both in English and in mathematics a *phrase* is an expression that is only part of a sentence. Because a phrase does not contain a complete idea, we cannot judge if it is true or false. A phrase is not a mathematical sentence. The following examples are not mathematical sentences:

1. "Did you do your homework?"   This is not a mathematical sentence because it asks a question.

2. "Get home early."   This is not a mathematical sentence because it gives a command.

3. "Every triangle"   This is not a mathematical sentence because it is a phrase.

4. "4 + 5"   This is not a mathematical sentence because it is a phrase.

Sentences With Uncertain Truth Value

In reasoning we try to judge whether sentences are true or false. Sometimes we are faced with difficult sentences. Although these sentences contain complete thoughts, they are true for some people and false for other people. For example:

> 1. "It's hot in this room."
> 2. "That sound is too loud."
> 3. "Liver really tastes good."

In other cases it is impossible to tell whether the sentence is true or false because more information is needed. These sentences contain *variables* or unknowns. We have seen that a variable may be a symbol such as "n" or "x," but a variable may also be a pronoun like "he" or "it." Any sentence that contains a variable is called an *open sentence*.

For example:

1. "$x + 3 = 7$"   *Open* sentence; the variable is "x."

2. "She is my sister."   *Open* sentence; the variable is "she."

3. "It's on TV at 8 o'clock."   *Open* sentence; the variable is "it."

In studying equations we have seen that a variable is a placeholder for a set of replacements called the *domain* or *replacement set*. The set of all replacements that will change the open sentence into true sentences is called the *solution set* or *truth set*.

For example:

Open sentence: $x + 10 = 13$

Variable: x

Domain: $\{1, 2, 3, 4\}$

When $x = 3$, then $3 + 10 = 13$ is a true sentence.

Solution set: $\{3\}$

The concepts that we apply to sentences in algebra are exactly the same as those we apply to sentences that we speak to one another. Of course, we would not use a domain like {1, 2, 3, 4} for the open sentence "She is my sister." Common sense tells us to use a domain of girls' names. Look at how sentences are used in the conversation that follows:

In this column, Mary and David are talking to each other.

In this column, we see the *mathematical reasoning* in the conversation taking place.

1. Mary: "She's my sister."

1. "She is my sister" is an *open sentence*; the variable is "she."

2. David: "Who? Is it Abby?"

2. "Is it Abby?" is *not* a mathematical sentence because it asks a question. However, David has chosen a girl's name from a "commonsense" *domain*.

3. Mary: "No."

3. This means that the variable, "she," is replaced by "Abby." Then, "Abby is my sister" is a *false sentence*.

4. David: "Is it Joanna?"

4. This is not a mathematical sentence because it asks a question. But David has chosen another name from the *domain*.

5. Mary: "Yes. Joanna is my sister."

5. The variable, "she," is replaced by "Joanna." Then "Joanna is my sister" is a *true sentence*.

In the following example, we compare this conversation with the use of sentences in algebra. Open sentences, variables, domains, and solution sets behave in exactly the same way.

Open sentence: She is my sister.

Variable: She

Domain: {Girls' names}

When "she" is "Joanna," then "Joanna is my sister" is a true sentence.

Solution set: {Joanna}

Sometimes a solution set contains more than one element. If Mary has two sisters, then the solution set may be {Joanna, Jennifer}. Some people have no sisters. For them the solution set for the open sentence "She is my sister" is the *empty set* or *null set*, written as { } or as $\emptyset$.

Statements

A sentence that can be judged to be true or false is called a *statement* or a *closed sentence*. In a statement there are no variables.

The following diagram shows how different kinds of sentences are related to one another. This diagram should help in beginning a study of logic.

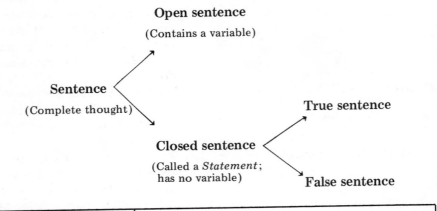

```
                    Open sentence
                 (Contains a variable)


    Sentence
(Complete thought)                      True sentence


                  Closed sentence
                (Called a Statement;
                  has no variable)      False sentence
```

MODEL PROBLEMS

Identify each of the following as a true sentence, false sentence, open sentence, or not a mathematical sentence at all.

Answers

1. John Wayne was a U.S. President.
2. John Wayne was a movie star.
3. He acted in many Westerns.

4. Do you like Westerns?

5. Read this book.

6. $3x + 5 < 26$

7. $5 + 7 + 8$

1. False sentence
2. True sentence
3. Open sentence (The variable is "He.")

4. Not a mathematical sentence (It asks a question.)

5. Not a mathematical sentence (It gives a command.)

6. Open sentence (The variable is "x.")

7. Not a mathematical sentence (It is a phrase.)

| EXERCISES |

In 1–8, tell whether each is or is not a mathematical sentence.

1. The school day ends at 3:15.
2. Take the bus.
3. Are you going?
4. If John goes.
5. Atlanta is a city in Alaska.
6. $x + 3 = 2x + 1$
7. Two teaspoons, three times a day.
8. Do the next seven problems.

In 9–15, all of the sentences are open sentences. Find the variable in every sentence.

9. She is smart.
10. We should not waste electricity.
11. It is my favorite color.
12. $4y < 20$
13. This is a great country.
14. You could do much better.
15. He was the most valuable player in the World Series.

In 16–23: a. Tell whether the sentence is true, false, or open. b. If the sentence is an open sentence, identify the variable.

16. The United States of America declared independence in 1776.
17. We celebrate Independence Day on June 14 every year.
18. San Francisco is a city in New York State.
19. A rectangle is a four-sided polygon.
20. $5x + 2 = 17$
21. $5(10) + 2 = 17$
22. $5(3) + 2 = 17$
23. $2^3 = 3^2$

In 24–28, use the replacement set {New York, Florida, California, Hawaii, Kansas} to find the truth set or solution set for each open sentence.

24. It was one of the last two states admitted to the U.S.A.
25. It does not border on or touch an ocean.
26. It is on the east coast of the United States.
27. Its capital is Sacramento.
28. It is one of the states of the United States of America.

In 29–40, use the domain of natural numbers to find the truth set or solution set for each open sentence. If no replacements make true sentences, write { }.

29. $x + 5 = 17$
30. $x - 5 = 17$
31. $\dfrac{2x}{3} = 12$
32. $56 = 3x - 4$

33. $2x + x = 6$ 34. $2x - x = 1$ 35. $x < 3$ 36. $x + 1 < 6$

37. $\dfrac{x}{8} = \dfrac{1}{2}$ 38. $\dfrac{2}{3} = \dfrac{x}{6}$ 39. $.2x + 3 = 6$ 40. $x + \dfrac{1}{3} = 3$

In 41–48, use the domain {square, triangle, rectangle, parallelogram, rhombus, trapezoid} to find the truth set for each open sentence. Identify an empty solution set by writing { }.

41. It has three and only three sides.
42. It has two pairs of opposite sides that are parallel.
43. It has four sides that are all equal in measure.
44. It must contain only right angles.
45. It has exactly six sides.
46. It has less than four sides.
47. It has exactly one pair of opposite sides that are parallel.
48. It has four angles that are equal in measure and four sides that are equal in measure.

2 NEGATIONS AND SYMBOLS

A sentence that has a *truth value* is called a statement. There are two truth values: *true* and *false*, shown by the symbols T and F. Every statement is either true or false. A statement cannot be both true and false at the same time.

In reasoning we learn how to make new statements based upon statements that we already know. One of the simplest examples of this type of reasoning is found in negating a statement.

The *negation* of a statement is formed by placing the word *"not"* within the original or given statement. The negation will always have the opposite truth value of the original statement.

For example:

1. Original: "John Kennedy was a U.S. President" is a true statement.
   Negation: "John Kennedy was *not* a U.S. President" is a false statement.

2. Original: "An owl is a fish" is a false statement.
   Negation: "An owl is *not* a fish" is a true statement.

There are many ways to place the word "not" into a statement to form its negation. One method starts the negation with the phrase "It is not true that . . .".

For example:

3. Original: "The post office handles mail." (True)
   Negation: "It is *not* true that the post office handles mail." (False)
   Negation: "The post office does *not* handle mail." (False)

Both negations here express the same false statement.

The First Symbols in Logic

In logic we use a single letter to represent a single complete thought. This means that an entire sentence may be replaced by a single letter of the alphabet. Although we can use any letter to represent a simple statement, the letters most often used in logic are *p*, *q*, and *r*. For example, let "*p*" represent "John Kennedy was a U.S. President."

To show a negation of a simple statement, we can place the symbol "~" before the letter for the original or given statement. Then "~*p*" would represent "John Kennedy was *not* a U.S. President." We read the symbol "~*p*" as "*not p*."

Here are some statements, both in words and in symbols. The symbolic form is written first in every example. Truth values are listed to the right.

1. *p*: There are twelve months in every year. (True)
   ~*p*: There are *not* twelve months in every year. (False)

2. *q*: 8 + 9 = 10 (False)
   ~*q*: 8 + 9 ≠ 10 (True)

These examples are clear because they are statements with known truth values. When *p* is true, then its negation, ~*p*, is false. When *q* is false, then its negation, ~*q*, is true. **A statement and its negation have opposite truth values.**

However, every sentence is not necessarily a statement with a known truth value. Questions arise in reasoning when we must deal with sentences having an uncertain truth value, such as "The radio is too loud."

The First Truth Table in Logic

To study sentences where we are uncertain of the truth value to be assigned, we use a device called a truth table. A *truth table* is a compact way of listing symbols to show all possible truth values for a set of sentences. The truth table for "negation" is very simple. We will see more complicated truth tables as we continue our study of logic.

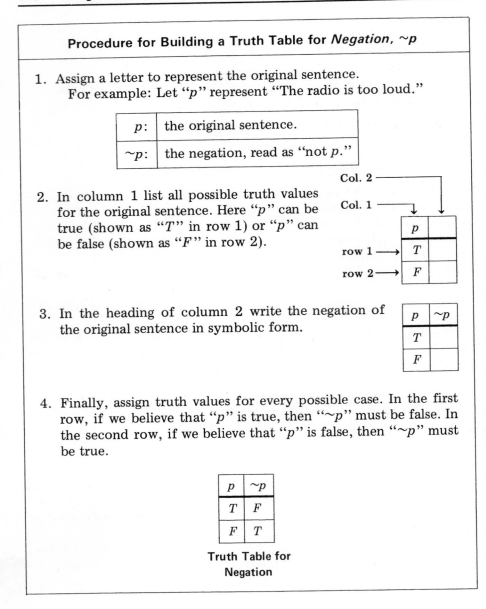

Procedure for Building a Truth Table for *Negation*, ~p

1. Assign a letter to represent the original sentence.
   For example: Let "*p*" represent "The radio is too loud."

p:	the original sentence.
~p:	the negation, read as "not *p*."

2. In column 1 list all possible truth values for the original sentence. Here "*p*" can be true (shown as "*T*" in row 1) or "*p*" can be false (shown as "*F*" in row 2).

   Col. 2 ——
   Col. 1 ——

p	
T	
F	

   row 1 ——→
   row 2 ——→

3. In the heading of column 2 write the negation of the original sentence in symbolic form.

p	~p
T	
F	

4. Finally, assign truth values for every possible case. In the first row, if we believe that "*p*" is true, then "*~p*" must be false. In the second row, if we believe that "*p*" is false, then "*~p*" must be true.

p	~p
T	F
F	T

   Truth Table for
   Negation

As a final note, we must be aware that many negations can be given in a statement. Each time another negation is included, the truth value of the statement will change.

For example,

1. *k*:   "A dime is a coin."   (True)

2. ~*k*:   "A dime is not a coin."   (False)

3. ~(~k):   "It is not true that a dime is not a coin."   (True)

4. ~(~(~k)):   "It is not the case that it is not true that a dime is not a coin."   (False)

Of course, we don't usually talk like this because it is too confusing. But we must be alert to someone who tries to win an argument by using many negations at the same time.

| MODEL PROBLEMS |

In 1–6: Let "q" represent "Oatmeal is a cereal."

Let "r" represent "She has cereal every morning."

For each given sentence: **a.** Write the sentence in symbolic form. **b.** Tell whether the sentence is true, false, or open.

Answers

1. Oatmeal is a cereal.   **a.** q   **b.** True
2. Oatmeal is not a cereal.   **a.** ~q   **b.** False
3. It is not true that oatmeal is a cereal.   **a.** ~q   **b.** False
4. She has cereal every morning.   **a.** r   **b.** Open
5. She does not have cereal every morning.   **a.** ~r   **b.** Open
6. It is not true that oatmeal is not a cereal.   **a.** ~(~q)   **b.** True

In 7 and 8, examine the following symbols used to represent statements and the truth value of each statement:

K: An obtuse triangle contains exactly one obtuse angle.   (True)

M: An acute triangle contains exactly one acute angle.   (False)

For each sentence given in symbolic form: **a.** Write a complete sentence in words to show what the symbols represent. **b.** Tell if the statements are true or false.

Answers

7. ~K   **a.** "An obtuse triangle does *not* contain exactly one obtuse angle." Or, "It is *not* true that an obtuse triangle contains exactly one obtuse angle."
           b. False

8. ~M   **a.** "An acute triangle does *not* contain exactly one acute angle."
           b. True

EXERCISES

In 1–8, write the negation of each sentence.

1. The school has a cafeteria.
2. Georgia is not a city.
3. A school bus is painted yellow.
4. $18 + 20 \div 2 = 28$
5. The measure of a right angle is $90°$.
6. $1 + 2 + 3 \neq 4$
7. There are 100 centimeters in a meter.
8. Today is not Saturday.

In 9–18, for each given sentence: **a.** Write the sentence in symbolic form, using the symbols shown below. **b.** Then tell if the sentence is true, false, or open.

> Let "p" represent "The library contains books."
> Let "q" represent "The library sells sandwiches."
> Let "r" represent "We have a good library."

9. The library contains books.
10. The library sells sandwiches.
11. The library does not sell sandwiches.
12. The library does not contain books.
13. We have a good library.
14. We do not have a good library.
15. It is not true that the library sells sandwiches.
16. It is not the case that the library contains books.
17. It is not true that the library does not contain books.
18. It is not the case that the library does not sell sandwiches.

In 19–22, copy the truth table for negation and fill in all missing symbols.

19.

p	$\sim p$
T	
F	

20.

q	$\sim q$
T	
	T

21.

r	$\sim r$
	F
	T

22.

k	$\sim k$

23. Copy the truth table and fill in all missing symbols.

q	$\sim q$	$\sim(\sim q)$	$\sim(\sim(\sim q))$
T			
F			

24. A truth table is shown for a sentence and its negation.

q	$\sim q$
T	F
F	T

Let "q" represent "$x + 3 > 8$."

Tell which row of the truth table shows the correct truth values when:

a. $x = 2$ b. $x = 9$ c. $x = 0$ d. $x = 5$ e. $x = \frac{1}{2}(12)$
f. $x =$ the sum of 8 and 3   g. $x =$ the difference of 8 and 3
h. $x =$ the product of 8 and 3   i. $x =$ the quotient of 8 and 3

In 25–32, examine the symbols used to represent sentences.

p: Summer follows spring. r: Baseball is a summer sport.
q: Baseball is a sport. s: He likes baseball.

Then for each sentence given in symbolic form: **a.** Write a complete sentence in words to show what the symbols represent. **b.** Tell if the sentence is true, false, or open.

25. $\sim p$ 26. $\sim q$ 27. $\sim r$ 28. $\sim s$
29. $\sim(\sim q)$ 30. $\sim(\sim p)$ 31. $\sim(\sim r)$ 32. $\sim(\sim s)$

In 33–36, state a word, a phrase, or a symbol that can be placed in the blank to make the resulting sentence true.

33. When "p" is true, then "$\sim p$" is ____.
34. When "p" is false, then "$\sim p$" is ____.
35. $\sim(\sim p)$ has the same truth value as ____.
36. A sentence that has a truth value is called a ____.

3 CONJUNCTION

We have seen that a single letter can be used in logic to represent a single complete thought. Sometimes a sentence contains more than one thought. In English we use connectives to form compound sentences that have two or more thoughts. One of the simplest connectives is the word "and."

In logic a *conjunction* is a compound sentence formed by combining two simple sentences, using the word "*and.*" When "p" and "q" represent simple sentences, the conjunction "p and q" is written in symbols as "$p \wedge q$." For example:

p: There is no school on Saturday.

q: I sleep late.

$p \wedge q$: There is no school on Saturday and I sleep late.

The truth table for a compound sentence contains more than two rows. The first thought (p) can be true or false, and the second thought (q) can be true or false. We must consider every possible combination of these true and false statements. The diagram shown below is called a *tree diagram*. By following its "branches" we can see that there are four possible "true-false" combinations for every two simple statements.

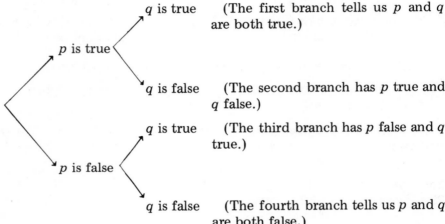

q is true   (The first branch tells us p and q are both true.)

p is true

q is false   (The second branch has p true and q false.)

q is true   (The third branch has p false and q true.)

p is false

q is false   (The fourth branch tells us p and q are both false.)

p	q
T	T
T	F
F	T
F	F

We will use this same order to set up the first two columns in every truth table containing two thoughts, p and q. By using the same order all the time, we can find specific cases quickly and we will reduce our chances of making errors.

The truth value of every compound sentence depends upon the truth value of the simple sentences used within the compound sentence. **The conjunction "p and q" is true only when both parts are true: "p"** must be true, and "q" must be true. If "p" is false, or if "q" is false, or if both are false, then the conjunction "p and q" must be false.

Consider these open sentences:

Let "p" represent "x is an even number."
Let "q" represent "$x < 8$."
Then "$p \wedge q$" represents "x is an even number and $x < 8$."

1. Let $x = 6$. p: 6 is an even number   (True)
                        q: $6 < 8$ (True)
           $p \wedge q$: 6 is an even number and $6 < 8$.   (True)
When both parts of the conjunction are true, then "p and q" is true.

2. Let $x = 10$. p: 10 is an even number   (True)

                          q: $10 < 8$ (False)

          $p \wedge q$: 10 is an even number and $10 < 8$.   (False)

      If any part of the conjunction is false, then "p and q" is false.

3. Let $x = 7$. p: 7 is an even number   (False)

                          q: $7 < 8$ (True)

          $p \wedge q$: 7 is an even number and $7 < 8$.   (False)

      If any part of the conjunction is false, then "p and q" is false.

4. Let $x = 13$. p: 13 is an even number   (False)

                          q: $13 < 8$ (False)

          $p \wedge q$: 13 is an even number and $13 < 8$.   (False)

      When both parts of the conjunction are false, then "p and q" is false.

Procedure for Building a Truth Table for *Conjunction, p ∧ q*

1. Assign two letters, each letter to serve as a symbol for a different simple sentence.

    For example: Let "p" represent "It is cold."
                   Let "q" represent "It is snowing."

2. List all possible truth values for the simple sentences "p" and "q" in the first two columns. Try to follow the same order as shown.

p	q
T	T
T	F
F	T
F	F

3. In the heading of the third column write the conjunction of the statements in symbolic form.

p	q	$p \wedge q$
T	T	
T	F	
F	T	
F	F	

4. Finally, assign truth values for the conjunction. When both simple statements "*p*" and "*q*" are true, then the conjunction "*p* and *q*" is true. In all other cases, the conjunction is false.

$p \wedge q$: "It is cold and it is snowing" will be true only when both parts are true.

p	q	$p \wedge q$
T	T	T
T	F	F
F	T	F
F	F	F

**Truth Table for
Conjunction**

A compound sentence may contain both conjunctions and negations at the same time. The truth table for such a sentence is developed in model problem 12 on page 134.

To build any truth table, work from the innermost parentheses first, or from the simplest level of thinking. This is very much like the order of operations we use in arithmetic and in solving equations.

MODEL PROBLEMS

In 1–6: Let "*p*" represent "Coffee is a beverage."   (True)
Let "*q*" represent "Toast is a beverage."   (False)
Let "*r*" represent "10 is divisible by 2."   (True)
Let "*s*" represent "10 is divisible by 3."   (False)

For each given sentence: **a.** Write the sentence in symbolic form. **b.** Tell whether the statement is true or false.

1. Coffee is a beverage and 10 is divisible by 2.

   Answer: **a.** $p \wedge r$ **b.** $T \wedge T$ = True

2. Coffee and toast are beverages.

   Answer: **a.** $p \wedge q$ **b.** $T \wedge F$ = False

3. Toast is a beverage and 10 is divisible by 2.

   Answer: **a.** $q \wedge r$ **b.** $F \wedge T$ = False

4. 10 is divisible by 2 and 10 is not divisible by 3.

   Answer: **a.** $r \wedge \sim s$ **b.** $T \wedge \sim F = T \wedge T =$ True

5. 10 is divisible by 2 and by 3.

   Answer: **a.** $r \wedge s$ **b.** $T \wedge F =$ False

6. Toast is not a beverage and 10 is not divisible by 3.

   Answer: **a.** $\sim q \wedge \sim s$ **b.** $\sim F \wedge \sim F = T \wedge T =$ True

7. Use the domain $\{1, 2, 3\}$ to find the truth set for the open sentence: $(x > 1) \wedge (x < 4)$.

   Solution: Let $x = 1$. $(1 > 1) \wedge (1 < 4)$
   False *and* true; conjunction is false.

   Let $x = 2$. $(2 > 1) \wedge (2 < 4)$
   True *and* true; conjunction is true.

   Let $x = 3$. $(3 > 1) \wedge (3 < 4)$
   True *and* true; conjunction is true.

Since a conjunction is true only when both simple sentences are true, the truth set or solution set is $\{2, 3\}$.

Answer: $\{2, 3\}$

In 8–11, examine the symbols used to represent statements about a rectangle with length *l* and width *w*. For each statement made, its truth value is noted.

Let "*p*" represent "Area = *lw*."   (True)

Let "*q*" represent "Perimeter = *l* + *w*."   (False)

Let "*r*" represent "Perimeter = 2*l* + 2*w*."   (True)

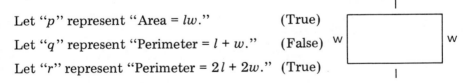

For each sentence given in symbolic form: **a.** Write a complete sentence in words to show what the symbols represent. **b.** Tell if the statement is true or false.

8. $p \wedge q$

   Answer: **a.** Area = *lw and* Perimeter = *l* + *w*.
   b. $T \wedge F =$ False statement.

9. $p \wedge r$

   Answer: **a.** Area = *lw and* Perimeter = 2*l* + 2*w*.
   b. $T \wedge T =$ True statement.

10. $\sim q \wedge p$

> *Answer:* **a.** Perimeter $\neq l + w$ *and* Area $= lw$.
> **b.** $\sim F \wedge T = T \wedge T =$ True statement.

11. $\sim(q \wedge p)$

> *Answer:* **a.** It is *not* the case that Perimeter $= l + w$ *and* Area $= lw$.
> **b.** $\sim(F \wedge T) = \sim(F) =$ True statement.

12. Build a truth table for the sentence $\sim(\sim p \wedge q)$.

Solution

(1) First, write all possible combinations of true-false statements for "p" and "q."

p	q
T	T
T	F
F	T
F	F

(2) Then, working inside the parentheses, we see that we first need "$\sim p$." Write "$\sim p$" in column 3 and negate the truth values for "p" found in column 1.

p	q	$\sim p$
T	T	F
T	F	F
F	T	T
F	F	T

(3) Next, to get "$\sim p \wedge q$," use the truth values found in columns 2 and 3 to write the truth values for the conjunction. Since "q" and "$\sim p$" are both true in the third row, this is the only conjunction that is true. All other rows are false.

p	q	$\sim p$	$\sim p \wedge q$
T	T	F	F
T	F	F	F
F	T	T	T
F	F	T	F

(4) Finally, negate the truth values for "$\sim p \wedge q$" found in column 4 to find the truth values of "$\sim(\sim p \wedge q)$" to be written in column 5.

p	q	$\sim p$	$\sim p \wedge q$	$\sim(\sim p \wedge q)$
T	T	F	F	T
T	F	F	F	T
F	T	T	T	F
F	F	T	F	T

13. Three sentences are written. The truth values are given for the first two sentences. Determine if the third sentence is true, is false, or has an uncertain truth value.

> "Trudie likes steak and Phil likes fish."   (False)
> "Trudie likes steak."   (True)
> "Phil likes fish."   (?)

Solution:

(1) Use symbols to represent the sentences. Indicate their truth values.

> $p \wedge q$ (False): "Trudie likes steak and Phil likes fish."
> p (True): "Trudie likes steak."
> q (?): "Phil likes fish."

(2) Construct a truth table for conjunction as follows:

The first sentence ($p \wedge q$) is given as false. In the truth table we see that $p \wedge q$ is false in rows 2, 3, and 4. Therefore, we can eliminate the case where $p \wedge q$ is true by crossing out row 1 of the truth table.

p	q	$p \wedge q$
~~T~~	~~T~~	~~T~~
T	F	F
F	T	F
F	F	F

(3) The second sentence (p) is given as true. In the three rows remaining in our truth table, p is true only in row 2. We eliminate the cases where p is false by crossing out rows 3 and 4 in the truth table.

p	q	$p \wedge q$
~~T~~	~~T~~	~~T~~
T	F	F
~~F~~	~~T~~	~~F~~
~~F~~	~~F~~	~~F~~

(4) There is only one case where $p \wedge q$ is false and where p is true. This occurs in row 2 of the truth table. In row 2, q is false. We can conclude that the statement q, representing "Phil likes fish," is false.

Answer: "Phil likes fish" is false.

14. Three sentences are given; the truth values are noted for the first two sentences. Determine if the third sentence is true, is false, or has an uncertain truth value.

"Jean likes hot weather and Bob likes cold weather."   (False)
"Jean likes hot weather."   (False)
"Bob likes cold weather."   (?)

Solution:

(1) Use symbols to represent the sentences. Include their truth values.

      $p \wedge q$ (False): "Jean likes hot weather and Bob likes cold weather."
        p (False): "Jean likes hot weather."
        q (?): "Bob likes cold weather."

(2) Construct a truth table for conjunction as follows:

The first sentence ($p \wedge q$) is false. We eliminate the case where $p \wedge q$ is true by crossing out row 1 of the truth table.

p	q	$p \wedge q$
~~T~~	~~T~~	~~T~~
T	F	F
F	T	F
F	F	F

(3) The second sentence (p) is false. This occurs in rows 3 and 4 of the truth table. We eliminate the case where p is true by crossing out row 2 of the truth table.

p	q	$p \wedge q$
~~T~~	~~T~~	~~T~~
~~T~~	~~F~~	~~F~~
F	T	F
F	F	F

(4) The remaining rows of the truth table show us that there are *two* cases where $p \wedge q$ is false and where p is false: rows 3 and 4. We see that q could be true, as in row 3, or that q could be false, as in row 4. Since we cannot place a single truth value on q, we conclude that q has an uncertain truth value.

Answer: "Bob likes cold weather" is uncertain.

| EXERCISES |

In 1–10, write each sentence in symbolic form, using the given symbols.

Let "p" represent "It is cold."
Let "q" represent "It is snowing."
Let "r" represent "The sun is shining."

1. It is cold and it is snowing.
2. It is cold and the sun is shining.
3. It is not cold.
4. It is not cold and the sun is shining.
5. It is snowing and the sun is not shining.
6. It is not cold and it is not snowing.
7. The sun is not shining and it is not cold.
8. The sun is not shining and it is cold.
9. It is not the case both that it is cold and it is snowing.
10. It is not the case both that it is snowing and it is not cold.

In 11–20, for each given statement: **a.** Write the statement in symbolic form, using the symbols shown below. **b.** Tell whether the statement is true or false.

Let "b" represent "Water boils at 100°C."   (True)
Let "f" represent "Water freezes at 0°C."   (True)
Let "t" represent "Normal body temperature is 37°C."   (True)
Let "r" represent "Room temperature is 60°C."   (False)

11. Normal body temperature is 37°C and water boils at 100°C.
12. Normal body temperature is 37°C and room temperature is 60°C.
13. Water freezes at 0°C and boils at 100°C.
14. Water freezes at 0°C and room temperature is 60°C.
15. Water does not boil at 100°C and water does not freeze at 0°C.
16. Room temperature is not 60°C and water boils at 100°C.
17. Normal body temperature is not 37°C and room temperature is 60°C.
18. It is not the case that water does not boil at 100°C.
19. It is not true that water boils at 100°C and freezes at 0°C.
20. It is not the case both that water boils at 100°C and room temperture is 60°C.

In 21–27, tell if the sentence is true, false, or open.

21. People wear gloves on their feet and shoes on their hands.
22. A square contains 4 right angles and a triangle contains 1 right angle.

23. Tuesday follows Monday and $1 + 2 = 3$.
24. This is a math book and it contains problems.
25. Most math books contain problems and $\frac{2}{3}$ of 12 is 8.
26. $x = 28 - 17$ and $x = 11$
27. The surgeon general of the U.S. has determined that cigarette smoking is dangerous to your health and warning labels are printed on cigarette packs.

In 28-30, copy the truth table for conjunction and fill in all missing symbols.

28.

p	q	$p \wedge q$
T	T	
T	F	
F	T	
F	F	

29.

m	r	$m \wedge r$
T	T	T
T		F
	T	F
		F

30.

f	g	$f \wedge g$

In 31-36, copy the truth table and fill in all missing symbols. (*Note:* In 32-36, prepare a complete truth table similar to the one shown in exercise 31.)

31.

p	q	$\sim p$	$\sim q$	$\sim p \wedge \sim q$
T	T			
T	F			
F	T			
F	F			

32.

p	q	$p \wedge q$	$\sim(p \wedge q)$

33.

p	q	$\sim q$	$p \wedge \sim q$

34.

p	q	$\sim p$	$\sim p \wedge q$

35.

p	q	$\sim q$	$q \wedge \sim q$	$\sim(q \wedge \sim q)$

36.

p	q	$\sim q$	$p \wedge \sim q$	$\sim(p \wedge \sim q)$

37. Use the domain of whole numbers to find the truth set for each compound open sentence.

    a. $(x > 5) \wedge (x < 8)$ b. $(x > 4) \wedge (x \leq 6)$ c. $(x \geq 3) \wedge (x < 7)$
    d. $(x < 5) \wedge (x < 2)$ e. $(x \leq 3) \wedge (x < 4)$ f. $(x > 8) \wedge (x > 3)$
    g. $(x \geq 3) \wedge (x + 5 < 7)$ h. $(x - 8 \leq 2) \wedge (3x > 24)$

In 38–49, examine the symbols assigned to represent sentences.

Let "*b*" represent "A banjo is a stringed instrument."
Let "*d*" represent "A drum is a stringed instrument."
Let "*g*" represent "A guitar is a stringed instrument."
Let "*s*" represent "She plays a guitar."

Then, for each sentence given in symbolic form: **a.** Write a complete sentence in words to show what the symbols represent. **b.** Tell if the sentence is true, false, or open.

38. $b \wedge g$ **39.** $b \wedge d$ **40.** $g \wedge s$ **41.** $b \wedge \sim d$
42. $b \wedge \sim g$ **43.** $b \wedge \sim s$ **44.** $g \wedge \sim d$ **45.** $\sim s \wedge g$
46. $\sim d \wedge \sim b$ **47.** $\sim (d \wedge b)$ **48.** $\sim (b \wedge g)$ **49.** $\sim (g \wedge s)$

In 50–57, state the word, phrase, or symbol that can be placed in the blank to make the resulting sentence true.

50. When p is true and q is true, then $p \wedge q$ is ____.
51. When p is false, then $p \wedge q$ is ____.
52. If p is true, or q is true, but not both, then $p \wedge q$ is ____.
53. When $p \wedge q$ is true, then p is ____ and q is ____.
54. When $p \wedge \sim q$ is true, then p is ____ and q is ____.
55. When $\sim p \wedge q$ is true, then p is ____ and q is ____.
56. When p is false and q is true, then $\sim (p \wedge q)$ is ____.
57. If both p and q are false, then $\sim p \wedge \sim q$ is ____.

In 58–64, three sentences are written. The truth values are given for the first two sentences. Determine if the third sentence is true, is false, or has an uncertain truth value.

58. "It is raining and I get wet."   (True)
     "It is raining."   (True)
     "I get wet."   (?)
59. "I have a headache and I take aspirin."   (False)
     "I have a headache."   (True)
     "I take aspirin."   (?)
60. "I have a headache and I take aspirin."   (False)
     "I have a headache."   (False)
     "I take aspirin."   (?)
61. "Both a potato and a hurricane have many eyes."   (False)
     "A potato has many eyes."   (True)
     "A hurricane has many eyes."   (?)
62. "Anna loves TV and Anna loves to stay home."   (True)
     "Anna loves TV."   (True)
     "Anna loves to stay home."   (?)

63. "Joe and Edna like to stay at home."   (False)
    "Joe likes to stay at home."   (True)
    "Edna likes to stay at home."   (?)
64. "Juan takes the train and the bus to go to work."   (False)
    "Juan takes the bus to go to work."   (False)
    "Juan takes the train to go to work."   (?)

In 65 and 66, a compound sentence is given using a conjunction. After examining the truth value of the compound sentence, determine if the truth value for each sentence that follows is true or false.

65. "Most plants need light and water to grow."   (True)
    a. Most plants need light to grow.
    b. Most plants need water to grow.
    c. Most plants do not need light to grow.
66. "I do not exercise and I know that I should."   (True)
    a. I do not exercise.
    b. I know that I should exercise.
    c. I exercise.

4   DISJUNCTION

We use many different connectives in our everyday conversation. Some connectives that might be heard at the local diner include: "Bacon and eggs"; "Lettuce and tomato"; "White bread or rye"; "Tea or coffee"; "Mustard or catsup." It should be clear that another common connective in our language is the word "or."

In logic, a *disjunction* is a compound sentence formed by combining two simple sentences using the word "or." When "p" and "q" represent simple sentences, the disjunction "p or q" is written in symbols as "p ∨ q." For example:

   p: You can use pencil to answer the test.

   q: You can use pen to answer the test.

   p ∨ q: You can use pencil or you can use pen to answer the test.

In this example the compound sentence "p or q" is true in many cases:

1. You answer in pencil. Here "p" is true and "q" is false. The disjunction "p ∨ q" is true.

2. You answer in pen. Here "*p*" is false while "*q*" is true. The disjunction "*p* ∨ *q*" is true.

3. You answer in pen but soon you run out of ink. You finish the test in pencil. Here "*p*" is true and "*q*" is true. Since you obeyed the rules and did nothing false, the disjunction "*p* ∨ *q*" is true.

The disjunction "*p* or *q*" is true when any part of the compound sentence is true: "*p*" is true, or "*q*" is true, or both "*p*" and "*q*" are true.

In fact, there is only one case where the disjunction "*p* or *q*" is false: Both "*p*" and "*q*" are false.

Procedure for Building a Truth Table for *Disjunction, p* ∨ *q*

1. Assign two letters; each letter is to serve as a symbol for a different simple sentence.

   For example,

   > Let "*p*" represent "The battery is dead."
   > Let "*q*" represent "We are out of gas."

2. List all possible truth values for the simple sentences "*p*" and "*q*" in the first two columns. Use the same order that was established for conjunction.

p	*q*
T	T
T	F
F	T
F	F

3. In the heading of the third column write the disjunction of the statements in symbolic form.

p	*q*	*p* ∨ *q*
T	T	
T	F	
F	T	
F	F	

4. Finally, assign truth values for the disjunction. All cases will be true except for the last row. When both "*p*" and "*q*" are false, the disjunction is false.

$p \vee q$: "The battery is dead or we are out of gas" will be true when the battery is dead, or when there is no gas, or when both problems exist.

p	q	$p \vee q$
T	T	T
T	F	T
F	T	T
F	F	F

**Truth Table for
Disjunction**

Two Uses of the Word "Or"

When we use the word "or" to mean that *one or both* of the simple sentences are true, we call this the *inclusive or*. The truth table we have just developed shows the truth values for the "inclusive or."

There are times when the word "or" is used in a different way, as in "He is in grade 9 or he is in grade 10." Here it is not possible for both simple sentences to be true at the same time. When we use the word "or" to mean that *one and only one* of the simple sentences is true, we call this the *exclusive or*. The truth table for the "exclusive or" will be different from the table shown for disjunction. In the "exclusive or" the disjunction "*p* or *q*" will be true when *p* is true, or when *q* is true, but not both.

We will use only the "inclusive or" in this book. Whenever we speak of disjunction, "*p or q*" will be true when *p* is true, or when *q* is true, or when *both p* and *q* are true.

Logic and Sets

Some people believe that logic is not like any other kind of mathematics that they have ever seen. This is not true. Conjunction and disjunction behave in exactly the same way as operations we have seen with sets. Consider this example in logic:

Let *p* represent "$x < 4$."
Let *q* represent "$x > 1$."
Let the domain = {1, 2, 3, 4, 5}.
What is the truth set of the conjunction $p \wedge q$?
What is the truth set of the disjunction $p \vee q$?

The conjunction is true only when both "*p*" and "*q*" are true.

This is seen when $x = 2$ and $x = 3$. So, $p \land q = \{2, 3\}$. The disjunction is true when "p" is true, or "q" is true, or both are true. This is seen for all values of the domain. So, $p \lor q = \{1, 2, 3, 4, 5\}$.

We can think of this problem in terms of sets: For the domain $\{1, 2, 3, 4, 5\}$ the solution set of "$x < 4$" is $\{1, 2, 3\}$. For the domain $\{1, 2, 3, 4, 5\}$ the solution set of "$x > 1$" is $\{2, 3, 4, 5\}$. Let set $A = \{1, 2, 3\}$ and set $B = \{2, 3, 4, 5\}$, as pictured in the diagram.

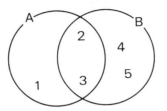

The intersection of two sets contains only those elements common to both. So, $A \cap B = \{2, 3\}$. The union of two sets contains the elements found in one set, or the other, or both. So, $A \cup B = \{1, 2, 3, 4, 5\}$.

By comparing these two approaches, we observe that:

1. **Conjunction ($p \land q$) behaves exactly like intersection ($A \cap B$).**

2. **Disjunction ($p \lor q$) behaves exactly like union ($A \cup B$).**

It is also possible to compare the negation of a statement with the complement of a set.

a. When p is true, then $\sim p$ is false. When an element of the domain is in set A, then it is not in the complement $\overline{A}$.

b. When p is false, then $\sim p$ is true. When an element of the domain is not in set A, then it is in its complement $\overline{A}$.

This leads us to the third observation:

3. **Negation ($\sim p$) behaves exactly like the complement ($\overline{A}$).**

MODEL PROBLEMS	

In 1–6: Let "k" represent "Kevin won the play-off."
        Let "a" represent "Alexis won the play-off."
        Let "n" represent "Nobody won."

Write each given sentence in symbolic form.

1. Kevin or Alexis won the play-off. $k \lor a$ *Ans.*
2. Kevin won the play-off or nobody won. $k \lor n$ *Ans.*

3. Alexis won the play-off or Alexis didn't win. $a \lor \sim a$ *Ans.*
4. It is not true that Kevin or Alexis won the play-off.
$$\sim(k \lor a) \quad Ans.$$
5. Either Kevin did not win the play-off or Alexis did not win.
$$\sim k \lor \sim a \quad Ans.$$
6. It's not the case that Alexis and Kevin won the play-off.
$$\sim(a \land k) \quad Ans.$$

In 7–10, examine the symbols used to represent the statements as shown. For each statement, its truth value is noted.

Let "k" represent "Every square is a rhombus."   (True)
Let "m" represent "Every rhombus is a square."   (False)
Let "t" represent "Every square is a parallelogram."   (True)

For each sentence given in symbolic form: a. Write a complete sentence in words to show what the symbols represent. b. Tell if the statement is true or false.

Answers

7. $k \lor t$ a. Every square is a rhombus or every square is a parallelogram.
    b. $T \lor T$ is a true disjunction.

8. $k \lor m$ a. Every square is a rhombus or every rhombus is a square.
    b. $T \lor F$ is a true disjunction.

9. $m \lor \sim t$ a. Every rhombus is a square or every square is not a parallelogram.
    b. $F \lor \sim T = F \lor F$ = a false disjunction.

10. $\sim(m \lor t)$ a. It is not the case that every rhombus is a square or every square is a parallelogram.
    b. $\sim(F \lor T) = \sim(T)$ = a false statement.

| EXERCISES |

In 1–10, write each sentence in symbolic form, using the given symbols.

Let "s" represent "I will study."
Let "p" represent "I will pass the test."
Let "f" represent "I am foolish."

1. I will study or I am foolish.
2. I will study or I will not pass the test.
3. I will study and I will pass the test.
4. I will pass the test or I am foolish.
5. I am not foolish and I will pass the test.
6. I will not study or I am foolish.
7. I will study or I will not study.
8. I will study and I will pass the test, or I am foolish.
9. It is not true that I will study or I am foolish.
10. It is not the case that I will not study or I am not foolish.

In 11-20, for each given statement: a. Write the statement in symbolic form, using the symbols given below. b. Tell whether the statement is true or false.

Let "*c*" represent "A meter contains 100 centimeters."   (True)
Let "*m*" represent "A meter contains 1000 millimeters."   (True)
Let "*k*" represent "A kilometer is 1000 meters."   (True)
Let "*l*" represent "A meter is a liquid measure."   (False)

11. A meter contains 1000 millimeters or a kilometer is 1000 meters.
12. A meter contains 100 centimeters or a meter is a liquid measure.
13. A meter contains 100 centimeters or 1000 millimeters.
14. A kilometer is not 1000 meters or a meter does not contain 100 centimeters.
15. A meter is a liquid measure or a kilometer is 1000 meters.
16. A meter is a liquid measure and a meter contains 100 centimeters.
17. It is not the case that a meter contains 100 centimeters or 1000 millimeters.
18. It is false that a kilometer is not 1000 meters or a meter is a liquid measure.
19. A meter contains 100 centimeters and 1000 millimeters or a meter is a liquid measure.
20. It is not true that a meter contains 100 centimeters or a meter is a liquid measure.

In 21-23, copy the truth table for disjunction and fill in the missing symbols.

21.

p	q	$p \lor q$
T	T	
T	F	
F	T	
F	F	

22.

k	t	$k \lor t$
T		
T		
F		
F	F	F

23.

p	r	$p \lor r$

In 24–29, copy the truth table and fill in all missing symbols. (*Note:* In 24–29, prepare a complete truth table similar to the one shown in exercise 21.)

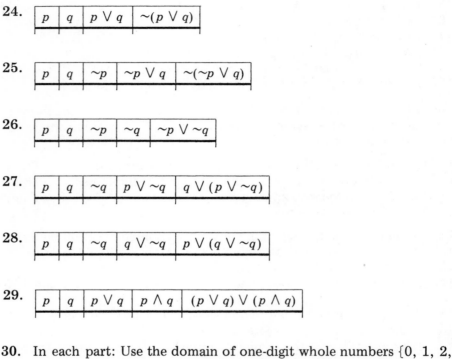

24.

p	q	$p \lor q$	$\sim(p \lor q)$

25.

p	q	$\sim p$	$\sim p \lor q$	$\sim(\sim p \lor q)$

26.

p	q	$\sim p$	$\sim q$	$\sim p \lor \sim q$

27.

p	q	$\sim q$	$p \lor \sim q$	$q \lor (p \lor \sim q)$

28.

p	q	$\sim q$	$q \lor \sim q$	$p \lor (q \lor \sim q)$

29.

p	q	$p \lor q$	$p \land q$	$(p \lor q) \lor (p \land q)$

30. In each part: Use the domain of one-digit whole numbers $\{0, 1, 2, \ldots, 9\}$ to find the truth set of the compound open sentence.

　　a. $(x < 3) \lor (x < 2)$　　b. $(x \geq 8) \lor (x < 1)$　c. $(x > 9) \lor (x \leq 3)$

　　d. $(x > 12) \lor (x < 4)$　e. $(x < 5) \lor (x > 9)$　f. $(x > 2) \lor (x < 7)$

In 31–42, examine the symbols assigned to represent sentences.

　　Let "b" represent "Biology is a science."
　　Let "s" represent "Spanish is a language."
　　Let "h" represent "Homemaking is a language."
　　Let "d" represent "It's a difficult course."

Then, for each sentence given in symbolic form: a. Write a complete sentence in words to show what the symbols represent. b. Tell if the sentence is true, false, or open.

31. $s \lor h$	32. $b \lor s$	33. d	34. $\sim s \lor h$
35. $\sim d$	36. $b \lor \sim h$	37. $\sim b \lor \sim s$	38. $\sim(s \lor h)$
39. $s \land h$	40. $s \land b$	41. $\sim(\sim b \lor s)$	42. $\sim(\sim s \lor h)$

In 43–49, state the word, phrase, or symbol that can be placed in the blank to make the resulting sentence true.

43. When p is true, then $p \lor q$ is ___.
44. When q is true, then $p \lor q$ is ___.
45. When p is false and q is false, then $p \lor q$ is ___.
46. When $p \lor \sim q$ is false, then p is ___ and q is ___.
47. When $\sim p \lor q$ is false, then p is ___ and q is ___.
48. When p is false and q is true, then $\sim(p \lor q)$ is ___.
49. When p is false and q is true, then $\sim p \lor \sim q$ is ___.

In 50–54, three sentences are written. The truth values are given for the first two sentences. Determine whether the third sentence is true, is false, or has an uncertain truth value.

50. "She will sink." (False)
 "She will swim." (True)
 "She will sink or she will swim." (?)

51. "I will work after school or I will study more." (True)
 "I will work after school." (False)
 "I will study more." (?)

52. "Michael cannot swim or skate." (False)
 "Michael cannot swim." (False)
 "Michael cannot skate." (?)

53. "Nicolette is my friend or I have two left feet." (True)
 "Nicolette is my friend." (True)
 "I have two left feet." (?)

54. "Jennifer draws well or plays the cello." (True)
 "Jennifer does not draw well." (False)
 "Jennifer plays the cello." (?)

5 THE CONDITIONAL

The connective that we use most often in reasoning can be found in the following sentence:

"If the fever continues, then he should see a doctor."

To find the connective, first list the simple sentences using "p" and "q."

p: The fever continues.
q: He should see a doctor.

The connective is seen in the words that remain, "If . . . then."

In English such a sentence is called a complex sentence. In mathematics, however, all sentences formed by connectives are called compound sentences.

In logic a *conditional* is a compound sentence formed by combining two simple sentences using the words *"if . . . then."* When *"p"* and *"q"* represent simple sentences, the conditional "if *p* then *q*" is written in symbols as *"p → q."*

A conditional is sometimes called an *implication*. This allows us to read the symbols for the conditional *p → q* as *"p implies q."* Let us look at another example.

> p: It is snowing.
> q: The temperature is below freezing.
> $p → q$: *If* it is snowing, *then* the temperature is below freezing.

or

> $p → q$: It is snowing *implies* that the temperature is below freezing.

Certainly we would agree that the compound sentence "If *p* then *q*" is true for this example: "If it is snowing, then the temperature must be below freezing." However, if we reverse the order of the simple sentences to form the compound "If *q* then *p*," we will get a sentence with a completely different meaning:

> $q → p$: *If* the temperature is below freezing, *then* it is snowing.

When the temperature is below freezing, it does not necessarily follow that it must be snowing. The conditional "If *q* then *p*" is not necessarily a true statement. We must be very careful. The *order* in which we connect the two simple sentences can *sometimes* result in forming two conditionals with *different truth values*.

The Parts of a Conditional

The parts of the conditional *if p then q* can be identified by name:

> *p* is called the *premise*, the *hypothesis*, or the *antecedent*. It is an assertion or a sentence that begins our argument. The antecedent is usually connected to the word "if."

q is called the *conclusion* or the *consequent*. It is an ending or a sentence that closes our argument. The consequent is usually connected to the word "then."

There are different ways to write the conditional "if p then q." Notice that the antecedent p is connected to the word "if" in the examples shown:

$p \to q$: "If $\underbrace{\text{Alice scores one more point,}}_{\substack{\text{antecedent} \\ \text{or} \\ \text{hypothesis}}}$ then $\underbrace{\text{our team will win.}}_{\substack{\text{consequent} \\ \text{or} \\ \text{conclusion}}}$"

$p \to q$: "$\underbrace{\text{Our team will win}}_{\substack{\text{consequent} \\ \text{or} \\ \text{conclusion}}}$ if $\underbrace{\text{Alice scores one more point.}}_{\substack{\text{antecedent} \\ \text{or} \\ \text{hypothesis}}}$"

Both sentences say the same thing: We hypothesize or hope that Alice scores one more point. When that happens, we can conclude that our team will win. Although the conditional may be written in different forms "using words," notice that the antecedent p is always written first when "using symbols" as in $p \to q$.

Procedure for Building a Truth Table for the *Conditional, $p \to q$*

1. Let p serve as the symbol for the antecedent and let q serve as the symbol for the consequent.

   For example: Dr. Cathy Russo told her patient, Bill, "If you take the medicine, then you'll feel better in 24 hours."

   p: You take the medicine.
   q: You'll feel better in 24 hours.

2. List all possible truth values for the antecedent p and the consequent q in the first two columns. Use the same order established for the other connectives.

p	q
T	T
T	F
F	T
F	F

p	q	p → q
T	T	
T	F	
F	T	
F	F	

3. In the heading of the third column, write the conditional *"if p then q"* in symbolic form.

4. Assign truth values to the conditional by considering the truth values for *p* and *q* in each row.

Row 1: *p* is true, Bill does take the medicine. *q* is true, he does feel better in 24 hours. It appears that Dr. Russo has told Bill the truth and so we can assign "true" to the conditional statement, "If you take the medicine, then you will feel better in 24 hours."

p	q	p → q
T	T	T
T	F	
F	T	
F	F	

Row 2: *p* is true, Bill does take the medicine. But *q* is false, he does *not* feel better in 24 hours. Because the medicine did *not* make Bill feel better, Dr. Russo did not tell Bill the truth. We can assign "false" to Dr. Russo's conditional statement, "If you take the medicine, then you will feel better in 24 hours."

p	q	p → q
T	T	T
T	F	F
F	T	
F	F	

Rows 3 and 4: In the last two rows, the antecedent *p* is false; Bill does *not* take the medicine. Remember, we are trying to place a truth value on the conditional statement made by Dr. Russo, "If you take the medicine, then you'll feel better in 24 hours."

p	q	p → q
T	T	T
T	F	F
F	T	?
F	F	?

If Bill does *not* take the medicine, it is possible that he could feel better (the consequent *q* is true, as in Row 3) or that he could *not* feel better (the consequent *q* is false, as in Row 4). In both cases, there is no way to test the statement made by Dr. Russo. We cannot say that the doctor told Bill a lie because she told him only what would happen if he *did* take the medicine.

Since we cannot accuse the doctor of making a false statement to Bill in these two cases, we will assign *"true"* to Dr. Russo's conditional statement, "If you take the medicine, then you'll feel better in 24 hours."

$p \rightarrow q$: "If you take the medicine, then you'll feel better in 24 hours" will be true in all cases except one: when the medicine is taken and Bill does not feel better in 24 hours.

p	q	$p \rightarrow q$
T	T	T
T	F	F
F	T	T
F	F	T

Truth Table for Conditional

■ **The conditional "if p then q" is false when a true hypothesis "p" leads to a false conclusion "q."** In all other cases, the conditional "if p then q" will be true.

The Hidden Conditional

We are constantly faced with the use of conditionals in our everyday lives. Often the words "if . . . then" do not appear in a sentence. In such a case, we say that the sentence has a hidden conditional. We can still understand that the sentence is a conditional because it contains an antecedent p and a consequent q. We can rewrite the words in the sentence so that the conditional form "if p then q" becomes more obvious.

For example:

1. "When this assignment has been written, you should hand it in" becomes:

   $p \rightarrow q$: "*If* the assignment has been written, *then* you should hand it in."

2. "For upset stomach, take Brand A pills" becomes:

   $p \rightarrow q$: "*If* you have an upset stomach, *then* you should take Brand A pills."

3. "Vote for me and I'll whip unemployment" becomes:

   $p \rightarrow q$: "*If* you vote for me, *then* I'll whip unemployment."

4. "$x + 3 = 10$, therefore $x = 7$" becomes:

   $p \rightarrow q$: "*If* $x + 3 = 10$, *then* $x = 7$."

| MODEL PROBLEMS |

In 1 and 2, for each given sentence: **a.** Identify the hypothesis p. **b.** identify the conclusion q.

1. If Mrs. Garbowski assigns homework, then you'd better do it.

   Answer: **a.** p: Mrs. Garbowski assigns homework.
   b. q: You'd better do the homework.

2. You can assemble the bicycle if you follow these easy directions.

   Answer: **a.** p: You follow these easy directions.
   b. q: You can assemble the bicycle.

In 3–6, identify the truth value to be assigned to each conditional statement.

3. If $2^2 = 4$, then $2^3 = 8$.

   Solution: The hypothesis p is "$2^2 = 4$," which is true.
   The conclusion q is "$2^3 = 8$," which is true.
   The conditional $p \rightarrow q$ $(T \rightarrow T)$ is true. *Answer:* True

4. If 9 is an odd number, then 9 is prime.

   Solution: The hypothesis p is "9 is an odd number," which is true.
   The conclusion q is "9 is prime," which is false because 9 is divisible by 3.
   The conditional $p \rightarrow q$ $(T \rightarrow F)$ is false. *Answer:* False

5. If a square has 5 sides, then $5 + 5 = 10$.

   Solution: The antecedent p is "A square has 5 sides," which is false.
   The consequent q is "$5 + 5 = 10$," which is true.
   The conditional $p \rightarrow q$ $(F \rightarrow T)$ is true. When we start with a false antecedent, we cannot prove that the conditional is false. *Answer:* True

6. If time goes backward, then I'll get younger every day.

   Solution: The antecedent *p* is "Time goes backward," which is false.
   The consequent *q* is "I'll get younger every day," which is false.
   The conditional $p \rightarrow q$ $(F \rightarrow F)$ is true. *Answer:* True

In 7–10, for each given statement: **a.** Write the statement in symbolic form, using the symbols given below. **b.** Tell whether the statement is true or false.

Let "*m*" represent "Tuesday follows Monday."   (True)
Let "*w*" represent "There are seven days in one week."   (True)
Let "*h*" represent "There are 40 hours in a day."   (False)

Answers

7. If Tuesday follows Monday, then there are seven days in one week.
   a. $m \rightarrow w$
   b. $T \rightarrow T$ is true.

8. If there are seven days in one week, then there are 40 hours in a day.
   a. $w \rightarrow h$
   b. $T \rightarrow F$ is false.

9. If Tuesday does not follow Monday, then there are not seven days in one week.
   a. $\sim m \rightarrow \sim w$
   b. $F \rightarrow F$ is true.

10. Tuesday follows Monday if there are not seven days in one week.
    a. $\sim w \rightarrow m$
    b. $F \rightarrow T$ is true.

EXERCISES

In 1–8, for each given sentence: **a.** Identify the hypothesis *p*. **b.** Identify the conclusion *q*.

1. If it rains, then the game is cancelled.
2. If it is 9:05 a.m., then I'm late to class.
3. When it rains, then I do not have to water the lawn.
4. You can get to the stadium if you take the Third Avenue bus.
5. The perimeter of a square is $4x + 8$ if one side of the square is $x + 2$.
6. If a polygon has exactly three sides, it is a triangle.
7. If the shoe fits, wear it.
8. When you have a headache, you should take aspirin and get some rest.

In 9–14, write each sentence in symbolic form, using the given symbols.

p: The test is easy.   *q*: Sam studies.   *r*: Sam passes the test.

   9. If the test is easy, then Sam will pass the test.
  10. If Sam studies, then Sam will pass the test.
  11. If the test is not easy, then Sam will not pass the test.
  12. The test is easy if Sam studies.
  13. Sam will not pass the test if Sam doesn't study.
  14. Sam passes the test if the test is easy.

In 15–22, for each given statement: **a.** Write the statement in symbolic form, using the symbols given below. **b.** Tell whether the conditional statement is true or false, based upon the truth values given below.

r: The race is difficult. (True)   *p*: Karen practices. (False)
w: Karen wins the race. (True)

  15. If Karen practices, then Karen will win the race.
  16. If Karen wins the race, then Karen has practiced.
  17. If Karen wins the race, the race is difficult.
  18. Karen wins the race if the race is not difficult.
  19. Karen will not win the race if Karen does not practice.
  20. Karen practices if the race is difficult.
  21. If the race is not difficult and Karen practices, then Karen will win the race.
  22. If the race is difficult and Karen does not practice, then Karen will not win the race.

In 23–25, copy the truth table for the conditional and fill in the missing symbols.

23.

r	*t*	*r* → *t*
T	*T*	*T*
T	*F*	*F*
F	*T*	
F	*F*	

24.

k	*m*	*k* → *m*
T	*T*	*T*
F	*T*	*T*
F	*F*	*T*

25.

q	*r*	*q* → *r*

In 26–33, find the truth value to be assigned to the conditional statement.

  26. If $5 + 7 = 12$, then $7 + 5 = 12$.   27. If $3 > 10$, then $10 > 13$.
  28. If $1 \cdot 1 = 1$, then $1 \cdot 1 \cdot 1 = 1$.

29. If $1 + 2 + 3 = 1 \cdot 2 \cdot 3$, then $1 + 2 = 1 \cdot 2$.

30. $12 \div 3 = 9$ if $12 \div 9 = 3$.

31. $2 + 2 = 2^2$ if $3 + 3 = 3^2$.   **32.** $2^3 = 3^2$ if $2^4 = 4^2$.

33. If every square is a rectangle, then every rectangle is a square.

In 34–49, examine the symbols assigned to represent sentences and the truth values assigned to these sentences.

Let "*j*" represent "I jog."   (True)
Let "*d*" represent "I diet."   (False)
Let "*g*" represent "I feel well."   (True)
Let "*h*" represent "I get hungry."   (True)

For the compound sentences in symbolic form: **a.** Write a complete sentence in words to show what the symbols represent. **b.** Tell whether the compound sentence is true or false.

34. $j \rightarrow g$ **35.** $d \rightarrow h$ **36.** $h \rightarrow d$ **37.** $\sim g \rightarrow j$

38. $\sim g \rightarrow \sim j$ **39.** $g \rightarrow \sim h$ **40.** $h \rightarrow \sim d$ **41.** $\sim d \rightarrow \sim h$

42. $\sim j \rightarrow \sim g$ **43.** $j \rightarrow d$ **44.** $(j \wedge h) \rightarrow g$ **45.** $j \rightarrow (h \wedge g)$

46. $(j \vee d) \rightarrow h$ **47.** $d \rightarrow (h \wedge \sim g)$ **48.** $\sim j \rightarrow (d \wedge h)$ **49.** $(j \wedge h) \rightarrow d$

In 50–55, state the word, phrase, or symbol that can be placed in the blank to make the resulting sentence true.

50. When "*p*" and "*q*" represent two simple sentences, the conditional "if *p* then *q*" is written symbolically as ____.

51. The conditional "if *q* then *p*" is written symbolically as ____.

52. The conditional $p \rightarrow q$ is false only when *p* is ____ and *q* is ____.

53. When the conclusion *q* is true, then $p \rightarrow q$ must be ____.

54. When the hypothesis *p* is false, then $p \rightarrow q$ must be ____.

55. If the hypothesis *p* is true and the conditional $p \rightarrow q$ is true, then the conclusion *q* must be ____.

In 56–60, three sentences are written. The truth values are given for the first two sentences. Determine if the third sentence is true, is false, or has an uncertain truth value.

56. "If you read in dim light, then you can strain your eyes."   (True)
"You read in dim light."   (True)
"You can strain your eyes."   (?)

57. "If the quadrilateral has 4 right angles, then the quadrilateral is a square."   (False)
"The quadrilateral has 4 right angles."   (True)
"The quadrilateral is a square."   (?)

58. "If n is an odd number, then $2 \cdot n$ is an even number."   (True)
    "$2 \cdot n$ is an even number."   (True)
    "n is an odd number."   (?)

59. "If the report is late, then you will not get an A."   (True)
    "The report is late."   (False)
    "You will not get an A."   (?)

60. "Area $= \frac{1}{2} bh$, if the polygon is a triangle."   (True)
    "The polygon is a triangle."   (True)
    "Area $= \frac{1}{2} bh$."   (?)

6 COMPOUND STATEMENTS AND TRUTH VALUES

Our study of logic to this point has included negation, conjunction, disjunction, and the conditional, as shown in the following truth tables:

p	q	Negations $\sim p$	$\sim q$	Conjunction $p \wedge q$	Disjunction $p \vee q$	Conditional $p \to q$
T	T	F	F	T	T	T
T	F	F	T	F	T	F
F	T	T	F	F	T	T
F	F	T	T	F	F	T

A compound sentence often contains more than one connective. To judge the truth value of any compound sentence, we examine the truth values of its component parts. When the truth value of every simple sentence is known within the compound being formed, we have a *compound statement*.

For example, "8 is an even number *and* 8 is *not* prime."

We may express this compound statement in symbolic form, assigning a letter to represent every "simple *positive* statement."

Let "e" represent "8 is an even number."
Let "p" represent "8 is prime."
Then "$\sim p$" represents "8 is *not* prime."
While "$e \wedge \sim p$" represents "8 is an even number *and* 8 is *not* prime."

Substituting truth values directly into the statement "$e \wedge \sim p$," we get "$T \wedge \sim F$," which reduces to "$T \wedge T$," or simply T. The compound statement is true. Other examples appear in the model problems.

■ **PROCEDURE.**   To find the truth value of a compound statement:

1. Simplify the truth values within parentheses or other groupings, always working from the innermost group first.

2. Simplify negations.

3. Simplify other connectives, working from left to right.

MODEL PROBLEMS

1. Let p represent "$7^2 = 49$" and let q represent "a rectangle is a parallelogram."

   a. Write in symbolic form using p and q: "$7^2 = 49$ *or* a rectangle is *not* a parallelogram."
   b. Find the truth value of this compound sentence.

   Solution:

   a. $p \lor \sim q$
   b. Substitute the truth values for p and q: $T \lor \sim T$
      Simplify the negation: $T \lor F$
      Simplify the disjunction: T *Ans.*

In 2 and 3, find the truth value of the compound statement when p, q, and r are all true.

2. $(\sim p \land r) \to q$

   Solution: Substitute the truth values: $(\sim T \land T) \to T$
              Within parentheses, negate: $(F \land T) \to T$
              Simplify parentheses: $F \to T$
              Simplify the conditional: T *Ans.*

3. $(p \to \sim q) \lor \sim r$

   Solution: Substitute the truth values: $(T \to \sim T) \lor \sim T$
              Within parentheses, negate: $(T \to F) \lor \sim T$
              Simplify parentheses: $F \lor \sim T$
              Simplify the negation: $F \lor F$
              Simplify the disjunction: F *Ans.*

| EXERCISES |

In 1-4, write a statement in symbolic form to show the correct heading for column 3.

1.		Col. 3	2.		Col. 3	3.		Col. 3	4.		Col. 3
p	q		p	q		p	q		p	q	
T	T	T	T	T	T	T	T	T	T	T	F
T	F	F	T	F	F	T	F	T	T	F	T
F	T	F	F	T	T	F	T	T	F	T	F
F	F	F	F	F	T	F	F	F	F	F	T

In 5-12, select the numeral preceding the word or expression that best completes the statement or answers the question.

5. When $p \lor q$ is false, then:
    (1) p is true and q is false.   (3) p and q are both false.
    (2) p is false and q is true.   (4) p and q are both true.

6. When $p \to q$ is false, then:
    (1) p is true and q is false.   (3) p and q are both false.
    (2) p is false and q is true.   (4) p and q are both true.

7. If p represents "x is divisible by 2" and q represents "x is divisible by 5," then which is true when $x = 14$?
    (1) $p \land q$ (2) $p \lor q$ (3) $\sim p$ (4) q

8. If p represents "the polygon has 4 sides" and q represents "opposite sides of the polygon are parallel," then which is true when the polygon is a triangle?
    (1) $p \land q$ (2) $p \lor q$ (3) $\sim p$ (4) q

9. If p represents "x is a prime number" and q represents "x is divisible by 3," then which is true when $x = 9$?
    (1) $p \land q$ (2) $p \lor q$ (3) $\sim q$ (4) p

10. If $p \land q$ is true, then:
    (1) $p \lor q$ is false.   (3) $p \lor q$ is true.
    (2) $p \to q$ is false.   (4) $\sim(p \land q)$ is true.

11. When p is true and q is false, then:
    (1) $p \land q$ is true.   (3) $p \lor q$ is false.
    (2) $p \to q$ is false.   (4) $\sim p \land \sim q$ is true.

12. Let p represent "$3x + 1 = 13$" and let q represent "$2x + 3x = 25$."
Which is true when $x = 4$?

(1) $p \wedge q$ (2) $p \rightarrow q$ (3) $p \vee q$ (4) $\sim p$

In 13–24: Let m represent "28 is a multiple of 7."   (True)
Let s represent "28 is the square of an integer."   (False)
Let f represent "7 is a factor of 28."   (True)

a. Write a correct translation in words for the statement given in symbolic form.
b. Tell the truth value of the compound statement.

13. $m \wedge \sim s$ 14. $f \vee \sim m$ 15. $\sim m \rightarrow s$ 16. $\sim(f \wedge s)$
17. $s \vee \sim f$ 18. $\sim(m \vee s)$ 19. $\sim f \rightarrow \sim m$ 20. $s \rightarrow \sim m$
21. $(m \wedge f) \rightarrow s$ 22. $m \rightarrow (s \vee f)$ 23. $(m \vee s) \rightarrow f$ 24. $f \rightarrow (s \vee m)$

In 25–32, find the truth value for the given statement.

25. If $2 + 3 = 5$ and $3 + 5 = 8$, then $5 + 8 = 13$.
26. If $2^2 = 4$ and $2 + 2 = 4$, then $3^2 = 3 + 3$.
27. If $2^2 = 4$, then $3^2 = 6$ and $4^2 = 8$.
28. If $4 + 8 = 10$ or $4 + 8 = 32$, then $10 - 8 = 4$ or $32 - 8 = 4$.
29. If $2(3) = 5$ and $3(2) = 5$, then $2(3) = 3(2)$.
30. $2^3 = 3^2$ if $2^3 = 6$ and $3^2 = 6$.
31. It is not true that $3 + 10 = 13$ and $3 - 10 = 7$.
32. It is not true that 12 is even and prime.

In 33–44, find the truth value of the compound sentence when p, q, and r are all true.

33. $p \rightarrow \sim q$ 34. $p \wedge \sim r$ 35. $q \vee \sim p$ 36. $p \wedge \sim p$
37. $\sim(p \vee q)$ 38. $\sim q \rightarrow r$ 39. $\sim r \rightarrow \sim p$ 40. $p \vee \sim p$
41. $\sim p \vee \sim q$ 42. $(p \wedge q) \rightarrow r$ 43. $(p \vee q) \vee r$ 44. $(p \wedge q) \vee \sim r$

7   COMPOUND SENTENCES   AND TRUTH TABLES

When the truth value of one or more of the simple sentences used to form the compound sentence is not known, we must consider cases where the simple sentences are true and where they are false in order to discover the truth value of the compound sentence. A truth table will show all possible truth values.

MODEL PROBLEM

Construct a truth table for the sentence $q \rightarrow \sim(p \lor \sim q)$.

Solution:

(1) List truth values for p and q in the first two columns.

p	q
T	T
T	F
F	T
F	F

(2) Working within parentheses, we see $(p \lor \sim q)$. We first get the negation of q by negating column 2.

p	q	$\sim q$
T	T	F
T	F	T
F	T	F
F	F	T

(3) Then we must find the truth values for $(p \lor \sim q)$ by combining columns 1 and 3 under disjunction.

p	q	$\sim q$	$p \lor \sim q$
T	T	F	T
T	F	T	T
F	T	F	F
F	F	T	T

(4) We negate column 4 to find the truth values for $\sim(p \lor \sim q)$.

p	q	$\sim q$	$p \lor \sim q$	$\sim(p \lor \sim q)$
T	T	F	T	F
T	F	T	T	F
F	T	F	F	T
F	F	T	T	F

(5) Using column 2 as the hypothesis and column 5 as the conclusion, we arrive at the truth values for the conditional sentence.

p	q	$\sim q$	$p \vee \sim q$	$\sim(p \vee \sim q)$	$q \to \sim(p \vee \sim q)$
T	T	F	T	F	F
T	F	T	T	F	T
F	T	F	F	T	T
F	F	T	T	F	T

We observe that the compound sentence, $q \to \sim(p \vee \sim q)$, is sometimes true and sometimes false, depending upon the truth values of p and q.

EXERCISES

In 1-8, copy and complete the truth table for the given sentence which is the last column head on the right. (In 2-8, prepare a truth table similar to the one shown in exercise 1.)

1.

p	q	$p \vee q$	$\sim q$	$(p \vee q) \to \sim q$
T	T			
T	F			
F	T			
F	F			

2.

p	q	$p \wedge q$	$p \vee q$	$(p \wedge q) \to (p \vee q)$

3.

p	q	$\sim p$	$q \to \sim p$	$(q \to \sim p) \wedge p$

4.

p	q	$\sim p$	$\sim p \wedge q$	$p \vee (\sim p \wedge q)$

5.

p	q	$\sim p$	$p \vee \sim p$	$q \to (p \vee \sim p)$

6.

p	q	$p \to q$	$\sim q$	$(p \to q) \to \sim q$

7.

p	q	$\sim p$	$\sim p \lor q$	$p \land q$	$(\sim p \lor q) \to (p \land q)$

8.

p	q	$p \land q$	$\sim(p \land q)$	$\sim p$	$\sim q$	$\sim p \land \sim q$	$\sim(p \land q) \to (\sim p \land \sim q)$

In 9–14, construct a truth table for the given sentence.

9. $\sim q \to (\sim q \land p)$ **10.** $p \to \sim(p \lor q)$

11. $\sim(p \land q) \lor p$ **12.** $(\sim p \land q) \lor p$

13. $(p \to \sim q) \land q$ **14.** $(\sim p \land \sim q) \lor (p \land q)$

15. Given the sentence: "*If* a number is *not* even, *then* it is even *or* it is prime."

Let e represent "A number is even."

Let p represent "A number is prime."

a. Write the compound sentence in symbolic form, using e and p.

b. Construct a truth table for the compound sentence.

c. For any case where the compound sentence is false, give the truth values of e and of p.

d. Find a whole number that fits the truth values listed in part c.

8 THE BICONDITIONAL

Hypothesis

Conclusion

p	q	$p \to q$
T	T	T
T	F	F
F	T	T
F	F	T

The truth table for the **conditional** $p \to q$ is shown at the right. The conditional $p \to q$ is false when the hypothesis p is true and the conclusion q is false: $(p \to q)$ becomes $(T \to F = F)$ in row 2. In all other cases, the conditional $p \to q$ is true.

Conclusion

Hypothesis

p	q	$q \to p$
T	T	T
T	F	T
F	T	F
F	F	T

When we reverse the order of the sentences p and q, we form a new **conditional** $q \to p$. Since $(T \to F = F)$ is correct for any conditional, the table will change. Here the hypothesis q is true and the conclusion p is false in row 3. In all other cases, the conditional $q \to p$ is true.

The prefix "bi-" means two as in bicycle, binary, and bifocals. The biconditional consists of two conditionals. In logic the *biconditional* is a compound sentence formed by combining the two conditionals $p \rightarrow q$ and $q \rightarrow p$ under a conjunction "and." To find the truth value of the biconditional, we can construct a truth table for the sentence $(p \rightarrow q) \wedge (q \rightarrow p)$.

p	q	$p \rightarrow q$	$q \rightarrow p$	$(p \rightarrow q) \wedge (q \rightarrow p)$
T	T	T	T	T
T	F	F	T	F
F	T	T	F	F
F	F	T	T	T

The compound sentence formed in the truth table is both lengthy to read and to write.

$(p \rightarrow q) \wedge (q \rightarrow p)$: **"If p then q, and if q then p"**

or

"p implies q, and q implies p."

We shorten the writing of the biconditional by introducing the symbol, "$p \leftrightarrow q$," to replace the compound sentence. We shorten the reading of the biconditional by using the words "p if and only if q." These abbreviated versions, as well as the lengthy ones, are all acceptable ways of indicating the biconditional. From the truth table we observe that:

The biconditional "p if and only if q" is true when p and q are both true or both false.

In other words, "$p \leftrightarrow q$" is true when p and q have the same truth value. When p and q have different truth values, the biconditional is false.

Procedure for Building the Truth Table for the *Biconditional*, $p \leftrightarrow q$

1. Assign two letters, each to serve as a symbol for a different simple sentence, say p and q.

2. List all possible truth values for p and q in columns 1 and 2.

p	q	$p \longleftrightarrow q$
T	T	
T	F	
F	T	
F	F	

3. In the third column, write the biconditional in symbolic form.

4. Finally, assign truth values for the biconditional. When p and q have the same truth value, as in rows 1 and 4, the biconditional is true. When p and q have different truth values, as in rows 2 and 3, the biconditional is false.

p	q	$p \longleftrightarrow q$
T	T	T
T	F	F
F	T	F
F	F	T

**Truth Table for
Biconditional**

Applications of the Biconditional

The truth table shows us that the biconditional is not true in all cases. For example,

$$p \leftrightarrow q: \text{ ``}x > 5 \text{ } if \text{ } and \text{ } only \text{ } if \text{ } x > 3.\text{''}$$

or

$$p \leftrightarrow q: \text{ ``If } x > 5, \text{ then } x > 3, and$$
$$\text{if } x > 3, \text{ then } x > 5.\text{''}$$

This biconditional is *false* because it fails for certain numbers. Let $x = 4$. Then p: "$x > 5$" is false while q: "$x > 3$" is true. Since the truth values are not the same, the biconditional is not true.

However, there are many examples where the biconditional is always true.

■ EXAMPLE 1. Definitions

Two conditionals are stated.

$p \rightarrow t$: "If a polygon has exactly 3 sides, then it is a triangle."

$t \rightarrow p$: "If a polygon is a triangle, then it has exactly 3 sides."

Together, $(p \rightarrow t) \wedge (t \rightarrow p)$ become the biconditional $(p \leftrightarrow t)$. When p is true, t is true. When p is false, t is false. Since the truth values are the same, the biconditional is always true. *We use the biconditional to serve as a definition.*

$p \leftrightarrow t$:   "A polygon is a triangle *if and only if* it has exactly three sides."

Precise definitions in mathematics include the words *"if and only if."* The "if" tells us what we must include, as in "exactly three sides." The "only if" tells us what to exclude, as in "all cases that do not have exactly three sides."

■ **EXAMPLE 2. Equations**

$$2x + 1 = 17$$
$$2x = 16$$
$$x = 8$$

In simplifying equations we follow a process as shown at the left. We can reverse this process since $x = 8$ will be true in every equation listed here and any other value will be false.

$a \rightarrow b$:   "$2x + 1 = 17$ implies $2x = 16$."
$b \rightarrow a$:   "$2x = 16$ implies $2x + 1 = 17$."

Therefore, we realize that equations of this type form biconditional statements.

$a \leftrightarrow b$:   "$2x + 1 = 17$ *if and only if* $2x = 16$."
$b \leftrightarrow c$:   "$2x = 16$ *if and only if* $x = 8$."

■ **EXAMPLE 3. Equivalences**

When any two statements have the same truth value, we can substitute one statement for another. The statements are said to be *logically equivalent*. We will see examples of equivalences in the next section.

| MODEL PROBLEMS |

In 1 and 2, identify the truth value to be assigned to each biconditional.

1. Cars stop if and only if there is a red light.

    Solution: Let "p" represent "Cars stop."
                Let "q" represent "There is a red light."

    When p is true, it does not follow that q must be true. Cars stop at stop signs, railroad crossings, when parking. Since p and q do not have the same truth value, the biconditional $p \leftrightarrow q$ is false.

    Answer: False

2. $x + 2 = 7$ if and only if $x = 5$.

   Solution: Let "p" represent "$x + 2 = 7$."
   Let "q" represent "$x = 5$."

   When $x = 5$, both p and q are true. When $x \neq 5$, both p and q are false. In any event, p and q have the same truth value. Thus, the biconditional $p \leftrightarrow q$ is true.   *Answer:* True

EXERCISES

In 1–5, write each biconditional in symbolic form, using the symbols given.

   t: The triangle is right.
   r: The triangle contains a right angle.
   n: The triangle contains a 90° angle.

1. A triangle is right if and only if it contains a right angle.
2. A triangle contains a 90° angle if and only if it is a right triangle.
3. A triangle contains a 90° angle if and only if it contains a right angle.
4. If a triangle is right, then it contains a 90° angle, and if the triangle contains a 90° angle, then it is right.
5. A triangle is not right if and only if it does not contain a 90° angle.

In 6–8, copy the truth table for the biconditional and fill in the missing symbols.

6.

p	q	$p \leftrightarrow q$
T	T	
T	F	
F	T	
F	F	

7.

r	s	$r \leftrightarrow s$
T	T	
T	F	F
F	T	F
F	F	

8.

d	k	$d \leftrightarrow k$

In 9–15, complete the truth tables, filling in all missing symbols. (In 10–15, prepare a truth table similar to the one shown in exercise 9.)

9.

p	q	$q \rightarrow p$
T	T	
T	F	
F	T	
F	F	

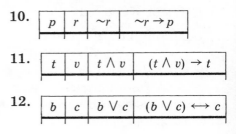

10.

p	r	$\sim r$	$\sim r \rightarrow p$

11.

t	v	$t \wedge v$	$(t \wedge v) \rightarrow t$

12.

b	c	$b \vee c$	$(b \vee c) \leftrightarrow c$

13.

p	t	$t \to p$	$p \to t$	$(t \to p) \wedge (p \to t)$

14.

p	q	$q \to p$	$(q \to p) \to q$

15.

r	s	$\sim r$	$\sim r \to s$	$(\sim r \to s) \leftrightarrow r$

In 16–25, identify the truth value to be assigned to each biconditional.

16. $x + 3 = 30$ if and only if $x = 27$.
17. A polygon is a pentagon if and only if it has exactly 3 sides.
18. $x + 4 = 12$ if and only if $x + 6 = 14$.
19. A rectangle is a square if and only if the rectangle has all sides of equal length.
20. The refrigerator runs if and only if the electricity is on.
21. An angle is right if and only if it contains 90°.
22. A set is empty if and only if it contains no elements.
23. A number is even if and only if it is exactly divisible by 2.
24. Two angles have the same measure if and only if they are right angles.
25. A sentence is a statement if and only if it has truth values.

26. Using the symbols p and q, write each compound sentence in symbolic form.
  a. p if and only if q.
  b. if p then q and if q then p.
  c. p implies q and q implies p.
  d. q if and only if p.
  e. if p then q or if q then p.

27. Of the five responses given in exercise 26, four of the answers name the biconditional, $p \leftrightarrow q$. Which choice does *not* represent the biconditional?

9 TAUTOLOGIES

We have seen many compound sentences that are sometimes true and sometimes false.

In logic a *tautology* is a compound sentence that is *always true*, regardless of the truth values assigned to the simple sentences within the compound. For example, $(p \wedge q) \to p$ is a tautology.

To demonstrate that the compound $(p \wedge q) \to p$ will always be true, we build a truth table. No matter what truth values p and q have, every element in the last column is true. This tells us that we have a tautology, or a basic truth in logic.

p	q	$p \wedge q$	$(p \wedge q) \rightarrow p$
T	T	T	T
T	F	F	T
F	T	F	T
F	F	F	T

Tautology

Examples of Tautologies

■ **EXAMPLE 1.** The *simplest tautology* is seen in the statement $p \vee \sim p$. Its truth table is shown at the right. We may replace the symbol p with any simple sentence, whether its truth values are known or not.

p	$\sim p$	$p \vee \sim p$
T	F	T
F	T	T

Tautology

$p \vee \sim p$: A number is odd or a number is not odd.
$p \vee \sim p$: A square is a triangle or a square is not a triangle.
$p \vee \sim p$: It will rain or it will not rain.
$p \vee \sim p$: $x + 3 = 15$ or $x + 3 \neq 15$.
$p \vee \sim p$: A statement is true or a statement is not true.

This last interpretation of $p \vee \sim p$ can also be read as "A statement is true or false."

■ **EXAMPLE 2.** Tautologies are used to develop *good powers of reasoning* and strong arguments. For example, these two statements are made:

$r \rightarrow m$: "If it rains, then we'll go to the movies."
r: "It rains."

Can we conclude that we'll go to the movies?

m: "We'll go to the movies."

To check our reasoning we combine the first two sentences under a conjunction "and." This compound sentence will be used as the hypothesis, while we test our conclusion under a conditional, "if . . . then."
The reasoning becomes: "*If* $r \rightarrow m$ *and* r, then m."
Written symbolically: $[(r \rightarrow m) \wedge r] \rightarrow m$
Test the reasoning in a truth table, working from the innermost parentheses first. Since the last column contains only "true" values, this is a tautology. Our reasoning is correct: "We will go to the movies."

r	m	$r \to m$	$(r \to m) \wedge r$	$[(r \to m) \wedge r] \to m$
T	T	T	T	T
T	F	F	F	T
F	T	T	F	T
F	F	T	F	T

Tautology

■ **EXAMPLE 3.** When two statements have the exact same truth values we have an *equivalence*. We can say that the two statements are logically equivalent.

To show that an equivalence exists we compare the two statements, using the biconditional. If the statements have the same truth values, then the biconditional will be true in every case. This will result in a tautology.

Let p represent "I study."
Let q represent "I fail."

The two statements being tested for an equivalence follow.

$\sim p \to q$: "If I don't study, then I'll fail."
$p \vee q$: "I study or I fail."

Using the biconditional, we wish to test the statement:

$$(\sim p \to q) \leftrightarrow (p \vee q)$$

In the truth table, we work within parentheses first to find $\sim p$, then $\sim p \to q$. Notice that the truth values of $\sim p \to q$ in column 4 match exactly with the truth values of $p \vee q$ in column 5. In the last column, the biconditional will always be true because the truth values are exactly the same.

p	q	$\sim p$	$\sim p \to q$	$p \vee q$	$(\sim p \to q) \leftrightarrow (p \vee q)$
T	T	F	T	T	T
T	F	F	T	T	T
F	T	T	T	T	T
F	F	T	F	F	T

Tautology

We see why "$p \vee q$" and "$\sim p \to q$" are called *equivalent statements*; they say the same thing in two different ways and this is verified by their matching truth values.

| MODEL PROBLEMS |

1. a. On your paper, copy and complete the truth table for the statement:

$$(p \rightarrow \sim q) \leftrightarrow (\sim p \vee \sim q)$$

p	q	$\sim p$	$\sim q$	$p \rightarrow \sim q$	$\sim p \vee \sim q$	$(p \rightarrow \sim q) \leftrightarrow (\sim p \vee \sim q)$

   b. Is $(p \rightarrow \sim q) \leftrightarrow (\sim p \vee \sim q)$ a tautology?

   c. Let p represent "I get a job."
       Let q represent "I go to the dance."
       Which sentence is equivalent to $(p \rightarrow \sim q)$?

       (1) If I don't get a job, then I won't go to the dance.
       (2) I get a job or I don't go to the dance.
       (3) I don't get a job or I don't go to the dance.
       (4) If I get a job, then I'll go to the dance.

Solution

a.

p	q	$\sim p$	$\sim q$	$p \rightarrow \sim q$	$\sim p \vee \sim q$	$(p \rightarrow \sim q) \leftrightarrow (\sim p \vee \sim q)$
T	T	F	F	F	F	T
T	F	F	T	T	T	T
F	T	T	F	T	T	T
F	F	T	T	T	T	T

   b. Since $(p \rightarrow \sim q) \leftrightarrow (\sim p \vee \sim q)$ is always true, this is a tautology.   *Answer:* Yes

   c. Because the compound sentence $(p \rightarrow \sim q) \leftrightarrow (\sim p \vee \sim q)$ is a tautology, $(p \rightarrow \sim q)$ and $(\sim p \vee \sim q)$ are logically equivalent statements. Given $(p \rightarrow \sim q)$, look for $(\sim p \vee \sim q)$. In choice 3, $(\sim p \vee \sim q)$: "I don't get a job or I don't go to the dance."

       Answer: (3)

2. a. Find the truth values for each of the following statements:

       1. $\sim q \rightarrow p$ 2. $\sim(p \rightarrow q)$ 3. $p \vee q$

   b. Which statements, if any, in part a are logically equivalent? State a tautology to show this equivalence or give a reason why there is no equivalence.

Solution

a. 1.

p	q	$\sim q$	$\sim q \to p$
T	T	F	T
T	F	T	T
F	T	F	T
F	F	T	F

a. 2.

p	q	$p \to q$	$\sim(p \to q)$
T	T	T	F
T	F	F	T
F	T	T	F
F	F	T	F

a. 3.

p	q	$p \vee q$
T	T	T
T	F	T
F	T	T
F	F	F

b. Because the truth tables for $(\sim q \to p)$ and $(p \vee q)$ have the same truth values, statement 1 and statement 3 are logically equivalent. We can write the tautology:

$$(\sim q \to p) \leftrightarrow (p \vee q)$$

3. Is $[(p \wedge q) \vee \sim q] \to \sim p$ a tautology? Give a reason why.

Solution

p	q	$p \wedge q$	$\sim q$	$(p \wedge q) \vee \sim q$	$\sim p$	$[(p \wedge q) \vee \sim q] \to \sim p$
T	T	T	F	T	F	F
T	F	F	T	T	F	F
F	T	F	F	F	T	T
F	F	F	T	T	T	T

Answer: No. This is not a tautology because the statement is false in rows 1 and 2.

| EXERCISES |

In 1–10: **a.** Copy and complete the truth table for the given statement. (*Note:* In 6–10, prepare a complete truth table similar to the one shown in exercise 5.) **b.** Indicate if the statement is or is not a tautology.

1.

p	$\sim p$	$\sim(\sim p)$	$p \leftrightarrow \sim(\sim p)$
T			
F			

2.

p	$\sim p$	$\sim p \wedge p$	$\sim(\sim p \wedge p)$
T			
F			

3.

p	$\sim p$	$p \to \sim p$	$(p \to \sim p) \leftrightarrow \sim p$
T			
F			

4.

q	$\sim q$	$\sim q \to q$
T		
F		

5.

p	q	$\sim p$	$\sim p \lor q$	$p \lor (\sim p \lor q)$
T	T			
T	F			
F	T			
F	F			

6.

p	q	$p \land q$	$p \lor q$	$(p \land q) \to (p \lor q)$

7.

p	q	$p \lor q$	$p \land q$	$(p \lor q) \to (p \land q)$

8.

p	q	$p \lor q$	$p \to (p \lor q)$

9.

p	q	$\sim p$	$\sim p \land q$	$p \land (\sim p \land q)$	$\sim[p \land (\sim p \land q)]$

10.

p	q	$\sim q$	$p \to \sim q$	$\sim(p \to \sim q)$	$p \land q$	$\sim(p \to \sim q) \leftrightarrow (p \land q)$

In 11–20, construct truth tables for the given tautologies.

11. $p \to (p \lor q)$
13. $(p \lor p) \to p$
15. $[p \lor (p \land q)] \leftrightarrow p$
17. $[(p \to q) \land \sim q] \to \sim p$
19. $\sim(p \lor q) \leftrightarrow (\sim p \land \sim q)$

12. $(p \land q) \leftrightarrow (q \land p)$
14. $(p \land q) \to q$
16. $(\sim p \lor q) \to (p \to q)$
18. $\sim[(\sim p \lor q) \lor \sim q] \to (p \land q)$
20. $[p \land (\sim p \lor q)] \leftrightarrow (p \land q)$

In 21–25: **a.** Find the truth values for each of the three statements in the row. **b.** Using the results from part a, either write a tautology for any two of the three statements that are logically equivalent, or tell why no tautology exists.

21. (1) $q \to \sim p$ (2) $\sim p \lor \sim q$ (3) $\sim q \to \sim p$
22. (1) $q \lor \sim p$ (2) $p \lor \sim q$ (3) $p \to q$
23. (1) $\sim p \to q$ (2) $q \land \sim p$ (3) $\sim q \to p$
24. (1) $p \land q$ (2) $p \leftrightarrow q$ (3) $\sim p \leftrightarrow \sim q$
25. (1) $p \to \sim q$ (2) $\sim(p \land q)$ (3) $p \leftrightarrow \sim q$

26. a. Construct a truth table for the statement $(p \to q) \leftrightarrow (\sim p \lor q)$.
    b. Let p: "I like baseball."   Let q: "I join the team."
       Which sentence, if any, is logically equivalent to $(p \to q)$?
       (1) I like baseball or I join the team.
       (2) I don't like baseball or I join the team.
       (3) If I like baseball, then I don't join the team.
       (4) If I don't like baseball, then I join the team.

27. a. Construct a truth table for the statement
       $\sim(p \lor \sim q) \leftrightarrow (\sim p \land q)$.
    b. Let p: "I save money."   Let q: "I work."
       Which sentence, if any, is logically equivalent to $\sim(p \lor \sim q)$?
       (1) I don't save money and I work.
       (2) If I don't save money, then I don't work.
       (3) I save money or I don't work.
       (4) I don't work and I save money.

28. a. Construct a truth table for the statement $(\sim p \to q) \leftrightarrow (p \lor q)$.
    b. Let p represent "I get home late."
       Let q represent "We'll go out."
       Tell which sentence, if any, is logically equivalent to "If I don't get home late, then we'll go out."
       (1) "If I get home late, then we'll go out."
       (2) "If I get home late, then we won't go out."
       (3) "I get home late and we go out."
       (4) "I get home late or we'll go out."

29. a. Construct a truth table for the statement
       $[p \lor (q \land \sim p)] \leftrightarrow (p \lor q)$.
    b. Let p represent "I'll go to college."
       Let q represent "I'll go to work."
       Which sentence, if any, is logically equivalent to $(p \lor q)$?
       (1) I'll go to college or I won't go to work.
       (2) I'll go to work or I won't go to college.
       (3) I'll go to college or I'll go to work and not college.
       (4) I'll go to work or I'll go to college and work.

30. Let "l" represent "Mark stays up late at night."
    Let "t" represent "Mark is tired in the morning."
    a. Write the symbolic form of the sentence "If Mark stays up late at night, then he is tired in the morning."
    b. Write the symbolic form of the sentence "If Mark is not tired in the morning, then he did not stay up late at night."
    c. Test to see if these sentences in a and b are equivalences by constructing a truth table, using the biconditional.

31. George made two statements, shown symbolically below.
    Let "$f \lor s$" represent "I will see you on Friday or Saturday."
    Let "$\sim f$" represent "I won't see you on Friday."
    Can we conclude that "s" is true? (*Hint:* Let "s" represent "I will see you on Saturday.") Answer the question by constructing a truth table for the compound statement $[(f \lor s) \land \sim f] \rightarrow s$.

10   INVERSE, CONVERSE, AND CONTRAPOSITIVE

We have seen that the conditional "if p then q" is the connective most often used in reasoning. Too often, people attempt to win an argument or to make a point by "twisting words around." In order to help you avoid becoming the victim of this kind of argument, we will study three new conditionals, each of which is formed by making some changes in an original conditional statement. These new conditionals are called the *inverse*, the *converse*, and the *contrapositive*.

The Inverse

Starting with an original conditional ($p \rightarrow q$), we form the *inverse* ($\sim p \rightarrow \sim q$) by negating the hypothesis and negating the conclusion. The symbols for the inverse may be read as "not p implies not q," or "if not p, then not q."

■ **EXAMPLE 1.**   Let p represent "It has rained."
    Let q represent "The ground gets wet."

Conditional ($p \rightarrow q$): "If it has rained, then the ground gets wet."

Inverse ($\sim p \rightarrow \sim q$): "If it has *not* rained, then the ground does *not* get wet."

Does the inverse of a conditional have the same truth value as the conditional? To answer this question, we will construct a truth table.

We see that the conditional and its inverse are *not equivalent* statements because they do not have matching truth values in each and every row.

				Conditional	Inverse
p	q	$\sim p$	$\sim q$	$p \to q$	$\sim p \to \sim q$
T	T	F	F	T	T
T	F	F	T	F	T
F	T	T	F	T	F
F	F	T	T	T	T

In rows 1, 3, and 4, the conditional ($p \to q$) is *true*: "If it rains, then the ground gets wet." However, we notice that:

In row 4, the inverse ($\sim p \to \sim q$) is *true*. Suppose "it does not rain." The conclusion, "the ground does not get wet," is true.

In row 3, the inverse ($\sim p \to \sim q$) is *false*. Suppose "it does not rain." Here, the conclusion, "the ground does not get wet," is false. A lawn sprinkler may be turned on, an underground pipe may burst, or it may snow.

If we can find *one possible case* where an inverse is false, then we cannot say that the inverse is true. In this example, we must say that this inverse ($\sim p \to \sim q$) is *false*.

■ **EXAMPLE 2.** In advertising a product, the manufacturer sometimes would like the reader to assume the truth of the inverse of a true conditional statement. For example, the Spritz Company makes and sells root beer. We can agree that the conditional "If you have a Spritz, then you have a root beer" is true. Would it follow that the company's advertisement, "When you're out of Spritz, then you're out of root beer," is also true? Let us see.

Conditional ($s \to r$): "If you have a Spritz, then you have a root beer."

Inverse ($\sim s \to \sim r$): "If you do *not* have a Spritz, then you do *not* have a root beer."

Notice that the advertisement is a "hidden" form of the inverse.

Inverse ($\sim s \to \sim r$): "When you're out of Spritz, then you're out of root beer."

We must say that this inverse is false. We do not have a Spritz, but we could have a root beer from another manufacturer.

■ **EXAMPLE 3.**   There are instances in which a conditional and its inverse are both true, as we can see from the first row of the truth table.

Conditional ($e \to f$):   "If $x + 3 = 7$, then $x = 4$."

Inverse ($\sim e \to \sim f$):   "If $x + 3 \neq 7$, then $x \neq 4$."

Hence, we must judge the truth value of each inverse on its own merits.

■ **Conclusion: When a conditional ($p \to q$) is true, its inverse ($\sim p \to \sim q$) may be true or it may be false.**

In reasoning, it is normal to start with a true conditional. Observe that when we start with a false conditional, as is shown in the second row of the truth table on page 175, the inverse is true.

The Converse

Starting with an original conditional ($p \to q$), we form the *converse* ($q \to p$) by interchanging the hypothesis and the conclusion. The symbols for the converse may be read as "q implies p" or "if q, then p."

■ **EXAMPLE 1.**   Let p represent "It has rained."
Let q represent "The ground gets wet."

Conditional ($p \to q$):   "If it has rained, then the ground gets wet."

Converse ($q \to p$):   "If the ground gets wet, then it has rained."

Does the converse have the same truth value as the conditional? To answer this question, we will construct a truth table. We see that the conditional and its converse are *not equivalent* statements because they do not have matching truth values in each and every row.

		Conditional	Converse
p	q	$p \to q$	$q \to p$
T	T	T	T
T	F	F	T
F	T	T	F
F	F	T	T

In rows 1, 3, and 4, the conditional $(p \rightarrow q)$ is true. "If it rains, then the ground gets wet." However, we notice that:

In row 4, the converse $(q \rightarrow p)$ is true. Suppose "the ground is wet." The conclusion "it has rained" is true.

In row 3, the converse $(q \rightarrow p)$ is false. Suppose "the ground is wet." Here, the conclusion "it has rained" is false. Again, a sprinkler or a burst pipe or snow could have caused the ground to become wet.

Since we can find instances where the converse is not true, we must say that this converse $(q \rightarrow p)$ is false.

■ **EXAMPLE 2.** A television commercial shows a series of beautiful women, all of whom use Cleanse soap. Assuming that these models really do use the product, let us also assume that the following conditional is true.

Conditional $(b \rightarrow c)$: "If you are beautiful, then you use Cleanse soap." Of course, what the advertiser wants you to believe is that the converse is true. This is not necessarily so.

Converse $(c \rightarrow b)$: "If you use Cleanse soap, then you will be beautiful." This converse is false because using the soap will not guarantee that you will become beautiful.

■ **EXAMPLE 3.** There are instances in which a conditional and its converse are both true, as we can see from the first row of the truth table on page 176.

Conditional $(h \rightarrow s)$: "If a polygon is a hexagon, then the polygon has exactly six sides."

Converse $(s \rightarrow h)$: "If a polygon has exactly six sides, then the polygon is a hexagon."

We must judge the truth value of each converse on its own merits.

■ **Conclusion:** When a conditional $(p \rightarrow q)$ is true, its converse $(q \rightarrow p)$ may be true or it may be false.

Remember that we normally start with a true conditional when reasoning. Observe that when we start with a false conditional, as is shown in the second row of the truth table on page 176, the converse is true.

The Contrapositive

Starting with an original conditional $(p \rightarrow q)$, we form the *contrapositive* $(\sim q \rightarrow \sim p)$ by negating both the hypothesis and the conclusion, and then interchanging the resulting negations. The symbols for the contrapositive may be read as "not q implies not p" or "if not q, then not p."

■ **EXAMPLE 1.**   Let p represent "It has rained."
Let q represent "The ground gets wet."

Conditional $(p \to q)$: "If it has rained, then the ground gets wet."

Contrapositive $(\sim q \to \sim p)$: "If the ground does not get wet, then it has not rained."

Does the contrapositive have the same truth value as the conditional? To answer this question, we will construct a truth table.

				Conditional	Contrapositive
p	q	$\sim q$	$\sim p$	$p \to q$	$\sim q \to \sim p$
T	T	F	F	T	T
T	F	T	F	F	F
F	T	F	T	T	T
F	F	T	T	T	T

From the table we see that **the conditional and its contrapositive are logically equivalent statements.**

Because the conditional and its contrapositive have matching truth values in each and every row, we can write a *tautology*:

$$(p \to q) \leftrightarrow (\sim q \to \sim p)$$

To examine the contrapositive $(\sim q \to \sim p)$, let us suppose "the ground does not get wet." Since the ground is dry, we cannot look for excuses such as a broken pipe or a lawn sprinkler.

■ **EXAMPLE 2.**   Let us consider an example in which we start with a *false* conditional. We will see that the contrapositive, as in the second row of the previous truth table, must also be *false*.

Conditional $(o \to r)$: "If 15 is an odd number, then 15 is a prime number." Here $(o \to r)$ is false because $(T \to F)$ is false.

Contrapositive ($\sim r \rightarrow \sim o$): "If 15 is not a prime number, then 15 is not an odd number." Here ($\sim r \rightarrow \sim o$) is false because ($T \rightarrow F$) is false.

■ **Conclusion:**

When a conditional ($p \rightarrow q$) is true, its contrapositive ($\sim q \rightarrow \sim p$) must also be true.

When a conditional is false, its contrapositive must be false.

Logical Equivalents

We have just seen that a *conditional* and its *contrapositive* are *logical equivalents* because they have the same truth value.

If we write the converse of a conditional and the inverse of that same conditional, we will notice that one is the contrapositive of the other.

For example:

Conditional ($p \rightarrow q$): "If it snows, then it is cold."

Converse ($q \rightarrow p$): "If it is cold, then it snows."

Inverse ($\sim p \rightarrow \sim q$): "If it does not snow, then it is not cold."

Since the contrapositive of ($q \rightarrow p$) is ($\sim p \rightarrow \sim q$), we can say that a *converse* of a statement and an *inverse* of that same statement are *logical equivalents*. We may also verify that the converse and inverse are logically equivalent by examining their truth tables.

The relationships among a conditional, its inverse, its converse, and its contrapositive are summarized pictorially in the rectangle shown at the right.

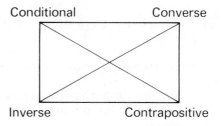

The statements that are connected by diagonals are logically equivalent. The conditional and the contrapositive are logically equivalent. The converse and the inverse are logically equivalent.

The statements that are connected by any one side of the rectangle are not logically equivalent. The conditional and the inverse are not logically equivalent, the inverse and the contrapositive are not logically equivalent, and so on.

Forming Related Statements

A conditional statement is not always formed by using a "positive" hypothesis and a "positive" conclusion. For example, "If it does not rain, then we'll go to the park." In this case,

r: "It rains."

$\sim r$: "It does *not* rain."

k: "We'll go to the park."

$\sim r \rightarrow k$: "If it does *not* rain, then we'll go to the park."

Using $(\sim r \rightarrow k)$ as the original conditional statement, we can form its inverse, its converse, and its contrapositive by following the rules established within each definition.

THE GENERAL CASE AND RULES	A SPECIFIC CASE
Conditional: $p \rightarrow q$ The hypothesis is p; the conclusion is q.	**Conditional:** $\sim r \rightarrow k$ "If it does not rain, then we'll go to the park."
Inverse: $\sim p \rightarrow \sim q$ Negate the hypothesis; negate the conclusion.	**Inverse:** $r \rightarrow \sim k$ "If it rains, then we will not go to the park."
Converse: $q \rightarrow p$ Interchange hypothesis and conclusion.	**Converse:** $k \rightarrow \sim r$ "If we go to the park, then it does not rain."
Contrapositive: $\sim q \rightarrow \sim p$ Negate hypothesis; negate conclusion; interchange these negations.	**Contrapositive:** $\sim k \rightarrow r$ "If we do not go to the park, then it rained."

Since the conditional $(\sim r \rightarrow k)$ and the contrapositive $(\sim k \rightarrow r)$ are logically equivalent, we can write the tautology $(\sim r \rightarrow k) \leftrightarrow (\sim k \rightarrow r)$.

Since the inverse $(r \rightarrow \sim k)$ and the converse $(k \rightarrow \sim r)$ are logically equivalent, we can write the tautology $(r \rightarrow \sim k) \leftrightarrow (k \rightarrow \sim r)$.

MODEL PROBLEMS

In 1–6, write the required statements in symbolic form.

Answers

1. the inverse of $k \rightarrow t$ $\sim k \rightarrow \sim t$
2. the inverse of $\sim m \rightarrow r$ $m \rightarrow \sim r$
3. the converse of $v \rightarrow y$ $y \rightarrow v$
4. the converse of $s \rightarrow \sim t$ $\sim t \rightarrow s$
5. the contrapositive of $l \rightarrow m$ $\sim m \rightarrow \sim l$
6. the contrapositive of $\sim c \rightarrow d$ $\sim d \rightarrow c$

7. Given the true statement: "If the polygon is a rectangle, then it has four sides." Which statement must also be true?

   (1) If the polygon has four sides, then it is a rectangle.
   (2) If the polygon is not a rectangle, then it does not have four sides.
   (3) If the polygon does not have four sides, then it is not a rectangle.
   (4) If the polygon has four sides, then it is not a rectangle.

   Solution: A conditional and its contrapositive always have the same truth value. When the conditional states "rectangle $\rightarrow$ four sides," the contrapositive is "not four sides $\rightarrow$ not rectangle."

   Answer: (3)

EXERCISES

In 1–4, write the inverse of the statement in symbolic form.

1. $p \rightarrow q$ 2. $t \rightarrow \sim w$ 3. $\sim m \rightarrow p$ 4. $\sim p \rightarrow \sim q$

In 5–8, write the converse of the statement in symbolic form.

5. $p \rightarrow q$ 6. $t \rightarrow \sim w$ 7. $\sim m \rightarrow p$ 8. $q \rightarrow p$

In 9–12, write the contrapositive of the statement in symbolic form.

9. $p \rightarrow q$ 10. $t \rightarrow \sim w$ 11. $\sim m \rightarrow p$ 12. $\sim q \rightarrow \sim p$

In 13–16, write the inverse of the statement in words.

13. If you use Charm face powder, then you will be beautiful.
14. If you buy Goal toothpaste, then your children will brush longer.
15. When you serve imported sparkling water, it shows that you have good taste.
16. The man who wears Cutrite clothes is well dressed.

In 17–20, (a) write the inverse of the conditional statement in words, (b) give the truth value of the conditional, and (c) give the truth value of the inverse.

17. If a polygon is a triangle, then the polygon has exactly three sides.
18. If a polygon is a trapezoid, then the polygon has exactly four sides.
19. If $2 \cdot 2 = 4$, then $2 \cdot 3 = 6$.
20. If $2^2 = 4$, then $3^2 = 6$.

In 21–24, write the converse of the statement in words.

21. If you live to an old age, then you eat Nano yogurt.
22. If you take pictures of your family with a Blinko camera, then you care about your family.
23. If you drive a Superb car, then you'll get good mileage.
24. If you use Dust and Roast, you'll make a better chicken dinner.

In 25–28, (a) write the converse of the conditional statement in words, (b) give the truth value of the conditional, and (c) give the truth value of the converse.

25. If a number is even, then the number is exactly divisible by 2.
26. If two segments are 5 cm each, then the two segments are equal in measure.
27. If $5 = 1 + 4$, then $5^2 = 1^2 + 4^2$.
28. If $2(5) + 3 = 10 + 3$, then $2(5) + 3 = 13$.

In 29–32, write the contrapositive of the statement in words.

29. If you care enough to send the best, then you send Trademark cards.
30. If you use Trickle deodorant, then you won't have body odor.
31. If you brush with Brite, then your teeth will be pearly white.
32. If you want a good job, then you'll get a high school diploma.

In 33–37, (a) write the contrapositive of the conditional statement in words, (b) give the truth value of the conditional, and (c) give the truth value of the contrapositive.

33. If opposite sides of a quadrilateral are parallel, then the quadrilateral is a parallelogram.
34. If two segments are 8 cm each, then the two segments are equal in measure.
35. If 1 + 2 = 3, then 2 + 3 = 4.
36. If all angles of a quadrilateral are equal in measure, then the quadrilateral is a rectangle.
37. If a number is prime, then it is not an even number.

In 38–42, write the numeral preceding the word or expression that best completes the statement or answers the question.

38. When $p \rightarrow q$ is true, which related conditional must be true?
    (1) $q \rightarrow p$ (2) $\sim p \rightarrow \sim q$ (3) $p \rightarrow \sim q$ (4) $\sim q \rightarrow \sim p$
39. Which is the contrapositive of "If winter comes, then spring is not far behind"?
    (1) If spring is not far behind, then winter comes.
    (2) If spring is far behind, then winter comes.
    (3) If spring is not far behind, then winter does not come.
    (4) If spring is far behind, then winter does not come.
40. Which is the converse of "If the polygon is a trapezoid, its area = $\frac{1}{2}(b + c) \cdot h$"?
    (1) If the polygon is not a trapezoid, then its area $\neq \frac{1}{2}(b + c) \cdot h$.
    (2) If the polygon has an area = $\frac{1}{2}(b + c) \cdot h$, then it is a trapezoid.
    (3) If the polygon has an area $\neq \frac{1}{2}(b + c) \cdot h$, then it is not a trapezoid.
    (4) If the area of a trapezoid is $\frac{1}{2}(b + c) \cdot h$, then it is a polygon.
41. Which is the inverse of "If $x = 2$, then $x + 3 \neq 9$"?
    (1) If $x + 3 \neq 9$, then $x = 2$.   (2) If $x + 3 = 9$, then $x \neq 2$.
    (3) If $x \neq 2$, then $x + 3 = 9$.   (4) If $x \neq 2$, then $x + 3 \neq 9$.
42. Which is the contrapositive of "If $x > 2$, then $3x + 5x \neq 16$"?
    (1) If $3x + 5x \neq 16$, then $x > 2$.
    (2) If $3x + 5x = 16$, then $x \not> 2$.
    (3) If $3x + 5x \neq 16$, then $x \not> 2$.
    (4) If $3x + 5x = 16$, then $x > 2$.

43. For a conditional statement $(p \rightarrow q)$:
    a. Write its inverse in symbolic form.
    b. Write the converse of this inverse in symbolic form.
    c. What is the relationship between the conditional statement $(p \rightarrow q)$ and the converse of the inverse of that statement?
    d. What might have been another way to define the contrapositive of a conditional statement?

In 44–51, a conditional statement is given. Write a sentence in words that describes (a) the inverse, (b) the converse, and (c) the contrapositive of that conditional.

44. If today is Friday, then tomorrow is Saturday.
45. If Douglas does well in college, then he will apply to medical school.
46. Arlette will get a role in the play if she auditions.
47. Dorothea will graduate from law school in January if she takes courses this summer.
48. If John is accepted at the Culinary Institute, then he has a chance of earning a high salary as a chef.
49. If a man is honest, he does not steal.
50. If Julia doesn't water the plants, then the plants will die.
51. Rachel will not get her allowance if she forgets to do her chores.

In 52–54, if the given statement is assumed to be true, which of the four statements that follow must also be true?

52. "If a figure is a square, then it is a polygon."
    (1) If the figure is a polygon, then it is a square.
    (2) If the figure is not a square, then it is not a polygon.
    (3) If the figure is not a polygon, then it is not a square.
    (4) If the figure is not a square, then it is a polygon.
53. "If $a = b$, then $b \neq d$."
    (1) If $a \neq b$, then $b \neq d$.   (2) If $b \neq d$, then $a = b$.
    (3) If $b = d$, then $a \neq b$.   (4) If $a \neq b$, then $b = d$.
54. "I'll get into shape if I exercise."
    (1) If I don't exercise, then I won't get into shape.
    (2) If I don't get into shape, then I do not exercise.
    (3) If I get into shape, then I exercise.
    (4) I exercise if I get into shape.

In 55–62, assume that the conditional statement is true. Then: a. Write its converse in words. b. Is the converse true, false, or uncertain? c. Write its inverse in words. d. Is the inverse true, false, or uncertain? e. Write its contrapositive in words. f. Is the contrapositive true, false, or uncertain?

55. If Eddie lives in San Francisco, then he lives in California.
56. If a number is divisible by 12, then it is divisible by 3.
57. If I have the flu, then I am ill.
58. If one pen costs 29 cents, then three pens cost 87 cents.
59. If a polygon is a rhombus, then it has four sides.
60. If Alex loves computers, then he will learn how to write programs.

chapter six

Signed Numbers

1 EXTENDING THE NUMBER LINE

Until now, we have dealt only with a number line like the one shown. It starts at zero and extends indefinitely to the right.

Since a line extends indefinitely in both directions, we can begin at zero and mark off unit intervals to the left as well as to the right. We label successive points to the right of zero, $^{+}1$, $^{+}2$, $^{+}3$, etc; we label successive points in the opposite direction, to the left of zero, $^{-}1$, $^{-}2$, $^{-}3$, etc.

The entire number line that extends both to the right of zero (in a positive direction) and to the left of zero (in a negative direction) is called the *real number line*. The coordinate of each point on the line is called a *real number*. Those numbers that are coordinates of points to the right of zero are called *positive real numbers*; those to the left are called *negative real numbers*. The numbers that are either 0 or positive are called *non-negative*; the numbers that are either 0 or negative are called *non-positive*. Since signs that indicate direction are used to distinguish between numerals that represent positive and negative numbers, these numbers are called *signed numbers*, or *directed numbers*. Although 0 is not written with a sign, we include it in the set of signed numbers.

There are points on the real number line that are associated with real numbers that we have not yet discussed, but which we will deal with in later chapters.

We will make frequent use of the set of signed numbers

$$\{\ldots, \ ^{-}4, \ ^{-}3, \ ^{-}2, \ ^{-}1, \ 0, \ ^{+}1, \ ^{+}2, \ ^{+}3, \ ^{+}4, \ldots\}$$

called the set of *integers*. The numbers $^{+}1$, $^{+}2$, $^{+}3$, . . . are called *positive integers*; the numbers $^{-}1$, $^{-}2$, $^{-}3$, . . . are called *negative integers*.

Observe that ⁺1 and 1 are considered as numerals that represent the same number, because they are associated with the same point on a number line. Likewise, 2 is another name for ⁺2, and ⁺3 is another name for 3. Actually, the positive numbers do not represent new numbers; only the negative numbers do.

We must be careful not to confuse the "+" and "−" with the "+" and "−." The "+" and "−," placed slightly above and to the left of the numerals, are used in signed numbers to indicate direction; the "+" and "−" are used to indicate addition and subtraction.

EXERCISES

In 1–3, draw a real number line. Then locate the points whose coordinates are given.

1. ⁺4, ⁻2, 0, ⁻5, ⁺3   2. ⁺$\frac{1}{2}$, 0, ⁻1$\frac{1}{2}$, ⁺3$\frac{1}{2}$, ⁻$\frac{3}{4}$ 3. ⁺1, ⁻$\frac{1}{3}$, 0, ⁺1$\frac{2}{3}$, ⁻$\frac{5}{6}$

In 4–11, state whether the signed numbers are on the same or opposite sides of the zero on a number line.

4. ⁺9, ⁺4   5. ⁻9, ⁻4   6. ⁺9, ⁻4   7. ⁻9, ⁺4
8. ⁺3, ⁺6   9. ⁻5, ⁻4   10. ⁺10, ⁻3   11. ⁻8, ⁺7

In 12–19, select the number which is farther from 0 on a number line.

12. ⁺10, ⁺4   13. ⁻10, ⁻4   14. ⁺10, ⁻4   15. ⁻10, ⁺4
16. ⁺9, ⁺3   17. ⁻6, ⁻8   18. ⁻7, ⁺5   19. ⁺8, ⁻1

In 20–25, graph the numbers on a number line. Then tell which point is to the right of the other.

20. ⁺5, ⁻2   21. ⁻5, ⁺2   22. ⁺7, ⁺3   23. ⁻7, ⁻3   24. 0, ⁻4   25. ⁺4, 0

In 26–32: a. Graph the number on a number line. b. Locate a point on the number line that is the same distance from 0 as the given point but on the opposite side of 0. c. Name the number located in b.

26. ⁺4   27. ⁻5   28. 7   29. ⁻3   30. 1$\frac{1}{2}$ 31. ⁻3$\frac{1}{4}$ 32. ⁺2.5

2 ORDERING SIGNED NUMBERS ON A NUMBER LINE

A Celsius temperature of ⁺4° is higher than a Celsius temperature of ⁺2°. That is, ⁺4 is greater than ⁺2, written ⁺4 > ⁺2. On a number line ⁺4 is to the right of ⁺2.

A Celsius temperature of ⁻3° is lower than a Celsius temperature of ⁻1°. That is, ⁻3 is less than ⁻1, written ⁻3 < ⁻1. On a number line ⁻3 is to the left of ⁻1.

These examples illustrate the fact that **all signed numbers are ordered on the real number line.** Any number is greater than every number to its left and is less than every number to its right.

To indicate that ⁻3 is between ⁻4 and ⁻2, we write ⁻4 < ⁻3 < ⁻2 or ⁻2 > ⁻3 > ⁻4. When we use the symbolism of logic we can indicate that ⁻3 is between ⁻4 and ⁻2 by writing:

$$(^-4 < {}^-3) \wedge (^-3 < {}^-2) \; or \; (^-2 > {}^-3) \wedge (^-3 > {}^-4)$$

MODEL PROBLEMS

State whether each of the sentences is true or false and give the reason for your answer:

Answers

1. ⁺7 > ⁻2   True because ⁺7 is to the right of ⁻2 on a number line.
2. ⁻5 > ⁻3   False because ⁻5 is to the left of ⁻3 on a number line.
3. ⁻4 < ⁺1   True because ⁻4 is to the left of ⁺1 on a number line.

EXERCISES

In 1–8, state whether the sentence is true or false. Give the reason for your answer.

1. ⁺5 > ⁺2   2. ⁻3 < 0   3. ⁺2 < 0   4. ⁺8 > ⁻2
5. ⁻7 > ⁻1   6. ⁻4 > ⁺2.5   7. $^-1\frac{3}{4} > {}^-1\frac{7}{8}$ 8. $0 < {}^-\frac{1}{4}$

In 9–14, use the symbol < to order the numbers.

9. ⁻4, ⁺8   10. ⁻3, ⁻6   11. $^+1\frac{1}{2}, {}^-1\frac{1}{2}$
12. ⁺3, ⁻2, ⁻4   13. ⁻2, ⁺8, 0   14. $^-3\frac{1}{2}, {}^+6, {}^+2\frac{1}{2}$

In 15–20, use the symbol > to order the numbers.

15. ⁺7, ⁻4   16. ⁻12, ⁺12   17. $^-1\frac{1}{2}, 0$
18. ⁺3, ⁻3, ⁺5   19. ⁻5, ⁻1, 0   20. $^-1.5, {}^+3\frac{1}{2}, {}^-2\frac{1}{2}$

In 21–23, state which number is between the other two.

21. ⁺8, ⁻2, ⁺2   22. ⁺9, ⁻9, ⁻4   23. ⁺.6, ⁺1.1, ⁻.8

In 24–27, state whether the sentence is true or false.

24. $^+5 \geq {}^+2$ 25. $^-2 \leq {}^+5$ 26. $^-9 \leq {}^-12$ 27. $^-3 \geq {}^+3$

28. If x is a positive number and y is a negative number ($x > 0$ and $y < 0$), tell whether each statement is true or false.
    a. $x = y$ b. $x > y$ c. $y > x$ d. $x < 0$ e. $y < 0 < x$
29. What is the smallest positive integer?
30. What is the greatest negative integer?
31. a. Is there a greatest positive integer?   b. Why?
32. a. Is there a least negative integer?   b. Why?

3 GRAPHING THE SOLUTION SET OF AN OPEN SENTENCE INVOLVING ONE VARIABLE ON A NUMBER LINE

■ **PROCEDURE.** To graph the solution set of an open sentence involving one variable on a number line:

1. Find the set of numbers that are solutions of the open sentence.

2. Graph the solution set on a number line.

| MODEL PROBLEMS |

1. If the domain of x is $\{^-3, {}^-2, {}^-1, 0, {}^+1, {}^+2, {}^+3\}$, graph the solution set for the sentence $x \geq {}^-2$.

    Solution: When any element of the domain except $^-3$ replaces x in the sentence $x \geq {}^-2$ (which means $x > {}^-2$ or $x = {}^-2$), the resulting statement is true. Therefore, the solution set of $x \geq {}^-2$ is $\{^-2, {}^-1, 0, {}^+1, {}^+2, {}^+3\}$.

2. Using the set of signed numbers as the replacement set, graph the solution set of each of the following sentences:
    a. $y > {}^-4$ b. $m \leq {}^-2$ c. $^-3 \leq t < {}^+2$

    Solution:

    a. The graph of $y > {}^-4$ consists of all points to the right of $^-4$. The non-darkened circle shows that $^-4$ is not included.
    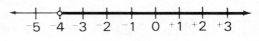

b. The graph of $m \leq {}^-2$ consists of the point $^-2$ and all points to the left of $^-2$. The darkened circle shows that $^-2$ is included.

c. The graph of $^-3 \leq t < {}^+2$ consists of the point $^-3$ and all points between $^-3$ and $^+2$. The point $^+2$ is not included.

3. Graph $\{x \mid x > {}^-2 \wedge x < {}^+3\}$

Solution:

$\{x \mid x > {}^-2 \wedge x < {}^+3\}$ is the set of all x's such that $x > {}^-2$ and $x < {}^+3$; that is, x is between $^-2$ and $^+3$, written $^-2 < x < {}^+3$. The graph of this set consists of all the points between $^-2$ and $^+3$. The points $^-2$ and $^+3$ are not included.

EXERCISES

In 1–12, if the replacement set is $\{{}^-4, {}^-3, {}^-2, {}^-1, 0, {}^+1, {}^+2, {}^+3, {}^+4\}$, graph the solution set of the open sentence.

1. $x > 0$
2. $x < 0$
3. $x \geq 0$
4. $x \leq 0$
5. $y > {}^-1$
6. $t < {}^+2$
7. $m \geq {}^+1$
8. $c \leq {}^-1$
9. $^-1 < d < {}^+3$
10. $^-1 \leq x < {}^+2$
11. $^-1 < y \leq {}^+2$
12. $^-3 \leq t \leq {}^+3$

In 13–24, if the domain is the set of signed numbers, graph the solution set of the sentence.

13. $x > {}^+6$
14. $y < {}^-3$
15. $r > 0$
16. $s \leq 0$
17. $m \geq {}^-1$
18. $m \leq {}^-4$
19. $x \neq {}^+2$
20. $z \geq {}^+2\frac{1}{2}$
21. $^-3 < x < {}^+2$
22. $^-2 \leq x < {}^+4$
23. $^-1 < y \leq {}^+3$
24. $^-3 \leq m \leq {}^+3$

In 25–30, choose the inequality that is represented by the accompanying graph.

25. (1) $^-3 < x \leq {}^+2$
    (2) $^-3 \leq x < {}^+2$
    (3) $^-3 \leq x \leq {}^+2$
    (4) $^-3 < x < {}^+2$

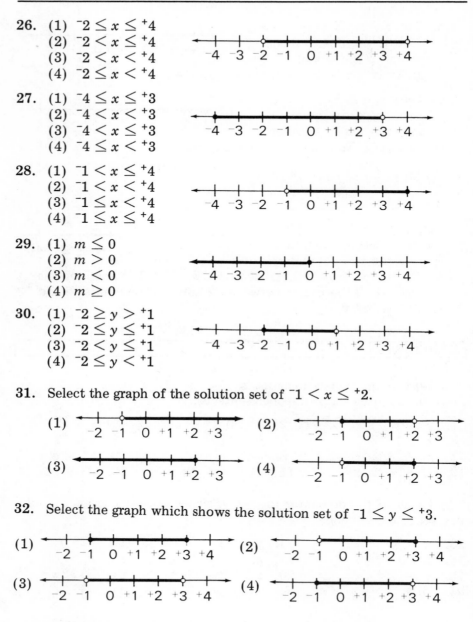

26. (1) $^-2 \leq x \leq {^+4}$
　　(2) $^-2 < x \leq {^+4}$
　　(3) $^-2 < x < {^+4}$
　　(4) $^-2 \leq x < {^+4}$

27. (1) $^-4 \leq x \leq {^+3}$
　　(2) $^-4 < x < {^+3}$
　　(3) $^-4 < x \leq {^+3}$
　　(4) $^-4 \leq x < {^+3}$

28. (1) $^-1 < x \leq {^+4}$
　　(2) $^-1 < x < {^+4}$
　　(3) $^-1 \leq x < {^+4}$
　　(4) $^-1 \leq x \leq {^+4}$

29. (1) $m \leq 0$
　　(2) $m > 0$
　　(3) $m < 0$
　　(4) $m \geq 0$

30. (1) $^-2 \geq y > {^+1}$
　　(2) $^-2 \leq y \leq {^+1}$
　　(3) $^-2 < y \leq {^+1}$
　　(4) $^-2 \leq y < {^+1}$

31. Select the graph of the solution set of $^-1 < x \leq {^+2}$.

　　(1) 　　　　　　　　　　　　(2)

　　(3) 　　　　　　　　　　　　(4)

32. Select the graph which shows the solution set of $^-1 \leq y \leq {^+3}$.

(1) 　　　　　　　　　　　　(2)

(3) 　　　　　　　　　　　　(4)

In 33–40, graph the given set.

33. $\{x \mid x < {^+2} \wedge x > {^-3}\}$　　　　**34.** $\{x \mid x \geq {^-1} \wedge x \leq {^+4}\}$
35. $\{x \mid x \geq {^-4} \wedge x < {^+1}\}$　　　　**36.** $\{x \mid x > 0 \wedge x \leq {^+3}\}$
37. $\{x \mid x \leq {^-1} \vee x \geq {^+2}\}$　　　　**38.** $\{x \mid x < {^-2} \vee x \geq {^+5}\}$
39. $\{x \mid x \leq {^-2} \vee x < {^+4}\}$　　　　**40.** $\{x \mid x \leq {^-3} \vee x \geq {^-3}\}$

4 THE OPPOSITE OF A DIRECTED NUMBER

On a real number line any number can be paired with another number that is the same distance from 0 and on the opposite side of 0. We call such a pair of numbers *opposites*. For example, ⁻1

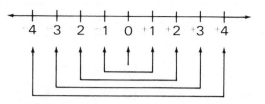

is the opposite of ⁺1, and ⁺2 is the opposite of ⁻2. We say that the opposite of 0 is 0. A centered dash "‐" placed before a numeral is used as a symbol for "the opposite of."

$-(^+1) = {}^-1$ is read, "the opposite of ⁺1 is ⁻1"
$-(^-2) = {}^+2$ is read, "the opposite of ⁻2 is ⁺2"

We know that ⁺4 and 4 name the same number. Hence, the opposite of ⁺4, written $-(^+4)$, and the opposite of 4, written -4, both name the same number. Since $-(^+4) = {}^-4$, then $-4 = {}^-4$. Notice that -4 and ⁻4 are really two different names for the same number. Therefore, we will use only one symbol, -4, to represent that number. Thus, we see that:

$$-4 \text{ can mean:} \begin{cases} \text{negative } 4 \\ \text{or} \\ \text{the opposite of } 4 \end{cases}$$

In the future, in order to simplify our mathematical notation, we will not use the symbols "⁺" and "⁻". The number represented by the symbol ⁺4 will be written 4 or $+4$. The number represented by the symbols ⁻4 and $-(^+4)$ will be written -4. The equation $-(^+4) = {}^-4$ will be written $-(+4) = -4$ or, even more simply, $-4 = -4$.

If y is a real number, the opposite of y is written $-y$, frequently read "negative y." However, this does not mean that $-y$ is always a negative number. For example, when $y = -6$, its opposite $-y$, $= -(-6) = +6$.

■ The opposite of the opposite of a number is always the number itself.

For example:

number	5	-6
opposite	$-(5) = -5$	$-(-6) = 6$
opposite of opposite	$-(-5) = 5$	$-[-(-6)] = -6$

In general, if y is a signed number, then:

$$-(-y) = y$$

Notice the following similarity. If p is a sentence, then $\sim(\sim p) = p$. And, if y is a signed number, then $-(-y) = y$.

MODEL PROBLEMS

In 1–4, write the simplest symbol that represents the opposite of the number.

1. 15 -15 *Ans.*   2. -10 10 *or* $+10$ *Ans.*
3. $(4 + 8)$ -12 *Ans.*   4. $-[-(9 - 3)]$ -6 *Ans.*

EXERCISES

In 1–12, write the simplest symbol that represents the opposite of the number.

1. 8   2. -8 3. $+3\frac{1}{2}$ 4. -6.5
5. $(10 + 9)$ 6. $(24 - 10)$ 7. $(9 - 9)$ 8. 8×0
9. $-(-7)$ 10. $-(-\frac{3}{4})$ 11. $-[-(+5)]$ 12. $-[-(6 + 8)]$

In 13–16, select the greater of the two numbers.

13. $10, -5$ 14. $-1, 7$ 15. $-8, -4$ 16. $-12, 0$

In 17–28, graph the solution set of the open sentence if the domain of the variable is the set of real numbers.

17. $x < -3$ 18. $y > -6$ 19. $m \geq -1$ 20. $y \leq -2$
21. $-t \geq 4$ 22. $-s \leq 0$ 23. $-c < -2$ 24. $-d > -3$
25. $-m \geq -2\frac{1}{2}$ 26. $-r \leq -4$ 27. $-8 < s < 3$ 28. $-3 < -y < 1$

In 29–35, tell whether the statement is true or false.

29. If a is a real number, then $-a$ is always a negative number.
30. If a is a negative number, then $-a$ is always a positive number.
31. The opposite of a number is always a different number.
32. On a number line the opposite of a positive number is to the left of the number.
33. On a number line the opposite of any number is always to the left of the number.
34. If x is a positive number, then x is greater than its opposite.
35. The opposite of the opposite of a number is that number itself.

5 THE ABSOLUTE VALUE OF A NUMBER

In every pair of opposite numbers, other than 0 and 0, the positive number is the greater. On a real number line the positive number is always to the right of the negative number that is its opposite. For example, 10 is greater than its opposite -10; on a number line 10 is to the right of -10.

The greater of a nonzero number and its opposite is called the *absolute value* of the number.

The absolute value of a number is symbolized by writing a name of the number between a pair of vertical bars, $|\ |$. For example, since 10 is the greater of the two opposite numbers 10 and -10, the absolute value of 10 is 10, written $|10| = 10$. Also, the absolute value of -10 is 10, written $|-10| = 10$.

We use the symbol "$|x|$" to represent the absolute value of the number x. The absolute value of 0 is defined as 0 itself, written $|0| = 0$. Since $|10| = 10$ and $|-10| = 10$, then $|-10| = |10| = 10$. Also, $|-8| = |+8| = 8$.

These examples illustrate that, for a pair of opposite numbers, the absolute value of one member of the pair is the same number as the absolute value of the second member. Notice that the absolute value of a positive number is the number itself; the absolute value of a negative number is always its opposite.

The absolute value of a number can also be considered as the distance between 0 and the graph of that number on the real number line. For example, $|3| = 3$, the distance from 0 to P, the graph of 3 on the real number line; $|-3| = 3$, the distance from 0 to S, the graph of -3, on the real number line.

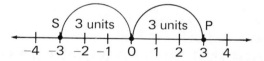

Observe too that the absolute value of any real number x may also be considered as the maximum of the number and its opposite, symbolized as follows:

$$|x| = x \ \text{max} \ (-x)$$

| MODEL PROBLEM |

Find the value of the number expression $|12| + |-3|$.

Solution:

Since $|12| = 12$, and $|-3| = 3$, $|12| + |-3| = 12 + 3 = 15$ *Ans.*

| **EXERCISES** |

In 1–10: **a.** Give the absolute value of the given number. **b.** Give another number that has the same absolute value.

1. 3   **2.** −5   **3.** +18   **4.** −13   **5.** −20
6. $1\frac{1}{2}$ **7.** $-3\frac{3}{4}$ **8.** $-1\frac{1}{2}$ **9.** +2.7   **10.** −1.4

In 11–18, state whether the sentence is true or false.

11. $|20| = 20$ **12.** $|-13| = 13$ **13.** $|-15| = -15$ **14.** $|-9| = |9|$
15. $|-7| < |7|$ **16.** $|-10| > |3|$ **17.** $|8| < |-19|$ **18.** $|-21| > 21$

In 19–33, find the value of the number expression.

19. $|9| + |3|$ **20.** $|+8| - |+2|$ **21.** $|-6| + |4|$
22. $|-10| - |-5|$ **23.** $|4.5| - |4.5|$ **24.** $|+6| + |-4|$
25. $|8 + 6|$ **26.** $|7 - 2|$ **27.** $|15 - 15|$
28. $|9| + |-3| - |-4|$ **29.** $|-8| - |-2| + |-3|$ **30.** $|10| - |-6| - |4|$
31. $|(8 - 4)| + |-3|$ **32.** $-(|-9| - |7|)$ **33.** $-(|-8| - 2)$

In 34–41, state whether the sentence is true or false.

34. $|+5| - |-5| = 0$ **35.** $|+9| + |-9| = 0$
36. $|3| \cdot |-3| = -9$ **37.** $2 \cdot |-4| = |-2| \cdot |-4|$
38. $\dfrac{|-8|}{|-4|} = -|+2|$ **39.** $|4| \cdot |-2| - \dfrac{|-16|}{|2|} = 0$
40. $|-6| \cdot |4| > 0$ **41.** $|6| + |-4| < 6 - 4$

6   ADDING SIGNED NUMBERS ON A NUMBER LINE

Addition of signed numbers may be interpreted on a number line as a sequence of directed moves. We will relate "moving to the right" with a positive number and "moving to the left" with a negative number.

| **MODEL PROBLEMS** |

1.   Add +3 and +2.

Solution: Start at 0 and move 3 units to the right to +3; then move 2 more units to the right, arriving at +5.

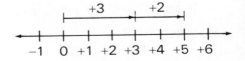

Answer: (+3) + (+2) = +5

2. Add – 3 and – 2.

Solution: Start at 0 and move
3 units to the left to – 3; then
move 2 more units to the left,
arriving at – 5.

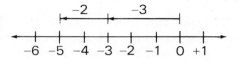

Answer: (– 3) + (– 2) = – 5

3. Add +3 and – 2.

Solution: Start at 0 and move 3
units to the right to +3; then move
2 units to the left, arriving at +1.

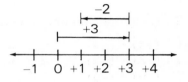

Answer: (+3) + (– 2) = +1

4. Add – 3 and +2.

Solution: Start at 0 and move 3
units to the left to – 3; then move
2 units to the right, arriving at – 1.

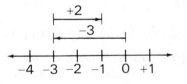

Answer: (– 3) + (+2) = – 1

5. Add +3 and – 3.

Solution: Start at 0 and move 3
units to the right to +3; then move
3 units to the left, arriving at 0.

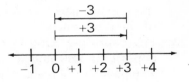

Answer: (+3) + (– 3) = 0

6. Add 0 and – 3.

Solution: Start at 0 and move
neither to the right nor to the left;
then move 3 units to the left,
arriving at – 3.

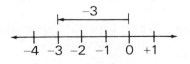

Answer: (0) + (– 3) = – 3

■ **PROCEDURE.**   To add two signed numbers on a number line:

1. Graph the first number.

2. From this point move to the right a number of units equal to the absolute value of the second number if the second number is positive; move to the left if the second number is negative; do not move if the second number is 0. The number at the point that is reached is the sum of the two signed numbers.

| EXERCISES |

In 1–19, use a number line to find the sum of the signed numbers.

 1. (+3) + (+4)   2. (+6) + (+8)   3. (−2) + (−4)
 4. (−5) + (−3)   5. (+7) + (−4)   6. (+4) + (−1)
 7. (−6) + (+5)   8. (−8) + (+10)   9. (+4) + (−4)
10. (−7) + (+7)   11. (−2) + (+2)   12. (0) + (+4)
13. (0) + (−6)   14. (+6) + (0)   15. (−8) + (0)
16. [(+3) + (+4)] + (+2)   17. [(+8) + (−4)] + (−6)
18. [(−7) + (−3)] + (+6)   19. [(−5) + (+2)] + (+3)

In 20–24, use signed numbers to solve the problem.

20. In one hour the Celsius temperature rose 4° and in the next hour the Celsius temperature rose 3°. What was the net change in temperature during the two-hour period?

21. An elevator started on the ground floor and rose 30 floors. Then it came down 12 floors. At which floor was it at that time?

22. A football team gained 7 yards on the first play, lost 2 yards on the second, and lost 8 yards on the third. What was the net result of the three plays?

23. Fay deposited $250 in a bank. During the next month she made a deposit of $60 and a withdrawal of $80. How much money did Fay have in the bank at that time?

24. During a four-day period the value of a share of stock rose $1\frac{1}{2}$ on the first day, dropped $\frac{5}{8}$ on the second day, rose $\frac{1}{8}$ on the third day, and dropped $1\frac{3}{4}$ on the fourth day. What was the net change in the stock during this period?

25. What type of number does the sum of two positive numbers always appear to be?

26. What type of number does the sum of two negative numbers always appear to be?

27. Is it possible for the sum of a positive and a negative number to be (a) a positive number? (b) a negative number?
28. If two given signed numbers (not opposites) are to be added, how can you tell whether the sum is a positive number or a negative number?
29. Is it possible for the sum of two numbers of arithmetic to be smaller than each of the numbers?
30. a. Is it possible for the sum of two signed numbers to be smaller than each of the numbers?
    b. If your answer in part a is yes, give an example.

7 ADDITION OF SIGNED NUMBERS

In Chapter 3 we learned that the numbers of arithmetic have various properties of addition. Now we will define the operation of addition so that these properties will also be true for signed numbers. By doing this we will be able to add signed numbers without the use of a number line.

Addition of Two Positive Numbers

If +2 and +4 are added on a number line, the sum is +6. We write (+2) + (+4) = +6, or 2 + 4 = 6. This example illustrates that we can add positive numbers in the same manner that we added the numbers of arithmetic.

The sum (+2) + (+4) can also be written vertically as shown at the right.

+2	The absolute value of +2 is 2.
+4	The absolute value of +4 is 4.
+6	The sum of the absolute values is 6.

Observe that the sum +6 is a positive number whose absolute value 6 is the sum of 2 and 4, the absolute values of +2 and +4.

■ **Rule 1.** The sum of two positive numbers is a positive number whose absolute value is found by adding the absolute values of the numbers.

In general, if both a and b are positive numbers:

$$a + b = |a| + |b|$$

| MODEL PROBLEMS |

In 1–4, add the two numbers.

1. $\begin{array}{r} +\ 8 \\ +10 \\ \hline +18 \end{array}$ 2. $\begin{array}{r} +\ 9.1 \\ +\ 7.5 \\ \hline +16.6 \end{array}$ 3. $(+7) + (+5) = +12$ 4. $\frac{3}{8} + \frac{4}{8} = \frac{7}{8}$

Addition of Two Negative Numbers

If -2 and -4 are added on a number line, the sum is -6. We can write $(-2) + (-4) = -6$, or we can arrange the addition vertically as shown at the right.

-2	The absolute value of -2 is 2.
-4	The absolute value of -4 is 4.
-6	The sum of the absolute values is 6.

Observe that the sum -6 is a negative number whose absolute value 6 is the sum of 2 and 4, the absolute values of -2 and -4.

■ **Rule 2.** The sum of two negative numbers is a negative number whose absolute value is found by adding the absolute values of the numbers.

In general, if both a and b are negative numbers:

$$a + b = -(|a| + |b|)$$

Observe that in effect rule 1 and rule 2 tell us that:

■ To add two numbers that have the same sign, add their absolute values and write the common sign before the sum of the absolute values.

| MODEL PROBLEMS |

In 1–6, add.

1. $\begin{array}{r} -4 \\ -3 \\ \hline -7 \end{array}$ 2. $\begin{array}{r} -10 \\ -\ 8 \\ \hline -18 \end{array}$ 3. $\begin{array}{r} -4.2 \\ -3.6 \\ \hline -7.8 \end{array}$ 4. $\begin{array}{r} -\ 7.4 \\ -\ 8.7 \\ \hline -16.1 \end{array}$

5. $(-\frac{3}{10}) + (-\frac{4}{10}) = -\frac{7}{10}$

6. $(-5\frac{1}{8}) + (-5\frac{7}{8}) = -11$

Addition of a Positive Number and a Negative Number

If +5 and -3 are added on a number line, the sum is +2. We can write this as (+5) + (-3) = +2, or

+5	The absolute value of +5 is 5.
-3	The absolute value of -3 is 3.
+2	The difference of the absolute values is 2.

we can arrange the addition vertically as shown above.

Observe that the sum +2 is a positive number; and +5, the number with the greater absolute value, is also a positive number. Considering only absolute values, observe that the difference of 5 and 3 is 2. The difference of two absolute values (unsigned numbers) is simply the greater minus the smaller.

If -5 and +3 are added on a number line, the sum is -2. We can write this as (-5) + (+3) = -2, or

-5	The absolute value of -5 is 5.
+3	The absolute value of +3 is 3.
-2	The difference of the absolute values is 2.

we can arrange the addition vertically as shown above.

Observe that the sum -2 is a negative number; and -5, the number with the greater absolute value, is also a negative number. Considering only absolute values, again observe that the difference of 5 and 3 is 2.

If +6 and -6 are added on a number line, the sum is 0. We write (+6) + (-6) = 0.

■ **Rule 3.** To find the sum of two numbers, one of which is positive or 0 and the other negative, find a number whose absolute value is the difference of the absolute values of the numbers.

The sum is positive when the positive number has the greater absolute value; the sum is negative when the negative number has the greater absolute value; the sum is 0 if both numbers have the same absolute value.

In general, if a is a positive number or 0, that is, $a \geq 0$; and if b is a negative number, that is, $b < 0$, then:

$$\text{if } |a| \geq |b|, \text{ then } a + b = |a| - |b|$$

$$and$$

$$\text{if } |b| > |a|, \text{ then } a + b = -(|b| - |a|)$$

If b is a positive number or 0, that is, $b \geq 0$; and if a is a negative number, that is, $a < 0$, then:

$$\text{if } |b| \geq |a|, \text{ then } a + b = |b| - |a|$$

$$and$$

$$\text{if } |a| > |b|, \text{ then } a + b = -(|a| - |b|)$$

Observe that in effect rule 3 tells us that:

■ To add two signed numbers that have different signs, find the difference of the absolute values of these numbers and write before this difference the sign of the number that has the greater absolute value; the sum is 0 if both numbers have the same absolute value.

| MODEL PROBLEMS |

In 1-6, add the numbers.

1.	+9	2.	-8	3.	-6	4.	-6.7	5.	-1.8	6.	$-7\frac{3}{4}$
	-2		$+3$		$+8$		$+4.2$		7.2		$5\frac{1}{4}$
	$+7$		-5		$+2$		-2.5		5.4		$-2\frac{1}{2}$

In Chapter 3 we studied addition properties of the numbers of arithmetic. These same properties apply to signed numbers.

Closure Property of Addition

The sum of two signed numbers is always a unique member of the set of signed numbers. Thus, addition is a binary operation for the set of signed numbers.

In general, for every signed number a and every signed number b:

a + b is a unique signed number

Commutative Property of Addition

In general, for every signed number a and every signed number b:

$$a + b = b + a$$

Associative Property of Addition

In general, for every signed number a, every signed number b, and every signed number c:

$$(a + b) + c = a + (b + c)$$

Addition Property of Zero

The sum of 0 and a signed number is that number itself. For this reason, 0 is called the *identity element of addition*, or the *additive identity*. In general, for every signed number a:

$$a + 0 = a \quad \text{and} \quad 0 + a = a$$

Other properties for signed numbers which we will assume are:

Addition Property of Opposites

Every signed number a has an *opposite* $-a$, such that their sum is 0. The opposite of a number is called the *additive inverse* of the number. In general, for every signed number a and its opposite $-a$:

$$a + (-a) = 0$$

Property of the Opposite of a Sum

The opposite of the sum of two signed numbers is equal to the sum of the opposites.

In general, for every signed number a and every signed number b:

$$-(a + b) = (-a) + (-b)$$

Note: When adding more than two signed numbers, the commutative and associative properties allow us to arrange them in any order and group them in any way. It may prove helpful to add the positive numbers first, to add the negative numbers second, and then to add these two results.

MODEL PROBLEM

Add: $(+6) + (-2) + (+7) + (-4)$

How to Proceed   *Solution*

(1) Write the expression.

$(+6) + (-2) + (+7) + (-4)$

(2) Use the commutative and associative properties and add the positive and negative numbers separately.

$[(+6) + (+7)] + [(-2) + (-4)]$

$\begin{array}{r} +6 \\ +7 \\ \hline +13 \end{array} \qquad \begin{array}{r} -2 \\ -4 \\ \hline -6 \end{array}$

(3) Add the positive and negative sums.

$(+13) + (-6) = +7$ *Ans.*

| EXERCISES |

In 1–76, add the numbers.

1. +6
   +4

2. +9
   +8

3. +7
   +6

4. -14
   -23

5. -14
   -9

6. -17
   -28

7. +8
   -6

8. -9
   +7

9. +8
   -4

10. +2
    -9

11. -13
    +7

12. +23
    -35

13. +6
    0

14. -5
    0

15. 0
    +4

16. 0
    -9

17. +5
    -5

18. -9
    +9

19. +15
    +9

20. -17
    -8

21. -28
    -38

22. +8
    +17

23. -15
    -15

24. 34
    66

25. $+6\frac{2}{3}$
    $+1\frac{1}{3}$

26. $-5\frac{1}{2}$
    $-3\frac{1}{2}$

27. $+3\frac{1}{4}$
    $+7\frac{1}{4}$

28. $-8\frac{2}{3}$
    $-4\frac{2}{3}$

29. $9\frac{1}{2}$
    $8\frac{3}{4}$

30. $-6\frac{5}{6}$
    $-1\frac{2}{3}$

31. -5.6
    -2.2

32. +6.8
    +3.2

33. +5.4
    +2.9

34. -8.8
    -7.5

35. 5.7
    8.3

36. -5.4
    -2.6

37. 7.9
    -5.6

38. -8.7
    +3.7

39. -6.9
    9.4

40. +7
    $-8\frac{3}{4}$

41. $-33\frac{1}{3}$
    $+19\frac{2}{3}$

42. $-5\frac{3}{4}$
    $8\frac{1}{2}$

43. (+8) + (-14)

44. (-12) + (+37)

45. (+40) + (-17)

46. (-18) + 0

47. 0 + (-28)

48. (+15) + (-15)

49. (-15) + 34

50. 14 + 17

51. (-19) + 7

52. |-34| + |+20|

53. -|7| + (-10)

54. |15| + (-|-15|)

55. +27
    -9
    -12

56. -45
    +12
    +13

57. 15
    -28
    13

58. +20
    -12
    -8

59. -1.5
    +3.7
    -8.3

60. $8\frac{1}{2}$
    $-4\frac{1}{4}$
    $7\frac{3}{4}$

61. +9
    +7
    -3
    -5

62. -21
    -13
    +17
    +10

63. 14
    -9
    -13
    +8

64. -24
    15
    19
    -12

65. -.7
    +3.1
    -9.6
    +.5

66. $8\frac{1}{6}$
    $-13\frac{1}{6}$
    $-3\frac{1}{3}$
    $-9\frac{5}{6}$

67. (+18) + (-15) + (+9)

68. 30 + (-18) + (-12)

69. (-19) + (+8) + (-15)

70. (-17) + (-19) + 40

71. (+12) + (-18) + (-4) + (+7)

72. (-19) + 8 + (-5) + 16

73. 48 + (-32) + 19 + (-41)

74. $(-4\frac{1}{3}) + 7 + 8\frac{1}{3} - 11$

75. |+7| + |-8| + |0|

76. |-13| + |7| + (-|-20|)

In 77–81, name the signed number that represents the sum of the quantities. Represent a rise or a profit by a positive number.

77. a rise of 4 meters and a rise of 6 meters
78. a loss of 6 yards and a loss of 2 yards
79. a rise of 7 meters and a fall of 5 meters
80. a loss of $20 and a profit of $20
81. a rise of 4°, a drop of 3°, and a drop of 5°

In 82–86, give the additive inverse of the given expression.

82. +10   83. −8   84. 15.5   85. C 86. $-d$

In 87–98, give a replacement for the question mark that will make the resulting sentence true.

87. $(+4) + (?) = 0$
89. $(0) + (?) = 0$
91. $(b) + (?) = 0$
93. $(+8) + (?) = (+12)$
95. $(6) + (?) = -4$
97. $(-\frac{6}{7}) + (?) = (+\frac{2}{7})$

88. $(-2) + (?) = 0$
90. $(12) + (?) = 0$
92. $(-y) + (?) = 0$
94. $(+10) + (?) = 7$
96. $(-4\frac{1}{2}) + (?) = -9\frac{1}{2}$
98. $(-3.75) + (?) = -3.75$

In 99–104, give a replacement for the variable that will make the resulting sentence true.

99. $9 + y = 0$ 100. $x + (-12) = 0$ 101. $5 + c = 1$
102. $x + 4 = -2$ 103. $x + (-6) = 8$ 104. $d + (-5) = -3$

In 105–109, name the addition property that makes each sentence true.

105. $(-3) + (+8) = (+8) + (-3)$
107. $(-8) + 0 = -8$
109. $(-6) + [(-4) + (+2)] = [(-6) + (-4)] + (+2)$

106. $(+50) + (-50) = 0$
108. $-[8 + 9] = (-8) + (-9)$

In 110–113, state whether the sentence is true or false.

110. $|x| + |-x| = 0$ $(x \neq 0)$
112. $-(-b) = b$

111. $(-c) + (-d) = -(c + d)$
113. $(a + b) + [-(a + b)] = 0$

8 SUBTRACTION OF SIGNED NUMBERS

When we were dealing with the numbers of arithmetic, we were able to subtract 3 from 7. The result was 4. We wrote $7 - 3 = 4$. However, we were not able to subtract 7 from 3 because we had no number to represent $3 - 7$. The set of numbers of arithmetic was not closed with respect to subtraction. In other words, for the set of numbers of arithmetic, we saw that subtraction was not a binary operation.

Now we will learn that we can always subtract one number from another when we are dealing with the set of signed numbers.

In arithmetic, to subtract 3 from 7, we find a number which, when added to 3, will give 7. That number is 4. We know that $7 - 3 = 4$ because $3 + 4 = 7$.

Subtraction in the set of numbers of arithmetic is defined as the inverse operation of addition.

In general, for every number c and every number b, the expression $c - b$ means to find a number a such that $b + a = c$.

We use the same definition of subtraction in the set of signed numbers. To subtract (-2) from $(+3)$, written $(+3) - (-2)$, we must find a number which, when added to -2, will give $+3$. We write $(-2) + (?) = +3$.

We can use a number line to help us find the answer to $(-2) + (?) = +3$. Think as follows: From a point 2 units to the left of 0, what motion must be made to

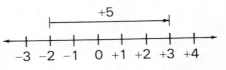

arrive at a point 3 units to the right of 0? We must move 5 units to the right. This motion is represented by $+5$.

Therefore, $(+3) - (-2) = +5$ because $(-2) + (+5) = +3$. We can write $(+3) - (-2) = +5$ vertically as follows:

$$\begin{array}{cl} (+3) & or \quad Subtract: \quad (+3) \quad \text{minuend} \\ \underline{-(-2)} & \quad \underline{(-2)} \quad \text{subtrahend} \\ +5 & \quad +5 \quad \text{difference} \end{array}$$

Check each of the following examples by using a number line to answer the related question: subtrahend + (?) = minuend.

$$\begin{array}{ccccc} Subtract: & +9 & -7 & +5 & -3 \\ & \underline{+6} & \underline{-2} & \underline{-2} & \underline{+1} \\ & +3 & -5 & +7 & -4 \end{array}$$

Now we will consider another way in which addition and subtraction are related. In each of the following examples compare the result obtained when subtracting the signed number with the result obtained when adding the opposite of that signed number:

Subtract	Add	Subtract	Add	Subtract	Add	Subtract	Add
+9	+9	-7	-7	+5	+5	-3	-3
+6	-6	-2	+2	-2	+2	+1	-1
+3	+3	-5	-5	+7	+7	-4	-4

Observe that in each example adding the opposite (the additive inverse) of a signed number gives the same result as subtracting that signed number. It therefore seems reasonable to define subtraction as follows:

If a is any signed number and b is any signed number, then:

$$a - b = a + (-b)$$

■ **PROCEDURE.** To subtract one signed number from another, add the opposite (additive inverse) of the subtrahend to the minuend.

Notice that it is always possible to subtract one signed number from another and obtain a unique signed number as the result. Therefore, the set of signed numbers is closed with respect to subtraction. In other words, for the set of signed numbers, subtraction is a binary operation.

Uses of the Symbol "-"

In the expression $7 - (-5)$, the symbol "-" is used in two different ways. The first "-", which stands between the two numerals 7 and (-5), indicates the operation of subtraction. The second "-", which is part of the numeral (-5), indicates the opposite of 5.

Since $7 - 4 = 7 + (-4)$, the symbol $7 + (-4)$ is sometimes written $7 - 4$.

Similarly, $(+9) + (-2) + (-4)$ is sometimes written $9 - 2 - 4$.

Likewise, $-3 - 4 - 2$ can mean the sum of $-3, -4,$ and -2; this may be written $(-3) + (-4) + (-2)$.

MODEL PROBLEMS

In 1–4, perform the indicated subtraction.

1. $(+30) - (+12) = (+30) + (-12) = +18$ *Ans.*
2. $(-19) - (-7) = (-19) + (+7) = -12$ *Ans.*
3. $(-4) - (0) = (-4) + (0) = -4$ *Ans.*
4. $0 - 8 = 0 + (-8) = -8$ *Ans.*

In 5–11, subtract the lower number from the upper number.

5.	+45	6.	-19	7.	-19	8.	+25	9.	0	10.	-8	11.	-8
	+20		-14		+17		-18		-6		-8		+8
	+25		-5		-36		+43		+6		0		-16

Note: In each problem the signed number is subtracted by adding its opposite to the minuend.

EXERCISES

In 1–6, use a number line to do the subtraction.

1. $(+6) - (+2)$ **2.** $(+5) - (-3)$ **3.** $(-1) - (+2)$
4. $(-3) - (-4)$ **5.** $(-3) - (+3)$ **6.** $(-3) - (-3)$

In 7–42, subtract the lower number from the upper number.

7. $+9$	**8.** $+25$	**9.** $+6$	**10.** $+16$	**11.** -7	**12.** -26
$+3$	$+18$	$+8$	$+24$	-3	-12

13. -2	**14.** -34	**15.** $+5$	**16.** $+26$	**17.** $+4$	**18.** $+65$
-6	-50	-1	-19	-9	-75

19. -6	**20.** -63	**21.** -5	**22.** -36	**23.** $+10$	**24.** 0
$+2$	$+29$	$+7$	$+50$	0	$+7$

25. 0	**26.** -19	**27.** $+18$	**28.** $+15$	**29.** $+36$	**30.** -39
-20	-19	$+29$	$+15$	-15	$+15$

31. -45	**32.** -6	**33.** -8	**34.** 0	**35.** $+8.7$	**36.** $+8.3$
$+17$	$+6$	-8	-15	$+6.5$	-6.2

37. -6.9	**38.** 5.9	**39.** $+9\frac{1}{2}$	**40.** $-3\frac{1}{4}$	**41.** $7\frac{3}{4}$	**42.** $-6\frac{5}{6}$
$+3.7$	7.2	$+6\frac{1}{2}$	$-7\frac{3}{4}$	$-2\frac{1}{4}$	$+3\frac{1}{3}$

In 43–48, perform the indicated subtraction.

43. $(+19) - (+30)$ **44.** $(-12) - (-25)$ **45.** $22 - (-8)$
46. $(+6.4) - (+8.1)$ **47.** $(-3.7) - (-5.2)$ **48.** $(-9.2) - 8.3$

49. How much is 18 decreased by -7?
50. How much greater than -15 is 12?
51. How much greater than -4 is -1?
52. How much less than 6 is -3?
53. What number is 6 less than -6?
54. From the sum of 25 and -10, subtract -4.
55. Subtract 8 from the sum of -6 and -12.

In 56–61, state the number that must be added to the given number to make the result equal to 0.

56. $+5$ **57.** -3 **58.** $+8.5$ **59.** -3.7 **60.** $+1\frac{7}{8}$ **61.** $-\frac{9}{2}$

In 62–67, find the value of the given expression.

62. $(+7) + (+9) - (-4)$ **63.** $(-12) - (+9) + (-20)$

64. $32 - 49 - 21 + 10$ **65.** $-15 + 8 - 5 + 12$

66. $6\frac{1}{4} - 5 + 7\frac{3}{4} - 1\frac{1}{2}$ **67.** $-5\frac{1}{3} + 8 + 9\frac{1}{3} - 12$

In 68–70, use signed numbers to do the problem.

68. Find the change when the Celsius temperature changes from:
  a. $+5°$ to $+8°$ **b.** $-10°$ to $+18°$ **c.** $-6°$ to $-18°$ **d.** $+12°$ to $-4°$

69. Find the change in altitude when you go from a place that is 15 meters below sea level to a place that is 95 meters above sea level.

70. In a game, Sid was 35 points "in the hole." How many points must he make in order to have a score of 150 points?

71. The record high Fahrenheit temperature in New City is $105°$; the record low is $-9°$. Find the difference between these temperatures.

72. At one point the Pacific Ocean is .5 kilometer in depth; at another point it is .25 kilometer in depth. Find the difference between these depths.

73. State whether the following sentences are true or false:
  a. $(+5) - (-3) = (-3) - (+5)$
  b. $(-7) - (-4) = (-4) - (-7)$

74. If x and y represent numbers:
  a. Does $x - y = y - x$ for all replacements of x and y?
  b. Does $x - y = y - x$ for any replacements of x and y? For which values of x and y?
  c. What is the relation between $x - y$ and $y - x$ for all replacements of x and y?
  d. Is the operation of subtraction commutative? That is, does $x - y = y - x$ for all signed numbers x and y?

75. State whether the following sentences are true or false:
  a. $(15 - 9) - 6 = 15 - (9 - 6)$
  b. $[(-10) - (+4)] - (+8) = (-10) - [(+4) - (+8)]$

76. Is the operation of subtraction associative? That is, does $(x - y) - z = x - (y - z)$ for all signed numbers x, y, and z?

9   MULTIPLICATION OF SIGNED NUMBERS

We will define multiplication of signed numbers in such a way that the properties of multiplication of numbers of arithmetic will still hold. Our own experiences will be used to illustrate the various situations that arise in the multiplication of signed numbers. We will represent a gain of weight by a positive number and a loss of weight by a negative number, a number of weeks in the future by a positive number, and a number of weeks in the past by a negative number.

Case 1. Multiplying a Positive Number by a Positive Number

If a girl gains 1 kilogram each week, 4 weeks from now she will be 4 kilograms heavier. Using signed numbers, we may write:

$$(+4) \cdot (+1) = +4$$

Notice that the product of the two positive numbers is a positive number.

Case 2. Multiplying a Negative Number by a Positive Number

If a girl loses 1 kilogram each week, 4 weeks from now she will be 4 kilograms lighter than she is now. Using signed numbers, we may write:

$$(+4) \cdot (-1) = -4$$

Notice that the product of the negative number and the positive number is a negative number.

Case 3. Multiplying a Positive Number by a Negative Number

If a girl has gained 1 kilogram each week, 4 weeks ago she was 4 kilograms lighter than she is now. Using signed numbers, we may write:

$$(-4) \cdot (+1) = -4$$

Notice that the product of the positive number and the negative number is a negative number.

Case 4. Multiplying a Negative Number by a Negative Number

If a girl has lost 1 kilogram each week, 4 weeks ago she was 4 kilograms heavier than she is now. Using signed numbers, we may write:

$$(-4) \cdot (-1) = +4$$

Notice that the product of the two negative numbers is a positive number.

Observe that in all four cases the absolute value of the product, 4, is equal to the product of the absolute values of the factors, 4 and 1.

These four examples illustrate the reasonableness of the following rules:

Rules for Multiplying Signed Numbers

■ **Rule 1.** The product of two positive numbers or of two negative numbers is a positive number whose absolute value is the product of the absolute values of the numbers.

■ **Rule 2.** The product of a positive number and a negative number is a negative number whose absolute value is the product of the absolute values of the numbers.

In general, if a and b are both positive or are both negative, then:

$$ab = |a| \cdot |b|$$

If one of the numbers a and b is positive and the other is negative, then:

$$ab = -(|a| \cdot |b|)$$

Notice that in effect rule 1 and rule 2 tell us that:

■ To multiply two signed numbers, multiply their absolute values and write a plus sign before this product when the two numbers have the same sign; write a minus sign before this product when the two numbers have different signs.

MODEL PROBLEMS

In 1–6, multiply the two numbers.

1. $+12$	2. -13	3. $+18$	4. -15	5. $+3.4$	6. $-7\frac{1}{8}$
$+4$	-5	$-3.$	6	-3	-3
$+48$	$+65$	-54	-90	-10.2	$+21\frac{3}{8}$

In Chapter 3 we studied multiplication properties of the numbers of arithmetic. These same properties also apply to signed numbers.

Closure Property of Multiplication

The product of two signed numbers is always a unique member of the set of signed numbers. Thus, multiplication is a binary operation for the set of signed numbers.

In general, for every signed number a and every signed number b:

$$ab \text{ is a unique signed number}$$

Commutative Property of Multiplication

In general, for every signed number a and every signed number b:

$$ab = ba$$

Associative Property of Multiplication

In general, for every signed number a, every signed number b, and every signed number c:

$$(ab)c = a(bc)$$

Distributive Property of Multiplication

In general, for every signed number a, every signed number b, and every signed number c:

$$a(b + c) = ab + ac \quad \text{and} \quad ab + ac = a(b + c)$$

Also:

$$a(b - c) = ab - ac \quad \text{and} \quad ab - ac = a(b - c)$$

Multiplication Property of One

The product of 1 and a signed number is that number itself. For this reason, 1 is called the *identity element of multiplication*, or the *multiplicative identity*.

In general, for every signed number a:

$$a \cdot 1 = a \quad \text{and} \quad 1 \cdot a = a$$

Multiplication Property of Zero

In general, for every signed number a:

$$a \cdot 0 = 0 \quad \text{and} \quad 0 \cdot a = 0$$

We may also note one new property that we will assume for signed numbers:

Multiplication Property of the Number "Negative One"

In general, for every signed number a:

$$(a) \cdot (-1) = -a \quad \text{and} \quad (-1) \cdot (a) = -a$$

| MODEL PROBLEMS |

1. Find the value of $(-2)^3$.

    Solution: $(-2)^3 = (-2)(-2)(-2) = -8$ *Ans.*

    Note: The answer is negative because there is an odd number of negative factors (3 negative factors).

2. Find the value of $(-3)^4$.

Solution: $(-3)^4 = (-3)(-3)(-3)(-3) = +81$ *Ans.*

Note: The answer is positive because there is an even number of negative factors (4 negative factors).

EXERCISES

In 1–36, find the product of the numbers.

1. +6 +4	**2.** +3 +8	**3.** +23 +6	**4.** -7 -1	**5.** -6 -8	**6.** -15 -7
7. -8 +4	**8.** -9 +7	**9.** +15 -8	**10.** 24 -6	**11.** 0 +3	**12.** -12 0
13. -25 -4	**14.** -24 +8	**15.** 0 -5	**16.** -75 -3	**17.** 15 -9	**18.** +9 0
19. +1.5 -2.4	**20.** -.25 80	**21.** +8 $+\frac{1}{2}$	**22.** -15 $+\frac{3}{5}$	**23.** $-\frac{1}{2}$ $-\frac{1}{3}$	**24.** +16 $-2\frac{1}{4}$

25. $(+8) \times (+6)$ **26.** $(-12) \times (-5)$ **27.** $(+11) \times (-7)$
28. $(+8)(+\frac{1}{4})$ **29.** $(-\frac{3}{5})(-20)$ **30.** $(2)(\frac{1}{2})$
31. $(+4)(+3)(+2)$ **32.** $(-1)(-7)(-8)$ **33.** $(-3)(-5)(+4)(-1)$
34. $(-7)(+2)(0)$ **35.** $|+10| \cdot |-3| \cdot (-4)$ **36.** $(+8)(-9)(0)(-10)$

In 37–48, find the value of the expression.

37. $(+4)^2$ **38.** $(-3)^2$ **39.** $(+5)^3$ **40.** $(-4)^3$
41. $(-5)^3$ **42.** $(-1)^4$ **43.** $(+\frac{1}{2})^2$ **44.** $(-\frac{1}{2})^2$
45. $(+\frac{2}{3})^3$ **46.** $(-\frac{3}{5})^3$ **47.** $(-\frac{1}{4})^3$ **48.** $(-\frac{1}{5})^4$

In 49–53, fill in the blanks so that the resulting sentence is an illustration of the distributive property.

49. $5 \cdot (9 + 7) =$ ___   **50.** $-4(x + y) =$ ___
51. ___ $= (6) \cdot (-3) + 6 \cdot (-5)$ **52.** ___ $= 7a + 7b$
53. $8 \cdot ($___$) = ($___$) \cdot 5 + ($___$) \cdot (-3)$

In 54–57, name the multiplication property illustrated.

54. $(-6) \cdot (-5) = (-5) \cdot (-6)$ **55.** $[(-3) \cdot 4] \cdot 7 = (-3) \cdot [4 \cdot 7]$
56. $-8 \cdot [4 + (-1)] = (-8) \cdot (4) + (-8) \cdot (-1)$
57. $5x + 5 \cdot (-y) = 5 \cdot [x + (-y)]$

58. Write the number property of the set of signed numbers that justifies each of the statements a through e.

   a. $2(1 + 3) = 2(1) + 2(3)$ b. $(-2) + (-1) = (-1) + (-2)$
   c. $(1 + 2) + 3 = 1 + (2 + 3)$ d. $2 + 0 = 2$
   e. $(-5) \times 7 = 7 \times (-5)$

59. State whether the following sentences are true or false:

   a. $5(7 - 3) = 5 \cdot 7 - 5 \cdot 3$
   b. $8[(+4) - (-2)] = 8 \cdot (+4) - 8 \cdot (-2)$

60. Is the operation of multiplication distributive over subtraction? That is, does $x(y - z) = xy - xz$ for all signed numbers x, y, and z?

61. a. Complete the first table, showing the product ab for each pair of numbers a and b.
    b. In the second table, what is the heading for the third column, written in symbolic logic?
    c. What similarities, if any, can you find when comparing the two tables?

a	b	ab
+5	+2	
+5	-2	
-5	+2	
-5	-2	

Table 1

p	q	
T	T	T
T	F	F
F	T	F
F	F	T

Table 2

10   DIVISION OF SIGNED NUMBERS

Using the Inverse Operation in Dividing Signed Numbers

Division may be defined as the inverse operation of multiplication, just as subtraction is defined as the inverse operation of addition. To divide 6 by 2 means to find a number which, when multiplied by 2, gives 6. The number is 3 because $3 \times 2 = 6$. We write $\frac{6}{2} = 3$, or $6 \div 2 = 3$. The number 6 is the *dividend*, 2 is the *divisor*, and 3 is the *quotient*.

It is impossible to divide a signed number by 0. That is, division by 0 is undefined. For example, to solve $(-9) \div 0 = ?$, we would have to find a number which, when multiplied by 0, would give -9. There is no such number since the product of any signed number and 0 is 0.

In general, for every signed number a and every signed number b $(b \neq 0)$:

$$a \div b, \text{ or } \frac{a}{b}, \text{ means to find a unique number } c \text{ such that } cb = a$$

In dividing nonzero signed numbers, there are four possible cases. Consider the following examples:

Case 1. $\dfrac{+6}{+3}$ means $(?)(+3) = +6$.   Since ? is $+2$, $\dfrac{+6}{+3} = +2$.

Case 2. $\dfrac{-6}{-3}$ means $(?)(-3) = -6$.   Since ? is $+2$, $\dfrac{-6}{-3} = +2$.

Case 3. $\dfrac{-6}{+3}$ means $(?)(+3) = -6$.   Since ? is -2, $\dfrac{-6}{+3} = -2$.

Case 4. $\dfrac{+6}{-3}$ means $(?)(-3) = +6$.   Since ? is -2, $\dfrac{+6}{-3} = -2$.

■ In the preceding examples, observe:

1. When the dividend and divisor are both positive, the quotient is positive; when the dividend and divisor are both negative, the quotient is positive.

2. When the dividend is positive and the divisor is negative, or when the dividend is negative and the divisor is positive, the quotient is negative.

3. In all cases, the absolute value of the quotient is the absolute value of the dividend divided by the absolute value of the divisor.

The previous examples illustrate the following rules of division:

Rules for Dividing Signed Numbers

■ **Rule 1.** The quotient of two positive numbers, or of two negative numbers, is a positive number whose absolute value is the absolute value of the dividend divided by the absolute value of the divisor.

■ **Rule 2.** The quotient of a positive number and a negative number is a negative number whose absolute value is the absolute value of the dividend divided by the absolute value of the divisor.

In general:

For every signed number a and every signed number b such that $a > 0$ and $b > 0$, or $a < 0$ and $b < 0$:

$$\frac{a}{b} = \frac{|a|}{|b|}$$

For every signed number a and every signed number b such that $a > 0$ and $b < 0$, or $a < 0$ and $b > 0$:

$$\frac{a}{b} = -\left(\frac{|a|}{|b|}\right)$$

Notice that in effect rule 1 and rule 2 tell us that:

■ To divide one signed number by another signed number, divide the absolute value of the dividend by the absolute value of the divisor and write a plus sign before this quotient when the two numbers have the same sign; write a minus sign before the quotient when the two numbers have different signs.

Rule for Dividing Zero by a Nonzero Number

The expression $\frac{0}{-5}$ means $(?)(-5) = 0$. Since 0 is the only number that can replace ? and result in a true statement, $\frac{0}{-5} = 0$. This illustrates that zero divided by any nonzero number is zero.

In general, if a is a nonzero number $(a \neq 0)$:

$$\frac{0}{a} = 0$$

| MODEL PROBLEMS |

In 1–6, perform the indicated division.

1. $\dfrac{+60}{+15} = +\left(\dfrac{60}{15}\right) = +4$

2. $\dfrac{+90}{-10} = -\left(\dfrac{90}{10}\right) = -9$

3. $\dfrac{-27}{-3} = +\left(\dfrac{27}{3}\right) = +9$

4. $(-45) \div 9 = -(45 \div 9) = -5$

5. $0 \div 9 = 0$

6. $0 \div (-3) = 0$

Using the Reciprocal in Dividing Signed Numbers

When the product of two numbers is 1, one number is called the *reciprocal* or *multiplicative inverse* of the other. For example, since $(+8) \cdot (+\frac{1}{8}) = 1$, we say $+\frac{1}{8}$ is the reciprocal or multiplicative inverse of $+8$. Also, $+8$ is the reciprocal or multiplicative inverse of $+\frac{1}{8}$.

Since $(\frac{3}{5}) \cdot (\frac{5}{3}) = 1$, we say $\frac{5}{3}$ is the reciprocal or multiplicative inverse of $\frac{3}{5}$. Also, $\frac{3}{5}$ is the reciprocal or multiplicative inverse of $\frac{5}{3}$.

Since $\left(-\frac{1}{2}\right) \cdot (-2) = 1$, we say -2 is the reciprocal or multiplicative inverse of $-\frac{1}{2}$. Also, $-\frac{1}{2}$ is the reciprocal or multiplicative inverse of -2.

Since there is no number which, when multiplied by 0, gives 1, the number 0 has no reciprocal.

In general, for every nonzero signed number a ($a \neq 0$), there is a unique signed number such that:

$$a \cdot \frac{1}{a} = 1$$

Notice that if a number is positive, its reciprocal is positive; if a number is negative, its reciprocal is negative.

Using the reciprocal of a number, we can define division in terms of multiplication as follows:

For every signed number a and every nonzero signed number b ($b \neq 0$), "a (the dividend) divided by b (the divisor)" means "a multiplied by the reciprocal of b," or:

$$\frac{a}{b} = a \cdot \frac{1}{b} \quad (b \neq 0)$$

■ **PROCEDURE.** To divide a signed number by another nonzero signed number, multiply the dividend by the reciprocal of the divisor.

Notice that if we exclude division by 0, the set of signed numbers is closed with respect to division because every nonzero signed number has a unique reciprocal, and multiplication is always possible. This is to say that if division by zero is excluded, division is a binary operation for the set of signed numbers.

| MODEL PROBLEMS |

In 1–5, perform the indicated division.

1. $\dfrac{+10}{+2} = (+10)\left(+\dfrac{1}{2}\right) = +(10)\left(\dfrac{1}{2}\right) = +5$

2. $\dfrac{-12}{+6} = (-12)\left(+\dfrac{1}{6}\right) = -(12)\left(\dfrac{1}{6}\right) = -2$

3. $\dfrac{-28}{-7} = (-28)\left(-\dfrac{1}{7}\right) = +(28)\left(\dfrac{1}{7}\right) = +4$ 4. $\dfrac{0}{-3} = (0)\left(-\dfrac{1}{3}\right) = 0$

5. $(+18) \div \left(-\dfrac{1}{2}\right) = (+18)(-2) = -(18)(2) = -36$

EXERCISES

In 1–12, name the reciprocal (the multiplicative inverse) of the given number.

1. 6   2. -5 3. 9   4. -7

5. 1   6. -1 7. $\frac{1}{5}$ 8. $-\frac{1}{10}$

9. $\frac{3}{4}$ 10. $-\frac{2}{3}$ 11. $x \ (x \neq 0)$ 12. $-x \ (x \neq 0)$

In 13–54, find the indicated quotients.

13. $\frac{+10}{+2}$ 14. $\frac{+36}{+9}$ 15. $\frac{-63}{-9}$ 16. $\frac{-80}{-16}$ 17. $\frac{-8}{+4}$ 18. $\frac{-48}{+16}$

19. $\frac{+25}{-1}$ 20. $\frac{+84}{-14}$ 21. $\frac{-1}{-1}$ 22. $\frac{-10}{+10}$ 23. $\frac{0}{+6}$ 24. $\frac{0}{-12}$

25. $\frac{+18}{+6}$ 26. $\frac{-36}{-3}$ 27. $\frac{+52}{-4}$ 28. $\frac{+84}{-12}$ 29. $\frac{-30}{-6}$ 30. $\frac{+100}{-25}$

31. $\frac{-108}{+9}$ 32. $\frac{-65}{+5}$ 33. $\frac{0}{3}$ 34. $\frac{+4}{-8}$ 35. $\frac{-6}{-9}$ 36. $\frac{-15}{-12}$

37. $\frac{+18}{-4}$ 38. $\frac{-16}{+6}$ 39. $\frac{-34}{4}$ 40. $\frac{+100}{-8}$ 41. $\frac{-36}{-8}$ 42. $\frac{0}{-4}$

43. $\frac{-5}{-9}$ 44. $\frac{3}{-7}$ 45. $\frac{20}{-8}$ 46. $\frac{8.4}{-4}$ 47. $\frac{-9.6}{-.3}$ 48. $\frac{-3.6}{1.2}$

49. $(+48) \div (-6)$ 50. $(-75) \div (-15)$ 51. $(-50) \div (+10)$

52. $(+12) \div (-\frac{1}{3})$ 53. $(-\frac{3}{4}) \div (+6)$ 54. $(-\frac{3}{4}) \div (-\frac{2}{3})$

55. a. Find the value of x for which the denominator of the fraction
    $\frac{1}{x-2}$ has a value of 0.

    b. State the value of x for which the multiplicative inverse of $(x-2)$ is not defined.

In 56–59, give the multiplicative inverse of the expression and state the value of x for which the multiplicative inverse is not defined.

56. $x-5$ 57. $x+3$ 58. $2x-1$ 59. $3x+1$

60. State whether the following sentences are true or false:

    a. $(+10) \div (-5) = (-5) \div (+10)$
    b. $(-16) \div (-2) = (-2) \div (-16)$

61. If x and y represent signed numbers:
    a. Does $x \div y = y \div x$ for all replacements of x and y?

   b. Does $x \div y = y \div x$ for any replacements of x and y? If your answer is yes, give an example.

   c. What is the relation between $x \div y$ and $y \div x$ when $x \neq 0$ and $y \neq 0$?

   d. Is the operation of division commutative? That is, does $x \div y = y \div x$ for every nonzero signed number x and every nonzero signed number y?

62. State whether the following sentences are true or false:
   a. $[(+16) \div (+4)] \div (+2) = (+16) \div [(+4) \div (+2)]$
   b. $[(-36) \div (+6)] \div (-2) = (-36) \div [(+6) \div (-2)]$

63. Is the operation of division associative? That is, does $(x \div y) \div z = x \div (y \div z)$ for every signed number x, y, and z, when $y \neq 0$ and $z \neq 0$?

64. State whether the following sentences are true or false:
   a. $(12 + 6) \div 2 = 12 \div 2 + 6 \div 2$
   b. $[(+25) - (-10)] \div (+5) = (+25) \div (+5) - (-10) \div (+5)$

65. Does it appear that the operation of division is distributive over addition? That is, does $(x + y) \div z = x \div z + y \div z$ for every signed number x, y, and z when $z \neq 0$?

66. a. What is the additive identity for the set of signed numbers?
   b. What is the multiplicative identity for the set of signed numbers?
   c. What is the additive inverse of 3?
   d. What is the multiplicative inverse of -6?
   e. What positive number is its own multiplicative inverse?

11 EVALUATING ALGEBRAIC EXPRESSIONS BY USING SIGNED NUMBERS

When we evaluate an algebraic expression by replacing the variables by signed numbers, we follow the same procedure that we used when we evaluated algebraic expressions by replacing the variables by the numbers of arithmetic.

| MODEL PROBLEMS |

1. Find the value of $-3x^2y^3$ when $x = +2$ and $y = -1$.

How to Proceed	*Solution*
(1) Write the expression.	$-3x^2y^3$
(2) Replace the variables by the given values.	$= -3(+2)^2(-1)^3$
(3) Evaluate the powers.	$= -3(+4)(-1)$
(4) Multiply the signed numbers.	$= +12$ *Ans.*

2. Find the value of $x^2 - 3x - 54$ when $x = -5$.

How to Proceed	*Solution*
(1) Write the expression.	$x^2 - 3x - 54$
(2) Replace the variable by its given value.	$= (-5)^2 - 3(-5) - 54$
(3) Evaluate the power.	$= 25 - 3(-5) - 54$
(4) Do the multiplication.	$= 25 + 15 - 54$
(5) Do the addition and subtraction.	$= -14$ *Ans.*

EXERCISES

In 1–52, find the numerical value of the expression. Use $a = -8$, $b = +6$, $d = -3$, $x = -4$, $y = 5$, and $z = -1$.

1. $6a$ 2. $-5b$ 3. ab 4. $2xy$

5. $-4bz$ 6. $\frac{1}{3}d$ 7. $-\frac{2}{3}b$ 8. $\frac{3}{8}a$

9. $\frac{1}{2}xy$ 10. $-\frac{3}{4}ab$ 11. a^2 12. d^3

13. $-y^2$ 14. $-d^2$ 15. $-z^3$ 16. $2x^2$

17. $-3y^2$ 18. $-3b^2$ 19. $4d^2$ 20. $-2z^3$

21. xy^2 22. a^2b 23. $2d^2y^2$ 24. $\frac{1}{2}db^2$

25. $-2d^3z^2$ 26. $a + b$ 27. $a - x$ 28. $2x + z$

29. $3y - b$ 30. $a - 2d$ 31. $b - 4d$ 32. $5x + 2y$

33. $7b - 5x$ 34. $x^2 + x$ 35. $2b^2 + b$ 36. $y^2 - y$

37. $2d^2 - d$ 38. $2a + 5d + 3x$ 39. $8y + 5b - 6d$ 40. $9b - 3z - 2x$

41. $x^2 + 3x + 5$ 42. $z^2 + 2z - 7$ 43. $a^2 - 5a - 6$

44. $d^2 - 4d + 6$ 45. $2x^2 - 3x + 5$ 46. $15 + 5z - z^2$

47. $2(a + b)$ 48. $3(2x - 1) + 6$ 49. $10 - 3(x - 4)$

50. $(x + 2)(x - 1)$ 51. $(a - b)(a + b)$ 52. $(x + d)(x - 4z)$

53. Find the value of $a^2 - 9b$ when $a = 4$ and $b = \frac{1}{3}$.

54. Find the value of $9x^2 - 4y^2$ when $x = \frac{1}{3}$ and $y = \frac{1}{2}$.

55. If $x = 4$, find the value of (a) $2x^2$ and (b) $(2x)^2$.

56. If $y = -2$, find the value of (a) $3y^2$ and (b) $(3y)^2$.

57. If $z = -\frac{1}{2}$, find the value of (a) $4z^2$ and (b) $(4z)^2$.

In 58–62, find the value of the expression. Use $a = -12$, $b = +6$, and $c = -1$.

58. $\dfrac{ac}{-3b}$ 59. $\dfrac{b^2c}{a}$ 60. $\dfrac{3a^2c^3}{b^3}$ 61. $\dfrac{a - b^2}{-2c^2}$ 62. $\dfrac{b^2 - a^2}{b^2 + a^2}$

chapter seven

Operations With Monomials

1 ADDING LIKE MONOMIALS

An algebraic expression that has one term is called a *monomial*. Examples of monomials are:

$$5 \qquad x \qquad 8z \qquad -4y^2 \qquad 7a^2b^3$$

To add like monomials, we use the distributive property of multiplication. For example:

$$(+9t) + (-3t) = [(+9) + (-3)]t = +6t$$
$$-3ab + 7ab - 2ab = (-3 + 7 - 2)ab = +2ab$$

In the preceding examples the middle step may be done mentally.

■ **PROCEDURE.** To add like monomials, use the distributive property of multiplication; or find the sum of the numerical coefficients and multiply this sum by the common variable factors.

We often represent the measures of sides and the measures of angles of geometric figures in algebraic terms. For example, if the length of each side of a square is represented by s, the perimeter of the square will be represented by $s + s + s + s$, or $4s$. Note that the variable s cannot have a non-positive value because the length of a line is always a positive number.

When an algebraic expression involving a variable is used to represent the measure of a line or the measure of an angle of a geometric figure, the domain of the variable must be restricted to such values that result in a positive value for the measure involved.

MODEL PROBLEMS

In 1–6, add.

1.	2.	3.	4.	5.	6.
$+7x$	$-3y^2$	$-15abc$	$+8x^2y$	$-9y$	$+2(a + b)$
$-3x$	$-5y^2$	$+6abc$	$-x^2y$	$+9y$	$+6(a + b)$
$+4x$	$-8y^2$	$-9abc$	$+7x^2y$	0	$+8(a + b)$

| EXERCISES |

In 1–6, simplify the expression by adding the monomials.

1. $(+8c) + (+7c)$ 2. $(+10t) + (-3t)$ 3. $(-4a) + (-6a)$
4. $(-20r) + (5r)$ 5. $(-7w) + (+7w)$ 6. $(5ab) + (-9ab)$

In 7–31, add:

7. $+7c$
   $+8c$

8. $-39r$
   $-22r$

9. $-19t$
   $+6t$

10. $+14c$
    $-c$

11. $-1.5m$
    $+1.2m$

12. $+3e$
    $-3e$

13. $+2x^2$
    $+9x^2$

14. $-48y^2$
    $-13y^2$

15. $-d^2$
    $+7d^2$

16. $.5y^3$
    $.8y^3$

17. $+\frac{5}{3}c^4$
    $-\frac{7}{3}c^4$

18. $-10r^3$
    $10r^3$

19. $8rs$
    $6rs$

20. $-6mn$
    $-mn$

21. $-4xyz$
    $+5xyz$

22. $+.4cd$
    $-.8cd$

23. $-8xy$
    $+8xy$

24. $+3(x+y)$
    $+9(x+y)$

25. $+6a^2b$
    $+7a^2b$

26. $-xy^2$
    $-3xy^2$

27. $-16x^2$
    $-x^2$
    $+15x^2$

28. $-4rst$
    $+8rst$
    $+9rst$

29. $-6xy^2$
    $+9xy^2$
    $-3xy^2$

30. $9c^2d^2$
    $3c^2d^2$
    $-7c^2d^2$

31. $+5(r+s)$
    $-6(r+s)$
    $+(r+s)$

In 32–37, simplify the expression by combining like terms.

32. $(+6x) + (-4x) + (-5x) + (+10x)$
33. $-5y + 6y + 9y - 14y$
34. $(+7c) + (-15c) + (+2c) + (+12c)$
35. $4m + 9m - 12m - m$
36. $(+8x^2) + (-x^2) + (-12x^2) + (+2x^2)$
37. $13y^2 - 15y^2 - y^2 + 8y^2$

38. Express the perimeter of a rectangle whose width is represented by $2y$ and whose length is represented by

    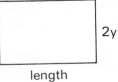

    2y

    length

    a. $6y$ b. $10y$ c. $7.5y$
    d. $1.8y$ e. $2\frac{1}{4}y$ f. $7\frac{3}{4}y$

2 SUBTRACTING LIKE MONOMIALS

We can subtract like monomials by using the same method that we used to subtract signed numbers; we add the opposite (additive inverse) of the subtrahend to the minuend.

$$(+7) - (-3) = (+7) + (+3) = +10$$

$$(+7x) - (-3x) = (+7x) + (+3x) = +10x$$

■ **PROCEDURE.** To subtract one monomial from another like monomial, add the opposite (additive inverse) of the subtrahend to the minuend.

MODEL PROBLEMS

In 1–6, subtract.

1. $+8y$ $+3y$ $\overline{+5y}$	2. $-5x^2$ $-3x^2$ $\overline{-2x^2}$	3. $+15rst$ $+14rst$ $\overline{+rst}$	4. 0 $-5t$ $\overline{+5t}$	5. $-8m$ $-8m$ $\overline{0}$	6. $+4(m+n)$ $-5(m+n)$ $\overline{+9(m+n)}$

EXERCISES

In 1–35, subtract.

1. $+9x$ $+3x$	2. $+12c$ $+9c$	3. $+7ab$ $+8ab$	4. $+12cd^2$ $+8cd^2$	5. $-7x$ $-9x$
6. $-12y$ $-8y$	7. $-6xy$ $-4xy$	8. $-5a^2b^2$ $-a^2b^2$	9. $+15c$ $-3c$	10. $-8x$ $+3x$
11. $-7xyz$ $+9xyz$	12. $+7z$ 0	13. 0 $-5x^2$	14. $3m$ $-3m$	15. $-5m$ $-5m$
16. $+9a$ $+7a$	17. $-9b$ $-3b$	18. $-8c$ $+2c$	19. $+7d$ $-d$	20. $-5.1x$ $+2.3x$
21. $-7r$ $-7r$	22. $3x^2$ $5x^2$	23. $-9y^2$ $-6y^2$	24. $7d^2$ $-3d^2$	25. $-8t^3$ $+t^3$
26. $-1.5y^3$ $+.7y^3$	27. $+9(m+n)$ $+5(m+n)$	28. $+7cd$ $+9cd$	29. $-8mn$ $-9mn$	30. $-6rs$ $+5rs$
31. $-3ab$ $7ab$	32. $.4cd$ $-.9cd$	33. $-5(x+y)$ $-3(x+y)$	34. $+3y^2z^2$ $+2y^2z^2$	35. $-5xy^2$ $+2xy^2$

In 36–47, simplify the expression by subtracting the monomials.

36. $(+9r) - (+2r)$

37. $(+15s) - (-5s)$

38. $(-17n) - (11n)$

39. $(-15t) - (-15t)$

40. $(+8x) - (0)$

41. $(0) - (+8x)$

42. $(+9x^2) - (-3x^2)$

43. $(-3y^2) - (+7y^2)$

44. $(+5ab) - (+2ab)$

45. $(-12xy) - (+3xy)$

46. $(-4rs^2) - (2rs^2)$

47. $(+7x^2y) - (9x^2y)$

48. Subtract $-2x$ from $-8x$.

49. From 0 take $-5x$.

50. From $+3xy^2$ subtract 0.

51. Take $-7x$ from 0.

52. What must be added to $+6x$ to give the result $+10x$?

53. What must be subtracted from $+9d$ to give the result $+5d$?

54. What must be subtracted from $-8z$ to give the result $+3z$?

55. From the sum of $-5xy$ and $+12xy$ subtract the sum of $+9xy$ and $-15xy$.

In 56–59, the representations of the perimeter of triangle ABC and the lengths of sides $\overline{AB}$ and $\overline{BC}$ are given. Find the representation of side $\overline{AC}$.

56. Perimeter $= 18x$, $AB = 6x$, $BC = 4x$

57. Perimeter $= 15y$, $AB = y$, $BC = 7y$

58. Perimeter $= 35k$, $AB = 3k$, $BC = 15k$

59. Perimeter $= x$, $AB = \frac{1}{3}x$, $BC = \frac{1}{3}x$

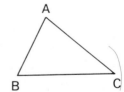

In 60–63, in triangle ABC, two sides have equal measures. The representations of the perimeter of triangle ABC and of the measure of each of the equal sides are given. Find the representation of the third side.

60. Perimeter $= 13c$, side $= 4c$

61. Perimeter $= 20bc$, side $= 6bc$

62. Perimeter $= 12.8d$, side $= 5.2d$

63. Perimeter $= 10x$, side $= 3\frac{1}{4}x$

3 MULTIPLYING POWERS OF THE SAME BASE

Finding the Product of Powers

We know that y^2 means $y \cdot y$ and y^3 means $y \cdot y \cdot y$. Therefore:

$$y^2 \cdot y^3 = \overbrace{(y \cdot y)}^{2} \cdot \overbrace{(y \cdot y \cdot y)}^{3} = \overbrace{y \cdot y \cdot y \cdot y \cdot y}^{5} = y^5$$

Similarly, $c^2 \cdot c^4 = \overbrace{(c \cdot c)}^{2} \cdot \overbrace{(c \cdot c \cdot c \cdot c)}^{4} = \overbrace{c \cdot c \cdot c \cdot c \cdot c \cdot c}^{6} = c^6$, and

$x \cdot x^3 = \overbrace{(x)}^{1} \cdot \overbrace{(x \cdot x \cdot x)}^{3} = x^4$ (Remember that x means x^1.)

Observe that the exponent in each product is the sum of the exponents in the factors. These examples illustrate how the exponent of a product is obtained from the exponents of the factors.

In general, when x is a signed number and a and b are positive integers:

$$x^a \cdot x^b = x^{a+b}$$

■ **PROCEDURE.** In multiplying powers of the same base, find the exponent of the product by adding the exponents of the factors. The base of the power that is the product is the same as the base of the factors.

Note that this procedure does not apply to the product of powers that have different bases. For example, $c^2 \cdot d^3$ cannot be simplified because $c^2 \cdot d^3 = c \cdot c \cdot d \cdot d \cdot d$, an expression that does not have 5 identical factors.

Finding a Power of a Power

Since $(x^3)^4 = x^3 \cdot x^3 \cdot x^3 \cdot x^3$, then $(x^3)^4 = x^{12}$. Observe that the exponent 12 can be obtained by addition, $3 + 3 + 3 + 3 = 12$, or by multiplication, $4 \times 3 = 12$. Likewise, we can show that $(x^3y^2)^4 = x^{12}y^8$.

In general, when x is a signed number and a and c are positive integers:

$$(x^a)^c = x^{ac}$$

MODEL PROBLEMS

In 1–5, simplify the expression by multiplying the powers.

1. $x^5 \cdot x^4 = x^{5+4} = x^9$ 2. $m^6 \cdot m = m^6 \cdot m^1 = m^{6+1} = m^7$

3. $10^3 \cdot 10^2 = 10^{3+2} = 10^5$ 4. $m^{4a} \cdot m^{3a} = m^{4a+3a} = m^{7a}$

5. $(a^2)^3 = a^2 \cdot a^2 \cdot a^2 = a^{2+2+2} = a^6$ or $(a^2)^3 = a^{2 \cdot 3} = a^6$

| EXERCISES |

In 1–35, multiply.

1. $a^2 \cdot a^3$ 2. $b^3 \cdot b^4$ 3. $c^2 \cdot c^5$ 4. $d^4 \cdot d^6$ 5. $r^2 \cdot r^4 \cdot r^5$
6. $t^2 \cdot t^2$ 7. $r^3 \cdot r^3$ 8. $s^4 \cdot s^4$ 9. $e^5 \cdot e^5$ 10. $z^3 \cdot z^3 \cdot z^5$
11. $x^3 \cdot x^2$ 12. $a^5 \cdot a^2$ 13. $s^6 \cdot s^3$ 14. $y^4 \cdot y^2$ 15. $t^8 \cdot t^4 \cdot t^2$
16. $x \cdot x$ 17. $a^2 \cdot a$ 18. $b^4 \cdot b$ 19. $c \cdot c^5$ 20. $e^4 \cdot e \cdot e^5$
21. $2^3 \cdot 2^2$ 22. $3^4 \cdot 3^3$ 23. $5^2 \cdot 5^4$ 24. $4^3 \cdot 4$ 25. $2^4 \cdot 2^5 \cdot 2$
26. $(x^3)^2$ 27. $(a^4)^2$ 28. $(y^2)^4$ 29. $(y^5)^2$ 30. $(z^3)^2 \cdot (z^4)^2$
31. $(x^2y^3)^2$ 32. $(ab^2)^4$ 33. $(rs)^3$ 34. $(2^2 \cdot 3^2)^3$ 35. $(5 \cdot 2^3)^4$

In 36–40, multiply. (The exponents in each exercise are positive integers.)

36. $x^a \cdot x^{2a}$ 37. $y^c \cdot y^2$ 38. $c^r \cdot c^2$ 39. $x^m \cdot x$ 40. $(3y)^a \cdot (3y)^b$

In 41–48, state whether the sentence is true or false.

41. $10^4 \cdot 10^3 = 10^7$ 42. $2^4 \cdot 2^2 = 2^8$ 43. $3^3 \cdot 2^2 = 6^5$
44. $3^3 \cdot 2^2 = 6^6$ 45. $5^4 \cdot 5 = 5^5$ 46. $2^2 + 2^2 = 2^3$
47. $(2^2)^3 = 2^5$ 48. $(2^3)^5 = 2^{15}$

In 49–51, the representations of the length, l, width, w, and height, h, of a rectangular solid are given. Represent the volume, V, of the rectangular solid. (Remember: $V = l \cdot w \cdot h$)

49. $l = x, w = x, h = x$ 50. $l = y, w = x, h = x$
51. $l = z, w = z, h = y$

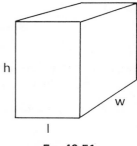

Ex. 49-51

4   MULTIPLYING A MONOMIAL BY A MONOMIAL

We know that the commutative property of multiplication makes it possible to rearrange the factors of a product and that the associative property of multiplication makes it possible to multiply the factors in any order. For example:

$$(5x)(6y) = (5)(6)(x)(y) = (5 \cdot 6)(x \cdot y) = 30xy$$
$$(3x)(7x) = (3)(7)(x)(x) = (3 \cdot 7)(x \cdot x) = 21x^2$$

$(-2x^2)(+5x^4) = (-2)(x^2)(+5)(x^4) = [(-2) \cdot (+5)][(x^2) \cdot (x^4)] = -10x^6$

$(-3a^2b^3)(-4a^4b) = (-3)(a^2)(b^3)(-4)(a^4)(b)$

$$= [(-3) \cdot (-4)][(a^2) \cdot (a^4)][(b^3) \cdot (b)] = +12a^6b^4$$

In the preceding examples the factors may be rearranged and grouped mentally.

■ **PROCEDURE.** To multiply monomials:

1. Use the commutative and associative properties to rearrange and group the factors. This may be done mentally.

2. Multiply the numerical coefficients.

3. Multiply the variable factors that are powers having the same base.

4. Multiply the products previously obtained in steps 2 and 3.

MODEL PROBLEMS

In 1–7, multiply.

1. $(+8xy)(+3z) = +24xyz$

2. $(-4a^3)(-5a^5) = +20a^8$

3. $(-6y^3)(y) = -6y^4$

4. $(+3a^2b^3)(+4a^3b^4) = +12a^5b^7$

5. $(-5x^2y^3)(-2xy^2) = +10x^3y^5$

6. $(+6c^2d^3)(-\frac{1}{2}d) = -3c^2d^4$

7. $(-3x^2)^3 = (-3x^2)(-3x^2)(-3x^2) = -27x^6$ or
$(-3x^2)^3 = (-3)^3(x^2)^3 = -27x^6$

8. Represent the area of a rectangle whose length is represented by $3x$ and whose width is represented by $2x$.

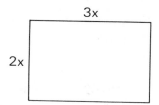

How to Proceed

(1) Write the area formula.
(2) Substitute the values of l and w.
(3) Perform the multiplication.

Solution

$A = l \cdot w$
$A = (3x) \cdot (2x)$
$A = (3 \cdot 2) \cdot (x \cdot x)$
$A = 6x^2$ *Ans.*

Notice that the same answer can be obtained by using the following set of geometric models:

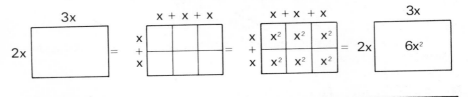

| EXERCISES |

In 1–12, multiply.

1. $4x^2$
   $3x^3$

2. $7c^2$
   $4c^4$

3. $8z^4$
   $3z$

4. $5w$
   $3w$

5. $-4x^3$
   $-7x^4$

6. $-3t^2$
   $-t$

7. $-8x^3$
   $-3x^5$

8. $+3y^4$
   $-6y^2$

9. $-5d^3$
   $+5d^3$

10. $+6y$
    $-7y^4$

11. $6d^5$
    $-3d$

12. $-9c$
    $12c$

In 13–48, find the product.

13. $(+6)(-2a)$
14. $(-4)(-6b)$
15. $(+5)(-2)(-3y)$
16. $(4a)(5b)$
17. $(-8r)(-2s)$
18. $(+7x)(-2y)(3z)$
19. $(+6x)(-\frac{1}{2}y)$
20. $(-\frac{3}{4}a)(+8b)$
21. $(-6x)(\frac{1}{2}y)(-\frac{1}{3}z)$
22. $(+5ab)(-3c)$
23. $(-7r)(5st)$
24. $(-2)(+6cd)(-e)$
25. $(+9xy)(-2cd)$
26. $(3s)(-4m)(5cd)$
27. $(+5a^2)(-4a^2)$
28. $(-6x^4)(-3x^3)$
29. $(20y^3)(-7y^2)$
30. $(18r^5)(-5r^2)$
31. $(+3z^2)(+4z)$
32. $(-8y^5)(+5y)$
33. $(-9z)(8z^4)(z^3)$
34. $(+6x^2y^3)(-4x^4y^2)$
35. $(-7a^3b)(+5a^2b^2)$
36. $(+4ab^2)(-2a^2b^3)$
37. $(-2r^4s)(+8rs)$
38. $(-9c)(+8cd^2)$
39. $(-3y)(5xy)(15xy^2)$
40. $(+\frac{2}{3}x^2)(-6x)$
41. $(+7a)^2$
42. $(-.5x)^2$
43. $(-2x^2)^3$
44. $(-\frac{2}{5}r^2s^2)^2$
45. $(+2x)^2(+3y)^2$
46. $(\frac{1}{2}x^2)^3(-4y^3)^2$
47. $5x(4x)^2$
48. $10(2x)^2(-y^2)^3$

In 49–52, represent the area of the rectangle whose length and width are given.

49. $l = 5y, w = 3y$

50. $l = x, w = 6x$

51. $l = 3x, w = 5y$

52. $l = 3cd^2, w = 8cd$

In 53–56, represent the area of the square the length of each of whose sides is given.

53. $2x$

54. $\frac{1}{2}y$

55. $3xy$

56. $5x^2$

In 57–60, represent the volume of the rectangular solid whose length, l, width, w, and height, h, are given.

57. $l = 4x, w = 2x, h = 5x$

58. $l = 4x, w = 2x, h = 5$

59. $l = 4x, w = 2y, h = 5z$

60. $l = b, w = 2a, h = d$

In 61–64, represent the volume of a cube the length of each of whose edges, e, is given. [Remember: $V = e^3$]

61. $e = w$

62. $e = 3x$

63. $e = 5y$

64. $e = \frac{1}{2}k$

In 65–67, select the correct answer.

65. The product of $(5x^3)$ and $(3x^5)$ is:
  (1) $8x^{15}$ (2) $15x^{15}$ (3) $15x^8$ (4) $8x^8$

66. The product of $(-3a^3)$ and $(4a^2)$ is:
  (1) $12a^5$ (2) $-12a^6$ (3) $-12a^5$ (4) $7a^5$

67. When $4rs^2$ is multiplied by $3r^3s^5$, the product is:
  (1) $12r^3s^{10}$ (2) $7r^4s^{10}$ (3) $12r^4s^7$ (4) $7r^3s^7$

5 DIVIDING POWERS OF THE SAME BASE

We know that division and multiplication are inverse operations.

Since $x^2 \cdot x^3 = x^5$, then $x^5 \div x^3 = x^2$.

Since $y^5 \cdot y^4 = y^9$, then $y^9 \div y^4 = y^5$.

Since $c^4 \cdot c = c^5$, then $c^5 \div c = c^4$. (Remember: c means c^1)

Observe that the exponent in each quotient is the difference between the exponent of the dividend and the exponent of the divisor.

In general, when $x \neq 0$ and a and b are positive integers with $a > b$:

$$x^a \div x^b = x^{a-b}$$

■ **PROCEDURE.** In dividing powers of the same base, find the exponent of the quotient by subtracting the exponent of the divisor from the exponent of the dividend. The base of the power that is the quotient is the same as the base of the dividend and the base of the divisor.

We know that any nonzero number divided by itself is 1. Therefore, $x \div x = 1$ and $y^3 \div y^3 = 1$.

In general, when $x \neq 0$ and a is a positive integer:

$$x^a \div x^a = 1$$

| MODEL PROBLEMS |

In 1–5, simplify by performing the indicated division.

1. $x^9 \div x^5 = x^{9-5} = x^4$ 2. $y^5 \div y = y^{5-1} = y^4$ 3. $c^5 \div c^5 = 1$

4. $10^5 \div 10^3 = 10^{5-3} = 10^2$ 5. $y^{6b} \div y^{4b} = y^{6b-4b} = y^{2b}$
(b is a positive integer.)

| EXERCISES |

In 1–20, divide.

1. $x^8 \div x^2$ 2. $a^{10} \div a^5$ 3. $b^7 \div b^3$ 4. $c^5 \div c^4$

5. $d^7 \div d^7$ 6. $\dfrac{d^4}{d^2}$ 7. $\dfrac{e^9}{e^3}$ 8. $\dfrac{m^{12}}{m^4}$

9. $\dfrac{n^{10}}{n^9}$ 10. $\dfrac{r^6}{r^6}$ 11. $x^8 \div x$ 12. $y^7 \div y$

13. $z^{10} \div z$ 14. $t^5 \div t$ 15. $m \div m$ 16. $2^5 \div 2^2$

17. $10^6 \div 10^4$ 18. $3^4 \div 3^2$ 19. $5^3 \div 5$ 20. $10^4 \div 10$

In 21–25, divide. (The exponents in each exercise are positive integers.)

21. $x^{5a} \div x^{2a}$ 22. $y^{10b} \div y^{2b}$ 23. $r^c \div r^d$ $(c > d)$

24. $s^x \div s^2$ $(x > 2)$ 25. $a^b \div a^b$

In 26–30, simplify the expression.

26. $\dfrac{2^3 \cdot 2^4}{2^2}$ 27. $\dfrac{5^8}{5^4 \cdot 5}$ 28. $\dfrac{10^2 \cdot 10^3}{10^4}$

29. $\dfrac{10^6}{10^2 \cdot 10^4}$ 30. $\dfrac{10^8 \cdot 10^2}{(10^5)^2}$

In 31–34, tell whether the sentence is true or false.

31. $4^5 \div 2^3 = 2^2$ 32. $5^6 \div 5^2 = 5^4$

33. $5^6 \div 5^2 = 5^3$ 34. $3^8 \div 3^4 = 1^4$

6 DIVIDING A MONOMIAL BY A MONOMIAL

We know that division and multiplication are inverse operations.

Since $(-5x^2)(+4x^4) = -20x^6$, then $(-20x^6) \div (+4x^4) = -5x^2$. Observe that -20 divided by $+4$ equals -5 and that x^6 divided by x^4 equals x^2.

Since $(+7a^2b^3)(-3a^3b) = -21a^5b^4$, then $\dfrac{-21a^5b^4}{-3a^3b} = +7a^2b^3$. Observe that $(-21) \div (-3) = +7$, that $a^5 \div a^3 = a^2$, and that $b^4 \div b = b^3$.

If the area of a rectangle is 42 and its length is 6, we can find its width by dividing the area 42 by the length 6. Thus, $42 \div 6 = 7$, which is the width. Similarly, if the area of a rectangle is represented by $42x^2$ and its length is represented by $6x$, we can represent the width by dividing the area $42x^2$ by the length $6x$. We get $(42x^2) \div (6x) = 7x$, which represents the width.

■ **PROCEDURE.** To divide monomials:
1. Divide their numerical coefficients.
2. Divide variable factors that are powers having the same base.
3. Multiply the quotients previously obtained.

MODEL PROBLEMS

In 1–5, divide:

1. $(+24a^5) \div (+3a^2) = +8a^3$

2. $(-15x^6y^5) \div (-3x^3y^2) = +5x^3y^3$

3. $\dfrac{-18x^3y^2}{+6x^2y} = -3xy$

4. $\dfrac{+20a^3c^4d^2}{-5a^3c^3} = -4cd^2$

5. $\dfrac{3r^2s^3}{3r^2s^3} = 1$

EXERCISES

In 1–19, divide.

1. $18x$ by 2
2. $14x^2y^2$ by -7
3. $-36y^{10}$ by $+6y^2$
4. $40a^4$ by $-4a$
5. $24a^2b^2$ by $-8b^2$
6. $15c^4d$ by $-5c^3d$
7. $7r^4c$ by $-7r^4c$
8. $-28c^2d$ by $7cd$
9. $30de^3$ by $5de^2$
10. $(+8cd) \div (-4c)$
11. $(-14xy^3) \div (-7xy^3)$
12. $\dfrac{18x^6}{2x^2}$
13. $\dfrac{-8c^3}{2c}$
14. $\dfrac{5x^2y^3}{-5y^3}$
15. $\dfrac{-49c^4b^3}{7c^2b^2}$
16. $\dfrac{-24x^2y}{-3xy}$
17. $\dfrac{-27xyz}{9xz}$
18. $\dfrac{-56abc}{8abc}$
19. $\dfrac{15(c-d)}{-5(c-d)}$

20. If $3y$ pens cost $12y^3$ dollars, represent the cost of a pen.

21. If the area of a rectangle is $35x^4$ and the length is $7x^2$, represent the width in simplest form.

In 22–24, represent the width of a rectangle whose area is represented by $24x^3y^2$ and whose length is given.

22. length = $8x^3$ 23. length = $24y^2$ 24. length = $2x^2y$

7   NON-POSITIVE INTEGRAL EXPONENTS

Now we will see that non-positive integers such as 0, -1, and -2 can also be used as exponents. We will define powers having zero and negative integral exponents in such a way that the properties that were valid for positive integral exponents will also be valid for non-positive integral exponents. Hence, the following properties will be valid for all integral exponents:

1. $x^a \cdot x^b = x^{a+b}$ 2. $x^a \div x^b = x^{a-b}$ $(x \neq 0)$ 3. $(x^a)^b = x^{a \cdot b}$

The Zero Exponent

We know that $\dfrac{x^3}{x^3} = 1$ $(x \neq 0)$. If we wish $\dfrac{x^3}{x^3} = x^{3-3}$, that is, $\dfrac{x^3}{x^3} = x^0$, to be a true meaningful statement, then we must say that $x^0 = 1$, since both x^0 and 1 are each equal to $\dfrac{x^3}{x^3}$. This leads us to make the following definition:

$$x^0 = 1 \text{ if } x \text{ is a number such that } x \neq 0$$

It can be shown that all the laws of exponents remain valid when x^0 is defined as 1. For example:

Using the definition $10^0 = 1$, $10^3 \cdot 10^0 = 10^3 \cdot 1 = 10^3$.

Using the law of exponents, $10^3 \cdot 10^0 = 10^{3+0} = 10^3$, the same as the previous result.

The definition $x^0 = 1$ $(x \neq 0)$ permits us to say that the zero power of any number, except zero, equals 1. Thus, $4^0 = 1$, $(-4)^0 = 1$, $(4x)^0 = 1$, $(-4x)^0 = 1$. Observe that $(4x)^0 = 1$. However, $4x^0 = 4$, because $4x^0 = 4 \cdot (x^0) = 4 \cdot (1) = 4$. In this book, whenever we write x^0, it is assumed that $x \neq 0$.

The Negative Integral Exponent

We know that $\dfrac{x^3}{x^5} = \dfrac{x \cdot x \cdot x}{x \cdot x \cdot x \cdot x \cdot x} = \dfrac{1}{x \cdot x} = \dfrac{1}{x^2}$. If we wish $\dfrac{x^3}{x^5} = x^{3-5}$,

that is, $\dfrac{x^3}{x^5} = x^{-2}$, to be a true meaningful statement, then we must say

that $x^{-2} = \dfrac{1}{x^2}$, since x^{-2} and $\dfrac{1}{x^2}$ are each equal to $\dfrac{x^3}{x^5}$. This leads us to

make the following definition:

$$x^{-n} = \frac{1}{x^n} \text{ if } x \text{ is a number such that } x \neq 0$$

Now we can say that for all integral values of a and b,

$$\frac{x^a}{x^b} = x^{a-b} \quad (x \neq 0)$$

It can be shown that all the laws of exponents remain valid if x^{-n} is

defined as $\dfrac{1}{x^n}$. For example:

Using the definition $2^{-4} = \dfrac{1}{2^4}$, $2^2 \cdot 2^{-4} = 2^2 \cdot \dfrac{1}{2^4} = \dfrac{2^2}{2^4} = \dfrac{2 \cdot 2}{2 \cdot 2 \cdot 2 \cdot 2}$

$= \dfrac{1}{2 \cdot 2} = \dfrac{1}{2^2} = 2^{-2}$.

Using the law of exponents, $2^2 \cdot 2^{-4} = 2^{2+(-4)} = 2^{-2}$, the same as the
previous result.

| MODEL PROBLEMS |

In 1–3, transform the given expression into an equivalent expression
involving a positive exponent.

1. $4^{-3} = \dfrac{1}{4^3}$
2. $10^{-1} = \dfrac{1}{10^1}$
3. $\left(-\dfrac{1}{2}\right)^{-4} = \dfrac{1}{\left(-\dfrac{1}{2}\right)^4}$

In 4–6, compute the value of the expression.

4. $3^0 = 1$
5. $10^{-2} = \dfrac{1}{10^2} = \dfrac{1}{100}$

6. $(-5)^0 + 2^{-4} = 1 + \dfrac{1}{2^4} = 1 + \dfrac{1}{16} = 1\dfrac{1}{16}$

In 7–9, use the laws of exponents to perform the indicated operation.

7. $2^7 \cdot 2^{-3} = (2)^{7+(-3)} = 2^4$ 8. $3^{-6} \div 3^{-2} = (3)^{-6-(-2)} = 3^{-4}$

9. $(x^4)^{-3} = x^{(4)(-3)} = x^{-12}$

EXERCISES

In 1–5, transform the given expression into an equivalent expression involving a positive exponent.

1. 10^{-4} 2. 2^{-1} 3. $\left(\frac{2}{3}\right)^{-2}$ 4. m^{-6} 5. r^{-3}

In 6–21, compute the value of the expression.

6. 10^0 7. $(-4)^0$ 8. y^0 9. $(2K)^0$
10. 3^{-2} 11. 2^{-4} 12. $(-6)^{-1}$ 13. $(-1)^{-5}$
14. 10^{-1} 15. 10^{-2} 16. 10^{-3} 17. 10^{-4}
18. $4(10)^{-2}$ 19. $1.5(10)^{-3}$ 20. $7^0 + 6^{-2}$ 21. $\left(\frac{1}{2}\right)^0 + 3^{-3}$

In 22–33, use the laws of exponents to perform the indicated operation.

22. $10^{-2} \cdot 10^5$ 23. $3^{-4} \cdot 3^{-2}$ 24. $10^{-3} \div 10^{-5}$ 25. $3^4 \div 3^0$
26. $(4^{-1})^2$ 27. $(3^{-3})^{-2}$ 28. $a^0 \cdot a^4$ 29. $x^{-5} \cdot x$
30. $m^2 \div m^7$ 31. $t^{-6} \div t^2$ 32. $(a^{-4})^3$ 33. $(x^{-2})^0$

34. Find the value of $7x^0 - (6x)^0$.

35. Find the value of $5x^0 + 2x^{-1}$ when $x = 4$.

8 EXPRESSING LARGE NUMBERS IN SCIENTIFIC NOTATION

Scientists frequently deal with very large numbers that have been rounded. In order to be able to write and to compute with such numbers more easily, the *scientific* (or *standard*) *notation* system was developed.

Scientific notation of a number is defined as follows:

■ **The number is expressed as a product of two quantities: The first is a number equal to or greater than 1, but less than 10, and the second is an integral power of 10.**

For example, to express 3,000,000,000 in scientific notation, we write 3×10^9. Let us learn how to do this.

The table at the right lists positive integral powers of ten.

Notice that the number of zeros following the 1 in the value of an integral power of 10 is equal to the exponent of 10. For example, in $10^3 = 1000$, the exponent is 3 and there are 3 zeros following 1 in 1000.

Positive Integral Powers of Ten	
$10^1 = 10$	$10^5 = 100,000$
$10^2 = 100$	$10^6 = 1,000,000$
$10^3 = 1000$	$10^7 = 10,000,000$
$10^4 = 10000$	$10^8 = 100,000,000$

If we wish to express 3,000,000,000 in scientific notation, we must express the number as the product of two numbers that fit the definition. Here,

$$3,000,000,000 = 3 \times 1,000,000,000$$

$$3,000,000,000 = 3 \times 10^9$$

MODEL PROBLEMS

1. The distance from the earth to the sun is approximately 93,000,000 miles. Write this number in scientific notation.

How to Proceed

(1) Express the number as a product of two factors that fit the definition. (Here, 9.3 is between 1 and 10.)
(2) Express the second factor as a power of 10, using an exponent.

Solution

$$93,000,000 = 9.3 \times 10,000,000$$

$$93,000,000 = 9.3 \times 10^7 \quad Ans.$$

2. The approximate population of the United States in 1970 was 2.03×10^8. Find the approximate number of people in the United States at that time.

How to Proceed

(1) Evaluate the second factor, which is a power of 10.
(2) Multiply the factors.

Solution

$$2.03 \times 10^8 = 2.03 \times 100,000,000$$

$$2.03 \times 10^8 = 203,000,000 \quad Ans.$$

Notice that we could have multiplied 2.03 by 10^8 quickly by moving the decimal point in 2.03 eight places to the right.

3. Express $(2 \times 10^4)(3.5 \times 10^5)$ **(a)** in scientific notation and **(b)** as an integer.

   a. $(2 \times 10^4)(3.5 \times 10^5) = (2 \times 3.5)(10^4 \times 10^5)$ (Associative
                 $= 7 \times 10^9$ property)

   b. $7 \times 10^9 = 7{,}000{,}000{,}000$

EXERCISES

In 1–3, write the number as a power of 10 using a positive exponent.

1. 100,000   **2.** 1,000,000,000   **3.** 1,000,000,000,000

In 4–15, find the number that is expressed by the numeral.

4. 10^7 **5.** 10^{10} **6.** 10^{13} **7.** 10^{15}
8. 3×10^5 **9.** 4×10^8 **10.** 6×10^{14} **11.** 9×10^9
12. 1.3×10^4 **13.** 8.3×10^{12} **14.** 1.27×10^3 **15.** 6.14×10^{10}

In 16–23, express the number in scientific notation.

16. 400   **17.** 6000   **18.** 30,000   **19.** 400,000   **20.** 7,000,000
21. 300,000,000   **22.** 80,000,000   **23.** 20,000,000,000

In 24–31, find the number that can replace the question mark and make the resulting statement true.

24. $120 = 1.2 \times 10^?$ **25.** $760 = 7.6 \times 10^?$
26. $9300 = 9.3 \times 10^?$ **27.** $52{,}000 = 5.2 \times 10^?$
28. $5280 = 5.28 \times 10^?$ **29.** $375{,}000 = 3.75 \times 10^?$
30. $1{,}610{,}000 = 1.61 \times 10^?$ **31.** $872{,}000{,}000 = 8.72 \times 10^?$

In 32–39, express the number in scientific notation.

32. 8400   **33.** 27,000   **34.** 54,000,000   **35.** 320,000,000
36. 6750   **37.** 81,600   **38.** 453,000   **39.** 375,000,000

In 40–43, compute the result applying the laws of exponents. Represent the result **(a)** in scientific notation and **(b)** as an integer.

40. $(3 \times 10^4)(2 \times 10^3)$ **41.** $(1.5 \times 10^6)(8 \times 10^7)$
42. $(8 \times 10^{15}) \div (4 \times 10^5)$ **43.** $(9.3 \times 10^8) \div (3.1 \times 10^2)$

In 44–48, express the number in scientific notation.

44. The planet Uranus is approximately 2,000,000,000 miles from the sun.

45. The velocity of light is 30,000,000,000 centimeters per second.
46. The distance between the earth and its nearest star, other than the sun, is 26,000,000,000,000 miles.
47. A light year, which is the distance light travels in one year, is approximately 9,500,000,000,000 kilometers.
48. A star that is about 12,000,000,000,000,000,000,000 miles away can be revealed by the Palomar telescope.

In 49–52, express the number as an integer.

49. The diameter of the universe is 2×10^9 light years.
50. The distance from the earth to the moon is 2.4×10^5 miles.
51. The sun weighs about 1.8×10^{27} tons.
52. The mass of the earth is approximately 5.9×10^{24} kilograms.

9 EXPRESSING SMALL NUMBERS IN SCIENTIFIC NOTATION

Scientists also deal with very small numbers that have been rounded. We may express such numbers in scientific notation. Let us learn how to do this.

The table below lists negative integral powers of ten.

Negative Integral Powers of Ten	
$.1 = \dfrac{1}{10^1} = 10^{-1}$	$.00001 = \dfrac{1}{10^5} = 10^{-5}$
$.01 = \dfrac{1}{10^2} = 10^{-2}$	$.000001 = \dfrac{1}{10^6} = 10^{-6}$
$.001 = \dfrac{1}{10^3} = 10^{-3}$	$.0000001 = \dfrac{1}{10^7} = 10^{-7}$
$.0001 = \dfrac{1}{10^4} = 10^{-4}$	$.00000001 = \dfrac{1}{10^8} = 10^{-8}$

Notice that in each case the absolute value of the negative exponent of 10 is equal to the number of places to the right of the decimal point.

If we wish to express .0003 in scientific notation, we must first express the number as a product of two numbers to fit the definition. Here,

$$.0003 = 3. \times .0001$$

$$.0003 = 3 \times 10^{-4}$$

| MODEL PROBLEMS |

1. Express .0000029 in scientific notation.

How to Proceed   *Solution*

(1) Express the number as the product of two factors that fit the definition. (Here 2.9 is between 1 and 10.)

.0000029 = 2.9 × .000001

(2) Express the second factor as a power of 10, using exponents.

.0000029 = 2.9 × 10^{-6} *Ans.*

2. The diameter of a red blood corpuscle expressed in scientific notation is 7.5 × (10^{-4}) centimeter. Find the number of centimeters in the diameter.

How to Proceed   *Solution*

(1) Evaluate the second factor, which is a power of 10.

7.5 × 10^{-4} = 7.5 × .0001

(2) Multiply the factors.

7.5 × 10^{-4} = .00075   *Ans.*

Notice that we could have multiplied 7.5 by 10^{-4} quickly by moving the decimal point in 7.5 four places to the left.

| EXERCISES |

In 1–4, write the number as a power of 10 involving a negative exponent.

1. .01   2. .00001   3. .00000001   4. .0000000001

In 5–16, express the given symbol as a decimal fraction.

5. 10^{-6} 6. 10^{-8} 7. 10^{-15}

8. 10^{-18} 9. 4×10^{-3} 10. $7 \times (10^{-9})$

11. 8×10^{-10} 12. $9 \times (10^{-13})$ 13. 1.2×10^{-4}

14. $3.6 \times (10^{-5})$ 15. 7.4×10^{-11} 16. $3.14 \times (10^{-14})$

In 17–20, express the number in scientific notation.

17. .002   18. .0005   19. .000003   20. .00000009

In 21–26, state the number that can replace the question mark to make the statement true.

21. $.023 = 2.3 \times 10^?$ 22. $.000086 = 8.6 \times 10^?$
23. $.000000019 = 1.9 \times 10^?$ 24. $.000000000041 = 4.1 \times 10^?$
25. $.00156 = 1.56 \times 10^?$ 26. $.000000873 = 8.73 \times 10^?$

In 27–34, express the number in scientific notation.

27. $.0052$ 28. $.00061$ 29. $.0000039$ 30. $.000000014$
31. $.156$ 32. $.00381$ 33. $.0000763$ 34. $.000000917$

In 35–38, compute the result applying the law of exponents. Represent the result **(a)** in scientific notation and **(b)** as a decimal.

35. $(2 \times 10^{-5})(3 \times 10^2)$ 36. $(2.5 \times 10^{-2})(3 \times 10^{-3})$
37. $(7.5 \times 10^{-4}) \div (2.5 \times 10^3)$ 38. $(6.8 \times 10^{-5}) \div (3.4 \times 10^{-8})$

In 39–44, express each decimal fraction in scientific notation.

39. The approximate diameter of the smallest particle visible to the naked eye is .004 inch.
40. A micro-ampere is .000001 of an ampere.
41. The radius of an electron is about .0000000000005 centimeter.
42. The diameter of some white blood corpuscles is approximately .0008 inch.
43. The wavelength of red light is .000065 centimeter.
44. The mass of a hydrogen atom is approximately .00000000000000000000000167 gram.

In 45–48, express the number as a decimal.

45. In a motion-picture film, the image of each picture remains on the screen approximately 6×10^{-2} second.
46. It takes light about 2×10^{-8} second to cross a room.
47. The density of dry air is approximately 1.3×10^{-3} gram per centimeter.
48. An atomic mass unit is 1.66×10^{-24} gram.

chapter eight

Operations With Polynomials

1 ADDING POLYNOMIALS

We have already learned that terms like 5, x, z^2, $4y^3$ are called *monomials*. The degree of a monomial in one variable is the exponent of the variable.

The degree of x or x^1 is 1; the degree of z^2 is 2; the degree of $4y^3$ is 3.

We will say that the degree of a nonzero constant such as 5 is zero. We will also say that the monomial 0 has no degree.

■ **A polynomial is a sum of monomials.**

A monomial such as $4x^2$ may be considered to be a polynomial of one term. (*Mono* means "one", *poly* means "many.")

A polynomial of two unlike terms such as $10a + 12b$ is called a *binomial*. (*Bi* means "two.")

A polynomial of three unlike terms such as $x^2 + 3x + 2$ is called a *trinomial*. (*Tri* means "three.")

A polynomial such as $5x^2 + (-2x) + (-4)$ is usually written as $5x^2 - 2x - 4$.

We say that a polynomial has been simplified or is in *simplest form* when no two terms in it are alike. For example, $5x^3 + 8x^2 - 5x^3 + 7$, when expressed in simplest form, becomes $8x^2 + 7$.

The *degree of a polynomial* is the greatest of the degrees of its terms after the polynomial has been simplified. For example, the degree of $5x^3 + 8x^2 - 5x^3 + 7$, which when simplified becomes $8x^2 + 7$, is 2 (not 3).

A polynomial is arranged in *descending powers* when the exponents of a particular variable decrease as we move from left to right. Thus, $x^3 - 3x^2 + 5x - 7$ is arranged in descending powers of x.

A polynomial is arranged in *ascending powers* when the exponents of a particular variable increase as we move from left to right. Thus, $y - 4y^2 + 5y^3$ is arranged in ascending powers of y. The polynomial $x^2 + 2xy + y^2$ is arranged in descending powers of x, whereas it is arranged in ascending powers of y.

A polynomial in one variable is written in *standard form* when its terms are arranged in descending order. The polynomial $3x^2 - 7x + 3$ is in standard form, whereas the polynomial $4z^2 - 2z + 5z^3$ is not in standard form.

To add two polynomials, we use the commutative, associative, and distributive properties to combine like terms. For example, we can add $3x^2 + 5$ and $6x^2 + 8$ as follows:

Step	*Reason*
(1) $(3x^2 + 5) + (6x^2 + 8) = (3x^2 + 6x^2) + (5 + 8)$	(1) Commutative and associative properties
(2) $ = (3 + 6)x^2 + (5 + 8)$	(2) Distributive property
(3) $ = 9x^2 + 13$	(3) Substitution principle

To find the sum of the polynomials $4x^2 + 3x - 5$, $3x^2 - 6 - 5x$, and $-x + 3 - 2x^2$, we can write the polynomials vertically, first arranging them in descending (or ascending) powers of x. Then we can add the like terms in each column. As shown at the right, the sum is $5x^2 - 3x - 8$.

$$\begin{array}{r} 4x^2 + 3x - 5 \\ 3x^2 - 5x - 6 \\ -2x^2 - x + 3 \\ \hline 5x^2 - 3x - 8 \end{array}$$

■ **PROCEDURE.** To add polynomials, combine like terms by adding their numerical coefficients. For convenience, arrange the polynomials in descending or ascending powers of a particular variable so that like terms are in vertical columns. Then add each column separately.

Addition can be checked by adding again in the opposite direction. Addition can also be checked by substituting convenient values for the variables and evaluating the polynomials and the sum. The sum of the values of the polynomials should be equal to the value of the polynomial that is the sum of the polynomials.

■ Do not use 0 or 1 as values for checking the addition of polynomials.

To represent the perimeter of a rectangle whose length is represented by $x + 6$ and whose width is represented by $x - 2$, we would add the measures of the four sides.

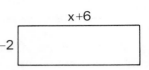

$$P = (x + 6) + (x - 2) + (x + 6) + (x - 2) = 4x + 8$$

Since the width $x - 2$ must be a positive number, the value of the variable x cannot be 2 or less than 2.

MODEL PROBLEMS

1. Add and check: $4x + 3y - 5z, 3x - 5y - 6z, -2x - y + 3z$

    Solution: *Check:* Let $x = 4, y = 3, z = 2$.

    $\begin{array}{l} 4x + 3y - 5z \\ 3x - 5y - 6z \\ -2x - y + 3z \\ \hline 5x - 3y - 8z \end{array}$
    $\begin{array}{lr} 16 + 9 - 10 & = 15 \\ 12 - 15 - 12 & = -15 \\ -8 - 3 + 6 & = -5 \\ \hline 20 - 9 - 16 = -5 \longleftrightarrow & -5 \end{array}$

    Answer: $5x - 3y - 8z$

2. Add: $+7x^2 - 5xy + 4y^2, +3xy - x^2, -9y^2 + 2xy$

How to Proceed	*Solution*
(1) Arrange in descending powers of x.	$+7x^2 - 5xy + 4y^2$
(2) Arrange like terms in the same column.	$- x^2 + 3xy$
(3) Add like terms in each column.	$+ 2xy - 9y^2$
	$\overline{+6x^2 + 0 - 5y^2}$

    Answer: $6x^2 - 5y^2$. Check by adding in the opposite direction.

3. Simplify: $6a + [5a + (6 - 3a)]$

    Solution: When one grouping symbol appears within another grouping symbol, first perform the operation involving the algebraic expression within the innermost grouping symbol.

    $$\begin{aligned} 6a + [5a + (6 - 3a)] &= 6a + [5a + 6 - 3a] \\ &= 6a + [2a + 6] \\ &= 6a + 2a + 6 \\ &= 8a + 6 \quad Ans. \end{aligned}$$

| EXERCISES |

In 1–5, state the degree of the monomial.

1. x^2 2. $4y^5$ 3. $\frac{1}{2}c^3$ 4. $5x$ 5. 0

In 6–10, state the degree of the polynomial.

6. $2x^3 + 7x - 4$ 7. $\frac{1}{2} + 5x^2$ 8. $x^3 - 4$
9. $a^2 + 7a^4 - 9$ 10. 8

In 11–14, state whether the expression is a monomial, a binomial, a trinomial, or none of these.

11. $8x + 3$ 12. $7y$ 13. $-2a^2 + 3a - 6$ 14. $x^3 + 2x^2 + x - 7$

In 15–18: **a.** Arrange the polynomial in descending powers of the variable (standard form). **b.** Arrange the polynomial in ascending powers of the variable. **c.** State the degree of the polynomial.

15. $5 + 2x^2 - 3x$ 16. $y^4 - 9 + y^3$
17. $6 + x^4 - \frac{1}{2}x^3$ 18. $2a^2 - 3a + a^4$

In 19–26, simplify the polynomials.

19. $5c + 3d + 2c + 8d$ 20. $9y + 6w + 3w + y$
21. $8x + 9y - 3x - 6y$ 22. $-4a + 6b + 3a - b$
23. $3r + 2s + 9t + 4r - 5s + t$ 24. $-5m + 6n + 8p - 6n + 3m$
25. $3x^2 - 5x + 7 + 2x^2 + 3x - 9$ 26. $2x + 4x^2 - 7 - x^2 + 7 - 8x$

In 27–36, add and check the result.

27. $5x + 3y$ 28. $4a - 6b$ 29. $-6m + n$ 30. $-9ab + 8cd$
     $6x + 9y$ $9a + 3b$ $-4m - 5n$ $3ab - 8cd$

31. $15x - 26y + 8z$ 32. $x^2 - 33x + 15$ 33. $-5a^2 - 6ab - 4b^2$
     $3x - 14y - 3z$ $-4x^2 + 18x - 36$ $+7a^2 + 6ab - 3b^2$

34. $x^2 + 3x + 5$ 35. $5c^2 - 4cd + 6d^2$ 36. $2.1 + .9z + z^2$
     $2x^2 - 4x - 1$ $-c^2 + 3cd + 2d^2$ $ - .7z - .2z^2$
     $-5x^2 + 2x + 4$ $-3c^2 + cd - 8d^2$ $ - .9 + .2z$

In 37–53, simplify the expression.

37. $4a + (9a + 3)$ 38. $7b + (4b - 6)$ 39. $8c + (7 - 9c)$
40. $(-6x - 4) + 6x$ 41. $r + (s + 2r)$ 42. $8d^2 + (6d^2 - 4d)$

43. $(5x + 3) + (6x - 5)$
44. $(-6y + 7) + (+6y - 7)$
45. $(5 - 6y) + (-9y + 2)$
46. $(5a + 3b) + (-2a + 4d)$
47. $(5x^2 + 4) + (-3x^2 - 4)$
48. $(3y^2 - 6y) + (3y - 4)$
49. $(x^3 + 3x^2) + (-2x^2 - 9)$
50. $(d^2 + 9d + 2) + (-4d - d^2)$
51. $(x^2 + 5x - 24) + (-x^2 - 4x + 9)$
52. $(-r^3 + 5r^2 + 6r + 8) + (4r^3 - 6r + 2)$
53. $(x^3 + 9x - 5) + (-4x^2 - 12x + 5)$

54. Add: $6c - 3d, d - 2c, 2d - c$
55. Add: $3x - 5, -2x + 3, 2 - x$
56. Add: $9a - 4b + c$ and $-5a + 3c + 4b$
57. Find the sum of $3c - 7d, -2c + 5d, -c + 8d$, and $4c - 6d$.
58. Find the sum of $6p - 3q + z, -3p + 2q - z$, and $-p + q$.
59. Find the sum of $4x^2 - 6x - 3$ and $3x^2 - 5x + 7$.
60. Add: $3y^2 + 7 - 5y$ and $9 + 4y - 5y^2$
61. Add: $2c^2 + 5c - 3, 4c^2 - 5, 6 - 5c$
62. Add: $x^2 - 7xy + 3y^2, -2y^2 + 3x^2 - 4xy, xy - 2x^2 - 4y^2$

In 63–68: **a.** Express the perimeter of the rectangle in simplest form. **b.** Name one value for x that is possible. **c.** Name one value for x that is not possible.

63. length = $2x$, width = x
64. length = $3x$, width = $x + 2$
65. length = x, width = $x - 3$
66. length = $x + 3$, width = $x - 8$
67. length = x, width = $3x - 4$
68. length = $x - 4$, width = $x - 6$

In 69–72, **(a)** express the perimeter of the figure as a polynomial in simplest form and **(b)** name one value for x that is not possible.

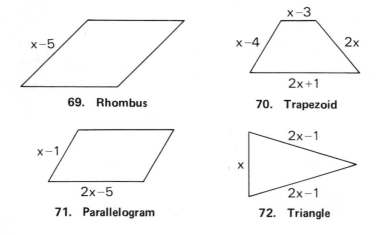

69. Rhombus

70. Trapezoid

71. Parallelogram

72. Triangle

73. Represent the perimeter of a square each of whose sides is represented by:

a. $3x + 5$ b. $4x - 1$ c. $x^2 + 4x - 3$ d. $x^2 + 2xy + y^2$

2 SUBTRACTING POLYNOMIALS

To subtract one polynomial from another, we use a procedure similar to that used to subtract like terms; we add the opposite of the subtrahend to the minuend.

We can write the opposite of a polynomial using the symbol "-." For example, the opposite of $2x^2 - 5x - 3$ can be written $-(2x^2 - 5x - 3)$.

We can also write the opposite of a polynomial by forming a polynomial each of whose terms is the opposite of the corresponding terms of the original polynomial. For example:

If the original polynomial is $2x^2 - 5x - 3,$

the opposite of this polynomial is $-2x^2 + 5x + 3.$

In general, for any x, y, and z,

$$-(x + y + z) = (-x) + (-y) + (-z)$$

Now let us subtract $2x^2 - 5x - 3$ from $5x^2 + 8x - 7$ in the following manner:

$$
\begin{aligned}
(5x^2 + 8x - 7) - (2x^2 - 5x - 3) &= (5x^2 + 8x - 7) + (-2x^2 + 5x + 3) \\
&= 5x^2 + 8x - 7 - 2x^2 + 5x + 3 \\
&= (5 - 2)x^2 + (8 + 5)x + (-7 + 3) \\
&= 3x^2 + 13x - 4
\end{aligned}
$$

The solution of a subtraction example can also be arranged vertically as shown at the right. We mentally add the opposite of each term of the subtrahend to the corresponding term of the minuend.

$$
\begin{array}{r}
5x^2 + 8x - 7 \\
2x^2 - 5x - 3 \\
\hline
3x^2 + 13x - 4
\end{array}
$$

■ **PROCEDURE.** To subtract one polynomial from another, add the opposite (additive inverse) of the subtrahend to the minuend.

For convenience, place the subtrahend under the minuend, arranging the polynomials in descending or ascending powers of a particular variable, so that like terms are in vertical columns.

Then subtract the like terms in each column separately.

Subtraction can be checked by adding the subtrahend and the difference. The result should equal the minuend.

| MODEL PROBLEMS |

1. Subtract and check: $(5x^2 - 6x + 3) - (2x^2 - 9x - 6)$

Solution:

		Check:	
$5x^2 - 6x + 3$	Minuend	$2x^2 - 9x - 6$	Subtrahend
$2x^2 - 9x - 6$	Subtrahend	$3x^2 + 3x + 9$	Difference
$3x^2 + 3x + 9$	Difference	$5x^2 - 6x + 3$	Minuend

Answer: $3x^2 + 3x + 9$

2. Simplify the expression $9x - [7 - (4 - 2x)]$

Solution:

$$
\begin{aligned}
9x - [7 - (4 - 2x)] &= 9x - [7 + (-4 + 2x)] \\
&= 9x - [7 - 4 + 2x] \\
&= 9x - [3 + 2x] \\
&= 9x + [-3 - 2x] \\
&= 9x - 3 - 2x \\
&= 7x - 3
\end{aligned}
$$

(First perform the subtraction involving the expression within the innermost grouping symbol.)

Answer: $7x - 3$

| EXERCISES |

In 1–6, write the opposite (additive inverse) of the expression.

1. $9x + 6$ 2. $-5x + 3$ 3. $-6x - 6y$
4. $2x^2 - 3x + 2$ 5. $-y^2 + 5y - 4$ 6. $7ab - 3bc$

In 7–20, subtract and check the result.

7. $\begin{aligned}10a + 8b \\ 4a + 5b\end{aligned}$ 8. $\begin{aligned}5b + 3c \\ 4b + c\end{aligned}$ 9. $\begin{aligned}6d + 6e \\ 9d - 8e\end{aligned}$ 10. $\begin{aligned}8x - 3y \\ -4x + 8y\end{aligned}$

11. $\begin{aligned}4r - 7s \\ 5r - 7s\end{aligned}$ 12. $\begin{aligned}0 \\ 8a - 6b\end{aligned}$ 13. $\begin{aligned}6rs - 7bc \\ 9rs - 7bc\end{aligned}$ 14. $\begin{aligned}5xy - 9cd \\ -3xy + cd\end{aligned}$

15. $\begin{aligned}x^2 - 6x + 5 \\ 3x^2 - 2x - 2\end{aligned}$ 16. $\begin{aligned}3y^2 - 2y - 1 \\ -5y^2 - 2y + 6\end{aligned}$ 17. $\begin{aligned}3a^2 - 2ab + 3b^2 \\ -a^2 - 5ab + 3b^2\end{aligned}$

18. $\begin{aligned}7a + 6b - 9c \\ 3a - 6c\end{aligned}$ 19. $\begin{aligned}x^2 - 9 \\ -2x^2 + 5x - 3\end{aligned}$ 20. $\begin{aligned}5 - 6d - d^2 \\ - 4d - d^2\end{aligned}$

In 21–46, simplify the expression.

21. $(3y - 6) - (8 - 9y)$　　　　　**22.** $(-4x + 7) - (3x - 7)$

23. $(4a - 3b) - (5a - 2b)$　　　　**24.** $(2c + 3d) - (-6d - 5c)$

25. $(5x^2 + 6x - 9) - (x^2 - 3x + 7)$　**26.** $(2x^2 - 3x - 1) - (2x^2 + 5x)$

27. $5x - (2x + 5)$　　**28.** $3y - (5y - 4)$　　**29.** $4z - (6z - 2)$

30. $9m - (6 + 6m)$　　**31.** $m - (m - n)$　　**32.** $4d - (5c + 4d)$

33. $5c - (4c - 6c^2)$　　**34.** $8r - (-6s - 8r)$　　**35.** $-2x - (5x + 8)$

36. $-9d - (2c - 4d) + 4c$　　　**37.** $(3y + z) + (z - 5y) - (2z - 2y)$

38. $(a - b) - (a + b) - (-a - b)$　**39.** $(x^2 - 3x) + (5 - 9x) - (5x^2 - 7)$

40. $5c - [8c - (6 - 3c)]$　　　**41.** $12 - [-3 + (6x - 9)]$

42. $10x + [3x - (5x - 4)]$　　　**43.** $x^2 - [-3x + (4 - 7x)]$

44. $3x^2 - [7x - (4x - x^2) + 3]$　**45.** $9a - [5a^2 - (7 + 9a - 2a^2)]$

46. $4y^2 - \{4y + [3y^2 - (6y + 2) + 6]\}$

47. From $4x + 2y$, subtract $x - 4y$.

48. Subtract $5a - 7b$ from $3a - 9b$.

49. From $5x^2 + 5x - 4$, subtract $x^2 - 3x + 5$.

50. Subtract $7r^2 + 3r - 8$ from $10r^2 - 3r - 7$.

51. From $m^2 + 5m - 7$, subtract $m^2 - 3m - 4$.

52. From $12x - 6y + 9z$, subtract $-x - 3z + 6y$.

53. Subtract $2x^2 - 3x + 7$ from $x^2 + 6x - 12$.

54. The sum of two binomials is $6y^2 + 9y$. One of the binomials is $4y^2 + 5y$. What is the other binomial?

55. The sum of two trinomials is $15x^2 - 7x + 3$. One of the trinomials is $8x^2 + 9x - 7$. What is the other trinomial?

56. Subtract $2c^2 + 3c - 4$ from 0.

57. How much greater than $a^2 + 3ab + b^2$ is $4a^2 + 9ab - 2b^2$?

58. a. How much less than 25 is 15?

　　b. How much less than $5x + 3y$ is $2x + y$?

59. How much less than $4x^2 - 5$ is $3x^2 + 2$?

60. a. By how much does 13 exceed 10?

　　b. By how much does $7x + 5$ exceed $4x - 3$?

61. By how much does $a + b + c$ exceed $a + b - c$?

62. What algebraic expression must be added to $2x^2 + 5x + 7$ to give $8x^2 - 4x - 5$ as the result?

63. What algebraic expression must be added to $4x^2 - 8$ to make the result equal to 0?

64. What algebraic expression must be added to $-3x^2 + 7x - 5$ to give 0 as the result?

65. From the sum of $y^2 + 2y - 7$ and $2y^2 - 4y + 3$, subtract $3y^2 - 8y - 10$.

66. Subtract the sum of $c^2 - 5$ and $-2c^2 + 3c$ from $4c^2 - 6c + 7$.

3 MULTIPLYING A POLYNOMIAL BY A MONOMIAL

We know that the distributive property of multiplication states:

$$a(b + c) = ab + ac$$

Therefore, $x(4x + 3) = (x)(4x) + (x)(3)$

$$x(4x + 3) = 4x^2 + 3x$$

This result can be illustrated geometrically. Let us separate a rectangle whose length is $4x + 3$ and whose width is x into two smaller rectangles such that the length of one rectangle is $4x$ and the length of the other is 3.

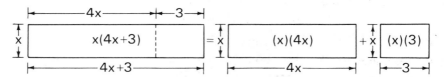

Since the area of the largest rectangle is equal to the sum of the areas of the two smaller rectangles, we see that $x(4x + 3) = (x)(4x) + (x)(3) = 4x^2 + 3x$.

To find the product $5(3x + 2y)$, we apply the distributive property of multiplication:

$$5(3x + 2y) = 5(3x) + 5(2y)$$

$$5(3x + 2y) = 15x + 10y$$

The multiplication may also be arranged vertically as shown at the right.

$$\begin{array}{r} 3x + \ \ 2y \\ 5 \\ \hline 15x + 10y \end{array}$$

■ **PROCEDURE.** To multiply a polynomial by a monomial, use the distributive property: multiply each term of the polynomial by the monomial and add the resulting products.

MODEL PROBLEMS

In 1–4, multiply.

1. $5(r - 7) = 5r - 35$
2. $8(3x - 2y + 4z) = 24x - 16y + 32z$
3. $-5x(x^2 - 2x + 4) = -5x^3 + 10x^2 - 20x$
4. $-3a^2b^2(4ab^2 - 3b^2) = -12a^3b^4 + 9a^2b^4$

EXERCISES

In 1–18, multiply.

1. $3(6c + 3d)$
2. $-5(4m - 6n)$
3. $-2(8a + 6b)$
4. $10(2x - \frac{1}{5}y)$
5. $12(\frac{2}{3}m - 4n)$
6. $-8(4r - \frac{1}{4}s)$
7. $-16(\frac{3}{4}c - \frac{5}{8}d)$
8. $4x(5x + 6)$
9. $5d(d^2 - 3d)$
10. $-5c^2(15c - 4c^2)$
11. $mn(m + n)$
12. $-ab(a - b)$
13. $3ab(5a^2 - 7b^2)$
14. $-r^3s^3(6r^4s - 3s^4)$
15. $10d(2a - 3c + 4b)$
16. $-8(2x^2 - 3x - 5)$
17. $3xy(x^2 + xy + y^2)$
18. $5r^2s^2(-2r^2 + 3rs - 4s^2)$

4   USING MULTIPLICATION TO SIMPLIFY ALGEBRAIC EXPRESSIONS CONTAINING SYMBOLS OF GROUPING

To simplify the expression $3x + 7(2x + 3)$, we use the distributive property and then collect like terms. Thus:

$$3x + 7(2x + 3) = 3x + 7(2x) + 7(3) = 3x + 14x + 21 = 17x + 21$$

By using addition we can simplify the expression $5 + (2x - 3)$ as shown at the right.

Since the multiplication property of 1 states that $1 \cdot x = x$ and $1 \cdot (2x - 3) = 2x - 3$, we can also simplify $5 + (2x - 3)$ using multiplication:

$$\begin{array}{r} 5 \\ 2x - 3 \\ \hline 2x + 2 \end{array}$$

$$5 + (2x - 3) = 5 + 1 \cdot (2x - 3) = 5 + 2x - 3 = 2x + 2$$

Likewise, we can simplify $5y - (2 - 7y)$ using multiplication:

$$5y - (2 - 7y) = 5y - 1 \cdot (2 - 7y) = 5y - 2 + 7y = 12y - 2$$

MODEL PROBLEMS

In 1–3, simplify the expression by using the distributive property of multiplication and collecting like terms.

1. $3(x + 5) - 10$ **2.** $2c + (7c - 4)$ **3.** $-2(3 - 2x) - (6 - 5x)$

Solution	*Solution*	*Solution*
$3(x + 5) - 10$	$2c + (7c - 4)$	$-2(3 - 2x) - (6 - 5x)$
$= 3x + 15 - 10$	$= 2c + 1(7c - 4)$	$= -2(3 - 2x) - 1 \cdot (6 - 5x)$
$= 3x + 5$ *Ans.*	$= 2c + 7c - 4$	$= -6 + 4x - 6 + 5x$
	$= 9c - 4$ *Ans.*	$= 9x - 12$ *Ans.*

EXERCISES

In 1–30, simplify the expression.

1. $5(d + 3) - 10$ **2.** $3(2 - 3c) + 5c$ **3.** $7 + 2(7x - 5)$
4. $-2(x - 1) + 6$ **5.** $-4(3 - 6a) - 7a$ **6.** $5 - 4(3e - 5)$
7. $8 + (4e - 2)$ **8.** $a + (b - a)$ **9.** $(6b + 4) - 2b$
10. $9 - (5t + 6)$ **11.** $4 - (2 - 8s)$ **12.** $-(6x - 7) + 14$
13. $5x(2x - 3) + 9x$ **14.** $12y - 3y(2y - 4)$
15. $7x + 3(2x - 1) - 8$ **16.** $7c - 4d - 2(4c - 3d)$
17. $3a - 2a(5a - a) + a^2$ **18.** $(a + 3b) - (a - 3b)$
19. $4(2x + 5) - 3(2 - 7x)$ **20.** $3(x + y) + 2(x - 3y)$
21. $5x(2 - 3x) - x(3x - 1)$ **22.** $y(y + 4) - y(y - 3) - 9y$
23. $7x(x + 3y) - 4y(-4x - y)$ **24.** $-2c(c + 2d) + 4d(2c - 3d)$
25. $ab(7a - 3c) - bc(2a - b)$ **26.** $mn(4m^2 - 2n^2) - 2mn(2m^2 - n^2)$
27. $7[5x + 2(x - 3) + 4]$ **28.** $-4[8y - 7 - 3(2y - 1)]$
29. $4x[2x^2 - 2x(x + 3) - 5]$ **30.** $x^2z - x[xy - x(y - z)]$

31. **a.** Express the area of the outer rectangle pictured at the right.
 b. Express the area of the inner rectangle pictured at the right.
 c. Express as a polynomial in simplest form the area of the shaded region.

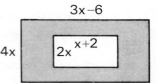

5 MULTIPLYING A POLYNOMIAL BY A POLYNOMIAL

To find the product $a(x + 3)$, we used the distributive property of multiplication: $a(x + 3) = a(x) + a(3)$. Now let us use this property to find the product of two polynomials: $(x + 4)(x + 3)$.

Since $a(x + 3)$ $=$ $a(x)$ $+$ $a(3)$, if we replace a by $x + 4$, then

$$(x + 4)(x + 3) = (x + 4)(x) + (x + 4)(3) \quad \text{Distributive property}$$
$$= x^2 + 4x \quad + 3x + 12 \quad \text{Distributive property}$$
$$= x^2 + 7x + 12 \quad \text{Combining like terms}$$

This result can also be illustrated geometrically.

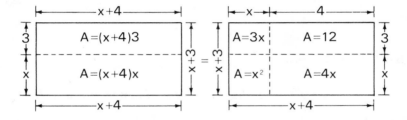

Observe that the area of the large rectangle is equal to the sum of the areas of the two small rectangles.

Observe that the area of the large rectangle is equal to the sum of the four small rectangles.

Therefore, we see that:

$$(x + 4)(x + 3)$$
$$= (x + 4)(x) + (x + 4)(3)$$
$$= x^2 + 4x + 3x + 12$$
$$= x^2 + 7x + 12$$

In general, for all numbers a, b, c, and d:

$$(a + b)(c + d) = (a + b)c + (a + b)d$$

$$or$$

$$(a + b)(c + d) = ac + bc + ad + bd$$

Notice that each term of the first polynomial is multiplied by each term of the second.

At the right we see a convenient vertical arrangement of the previous multiplication, similar to the arrangement used in arithmetic multiplication. Multiply from left to right.

$$\begin{array}{r} x \ + 4 \\ x \ + 3 \end{array}$$

$(x + 4)x \longrightarrow x^2 + 4x$
$(x + 4)3 \longrightarrow + 3x + 12$

Add like terms: $x^2 + 7x + 12$

■ **PROCEDURE.** To multiply a polynomial by a polynomial, first arrange the multiplicand and multiplier according to descending or ascending powers of a common variable. Then use the distributive property: multiply each term of the multiplicand by each term of the multiplier. Finally, combine like terms.

Multiplication can be checked by interchanging the multiplicand and the multiplier and multiplying again. The product should remain the same.

MODEL PROBLEMS

In 1 and 2, express the product as a polynomial in simplest form.

1. $(3x - 4)(4x + 5)$

Solution:

$3x \ - \ 4$	Multiplicand
$4x \ + \ 5$	Multiplier
$12x^2 - 16x$	Partial product
$ + 15x - 20$	Partial product
$12x^2 - x - 20$	Product

Answer: $12x^2 - x - 20$

2. $(x^2 + 3xy + 9y^2)(x - 3y)$

Solution:

$x^2 + 3xy \ + 9y^2$
$x \ - 3y$
$x^3 + 3x^2y + 9xy^2$
$ - 3x^2y - 9xy^2 - 27y^3$
$x^3 + 0 + 0 - 27y^3$

Answer: $x^3 - 27y^3$

The check is left to the student.

EXERCISES

In 1–52, multiply.

1. $(a + 2)(a + 3)$ **2.** $(c + 6)(c + 1)$ **3.** $(x - 5)(x - 3)$

4. $(d - 6)(d - 5)$ **5.** $(d + 9)(d - 3)$ **6.** $(x - 7)(x + 2)$

7. $(m + 3)(m - 7)$ **8.** $(z - 5)(z + 8)$ **9.** $(f + 10)(f - 8)$

10. $(t + 15)(t - 6)$ **11.** $(b - 8)(b - 10)$ **12.** $(w - 13)(w + 7)$

13. $(6 + y)(5 + y)$ **14.** $(8 - e)(6 - e)$ **15.** $(12 - r)(6 + r)$

16. $(x + 5)(x - 5)$ **17.** $(y + 7)(y - 7)$ **18.** $(a + 9)(a - 9)$

19. $(2x + 1)(x - 6)$ **20.** $(c - 5)(2c - 4)$ **21.** $(2a + 9)(3a + 1)$

22. $(5y - 2)(3y - 1)$ **23.** $(2x + 3)(2x - 3)$ **24.** $(3d + 8)(3d - 8)$

25. $(x + y)(x + y)$ **26.** $(a - b)(a - b)$ **27.** $(a + b)(a - b)$

28. $(a + 2b)(a + 3b)$ **29.** $(2c - d)(3c + d)$ **30.** $(x - 4y)(x + 4y)$

31. $(2z + 5w)(3z - 4w)$ **32.** $(9x - 5y)(2x + 3y)$

33. $(5k + 2m)(3r + 4s)$ **34.** $(3x + 4y)(3x - 4y)$

35. $(r^2 + 5)(r^2 - 2)$ **36.** $(x^2 - y^2)(x^2 + y^2)$

37. $(x^2 + 3x + 5)(x + 2)$ **38.** $(2c^2 - 3c - 1)(2c + 1)$

39. $(3 - 2d - d^2)(5 - 2d)$ **40.** $(c^2 - 2c + 4)(c + 2)$

41. $(2x^2 - 3x + 1)(3x - 2)$ **42.** $(3x^2 - 4xy + y^2)(4x + 3y)$

43. $(x^3 - 3x^2 + 2x - 4)(3x - 1)$ **44.** $(2x + 1)(3x - 4)(x + 3)$

45. $(x^2 - 4x + 1)(x^2 + 5x - 2)$ **46.** $(x + 4)(x + 4)(x + 4)$

47. $(a + 5)^3$ **48.** $(x - y)^3$

49. $(5 + x^2 - 2x)(2x - 3)$ **50.** $(5x - 4 + 2x^2)(3 + 4x)$

51. $(2xy + x^2 + y^2)(x + y)$ **52.** $a(a + b)(a - b)$

In 53–59, simplify the expression.

53. $(x + 7)(x - 2) - x^2$

54. $2(3x + 1)(2x - 3) + 14x$

55. $8x^2 - (4x + 3)(2x - 1)$

56. $(x + 4)(x + 3) - (x - 2)(x - 5)$

57. $(3y + 5)(2y - 3) - (y + 7)(5y - 1)$

58. $(y + 4)^2 - (y - 3)^2$

59. $r(r - 2s) - (r - s)$

In 60–62, use symbols of grouping to write an algebraic expression that represents the answer. Then express the answer as a polynomial in simplest form.

60. The length of a rectangle is $2x - 5$ and its width is $x + 7$. Express the area of the rectangle.

61. The dimensions of a rectangle are represented by $11x - 8$ and $3x + 5$. Represent the area of the rectangle.

62. A plane travels at a rate represented by $(x + 100)$ kilometers per hour. Represent the distance it can travel in $(2x + 3)$ hours.

In 63–68: **a.** Find the area of the rectangle whose length and width are given. **b.** Check the result found in part **a** as follows:

(1) Copy the rectangle that is shown.
(2) Represent the length and width of each of the four small rectangles.
(3) Represent the area of each of the four small rectangles.
(4) Add the four areas found in step 3 to find the area of the original given rectangle.

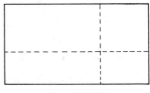

63. length = $x + 2$, width = $x + 3$
64. length = $x + 6$, width = $x + 5$
65. length = $2x + 5$, width = $5x + 3$
66. length = $3x + 1$, width = $3x + 1$
67. length = $x + y$, width = $2x + 3y$
68. length = $2x + 5y$, width = $3x + 4y$

Ex. 63–68

6   DIVIDING A POLYNOMIAL BY A MONOMIAL

Since division is the inverse operation of multiplication, if

$(x + y)2 = 2x + 2y$, then $\dfrac{2x + 2y}{2} = x + y$.

We can obtain the same result by using the multiplicative inverse and the distributive property. Recall that, to divide by 2, we can multiply by its multiplicative inverse, $\frac{1}{2}$.

$$\frac{2x + 2y}{2} = \frac{1}{2}(2x + 2y) = \frac{1}{2}(2x) + \frac{1}{2}(2y) = x + y$$

Observe that the quotient $x + y$ can also be obtained by dividing each

term of $2x + 2y$ by 2. Thus, $\dfrac{2x + 2y}{2} = \dfrac{2x}{2} + \dfrac{2y}{2} = x + y$.

In general, for all numbers a, x, and y $(a \neq 0)$:

$$\frac{ax + ay}{a} = \frac{ax}{a} + \frac{ay}{a} = x + y$$

Usually, the middle step $\dfrac{ax}{a} + \dfrac{ay}{a}$ is done mentally.

■ **PROCEDURE.**   To divide a polynomial by a monomial, divide each term of the polynomial by the monomial.

MODEL PROBLEMS

In 1 and 2, divide.

1. $(8a^5 - 6a^4) \div 2a^2 = 4a^3 - 3a^2$

2. $\dfrac{24x^3y^4 - 18x^2y^2 - 6xy}{-6xy} = -4x^2y^3 + 3xy + 1$

EXERCISES

In 1–31, divide.

1. $(10x + 20y) \div 5$ 2. $(18r - 27s) \div 9$ 3. $(14x + 7) \div 7$

4. $(cm + cn) \div c$ 5. $(tr - r) \div r$ 6. $\dfrac{12a - 6b}{-2}$

7. $\dfrac{8c^2 - 12d^2}{-4}$ 8. $\dfrac{m^2 + 8m}{m}$ 9. $\dfrac{p + prt}{p}$

10. $\dfrac{y^2 - 5y}{-y}$ 11. $\dfrac{18d^3 + 12d^2}{6d}$ 12. $\dfrac{20x^2 + 15x}{5x}$

13. $\dfrac{18r^5 + 12r^3}{6r^2}$ 14. $\dfrac{16t^5 - 8t^4}{4t^2}$ 15. $\dfrac{9y^9 - 6y^6}{-3y^3}$

16. $\dfrac{8a^3 - 4a^2}{-4a^2}$ 17. $\dfrac{3ab^2 - 4a^2b}{ab}$ 18. $\dfrac{4c^2d - 12cd^2}{4cd}$

19. $\dfrac{2\pi r^2 + 2\pi rh}{2\pi r}$ 20. $\dfrac{-6a^2b - 12ab^2}{-2ab}$ 21. $\dfrac{36a^4b^2 - 18a^2b^2}{-18a^2b^2}$

22. $\dfrac{-5y^5 + 15y - 25}{-5}$ 23. $\dfrac{-2a^2 - 3a + 1}{-1}$

24. $\dfrac{2.4y^5 + 1.2y^4 - .6y^3}{-.6y^3}$ 25. $\dfrac{15r^4s^4 + 20r^3s^3 - 5r^2s^2}{-5r^2s^2}$

26. $(8y^2 + 6y) \div 2y$ 27. $(9c^3 - 6c^2 + 3c) \div 3c$

28. $(5ab - 10ac) \div 5a$ 29. $(y^3 - y^2 + y) \div -y$

30. Divide $12x^3 - 8x^2 + 4x$ by $4x$.   31. Divide $8d^3 - 6d^2 + 4d$ by $4d$.

7 DIVIDING A POLYNOMIAL BY A POLYNOMIAL

To divide one polynomial by another, we use a procedure similar to the one used when dividing one arithmetic number by another. When we divide 736 by 32, we discover through repeated subtractions how many times 32 is contained in 736. Likewise, when we divide $x^2 + 6x + 8$

by $x + 2$, we discover through repeated subtractions how many times $x + 2$ is contained in $x^2 + 6x + 8$.

See how dividing $x^2 + 6x + 8$ by $x + 2$ follows the same pattern as dividing 736 by 32:

How to Proceed	*Solution 1*	*Solution 2*
(1) Write the usual division form.	$32\overline{)736}$	$x + 2\overline{)x^2 + 6x + 8}$
(2) Divide the left number of the dividend by the left number of the divisor to obtain the first number of the quotient.	$\dfrac{2}{32\overline{)736}}$	$\dfrac{x}{x + 2\overline{)x^2 + 6x + 8}}$
(3) Multiply the whole divisor by the first number of the quotient.	$\begin{array}{r} 2 \\ 32\overline{)736} \\ \underline{64} \end{array}$	$\begin{array}{r} x \\ x + 2\overline{)x^2 + 6x + 8} \\ \underline{x^2 + 2x} \end{array}$
(4) Subtract this product from the dividend and bring down the next number of the dividend to obtain the new dividend.	$\begin{array}{r} 2 \\ 32\overline{)736} \\ \underline{64} \\ 96 \end{array}$	$\begin{array}{r} x \\ x + 2\overline{)x^2 + 6x + 8} \\ \underline{x^2 + 2x} \\ 4x + 8 \end{array}$
(5) Divide the left number of the new dividend by the left number of the divisor to obtain the next number of the quotient.	$\begin{array}{r} 23 \\ 32\overline{)736} \\ \underline{64} \\ 96 \end{array}$	$\begin{array}{r} x + 4 \\ x + 2\overline{)x^2 + 6x + 8} \\ \underline{x^2 + 2x} \\ 4x + 8 \end{array}$
(6) Repeat steps 3 and 4, multiplying the whole divisor by the second number of the quotient. Subtract the result from the new dividend. The last remainder is 0.	$\begin{array}{r} 23 \\ 32\overline{)736} \\ \underline{64} \\ 96 \\ \underline{96} \end{array}$	$\begin{array}{r} x + 4 \\ x + 2\overline{)x^2 + 6x + 8} \\ \underline{x^2 + 2x} \\ 4x + 8 \\ \underline{4x + 8} \end{array}$
	23 *Ans.*	$x + 4$ *Ans.*

Note: The division process comes to an end when the remainder is 0, or the degree of the remainder is less than the degree of the divisor.

To check the division, use the relationship:

quotient $\times$ divisor + remainder = dividend

Check 1	*Check 2*
23	$x + 4$
$\underline{32}$	$\underline{x + 2}$
46	$x^2 + 4x$
$\underline{69}$	$\underline{ + 2x + 8}$
736	$x^2 + 6x + 8$

Division becomes more convenient if the terms of both the divisor and the dividend are arranged in descending or ascending powers of one variable.

For example, if $3x - 1 + x^3 - 3x^2$ is to be divided by $x - 1$, write:

$$x - 1 \overline{)x^3 - 3x^2 + 3x - 1}$$

MODEL PROBLEM

Divide $5s + 6s^2 - 15$ by $2s + 3$.　Check.

Solution:　　　　　　　　　　　　　　　*Check:*

Arrange terms of dividend in descending powers of s.

$$\begin{array}{r} 3s - 2 \\ 2s + 3 \overline{)6s^2 + 5s - 15} \\ \underline{6s^2 + 9s} \\ -4s - 15 \\ \underline{-4s - 6} \\ -9 \end{array}$$

Answer: $3s - 2 + \dfrac{-9}{2s + 3}$

$$\begin{array}{ll} 2s \;\; +3 & \text{Divisor} \\ \underline{3s \;\; -2} & \text{Quotient} \\ 6s^2 + 9s \\ -4s - \;\;6 \\ \underline{6s^2 + 5s - \;\;6} \\ -\;\;9 & \text{Remainder} \\ 6s^2 + 5s - 15 & \text{Dividend} \end{array}$$

EXERCISES

In 1–14, divide and check.

1. $b^2 + 5b + 6$ by $b + 3$
2. $y^2 + 3y + 2$ by $y + 2$
3. $m^2 - 8m + 7$ by $m - 1$
4. $w^2 + 2w - 15$ by $w + 5$
5. $y^2 + 20y + 61$ by $y + 17$
6. $m^2 + 7m - 27$ by $m - 5$
7. $3x^2 - 8x + 4$ by $3x - 2$
8. $15t^2 - 19t - 56$ by $5t + 7$
9. $10r^2 - r - 24$ by $2r + 3$
10. $12c^2 - 22c + 8$ by $4c - 2$
11. $66 + 17x + x^2$ by $6 + x$
12. $30 - m - m^2$ by $5 - m$
13. $x^2 - 64$ by $x - 8$
14. $4y^2 - 49$ by $2y + 7$

15. One factor of $x^2 - 4x - 21$ is $x - 7$. Find the other factor.
16. The area of a rectangle is represented by $x^2 - 8x - 9$. If its length is represented by $x + 1$, how can its width be represented?
17. The area of a rectangle is represented by $3y^2 + 8y + 4$. If its width is represented by $3y + 2$, how can its length be represented?

chapter nine

First-Degree Equations and Inequalities in One Variable

1 USING THE ADDITIVE INVERSE IN SOLVING EQUATIONS

When we were dealing with the set of numbers of arithmetic, we used the addition property of equality to solve the first-degree equation $x - 4 = 7$ and the subtraction property to solve $x + 5 = 9$.

$$
\begin{array}{ll}
x - 4 = 7 & x + 5 = 9 \\
x - 4 + 4 = 7 + 4 & x + 5 - 5 = 9 - 5 \\
\quad\; x = 11 & \quad\; x = 4
\end{array}
$$

The addition and subtraction properties of equality also hold true in the set of signed numbers. When the same signed number is added to both members of an equation or subtracted from both members of an equation, the equality is retained. However, with our knowledge of signed numbers, we can solve equations such as $x - 4 = 7$ and $x + 5 = 9$ by using only the addition property of equality.

Remember that the sum of a number and its additive inverse (opposite) is 0; that is, $n + (-n) = 0$. The following model problems illustrate how the additive inverse is used in solving equations:

MODEL PROBLEMS

1. Solve and check: $x - 4 = 7$

How to Proceed	Solution	Check
To transform $x - 4$ to x, add $+4$, the additive inverse (opposite) of -4, to both members of the equation.	$x - 4 = 7$ $x - 4 + (+4) = 7 + (+4)$ $x + 0 = 11$ $x = 11$	$x - 4 = 7$ $11 - 4 \overset{?}{=} 7$ $7 = 7$ (True)

Answer: $x = 11$ *or* solution set is $\{11\}$

2. Solve and check: $x + 5 = 3$

How to Proceed	Solution	Check
To eliminate +5, add its additive inverse (opposite) -5 to both members of the equation.	$x + 5 = 3$ $x + 5 + (-5) = 3 + (-5)$ $x + 0 = -2$ $x = -2$	$x + 5 = 3$ $(-2) + 5 \overset{?}{=} 3$ $3 = 3$ (True)

Answer: $x = -2$ *or* solution set is $\{-2\}$

EXERCISES

In 1-20, solve for the variable and check.

1. $x - 5 = 13$ 2. $y + 8 = 12$ 3. $17 = t - 9$ 4. $36 = c + 20$
5. $x + 6 = 4$ 6. $x - 5 = -9$ 7. $n + 7 = 4$ 8. $3 = y + 12$
9. $5 + r = -9$ 10. $-5 = -7 + c$ 11. $-4 = d - 8$ 12. $s + 12 = 8$
13. $x + .9 = .5$ 14. $w - 1.6 = .3$ 15. $.6 + y = .2$ 16. $-.3 = s + .7$
17. $n + 3\frac{1}{2} = 2$ 18. $x - 2\frac{1}{3} = -5$ 19. $-\frac{1}{2} = n - 1\frac{3}{4}$ 20. $3\frac{1}{4} = y + 6\frac{1}{2}$

In 21-23, determine the element(s) of the set if $x \in \{$signed numbers$\}$.

21. $\{x \mid x + 7 = 2\}$ 22. $\{x \mid 9 = x + 15\}$ 23. $\{x \mid 10 = x + 10\}$

2 USING THE MULTIPLICATIVE INVERSE IN SOLVING EQUATIONS

The multiplication and division properties of equality hold true in the set of signed numbers as well as in the set of numbers of arithmetic. When both members of an equation are multiplied or divided by the same signed number (not zero), the equality is retained. However, with our knowledge of signed numbers, we can solve equations such as $5x = -20$ and $\frac{x}{3} = -2$ by using only the multiplication property of equality.

Remember that the product of a number and its multiplicative inverse (reciprocal) is 1; that is, $(n)\left(\dfrac{1}{n}\right) = 1$. The following model problems illustrate how the multiplicative inverse is used in solving equations:

| MODEL PROBLEMS |

1. Solve and check: $5x = -20$

How to Proceed	Solution	Check

To transform $5x$ to x, multiply both members of the equation by $\frac{1}{5}$, the multiplicative inverse (reciprocal) of the coefficient 5.

$$5x = -20$$
$$\tfrac{1}{5}(5x) = \tfrac{1}{5}(-20)$$
$$1 \cdot x = -4$$
$$x = -4$$

$$5x = -20$$
$$5(-4) \overset{?}{=} -20$$
$$-20 = -20$$
(True)

Answer: $x = -4$ *or solution set is* $\{-4\}$

2. Solve and check: $-\frac{2}{3}y = 18$

How to Proceed	Solution	Check

To transform $-\frac{2}{3}y$ to y, multiply both members of the equation by $-\frac{3}{2}$, the multiplicative inverse (reciprocal) of the coefficient $-\frac{2}{3}$.

$$-\tfrac{2}{3}y = 18$$
$$(-\tfrac{3}{2})(-\tfrac{2}{3}y) = (-\tfrac{3}{2})(18)$$
$$1 \cdot y = -27$$
$$y = -27$$

$$-\tfrac{2}{3}y = 18$$
$$(-\tfrac{2}{3})(-27) \overset{?}{=} 18$$
$$18 = 18$$
(True)

Answer: $y = -27$ *or solution set is* $\{-27\}$

| EXERCISES |

In 1–20, find the solution set of the sentence and check.

1. $3m = 15$
2. $15x = -45$
3. $-77 = 11k$
4. $-5 = 2y$

5. $-13a = 65$
6. $-8k = 8.8$
7. $-5m = -35$
8. $2x = -\frac{1}{9}$

9. $-x = 18$
10. $\frac{1}{3}z = 6$
11. $-20 = \frac{2}{5}d$
12. $\frac{5}{8}x = -10$

13. $\frac{1}{3}x = -1.8$
14. $\frac{3}{5}y = \frac{6}{8}$
15. $\frac{12}{9} = \frac{-4}{3}c$
16. $-\frac{3}{2}x = 1\frac{1}{2}$

17. $\frac{-25}{9} = 8\frac{1}{3}t$
18. $\frac{y}{3} = -15$
19. $\frac{c}{9} = -\frac{2}{3}$
20. $\frac{2x}{3} = \frac{4}{9}$

In 21–23, determine the elements of the set if $x \in \{$signed numbers$\}$.

21. $\left\{ x \,\middle|\, \dfrac{x}{5} = -20 \right\}$
22. $\left\{ x \,\middle|\, -\dfrac{4}{5}x = 40 \right\}$
23. $\left\{ x \,\middle|\, \dfrac{3}{10}x = 0 \right\}$

3 USING BOTH THE ADDITIVE AND MULTIPLICATIVE INVERSES IN SOLVING EQUATIONS

When the solution of an equation requires the use of both the additive and the multiplicative inverses, either inverse may be used first. However, the solution is usually easier when the additive inverse is used first.

MODEL PROBLEMS

1. Solve and check: $2x + 3x + 4 = -6$

How to Proceed	*Solution*
(1) Write the equation.	$2x + 3x + 4 = -6$
(2) Combine like terms.	$5x + 4 = -6$
(3) Add -4, the additive inverse of $+4$.	$5x + 4 + (-4) = -6 + (-4)$
	$5x = -10$
(4) Multiply by $\frac{1}{5}$, the multiplicative inverse of 5.	$\frac{1}{5}(5x) = \frac{1}{5}(-10)$
	$x = -2$

Check

$$2x + 3x + 4 = -6$$
$$2(-2) + 3(-2) + 4 \overset{?}{=} -6$$
$$(-4) + (-6) + 4 \overset{?}{=} -6$$
$$-6 = -6 \quad \text{(True)}$$

Answer: $x = -2$ *or* solution set is $\{-2\}$

2. Solve and check: $\frac{3}{4}x - 4 = 17$

How to Proceed	*Solution*	*Check*
(1) Write the equation.	$\frac{3}{4}x - 4 = 17$	$\frac{3}{4}x - 4 = 17$
(2) Add $+4$, the additive inverse of -4.	$\frac{3}{4}x - 4 + (+4) = 17 + (+4)$	$\frac{3}{4}(28) - 4 \overset{?}{=} 17$
	$\frac{3}{4}x = 21$	$21 - 4 \overset{?}{=} 17$
(3) Multiply by $\frac{4}{3}$, the multiplicative inverse of $\frac{3}{4}$.	$\frac{4}{3}(\frac{3}{4}x) = \frac{4}{3}(21)$	$17 = 17$
	$x = 28$	(True)

Answer: $x = 28$ *or* solution set is $\{28\}$

3. If 4 times a number is increased by 5, the result is 41. Find the number.

How to Proceed	*Solution*
(1) Represent the number by a letter.	Let x = the number.
(2) Write the word statement as an equation.	$4x + 5 = 41$
(3) Solve the equation.	$4x = 36$ A_{-5}
	$x = 9$ $M_{\frac{1}{4}}$

Check: Does 4×9 increased by 5 give a result of 41? Yes.

Answer: The number is 9.

Note: We can arrive at the same result geometrically, making use of the following models:

1. Draw two models to represent the equation.	2. Subtract 5 from each model.	3. Divide by 4 to find each of the equal parts.

$$4x+5 = 41 \qquad 4x = 36 \qquad x = 9$$

EXERCISES

In 1–21, solve the equation and check.

1. $3x + 4 = 16$
2. $35 = 21y - 7$
3. $2c + 1 = -31$
4. $2y + 18 = 8$
5. $2x + 9 = 37$
6. $4x + 2 = -34$
7. $-42 = 5x + 28$
8. $-34 = 2 - 6t$
9. $13 = 8x - 7$
10. $-32 = 24y - 20$
11. $\frac{1}{2}z + 6 = 15$
12. $\frac{1}{5}y - 3 = -4$
13. $\frac{2}{3}m + 7 = 29$
14. $\frac{2}{5}r - 9 = -19$
15. $\frac{3}{2}x - 14 = 16$
16. $-25 = \frac{7}{3}r - 11$
17. $-5.4 = 2.6 + 2x$
18. $9x - 5x + 9 = 1$
19. $5x + 2x - 17 = 53$
20. $2y - 8y + 29 = 5$
21. $8x - 21 - 5x = -15$

In 22–25, determine the element(s) of the set if $x \in$ {signed numbers}.

22. $\{x \mid 5x + 30 = 10\}$
23. $\{x \mid 15 = 6x - 15\}$
24. $\{x \mid \frac{2}{3}x - 12 = 60\}$
25. $\{x \mid 5x + 5 - 9x = -11\}$

26. The sum of 7 times a number and 5 is 47. Find the number.
27. If 10 times a number is decreased by 6, the result is 104. Find the number.
28. If $\frac{2}{3}$ of a number is diminished by 8, the result is 32. Find the number.
29. The Tigers played 78 games. If they won 8 games more than they lost, how many games did they lose?
30. A salesman receives a weekly salary of $150. He also receives $4 for each tire he sells. One week he earned $330. How many tires did he sell that week?
31. Rosita wishes to make a long-distance telephone call. The charges are $.75 for the first three minutes and 14 cents for each additional minute. If Rosita has $2.15, how many minutes can her call last?
32. Ray's father pays him $5 for cutting the grass and $3 an hour for cutting the hedges. One day Ray earned $15.50 for cutting the grass and cutting the hedges. How many hours did Ray spend cutting the hedges?

4 SOLVING EQUATIONS THAT HAVE THE VARIABLE IN BOTH MEMBERS

A variable represents a number; as we know, any number may be added to or subtracted from both members of an equation without changing the solution set. Therefore, the same variable (or the same multiple of the same variable) may be added to or subtracted from both members of an equation without changing the solution set.

To solve $8x = 30 + 5x$, we first eliminate $5x$ from the right member of the equation by either of the following two methods:

Method 1

Subtract $5x$ from both members of the equation, S_{5x}.

$$8x = 30 + 5x$$
$$8x - 5x = 30 + 5x - 5x$$
$$3x = 30$$
$$x = 10$$

Method 2

Add $-5x$, the additive inverse of $+5x$, to both members of the equation, A_{-5x}.

$$8x = 30 + 5x$$
$$8x + (-5x) = 30 + 5x + (-5x)$$
$$3x = 30$$
$$x = 10$$

The check is left to the student.

Answer: $x = 10$ *or* solution set is $\{10\}$

■ **PROCEDURE.** To solve an equation that has the variable in both members, transform it into an equivalent equation in which the variable appears only in one member. Then solve this equation.

MODEL PROBLEMS

1. Solve and check: $7x = 63 - 2x$

How to Proceed	*Solution*	*Check*
(1) Write the equation.	$7x = 63 - 2x$	$7x = 63 - 2x$
(2) A_{+2x}	$7x + (+2x) = 63 - 2x + (+2x)$	$7(7) \overset{?}{=} 63 - 2(7)$
(3) Collect like terms.	$9x = 63$	$49 \overset{?}{=} 63 - 14$
(4) D_9 *or* $M_{\frac{1}{9}}$	$x = 7$	$49 = 49$ (True)

Answer: $x = 7$ *or solution set is* {7}

2. If five times a number is decreased by 13, the result is equal to twice the number increased by 11. Find the number.

Solution:

Let x = the number.
Then $5x - 13$ = five times the number decreased by 13.
And $2x + 11$ = twice the number increased by 11.
        $5x - 13 = 2x + 11$ [Write the word statement as an equation.]
$5x - 2x - 13 = 2x - 2x + 11$ S_{2x} *or* A_{-2x}
        $3x - 13 = 11$ *Check*
$3x - 13 + 13 = 11 + 13$ A_{13} Show that 8 satisfies
        $3x = 24$ the original question:
        $x = 8$ D_3 *or* $M_{\frac{1}{3}}$ $5 \times 8 - 13 = 27$
                                                     $2 \times 8 + 11 = 27$

Answer: The number is 8.

EXERCISES

In 1–38, solve the equation and check.

1. $7x = 10 + 2x$ 2. $9x = 44 - 2x$ 3. $5c = 28 + c$

4. $y = 4y + 30$ 5. $2d = 36 + 5d$ 6. $2\frac{1}{4}y = 1\frac{1}{4}y - 8$

7. $.8m = .2m + 24$ 8. $8y = 90 - 2y$ 9. $2.3x + 36 = .3x$

10. $2\frac{3}{4}x + 24 = 3x$ 11. $5a - 40 = 3a$ 12. $5c = 2c - 81$

13. $x = 9x - 72$ 14. $.5m - 30 = 1.1m$ 15. $4\frac{1}{4}c = 9\frac{3}{4}c + 44$

16. $7r + 10 = 3r + 50$ 17. $4y + 20 = 5y + 9$ 18. $7x + 8 = 6x + 1$

19. $x + 4 = 9x + 4$

20. $9x - 3 = 2x + 46$

21. $y + 30 = 12y - 14$

22. $c + 20 = 55 - 4c$

23. $2d + 36 = -3d - 54$

24. $7y - 5 = 9y + 29$

25. $2m - 1 = 6m + 1$

26. $4x - 3 = 47 - x$

27. $3b - 8 = 14 - 8b$

28. $\frac{2}{3}t - 11 = 64 - 4\frac{1}{3}t$

29. $18 - 4n = 6 - 16n$

30. $-2y - 39 = 5y - 18$

31. $7x - 4 = 5x - x + 35$

32. $10 - x - 3x = 7x - 23$

33. $8a - 15 - 6a = 85 - 3a$

34. $8c + 1 = 7c - 14 - 2c$

35. $12x - 5 = 8x - x + 50$

36. $6d - 12 - d = 9d + 53 + d$

37. $3m - 5m - 12 = 7m - 88 - 5$

38. $5 - 3z - 18 = z - 1 + 8z$

39. Eight times a number equals 35 more than the number. Find the number.

40. Six times a number equals 3 times the number, increased by 24. Find the number.

41. Twice a number is equal to 35 more than 7 times the number. Find the number.

42. If a number is multiplied by 7, the result is the same as when 25 is added to twice the number. Find the number.

43. If twice a number is subtracted from 132, the result equals four times the number. Find the number.

44. If 3 is added to 5 times a number, the result is the same as when 15 is added to twice the number. Find the number.

45. If 4 times a number is decreased by 9, the result is the same as when 3 times the number is decreased by 1. Find the number.

46. If 3 times a number is increased by 5, the result is the same as when 77 is decreased by 9 times the number. Find the number.

5 SOLVING EQUATIONS CONTAINING PARENTHESES

■ PROCEDURE. To solve an equation containing parentheses, transform it into an equivalent equation that does not contain parentheses. Do this by performing the indicated operation on the numbers and variables contained within the parentheses. Then solve the transformed equation.

| MODEL PROBLEMS |

1. Solve and check: $8x + (2x - 3) = 2$

   Note: $8x + (2x - 3)$ means add $8x$ and $(2x - 3)$.

How to Proceed	*Solution*
(1) Write the equation.	$8x + (2x - 3) = 2$
(2) Perform the addition.	$8x + 2x - 3 = 2$
(3) Collect like terms.	$10x - 3 = 2$
(4) A_{+3}	$10x - 3 + (+3) = 2 + (+3)$
(5) Collect like terms.	$10x = 5$
(6) D_{10} or $M_{\frac{1}{10}}$	$x = \frac{1}{2}$

Check

$$8x + (2x - 3) = 2$$
$$8 \times \tfrac{1}{2} + (2 \times \tfrac{1}{2} - 3) \overset{?}{=} 2$$
$$8 \times \tfrac{1}{2} + (1 - 3) \overset{?}{=} 2$$
$$4 + (-2) \overset{?}{=} 2$$
$$2 = 2 \quad \text{(True)}$$

Answer: $x = \frac{1}{2}$ *or solution set is* $\{\frac{1}{2}\}$

2. Solve and check: $9t - (2t - 4) = 25$

   Note: $9t - (2t - 4)$ means from $9t$ subtract $(2t - 4)$.

How to Proceed	*Solution*	*Check*
(1) Write the equation.	$9t - (2t - 4) = 25$	$9t - (2t - 4) = 25$
		$9 \cdot 3 - (2 \cdot 3 - 4) \overset{?}{=} 25$
(2) To subtract $(2t - 4)$, add its opposite $(-2t + 4)$.	$9t + (-2t + 4) = 25$	$9 \cdot 3 - (6 - 4) \overset{?}{=} 25$
	$9t - 2t + 4 = 25$	$27 - (2) \overset{?}{=} 25$
(3) Collect like terms.	$7t + 4 = 25$	$25 = 25$
(4) S_4 or A_{-4}	$7t + 4 + (-4) = 25 + (-4)$	(True)
(5) Collect like terms.	$7t = 21$	
(6) D_7 or $M_{\frac{1}{7}}$	$t = 3$	

Answer: $t = 3$ *or solution set is* $\{3\}$

3. Solve and check: $27x - 3(x - 6) = 6$

Note: Since $3(x - 6)$ means that 3 and $(x - 6)$ are to be multiplied, we will use the distributive property of multiplication.

How to Proceed	*Solution*
(1) Write the equation.	$27x - 3(x - 6) = 6$
(2) Use the distributive property.	$27x - 3x + 18 = 6$
(3) Collect like terms.	$24x + 18 = 6$
(4) A_{-18}	$24x + 18 + (-18) = 6 + (-18)$
(5) Collect like terms.	$24x = -12$
(6) D_{24} or $M_{\frac{1}{24}}$	$x = \dfrac{-12}{24}$
	$x = -\frac{1}{2}$

The check is left to the student.

Answer: $x = -\frac{1}{2}$ or solution set is $\{-\frac{1}{2}\}$

EXERCISES

In 1–32, solve and check the equation.

1. $x + (x - 6) = 20$
2. $x - (12 - x) = 38$
3. $(15x + 7) - 12 = 4$
4. $(14 - 3c) + 7c = 94$
5. $x + (4x + 32) = 12$
6. $7x - (4x - 39) = 0$
7. $5(x + 2) = 20$
8. $3(y - 9) = 30$
9. $8(2c - 1) = 56$
10. $6(3c - 1) = -42$
11. $3y = 2(10 - y)$
12. $4(c + 1) = 32$
13. $5t - 2(t - 5) = 19$
14. $18 = -6x + 4(2x + 3)$
15. $5m - 4 = 3(m + 2)$
16. $5(x - 3) = 30 - 10x$
17. $7(x + 2) = 5(x + 4)$
18. $3(a - 5) = 2(2a + 1)$
19. $3(2b + 1) - 7 = 50$
20. $5(3c - 2) + 8 = 43$
21. $7r - (6r - 5) = 7$
22. $8y - (5y + 2) = 16$
23. $11x = 40 + (7x + 4)$
24. $10z - (3z - 11) = 17$
25. $8b - 4(b - 2) = 24$
26. $5m - 2(m - 5) = 17$
27. $9 + 2(5v + 3) = 13v$
28. $28r - 6(3r - 5) = 40$
29. $3a + (2a - 5) = 13 - 2(a + 2)$
30. $4(2r + 1) - 3(2r - 5) = 29$
31. $\frac{1}{2}(8x - 6) = 25$
32. $\frac{3}{4}(8 + 4x) - \frac{1}{3}(6x + 3) = 9$

33. The larger of two numbers is 5 more than the smaller. The smaller number plus twice the larger equals 100. Find the numbers.
34. One number is 2 less than another. If 4 times the larger is subtracted from 5 times the smaller, the result is 10. Find the numbers.

35. The perimeter of a rectangle is 54 cm. Find its length and its width when these measures are represented by the given expressions:

a. $l = 4x + 5, w = 3x + 1$ b. $l = 3x + 2, w = 2x - 5$

c. $l = 4x - 3, w = x - 1$ d. $l = 5x + 5, w = 5x - 3$

6 EVALUATING A FORMULA BY SOLVING AN EQUATION

If the values of the subject of a formula and all its other variables but one are known, the value of the remaining variable can be computed.

■ **PROCEDURE.** To find the value of a variable in a formula when the values of the other variables including the subject of the formula are given:

1. Substitute the given values in the formula.

2. Solve the resulting equation.

| MODEL PROBLEM |

The perimeter of a rectangle is 48 cm. If the length of the rectangle is 16 cm, find its width. (Use $P = 2l + 2w$.)

Solution

$P = 2l + 2w$
$48 = 2(16) + 2w$ $[P = 48, l = 16]$
$48 = 32 + 2w$
$16 = 2w$
$8 = w$ *Answer:* 8 cm

Check

$P = 2l + 2w$
$48 \overset{?}{=} 2(16) + 2(8)$
$48 \overset{?}{=} 32 + 16$
$48 = 48$ (True)

| EXERCISES |

1. If $P = a + b + c$, find c when $P = 80, a = 20$, and $b = 25$.
2. If $P = 4s$, find s when (a) $P = 20$; (b) $P = 32$; (c) $P = 6.4$.
3. If $A = lw$, find w when (a) $A = 100, l = 5$; (b) $A = 3.6, l = .9$.
4. If $A = \frac{1}{2}bh$, find h when (a) $A = 24, b = 8$; (b) $A = 12, b = 3$.
5. If $V = lwh$, find w when $V = 72, l = \frac{3}{4}$, and $h = 12$.
6. If $P = 2l + 2w$, find w when (a) $P = 20, l = 7$; (b) $P = 36, l = 9\frac{1}{2}$.
7. If $P = 2l + 2w$, find l when (a) $P = 28, w = 3$; (b) $P = 24.8, w = 4.7$.
8. If $P = 2a + b$, find b when $P = 80$ cm and $a = 30$ cm.

9. If $P = 2a + b$, find a when $P = 18.6$ cm and $b = 5.8$ cm.

10. If $A = \frac{1}{2}h(b + c)$, find h when $A = 30$, $b = 4$, and $c = 6$.

11. If $A = \frac{1}{2}h(b + c)$, find b when $A = 50$ cm^2, $h = 4$ cm, and $c = 11$ cm.

12. If $D = RT$, find R when **(a)** $D = 120$, $T = 3$; **(b)** $D = 40$, $T = \frac{1}{2}$.

13. If $I = prt$, find p when $I = \$135$, $r = 6\%$, and $t = 3$ yr.

14. If $F = \frac{9}{5}C + 32$, find C when **(a)** $F = 95°$; **(b)** $F = 68°$; **(c)** $F = 59°$; **(d)** $F = 32°$; **(e)** $F = 212°$; **(f)** $F = -13°$.

15. Find the length of a rectangle whose perimeter is 34.6 cm and whose width is 5.7 cm.

16. The area of a triangle is 36 cm^2. Find the measure of the altitude drawn to the base when the **(a)** base = 8 cm; **(b)** base = 12 cm.

In 17–20, the perimeter of a square is given. **a.** Find the length of each side of the square. **b.** Find the area of the square.

17. $P = 28$ cm   **18.** $P = 3$ in.   **19.** $P = 16.8$ cm   **20.** $P = 2$ ft.

7   SOLVING EQUATIONS CONTAINING MORE THAN ONE VARIABLE

An equation may contain more than one variable. Examples of such equations are $ax = b$, $x + c = d$, and $y - r = z$.

To solve such an equation for one of its variables means to express this particular variable in terms of the other variables. In order to plan the steps in the solution, it may be helpful to compare the equation with a similar equation that contains only the variable being solved for. For example, in solving $bx - c = d$ for x, compare it with $2x - 5 = 19$. The same operations are used in solving both equations.

| MODEL PROBLEMS |
---

1. Solve for x: $ax = b$ $[a \neq 0]$

Solution   *Check*

Compare with $2x = 7$. $ax = b$

$2x = 7$ $ax = b$ $a\left(\dfrac{b}{a}\right) \overset{?}{=} b$

$\dfrac{2x}{2} = \dfrac{7}{2}$ D$_2$ *or* M$_{\frac{1}{2}}$ $\dfrac{ax}{a} = \dfrac{b}{a}$ D$_a$ *or* M$_{\frac{1}{a}}$ $b = b$ (True)

$x = \dfrac{7}{2}$ *Ans.* $x = \dfrac{b}{a}$ *Ans.*

2. Solve for x: $x + a = b$

<table><tr><td>*Solution*</td><td>*Check*</td></tr></table>

Compare with $x + 5 = 9$.

$$x + a = b$$
$$x + a + (-a) = b + (-a) \quad \text{S}_a \text{ or A}_{-a}$$
$$x = b - a \quad Ans.$$

$$x + a = b$$
$$b - a + a \overset{?}{=} b$$
$$b = b \quad \text{(True)}$$

3. Solve for x: $2ax = 10a^2 - 3ax$

How to Proceed

Solution

Compare with $2x = 10 - 3x$.

(1) Write the equation. $\quad 2ax = 10a^2 - 3ax$

(2) A_{+3ax} $\quad 2ax + (+3ax) = 10a^2 - 3ax + (+3ax)$

(3) Collect like terms. $\quad 5ax = 10a^2$

(4) D_{5a} *or* $\text{M}_{\frac{1}{5}a}$ $\quad \dfrac{5ax}{5a} = \dfrac{10a^2}{5a}$

(5) Simplify. $\quad x = 2a \quad Ans.$

The check is left to the student.

EXERCISES

In 1–32, solve for x or y and check.

1. $5x = b$
2. $sx = 8$
3. $ry = s$
4. $3y = t$
5. $cy = 5$
6. $hy = m$
7. $x + 5 = r$
8. $x + a = 7$
9. $y + c = d$
10. $4 + x = k$
11. $d + y = 9$
12. $3x - q = p$
13. $x - 2 = r$
14. $y - a = 7$
15. $x - c = d$
16. $3x - e = r$
17. $cy - d = 4$
18. $ax + b = c$
19. $rx - s = 0$
20. $r + sy = t$
21. $m = 2(x + n)$
22. $4x - 5c = 3c$
23. $bx = 9b^2$
24. $cx + c^2 = 5c^2 - 3cx$
25. $bx - 5 = c$
26. $a = by + 6$
27. $ry + s = t$
28. $abx - d = 5d$
29. $rsx - rs^2 = 0$
30. $m^2x - 3m^2 = 12m^2$
31. $9x - 24a = 6a + 4x$
32. $8ax - 7a^2 = 19a^2 - 5ax$

8 TRANSFORMING FORMULAS

A formula may be expressed in more than one form. Sometimes we must solve a formula for a variable different from the one for which it is set up to be solved. This is called *transforming* the formula, or *changing the subject* of the formula. For example, the formula $D = 40t$ can be transformed into the equivalent formula $\dfrac{D}{40} = t$. In the formula $D = 40t$,

D is expressed in terms of t; in the formula $t = \dfrac{D}{40}$, t is expressed in terms of D. If we know the value of D and wish to find the value of t, the computation is more convenient when we use the formula $t = \dfrac{D}{40}$. (See the first model problem following the Procedure.)

■ **PROCEDURE.** To transform a formula so that it is solved for a particular variable, consider the formula as an equation with several variables and solve it for the indicated variable in terms of the others.

MODEL PROBLEMS

1. a. Solve the formula $D = 40t$ for t.
   b. Use the answer found in **a** to find the value of t when $D = 200$.

   Solution:

   a. $D = 40t$

   $\dfrac{D}{40} = \dfrac{40t}{40}$ D_{40}

   $\dfrac{D}{40} = t$

   $t = \dfrac{D}{40}$ *Ans.*

   b. $t = \dfrac{D}{40}$

   $t = \dfrac{200}{40}$ $(D = 200)$

   $t = 5$ *Ans.*

2. Solve the formula $V = \tfrac{1}{3}Bh$ for B.

   Solution

   $V = \tfrac{1}{3}Bh$

   $3V = 3 \cdot \tfrac{1}{3}Bh$ M_3

   $3V = Bh$

   $\dfrac{3V}{h} = \dfrac{Bh}{h}$ D_h

   $\dfrac{3V}{h} = B$ *Ans.*

3. Solve the formula $P = 2(L + W)$ for W.

   Solution

   $P = 2(L + W)$

   $P = 2L + 2W$ (Distributive property)

   $P + (-2L) = 2L + 2W + (-2L)$ A_{-2L}

   $P - 2L = 2W$

   $\dfrac{P - 2L}{2} = \dfrac{2W}{2}$ D_2.

   $\dfrac{P - 2L}{2} = W$ *Ans.*

EXERCISES

In 1–19, transform the given formula by solving for the indicated letter.

1. $A = 6h$ for h 2. $36 = bh$ for h 3. $P = 4s$ for s

4. $D = rt$ for t 5. $V = lwh$ for l 6. $p = br$ for r

7. $A = BH$ for B 8. $A = lw$ for l 9. $V = lwh$ for h

10. $V = 4bh$ for h 11. $i = prt$ for p 12. $400 = BH$ for B

13. $A = \frac{1}{2}bh$ for h 14. $V = \frac{1}{3}BH$ for H 15. $S = \frac{1}{2}gt^2$ for g

16. $l = c - s$ for c 17. $P = 2l + 2w$ for l 18. $F = \frac{9}{5}C + 32$ for C

19. $2S = n(a + l)$ for a

20. If $A = BH$, express H in terms of A and B. (Solve for H.)

21. If $P = 2a + b$, express b in terms of P and a.

22. If $P = 2a + b + c$, express a in terms of the other variables.

In 23–26: **a.** Transform the given formula by solving for the variable to be evaluated. **b.** Using the result obtained in part **a**, substitute the given values to find the value of this variable.

23. If $LWH = 144$, find W when $L = 3$ and $H = 6$.

24. If $A = \frac{1}{2}bh$, find h when $A = 15$ and $b = 5$.

25. If $F = \frac{9}{5}C + 32$, find C when $F = 95$.

26. If $P = 2L + 2W$, find L when $P = 64$ and $W = 13$.

27. The formula for finding the area of a rectangle is $A = bh$. Rewrite this formula if $b = 4h$.

28. The formula for the area of a triangle is $A = \frac{1}{2}bh$. Rewrite this formula if $h = 4b$.

9 USING FORMULAS TO STUDY RELATED CHANGES IN PERIMETERS, AREAS, AND VOLUMES

The formula $P = 4s$ states the relationship between the side of a square, s, and its perimeter, P. A change in the value of the variable s will bring about a change in the value of the variable P. For example:

If the side of a square is doubled, what change takes place in its perimeter?

We can use three different approaches to answer this question.

1. *Arithmetic*

Here we make use of a table of values.

(1) Choose any value for side s, say $s = 3$.
    Then $P = 4s = 4(3) = 12$.

(2) *Double* side s to get $s = 6$.
    Then $P = 4s = 4(6) = 24$.

(3) *Double* side s again to get $s = 12$.
    Then $P = 4s = 4(12) = 48$.

$$P = 4s$$

s	P
3	12
6	24
12	48

The table shows that each value of P appears to be *double* the previous value. Hence, it appears that when the side of a square is *doubled*, the perimeter is doubled.

If we were to use other values for s, might the result be different? The arithmetic approach is not foolproof in answering this question or others like it. Now we will consider a more general approach, an algebraic approach, which is foolproof.

2. *Algebraic*

The formula for the perimeter of a square is $P = 4s$. Since the side of the square, s, is to be doubled, the side of the new square can be represented by $2s$. The perimeter of the new square P', read "P prime," can be found by substituting $2s$ for s in the formula $P = 4s$.

$P' = 4(2s)$. Hence, $P' = 8s$.

Since $8s$ is twice $4s$, then P' is twice P.

Answer: The perimeter is doubled.

Notice that in this example the arithmetic solution did lead to a correct answer.

3. *Geometric*

(1) We draw a model of the original square whose side is s and whose perimeter is $4s$.

(2) We draw a second model each of whose sides is $2s$, which is double the side s of the original square.

(3) We find the perimeter of the new square to be $2s + 2s + 2s + 2s$, or $8s$.

(4) We compare the perimeters of the two squares and find that since $8s = 2(4s)$, the perimeter is doubled.

MODEL PROBLEMS

1. If the side of a square is doubled, what change takes place in its area?

    Solution: The formula for the area of a square is $A = s^2$. Since the side of the square is doubled, represent the side of the new square by $2s$. Find the area of the new square A' by substituting $2s$ for s in the formula $A = s^2$.

    $$A' = (2s)^2$$
    $$A' = (2s)(2s)$$
    $$A' = 4s^2$$

    Since $4s^2$ is 4 times s^2, then A' is 4 times A.

    Answer: The area is multiplied by 4.

    Note: We can arrive at the same result geometrically. The original area is s^2. By doubling each side, the new area is $4s^2$.

    Answer: The area is multiplied by 4.

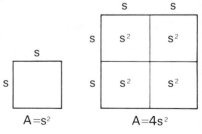

2. The length of a rectangle is doubled and its width is tripled. How is its area affected?

Solution: The formula for the area of a rectangle whose length is l and whose width is w is $A = lw$. Since the length is doubled, the length of the new rectangle can be represented by $2l$. Since the width is tripled, the new width can be represented by $3w$. We find the area of the new rectangle A' by substituting $2l$ for l and $3w$ for w in the formula $A = lw$.

$A' = (2l)(3w)$. Hence, $A' = 6lw$.

Since $6lw$ is 6 times lw, then A' is 6 times A.

Answer: The area is multiplied by 6.

Note: To solve geometrically, we draw models to show that the area is multiplied by 6.

$A = lw$ $\qquad\qquad$ $A = 6\,lw$

EXERCISES

In 1–6, state how the perimeter of a square is affected when each side is multiplied by the given number.

1. 3 $\qquad$ 2. 4 $\qquad$ 3. 6 $\qquad$ 4. 10 $\qquad$ 5. $\frac{1}{2}$ $\qquad$ 6. $\frac{1}{4}$

In 7–12, state how the area of a square is affected when each side is multiplied by the given number.

7. 3 $\qquad$ 8. 4 $\qquad$ 9. 5 $\qquad$ 10. 8 $\qquad$ 11. $\frac{1}{2}$ $\qquad$ 12. $\frac{1}{3}$

13. State how the area of a rectangle is affected when:
    a. The length is doubled and the width is multiplied by 5.
    b. The length is multiplied by 8 and the width is doubled.
    c. The length is doubled and the width is halved.
14. Tell how the volume of a rectangular solid is affected when:
    a. The length is multiplied by 3, the width is multiplied by 4, and the height is multiplied by 5.

b. The length is doubled, the width is doubled, and the height is tripled.

c. The length is doubled, the width is halved, and the height is unchanged.

15. State how the volume of a cube is affected when each side is:

a. multiplied by 2   b. multiplied by 3   c. halved

10 PROPERTIES OF INEQUALITIES

The Order Property of Number

If two signed numbers x and y are graphed on a number line, only one of the following situations can happen:

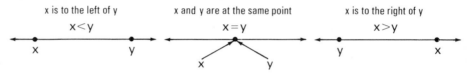

These graphs illustrate the *order property of number:*

■ If x and y are two signed numbers, then one and only one of the following sentences is true:

$$x < y \qquad x = y \qquad x > y$$

The Transitive Property of Inequalities

From the graph at the right, we see that if x lies to the left of y, or $x < y$, and if y lies to the left of z, or $y < z$, then x lies to the left of z, or $x < z$. Likewise, if z lies to the right of y, or $z > y$, and if y lies to the right of x, or $y > x$, then z lies to the right of x, or $z > x$.

This graph illustrates the *transitive property of inequalities:*

■ If x, y, and z are signed numbers, then:

If $x < y$ and $y < z$, then $x < z$.
If $z > y$ and $y > x$, then $z > x$.

The Addition Property of Inequalities

If 3 is added to both members of $9 > 2$, which is a true sentence, then $9 + (3) > 2 + (3)$, or $12 > 5$, is also a true sentence. Observe that $2 < 9$ is a true sentence and that $2 + (-3) < 9 + (-3)$, or $-1 < 6$, is also a true sentence.

These examples illustrate the *addition property of inequalities:*

■ If x, y, and z are signed numbers, then:

$$\text{If } x > y, \text{ then } x + z > y + z.$$
$$\text{If } x < y, \text{ then } x + z < y + z.$$

Since subtracting a signed number from both members of an inequality means adding its additive inverse to both members of the inequality, we can say:

■ When the same number is added to or subtracted from both members of an inequality, the order of the inequality remains unchanged.

The Multiplication Property of Inequalities

If we multiply both members of $5 > 3$, which is a true sentence, by 7, then $7 \times 5 > 7 \times 3$, or $35 > 21$, is also a true sentence. Observe that $-2 < 4$ is a true sentence and that $5(-2) < 5(4)$, or $-10 < 20$, is also a true sentence. Notice that when both members of an inequality were multiplied by the same positive number, the order of the inequality remained unchanged.

Now let us multiply both members of $5 > 3$ by -7. We see that $(-7)(5) > (-7)(3)$, or $-35 > -21$, is a false sentence. If we reverse the order in the resulting inequality $-35 > -21$, changing $>$ to $<$, we will have $-35 < -21$, a true sentence. Likewise, $-2 < 4$ is a true sentence, but $(-5)(-2) < (-5)(4)$, or $10 < -20$, is a false sentence. However, if we reverse the order in the resulting inequality $10 < -20$ and write $10 > -20$, we have a true sentence.

These examples illustrate the *multiplication property of inequalities:*

■ If x, y, and z are signed numbers, then:

$$\text{If } x > y, \text{ then } xz > yz \text{ when } z \text{ is positive } (z > 0).$$
$$\text{If } x < y, \text{ then } xz < yz \text{ when } z \text{ is positive } (z > 0).$$
$$\text{If } x > y, \text{ then } xz < yz \text{ when } z \text{ is negative } (z < 0).$$
$$\text{If } x < y, \text{ then } xz > yz \text{ when } z \text{ is negative } (z < 0).$$

Since dividing both members of an inequality by a nonzero signed number means to multiply by the reciprocal, or multiplicative inverse, of the number, we can say:

■ When both members of an inequality are multiplied or divided by a positive number, the order of the inequality remains unchanged; when both members are multiplied or divided by a negative number, the order of the inequality is reversed.

| EXERCISES |

In 1–25, replace the question mark with the symbol $>$ or the symbol $<$ so that the resulting sentence will be true. All variables in exercises 9–25 are nonzero signed numbers.

1. Since $8 > 2$, $8 + 1$? $2 + 1$.
2. Since $-6 < 2$, $-6 + (-4)$? $2 + (-4)$.
3. Since $9 > 5$, $9 - 2$? $5 - 2$.
4. Since $-2 > -8$, $-2 - (\frac{1}{4})$? $-8 - (\frac{1}{4})$.
5. Since $7 > 3$, $\frac{2}{3}(7)$? $\frac{2}{3}(3)$.
6. Since $-4 < 1$, $(-2)(-4)$? $(-2)(1)$.
7. Since $-8 < 4$, $(-8) \div (4)$? $(4) \div (4)$.
8. Since $9 > 6$, $(9) \div (-\frac{1}{3})$? $(6) \div (-\frac{1}{3})$.
9. If $5 > x$, then $5 + 7$? $x + 7$.
10. If $y < 6$, then $y - 2$? $6 - 2$.
11. If $20 > r$, then $4(20)$? $4(r)$.
12. If $t < 64$, then $t \div 8$? $64 \div 8$.
13. If $x > 8$, then $-2x$? $(-2)(8)$.
14. If $y < 8$, then $y \div (-4)$? $8 \div (-4)$.
15. If $x + 2 > 7$, then $x + 2 + (-2)$? $7 + (-2)$ and x ? 5.
16. If $y - 3 < 12$, then $y - 3 + 3$? $12 + 3$, or y ? 15.
17. If $x + 5 < 14$, then $x + 5 - 5$? $14 - 5$, or x ? 9.
18. If $2x > 8$, then $\dfrac{2x}{2}$? $\dfrac{8}{2}$, or x ? 4.
19. If $\frac{1}{3}y < 4$, then $3 \times \frac{1}{3}y$? 3×4, or y ? 12.
20. If $-3x < 36$, then $\dfrac{-3x}{-3}$? $\dfrac{36}{-3}$, or x ? -12.
21. If $-2x > 6$, then $(-\frac{1}{2})(-2x)$? $(-\frac{1}{2})(6)$, or x ? -3.
22. If $x < 5$ and $5 < y$, then x ? y.
23. If $m > -7$ and $-7 > a$, then m ? a.
24. If $x < 10$ and $z > 10$, then x ? z.
25. If $a > b$ and $c < b$, then a ? c.

In 26–33, tell whether the statement is always, sometimes, or never true.

26. If $c > d$, then $c + a > d + a$.

27. If $r < s$, then $r - t < s - t$.

28. If $a > b$, then $ac > bc$.

29. If $w < d$, then $-w < -d$.

30. If $x > y$ and $z < 0$, then $\frac{x}{z} < \frac{y}{z}$.

31. If $cd > 0$, then $c > 0$ and $d > 0$.

32. If $ab < 0$, then $a < 0$ and $b < 0$.

33. If $b > c$ and $c > d$, then $b > d$.

11 FINDING THE SOLUTION SETS OF INEQUALITIES CONTAINING ONE VARIABLE

Let us find the solution set of the inequality $2x > 8$, when x is a member of the set of signed numbers. To do this, we must find the set of all numbers each of which can replace x in the sentence $2x > 8$ and result in a true sentence.

$$2x > 8$$

If $x = 1$, then $2(1) > 8$, or $2 > 8$, is a false sentence.

If $x = 2\frac{1}{2}$, then $2(2\frac{1}{2}) > 8$, or $5 > 8$, is a false sentence.

If $x = 3\frac{3}{4}$, then $2(3\frac{3}{4}) > 8$, or $7\frac{1}{2} > 8$, is a false sentence.

If $x = 4$, then $2(4) > 8$, or $8 > 8$, is a false sentence.

If $x = 4.1$, then $2(4.1) > 8$, or $8.2 > 8$, is a *true* sentence.

If $x = 5$, then $2(5) > 8$, or $10 > 8$, is a *true* sentence.

Notice that if x is replaced by any number greater than 4, the resulting sentence is true. Therefore, the solution set of $2x > 8$ is the set of all signed numbers greater than 4, written {all signed numbers greater than 4}. The solution set can also be described by the symbol $\{x \mid x > 4\}$, which is read "the set of all x such that x is greater than 4."

Observe that every member of the solution set of $x > 4$ is also a member of the solution set of $2x > 8$. Therefore, we call $2x > 8$ and $x > 4$ *equivalent inequalities*.

To find the solution set of an inequality, we will solve the inequality by using methods similar to those used in solving an equation. We will use the properties of inequalities to transform the given inequality into a simpler equivalent inequality whose solution set is evident. Study the following model problems to learn how this is done.

| MODEL PROBLEMS |

In 1–4, the domain of the variable is the set of signed numbers.

1. Find and graph the solution set of the inequality $x - 4 > 1$.

How to Proceed	*Solution*
(1) Write the inequality.	$x - 4 > 1$
(2) Add 4 to both members, and use the addition property of inequalities.	$x - 4 + 4 > 1 + 4$ $x > 5$

Answer: The solution set is {all signed numbers greater than 5}
    or $\{x \mid x > 5\}$

The graph of the solution set is shown below. Note that 5 is not included in the graph.

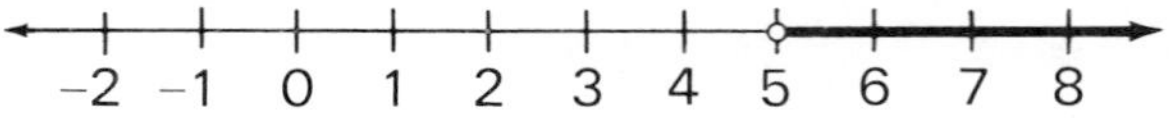

2. Find and graph the solution set of the inequality $x + 1 \le 4$. Remember that $x + 1 \le 4$ means $x + 1 < 4$ or $x + 1 = 4$. That is, $x + 1 \le 4$ is equivalent to the disjunction $(x + 1 < 4) \lor (x + 1 = 4)$.

How to Proceed	*Solution*	*Check*
(1) Write the inequality.	$x + 1 \le 4$	If $x = 3$, then $x + 1 = 4$.
(2) Subtract 1 from both members, and use the subtraction property of inequalities.	$x + 1 - 1 \le 4 - 1$ $x \le 3$	If $x < 3$, then $x + 1 < 4$.

Answer: The solution set is {all signed numbers less than or equal to 3}
    or $\{x \mid x \le 3\}$

Note: This problem can also be solved by adding -1, which is the opposite, or additive inverse, of +1, to both members of the inequality.

The graph of the solution set is shown at the right. Note that 3 is included in the graph.

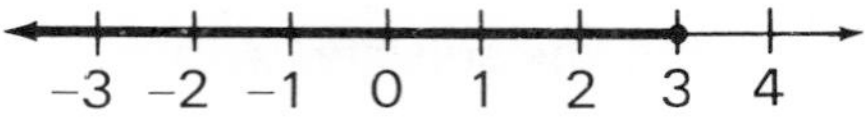

3. Find and graph the solution set of the inequality $5x + 4 \le 11 - 2x$.

How to Proceed	*Solution*
(1) Write the inequality.	$5x + 4 \leq 11 - 2x$
(2) Add $2x$ to each member, and use the addition property of inequalities.	$5x + 4 + 2x \leq 11 - 2x + 2x$ $7x + 4 \leq 11$
(3) Subtract 4 from both members, and use the subtraction property of inequalities.	$7x + 4 - 4 \leq 11 - 4$ $7x \leq 7$
(4) Divide both members by 7, and use the property of dividing by a positive number.	$\dfrac{7x}{7} \leq \dfrac{7}{7}$ $x \leq 1$

The check is left to the student.

Answer: The solution set is {all signed numbers less than or equal to 1} *or* $\{x \mid x \leq 1\}$

The graph of the solution set is shown at the right. Note that 1 is included in the graph.

4. Find and graph the solution set of the inequality $2(2x - 8) - 8x \leq 0$.

How to Proceed	*Solution*
(1) Write the inequality.	$2(2x - 8) - 8x \leq 0$
(2) Use the distributive property.	$4x - 16 - 8x \leq 0$
(3) Collect like terms.	$-4x - 16 \leq 0$
(4) Add 16 to both members, and use the addition property of inequalities.	$-4x - 16 + 16 \leq 0 + 16$ $-4x \leq 16$
(5) Divide both members by -4, and use the property of division by a negative number. Remember to reverse the order of the inequality.	$\dfrac{-4x}{-4} \geq \dfrac{16}{-4}$ $x \geq -4$

The check is left to the student.

Answer: The solution set is $\{x \mid x \geq -4\}$ *or* {all signed numbers greater than or equal to -4}

The graph of the solution set is shown at the right. Note that -4 is included in the graph.

| EXERCISES |

In 1–51, find and graph the solution set of the inequality. Use the set of signed numbers as the domain of the variable.

1. $x - 2 > 4$

2. $z - 6 < 4$

3. $y - \frac{1}{2} > 2$

4. $x - 1.5 < 3.5$

5. $x + 3 > 6$

6. $19 < y + 17$

7. $d + \frac{1}{4} > 3$

8. $-3\frac{1}{2} > c + \frac{1}{2}$

9. $y - 4 \geq 4$

10. $25 \leq d + 22$

11. $3t > 6$

12. $2x \leq 12$

13. $15 \leq 3y$

14. $-10 \leq 4h$

15. $-6y < 24$

16. $27 > -9y$

17. $-10x > -20$

18. $12 \leq -1.2r$

19. $\frac{1}{3}x > 2$

20. $-\frac{2}{3}z \geq 6$

21. $\frac{x}{2} > 1$

22. $\frac{y}{3} \leq -1$

23. $\frac{1}{2} \leq \frac{z}{4}$

24. $-.4y \leq 4$

25. $-10 \geq 2.5z$

26. $2x - 1 > 5$

27. $3y - 6 \geq 12$

28. $5x - 1 > -31$

29. $-5 \leq 3y - 2$

30. $3x + 4 > 10$

31. $5y + 3 \geq 13$

32. $6c + 1 > -11$

33. $4d + 3 \leq 17$

34. $5x + 3x - 4 > 4$

35. $8y - 3y - 1 \leq 29$

36. $6x + 2 - 8x < 14$

37. $3x + 1 > 2x + 7$

38. $7y - 4 < 6 + 2y$

39. $4 - 3x \geq 16 + x$

40. $2x - 1 > 4 - \frac{1}{2}x$

41. $2c + 5 \geq 14 + 2\frac{1}{3}c$

42. $\frac{x}{3} - 1 \leq \frac{x}{2} + 3$

43. $4(x - 1) > 16$

44. $8x < 5(2x + 4)$

45. $12\left(\frac{1}{4} + \frac{x}{3}\right) > 15$

46. $8m - 2(2m + 3) \geq 0$

47. $12r - (8r - 20) > 12$

48. $3y - 6 \leq 3(7 + 2y)$

49. $5x \leq 10 + 2(3x - 4)$

50. $-3(4x - 8) > 2(3 + 2x)$

51. $4 - 5(y - 2) \leq -2(-9 + 2y)$

52. To which of the following is $y + 4 \geq 9$ equivalent?

    (1) $y > 5$ (2) $y \geq 5$ (3) $y \geq 13$ (4) $y = 13$

53. To which of the following is $5x < 4x + 6$ equivalent?

    (1) $x > 6$ (2) $x = 6$ (3) $x = \frac{6}{5}$ (4) $x < 6$

54. Which of the following is the smallest member of the solution set of $3x - 7 \geq 8$?

    (1) 3   (2) 4   (3) 5   (4) 6

55. Which of the following is the largest member of the solution set of $4x \leq 3x + 2$?

    (1) 1   (2) 2   (3) 3   (4) 4

In 56–59, write an inequality for the graph that is shown.

56.

57.

58.

59.

60. Six times a number is less than 72. What numbers satisfy this condition?

61. A number increased by 10 is greater than 50. What numbers satisfy this condition?

62. A number decreased by 15 is less than 35. What numbers satisfy this condition?

63. Twice a number, increased by 6, is less than 48. What numbers satisfy this condition?

64. Five times a number, decreased by 24, is greater than 3 times the number. What numbers satisfy this condition?

65. Mr. Simpson paid off $1000 of a loan. He still owes $2500 or more on that loan. How much is the smallest amount that his loan might have been before he made the payment?

12 GRAPHING SOLUTION SETS OF CONJUNCTIONS AND DISJUNCTIONS

Graphing a Conjunction

When we say that x is between 3 and 6, symbolized $3 < x < 6$, we are saying that $3 < x$ and $x < 6$. Hence, we see that $3 < x < 6$ is equivalent to the conjunction $(3 < x) \wedge (x < 6)$. Since the solution set of a conjunction must contain all values of the variable that satisfy both open sentences, the graph of the conjunction $(3 < x) \wedge (x < 6)$ can be obtained in the following manner:

	Steps	*Solution*

Steps	*Solution*
(1) Graph the solution set of the first open sentence $3 < x$.	*Think* $3 < x$
(2) Graph on the same number line the solution set of the second open sentence $x < 6$.	*Think* $x < 6$ $3 < x$
(3) The graph of the solution set of the conjunction is the set of points common to the graphs made in steps (1) and (2), that is, the *intersection* of the two sets of points graphed in steps (1) and (2).	*Write* $3 < x < 6$

Graphing a Disjunction

The disjunction $(3 < x) \lor (x > 6)$ means $3 < x$ or $x > 6$. Since the solution set of a disjunction must contain all the values of the variable that satisfy at least one of the open sentences, the graph of the disjunction $(3 < x) \lor (x > 6)$ can be obtained in the following manner:

Steps	*Solution*
(1) Graph the solution set of the first open sentence $3 < x$.	*Think* $3 < x$
(2) Graph on the same number line the solution set of the second open sentence $x > 6$.	*Think* $x > 6$ $3 < x$
(3) The graph of the solution set of the disjunction is the set of points that are in at least one of the graphs made in step (1)	*Write* $(3 < x) \lor (x > 6)$

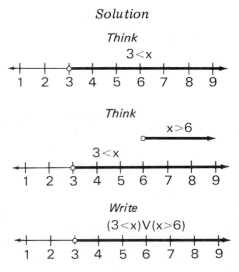

and step (2), that is, the *union* of the two sets of points graphed in step (1) and step (2).

It is possible that two open sentences that are involved in a disjunction have no elements in common. The graph of the disjunction still shows the union of both graphs. For example, the graph of $(x < 2) \lor (x \geq 5)$ is:

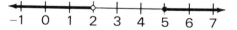

EXERCISES

In 1–6, graph the solution set of the given sentence on a number line.

1. $1 < x < 5$
2. $-1 < x \leq 4$
3. $-5 \leq x \leq -2$
4. $(-2 < y) \lor (y > 3)$
5. $(w \leq -1) \lor (w \geq 2)$
6. $(t \geq -3) \lor (t > 1)$

In 7–12, graph the set on a number line.

7. $\{x \mid -3 < x < 3\}$
8. $\{x \mid 0 \leq x \leq 6\}$
9. $\{y \mid -1 < y < 3\frac{1}{2}\}$
10. $\{x \mid (x < -3) \lor (x > 0)\}$
11. $\{a \mid (a \leq 2) \lor (a \leq 7)\}$
12. $\{d \mid (d \leq -5) \lor (d > -1)\}$

13. Which of the following is represented by the graph at the right?

    (1) $-2 < x < 4$
    (2) $4 \leq x < -2$
    (3) $-2 \leq x < 4$
    (4) $4 \leq x \leq -2$

14. Which of the following is represented by the graph at the right?

    (1) $(x > -3) \lor (x > 5)$
    (2) $(x \geq -3) \lor (x \geq 5)$
    (3) $(5 < x) \lor (x > -3)$
    (4) $(x \geq 5) \lor (x \leq -3)$

15. Which of the following is represented by the graph at the right?

    (1) $(x \leq -1) \lor (x \geq 2)$
    (2) $(x < -1) \lor (x \geq 2)$
    (3) $(x > -1) \lor (x > 2)$
    (4) $(x \leq -1) \lor (x > 2)$

chapter ten

Ratio and Proportion

1 RATIO

A *ratio* of one number to another (not zero) is the quotient of the first number divided by the second number.

For example, the ratio of 18 to 6 is $18 \div 6$ or $\frac{18}{6}$. The quotient $\frac{18}{6}$ is equivalent to $\frac{3}{1}$ or 3. We may say that the first number 18 is 3 times the second number 6. Notice that a ratio can be used to compare numbers.

Another way to express the ratio $\frac{18}{6}$ is to use the colon symbol ":" and write $18:6$.

In general, the ratio of a to b can be expressed as

$$\frac{a}{b} \quad or \quad a \div b \quad or \quad a:b$$

The numbers a and b are called the *terms* of the ratio.

A ratio is the quotient of two numbers in a definite order. The ratio of 3 to 1 is written $\frac{3}{1}$ or $3:1$, whereas the ratio of 1 to 3 is written $\frac{1}{3}$ or $1:3$. Therefore, a ratio may be considered as an ordered pair of numbers, and we can say that finding the ratio of two numbers is a binary operation.

To find the ratio of two quantities, both quantities must be expressed in the same unit of measure before we find their quotient. For example, to compare a nickel with a penny, we first convert the nickel to 5 pennies and then find the ratio, which is $\frac{5}{1}$ or $5:1$. Therefore, a nickel is worth 5 times as much as a penny.

Equivalent Ratios

Since the ratio $\frac{5}{1}$ is a fraction, we can use the multiplication property of 1 to find many equivalent ratios. For example:

$$\frac{5}{1} = \frac{5}{1} \cdot \frac{2}{2} = \frac{10}{2} \qquad \frac{5}{1} = \frac{5}{1} \cdot \frac{3}{3} = \frac{15}{3} \qquad \frac{5}{1} = \frac{5}{1} \cdot \frac{x}{x} = \frac{5x}{1x} \quad (x \neq 0)$$

From the last example we see that $5x$ and $1x$ represent two numbers whose ratio is $5:1$.

In general, if a, b, and x are numbers ($b \neq 0$, $x \neq 0$), ax and bx represent two numbers whose ratio is $a:b$ because:

$$\frac{a}{b} = \frac{a}{b} \cdot 1 = \frac{a}{b} \cdot \frac{x}{x} = \frac{ax}{bx}$$

Also, since a ratio such as $\frac{24}{16}$ is a fraction, we can use the division property of a fraction to find equivalent ratios. For example:

$$\frac{24}{16} = \frac{24 \div 2}{16 \div 2} = \frac{12}{8} \qquad \frac{24}{16} = \frac{24 \div 4}{16 \div 4} = \frac{6}{4} \qquad \frac{24}{16} = \frac{24 \div 8}{16 \div 8} = \frac{3}{2}$$

A ratio is expressed in *simplest form* when both terms of the ratio are whole numbers and when there is no whole number other than 1 that divides exactly into these terms. Thus, to express the ratio $\frac{24}{16}$ in simplest form, we divide both terms by 8, the greatest number that divides both 24 and 16 exactly. We obtain the ratio $\frac{3}{2}$ (as shown in the preceding example).

Continued Ratio

In a rectangular solid the length is 75 cm, the width is 60 cm, and the height is 45 cm. The ratio of the length to the width is $75:60$, and the ratio of the width to the height is $60:45$. We can write these two ratios in an abbreviated form as the continued ratio $75:60:45$. We say that the ratio of the measures of the length, width, and height of the rectangular solid is $75:60:45$, or, in simplest form, $5:4:3$.

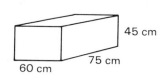

In general, the ratio of the numbers a, b, and c ($b \neq 0$, $c \neq 0$) is $a:b:c$.

MODEL PROBLEMS

1. An oil tank has a capacity of 200 gallons. There are 50 gallons of oil in the tank. **a.** Find the ratio of the number of gallons of oil in the tank to the capacity of the tank. **b.** What part of the tank is full?

Solution:

a. ratio = $\dfrac{\text{number of gallons of oil in the tank}}{\text{capacity of the tank}} = \dfrac{50}{200} = \dfrac{1}{4}$

Answer: The ratio is 1 to 4.

b. *Answer:* $\frac{1}{4}$ of the tank is full.

2. Compute the ratio of 6.4 ounces to 1 pound.

Solution: First we express both quantities in the same unit of measure.

$$1 \text{ pound} = 16 \text{ ounces}$$

$$\text{ratio} = \frac{6.4 \text{ ounces}}{1 \text{ pound}} = \frac{6.4 \text{ ounces}}{16 \text{ ounces}} = \frac{6.4}{16} = \frac{64}{160} = \frac{2}{5}$$

Answer: The ratio is $2:5$.

3. Express the ratio $1\frac{3}{4}$ to $1\frac{1}{2}$ in simplest form.

Solution: ratio = $1\frac{3}{4} : 1\frac{1}{2} = 1\frac{3}{4} \div 1\frac{1}{2} = \frac{7}{4} \div \frac{3}{2} = \frac{7}{4} \times \frac{2}{3} = \frac{14}{12} = \frac{7}{6}$ *Ans.*

EXERCISES

In 1–5, express each ratio (a) as a fraction and (b) using a colon.

1. 36 to 12   2. 48 to 24   3. 40 to 25   4. 2 to 3   5. 5 to 4

6. Express each ratio in simplest form.
   a. $\frac{8}{32}$ b. $\frac{40}{5}$ c. $\frac{12}{28}$ d. $\frac{36}{27}$ e. $\frac{36}{24}$
   f. $20:10$ g. $15:45$ h. $18:18$ i. $48:20$ j. $21:35$
   k. $3x:2x$ l. $1y:4y$ m. $3c:5c$ n. $7x:7y$ o. $12s:4s$

7. The larger number is how many times the smaller number?
   a. 10, 5   b. 18, 6   c. 12, 8   d. 25, 10   e. 15, 25

8. If the ratio of two numbers is $10:1$, how many times the smaller number is the larger number?

9. If the ratio of two numbers is $8:1$, the smaller number is what fractional part of the larger number?

10. In each part, tell whether the ratio is equal to $\frac{3}{2}$.
    a. $\frac{30}{20}$ b. $\frac{9}{4}$ c. $\frac{8}{12}$ d. $9:6$ e. $\frac{45}{30}$ f. $18:6$

11. In each part, name the ratios that are equal.
    a. $\frac{2}{3}, \frac{6}{9}, \frac{10}{30}, \frac{28}{36}, \frac{50}{75}$ b. $10:8, 20:16, 15:13, 4:5, 50:40$

12. Find three pairs of numbers, the ratio of each pair of numbers being:
    a. $\frac{1}{2}$ b. $\frac{1}{5}$ c. $3:1$ d. $4:1$ e. $\frac{3}{4}$ f. $2:3$

13. Using a colon, express in simplest form the ratio of all pairs of (a) equal numbers (not zero) and (b) nonzero numbers whose difference is 0.

14. Express each ratio in simplest form.
    a. $\frac{3}{4}$ to $\frac{1}{4}$ b. $1\frac{1}{8}$ to $\frac{3}{8}$ c. 1.2 to 2.4   d. .75 to .25   e. $6:.25$

15. Express each ratio in simplest form.
    a. 45 min. to 15 min.   b. 12 oz. to 16 oz.   c. \$75. to \$100.
    d. 100 mi. to 60 mi.   e. 50 gal. to 275 gal.   f. 15 hr. to 24 hr.

16. Express each ratio in simplest form.
    a. 80 m to 16 m   b. 75 g to 100 g   c. 36 cm to 72 cm
    d. 54 cg to 90 cg   e. 75 cl to 35 cl   f. 32 mm to 48 mm
    g. 36 ml to 63 ml   h. 150 km to 125 km   i. 54 kl to 81 kl

17. Express each ratio in simplest form.
    a. 25 cm to 1 m   b. 300 g to 1 kg   c. 30 cl to 1 l
    d. 500 g to 2 kg   e. 750 m to 3 km   f. 250 ml to 1 l
    g. 40 cm to 1.2 m   h. 50 mg to $\frac{1}{2}$ g   i. 350 m to 1.4 km

18. Express each ratio in simplest form.
    a. $1\frac{1}{2}$ hr. to $\frac{1}{2}$ hr.   b. 3 in. to $\frac{1}{2}$ in.   c. 1 ft. to 1 in.
    d. 1 yd. to 1 ft.   e. $\frac{1}{3}$ yd. to 6 in.   f. 12 oz. to 3 lb.
    g. 1 hr. to 15 min.   h. \$6 to 50 cents   i. 2 mi. to 880 yd.

19. A baseball team played 162 games and won 90.
    a. What is the ratio of the number of games won to the number of games played?
    b. For every 9 games played, how many games were won?

20. A student did 6 out of 10 problems correctly.
    a. What is the ratio of the number right to the number wrong?
    b. For every two answers that were wrong, how many answers were right?

21. A cake recipe calls for $1\frac{1}{2}$ cups of milk to $1\frac{3}{4}$ cups of flour. What is the ratio of the number of cups of milk to the number of cups of flour in this recipe?

22. The perimeter of a rectangle is 30 ft. and the width is 5 ft. Find the ratio of the length of the rectangle to its width.

23. In a freshman class there are b boys and g girls. Express the ratio of the number of boys to the total number of pupils.

24. The length of a rectangle is represented by $3x$ and its width by $2x$. Find the ratio of the width of the rectangle to its perimeter.

25. Represent in terms of x two numbers whose ratio is:
    a. 3 to 4   b. 5 to 3   c. 1 to 4   d. $1:2$ e. $3:5$

26. Represent in terms of x three numbers which have the continued ratio:
    a. 1 to 2 to 3   b. 3 to 4 to 5   c. $1:3:4$ d. $2:3:5$

2 USING A RATIO TO EXPRESS A RATE

We have learned how to use a ratio to compare two quantities that are measured in the same unit. It is also possible to compare two quantities of different types. For example, if 120 students of integrated mathematics course I are registered in 4 classes, the ratio of the number of students registered to the number of classes in course I is $\frac{120}{4}$, which is equal to 30. This tells us that the average number of students in a course I class is 30. We say that there are on the average 30 students per class. Similarly, if a plane flies 1920 kilometers in 3 hours, the ratio of the distance traveled to the time that the plane was in flight is

$$\frac{1920 \text{ kilometers}}{3 \text{ hours}} = 640 \text{ kilometers per hour.}$$ We say that the plane was

flying at the rate of 640 kilometers per hour. When the numbers in a ratio are expressed in simplest form to state a rate, we say that the rate is a ratio expressed in *lowest terms*.

| MODEL PROBLEMS |

1. Clyde Champion scored 175 points in 7 basketball games. Express, in lowest terms, the ratio of the number of points Clyde scored to the number of games Clyde played.

   Solution: ratio $= \frac{175}{7} = 25$ points per game   *Ans.*

2. There are 5 grams of salt in 100 cm^3 of a solution of salt and water. Express, in lowest terms, the ratio of the number of grams of salt to the number of cm^3 in the solution.

   Solution: ratio $= \frac{5}{100} = .05$ g per cm^3 *Ans.*

| EXERCISES |

In 1–6, express the ratio in lowest terms.

1. the ratio of 36 apples to 18 people
2. the ratio of 48 patients to 6 nurses
3. the ratio of $1.50 to 3 liters
4. the ratio of 96 cents to 16 grams
5. the ratio of 6.75 ounces to $2.25
6. the ratio of 62 miles to 100 kilometers

7. If there are 240 tennis balls in 80 cans, how many tennis balls are there in each can?
8. If an 11-ounce can of shaving cream costs 88 cents, what is the cost of each ounce of shaving cream in the can?
9. If, in traveling 31 miles, you travel 50 kilometers, how many miles are there in each kilometer?
10. In a supermarket the regular size of Cleanright cleanser contains 14 ounces and costs 49 cents. The giant size of Cleanright cleanser, which contains 20 ounces, costs 66 cents.
    a. Find, correct to the nearest tenth of a cent, the cost per ounce for the regular can.
    b. Find, correct to the nearest tenth of a cent, the cost per ounce for the giant can.
    c. Which is the better buy?
11. Sue types 1800 words in 30 minutes. Rita types 1000 words in 20 minutes. Which girl is the faster typist?
12. Ronald runs 300 meters in 40 seconds. Carlos runs 200 meters in 30 seconds. Which boy is the faster runner for short races?

3 SOLVING VERBAL PROBLEMS INVOLVING RATIOS

1. The perimeter of a triangle is 60 cm. If the sides are in the ratio $3:4:5$, find the length of each side of the triangle.

Solution: Let $3x$ = length of the first side.
Let $4x$ = length of the second side.
Let $5x$ = length of the third side.

The perimeter of the triangle is 60 cm.

$$3x + 4x + 5x = 60$$
$$12x = 60$$
$$x = 5$$
$$3x = 15$$
$$4x = 20$$
$$5x = 25$$

Check

$$15:20:25 = 3:4:5$$
$$15 + 20 + 25 = 60$$

Answer: The lengths of the sides are 15 cm, 20 cm, and 25 cm.

2. Two numbers have the ratio $2:3$. The larger is 30 more than $\frac{1}{2}$ of the smaller. Find the numbers.

Solution:

Let $2x$ = the smaller number.
Then $3x$ = the larger number.

The larger number is 30 more than $\frac{1}{2}$ of the smaller number.

$$3x = \frac{1}{2}(2x) + 30$$
$$3x = x + 30$$
$$3x - x = x + 30 - x$$
$$2x = 30$$
$$x = 15$$
$$2x = 30$$
$$3x = 45$$

Check

The ratio of 30 to 45 is $30:45$ or $2:3$. The larger number, 45, is 30 more than 15, which is $\frac{1}{2}$ of the smaller number.

Answer: The numbers are 30 and 45.

| EXERCISES |

1. Two numbers have the ratio $4:3$. Their sum is 70. Find the numbers.
2. Find two numbers whose sum is 160 and that have the ratio $5:3$.
3. Two numbers have the ratio $7:5$. Their difference is 12. Find the numbers.
4. Find two numbers whose ratio is $4:1$ and whose difference is 36.
5. A piece of wire 32 centimeters in length is divided into two parts that are in the ratio $3:5$. Find the length of each part.
6. The sides of a triangle are in the ratio of $6:6:5$. The perimeter of the triangle is 34 cm. Find the length of each side of the triangle.
7. The ratio of the number of boys in a school to the number of girls is 11 to 10. If there are 525 pupils in the school, how many of them are boys?

8. The perimeter of a triangle is 48 cm. The lengths of the sides are in the ratio $3:4:5$. Find the length of each side.

9. The ratio of the length of a rectangle to its width is $\frac{7}{2}$. If the width of the rectangle is 10 cm, find the length of the rectangle.

10. During a baseball season the ratio of the number of times that Reggie made a hit to the official number of times he went to bat was $3:10$. If Reggie had 480 official times at bat, how many hits did he have that season?

11. Miss Corliss is following a budget in which the ratio of the amount paid for rent to the total monthly income is $1:4$. If Miss Corliss earns \$1000 a month, what is her monthly rent?

12. The ratio of Carl's money to Donald's money is $7:3$. If Carl gives Donald \$20, the two then have equal amounts. Find the original amount that each one had.

13. Two numbers are in the ratio $3:7$. The larger exceeds the smaller by 12. Find the numbers.

14. Two numbers are in the ratio $3:5$. If 9 is added to their sum, the result is 41. Find the numbers.

15. In a basketball foul-shooting contest, the points made by Sam and Wilbur were in the ratio $7:9$. Wilbur made 6 more points than Sam. Find the number of points made by each.

16. A chemist wishes to make $12\frac{1}{2}$ liters of an acid solution by using water and acid in the ratio $3:2$. How many liters of each should he use?

17. The perimeter of a rectangle is 360 centimeters. If the ratio of its length to its width is $11:4$, find the dimensions of the rectangle.

18. In a triangle two sides have the same length. The ratio of each of these sides to the third side is $5:3$. If the perimeter of the triangle is 65 in., find the length of each side of the triangle.

4   PROPORTION

Since the ratio $\frac{4}{20}$ is equal to the ratio $\frac{1}{5}$, we may write $\frac{4}{20} = \frac{1}{5}$. The equation $\frac{4}{20} = \frac{1}{5}$ is called a *proportion*. A proportion is an equation that states that two ratios are equal.

Another way of writing the proportion $\frac{4}{20} = \frac{1}{5}$ is $4:20 = 1:5$. Both these equations are read "4 is to 20 as 1 is to 5."

The proportion $\frac{a}{b} = \frac{c}{d}$ $(b \neq 0, d \neq 0)$, or $a:b = c:d$, is read "a is to b as c is to d." There are four terms in this proportion, namely, a, b, c, and d. The first and fourth terms, a and d, are called the *extremes* of

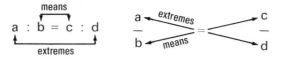

the proportion. The second and third terms, b and c, are called the *means*.

Observe that in the proportion $4:20 = 1:5$ the product of the two means, 20×1, is equal to the product of the two extremes, 4×5, because each product is 20.

In the proportion $\frac{5}{15} = \frac{10}{30}$ the product of the means, 15×10, is equal to the product of the extremes, 5×30, each product being 150.

In the proportion $\frac{a}{b} = \frac{c}{d}$ we can also show that the product of the means is equal to the product of the extremes, $ad = bc$.

Since $\frac{a}{b} = \frac{c}{d}$ is an equation, we can multiply both members by the L.C.D., bd, as follows:

$$\frac{a}{b} = \frac{c}{d}$$

$$bd\left(\frac{a}{b}\right) = bd\left(\frac{c}{d}\right)$$

$$bd\left(a \cdot \frac{1}{b}\right) = bd\left(c \cdot \frac{1}{d}\right)$$

$$\left(b \cdot \frac{1}{b}\right)(a \cdot d) = \left(d \cdot \frac{1}{d}\right)(bc) \quad \text{(Commutative}$$

$$\qquad\qquad\qquad\qquad\qquad\qquad\text{and associative}$$

$$1 \cdot (ad) = 1 \cdot (bc) \qquad \text{properties)}$$

$$ad = bc$$

Therefore, we have shown that the following statement is always true:

■ In a proportion the product of the means is equal to the product of the extremes.

If a sentence states that two ratios are equal, then:

1. When the product of the first and fourth terms is equal to the product of the second and third terms, the sentence is *true* and we have a *true proportion*.

2. When the product of the first and fourth terms is *not* equal to the product of the second and third terms, the sentence is *false* and we do *not* have a true proportion.

MODEL PROBLEMS

1. Tell whether $\frac{4}{16} = \frac{5}{20}$ is a true proportion.

Solution:

Method 1

Reduce each ratio to simplest form.

$$\frac{4}{16} = \frac{1}{4} \text{ and } \frac{5}{20} = \frac{1}{4}$$

Therefore, $\frac{4}{16}$ and $\frac{5}{20}$ are equal ratios and $\frac{4}{16} = \frac{5}{20}$ is a true proportion.

Method 2

In the equation $\frac{4}{16} = \frac{5}{20}$, the product of the second and third terms is 16×5, or 80. The product of the first and fourth terms, 4×20, is also 80. Therefore, $\frac{4}{16} = \frac{5}{20}$ is a true proportion.

Answer: Yes

2. Solve for q in the proportion $25:q = 5:2$.

Solution

If $25:q = 5:2$ is a true proportion, then $5q = 25 \times 2$ (the product of the means is equal to the product of the extremes).

$$5q = 25 \times 2$$
$$5q = 50$$
$$q = 10$$

Check

$$25:q = 5:2$$
$$25:10 \stackrel{?}{=} 5:2$$
$$5:2 = 5:2 \quad \text{(True)}$$

Answer: $q = 10$

3. Solve for x: $\dfrac{12}{x-2} = \dfrac{32}{x+8}$

Solution

$$\frac{12}{x-2} = \frac{32}{x+8}$$

In a proportion, the product of the means is equal to the product of the extremes.

$$32(x-2) = 12(x+8)$$
$$32x - 64 = 12x + 96$$
$$32x - 12x = 96 + 64$$
$$20x = 160$$
$$x = 8$$

Check

$$\frac{12}{x-2} = \frac{32}{x+8}$$
$$\frac{12}{8-2} \stackrel{?}{=} \frac{32}{8+8}$$
$$\frac{12}{6} \stackrel{?}{=} \frac{32}{16}$$
$$2 = 2 \quad \text{(True)}$$

Answer: $x = 8$

| EXERCISES |

In 1–6, state whether or not the given ratios may form a true proportion.

1. $\frac{3}{4}, \frac{30}{40}$

2. $\frac{2}{3}, \frac{10}{5}$

3. $\frac{4}{5}, \frac{16}{25}$

4. $\frac{2}{5}, \frac{5}{2}$

5. $\frac{14}{18}, \frac{28}{36}$

6. $\frac{36}{30}, \frac{18}{15}$

In 7–14, find the number that can replace the question mark and make the result a true proportion.

7. $\frac{1}{2} = \frac{?}{8}$

8. $\frac{3}{5} = \frac{18}{?}$

9. $1:4 = 6:?$

10. $4:6 = ?:42$

11. $\frac{4}{?} = \frac{12}{60}$

12. $\frac{?}{9} = \frac{35}{63}$

13. $?:60 = 6:10$

14. $16:? = 12:9$

In 15–23, solve the equation.

15. $\frac{x}{60} = \frac{3}{20}$

16. $\frac{5}{4} = \frac{x}{12}$

17. $\frac{30}{4x} = \frac{10}{24}$

18. $\frac{5}{15} = \frac{x}{x + 8}$

19. $\frac{x}{12 - x} = \frac{10}{30}$

20. $\frac{16}{8} = \frac{21 - x}{x}$

21. $12:15 = x:45$

22. $\frac{5}{x + 2} = \frac{4}{x}$

23. $\frac{3x + 3}{3} = \frac{7x - 1}{5}$

In 24–26, solve for x in terms of the other variables.

24. $a:b = c:x$

25. $2r:s = x:t$

26. $2x:m = 4r:s$

5 USING PROPORTIONS TO CONVERT UNITS OF MEASURE IN THE ENGLISH AND METRIC SYSTEMS

Most countries in the world have converted to the metric system. Some countries, like the United States, are in the process of converting from English to metric. During this period of transition we will see measurements in both systems. While it is correct to think in only one system of measurement at a time, we may face problems that involve both systems of measure.

Proportions can be used to convert units of measure from one system to another, for example, to convert miles to kilometers. The table of Metric–English equivalents shown on the next page contains only approximate measures.

Measures of Length

1 centimeter = .39 inch	1 inch = 2.54 centimeters
1 meter = 3.28 feet	1 foot = .3 meter
1 kilometer = .62 mile	1 mile = 1.6 kilometers

Measures of Weight or Mass

1 gram = .035 ounce	1 ounce = 28.35 grams
1 kilogram = 2.2 pounds	1 pound = .45 kilogram

Measures of Volume (Liquid)

1 liter = 1.06 quarts	1 quart = .95 liter
1 liter = .26 gallon	1 gallon = 3.8 liters

We will not stress extreme precision in converting from one system to another. While 1 kilometer = .62137 mile approximately, we will simply use 1 km = .62 mile, or even 1 km = .6 mile.

MODEL PROBLEM

A motorist passes a sign that says "Stratford, 40 km." His car registers distance traveled in miles, not in kilometers. How many miles will he have to travel to reach Stratford?

Solution

From the table we know that 1 kilometer = .62 mile approximately.

Let x = the number of miles in 40 kilometers.

We write a proportion to compare kilometers to miles; that is, 40 kilometers is to x miles as 1 kilometer is to .62 mile.

$$\frac{40}{x} = \frac{1}{.62} \quad \begin{array}{l}\leftarrow \text{ kilometers} \\ \leftarrow \text{ miles}\end{array}$$

Since, in a proportion, the product of the means is equal to the product of the extremes, we multiply.

$$1(x) = 40(.62)$$
$$x = 24.8$$

Answer: 40 kilometers is approximately equivalent to 24.8 miles.

Note: If we had used the equivalent of 1 kilometer = .6 mile, then $\frac{40}{x} = \frac{1}{.6}$ becomes $1x = 40(.6)$, and $x = 24$ miles. In any event, the motorist would know that the distance to Stratford is about 24 or 25 miles, a reasonable approximation.

EXERCISES

In 1–18: Find the appropriate values to use from the table of equivalent measures; set up a proportion to solve the conversion from one system to another; round off the approximate answer to the nearest whole number. (Some answers may vary slightly, depending upon the equivalent used in the proportion.)

In 1–10, convert:

1. 60 miles to kilometers
2. 45 kilometers to miles
3. 20 gallons to liters
4. 19 liters to quarts
5. 12 pounds to kilograms
6. 8 ounces to grams
7. 40 kilograms to pounds
8. 10 feet to meters
9. 30 centimeters to inches
10. 10 meters to feet
11. The speed limit in most states is 55 miles per hour. What should this speed limit be when signs are posted in kilometers per hour?
12. A subcompact car holds 10 gallons in its gasoline tank. When gasoline is sold by the liter, how many liters of gasoline will this tank hold?
13. On the average, a large family uses $2\frac{1}{2}$ gallons of milk each day. When milk is sold in metric measures only, how many liters of milk will this large family use daily?
14. How many grams are there in a one-pound loaf of bread? (Remember, 1 pound = 16 ounces.)
15. Mrs. Adasse bought a car that registers speed in kilometers per hour. She was driving at 45 kilometers per hour when she saw a sign that read "Speed Limit, 30 miles per hour." Is Mrs. Adasse driving over the speed limit? Explain your answer.
16. The blueprint of an apartment shows the living room to be 4.2 meters wide and 5.1 meters long. Miss Bagley has a rug that measures 12 feet by 15 feet. Will the rug fit into the living room? Explain your answer.
17. Grandma always cooks a 22-pound turkey when the family gathers together on Thanksgiving Day. What size turkey should she buy when meat is weighed in kilograms only?
18. Carissa Sue Jones is 5 ft. 2 in. tall and weighs 105 pounds. a. What is her height in centimeters? b. What is her weight in kilograms?

6 SOLVING VERBAL PROBLEMS BY USING PROPORTIONS

MODEL PROBLEM

There are about 90 calories in 20 grams of a cheese. Reggie ate 70 grams of this cheese. About how many calories were there in the cheese she ate?

Solution

Let x = the number of calories in 70 grams of cheese.

$$\frac{x}{70} = \frac{90}{20} \quad \begin{array}{l} \leftarrow \text{ number of calories} \\ \leftarrow \text{ number of grams of cheese} \end{array}$$

In a proportion the product of the means is equal to the product of the extremes.

$$
\begin{aligned}
20x &= 90(70) \\
20x &= 6300 \\
x &= 315
\end{aligned}
$$

Check

$$\frac{315}{70} \overset{?}{=} \frac{90}{20}$$

$$\frac{9}{2} = \frac{9}{2} \quad \text{(True)}$$

Answer: 315 calories

EXERCISES

Solve each of the following problems algebraically.

1. If 3 pounds of apples cost $.89, what is the cost of 15 pounds of apples at the same rate?
2. If 4 tickets to a show cost $17.60, what is the cost of 7 such tickets?
3. If 2 pounds of chopped meat sell for $3.50, how much chopped meat can be bought for $8.75?
4. Willis scores an average of 7 foul shots out of every 10 attempts. At the same rate, how many shots would he score in 200 attempts?
5. There are about 60 calories in 30 grams of canned salmon. About how many calories are there in a 210-gram can?
6. There are 81 calories in a slice of bread that weighs 30 grams. How many calories are there in a package of this bread that weighs 600 grams?

7. There are about 17 calories in three medium shelled peanuts. Joan ate 30 such peanuts. How many calories were there in the peanuts she ate?

8. A train traveled 90 miles in $1\frac{1}{2}$ hours. At the same rate, how long will it take the train to travel 330 miles?

9. The weight of 20 meters of copper wire is .9 kilogram. Find the weight of 170 meters of the same wire.

10. A recipe calls for $1\frac{1}{2}$ cups of sugar for a 3-pound cake. How many cups of sugar should be used for a 5-pound cake?

11. If a 7.5-pound breast of veal sells for $11.25, how much should Mr. Daniels pay for a 5.5-pound breast of veal?

12. A house that is assessed for $12,000 pays $960 in realty taxes. What should be the realty tax on a house that is assessed for $16,500?

13. The scale on a map is: 5 cm represents 3.5 km. How far apart are two towns if the distance between these two towns on the map is 8 cm?

14. David received $8.75 in dividends on 25 shares of a stock. How much should Marie receive in dividends on 60 shares of the same stock?

15. A picture $3\frac{1}{4}$ inches long and $2\frac{1}{8}$ inches wide is to be enlarged so that its length will become $6\frac{1}{2}$ inches. What will be the width of the enlarged picture?

16. In a certain concrete mixture, the ratio of cement to sand is $1:4$. How many bags of cement would be used with 100 bags of sand?

17. If a man can buy p kilograms of candy for d dollars, represent the cost of n kilograms of this candy.

18. If a family consumes q liters of milk in d days, represent the amount of milk consumed in h days.

chapter eleven

Geometry

1 POINTS, LINES, PLANES, AND SPACE
Undefined Terms

We ordinarily define a word by using a simpler term. The simpler term can be defined by using one or more still simpler terms. But this process cannot go on endlessly. There comes a time when the definition must use a term whose meaning is *assumed* to be clear to all people. Because the meaning is accepted without definition, such a term is called an ***undefined term***.

In geometry we are concerned with such ideas as *point*, *line*, and *plane*. Since we cannot give a satisfactory definition of these words using simpler defined words, we will consider them as *undefined terms*.

Although point, line, and plane are undefined words, we must have a clear understanding of what they mean. Knowing the properties and characteristics they possess helps us to do this.

1. The word "point" is often used to mean "place" or "position." In geometry a *point* is merely an idea. It has no length, no width, no thickness—only position. A point is represented by a small dot, and named by a capital letter. The point (at the right) is called "point P."

P
•

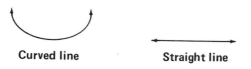

Curved line   Straight line

2. A *line* may be considered as a set of points. The set of points that is chosen may form a curved line or it may form a straight line as shown in the figure. If the set of points can be arranged along the edge of a ruler, the points form a straight line. Unless it is otherwise stated, the term *line* will mean *straight line*.

We can also think of a line as an infinite set of points that extends endlessly in both directions. Arrowheads are sometimes used in a geometric drawing that represents a line to emphasize the fact that there are no endpoints.

To name a line, we usually use two capital letters, which name two points on the line. The line pictured at the right may be named "line AB," written as $\overleftrightarrow{AB}$. It may also be named "line AC" or "line BC," written as $\overleftrightarrow{AC}$ or $\overleftrightarrow{BC}$.

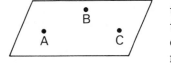 A line may also be named by placing a single small letter above it. The line at the left is called "line m."

3. A *plane* is a special set of points that forms a flat surface that extends in all directions without end. The figure at the right represents a plane, called "plane P." Actually, we have pictured only part of a plane because a plane has no boundaries.

A plane may also be named by using letters that name three points in the plane, provided that the points are not on the same line. For example, the plane pictured at the left may be named "plane ABC."

Now, making use of these undefined terms, we will define additional terms that we will use in our study of geometry.

Line Segment

A *line segment* or *segment* is a part of a line consisting of two endpoints and all points on the line between these endpoints.

At the right is pictured a line segment whose endpoints are points R and S. We use these endpoints to name this segment "segment RS," which may be written as $\overline{RS}$.

A line segment may also be named by placing a single small letter above it. The segment at the left is called "segment a."

Ray

A *ray* is a part of a line that consists of a point on the line, called an *endpoint*, and all the points on one side of the endpoint. To name a ray we use two capital letters and an arrow with one arrowhead. The first letter must be the letter that names the endpoint. The second letter may be the name of any other point on the ray.

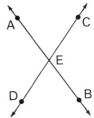

In the figure at the right the ray is named "ray AB," which is represented in symbols by $\overrightarrow{AB}$.

Any point on a line is the common endpoint of two different rays, which are called *opposite rays*. In the figure at the left $\overrightarrow{PS}$ and $\overrightarrow{PR}$ are called opposite rays.

Facts About Straight Lines

A statement that is accepted as true without proof is called an *axiom* or a *postulate*. We see examples of postulates in three statements about straight lines. If you examine the three figures pictured below, you will see that it is reasonable to accept the following three statements as postulates:

1. **In a plane an infinite number of straight lines can be drawn through a given point.**

2. **One and only one straight line can be drawn that contains two given points.** (We say that two points determine a straight line.)

3. **Two different straight lines can intersect in only one point.**

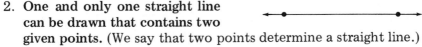

Operations Involving Sets

The *intersection* of two sets of points is the set of all points that belongs to both of those sets of points. For example, the intersection of the set of points contained in line AB and the set of points contained in line CD is the set that has one element, point E. We can write $\overleftrightarrow{AB} \cap \overleftrightarrow{CD} = \{E\}$.

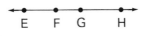

Since the intersection of segment EG and segment FH is segment FG, we can write $\overline{EG} \cap \overline{FH} = \overline{FG}$.

The *union* of two sets of points is the set of points that belongs to either or both of those sets of points. For example, the union of ray AB and ray AC is line BC. Hence, we can write $\overrightarrow{AB} \cup \overrightarrow{AC} = \overleftrightarrow{BC}$.

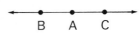

Since the union of segment EG and segment FH is segment EH, we can write $\overline{EG} \cup \overline{FH} = \overline{EH}$.

EXERCISES

In 1–5, write the meaning of the symbol.

1. $\overleftrightarrow{LM}$ 2. $\overline{LM}$ 3. $\overrightarrow{LM}$ 4. $\overrightarrow{RS}$ 5. $\overrightarrow{SR}$

In 6–14, use the following figure:

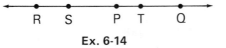

Ex. 6-14

6. Name two points on the same side of P.
7. Name two points on opposite sides of S.
8. Name the segment determined by point R and point Q.
9. Name two segments indicated on the line.
10. Name two rays each of which has point T as an endpoint.
11. Name the opposite ray of $\overrightarrow{TQ}$.
12. Does $\overrightarrow{ST}$ represent the same ray as $\overrightarrow{TS}$? Why?
13. Is $\overrightarrow{ST}$ the opposite ray of $\overrightarrow{TS}$? Why?
14. Is point R in $\overrightarrow{SP}$?

15. State the number of endpoints that there are for
    (a) a line segment   (b) a ray   (c) a line

In 16–27, name the set that is the result obtained when the indicated operation is performed on the two given sets.

16. $\overleftrightarrow{GC} \cap \overleftrightarrow{JE}$ 17. $\overline{HE} \cap \overline{JA}$

18. $\overline{JH} \cap \overrightarrow{HE}$ 19. $\overrightarrow{DJ} \cap \overline{HE}$

20. $\overline{AG} \cap \overline{AF}$ 21. $\overline{AG} \cap \overrightarrow{AF}$

22. $\overrightarrow{AD} \cup \overrightarrow{AJ}$ 23. $\overline{AB} \cup \overline{AG}$

24. $\overline{DJ} \cup \overline{HE}$ 25. $\overline{GA} \cup \overline{FC}$

26. $\overline{AG} \cup \overline{AF}$ 27. $\overrightarrow{AG} \cap \overrightarrow{GA}$

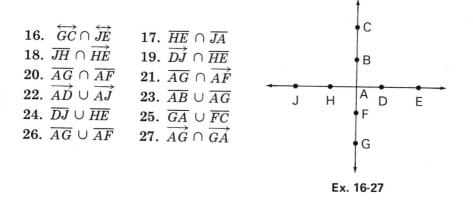

Ex. 16-27

In 28–34, tell whether the statement is always, sometimes, or never true.

28. The intersection of two lines is a segment.
29. The union of two segments is a segment.
30. The union of two rays that have the same endpoint is a line.
31. The union of two opposite rays is a line.
32. A segment is a subset of a line.
33. A line is a subset of a ray.   34. Two points determine a line.

2 ANGLES, ANGLE MEASURES, AND PERPENDICULARITY

An *angle* is a set of points which is the union of two rays having the same endpoint.

In the illustration, rays $\overrightarrow{AB}$ and $\overrightarrow{AC}$, which form an angle, are called the *sides* of the angle. A, the endpoint of each ray, is called the *vertex* of the angle. The symbol for angle is $\angle$ (plural, $\angle$s). The plural of vertex is *vertices*, as in the three vertices of a triangle.

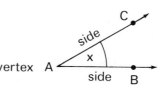

An angle, such as the one illustrated here, may be named in any of the following ways:

1. By a capital letter, which names its vertex. For example, $\angle A$.
2. By a lower case letter or by a number placed inside the angle. For example, $\angle x$.
3. By three capital letters, one naming the vertex of the angle and the others naming points on the two sides of the angle. The letter at the

vertex of the angle is always the middle letter. For example, $\angle BAC$ or $\angle CAB$.

In the figure at the right, we can think of $\angle TOS$ as having been formed by rotating $\overrightarrow{OT}$. If $\overrightarrow{OT}$ is rotated in a counterclockwise direction about vertex O, it will assume the position $\overrightarrow{OS}$, forming $\angle TOS$.

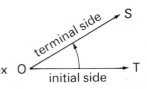

Measuring Angles

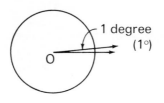

To measure an angle means to determine the number of units of measure it contains. A common standard unit of measure of an angle is a degree, written as $1°$. A degree is $\frac{1}{360}$ of a complete rotation of a ray about a point. Thus a complete rotation contains 360 degrees, written as $360°$.

The *protractor* is an instrument used to measure angles. Study the protractor shown here.

The two scales on the protractor show divisions starting at $0°$ and going up to $180°$. One scale starts at $0°$ at the right and continues around to $180°$ at the left. The other scale starts at $0°$ at the left and continues around to $180°$ at the right. These two scales make it convenient to measure an angle easily, regardless of its position.

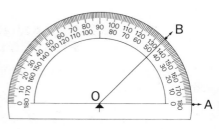

To measure an angle, place the center of the protractor on the vertex of the angle. At the same time let one side of the angle cut across $0°$ on one of the scales. The measure of the angle is read at the point where the second side of the angle cuts across the scale being used. If the sides of the angle do not reach the scale, extend them until they do.

In measuring angle AOB in the illustration, place the protractor so that side $\overrightarrow{OA}$ passes through the $0°$ reading on the inner scale. Side $\overrightarrow{OB}$ cuts across this scale at a point marked $45°$. Therefore, angle AOB contains $45°$. We will also say $m\angle AOB = 45°$, which is read "The measure of angle AOB is 45 degrees."

Types of Angles

Angles are classified according to their measures.

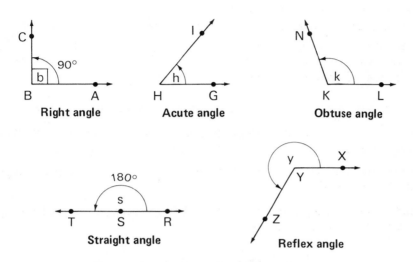

A *right angle* is an angle whose measure is 90°. $\angle ABC$ pictures a right angle. Hence, we can say that m$\angle ABC = 90°$, or m$\angle b = 90°$. Note that the symbol ⌐ at B is used to show that $\angle ABC$ is a right angle.

An *acute angle* is an angle whose measure is greater than 0° and less than 90°. That is, its measure is between 0° and 90°. $\angle GHI$ pictures an acute angle. Hence, $0° < $ m$\angle h < 90°$.

An *obtuse angle* is an angle whose measure is greater than 90° and less than 180°. That is, its measure is between 90° and 180°. $\angle LKN$ pictures an obtuse angle. Hence, $90° < $ m$\angle k < 180°$.

A *straight angle* is an angle whose measure is 180°. $\angle RST$ pictures a straight angle. Hence, m$\angle RST = 180°$, or m$\angle s = 180°$.

A *reflex angle* is an angle whose measure is greater than 180° and less than 360°. That is, its measure is between 180° and 360°. Hence, $180° < $ m$\angle y < 360°$.

Perpendicularity

Two lines are *perpendicular* if and only if the two lines or parts of the lines intersect to form right angles. The symbol for perpendicular is "⊥".

In the figures at the right $\overleftrightarrow{PR}$ is perpendicular to $\overleftrightarrow{AB}$, symbolized $\overleftrightarrow{PR} \perp \overleftrightarrow{AB}$. Also, segment PR is perpendicular to line AB, symbolized $\overline{PR} \perp \overleftrightarrow{AB}$. The symbol "⌐" is used to show that the lines indicated are perpendicular.

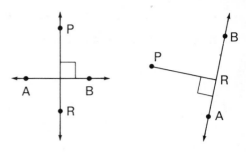

We can now realize the following truths about angles:

1. The measure of an angle depends only upon the amount of rotation, not upon the pictured lengths of the rays forming the angle.

2. Since every right angle measures 90°, we can say that all right angles are equal in measure.

3. Since every straight angle measures 180°, we can say that all straight angles are equal in measure.

Drawing Angles

The protractor is used not only for measuring angles, but also for drawing them. Let us draw an angle whose measure is 65°. (See the figure at the right.)

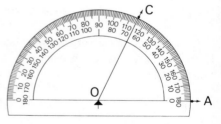

Draw a line and name it $\overleftrightarrow{OA}$. Place the protractor so that its center is at O and the zero on one of its scales lies on $\overrightarrow{OA}$. Place a point C next to the number 65 on that scale. Remove the protractor and draw $\overrightarrow{OC}$ from point O through the point C. The measure of angle AOC is 65°.

EXERCISES

In 1–9: a. Use a protractor to measure the angle. b. State what kind of angle it is.

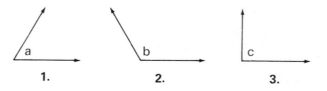

1.   2.   3.

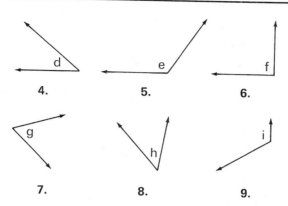

In 10–21, use a protractor to draw an angle whose measure is:

10. 30° **11.** 80° **12.** 90° **13.** 65° **14.** 48° **15.** 24°
16. 120° **17.** 150° **18.** 180° **19.** 115° **20.** 96° **21.** 138°

22. What kind of angle is each angle of a rectangle?
23. Use angle measures to help you name the following types of angles in order, starting with the smallest angle first: right angle, obtuse angle, acute angle, reflex angle, straight angle.

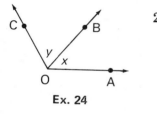

Ex. 24

24. Using the figure at the left:
  a. Name angle x, using three capital letters.
  b. Give the shorter name for angle COB.
  c. Name one acute angle.
  d. Name one obtuse angle.

25. In triangle RST, $\overline{TW}$ is perpendicular to $\overline{RS}$. Angle TWR is which of the following?
  (1) an acute angle
  (2) an obtuse angle
  (3) a right angle
  (4) a straight angle

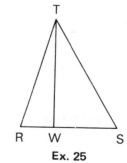

Ex. 25

26. Find the number of degrees in:
  a. $\frac{1}{2}$ of a complete rotation
  b. $\frac{1}{4}$ of a complete rotation
  c. $\frac{3}{4}$ of a complete rotation
  d. $\frac{1}{12}$ of a complete rotation
  e. $\frac{1}{3}$ of a right angle
  f. $\frac{3}{5}$ of a right angle
  g. $\frac{1}{4}$ of a straight angle
  h. $\frac{5}{6}$ of a straight angle

In 27–31, classify the angle whose measure is given as either acute, right, obtuse, straight, or reflex.

27. $135°$ **28.** $17°$ **29.** $90°$ **30.** $280°$ **31.** $180°$

In 32–41, state what part of a complete rotation the angle whose measure is given would be.

32. $60°$ **33.** $90°$ **34.** $135°$ **35.** $180°$ **36.** $225°$
37. $300°$ **38.** $25°$ **39.** $145°$ **40.** $m°$ **41.** $x°$

In 42–51, find the number of degrees in the angle formed by the hands of a clock at the given time.

42. 1 P.M.   **43.** 2 P.M.   **44.** 3 P.M.   **45.** 4 P.M.
46. 5 P.M.   **47.** 6 P.M.   **48.** 5:30 P.M.   **49.** 12:30 P.M.
50. 4:20 P.M.   **51.** 2:20 P.M.

52. Name a time when the hands of a clock form an angle of $0°$.

3 PAIRS OF ANGLES

An angle divides the points in a plane that are not on the angle into two sets of points called *regions*. One region is called the *interior of the angle*; the other is called the *exterior* of the angle as is illustrated in the figure at the right.

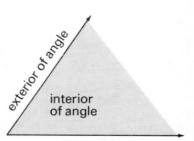

In geometry we often deal with situations that involve pairs of angles. We will now turn our attention to such pairs of angles.

Adjacent Angles

Adjacent angles are two angles in the same plane that have a common vertex and a common side but do not have any interior points in common. In the figure at the right $\angle ABC$ and $\angle CBD$ are adjacent angles.

Complementary Angles

Two angles are called *complementary angles* if and only if the sum of their measures is $90°$. Each angle is called the *complement* of the other. In the next figures, $\angle CAB$ and $\angle FDE$ are complementary angles

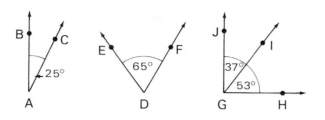

because m∠*CAB* + m∠*FDE* = 25° + 65° = 90°. Also, ∠*HGI* and ∠*IGJ* are complementary angles because m∠*HGI* + m∠*IGJ* = 53° + 37° = 90°. If an angle contains 50°, its complement contains 90° – 50°, or 40°. If an angle contains $x°$, its complement contains $(90 - x)°$.

Supplementary Angles

Two angles are called *supplementary angles* if and only if the sum of their measures is 180°. Each angle is called the *supplement* of the other. In the following figures ∠*LKM* and ∠*ONP* are supplementary angles because m∠*LKM* + m∠*ONP* = 50° + 130° = 180°. Also ∠*RQS* and ∠*SQT* are supplementary angles because m∠*RQS* + m∠*SQT* = 115° + 65° = 180°. If an angle contains 70°, its supplement contains 180° – 70°, or 110°. If an angle contains $x°$, its supplement contains $(180 - x)°$.

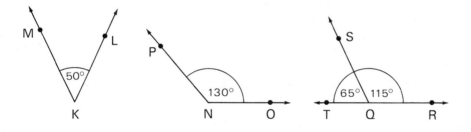

Linear Pair

Two angles are a *linear pair* if and only if they have a common side and their remaining sides are opposite rays. In the figure at the right, ∠*ABC* and ∠*CBD* share $\overrightarrow{BC}$ as a common side. The remaining sides of these angles are $\overrightarrow{BA}$ and $\overrightarrow{BD}$, opposite rays which together form the straight line $\overleftrightarrow{AD}$. Notice that the term "linear" tells us that a "line" exists.

We also observe that a linear pair can be described as two adjacent angles that are supplementary.

Vertical Angles

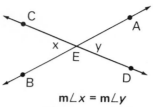

$m\angle x = m\angle y$

$m\angle CEA = m\angle BED$

If two straight lines $\overleftrightarrow{AB}$ and $\overleftrightarrow{CD}$ intersect at E, $\angle x$ and $\angle y$ are opposite each other and share a common vertex at E. They are called a pair of *vertical angles*. Two angles are *vertical angles* if and only if the sides of one angle are rays that are opposites to the sides of the second angle.

When we measure $\angle x$ and $\angle y$, we find that each angle measures $50°$. Therefore, $m\angle x = m\angle y$. Also, $\angle CEA$ and $\angle BED$ are a pair of vertical angles, each of which measures $130°$. Therefore, $m\angle CEA = m\angle BED$.

■ **When two angles have equal measure, we say the angles are congruent.**

We use the symbol "$\cong$" to represent "is congruent to." Here we would say $\angle CEA \cong \angle BED$, read as "angle CEA is congruent to angle BED." Notice the different correct ways to indicate angles with equal measures:

1. *The angle measures are equal:* $m\angle CEA = m\angle BED$ or $m\angle x = m\angle y$

2. *The angles are congruent:* $\angle CEA \cong \angle BED$ or $\angle x \cong \angle y$

It would not be correct to say that the angles are equal, or that the angle measures are congruent.

If we were to draw and measure additional pairs of vertical angles, we would find in each case that the vertical angles would be equal in measure. It appears reasonable to accept the truth of the following property of vertical angles:

■ **If two lines intersect, the vertical angles formed are equal in measure, that is, they are congruent.**

We have seen that in geometry we make use of undefined terms to develop definitions for other new terms. Similarly, in geometry we use statements whose truth we accept without proof (postulates) to develop logically or to prove the truth of other new statements called *theorems*. In this course we will deal with the procedure of proving theorems very informally. In higher-level courses, the treatment of "proof" will be on a more formal level.

We know that no matter how many examples of a given situation we consider, we cannot assume that a conclusion that we draw in these examples will always be true. We must prove the conclusion. Let us consider an informal proof of the statement:

■ If two lines intersect, the vertical angles formed are equal in measure, that is, they are congruent.

Step 1. If $\overleftrightarrow{AB}$ and $\overleftrightarrow{CD}$ intersect at E, then $\angle AEB$ is a straight angle whose measure is $180°$. Hence, $m\angle AEC + m\angle CEB = 180°$.

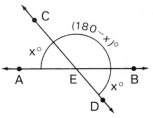

Step 2. If $m\angle AEC = x°$, then $m\angle CEB = (180 - x)°$.

Step 3. Likewise, $\angle CED$ is a straight angle whose measure is $180°$. Hence, $m\angle CEB + m\angle BED = 180°$.

Step 4. Since $m\angle CEB = (180 - x)°$, then $m\angle BED = x°$.

Step 5. Since both $m\angle AEC = x°$ and $m\angle BED = x°$, then $m\angle AEC = m\angle BED$, that is, $\angle AEC \cong \angle BED$.

MODEL PROBLEMS

1. The measure of the complement of an angle is four times the measure of the angle. Find the measure of the angle.

   Solution: Let x = the measure of the angle.
   Then $4x$ = the measure of the complement of the angle.

   The sum of the measures of an angle and its complement is 90.

   Step 1. $x + 4x = 90$

   Step 2. $5x = 90$

   Step 3. $x = 18$

   Check

   The measure of the first angle is $18°$.

   The measure of the second angle is $4(18°)$ or $72°$.

   The sum of the measures of the angles is $90°$. Hence, the angles are complementary.

   Answer: The measure of the angle is $18°$.

2. Find the measure of an angle if its measure is $40°$ more than the measure of its supplement.

   Solution: Let x = the measure of the supplement of the angle.
   Then $x + 40$ = the measure of the angle.

   The sum of the measures of an angle and its supplement is 180.

Step 1. $x + x + 40 = 180$
Step 2. $2x + 40 = 180$
Step 3. $2x = 140$
Step 4. $x = 70, x + 40 = 110$

Answer: The measure of the angle is $110°$.

| EXERCISES |

Complementary Angles

In 1–10, write the measure of the complement of the angle whose measure is given.

1. $40°$ 2. $25°$ 3. $45°$ 4. $69.5°$ 5. $87\frac{1}{3}°$
6. $m°$ 7. $d°$ 8. $(90 - y)°$ 9. $(x + 10°)$ 10. $(x - 20)°$

In 11–14, $\angle A$ and $\angle B$ are complementary. Find the measure of each angle if their measures are represented by the given expressions. Solve the problem algebraically using an equation.

11. $m\angle A = x°, m\angle B = (5x)°$ 12. $m\angle B = x°, m\angle A = (x + 50)°$
13. $m\angle A = x°, m\angle B = (x - 40)°$ 14. $m\angle B = y°, m\angle A = (2y + 30)°$

In 15–20, solve the problem algebraically using an equation.

15. Two angles are complementary. One angle is twice as large as the other. Find the number of degrees in each angle.
16. The complement of an angle is 8 times as large as the angle. Find the measure of the complement.
17. The complement of an angle is one-fifth of the measure of the angle. Find the measure of the angle.
18. The complement of an angle measures $20°$ more than the angle. Find the number of degrees in the angle.
19. Find the number of degrees in an angle that measures $8°$ less than its complement.
20. In each part find the measures of two complementary angles whose measures are in the given ratio.
    a. $1:2$ b. $1:4$ c. $8:1$ d. $2:3$ e. $5:4$ f. $3:1$ g. $3:5$

Supplementary Angles

In 21–30, write the measure of the supplement of the angle whose measure is given.

21. $40°$ 22. $69°$ 23. $90°$ 24. $110°$ 25. $167\frac{1}{2}°$

26. $m°$ **27.** $c°$ **28.** $(2y)°$ **29.** $(180 - t)°$ **30.** $(x + 40)°$

In 31–34, $\angle A$ and $\angle B$ form a linear pair. (They are supplementary.) Find the measure of each angle if their measures are represented by the given expressions. Solve the problem algebraically using an equation.

31. $m\angle A = x°$, $m\angle B = (3x)°$ **32.** $m\angle B = y°$, $m\angle A = (\frac{1}{2}y)°$

33. $m\angle A = w°$, $m\angle B = (w - 30)°$ **34.** $m\angle B = x°$, $m\angle A = (x + 80)°$

In 35–39, solve the problem algebraically using an equation.

35. Two angles are supplementary. The measure of one angle is twice as large as the measure of the other. Find the number of degrees in each angle.

36. In each part find the measures of two supplementary angles whose measures are in the given ratio.
    a. $1:3$ **b.** $1:5$ **c.** $8:1$ **d.** $3:2$ **e.** $4:5$ **f.** $7:1$ **g.** $5:3$

37. The measure of the supplement of an angle is $40°$ more than the measure of the angle. Find the number of degrees in the supplement.

38. Find the number of degrees in the measure of an angle that is $20°$ less than 4 times the measure of its supplement.

39. The difference between the measures of two supplementary angles is $80°$. Find the measure of the larger of the two angles.

40. The supplement of the complement of an acute angle is always (1) an acute angle (2) a right angle (3) an obtuse angle (4) a straight angle.

Vertical Angles

In 41–45, $\overleftrightarrow{AB}$ and $\overleftrightarrow{CD}$ intersect at E. Find the measure of angle BEC when angle AED measures:

41. $30°$ **42.** $65°$ **43.** $90°$ **44.** $128.4°$ **45.** $175\frac{1}{2}°$

In 46–48, $\overleftrightarrow{MN}$ and $\overleftrightarrow{RS}$ intersect at T.

46. If $m\angle RTM = (5x)°$ and $m\angle NTS = (3x + 10)°$, find the number of degrees contained in $\angle RTM$.

47. If $m\angle MTS = (4x - 60)°$ and $m\angle NTR = (2x)°$, find the number of degrees contained in $\angle MTS$.

48. If $m\angle RTM = (7x + 16)°$ and $m\angle NTS = (3x + 48)°$, find the number of degrees contained in $\angle NTS$.

Miscellaneous

In 49–56, based on the given conditions, find the measure of each angle named.

49. Given: $\overleftrightarrow{EF} \perp \overrightarrow{GH}$;
m$\angle EGI = 62°$.

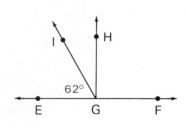

Find: m$\angle FGH$; m$\angle HGI$.

50. Given: $\overleftrightarrow{JK} \perp \overline{LM}$; $\overleftrightarrow{NLO}$ is a line; m$\angle NLM = 48°$.

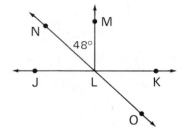

Find: m$\angle JLN$; m$\angle MLK$; m$\angle KLO$; m$\angle JLO$.

51. Given: $\angle GKH$ and $\angle HKI$ are a linear pair; $\overrightarrow{KH} \perp \overrightarrow{KJ}$; m$\angle IKJ = 34°$.

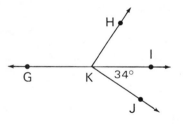

Find: m$\angle HKI$; m$\angle HKG$; m$\angle GKJ$.

52. Given: $\overrightarrow{MO} \perp \overrightarrow{MP}$; $\overleftrightarrow{LMN}$ is a line; m$\angle PMN = 40°$.

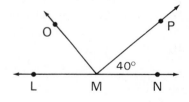

Find: m$\angle PMO$; m$\angle OML$.

53. Given: $\overleftrightarrow{RST} \perp \overrightarrow{SQ}$;
m$\angle RSU = 89°$.

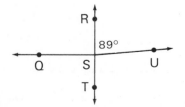

Find: m$\angle RSQ$; m$\angle QST$; m$\angle TSU$.

54. Given: lines $\overleftrightarrow{VWX}$ and $\overleftrightarrow{YWZ}$;
m$\angle VWZ = 89°$.

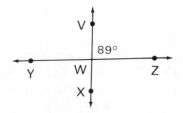

Find: m$\angle VWY$; m$\angle YWX$; m$\angle XWZ$.

55. Given: $\angle ABE$ and $\angle EBC$ form a linear pair; m$\angle EBC$ = 40°; $\angle ABD \cong \angle DBE$.

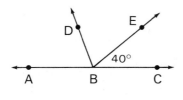

Find: m$\angle ABD$; m$\angle DBE$.

56. Given: $\overleftrightarrow{FI}$ intersects $\overleftrightarrow{JH}$ at K; m$\angle HKI$ = 40°; $\angle FKG \cong$ $\angle FKJ$.

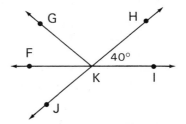

Find: m$\angle FKJ$; m$\angle FKG$; m$\angle GKH$; m$\angle JKI$.

57. Given: $\overleftrightarrow{AB}$ intersects $\overleftrightarrow{CD}$ at E; m$\angle AED$ = 20°. (Sketch and label the diagram.)
    Find: m$\angle CEB$; m$\angle BED$; m$\angle CEA$.

58. Given: $\angle PQR$ and $\angle RQS$ are complementary; m$\angle PQR$ = 30°; $\overleftrightarrow{RQT}$ is a line. (Sketch and label the diagram.)
    Find: m$\angle RQS$; m$\angle SQT$; m$\angle PQT$.

4 ANGLES AND PARALLEL LINES

We have studied situations involving intersecting lines that lie in the same plane. Not all lines in the same plane intersect. Two or more lines are called *parallel lines* if and only if the lines lie in the same plane and do not intersect.

In the figures at the right, $\overleftrightarrow{AB}$ and $\overleftrightarrow{CD}$ lie in the same plane and do not intersect. Hence, we say that $\overleftrightarrow{AB}$ is parallel to $\overleftrightarrow{CD}$. Using the symbol "∥" for "is parallel to," we write $\overleftrightarrow{AB} \parallel \overleftrightarrow{CD}$. When we speak of two parallel lines, we will mean two *distinct* lines. In higher courses we will see that a line is parallel to itself.

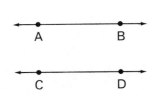

In the definition, "parallel lines are two or more lines that lie in the same plane and do not intersect," the word *lines* means straight lines of unlimited extent. We say that line segments and rays are parallel if the lines that contain them are parallel.

Observe that if two lines such as $\overleftrightarrow{AB}$ and $\overleftrightarrow{CD}$ lie in the same plane, they must be either intersecting lines or parallel lines as shown in the following figures.

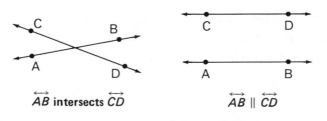

$\overleftrightarrow{AB}$ intersects $\overleftrightarrow{CD}$ $\overleftrightarrow{AB} \parallel \overleftrightarrow{CD}$

Notice that when two lines such as $\overleftrightarrow{AB}$ and $\overleftrightarrow{CD}$ are parallel, they have no points in common. Hence, the intersection set of $\overleftrightarrow{AB}$ and $\overleftrightarrow{CD}$ is the empty set symbolized as $\overleftrightarrow{AB} \cap \overleftrightarrow{CD} = \emptyset$.

When two lines are cut by a third line, called a *transversal*, two sets of angles, each containing four angles, are formed.

Angles 3, 4, 5, 6 are called *interior angles*.

Angles 1, 2, 7, 8 are called *exterior angles*.

Angles 4 and 5, which are interior angles on opposite sides of the transversal and do not have the same vertex, are called *alternate interior angles*. Angles 3 and 6 are another pair of alternate interior angles.

Angles 1 and 8, which are exterior angles on opposite sides of the transversal and do not have the same vertex, are called *alternate exterior angles*. Angles 2 and 7 are another pair of alternate exterior angles.

Angles 4 and 6 are *interior angles on the same side of the transversal*. Angles 3 and 5 are another pair of interior angles on the same side of the transversal.

Angles 1 and 5, one of which is an exterior angle and the other of which is an interior angle, both being on the same side of the transversal, are called *corresponding angles*. Other pairs of corresponding angles are 2 and 6, 3 and 7, 4 and 8.

Alternate Interior Angles and Parallel Lines

In the figure at the right we see a transversal that intersects two parallel lines forming a pair of alternate interior angles, $\angle 3$ and $\angle 6$.

If we measure $\angle 3$ and $\angle 6$ with a protractor, we will find each angle measures 60°. Hence, alternate interior angles 3 and 6 have equal measures, and $\angle 3 \cong \angle 6$. If we draw other pairs

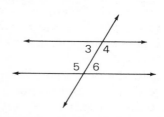

of parallel lines intersected by tranversals, we would find again that pairs of alternate interior angles have equal measures. Try it for yourself. Yet, we would be hard pressed to prove that this is *always* true. Hence we will accept, without proof, the following postulate:

■ If two parallel lines are cut by a transversal, then the alternate interior angles that are formed have equal measures, that is, they are congruent.

Note that ∠4 and ∠5 are another pair of alternate interior angles. Hence, ∠4 ≅ ∠5.

Corresponding Angles and Parallel Lines

If two parallel lines are cut by a transversal, we form many pairs of corresponding angles. One such pair of corresponding angles is ∠2 and ∠6, as shown in the figure at the right. Would these angles have equal measures? We could perform experiments and arrive at the conclusion, "yes." However, it is not necessary to do this because we are now ready to prove this conclusion in an informal manner.

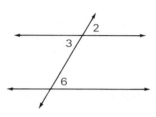

Step 1. Let $m\angle 2 = x°$.

Step 2. If $m\angle 2 = x°$, then $m\angle 3 = x°$ (because ∠2 and ∠3 are vertical angles, which we have previously shown must have equal measures).

Step 3. If $m\angle 3 = x°$, then $m\angle 6 = x°$ (because ∠3 and ∠6 are alternate interior angles of parallel lines, and we have just accepted the postulate that they have the same measure).

Step 4. Therefore $m\angle 2 = m\angle 6$ (because both angles have a measure of $x°$).

Hence we have proved informally the following theorem:

■ If two parallel lines are cut by a transversal, then the corresponding angles formed have equal measures, that is, they are congruent.

Note that this theorem is true for all pairs of corresponding angles: ∠1 ≅ ∠5; ∠2 ≅ ∠6; ∠3 ≅ ∠7; ∠4 ≅ ∠8.

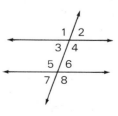

Alternate Exterior Angles and Parallel Lines

If two parallel lines are cut by a transversal, we can prove informally that the alternate exterior angles formed have equal measures. One such pair of alternate exterior angles is $\angle 2$ and $\angle 7$, as shown in the figure at the right.

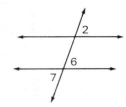

Step 1. Let $m\angle 2 = x°$.

Step 2. If $m\angle 2 = x°$, then $m\angle 6 = x°$ (because $\angle 2$ and $\angle 6$ are corresponding angles of parallel lines, proven to have the same measure).

Step 3. If $m\angle 6 = x°$, then $m\angle 7 = x°$ (because $\angle 6$ and $\angle 7$ are vertical angles, previously proven to have the same measure).

Step 4. Therefore $m\angle 2 = m\angle 7$ (because both angles have a measure of $x°$).

Hence we have proven informally the theorem:

■ If two parallel lines are cut by a transversal, then the alternate exterior angles formed have equal measures, that is, they are congruent.

Note that this theorem is true for all pairs of alternate exterior angles: $\angle 1 \cong \angle 8$; $\angle 2 \cong \angle 7$.

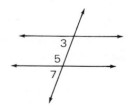

Interior Angles on the Same Side of the Transversal

When two parallel lines are cut by a transversal, we can prove informally that the sum of the measures of the interior angles on the same side of the transversal will be $180°$. One such pair of interior angles on the same side of the transversal is $\angle 3$ and $\angle 5$, as shown in the figure at the right.

Step 1. $m\angle 5 + m\angle 7 = 180°$ ($\angle 5$ and $\angle 7$ are supplementary angles).

Step 2. $m\angle 7 = m\angle 3$ ($\angle 7$ and $\angle 3$ are corresponding angles).

Step 3. $m\angle 5 + m\angle 3 = 180°$ (by substituting $m\angle 3$ for $m\angle 7$).

Hence we have proven informally the theorem:

■ **If two parallel lines are cut by a transversal, then the sum of the measures of the interior angles on the same side of the transversal is 180°.**

| MODEL PROBLEM |

In the figure the parallel lines are cut by a transversal. If $m\angle 1 = (5x - 10)°$ and $m\angle 2 = (3x + 60)°$, find the measures of $\angle 1$ and $\angle 2$.

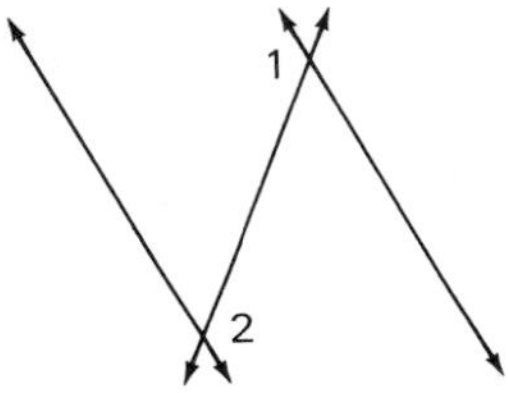

Solution

(1) Since the lines are parallel, the alternate interior angles, $\angle 1$ and $\angle 2$, have equal measures.

(2) Hence: $5x - 10 = 3x + 60$
(3) A_{10} $5x = 3x + 70$
(4) S_{3x} $2x = 70$
(5) D_2 $x = 35$

(6) Substitute: $5x - 10 = 5(35) - 10 = 175 - 10 = 165$
                $3x + 60 = 3(35) + 60 = 105 + 60 = 165$

Answer: $m\angle 1 = 165°$ and $m\angle 2 = 165°$.

| EXERCISES |

In 1–5, the figure at the right shows two parallel lines cut by a transversal. **a.** In each exercise find the measure of the remaining seven angles. **b.** Explain how you arrived at your answer.

1. $m\angle 3 = 80°$ 2. $m\angle 6 = 150°$
3. $m\angle 5 = 60°$ 4. $m\angle 1 = 75°$
5. $m\angle 3 = 65°$

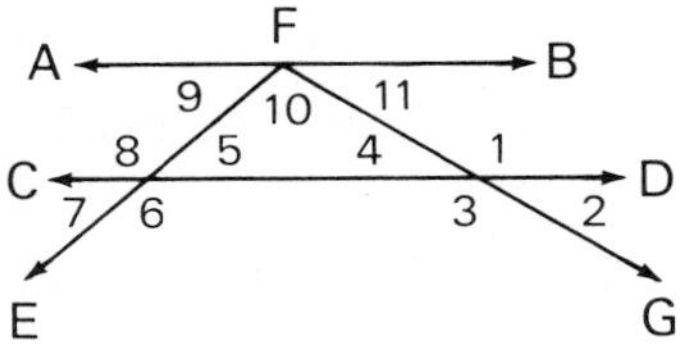

Ex. 1-5

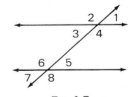

6. If $\overleftrightarrow{AB} \parallel \overleftrightarrow{CD}$, $m\angle 5 = 40°$, and $m\angle 4 = 30°$, find the measures of the remaining angles in the figure.

Ex. 6

In 7–12, the figure at the right shows two parallel lines cut by a transversal. In each exercise find the measures of all eight angles under the given conditions.

7. $m\angle 3 = (2x + 40)°$ and $m\angle 7 = (3x + 20)°$
8. $m\angle 4 = (4x - 10)°$ and $m\angle 6 = (x + 80)°$
9. $m\angle 4 = (3x + 40)°$ and $m\angle 5 = (2x)°$
10. $m\angle 3 = (2x - 10)°$ and $m\angle 1 = (x + 60)°$
11. $\angle 8 \cong \angle 3$
12. the ratio of $m\angle 3$ to $m\angle 6$ is $1:2$

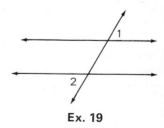

Ex. 7-12

In 13–18, tell whether the statement is always, sometimes, or never true.

13. If two distinct lines intersect, then they are parallel.
14. If two distinct lines do not intersect, then they are parallel.
15. If two angles are alternate interior angles, then they are on opposite sides of the transversal.
16. If two parallel lines are cut by a transversal, then the alternate interior angles are congruent.
17. If two parallel lines are cut by a transversal, then the alternate interior angles are complementary.
18. If two parallel lines are cut by a transversal, then the corresponding angles are supplementary.

19. In the figure at the right, two parallel lines are cut by a transversal. Write an informal proof that demonstrates that $\angle 1$ and $\angle 2$ have equal measures.

Ex. 19

5 GEOMETRIC FIGURES

Any set of points is a *geometric figure*. A geometric figure may be a set of one point or a set of many points.

Plane geometric figures are figures all of whose points are in the same plane. Plane geometric figures can be pictured on a flat surface.

Curves

If a picture of a set of points can be drawn without removing the pencil from the paper, the figure is called a *curve*. A curve that starts and ends at the same point is called a *closed curve*. Among the eight curves pictured at the right only curves (5), (6), (7), and (8) are closed curves. Observe that curves (7) and (8) cross themselves; curves (5) and (6) do not cross themselves. Closed curves that do not cross themselves are called *simple closed curves*.

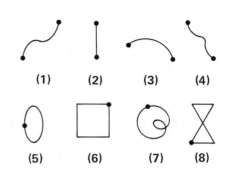

(1)   (2)   (3)   (4)

(5)   (6)   (7)   (8)

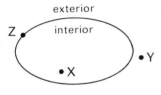

As shown in the figure at the left, a simple closed plane curve divides the plane into three sets of points:

1. The set of points *inside* the curve is called the *interior region*. For example, point X is in the interior of the curve.

2. The set of points *outside* the curve is called the *exterior region*. For example, point Y is in the exterior of the curve.

3. The set of points that are *in* the curve is called the *boundary* between the interior and the exterior. For example, point Z is in the boundary of the curve.

Polygons

A *polygon* is a simple closed plane curve that consists of line segments. We say that it is the union of line segments. In a polygon each line segment is called a *side* of the polygon. A common endpoint of two line segments is called a *vertex* of the polygon. We can name a polygon by naming each vertex with a capital letter. In the figure at the right, the polygon is named RST. Its sides are the line segments $\overline{RS}$, $\overline{ST}$, and $\overline{TR}$. Its vertices are R, S, and T.

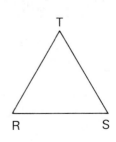

As shown in the following figures, polygons are classified according to the number of sides.

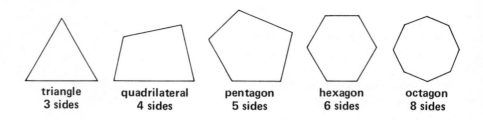

| triangle | quadrilateral | pentagon | hexagon | octagon |
| 3 sides | 4 sides | 5 sides | 6 sides | 8 sides |

A *regular polygon* is a polygon in which all of the sides have equal measures, that is, it is equilateral; and all of its angles have equal measures, that is, it is equiangular. For example, in the figures pictured above, the triangle, the hexagon, and the octagon are regular polygons; the quadrilateral and the pentagon are not regular polygons. Of course, there are regular pentagons and regular quadrilaterals. For example, a square is a regular quadrilateral.

Previously we said that two angles are congruent (≅) if their measures are equal. Similarly we say that two line segments are congruent (≅) if their measures are equal. Hence we can say that in a regular polygon all the sides are congruent and all the angles are congruent.

Notice the commonly accepted ways to indicate that two distinct line segments such as $\overline{AB}$ and $\overline{CD}$ have equal measures:

1. *The line segments are congruent:* $\overline{AB} \cong \overline{CD}$

2. *The measures of the segments are equal:* $AB = CD$

3. *The distances are equal:* $AB = CD$

It is correct to say that $m\overline{AB} = m\overline{CD}$, but this symbolism is cumbersome. It is not correct to say that line segments $\overline{AB}$ and $\overline{CD}$ are equal.

EXERCISES

1. Which of the figures pictured are (a) closed curves (b) simple closed curves?

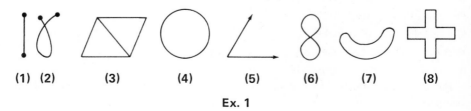

(1) (2)   (3)   (4)   (5)   (6)   (7)   (8)

Ex. 1

2. In the figure:

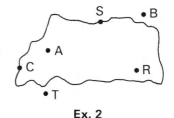

a. Name the points in the curve.
b. Name the points in the interior of the curve.
c. Name the points in the exterior of the curve.

Ex. 2

3. Which of the figures represent (a) polygons (b) a triangle (c) a quadrilateral (d) a pentagon (e) a hexagon (f) an octagon?

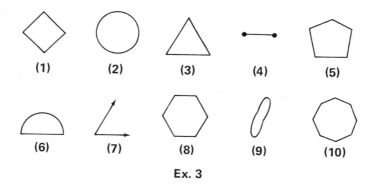

Ex. 3

4. Tell the number of sides each of the following polygons has:
   a. hexagon   b. quadrilateral   c. triangle   d. octagon   e. pentagon
5. Each of the following is shaped like a geometric plane figure. Name the figure.
   a. a door   b. a baseball diamond   c. a snowflake   d. a dollar bill
   e. the cells of a honeycomb   f. a newspaper page   g. a kite

6 THE TRIANGLE

We have seen that *two points determine a straight line*.

Now think of three points, not all on the same line. What do these three points determine? If you said "a triangle," you are correct; but there is a better answer to this question: *Three points, not all on the same line, determine a plane*. We will begin our study of polygons with a study of the triangle, which is the simplest polygon in a plane.

On a practical side, there are many uses of the triangle, especially in construction work such as the building of bridges, radio towers, and airplane wings because the triangle is a *rigid figure*. The shape of the triangle cannot be changed without changing the length of at least one of its sides.

Let us begin our study of the triangle by considering triangle ABC. The symbol for triangle ABC is $\triangle ABC$. In triangle ABC the points A, B, and C are the *vertices* of the triangle. Line segments $\overline{AB}$, $\overline{BC}$, and $\overline{CA}$ are the *sides* of the triangle. $\angle A$, $\angle B$, and $\angle C$ are the *angles* of the triangle.

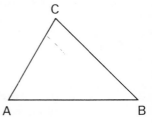

We make the following observations:

1. side $\overline{AB}$ is included between $\angle A$ and $\angle B$.
2. side $\overline{BC}$ is included between $\angle B$ and $\angle C$.
3. side $\overline{CA}$ is included between $\angle C$ and $\angle A$.
4. $\angle A$ is included between sides $\overline{AB}$ and $\overline{AC}$.
5. $\angle B$ is included between sides $\overline{BA}$ and $\overline{BC}$.
6. $\angle C$ is included between sides $\overline{CA}$ and $\overline{CB}$.

Classifying Triangles According to Angles

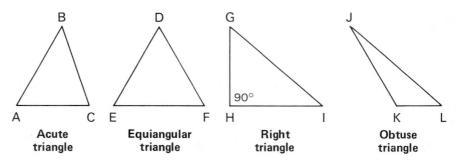

| Acute triangle | Equiangular triangle | Right triangle | Obtuse triangle |

An *acute triangle* is a triangle that has three acute angles.

An *equiangular triangle* is a triangle that has three angles equal in measure.

A *right triangle* is a triangle that has one right angle.

An *obtuse triangle* is a triangle that has one obtuse angle.

In right triangle GHI above, the two sides of the triangle that form the right angle, $\overline{GH}$ and $\overline{HI}$, are called the *legs* of the right triangle. $\overline{GI}$, the side opposite the right angle, is called the *hypotenuse*.

Classifying Triangles According to Sides

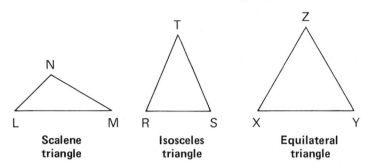

| Scalene triangle | Isosceles triangle | Equilateral triangle |

A *scalene triangle* is a triangle that has no sides equal in length.

An *isosceles triangle* is a triangle that has two sides equal in length.

An *equilateral triangle* is a triangle that has three sides equal in length.

The Sum of the Measures of the Angles of a Triangle

When we change the shape of a triangle, changes take place in the measures of its angles. Is there any relationship among the measures of the triangle that does not change? Let us see.

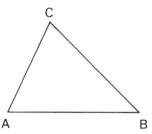

Draw several triangles of different shapes. In each triangle measure the three angles and find the sum of the three measures. For example, in $\triangle ABC$, $m\angle A + m\angle B + m\angle C = 65° + 45° + 70° = 180°$.

If you measured accurately, you should have found that in each triangle the sum of the measures of the three angles is 180°.

You can see that this is so by tearing off two angles of any triangle and placing them adjacent to the third angle as is shown in the figures below.

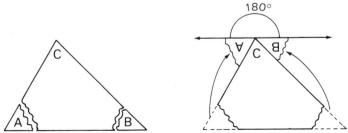

For these reasons we will accept the truth of the following statement which will be proved in a higher-level course as a theorem:

■ The sum of the measures of the angles of a triangle is 180°.

| MODEL PROBLEM |

In triangle ABC the measure of angle B is twice the measure of angle A, and the measure of angle C is three times the measure of angle A. Find the number of degrees in each angle of the triangle.

Solution:

Let x = the number of degrees in angle A.
Then $2x$ = the number of degrees in angle B.
Then $3x$ = the number of degrees in angle C.

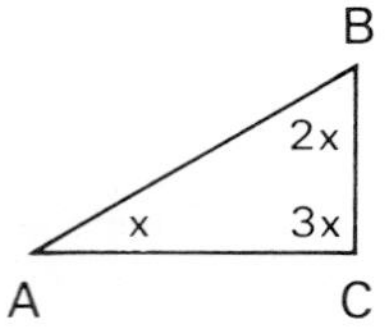

The sum of the measures of the angles of a triangle is 180°.

$$x + 2x + 3x = 180$$
$$6x = 180$$
$$x = 30$$
$$2x = 60$$
$$3x = 90$$

Check

$60° = 2 \times 30°$
$90° = 3 \times 30°$
$30° + 60° + 90° = 180°$

Answer: $m\angle A = 30°, m\angle B = 60°, m\angle C = 90°$

| EXERCISES |

In 1–3, discover whether the three angles can be the three angles of a triangle.

1. $30°, 70°, 80°$ 2. $70°, 80°, 90°$ 3. $30°, 110°, 40°$

In 4–7, find the measure of the third angle of the triangle if the first two angles contain:

4. $60°, 40°$ 5. $100°, 20°$ 6. $54.5°, 82.3°$ 7. $24\frac{1}{4}°, 81\frac{3}{4}°$

8. Find the number of degrees in each angle of an equiangular triangle.
9. Can a triangle have: **(a)** two right angles? **(b)** two obtuse angles? **(c)** one right and one obtuse angle? Why?
10. What is the sum of the measures of the two acute angles of a right triangle?
11. If two angles in one triangle contain the same number of degrees as two angles in another triangle, what must be true of the third pair of angles in the two triangles? Why?

12. In a triangle the measure of the second angle is 3 times the measure of the first angle, and the measure of the third angle is 5 times the measure of the first angle. Find the number of degrees in each angle of the triangle.

13. In each part find the measures of the three angles of a triangle whose measures are in the given continued ratio.
    a. $1:2:3$ **b.** $1:4:7$ **c.** $2:3:4$ **d.** $4:5:9$ **e.** $1:3:4$

14. In a triangle the measure of the second angle is 4 times the measure of the first angle. The measure of the third angle is equal to the sum of the measures of the first two angles. Find the number of degrees in each angle of the triangle.

15. In a triangle the measure of the second angle is 30° more than the measure of the first angle, and the measure of the third angle is 45° more than the measure of the first angle. Find the number of degrees in each angle of the triangle.

16. In a triangle the measure of the second angle is 5° more than twice the measure of the first angle. The measure of the third angle is 35° less than 3 times the measure of the first angle. Find the number of degrees in each angle of the triangle.

17. $\overleftrightarrow{AEFB}$ is a straight line; $m\angle AEG = 120°$; $m\angle BFG = 150°$.
    a. Find $m\angle x$, $m\angle y$, and $m\angle z$.
    b. What kind of triangle is triangle EFG?

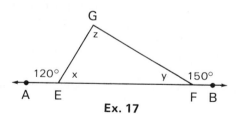

Ex. 17

18. In $\triangle RST$, $m\angle R = x$, $m\angle S = x + 30$, $m\angle T = x - 30$.
    a. Find the measures of the three angles.
    b. What kind of triangle is $\triangle RST$?

19. In $\triangle KLM$, $m\angle K = 2x$, $m\angle L = x + 30$, $m\angle M = 3x - 30$.
    a. Find the measures of the three angles.
    b. What kind of triangle is $\triangle KLM$?

The Exterior Angle of a Triangle

In the figure at the right, side $\overline{AC}$ is extended to form $\angle BCE$ at vertex C. Notice that $\angle BCE$ is in the *exterior* of triangle ABC. Also notice that $\angle BCE$ and $\angle BCA$ are supplementary, forming a linear pair. We call $\angle BCE$ an *exterior angle* of $\triangle ABC$, drawn at vertex C.

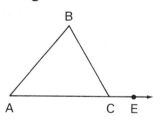

■ An exterior angle of a triangle is an angle that forms a linear pair with one of the angles of the triangle.

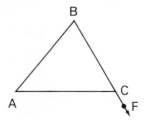

We could have formed another exterior angle at vertex C by extending side $\overline{BC}$, as shown at the left. Notice that $\angle ACF$ and $\angle BCA$ form a linear pair, and that $\angle ACF$ is in the exterior of $\triangle ABC$.

In the two figures we have just seen, let $m\angle BCA = x°$. For the first figure, $m\angle BCE = (180 - x)°$ and, for the second figure, $m\angle ACF = (180 - x)°$. We see that in both cases the exterior angle has a measure of $(180 - x)°$. This tells us that either side of $\angle BCA$ can be extended to form the exterior angle at vertex C.

In the figure at the right, $\triangle DEF$ is shown with exterior $\angle EFG$ at vertex F. There are three angles found in the *interior* of $\triangle DEF$. We know that $\angle EFD$ is *adjacent* to exterior $\angle EFG$ because these angles form a linear pair. The two angles at the remaining vertices, $\angle D$ and $\angle E$, are called *remote interior angles* to the exterior $\angle EFG$. Using this triangle and exterior $\angle EFG$, we observe:

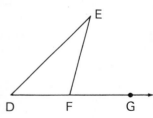

(1) If $m\angle D = 45°$ and $m\angle E = 30°$, then $m\angle EFD = 180° - (45° + 30°) = 180° - 75° = 105°$.

(2) If $m\angle EFD = 105°$ and this angle forms a linear pair with exterior $\angle EFG$, then $m\angle EFG = 180° - 105° = 75°$.

(3) We conclude that $m\angle D + m\angle E = m\angle EFG$, since $45° + 30° = 75°$.

This example illustrates the truth of the following statement, which you can try to prove informally:

■ The measure of an exterior angle of a triangle is equal to the sum of the measures of the two remote interior angles.

| EXERCISES |

In 1–5, **(a)** name the given exterior angle of the triangle; **(b)** name the two remote interior angles to that exterior angle.

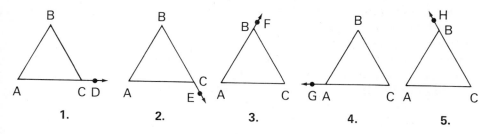

1.　　　2.　　　3.　　　4.　　　5.

In 6–15, find the number of degrees in the value of x.

6.　　　7.　　　8.　　　9.　　　10.

11.　　　12.　　　13.　　　14.　　　15.

16. In an equiangular triangle what is the degree measure of any one of its exterior angles?
17. In a right triangle what is the degree measure of the exterior angle to the right angle?
18. An exterior angle is drawn to a triangle. If this exterior angle is acute, then the triangle must be: (1) acute　(2) right　(3) obtuse (4) equilateral.

19. In the figure at the right, three exterior angles are drawn to $\triangle ABC$.
    a. What is the sum of the measures of the three exterior angles of $\triangle ABC$?
    b. Will the answer to part **a** be true for the sum of the measures of the exterior angles of any triangle?

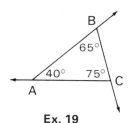

Ex. 19

The Isosceles Triangle

In isosceles triangle *ABC,* the two sides which are equal in measure, $\overline{AC}$ and $\overline{BC}$, are called the *legs*. The remaining side, $\overline{AB}$, is called the *base*. The angle formed by the two congruent sides, $\angle C$, is called the *vertex angle*. The two angles at the endpoints of the base, $\angle A$ and $\angle B$, are called the *base angles*.

In isosceles triangle *ABC,* if we measure the base angles, $\angle A$ and $\angle B$, we find that each angle contains $65°$. Therefore, $m\angle A = m\angle B$. If you measure the base angles in any other isosceles triangle, you will find that they are again equal in measure. Try it yourself. For this reason we will accept the truth of the following statement which will be proved in a higher-level course as a theorem:

■ **The base angles of an isosceles triangle are equal in measure, that is, they are congruent.**

This statement may be rephrased in a variety of ways. For example:

1. "If a triangle is isosceles, then its two base angles are equal in measure."

2. "If two sides of a triangle are congruent, then the angles opposite these sides are congruent."

Note: The following, which is the *converse* of the previous statement, can be proved in a higher-level course:

■ **If two angles of a triangle are equal in measure, then the triangle is an isosceles triangle.**

This statement may also be rephrased as follows:

"If two angles of a triangle are congruent, then the sides opposite these angles are congruent."

Properties of Triangles

1. The sum of the measures of the angles of a triangle is $180°$.

2. The acute angles of a right triangle are complementary.

3. If the measures of two angles of one triangle are equal, respectively, to the measures of two angles of another triangle, then the remaining angles are equal in measure.

4. If two sides of a triangle are equal in measure, the angles opposite these sides are equal in measure. (Base angles of an isosceles triangle are equal in measure.)

5. If two angles of a triangle are equal in measure, the sides opposite these angles are equal in measure and the triangle is an isosceles triangle.

6. The measure of an exterior angle of a triangle is equal to the sum of the measures of the two remote interior angles.

MODEL PROBLEM

In isosceles triangle ABC the measure of vertex angle C is 30° more than the measure of each base angle. Find the number of degrees in each angle of the triangle.

Solution:

Let x = the number of degrees in one base angle, A.

Then x = the number of degrees in the other base angle, B.

Then $x + 30$ = the number of degrees in the vertex angle, C.

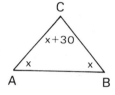

The sum of the measures of the angles of a triangle is 180°.

$$x + x + x + 30 = 180$$
$$3x + 30 = 180$$
$$3x = 150$$
$$x = 50$$
$$x + 30 = 80$$

Check

$$50° + 50° + 80° = 180°$$

Answer: $m\angle A = 50°$, $m\angle B = 50°$, $m\angle C = 80°$

EXERCISES

1. Name the legs, base, vertex angle, and base angles in each of the following isosceles triangles:

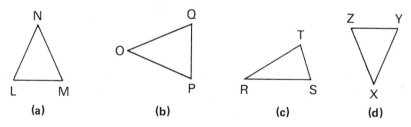

(a)   (b)   (c)   (d)

2. In $\triangle ABC$, AC = 4 cm, CB = 6 cm, and
AB = 6 cm.
   a. What type of triangle is $\triangle ABC$?
   b. Name two angles in $\triangle ABC$ whose measures
      are equal.
   c. Why are they equal in measure?

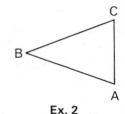

Ex. 2

3. In $\triangle RST$, $m\angle R$ = 70° and $m\angle T$ = 40°.
   a. Find the measure of $\angle S$.
   b. Name two sides in $\triangle RST$ that are
      congruent.
   c. Why are the two sides congruent?
   d. What type of triangle is $\triangle RST$?

Ex. 3

4. Draw an isosceles triangle that is **(a)** an acute triangle, **(b)** a right triangle, and **(c)** an obtuse triangle.

5. Can a base angle of an isosceles triangle be **(a)** a right angle **(b)** an obtuse angle? Why?

6. Find the measure of the vertex angle of an isosceles triangle if the measure of each base angle is:
   a. 80°   **b.** 55°   **c.** 42°   **d.** $22\frac{1}{2}$°   **e.** 51.5°

7. Find the measure of each base angle of an isosceles triangle if the vertex angle measures:
   a. 40°   **b.** 50°   **c.** 76°   **d.** 100°   **e.** 65°

8. What is the number of degrees in each acute angle of an isosceles right triangle?

9. The measure of each base angle of an isosceles triangle is seven times the measure of the vertex angle. Find the measure of each angle of the triangle.

10. The measure of each of the congruent angles of an isosceles triangle is one-half of the measure of the vertex angle. Find the measure of each angle of the triangle.

11. The measure of the vertex angle of an isosceles triangle is 3 times as large as the measure of each base angle. Find the number of degrees in each angle of the triangle.

12. The measure of the vertex angle of an isosceles triangle is 15° more than the measure of each base angle. Find the number of degrees in each angle of the triangle.

13. The measure of each of the congruent angles of an isosceles triangle is 6° less than the measure of the vertex angle. Find the measure of each angle of the triangle.

14. The measure of each of the equal angles of an isosceles triangle is 9° less than 4 times the vertex angle. Find the measure of each angle of the triangle.

15. In $\triangle ABC$, $m\angle A = x$, $m\angle B = x + 30$, and $m\angle C = 2x - 10$.
    a. Find the measures of the three angles.
    b. What kind of triangle is $\triangle ABC$?

16. In $\triangle DEF$ the ratio of the measures of the three angles is $2:2:5$.
    a. Find the measures of the three angles.
    b. What kind of triangle is $\triangle DEF$?

17. The vertex angle of an isosceles triangle is 80° in measure. What is the measure of an exterior angle to one of the base angles of this triangle?

18. The measure of an exterior angle to a base angle of an isosceles triangle is 115°. What is the measure of the vertex angle of the triangle?

19. The measure of an exterior angle to the vertex angle of an isosceles triangle is 60°. What is the measure of one of the base angles of the triangle?

20. Given the statement: "If two sides of a triangle are equal in measure, then the angles opposite these sides are equal in measure."
    a. What is the truth value of the statement?
    b. Write the converse of the statement.
    c. What is the truth value of the converse?
    d. Using the statement and its converse, write a biconditional statement.
    e. What is the truth value of this biconditional?

7 THE QUADRILATERAL

A *quadrilateral* is a polygon that has four sides. A point at which any two sides of the quadrilateral meet is called a *vertex* of the quadrilateral. At each vertex the two sides that meet form an angle of the quadrilateral. Thus, $ABCD$ is a quadrilateral whose sides are $\overline{AB}$, $\overline{BC}$, $\overline{CD}$, and $\overline{DA}$. Its vertices are A, B, C, and D. Its angles are $\angle ABC$, $\angle BCD$, $\angle CDA$, and $\angle DAB$.

In a quadrilateral two angles whose vertices are the endpoints of a side are called *consecutive angles*. For example, in quadrilateral $ABCD$, $\angle A$ and $\angle B$ are consecutive angles; $\angle B$ and $\angle C$ are consecutive angles; and so on. Two angles that are not consecutive angles are called *oppo-*

site angles. For example, $\angle A$ and $\angle C$ are opposite angles; $\angle B$ and $\angle D$ are opposite angles.

When we vary the shape of the quadrilateral by making some of its sides parallel, by making some of its sides equal in length, or by making its angles become right angles, we get different members of the family of quadrilaterals, as shown below:

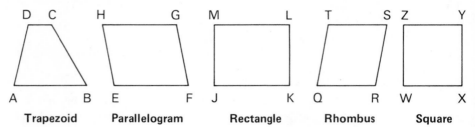

| Trapezoid | Parallelogram | Rectangle | Rhombus | Square |

A *trapezoid* is a quadrilateral in which two and only two opposite sides are parallel. In trapezoid $ABCD$, $\overline{AB} \parallel \overline{CD}$. The parallel sides $\overline{AB}$ and $\overline{CD}$ are called the *bases* of the trapezoid.

A *parallelogram* is a quadrilateral in which both pairs of opposite sides are parallel. In parallelogram $EFGH$, $\overline{EF} \parallel \overline{GH}$ and $\overline{EH} \parallel \overline{FG}$. The symbol for parallelogram is $\square$.

A *rectangle* is a parallelogram in which all four angles are right angles. Rectangle $JKLM$ is a parallelogram in which $\angle J$, $\angle K$, $\angle L$, and $\angle M$ are right angles. The symbol for rectangle is $\square$.

A *rhombus* is a parallelogram in which all the sides are equal in length. Rhombus $QRST$ is a parallelogram in which $QR = RS = ST = TQ$.

A *square* is a rectangle all of whose sides are equal in length. Therefore, square $WXYZ$ is also a parallelogram in which $\angle W$, $\angle X$, $\angle Y$, and $\angle Z$ are right angles, and $WX = XY = YZ = ZW$.

Draw a large quadrilateral like the one shown at the right. Measure each of its four angles. Is the sum 360°? It should be. Do the same with several other quadrilaterals of different shapes and sizes. Is the sum of the four measures 360° in each case? It should be. Now we are ready to understand the truth of the following statement whose truth will be proved in a higher-level course:

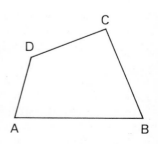

■ **The sum of the measures of the angles of a quadrilateral is 360°.**

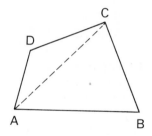

In order to help us prove informally that this statement is true, we draw diagonal $\overline{AC}$, which is a line segment whose endpoints are the vertices of the two opposite angles, $\angle A$ and $\angle C$.

Step 1. Diagonal $\overline{AC}$ divides quadrilateral $ABCD$ into two triangles, $\triangle ABC$ and $\triangle ADC$.

Step 2. The sum of the measures of the angles of $\triangle ABC$ is $180°$ and the sum of the measures of the angles of $\triangle ADC = 180°$.

Step 3. The sum of the measures of all the angles of $\triangle ABC$ and $\triangle ADC$ together is $360°$.

Step 4. Hence, $m\angle A + m\angle B + m\angle C + m\angle D$ is $360°$.

The Family of Parallelograms

Let us discover some of the relationships that hold true in parallelograms, rectangles, rhombuses, and squares.

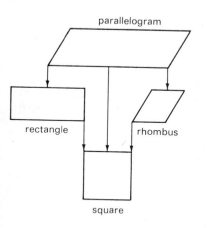

1. Rectangles, rhombuses, and squares are members of the family of parallelograms. Therefore, any property of the family of parallelograms must also be a property of rectangles, rhombuses, and squares.

2. A square is a member of the family of rectangles. Therefore, any property of the family of rectangles must also be a property of squares.

3. A square is a member of the family of rhombuses. Therefore, any property of the family of rhombuses must also be a property of squares.

In parallelogram $ABCD$, as shown at the right, opposite sides are parallel. Thus, $\overline{AB} \parallel \overline{DC}$ and $\overline{AD} \parallel \overline{BC}$. The following statements, which will be proved in a higher-level course, are true for any parallelogram:

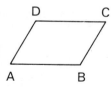

1. Opposite sides of a parallelogram are equal in length (or congruent). Here, $AB = DC$ and $AD = BC$. (We also say $\overline{AB} \cong \overline{DC}$ and $\overline{AD} \cong \overline{BC}$.)

2. Opposite angles of a parallelogram are equal in measure (or congruent). Here, $m\angle A = m\angle C$ and $m\angle B = m\angle D$. (We also say $\angle A \cong \angle C$ and $\angle B \cong \angle D$.)

3. Consecutive angles of a parallelogram are supplementary. Here, $\angle A$ and $\angle B$ are supplementary. Thus, $m\angle A + m\angle B = 180°$. Also, $\angle B$ and $\angle C$ are supplementary. Thus, $m\angle B + m\angle C = 180°$. And so forth.

Since rhombuses, rectangles, and squares are members of the family of parallelograms, these statements will be true for any rhombus, any rectangle, and any square.

Informal Proofs for Angles in a Parallelogram

Let us consider parallelogram $ABCD$. The following statements can help us to prove informally that "consecutive angles of a parallelogram are supplementary."

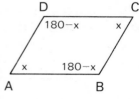

Step 1. $\overline{DC} \parallel \overline{AB}$ and $\overline{AD}$ is a transversal (because opposite sides of a parallelogram are parallel and a transversal intersects these lines).

Step 2. If $m\angle A = x°$, then $m\angle D = (180 - x)°$ (since $\angle A$ and $\angle D$ are interior angles on the same side of a transversal, previously shown to be supplementary).

Step 3. Similarly, in looking at $\overline{AD} \parallel \overline{BC}$ and the transversal $\overline{AB}$, we can say: If $m\angle A = x°$, then $m\angle B = (180 - x)°$ for the same reason as step 2.

Step 4. Also, in looking at $\overline{AB} \parallel \overline{DC}$ and the transversal $\overline{BC}$, we say: If $m\angle B = (180 - x)°$, then $m\angle C = x°$. Therefore, we have proved:

Consecutive angles of a parallelogram are supplementary.

We use this statement to prove informally that:

Opposite angles of a parallelogram are equal in measure.

Step 1. In parallelogram $ABCD$ we have shown that:
$$m\angle A = x°; m\angle B = (180 - x)°; m\angle C = x°; m\angle D = (180 - x)°.$$

Step 2. Thus, $m\angle A = m\angle C$ and $m\angle B = m\angle D$.

Remember that these statements are also true for any rhombus, any rectangle, and any square.

MODEL PROBLEM

$ABCD$ is a parallelogram where $m\angle A = 2x + 50$ and $m\angle C = 3x + 40$.

a. Find the value of x.
b. Find the measure of each angle.

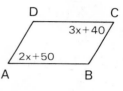

Solution:

a. In $\square ABCD$ $m\angle C = m\angle A$ because the opposite angles of a parallelogram are equal in measure. Thus:
$$3x + 40 = 2x + 50$$
$$x = 10$$

b. By substitution:
$m\angle A = 2x + 50 = 2(10) + 50 = 70$ and $m\angle C = 3x + 40$
$= 3(10) + 40 = 70$.
Since $m\angle B + m\angle A = 180°$, $m\angle B + 70 = 180$, and $m\angle B = 110$.
Since $m\angle D = m\angle B$, $m\angle D = 110$.

Answer: $m\angle A = 70°, m\angle B = 110°, m\angle C = 70°, m\angle D = 110°$

EXERCISES

In 1-6:

a. Copy the given statement. Is it true or false?
b. Write the converse of the given statement. Is it true or false?
c. Write the inverse of the given statement. Is it true or false?
d. Write the contrapositive of the given statement. Is it true or false?

1. If a polygon is a trapezoid, it is a quadrilateral.
2. If a polygon is a rectangle, it is a parallelogram.
3. If a polygon is a rhombus, it is a parallelogram.
4. If a polygon is a rhombus, it is a square.
5. If a polygon is a parallelogram, it is a square.
6. If two angles are opposite angles of a parallelogram, they are congruent.

In 7-10, the angle measures are given in each quadrilateral. **a.** Find the value of x. **b.** State the measure of each angle of the quadrilateral.

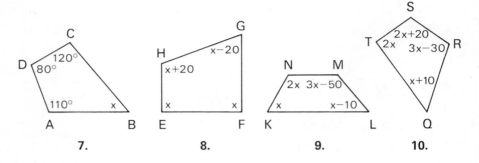

| 7. | 8. | 9. | 10. |

In 11-13, polygon $ABCD$ is a parallelogram.

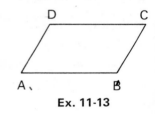

11. $AB = 3x + 8; DC = x + 12$.   Find AB and DC.
12. $m\angle A = 5x - 40; m\angle C = 3x + 20$. Find $m\angle A, m\angle B, m\angle C, m\angle D$.
13. The ratio of $m\angle A : m\angle B = 1:3$. Find $m\angle A, m\angle B, m\angle C, m\angle D$.

Ex. 11-13

In 14 and 15, polygon $ABCD$ is a rectangle.

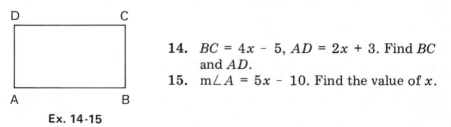

Ex. 14-15

14. $BC = 4x - 5, AD = 2x + 3$. Find BC and AD.
15. $m\angle A = 5x - 10$. Find the value of x.

16. $ABCD$ is a square. If $AB = 8x - 6$ and $BC = 5x + 12$, find the length of each side of the square.

In 17 and 18, polygon $KLMN$ is a rhombus.

17. The ratio of $m\angle N$ to $m\angle M$ is $3:2$. Find the measure of each angle of the rhombus.
18. $KL = 3x$, $LM = 2(x + 3)$. Find the length of each side of the rhombus.

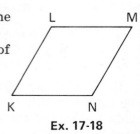

Ex. 17-18

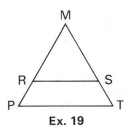

M

R ___ S

P _____ T

Ex. 19

19. In the figure at the left △*MPT* is an isosceles triangle in which *PM* = *TM*. $\overline{RS}$ is drawn parallel to $\overline{PT}$ forming an *isosceles trapezoid* in which *PR* = *TS*. (In an *isosceles trapezoid* exactly one pair of opposite sides is parallel, while the sides that are not parallel are congruent.)

a. If *PR* = *x* + 3, *TS* = 2*x* + 2, *RS* = *x* + 6, and *PT* = 8*x* + 3, find the length of each side.

b. If m∠*P* = 60°, find the measures of all four angles in the isosceles trapezoid.

20. In the figure at the right four exterior angles are drawn to quadrilateral *ABCD*, one at each vertex. The angle measures are 70°, 65°, 85°, and 140°.

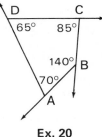

Ex. 20

a. What is the sum of the interior angles of the quadrilateral?

b. What is the sum of the exterior angles of the quadrilateral?

c. Will the answer to part *b* be true for the sum of the exterior angles of any quadrilateral?

8 SYMMETRY

In nature, in art, and in industry, we find many forms that have a pleasing and attractive appearance because of the *balanced* arrangement of their parts. We say that such forms have *symmetry*.

Line Symmetry

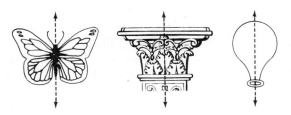

In each of the figures above there is a line on which the figure may be folded so that the two parts of the figure will coincide. This line is called a *line of reflection* or an *axis of symmetry*, and each figure is said to have *line symmetry*.

An isosceles triangle ABC is shown at the right. The line of symmetry, called line k, passes through the vertex angle B. If this triangle were folded, point A would fall on top of point C. We can say that the *image* of A, under the line reflection through k, is point C. In the same way, the *image* of C is point A. We can see that when folded on the line of reflection, the image of B is B, and the image of D is D. Points B and D are called ***fixed points*** because they are on the line of reflection. In other words, a reflection line acts "like a mirror." We may symbolize a point P and its image P' by use of an arrow, $P \to P'$. Hence, under the line reflection k, $A \to C$, $C \to A$, $B \to B$, and $D \to D$.

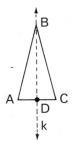

Using this same notation, we can show that the image of side $\overline{AB}$ is side $\overline{CB}$ by writing $\overline{AB} \to \overline{CB}$. Also, the image of $\angle BAD$ is $\angle BCD$, shown as $\angle BAD \to \angle BCD$. We feel that this is true because base angles of an isosceles triangle are congruent and the sides opposite them are congruent.

Looking at isosceles triangle ABC and the reflection line k, we can note some of the *properties of a line reflection* without proving them:

1. Distance is preserved. $AB = CB$ since $\overline{AB} \to \overline{CB}$. Similarly the image of $\overline{AD}$ is $\overline{CD}$, so their lengths or distances are equal, namely $AD = DC$.

2. Angle measure is preserved. $m\angle BAD = m\angle BCD$ since $\angle BAD \to \angle BCD$. Similarly we can see that $m\angle BDA = m\angle BDC$.

3. The line of reflection is a ***perpendicular bisector*** to every segment formed by joining a point to its image. For example, the image of A is C. Hence, we form segment AC.

   (1) $\angle BDA$ and $\angle BDC$ are a linear pair where $m\angle BDA = m\angle BDC$. From $x + x = 180°$, we see that $2x = 180°$ or $x = 90°$. Each angle formed is a right angle. Thus, line k is *perpendicular* to segment AC.

   (2) Since $AD = CD$ under the line reflection, D is the midpoint of segment AC. Line k passes through segment AC at point D. Thus, line k bisects segment AC or divides the segment into two congruent parts.

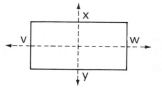

It is possible for a figure to have more than one axis of symmetry or reflection line. In the rectangle at the left, the line XY is a line of reflection, and the line VW is a second line of reflection.

Lines of symmetry may be found for letters and for words as seen to the right.

Point Symmetry

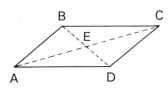

In each of the figures shown above, the design is built around a single point called the *center* of the figure, or the *point of symmetry*, or the *point of reflection*. For every point in the figure, there is another point found directly opposite it on the other side of the center. Each design is an example of *point symmetry*.

None of the figures just pictured has line symmetry; there is no way to fold the pictures over a line so that all the points coincide.

A parallelogram $ABCD$ is shown at the left. Diagonals $\overline{AC}$ and $\overline{BD}$ intersect at point E, which is the point of symmetry. On $\overline{BD}$ the point opposite B, through the center E, is point D. We say that the image of B is D, or simply $B \to D$. In the same way, reflecting through the point of symmetry E, we see that $A \to C$, $C \to A$ and $D \to B$. The only point that does not change in a point symmetry is the center point itself; we say that $E \to E$ and the point of symmetry E is a *fixed point*.

While we may think of a line reflection as looking through a mirror, this idea does not work with a point symmetry. We can think of a point symmetry as "turning the picture around." Try it. Turn the book upside down. Do the pictures look the same? They should, if they have point symmetry.

In the parallelogram $ABCD$ we can now see that the image of side $\overline{AB}$ is side $\overline{CD}$, or simply $\overline{AB} \to \overline{CD}$. Also the image of $\angle BAD$ is $\angle DCB$, shown as $\angle BAD \to \angle DCB$. We feel that this is true because opposite sides of a parallelogram are congruent and opposite angles of a parallelogram are congruent.

Looking at the parallelogram $ABCD$ and the point of reflection E, we can note some of the *properties of a point symmetry* without proving them:

1. Distance is preserved. $AB = CD$ since $\overline{AB} \to \overline{CD}$. Similarly the image of $\overline{AD}$ is $\overline{CB}$, so their lengths or distances are equal, namely, $AD = CB$.

2. Angle measure is preserved. $m\angle BAD = m\angle DCB$ since $\angle BAD \to \angle DCB$. Similarly we can see that $m\angle ABC = m\angle CDA$.

3. The point of reflection is a **midpoint** to every segment formed by joining a point to its image. For example, the image of A is C. Hence, we form $\overline{AC}$.

   (1) Since distance is preserved, then $AE = EC$ under the point symmetry. Thus, E is the midpoint of $\overline{AC}$.

   (2) In the same way, $BE = ED$ and E is the midpoint of $\overline{BD}$.

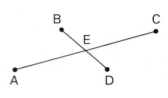

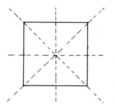

It is possible for a figure to have both line symmetry and point symmetry at the same time. In the square at the left there are 4 lines of symmetry. Note that the point of symmetry lies at the intersection of these 4 lines.

Points of symmetry may be found for letters and for words as seen below.

Z M⊙W

| EXERCISES |

1. Using the printed capital letters of the alphabet: **a.** Find all the letters that have *line symmetry* and copy these letters on your paper with one or more lines of reflection drawn over the letters. **b.** Find all the letters that have *point symmetry* and copy these letters on your paper with the point of reflection marked on the letter. **c.** Which letters have *both* line symmetry and point symmetry? **d.** Which letters have *neither* line nor point symmetry?

2. Tell whether each of the following words has line symmetry, point symmetry, both types of symmetry, or neither.

   a. MOM   b. DAD   c. SIS   d. OTTO
   e. BOOK   f. RADAR   g. NO   h. NOON
   i. HIKE   j. MATH   k. OHHO   l. CHOKED

In 3–14, for each geometric figure named: **a.** Sketch the figure. **b.** Tell the number of lines of symmetry the figure has, if any, and sketch them on your drawing. **c.** Tell if the figure has point symmetry and sketch the point if it exists.

3. rectangle   4. equilateral triangle   5. parallelogram
6. isosceles triangle   7. rhombus   8. regular hexagon
9. trapezoid   10. scalene triangle   11. circle
12. regular octagon   13. square   14. regular pentagon

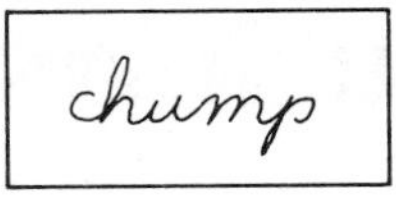

15. Look at the handwritten word "chump" in the box at the left. Does it have any type of symmetry?

chump

Ex. 15

chapter twelve

Similarity, Congruence, and Constructions

1 SIMILAR POLYGONS

In modern-day living it is often necessary to deal with geometric figures that have the "same shape" but do not have the "same size." For example, a photographer will make an enlargement of a small picture; an architect will make a small scale drawing of the floor plan of a room in a house. There are many other examples of situations that involve polygons that have the same shape but do not have the same size. We call such polygons *similar polygons*. The symbol for "similar" and "is similar to" is "~."

Below we see two similar polygons. Let us study these figures to discover what causes them to appear to be similar. We will pair vertex A with vertex A', vertex B with vertex B', vertex C with vertex C', and vertex D with vertex D'. Here we say that polygon $ABCD$ is similar to polygon $A'B'C'D'$, written symbolically as $ABCD \sim A'B'C'D'$.

Every two angles whose vertices we have paired are called a pair of *corresponding angles*. For example, pairs of corresponding angles here are $\angle A$ and $\angle A'$, $\angle B$ and $\angle B'$, $\angle C$ and $\angle C'$, $\angle D$ and $\angle D'$.

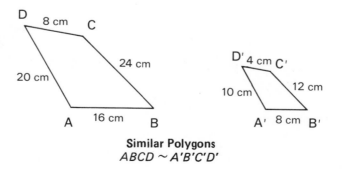

Similar Polygons
$ABCD \sim A'B'C'D'$

The sides that join two pairs of corresponding vertices are called *corresponding sides*. For example, pairs of corresponding sides here are: $\overline{AB}$ and $\overline{A'B'}$; $\overline{BC}$ and $\overline{B'C'}$; $\overline{CD}$ and $\overline{C'D'}$; $\overline{DA}$ and $\overline{D'A'}$.

Measure $\angle A$ and the corresponding $\angle A'$. How do they compare? Also measure $\angle B$ and $\angle B'$, $\angle C$ and $\angle C'$, $\angle D$ and $\angle D'$. What do you notice about all pairs of corresponding angles? They should be equal in measure, that is, congruent.

Examine the ratio of the lengths of each pair of corresponding sides.

For sides $\overline{AB}$ and $\overline{A'B'}$, the ratio of their lengths $= \dfrac{AB}{A'B'} = \dfrac{16}{8} = \dfrac{2}{1}$.

For sides $\overline{BC}$ and $\overline{B'C'}$, the ratio of their lengths $= \dfrac{BC}{B'C'} = \dfrac{24}{12} = \dfrac{2}{1}$.

For the remaining sides, what is $\dfrac{CD}{C'D'}$?   What is $\dfrac{DA}{D'A'}$?

What do you notice about the ratios of the measures of all pairs of corresponding sides? They should all be equal. We are now ready to understand the following:

■ Two polygons are similar if the measures of their corresponding angles are equal and the ratio of the measures of any pair of corresponding sides is equal to the ratio of the measures of all the other pairs of corresponding sides.

Another way of stating this is:

■ Two polygons are similar if their corresponding angles are congruent and corresponding sides are in proportion.

Conversely, we may also say:

■ If two polygons are similar, then corresponding angles are congruent and corresponding sides are in proportion.

| MODEL PROBLEM |

If rectangle $ABCD$ is similar to rectangle $A'B'C'D'$, find the length of $\overline{A'D'}$.

Solution:

Let x represent the length of $\overline{A'D'}$.

The ratio of $A'D'$ to $AD = \dfrac{x}{12}$.

The ratio of $A'B'$ to $AB = \dfrac{8}{16}$.

Since the figures are similar,

$\dfrac{x}{12} = \dfrac{8}{16}$. Why?

Then $16(x) = 8(12)$. Why?

And $16x = 96$

$x = 6$

Check

$\dfrac{6}{12} \stackrel{?}{=} \dfrac{8}{16}$

$\dfrac{1}{2} = \dfrac{1}{2}$ (True)

Answer: $A'D' = 6$ cm

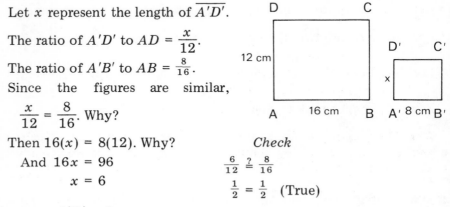

| EXERCISES |

1. Is square $ABCD$ similar to rectangle $EFGH$? Why?

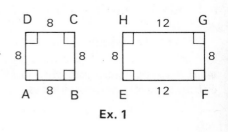

Ex. 1

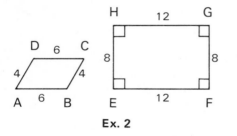

Ex. 2

2. Is parallelogram $ABCD$ similar to rectangle $EFGH$? Why?

3. Is square $WXYZ$ similar to square $QRST$? Why?

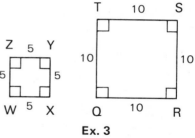

Ex. 3

4. Are all squares similar? Why?
5. Are all rectangles similar? Why?
6. Are all parallelograms similar? Why?
7. Are all rhombuses similar? Why?

8. Using the dimensions given on the similar rectangles at the right, find the number of centimeters in the length of the longer side $\overline{ZY}$.

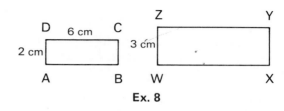

Ex. 8

9. A picture 12 centimeters long and 9 centimeters wide is to be enlarged so that its length will be 16 centimeters. How wide will the enlarged picture be?
10. Jenny wishes to enlarge a rectangular photograph that is $4\frac{1}{2}$ inches long and $2\frac{3}{4}$ inches wide so that it will be 9 inches long. How wide will the enlargement be?

In 11–14, the two polygons are similar. Pairs of corresponding sides are noted by using primes, such as $\overline{AB}$ and $\overline{A'B'}$. Find the length of every side in each polygon.

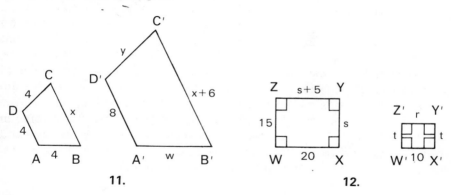

11.

12.

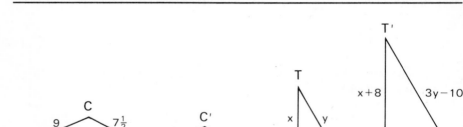

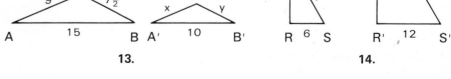

13.   **14.**

2 SIMILAR TRIANGLES

Since similar triangles are often used to solve problems in measurement, let us see whether we can discover a short method of showing that two triangles are similar.

In triangle ABC, the figure at the right, m$\angle A$ = 27° and m$\angle B$ = 63°.

Let us construct another triangle in which the measures of two angles are also 27° and 63°.

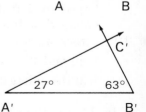

(1) We draw any line segment $\overline{A'B'}$. Let us make it twice as large as side $\overline{AB}$ in triangle ABC. (2) Using a protractor, we measure an angle of 27° at A'. (3) Using a protractor, we measure an angle of 63° at B'. (4) We let C' name the point of intersection of the two rays just drawn.

Observe that triangle $A'B'C'$ appears to be similar to triangle ABC. If we wish to be more certain of this, we measure $\angle C$ and $\angle C'$. How do their measures compare? They should be equal in measure. Recall that the sum of the measures of the angles of a triangle is always 180°. Hence, if two angles in one triangle are equal in measure to two angles in another triangle, the third pair of angles must also be equal in measure.

How do the ratios of the measures of the corresponding sides of the two triangles compare? They should be equal to 2:1. Therefore, in $\triangle ABC$ and $\triangle A'B'C'$, the corresponding angles are equal in measure and the measures of corresponding sides are in proportion. Now it seems reasonable to accept the truth of the following statement:

■ Two triangles are similar if two angles of one triangle are equal in measure to two corresponding angles of the other triangle.

or

■ Two triangles are similar if two angles of one triangle are congruent to two corresponding angles of the other triangle.

Since two right triangles have a pair of congruent right angles, we can say:

■ Two right triangles are similar if an acute angle in one triangle is equal in measure to an acute angle in the other triangle.

MODEL PROBLEMS

1. $\triangle ABC$ and $\triangle DEF$ are similar.

    a. Name three pairs of corresponding angles.

    b. Name three pairs of corresponding sides.

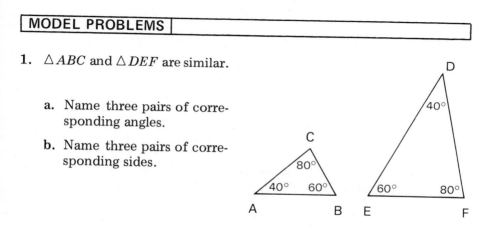

Solution

a. The corresponding angles are the pairs of angles whose measures are equal, that is, the angles which are congruent.

Since $m\angle A = 40°$ and $m\angle D = 40°$, $\angle D$ corresponds to $\angle A$.

Since $m\angle B = 60°$ and $m\angle E = 60°$, $\angle E$ corresponds to $\angle B$.

Since $m\angle C = 80°$ and $m\angle F = 80°$, $\angle F$ corresponds to $\angle C$.

b. The sides which join the vertices of two pairs of congruent angles are corresponding sides.

Since $\angle A \cong \angle D$ and $\angle B \cong \angle E$, $\overline{AB}$ corresponds to $\overline{DE}$.

Since $\angle B \cong \angle E$ and $\angle C \cong \angle F$, $\overline{BC}$ corresponds to $\overline{EF}$.

Since $\angle C \cong \angle F$ and $\angle A \cong \angle D$, $\overline{CA}$ corresponds to $\overline{FD}$.

2. In $\triangle ABC$, $AB = \frac{3}{4}''$, $m\angle A = 40°$, $m\angle B = 45°$. Use a ruler and a protractor to draw $\triangle DEF$ similar to $\triangle ABC$ so that $\overline{DE}$, which corresponds to $\overline{AB}$, measures $1''$.

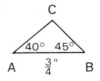

Solution

$\triangle DEF$ will be similar to $\triangle ABC$ if two angles in $\triangle DEF$ are equal in measure to two corresponding angles in $\triangle ABC$.

Step 1. Use a ruler to draw segment $\overline{DE}$ whose length is 1 inch.

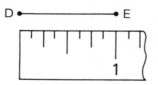

Step 2. Since point D corresponds to point A and $m\angle A = 40°$, use a protractor to draw an angle of $40°$ at D.

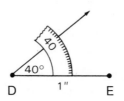

Step 3. Since point E corresponds to point B and $m\angle B = 45°$, use a protractor to draw an angle of $45°$ at E. Then name with the letter F the point of intersection of the two rays that were drawn to form $\angle D$ and $\angle E$.

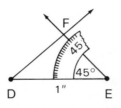

Answer: $\triangle DEF$ is the required triangle that is similar to $\triangle ABC$.

3. The sides of a triangle are 2, 8, and 7. If the longest side of a similar triangle is 4, find the length of the shortest side of that triangle.

Solution

If $\triangle RST \sim \triangle DEF$, their corresponding sides are in proportion. The longest sides $\overline{RS}$ and $\overline{DE}$ are corresponding sides; the shortest sides $\overline{RT}$ and $\overline{DF}$ are corresponding sides.

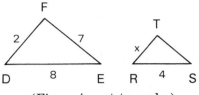

(Figure is not to scale.)

(1) $\dfrac{RT}{DF} = \dfrac{RS}{DE}$ [$RS = 4$, $DE = 8$, $DF = 2$]

(2) $\dfrac{x}{2} = \dfrac{4}{8}$ Let x = the length, RT.

(3) $8(x) = 2(4)$

(4) $8x = 8$

(5) $x = 1$

Answer: The length of the shortest side of $\triangle RST$ is 1.

4. At the same time that a vertical flagpole casts a shadow 15 feet long, a vertical pole that is 6 feet high casts a shadow that is 5 feet long. Find the length of the flagpole.

Solution

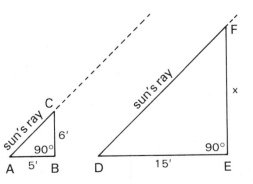

(1) Since the poles represented by $\overline{BC}$ and $\overline{EF}$ are vertical, $m\angle ABC = 90°$ and $m\angle DEF = 90°$.

(2) We will say that the sun's rays are parallel. Hence the angles that the sun's rays make with the ground, $\angle A$ and $\angle D$, have equal measures.

(3) Hence $\triangle DEF \sim \triangle ABC$ because two angles in one triangle are equal in measure to two corresponding angles in the other triangle.

(4) The corresponding sides of $\triangle DEF$ and $\triangle ABC$ are in proportion. Therefore:

$$\frac{EF}{BC} = \frac{DE}{AB} \quad (DE = 15 \text{ ft.}, AB = 5 \text{ ft.}, BC = 6 \text{ ft.})$$

$$\frac{x}{6} = \frac{15}{5} \quad \text{Let } x = \text{length } EF.$$

$$5(x) = 6(15)$$

$$5x = 90$$

$$x = 18$$

Answer: The length of the flagpole is 18 feet.

5. In the diagram at the right $\angle ADE$ and $\angle ABC$ are right angles, $\triangle ADE \sim \triangle ABC$, $AB = 24$, $BC = 18$, and $AD = 16$.
   a. Find DE.
   b. Find the area of $\triangle ABC$.
   c. Find the area of $\triangle ADE$.
   d. Find the area of trapezoid $BCED$.

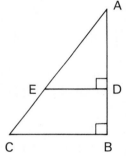

Solution

a. Since $\triangle ADE \sim \triangle ABC$, $\dfrac{DE}{BC} = \dfrac{AD}{AB}$.

   Let $DE = x$. Then:

$$\frac{x}{18} = \frac{16}{24} \quad (BC = 18, AD = 16, AB = 24)$$

$$24x = 16(18)$$

$$24x = 288$$

$$x = 12$$

Answer: $DE = 12$

b. Area of $\triangle ABC = \frac{1}{2}$ base $\cdot$ height

$$= \frac{1}{2} \cdot BC \cdot AB$$

$$= \frac{1}{2}(18)(24)$$

$$= \frac{1}{2}(432) = 216$$

   Area of $\triangle ABC = 216$ *Ans.*

c. Area of $\triangle ADE = \frac{1}{2}$ base · height

$$= \frac{1}{2} \cdot DE \cdot AD$$

$$= \frac{1}{2} (12)(16)$$

$$= \frac{1}{2} (192) = 96$$

Area of $\triangle ADE = 96$ *Ans.*

d. Area of trapezoid $BCED$ = area of $\triangle ABC$ - area of $\triangle ADE$. Thus:

area of trapezoid $BCED$ = 216 - 96 = 120

Answer: Area of trapezoid $BCED$ = 120

EXERCISES

In 1-4, the two triangles are similar. **a.** Name three pairs of corresponding angles. **b.** Name three pairs of corresponding sides.

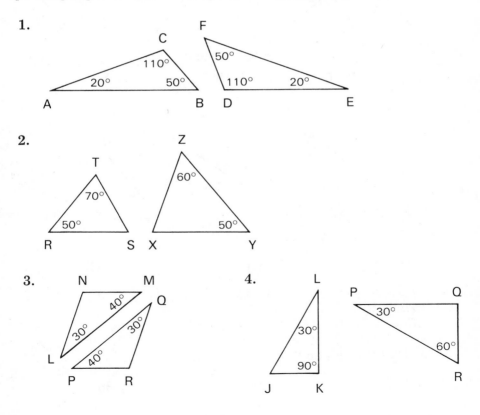

1.

2.

3.

4.

In 5 and 6, use a ruler and a protractor to draw the triangles involved in the question.

5. a. Draw triangle ABC in which $AB = 2$ in., $m\angle A = 50°$, and $m\angle B = 70°$.

    b. Draw triangle $A'B'C'$ similar to triangle ABC so that $\angle A'$ corresponds to $\angle A$, $\angle B'$ corresponds to $\angle B$, and $A'B' = 3$ inches.

6. a. Draw right triangle RST in which $\angle S$ is a right angle, $m\angle R = 70°$, and $RS = 3$ inches.

    b. Draw $\triangle R'S'T' \sim \triangle RST$ so that $\overline{R'S'}$ corresponds to $\overline{RS}$ and $R'S' = 1\frac{1}{2}$ inches.

7. In triangle RST, $m\angle R = 90°$ and $m\angle S = 40°$.
    In triangle XYZ, $m\angle Y = 40°$ and $m\angle Z = 50°$.
    a. Is triangle RST similar to triangle XYZ?   b. Why?

In 8 and 9, select the triangles that are similar and tell why they are similar.

8.

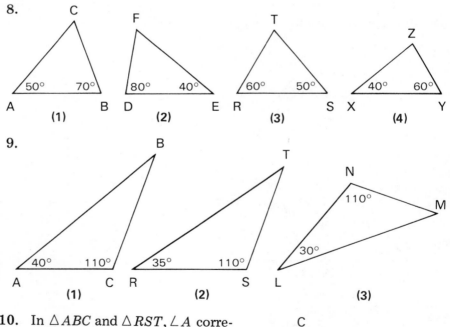

9.

10. In $\triangle ABC$ and $\triangle RST$, $\angle A$ corresponds to $\angle R$, $\angle B$ to $\angle S$, and $\angle C$ to $\angle T$. If $\triangle ABC \sim \triangle RST$, and if $AB = 9$ cm, $AC = 6$ cm, and $RS = 3$ cm, find RT.

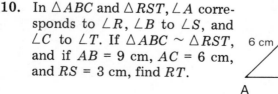

Ex. 10

11. **a.** Is triangle ABC similar to triangle DEF?
    b. State the reason for the answer given in part **a.**
    c. Find BC.

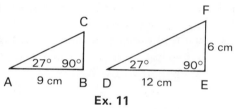

Ex. 11

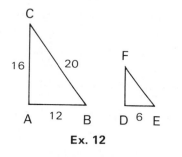

Ex. 12

12. In the figure, $m\angle A = m\angle D$ and $m\angle C = m\angle F$. If $AB = 12$, $AC = 16$, $BC = 20$, and $DE = 6$, find DF and EF.

13. In right triangles ABC and RST, $m\angle A = m\angle S$.
    a. Why is triangle ABC similar to triangle SRT?
    b. Find the value of x.

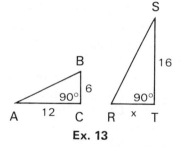

Ex. 13

14. The lengths of the sides of a triangle are 24, 16, and 12. If the shortest side of a similar triangle is 6, what is the length of the longest side of this triangle?

15. The lengths of the sides of a triangle are 36, 30, and 18. If the longest side of a similar triangle is 9, what is the length of the shortest side of this triangle?

16. To find the height of a tree, a hiker measured its shadow and found it to be 12 feet. At the same time a vertical rod 8 feet high cast a shadow of 6 feet.
    a. Is triangle ABC similar to triangle DEF?
    b. Why?
    c. Find the height of the tree.

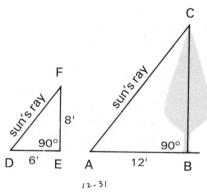

12-31

17. A certain tree casts a shadow 6 m long. At the same time a nearby boy 2 m tall casts a shadow 4 m long. Find the height of the tree.

18. A building casts a shadow 18 feet long. At the same time a woman 5 feet tall casts a shadow 3 feet long. Find the number of feet in the height of the building.

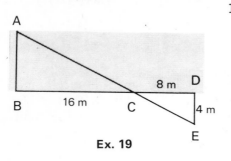

Ex. 19

19. In the figure, $\overline{AB}$ represents the width of a river. Angle B and angle D are right angles. $\overline{AE}$ and $\overline{BD}$ are line segments. m$\angle ACB$ = m$\angle DCE$. $BC = 16$ m, $CD = 8$ m, and $DE = 4$ m.
    a. Is triangle ABC similar to triangle EDC? Why?
    b. Find AB, the width of the river.

20. Using the figure in exercise 19, find AB, the width of the river, if $BC = 240$ ft., $CD = 80$ ft., and $DE = 25$ ft.

21. In the figure, $\overline{AD}$ and $\overline{CB}$ are line segments, m$\angle AEB$ = m$\angle DEC$, and m$\angle ABE$ = m$\angle DCE$. Find AB, the distance across the pond, if:
    a. $CE = 40$ m, $EB = 120$ m, and $CD = 50$ m
    b. $AE = 75$ m, $ED = 30$ m, and $CD = 36$ m

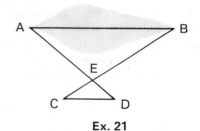

Ex. 21

In 22–26, use the figure at the right.

22. Prove informally that $\triangle ABC \sim \triangle AB'C'$.

23. $BC = 3$ in., $AC = 4$ in., and $AC' = 8$ in. Find $B'C'$.

24. $AC = 5$ m, $BC = 2$ m, and $B'C' = 8$ m. Find AC'.

25. $BC = 10$ cm and $AC = 8$ cm. Find the ratio of $B'C'$ to AC'.

26. $AC' = 48$, $B'C' = 36$, and $AC = 32$.
    a. Find BC.
    b. Find the area of triangle $AC'B'$.
    c. Find the area of triangle ACB.
    d. Find the area of trapezoid $BCC'B'$.

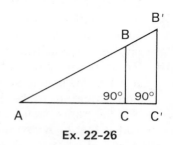

Ex. 22–26

3 CONGRUENT TRIANGLES

Congruent Polygons

In modern industry it is often necessary to make many copies of a part so that the original part and all copies will have the same size and shape. For example, a machine can stamp out many duplicates of a piece of metal, each copy having the same size and shape as the original. We say that the original and all its copies are *congruent*.

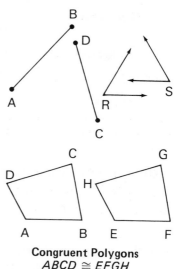

We have already talked about congruent segments such as $\overline{AB}$ and $\overline{CD}$, which are segments that are equal in length. We have also discussed congruent angles such as angles R and S, which are angles whose measures are equal. We have used the symbol "≅" to mean "is congruent to."

At the right we see two polygons that have the same size and shape. Such polygons are called *congruent polygons*. We say that polygon $ABCD$ is congruent to polygon $EFGH$, symbolized polygon $ABCD$ ≅ polygon $EFGH$.

Congruent Polygons
$ABCD \cong EFGH$

One way to discover whether or not two polygons have the same size and shape is to place one polygon upon the other. If the figures can be turned in such a way that the sides of one polygon *fit exactly* upon the sides of the other and the angles of one polygon *fit exactly* upon the angles of the other, we say that the polygons *coincide*. The sides that fit one upon the other are called *corresponding sides*. For example, in the given polygons $ABCD$ and $EFGH$, the pairs of corresponding sides are:

$$\overline{AB} \text{ and } \overline{EF} \quad \overline{BC} \text{ and } \overline{FG} \quad \overline{CD} \text{ and } \overline{GH} \quad \overline{DA} \text{ and } \overline{HE}$$

The angles that fit one upon the other are called *corresponding angles*. For example, in the given polygons $ABCD$ and $EFGH$, the pairs of corresponding angles are:

$$\angle A \text{ and } \angle E \quad \angle B \text{ and } \angle F \quad \angle C \text{ and } \angle G \quad \angle D \text{ and } \angle H$$

Now we can understand why we say:

If the sides of the first polygon are congruent to the corresponding sides of a second polygon, and if the angles of the first polygon are congruent to the corresponding angles of the second, then the two polygons are congruent.

Conversely, we can also say:

If two polygons are congruent, then their corresponding sides are congruent and their corresponding angles are congruent.

You can see that for two triangles to be proved congruent we would have to prove three pairs of corresponding sides congruent and three pairs of corresponding angles congruent. Let us see whether it is possible to prove two triangles congruent by proving fewer than three pairs of sides and three pairs of angles congruent.

Congruent Triangles Involving Two Sides and the Included Angle

Let us perform the following experiment:

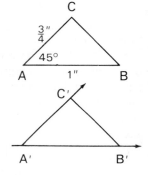

In $\triangle ABC$ we see that $AB = 1$ inch, $m\angle A = 45°$, and $AC = \frac{3}{4}$ inch. We say that $\angle A$ is *included* between side $\overline{AB}$ and side $\overline{AC}$ because these two segments are on the sides of the angle.

On a sheet of paper let us draw $\triangle A'B'C'$ so that $A'B' = 1$ inch, $A'C' = \frac{3}{4}$ inch, and the measure of the included angle A' is $45°$ ($m\angle A' = 45°$).

(1) We begin by drawing a working line on which we measure off 1 inch, the length of $\overline{A'B'}$.

(2) With a protractor we draw an angle of $45°$ whose vertex is at point A'.

(3) On the side of $\angle A'$ which was last drawn we measure off a line segment $\frac{3}{4}$ of an inch in length, beginning at point A' and ending at point C'.

(4) We then draw side $\overline{C'B'}$ to complete the triangle.

If we measure sides $\overline{CB}$ and $\overline{C'B'}$, we find the measures equal. Hence $\overline{CB} \cong \overline{C'B'}$. Also, if we measure $\angle C$ and $\angle C'$, we find their measures equal. $\angle B$ and $\angle B'$, if measured, are also found to have equal measures. Hence $\angle C \cong \angle C'$ and $\angle B \cong \angle B'$. Also, if we cut out $\triangle A'B'C'$, we can make it coincide with $\triangle ABC$. Thus $\triangle A'B'C'$ appears to be congruent to $\triangle ABC$.

If we repeat the same experiment several times with different sets of measurements for the two sides and the included angle, in each experiment the remaining pairs of corresponding parts of the triangles will appear to be congruent, and the triangles themselves will appear to be congruent. It seems reasonable, therefore, to accept the truth of the following statement:

■ Two triangles are congruent if two sides and the included angle of one triangle are congruent, respectively, to two sides and the included angle of the other. [s.a.s. ≅ s.a.s.]

In △ABC and △A'B'C' if $\overline{AB}$ ≅ $\overline{A'B'}$, ∠A ≅ ∠A', $\overline{AC}$ ≅ $\overline{A'C'}$, then △ABC ≅ △A'B'C'. [s.a.s. ≅ s.a.s.]

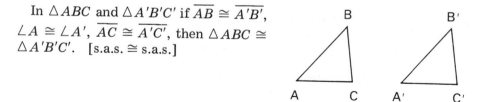

When the Angle Is Not Included Between the Sides

Let us see what happens when each of two triangles has one side 1″, a second side $\frac{3}{4}$″, and an angle that measures 45° is not included between these sides; that is, s.s.a. ≅ s.s.a. Must two such triangles always be congruent? With the use of a ruler and a protractor we can construct two different triangles that have the given measures as shown below.

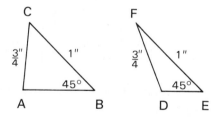

If we cut out triangle *ABC* and triangle *DEF*, we cannot make them coincide. Hence we see that when the angle is *not included* between the two sides, two triangles need not be congruent although two sides and an angle of one triangle are congruent to two sides and an angle in the other. Hence we see that proving s.s.a. ≅ s.s.a. in two triangles is *not sufficient* to prove the triangles congruent.

Congruent Triangles Involving Two Angles and the Included Side

Let us perform the following experiment:

In triangle *ABC* we see that m∠A = 60°, *AB* = 3 cm, and m∠B = 50°. We say that side $\overline{AB}$ is included between ∠A and ∠B because side $\overline{AB}$ is drawn between vertex *A* and vertex *B*.

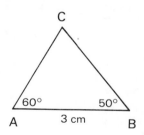

Let us construct $\triangle A'B'C'$ so that m$\angle A'$ = 60°, m$\angle B'$ = 50°, and the included side $\overline{A'B'}$ measures 3 cm. (See the figure at the right.)

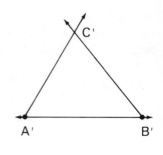

(1) We begin by drawing a working line on which we measure off 3 centimeters, the length of side $\overline{A'B'}$.

(2) With a protractor we measure an angle of 60° whose vertex is at point A'.

(3) We then measure an angle of 50° whose vertex is at point B'.

(4) To complete the triangle, we draw the sides of these angles so that they intersect at point C'.

We can see that $\triangle ABC$ and $\triangle A'B'C'$ appear to have the same size and shape.

Hence, $\triangle ABC$ appears to be congruent to $\triangle A'B'C'$.

If we repeat the same experiment several times with different sets of measurements for the two angles and the included side, the triangles in each experiment will appear to be congruent. Therefore, it seems reasonable to accept the truth of the following statement:

■ **Two triangles are congruent if two angles and the included side of one triangle are congruent respectively to two angles and the included side of the other triangle.   [a.s.a. $\cong$ a.s.a.]**

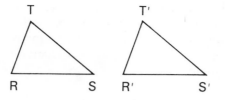

In $\triangle RST$ and $\triangle R'S'T'$: If $\angle R \cong \angle R'$, $\overline{RS} \cong \overline{R'S'}$, and $\angle S \cong \angle S'$, then $\triangle RST \cong \triangle R'S'T'$.   [a.s.a. $\cong$ a.s.a.]

| MODEL PROBLEMS |

1. In $\triangle ABC$: AB = 1", m$\angle A$ = 45°, and $AC = \frac{3}{4}''$. Use a ruler and a protractor to draw $\triangle DEF$ congruent to $\triangle ABC$.

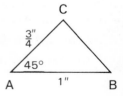

Solution

$\triangle DEF$ will be congruent to $\triangle ABC$ if two sides and an included angle in $\triangle DEF$ are congruent, respectively, to two sides and the included angle in $\triangle ABC$.   [s.a.s. $\cong$ s.a.s.]

Step 1. Use a ruler to draw segment $\overline{DE}$ whose length is 1 inch.

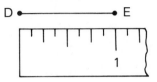

Step 2. Since point D corresponds to point A, and m$\angle A$ = 45°, draw, using a protractor, an angle of 45° at D.

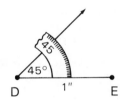

Step 3. Use a ruler to mark point F on this ray so that $DF = \frac{3}{4}''$, the length of the corresponding side $\overline{AC}$ in $\triangle ABC$.

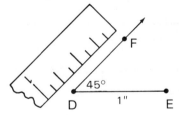

Step 4. Draw segment $\overline{EF}$ by connecting points E and F.

Answer: $\triangle DEF$ is the required triangle, which is congruent to $\triangle ABC$.

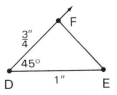

2. In the figure at the right, $\overline{AB}$ intersects $\overline{CD}$ at E, $\angle C$ and $\angle D$ are right angles, and $\overline{CE} \cong \overline{DE}$.

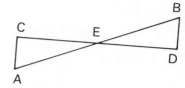

   a. Prove informally that $\triangle AEC \cong \triangle BED$.
   b. If $AE = 3x$ and $BE = 2x + 10$, find AE and BE.

Solution

a. (1) We are told that $\overline{CE} \cong \overline{DE}$.
   (2) We are told that $\angle C$ and $\angle D$ are right angles. Hence $\angle C \cong \angle D$ because all right angles are congruent.
   (3) Since $\angle CEA$ and $\angle DEB$ are a pair of vertical angles, $\angle CEA \cong \angle DEB$ because vertical angles are congruent.
   (4) $\triangle AEC \cong \triangle BED$ because two angles and the included side of one triangle are congruent to two angles and the included side of the other triangle. [a.s.a. $\cong$ a.s.a.]
b. (1) Since $\triangle AEC$ and $\triangle BED$ are congruent, their corresponding sides must be congruent. Therefore $\overline{AE} \cong \overline{BE}$.
   (2) Hence $AE = BE$.
   (3) Thus: $3x = 2x + 10$ S$_{2x}$
   $$x = 10$$
   $$3x = 30 \text{ and } 2x + 10 = 2(10) + 10 = 30$$

Answer: $AE = 30$ and $BE = 30$.

| EXERCISES |

In 1–3: Among figures **a, b, c, d,** and **e,** choose the figures that appear to be congruent.

1.

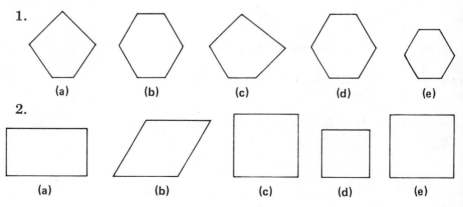

(a)   (b)   (c)   (d)   (e)

2.

(a)   (b)   (c)   (d)   (e)

3.

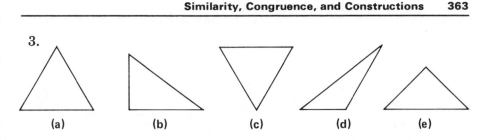

(a)   (b)   (c)   (d)   (e)

4. **a.** If several copies are made of the same photograph, will the figures in the original photograph and in the copies be congruent?
   b. Why?
5. **a.** If a photograph is enlarged, what can be said of the figures in the original and the figures in the enlargement? **b.** Why?
6. **a.** If two polygons are congruent, must they be similar? **b.** Why?
7. **a.** If two polygons are similar, must they be congruent? **b.** Why?

In 8–10, two triangles are to be drawn for each problem.   **a.** Use a ruler and protractor to draw $\triangle ABC$ and $\triangle DEF$, starting with the measures given for each triangle.   **b.** If the triangles are congruent, state the reason why they must be congruent. If the triangles are not congruent, explain why.

8. In $\triangle ABC$: $AB = 2''$, $m\angle B = 60°$, and $BC = 1\frac{1}{2}''$.
   In $\triangle DEF$: $DE = 1\frac{1}{2}''$, $m\angle E = 60°$, and $EF = 2''$.
9. In $\triangle ABC$: $AB = 3''$, $m\angle A = 40°$, and $m\angle B = 80°$.
   In $\triangle DEF$: $m\angle E = 80°$, $EF = 3''$, and $m\angle F = 40°$.
10. In $\triangle ABC$: $BC = 2.5$ cm, $m\angle C = 90°$, and $m\angle B = 60°$.
    In $\triangle DEF$: $EF = 2.5$ cm, $m\angle E = 60°$, and $\angle F$ is a right angle.

11. Sam and Rita each drew a triangle in which two sides and an angle measured, respectively, 5 cm, 8 cm, and 70°. The triangles were not congruent. Tell why this could have happened.
12. **a.** From the following triangles select pairs that are congruent. Tell why they are congruent. **b.** In each pair name the corresponding angles and the corresponding sides.

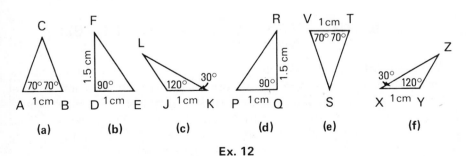

(a)   (b)   (c)   (d)   (e)   (f)

Ex. 12

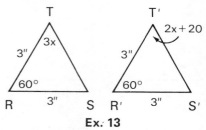

13. **a.** Tell why $\triangle RST \cong \triangle R'S'T'$.
    b. Find $m\angle RTS$ and $m\angle R'T'S'$.

Ex. 13

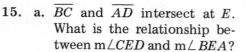

14. **a.** Tell why $\triangle ABC \cong \triangle A'B'C'$.

    b. Find BC and $B'C'$.

Ex. 14

15. **a.** $\overline{BC}$ and $\overline{AD}$ intersect at E. What is the relationship between $m\angle CED$ and $m\angle BEA$?
    b. Why is $\triangle CED \cong \triangle BEA$?
    c. What is the relationship between CD and BA?
    d. Find BA and CD.

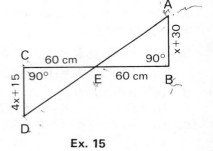

Ex. 15

16. In the figure at the right:
    a. What is the relationship that exists between $\triangle ABE$ and $\triangle CBE$? Why?
    b. Find AE and CE.

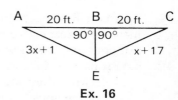

Ex. 16

4 CONSTRUCTIONS USING STRAIGHTEDGE AND COMPASS

When a draftsman draws a scale drawing for a blueprint, he may use a ruler to measure lengths, a protractor to measure angles, and parallel rulers to draw parallel lines. In our work in geometry, when we *draw* a figure, we may also use these instruments. However, when we *construct* a figure in geometry, we may use only the two tools of geometry: the straightedge, which is an unmarked ruler, and the compass.

To Construct a Segment Congruent to a Given Segment

Given: Line segment $\overline{AB}$

Required: To construct a line segment congruent to line segment $\overline{AB}$

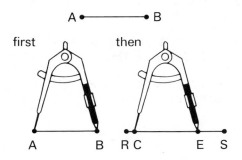

Construction: We begin by placing the point of the compass on point A and opening the compass so that the point of the pencil is on point B. Then we draw segment $\overline{RS}$, which is a longer segment than $\overline{AB}$. Choose any point on segment $\overline{RS}$ and mark it point C. Place the point of the compass on point C and swing the pencil point so that it cuts across segment $\overline{RS}$ at point E, being careful not to change the distance between the point of the compass and the point of the pencil. Segment $\overline{CE}$ and segment $\overline{AB}$ are congruent.

| EXERCISES |

In 1-4, use a straightedge and a compass only (no ruler) to construct a segment that is congruent to the given segment.

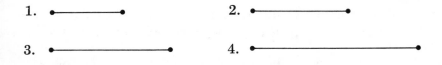

1. •————•   2. •————————•

3. •——————————•   4. •————————————•

In 5–7, use a straightedge and a compass to construct the required line segment. For each exercise use segment $\overline{AB}$, which is shown at the right.

5. Construct $\overline{RS}$ so that $\overline{RS} \cong \overline{AB}$.

6. Construct $\overline{DE}$ so that $\overline{DE}$ is twice as long as $\overline{AB}$.

7. Construct $\overline{JK}$ so that $\overline{JK}$ is three times the length of $\overline{AB}$.

A ———————————————— B

Ex. 5-7

To Construct a Triangle When the Three Sides Are Given [s.s.s.]

Given: Segments a, b, and c, which are the sides of $\triangle ABC$
Required: To construct $\triangle ABC$

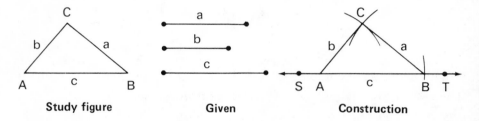

Study figure   Given   Construction

Construction: We begin with any line $\overleftrightarrow{ST}$.

(1) On line $\overleftrightarrow{ST}$ construct segment $\overline{AB}$ whose length is c. Mark the points A and B as shown above on the line $\overleftrightarrow{ST}$.

(2) With the compass opened to the length of b, place the compass point at A and draw an arc as shown above.

(3) With the compass opened to the length of a, place the compass point at B and draw an arc that intersects the previous arc at point C.

(4) Draw $\overline{AC}$ and $\overline{BC}$. The required triangle is $\triangle ABC$.

From this construction it appears that with three given segments to be used as the sides of a triangle, a triangle of only one shape and size can result.

Therefore it seems reasonable to believe the truth of the following statement:

■ **Two triangles are congruent if the three sides of one triangle are congruent respectively to the three sides of the other triangle. [s.s.s. $\cong$ s.s.s.]**

```
┌─────────────── KEEP IN MIND ───────────────┐
│                                             │
│  Two triangles are similar    when a.a.a. ≅ a.a.a.  │
│                               or    a.a. ≅ a.a.     │
│                                             │
├─────────────────────────────────────────────┤
│                                             │
│  Two triangles are congruent when s.s.s. ≅ s.s.s.  │
│                              or  s.a.s. ≅ s.a.s.    │
│                              or  a.s.a. ≅ a.s.a.    │
│                                             │
└─────────────────────────────────────────────┘
```

EXERCISES

1. Using only a straightedge and a compass, construct triangle RST in which RS = 1 in., ST = $1\frac{1}{2}$ in., and TR = 2 in.

In 2-4, use a straightedge and a compass to construct a triangle ABC whose sides have the same lengths as the given segments.

2. •——a——•   •————b————•   •—c—•

3. •——a——•   •——b——•   •————c————•

4. •——a——•   •——b——•   •————c————•

In 5-7, use only a straightedge and a compass to show that it is impossible to construct a triangle that has these segments as its sides:

5. 1 in., 2 in., 5 in.   6. $1\frac{1}{4}$ in., $1\frac{3}{4}$ in., $3\frac{1}{2}$ in.   7. 2 cm, 3 cm, 6 cm

8. What relationship does it appear must exist among the lengths of three given segments so that these three segments may be used as the sides in the construction of a triangle?

In 9-13, use a ruler to draw a segment that has the given length. Then construct an equilateral triangle, using straightedge and compass only, so that each of the sides of the equilateral triangle is congruent to the given segment.

9. 1 inch   10. $\frac{3}{4}$ inch   11. $1\frac{1}{2}$ inches   12. 3 cm   13. 2.5 cm

In 14–17, draw segments that have the given lengths. Then construct isosceles triangle ABC in which $\overline{AB}$ and $\overline{BC}$ are the congruent sides and $\overline{AC}$ is the base.

14. $AB = 1$ inch, $AC = \frac{3}{4}$ inch   **15.** $BC = 1\frac{1}{2}$ inches, $AC = 1$ inch
16. $AB = 2$ cm, $AC = 3$ cm   **17.** $BC = 3.5$ cm, $AC = 2.5$ cm

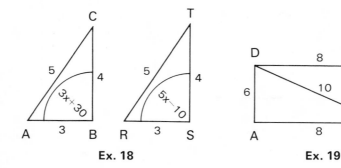

Ex. 18   Ex. 19

18. **a.** Is $\triangle ABC \cong \triangle RST$?   **b.** Why?   **c.** Find m$\angle B$ and m$\angle S$.
19. Prove informally that $\triangle ABD \cong \triangle CDB$.

To Construct an Angle Congruent to a Given Angle

Given: $\angle ABC$
Required: To construct an angle congruent to $\angle ABC$

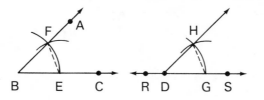

Construction: We begin with any line $\overleftrightarrow{RS}$.

(1) On line $\overleftrightarrow{RS}$ select and mark any point D.

(2) With the compass opened to any length, place the compass point at point B and draw an arc that intersects ray $\overrightarrow{BA}$ and ray $\overrightarrow{BC}$ in points F and E respectively as shown in the figure above.

(3) With the compass opened to the same length as in step (2), place the compass point at point D and draw an arc that intersects line $\overleftrightarrow{RS}$ at point G.

(4) Draw segment $\overline{EF}$ and open the compass to the length of $\overline{EF}$.

(5) With the compass opened to this length, place the compass point at point G and draw an arc that intersects the arc drawn in step (3) at point H.

(6) Draw ray $\overrightarrow{DH}$. Then, $\angle HDS$ will be congruent to $\angle ABC$.

   To prove that $\angle HDS$ is congruent to $\angle ABC$, we would draw segment $\overline{GH}$. Observe that $\triangle EBF$ would be congruent to $\triangle GDH$ because all pairs of corresponding sides were made congruent in the construction. Hence, $\angle HDS$ and $\angle ABC$ would be congruent because they are corresponding angles of congruent triangles.

EXERCISES

   In 1–5, draw an angle in the same position and having about the same measure as the given angle. Then, using a straightedge and compass, construct an angle congruent to the angle you have drawn.

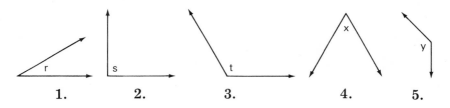

1.   2.   3.   4.   5.

To Construct a Triangle Similar to a Given Triangle on a Given Segment as a Base

   Given: $\triangle ABC$ and line segment $\overline{RS}$

   Required: On line segment $\overline{RS}$, corresponding to side $\overline{AB}$ of $\triangle ABC$, to construct a triangle similar to $\triangle ABC$

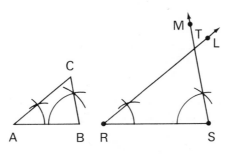

Construction:

(1) At R construct $\angle SRL$ congruent to $\angle BAC$.

(2) At S construct $\angle RSM$ congruent to $\angle ABC$.

(3) Represent by T the point of intersection of rays $\overrightarrow{RL}$ and $\overrightarrow{SM}$.

(4) The required triangle is $\triangle RST$.

It is a rather simple matter to explain why $\triangle RST \sim \triangle ABC$. The construction makes $\angle R \cong \angle A$ and $\angle S \cong \angle B$. Therefore, $\triangle RST \sim \triangle ABC$ because two angles of one triangle are congruent to two angles of the other triangle.   [a.a. $\cong$ a.a.]

EXERCISES

In 1–4, draw a triangle in the same position as the given triangle. Then use a straightedge and compass to construct a triangle similar to the triangle you drew.

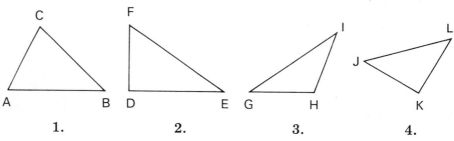

1.   2.   3.   4.

5. Draw a triangle like triangle XYZ. Then construct a triangle that will be similar to triangle XYZ and the ratio of whose sides to the corresponding sides in triangle XYZ will be:
   a. 2:1   b. 3:1   c. 1:1

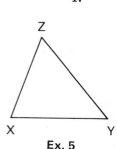

Ex. 5

6. What relationship will the triangle that was constructed in exercise 5, part c, have to triangle XYZ besides being similar to it?

To Construct a Triangle When Two Sides and the Included Angle Are Given [s.a.s.]

Given: Line segments b and c, and $\angle A$
Required: To construct $\triangle ABC$ with sides b and c, and included $\angle A$

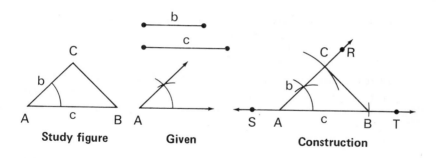

| Study figure | Given | Construction |

Construction: We begin with any line $\overleftrightarrow{ST}$.

(1) Select any point A on line $\overleftrightarrow{ST}$ and at A construct segment $\overline{AB} \cong$ segment c. Mark points A and B on $\overleftrightarrow{ST}$ as shown.

(2) At point A construct $\angle BAR \cong \angle A$.

(3) On ray $\overrightarrow{AR}$ construct segment $\overline{AC} \cong$ segment b.

(4) Construct segment $\overline{BC}$. The required triangle is $\triangle ABC$.

It is a rather simple matter to explain why $\triangle ABC$ is the required triangle. The construction makes $\overline{AB} \cong$ segment c, $\angle CAB \cong \angle A$, and $\overline{AC} \cong$ segment b. [s.a.s. $\cong$ s.a.s.]

EXERCISES

In 1–3, draw two segments and an angle that have about the same measures as those pictured. Then construct $\triangle ABC$ so that $\angle A$ will be included between segment b and segment c.

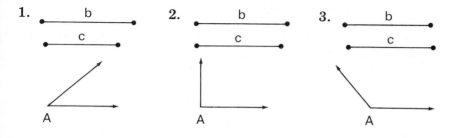

1. b   c   A

2. b   c   A

3. b   c   A

To Construct a Triangle When Two Angles and the Included Side Are Given [a.s.a.]

Given: Line segment c, $\angle A$, and $\angle B$
Required: To construct $\triangle ABC$ with $\angle A$, $\angle B$, and included side c

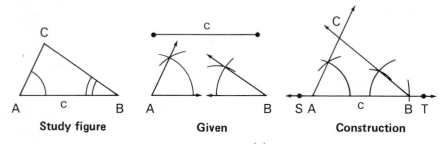

| Study figure | Given | Construction |

Construction: We begin with any line $\overleftrightarrow{ST}$.

(1) Select any point A on line $\overleftrightarrow{ST}$ and at A construct segment $\overline{AB} \cong$ segment c.

(2) At A construct an angle congruent to $\angle A$.

(3) At B construct an angle congruent to $\angle B$.

(4) Extend the sides of $\angle A$ and $\angle B$ constructed in steps (2) and (3) until they intersect at C.

(5) The required triangle is $\triangle ABC$.

It is rather a simple matter to explain why $\triangle ABC$ is the required triangle. The construction makes $\angle CAB \cong \angle A$, $\overline{AB} \cong$ segment c, and $\angle ABC \cong \angle B$. [a.s.a. $\cong$ a.s.a.]

EXERCISES

In 1–3, draw two angles and a segment that have about the same measures as those pictured. Then construct $\triangle ABC$ so that segment c will be included between $\angle A$ and $\angle B$.

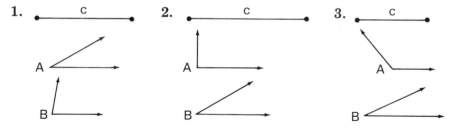

1.

2.

3.

chapter thirteen

Solving Problems by Using First-Degree Open Sentences in One Variable

We have already studied methods of solving number problems and geometric problems. Now we will learn how to solve more challenging problems that arise in a variety of situations. We will first translate the problem, which is stated in words, into an open sentence stated in algebraic language as an equation or an inequality. Then we will solve the open sentence.

1 NUMBER PROBLEMS

Preparing to Solve Number Problems

| EXERCISES |

In exercises 1–6, represent in terms of x:

1. twice the number represented by x increased by 8
2. three times the number represented by x decreased by 12
3. four times the number that is 3 more than x
4. three times the number that exceeds x by 5
5. twice the sum of the number represented by x and 5
6. ten times the number obtained when twice x is decreased by 10

7. If the smaller of two numbers is represented by x, represent the greater when their sum is:
   a. 10   b. 25   c. 36   d. 50   e. 100   f. 3000
8. If the sum of two numbers is represented by S, and the smaller number is represented by x, represent the greater in terms of S and x.
9. If the sum of two numbers is represented by S, and the greater number is represented by l, represent the smaller in terms of S and l.

Solving Number Problems

| MODEL PROBLEMS |

1. The greater of two numbers is twice the smaller. If the greater is decreased by 10, the result is 5 more than the smaller. Find the numbers.

How to Proceed   *Solution*

1. Represent the smaller number by a variable and all the other described numbers in terms of the same variable.

Let x = the smaller number.
Then $2x$ = the greater number.
Then $2x - 10$ = the greater decreased by 10.
Then $x + 5 = 5$ more than the smaller.

2. Write an open sentence that symbolizes the relationships stated in the problem.

The greater decreased by 10   *is*   *5 more than the smaller.*

$$2x - 10 = x + 5$$

3. Solve the open sentence.

$$2x - 10 + 10 = x + 5 + 10$$
$$2x = x + 15$$
$$2x + (-x) = x + 15 + (-x)$$
$$x = 15$$
$$2x = 30$$

4. Check the answers in the original problem.

The greater decreased by 10 = 30 - 10 = 20.
5 more than the smaller = 15 + 5 = 20.
The results are the same, 20.

Answer: The smaller number is 15; the greater number is 30.

2. The larger of two numbers is 4 times the smaller. If the larger number exceeds the smaller number by 15, find the number.

Note: When s represents the smaller number and $4s$ represents the larger number, "the larger exceeds the smaller by 15" has the following meanings. Use any one of them.

1. The larger equals 15 more than the smaller, written $4s = s + 15$.
2. The larger decreased by 15 equals the smaller, written $4s - 15 = s$.
3. The larger decreased by the smaller equals 15, written $4s - s = 15$.

Solution:

$$\text{Let } s = \text{the smaller number.}$$
$$\text{Then } 4s = \text{the larger number.}$$

The larger   is   15 more than the smaller.

$$4s \quad = \quad s + 15$$

$$4s = s + 15$$
$$4s + (-s) = s + 15 + (-s)$$
$$3s = 15$$
$$s = 5$$
$$4s = 20$$

Check: The larger number, 20, is 4 times the smaller number, 5. The larger number, 20, exceeds the smaller number, 5, by 15.

Answer: The larger number is 20; the smaller number is 5.

EXERCISES

1. The greater of two numbers is 12 more than the smaller. Their sum is 60. Find the numbers.
2. The smaller of two numbers is 8 less than the greater. The sum of these numbers is 28. Find the numbers.
3. The sum of two numbers is −35. Find these numbers if the second number is 4 more than two times the first number.

4. The greater of two numbers is 8 more than three times the smaller. Their sum is 28. Find the numbers.

5. The sum of two numbers is 65. The second is 10 less than four times the first. Find the numbers.

6. The sum of three numbers is 57. The first is 2 less than the second, and the third is 5 more than the second. Find the numbers.

7. If 5 times a number is increased by 50, the result is the same as when 200 is decreased by the number. Find the number.

8. If 10 times a certain number is increased by 4, the result is 12 more than 9 times the number. Find the number.

9. If 3 times a number is increased by 22, the result is 14 less than 7 times the number. Find the number.

10. The ratio of two numbers is 2:1. If the greater is diminished by 10, the result is 2 more than the smaller. Find the numbers.

11. The larger of two numbers is 20 more than the smaller. Four times the larger is 70 more than 5 times the smaller. Find the numbers.

12. If 14 is added to a certain number and the sum is multiplied by 2, the result is equal to 8 times the number decreased by 14. Find the number.

13. The difference between two numbers is 24. Find the numbers if their sum is 88.

14. Separate 144 people into two groups such that one group will be 12 less than twice the other.

15. Separate 45 into two parts such that 5 times the smaller is 6 less than twice the greater.

16. The greater of two numbers is 1 less than 3 times the smaller. If 3 times the greater is 5 more than 8 times the smaller, find the numbers.

17. The larger of two numbers is 1 more than 3 times the smaller. The difference between 8 times the smaller and 2 times the larger is 10. Find the numbers.

18. The ratio of two numbers is 8:1. If the larger number exceeds the smaller by 56, find the numbers.

19. The greater of two numbers is 1 more than twice the smaller. Three times the greater exceeds 5 times the smaller by 10. Find the numbers.

20. The second of three numbers is 2 more than the first. The third number is twice the first. The sum of the first and third exceeds the second by 2. Find the three numbers.

21. The second of three numbers is 1 less than the first. The third number is 5 less than twice the second. If the third number exceeds the first number by 12, find the three numbers.

2 CONSECUTIVE INTEGER PROBLEMS

Preparing to Solve Consecutive Integer Problems

As we know, an integer is any whole number, positive or negative, or zero. Examples of integers are 5, -3, and 0.

Consecutive integers are integers that follow one another in order. To obtain a set of consecutive integers, we start with any integer and count by ones. Each number in the set is 1 more than the previous number in the set. Each of the following is a set of consecutive integers:

1. $\{5, 6, 7, 8\}$ 2. $\{-5, -4, -3, -2\}$
3. $\{x, x + 1, x + 2, x + 3\}$ $x \in \{\text{integers}\}$

Consecutive even integers are even integers that follow one another in order. To obtain a set of consecutive even integers, we can start with any even integer and count by twos. Each number in the set is 2 more than the previous number in the set. Each of the following is a set of consecutive even integers:

1. $\{2, 4, 6, 8\}$ 2. $\{-12, -10, -8, -6\}$
3. $\{x, x + 2, x + 4, x + 6\}$ $x \in \{\text{even integers}\}$

Consecutive odd integers are odd integers that follow one another in order. To obtain a set of consecutive odd integers, we start with any odd integer and count by twos. Each number in the set is 2 more than the previous number in the set. Each of the following is a set of consecutive odd integers:

1. $\{3, 5, 7, 9\}$ 2. $\{-5, -3, -1, 1\}$
3. $\{x, x + 2, x + 4, x + 6\}$ $x \in \{\text{odd integers}\}$

```
┌──────────────────── KEEP IN MIND ────────────────────┐
│                                                       │
│  1.  Consecutive integers differ by 1.                │
│                                                       │
│  2.  Consecutive even integers and also consecutive odd│
│      integers differ by 2.                            │
│                                                       │
└───────────────────────────────────────────────────────┘
```

EXERCISES

1. a. If $x = 3$, what numbers do x, $x + 1$, $x + 2$, $x + 3$, and $x + 4$ represent? b. What kind of integers are these numbers?
2. a. If $n = -3$, what numbers do n, $n + 1$, $n + 2$, $n + 3$, and $n + 4$ represent? b. What kind of integers are these numbers?

3. a. If $x = -1$, what numbers do x, $x + 2$, $x + 4$, $x + 6$, and $x + 8$ represent? b. What kind of integers are these numbers?
4. Write 4 consecutive integers beginning with each of the following integers (y is an integer):
   a. 15   b. 31   c. -10 d. -2 e. y f. $2y + 1$ g. $3y - 2$
5. Write 4 consecutive even integers beginning with each of the following integers (y is an even integer):
   a. 8   b. 26   c. -20 d. -4 e. y f. $2y$ g. $2y - 6$
6. Write 4 consecutive odd integers beginning with each of the following integers (y is an odd integer):
   a. 9   b. 35   c. -15 d. -3 e. y f. $2y + 1$ g. $2y - 1$

In 7–10, tell whether the number represented is odd or even when n is: (a) an odd integer; (b) an even integer.

7. $n + 1$ 8. $n - 1$ 9. $n + 3$ 10. $n + 4$

11. State whether $x + y$ is odd or even when: (a) x and y are odd integers; (b) x is an odd integer and y is an even integer; (c) x and y are even integers.

In 12–14, replace the question mark with the word "odd" or the word "even" so that the resulting statement will be true.

12. The sum of an even number of consecutive odd integers is an __?__ integer.
13. The sum of an odd number of consecutive odd integers is an __?__ integer.
14. The sum of any number of consecutive even integers is an __?__ integer.

Solving Consecutive Integer Problems

| MODEL PROBLEMS |

1. Find two consecutive integers whose sum is 95.

   Solution:

   Let n = the first integer.
   Then $n + 1$ = the second integer.
   Then $2n + 1$ = the sum of the two integers.

$$\underbrace{\textit{The sum of the two integers}}\ \underbrace{\textit{is}}\ \underbrace{\textit{95.}}$$

$$n + (n + 1) \qquad\qquad = \quad 95$$

$$n + n + 1 = 95$$
$$2n + 1 = 95$$
$$2n + 1 - 1 = 95 - 1$$
$$2n = 94$$
$$n = 47, n + 1 = 48$$

Check: The sum of the consecutive integers, 47 and 48, is 95.

Answer: 47 and 48

2. Find 3 consecutive positive even integers such that 4 times the first decreased by the second is 12 more than twice the third.

Solution:

> Let n = the first even integer.
> Then $n + 2$ = the second even integer.
> Then $n + 4$ = the third even integer.

$$\underbrace{\textit{4 times the first decreased}\atop \textit{by the second}}\ \underbrace{\textit{is}}\ \underbrace{\textit{12 more than}\atop \textit{twice the third.}}$$

$$4n - (n + 2) \qquad\qquad = \quad 2(n + 4) + 12$$

$$4n - n - 2 = 2n + 8 + 12$$
$$3n - 2 = 2n + 20$$
$$3n - 2 + 2 = 2n + 20 + 2$$
$$3n = 2n + 22$$
$$3n + (-2n) = 2n + 22 + (-2n)$$
$$n = 22$$
$$n + 2 = 24, n + 4 = 26$$

Check: Show that 22, 24, and 26 satisfy the conditions in the given problem: $4(22) - 24$ is 12 more than $2(26)$.

Answer: 22, 24, 26

| EXERCISES |

1. Find two consecutive integers whose sum is:
   a. 61   b. 35   c. 91   d. 125   e. -17   f. -81
2. Find three consecutive integers whose sum is:
   a. 18   b. 48   c. 99   d. 0   e. -12   f. -57
3. Find four consecutive integers whose sum is 234.
4. Find two consecutive even integers whose sum is:
   a. 22   b. 38   c. 146   d. 206   e. -10   f. -34
5. Find three consecutive even integers whose sum is:
   a. 12   b. 48   c. 156   d. 258   e. -18   f. -60
6. Find four consecutive even integers whose sum is 60.
7. Find three consecutive odd integers whose sum is:
   a. 33   b. 45   c. 159   d. 615   e. -27   f. -105
8. Find four consecutive odd integers whose sum is 112.
9. Find three consecutive integers such that the sum of the first and the third is 40.
10. Find four consecutive integers such that the sum of the second and fourth is 132.
11. Find two consecutive odd integers such that four times the larger is 29 more than three times the smaller.
12. Find two consecutive even integers such that twice the smaller is 26 less than three times the larger.
13. In each part find two consecutive even integers whose ratio is given.
    a. $1:2$ b. $2:3$ c. $3:4$ d. $4:5$
14. In each part find two consecutive odd integers whose ratio is given.
    a. $1:3$ b. $3:5$ c. $5:7$ d. $11:13$
15. Find three consecutive integers such that twice the smallest is 12 more than the largest.
16. Find three consecutive integers such that the sum of the first two integers is 24 more than the third integer.
17. Find three consecutive even integers such that the sum of the smallest and twice the second is 20 more than the third.
18. Find two consecutive integers such that 4 times the larger exceeds 3 times the smaller by 23.
19. Find four consecutive odd integers such that the sum of the first three exceeds the fourth by 18.
20. Find three positive consecutive odd integers such that the largest decreased by three times the second is 47 less than the smallest.
21. Is it possible to find 3 consecutive even integers whose sum is 40? Why?
22. Is it possible to find 3 consecutive odd integers whose sum is 59? Why?

3 PERCENT AND PERCENTAGE PROBLEMS

You have learned that *percent* means *per hundred* or *hundredths*. For example, 13% is $\frac{13}{100}$ or .13. Likewise, 6% is $\frac{6}{100}$ or .06; 100% is $\frac{100}{100}$ or 1; 150% = $\frac{150}{100}$ or 1.50.

Problems dealing with discounts, commissions, and taxes frequently involve percents. For example, to find the amount of tax when $60 is taxed at a rate of 8%, we multiply $60 by 8%, .08(60), and get $4.80 as the result. In this case the three quantities related are:

1. the sum of money being taxed, the *base*, which is $60
2. the rate of tax, the *rate*, which is 8% or .08
3. the amount of tax, the *percentage*, which is $4.80

Hence, we see that:

$$\text{percentage} = \text{rate} \times \text{base}$$

The relation involving base, b, rate, r, and percentage, p, may be expressed as follows:

$$p = rb$$

Since $p = rb$, when we divide both sides of the equation by b, we get $\frac{p}{b} = \frac{rb}{b}$, or $\frac{p}{b} = r$. That is, $\frac{\text{percentage}}{\text{base}} = \text{rate}$.

Let us realize that a percent may be considered as the ratio of a number to 100. For example, 8%, which means $\frac{8}{100}$, is the ratio of 8 to 100. We can use this fact in the following manner to find how much an 8% tax on $60 is.

Let t = amount of the tax.

Then: $\dfrac{\text{amount of the tax}}{\text{sum to be taxed}} = \dfrac{8}{100}$ This is a proportion because it consists of two equal ratios.

$$\frac{t}{60} = \frac{8}{100}$$

$$100t = 480$$

$$t = 4.80$$

In a proportion the product of the means is equal to the product of the extremes.

Answer: The tax is $4.80.

Note: It may be helpful to think of the ratio as "*part is to whole*" when setting up the proportion. On one side the amount of the tax is a "part number" while the sum to be taxed is a "whole number." On the other side we write $\frac{8}{100}$ to show 8%. The 8 represents "how many percent in the part" and the 100 represents "how many percent in the whole."

Thus, $\overbrace{\dfrac{\text{Part}}{\text{Whole}}}^{\text{Number}} = \overbrace{\dfrac{\text{Part}}{\text{Whole}}}^{\text{Percent}}$, which represents a proportion.

| MODEL PROBLEMS |

1. Represent $\frac{3}{5}$ as a percent.

   Solution: Let x = the number of percent.

   $$\frac{3}{5} = \frac{x}{100}$$
   $$5x = 300$$
   $$x = 60 \quad \text{D}_5$$

   Check

   Does $\frac{3}{5} = \frac{60}{100}$? Yes.

   Answer: 60%

2. If 25% of a number is 80, find the number.

   Solution

Method 1	*Method 2*
[*Think:* 80 is "part" of some unknown "whole" number n; 25% = $\frac{25}{100}$]	[*Think:* percentage p = 80; rate r = 25% = .25; base b = unknown n]
Let n = the number.	Let n = the number.
$\dfrac{80}{n} = \dfrac{25}{100}$	$p = rb$
$25n = 8000$	$80 = .25n$
$n = 320 \quad \text{D}_{25}$	$\dfrac{80}{.25} = \dfrac{.25n}{.25} \quad \text{D}_{.25}$
	$320 = n$

   Check: 25% of 320 is 80.

   Answer: The number is 320.

3. Of the 560 seniors in Village High School, 476 attended the senior prom. What percent of the senior class attended the prom?

Solution

Let $\dfrac{x}{100}$ = the percent of the senior class that attended the dance.

Method 1

$$\dfrac{476}{560} = \dfrac{x}{100}$$

[476 = part; 560 = whole]

$$560x = 47{,}600$$

$$x = 85 \quad \mathrm{D}_{560}$$

$$\dfrac{x}{100} = \dfrac{85}{100} = 85\%$$

Method 2

$$p = br$$

$$[p = 476, \ b = 560]$$

$$476 = 560\left(\dfrac{x}{100}\right)$$

$$476 = \dfrac{560}{100}\,x$$

$$\dfrac{100}{560}\,(476) = \dfrac{100}{560}\left(\dfrac{560}{100}\,x\right) \quad \mathrm{M}_{\frac{100}{560}}$$

$$85 = x$$

$$\dfrac{x}{100} = \dfrac{85}{100} = 85\%$$

Check: 85% of 560 is 476.

Answer: 85% of the seniors attended.

EXERCISES

In 1–9, find the indicated percentage.

1. 2% of 36
2. 6% of 150
3. 15% of 48
4. 2.5% of 400
5. 60% of 56
6. 100% of 7.5
7. $12\frac{1}{2}\%$ of 128
8. $33\frac{1}{3}\%$ of 72
9. 150% of 18

In 10–17, find the number.

10. 20 is 10% of what number?
11. 64 is 80% of what number?
12. 8% of what number is 16?
13. 72 is 100% of what number?
14. 125% of what number is 45?
15. $37\frac{1}{2}\%$ of what number is 60?
16. $66\frac{2}{3}\%$ of what number is 54?
17. 3% of what number is 1.86?

In 18–25, find the percent.

18. 6 is what percent of 12?
19. 9 is what percent of 30?
20. What % of 10 is 6?
21. What % of 35 is 28?
22. 5 is what % of 15?
23. 22 is what % of 22?
24. 18 is what % of 12?
25. 2 is what percent of 400?

26. A newspaper has 80 pages. If 20 of the 80 pages are devoted to advertising, what percent of the newspaper is advertising?
27. A test was passed by 90% of a class. If 27 students passed the test, how many students were in the class?
28. Marie bought a dress that was marked $24. The sales tax is 8%. a. Find the sales tax. b. Find the total amount Marie had to pay.
29. There were 120 planes on an airfield. If 75% of the planes took off for a flight, how many planes took off?
30. One year the Ace Manufacturing Company made a profit of $480,000. This represented 6% of the volume of business for the year. What was the volume of business for the year?
31. The price of a new car is $5430. Mr. Klein made a down payment of 15% of the price of the car when he bought it. How much was his down payment?
32. How much silver is in 75 kilograms of an alloy that is 8% silver?
33. In a factory, 54,650 parts were made. When these were tested, 4% were found to be defective. How many parts were good?
34. A baseball team won 8 games, which was 50% of the total number of games it played. How many games did the team play?
35. Helen bought a coat at a "20% off" sale and saved $24. What was the marked price of the coat?
36. A businessman is required to collect an 8% sales tax. One day he collected $280 in taxes. Find the total amount of sales he made that day.
37. A merchant sold a television set for $150, which was 25% above its cost to him. Find the cost of the television set to the dealer.
38. Bill bought a set of golf clubs at a sale. The original price was $120; the sale price was $90. By what percent was the original price reduced?
39. If the sales tax on $150 is $7.50, what is the percent of the sales tax?
40. Mr. Tayler took a 2% discount on a bill. He paid the balance with a check for $76.44. What was the original amount of the bill?
41. After the price of a pound of meat was increased 10%, the new price was $1.98. What was the price of a pound of meat before the increase?
42. After Mrs. Sims lost 15% of her investment, she had $2550 left. How much did she invest originally?

43. When a salesman sold a vacuum cleaner for $110, he received a commission of $8.80. What was the rate of commission?
44. Alicia bought a car for $4800. At the end of a year, the value of the car had decreased $960. By what percent had the car decreased in value?
45. Mr. Brown's salary increased from $200 per week to $275 per week. Find the percent of increase in his salary.
46. At a sale a camera was reduced $8. This represented 10% of the original price. On the last day of the sale the camera was sold for 75% of the original price. What was the final selling price of the camera?

4   PERIMETER PROBLEMS

Preparing to Solve Perimeter Problems

KEEP IN MIND

The perimeter of a geometric plane figure is the sum of the lengths of all of its sides.

| EXERCISES |

1. Represent the perimeter of each of the following figures:

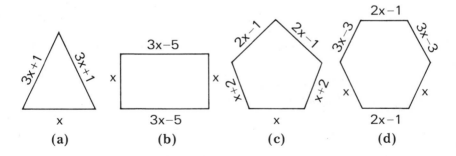

(a)   (b)   (c)   (d)

2. Represent the length and perimeter of a rectangle whose width is represented by x and whose length:
   a. is twice its width
   b. is 4 more than its width
   c. is 5 less than twice its width
   d. is 3 more than twice its width

3. A side of an equilateral triangle is represented by $x + 5$. Represent the perimeter of the triangle.

4. If each side of a square is represented by $2x - 1$, represent the perimeter of the square.

5. If each side of an equilateral pentagon (5 sides) is represented by $2x + 3$, represent the perimeter of the pentagon.

6. Each side of an equilateral hexagon (6 sides) is represented by $2x - 3$. Represent the perimeter of the hexagon.

7. The perimeter of an equilateral polygon is $12x - 24$. Express the length of one side if the polygon is:

   a. a triangle   b. a square   c. a hexagon

Solving Perimeter Problems

In solving problems dealing with the perimeters of geometric plane figures, it is helpful to draw the figures.

| MODEL PROBLEM |

The perimeter of a rectangle is 40 feet. The length is 2 more than 5 times the width. Find the dimensions of the rectangle.

Solution

Let w = the width of the rectangle.

Then $5w + 2$ = the length of the rectangle.

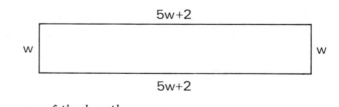

The sum of the lengths of all the sides *is 40.*

$$w + (5w + 2) + w + (5w + 2) = 40$$

$$w + 5w + 2 + w + 5w + 2 = 40$$
$$12w + 4 = 40$$
$$12w + 4 - 4 = 40 - 4$$
$$12w = 36$$
$$w = 3$$
$$5w + 2 = 17$$

Check

$$3 + 17 + 3 + 17 = 40$$
$$17 \stackrel{?}{=} 5(3) + 2$$
$$17 = 17 \quad \text{(True)}$$

Answer: The width is 3 feet; the length is 17 feet.

EXERCISES

1. The length of a rectangle is 3 times its width. The perimeter of the rectangle is 72 cm. Find the dimensions of the rectangle.

2. The ratio of the length of a rectangle to its width is $4:1$. The perimeter of the rectangle is 150 feet. Find the dimensions of the rectangle.

3. The length of a rectangle is $2\frac{1}{2}$ times its width. The perimeter of the rectangle is 84 cm. Find the dimensions of the rectangle.

4. In an isosceles triangle the ratio of one leg to the base is 4 to 1. The perimeter of the triangle is 144 meters. Find the length of each side of the triangle.

5. The length of the second side of a triangle is 8 inches less than the length of the first side. The length of the third side is 14 inches more than the length of the first side. The perimeter of the triangle is 63 inches. Find the length of each side of the triangle.

6. Two sides of a triangle are equal in length. The length of the third side exceeds the length of each of the congruent sides by 3 centimeters. The perimeter of the triangle is 93 centimeters. Find the length of each of the congruent sides of the triangle.

7. The length of a rectangle is 5 meters more than its width. The perimeter is 66 meters. Find the dimensions of the rectangle.

8. The width of a rectangle is 3 yards less than its length. The perimeter is 130 yards. Find the length and the width of the rectangle.

9. The perimeter of a rectangular parking lot is 146 meters. Find its dimensions if the length is 7 meters less than 4 times the width.

10. The perimeter of a rectangular tennis court is 228 feet. If the length of the court exceeds twice its width by 6 feet, find its dimensions.

11. The length of the base of an isosceles triangle is 10 less than twice the length of one of its legs. If the perimeter of the triangle is 50, find the length of the base of the triangle.

12. The base of an isosceles triangle and one of its legs have lengths that are consecutive integers. The leg is larger than the base. The perimeter of the triangle is 20. Find the length of each side of the triangle.

13. The length of a rectangle is twice the width. If the length is increased by 4 inches and the width is decreased by 1 inch, a new rectangle is formed whose perimeter is 198 inches. Find the dimensions of the original rectangle.

14. The length of a rectangle exceeds its width by 4 feet. If the width is doubled and the length is diminished by 2 feet, a new rectangle is formed whose perimeter is 8 feet more than the perimeter of the original rectangle. Find the dimensions of the original rectangle.

15. A side of a square is 10 meters longer than the side of an equilateral triangle. The perimeter of the square is 3 times the perimeter of the triangle. Find the length of each side of the triangle.
16. The length of each side of a hexagon is 4 inches less than the length of a side of a square. The perimeter of the hexagon is equal to the perimeter of the square. Find the length of a side of the hexagon and the length of a side of the square.

5   AREA PROBLEMS
Preparing to Solve Area Problems

KEEP IN MIND

Area of a rectangle = Length $\times$ Width

| EXERCISES |

1. Represent as a polynomial in terms of x the area of a rectangle whose length and width are represented by:
   a. $l = 7, w = x$ b. $l = 5, w = x + 2$ c. $l = 10, w = 2x - 3$
   d. $l = x, w = x - 1$ e. $l = x + 5, w = x$ f. $l = x + 3, w = x + 2$
2. The length of a rectangle is 10 more than its width, x. Represent the area of the rectangle as a binomial in terms of x.
3. The width of a rectangle is 8 less than twice its length, x. Represent the area of the rectangle as a binomial in terms of x.
4. The length of a rectangle exceeds 3 times its width, x, by 2. Represent the area of the rectangle.
5. The length of a rectangle is 2 cm more than the width, x. If the length of the rectangle is increased by 6 cm and the width is decreased by 3 cm, a new rectangle is formed.
   a. Represent the dimensions of the original rectangle.
   b. Represent the dimensions of the new rectangle.
   c. Represent the area of the original rectangle as a binomial in terms of x.
   d. Represent the area of the new rectangle as a trinomial in terms of x.
   e. Write an open sentence that would indicate that the area of the new rectangle is equal to the area of the original rectangle.
   f. Write an open sentence that would indicate that the area of the new rectangle is 6 square centimeters more than the area of the original rectangle.

Solving Area Problems

In solving problems dealing with areas of geometric figures, it is helpful to draw the figures.

| MODEL PROBLEM |

The length of a rectangle exceeds its width by 7 centimeters. If the length of the rectangle is decreased by 2 centimeters and the width is increased by 3 centimeters, a new rectangle is formed whose area is 20 square centimeters more than the area of the original rectangle. Find the dimensions of the original rectangle.

Solution: Let w = the width of the original rectangle.

Then $w + 7$ = the length of the original rectangle.

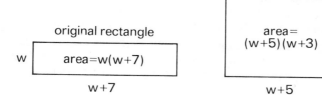

The area of the new rectangle ⌣ is 20 sq. cm more than the area of the old rectangle.

$$(w + 5)(w + 3) = w(w + 7) + 20$$

$$w^2 + 8w + 15 = w^2 + 7w + 20$$
$$w^2 + 8w + 15 + (-w^2) + (-7w) = w^2 + 7w + 20 + (-w^2) + (-7w)$$
$$w + 15 = 20$$
$$w + 15 + (-15) = 20 + (-15)$$
$$w = 5$$
$$w + 7 = 12$$

Check: In the old rectangle, $l = 12$, $w = 5$, and the area = $12(5) = 60$.

In the new rectangle, $l = 10$, $w = 8$, and the area = $10(8) = 80$.

80 is 20 more than 60.

Answer: The length of the original rectangle is 12 centimeters; the width is 5 centimeters.

| EXERCISES |

1. The length of a rectangle is 8 centimeters more than its width. If the length is increased by 4 centimeters and the width is decreased by 1 centimeter, the area is unchanged. Find the dimensions of the original rectangle.

2. The length of a rectangle exceeds 3 times the width by 1 foot. If the length is decreased by 5 feet and the width is increased by 2 feet, the area is unchanged. Find the dimensions of each rectangle.

3. If the length of one side of a square is increased by 3 inches and the length of an adjacent side is decreased by 2 inches, a rectangle is formed whose area is equal to the area of the square. Find the length of a side of the square.

4. A square and a rectangle are equal in area. The length of the rectangle is 8 meters more than a side of the square. The width of the rectangle is 4 meters less than a side of the square. Find the length of a side of the square.

5. Each side of a square is increased by 3 feet. The area of the new square that is formed is 39 square feet more than the area of the original square. Find the length of a side of the original square.

6. If the length of one side of a square is increased by 3 cm and the length of an adjacent side is decreased by 4 cm, a rectangle is formed whose area is 19 cm² less than the area of the square. Find the length of a side of the original square.

7. The length of a rectangular garden exceeds its width by 8 feet. If each side of the garden is increased by 2 feet, the area of the garden will be increased by 60 square feet. Find the dimensions of the original garden.

8. The length of a rectangle is 3 meters more than its width. The length of a side of a square is equal to the length of the rectangle. The area of the square exceeds the area of the rectangle by 24 square meters. Find the dimensions of the rectangle.

6 SOLVING VERBAL PROBLEMS BY USING INEQUALITIES

Preparing to Solve Problems Involving Inequalities

The following examples illustrate how to represent algebraically some sentences that involve relationships of inequality.

Sentence	*Meaning*	*Representation*
1. x is at least 25.	x is equal to 25, or x is greater than 25.	$x \geq 25$

2. The minimum value of x is 25.	x is equal to 25, or x is greater than 25.	$x \geq 25$
3. x is at most 25.	x is equal to 25, or x is less than 25.	$x \leq 25$
4. The maximum value of x is 25.	x is equal to 25, or x is less than 25.	$x \leq 25$
5. x is more than 25.	x is greater than 25.	$x > 25$
6. x is under 25.	x is less than 25.	$x < 25$

EXERCISES

In 1–9, represent the sentence as an algebraic inequality.

1. x is less than or equal to 15.
2. y is greater than or equal to 4.
3. x is at most 50.
4. x is more than 50.
5. The greatest possible value of $3y$ is 30.
6. The sum of $5x$ and $2x$ is at least 70.
7. The maximum value of $4x - 6$ is 54.
8. The minimum value of $2x + 1$ is 13.
9. The product of $3x$ and $x + 1$ is less than 35.

Solving Problems Involving Inequalities

MODEL PROBLEMS

1. Five times a number is less than 55. Find the greatest possible integer value for the number.

Solution:

Let x = the number.

$$\underbrace{\text{Five times a number}}_{5x} \underbrace{\text{ is less than }}_{<} \underbrace{55.}_{55}$$

$$x < 11$$

Check: If a number is less than 11, 5 times the number will be less than 5(11), which is 55. The greatest integer less than 11 is 10, and 5(10) = 50, which is less than 55.

Answer: 10

2. The length of a rectangle is 5 cm more than its width. The perimeter of the rectangle is at least 66 cm. Find the minimum measures of the length and the width.

Solution:

If the perimeter is at least 66 cm, then the sum of the measures of the four sides is either equal to 66 cm or is greater than 66 cm.

Let x = the width of the rectangle.

Then $x + 5$ = the length of the rectangle.

$$\underbrace{\textit{The perimeter of the rectangle}}\quad \underbrace{\textit{is at least}}\quad \underbrace{\textit{66 cm.}}$$

$$x + (x + 5) + x + (x + 5) \qquad \geq \qquad 66$$

$$x + x + 5 + x + x + 5 \geq 66$$
$$4x + 10 \geq 66$$
$$4x \geq 56$$
$$x \geq 14 \quad \text{(The width is at least 14 cm.)}$$
$$x + 5 \geq 19 \quad \text{(The length is at least 19 cm.)}$$

Answer: The length is at least 19 cm; the width is at least 14 cm.

(The check is left to the student.)

| EXERCISES |

1. Six more than 4 times a whole number is less than 60. Find the maximum value of the number.
2. 6 more than 2 times a certain number is less than the number increased by 20. Find the numbers that satisfy this condition.
3. Carol weighs 3 times as much as Sue. Both weights are whole numbers. The sum of their weights is less than 160 pounds. Find the greatest possible weight in pounds for each girl.
4. Mr. Burke had a sum of money in a bank. After he deposited an additional sum of $100, he had at least $550 in the bank. At least how much money did Mr. Burke have in the bank originally?
5. A club agreed to buy at least 250 tickets for a theatre party. If it agreed to buy 80 less orchestra tickets than balcony tickets, what was the least number of balcony tickets it could buy?

6. Mrs. Scott decided that she would spend no more than $120 to buy a coat and a dress. If the price of the coat was $20 more than 3 times the price of the dress, find the highest possible price of the dress.

7. Three times a number increased by 8 is at most 40 more than the number. Find the greatest value of the number.

8. The length of a rectangle is 8 meters less than 5 times its width. If the perimeter of the rectangle is at most 104 meters, find the greatest possible width of the rectangle.

9. The length of a rectangle is 10 cm less than 3 times its width. If the perimeter of the rectangle is at most 180 cm, find the greatest possible length of the rectangle.

10. Mrs. Diaz wishes to save at least $1500 in 12 months. If she saved $300 during the first 4 months, what is the least possible average amount that she must save in each of the remaining 8 months?

11. Two consecutive even numbers are such that their sum is greater than 98 decreased by twice the larger. Find the smallest possible values for the integers.

12. Joan needed $14 to buy some records. Her father agreed to pay her $3 an hour for gardening in addition to her $2 weekly allowance for helping around the house. What is the minimum number of hours Joan must work at gardening to earn $14 this week?

13. Fred bought 4 shirts, each at the same price, and received less than $2.00 change from a $20.00 bill. What is the minimum cost of one shirt?

14. Allison has between 2 and 3 hours to spend on her homework. She has work in math, English, and social studies. She plans to spend an equal amount of time studying English and studying social studies. Allison plans to spend twice as much time studying math as the time spent in doing English.
    a. What is the minimum time she can spend on English homework?
    b. What is the maximum time she can spend on social studies?
    c. What is the maximum time she can devote to math?

15. The measure of angle A is $40°$ more than 5 times the measure of angle B. If $\angle A$ is an obtuse angle, copy and complete the following sentence to describe the measure of $\angle B$: "The measure of $\angle B$ is less than ____ degrees and more than ____ degrees."

chapter fourteen

Special Products and Factoring

1 UNDERSTANDING THE MEANING OF FACTORING

When two integers are multiplied, the result is called their *product*. The integers being multiplied are called the *factors* of the product. Since $3 \times 5 = 15$, then 3 and 5 are factors of the product 15. Since $3 \times 5 = 15$, then $15 \div 3 = 5$ and $15 \div 5 = 3$.

This illustrates that over the set of integers a factor of an integer is an exact divisor of that integer.

In general, if an integer f is an exact divisor of an integer n, then $n \div f$ represents an integer.

Factors of a product can be discovered by using division. If the remainder is 0, then the divisor is a factor of the product. For example, $35 \div 5 = 7$. Hence, $35 = 5 \times 7$ and 5 is a factor of 35. When a product of two integers is divided by one of its factors, the quotient is the other factor. For example, since $35 \div 5 = 7$, 5 is one factor of 35 and the quotient 7 is the other factor of 35.

Factoring a number is the process of finding those numbers whose product is the given number. In our work, when we factor an integer, we will deal only with factors that are integers, that is, *integral factors*, unless we say otherwise. For example, when we factor the number 34 dealing only with integers, we say that $34 = 2 \cdot 17$, or $34 = 1 \cdot 34$.

When we factor, we will basically use the set of *prime numbers*, also called the set of *primes*.

Recall that we have said that a prime number is an integer greater than 1 that has no integral factors other than itself and 1. Examples of the first prime numbers are $2, 3, 5, 7, 11, 13, 17, \ldots$.

Every integer can be expressed as the product of prime factors. Although the factors may be written in any order, there is one and only one combination of prime factors whose product is a given integer. Study the examples at the right. Note that a prime factor may appear in the product more than once.

$$21 = 3 \times 7$$
$$20 = 2 \cdot 2 \cdot 5 \text{ or } 2^2 \cdot 5$$

To express an integer, for example 280, as a product of primes, we start with any pair of integers whose product is the given number.

At the right we see that $280 = 28 \cdot 10$. Then we continue to factor these factors: $28 = 2 \cdot 14$ and $10 = 2 \cdot 5$. This process continues until all the factors are primes. Notice that we must factor $14 = 2 \cdot 7$, while all other factors are primes.

Finally, we can rearrange these prime factors in numerical order.

$$280 = 28 \cdot 10$$
$$280 = 2 \cdot 14 \cdot 2 \cdot 5$$
$$280 = 2 \cdot 2 \cdot 7 \cdot 2 \cdot 5$$
$$280 = 2 \cdot 2 \cdot 2 \cdot 5 \cdot 7$$
$$\text{or}$$
$$280 = 2^3 \cdot 5 \cdot 7$$

Expressing each of two integers as the product of prime factors makes it possible to discover the greatest integer that is a factor of both of them. We call this factor their *greatest common factor*.

Let us find the greatest common factor of 180 and 54.

$$180 = 2 \cdot 2 \cdot 3 \cdot 3 \cdot 5 \text{ or } 2^2 \cdot 3^2 \cdot 5$$
$$54 = 2 \cdot 3 \cdot 3 \cdot 3 \quad\quad \text{or } 2 \cdot 3^3$$
$$\text{Greatest common factor} = 2 \cdot \quad 3 \cdot 3 \quad\quad \text{or } 2 \cdot 3^2 \quad\quad \text{or } 18$$

We see that the greatest number of times that 2 appears as a factor in both 180 and 54 is once; the greatest number of times that 3 appears as a factor in both 180 and 54 is twice. Therefore, the greatest common factor of 180 and 54 is $2 \cdot 3 \cdot 3$, or $2 \cdot 3^2$, or 18.

The *greatest common factor* of two or more monomials is the product of the greatest common factor of their numerical coefficients and the highest power of every variable that is a factor of each monomial.

For example, let us find the greatest common factor of $24a^3b^2$ and $18a^2b$. On the next page we see that the greatest common factor of the numerical coefficients is $2 \cdot 3$ or 6, and the highest powers of the variables that are factors of each monomial are a^2 and b.

$$
\begin{array}{l}
24a^3b^2 = 2 \cdot 2 \cdot 2 \cdot 3 \cdot \quad a \cdot a \cdot a \cdot b \cdot b \\
\quad\quad\quad \downarrow \quad\quad\quad\quad\quad \downarrow \quad \downarrow\ \downarrow \quad\quad \downarrow \\
18a^2b = 2 \cdot \quad\quad 3 \cdot 3 \cdot a \cdot a \cdot \quad\quad b \\
\quad\quad\quad \downarrow \quad\quad\quad\quad \downarrow \quad\quad \downarrow\ \downarrow \quad\quad \downarrow \\
\text{Greatest common factor} = 2 \cdot \quad\quad 3 \cdot \quad a \cdot a \cdot \quad b = 6a^2b
\end{array}
$$

Therefore the greatest common factor of $24a^3b^2$ and $18a^2b$ is $6a^2b$.

When we are expressing an algebraic factor, such as $6a^2b$, we will agree that:

■ **Numerical coefficients need not be factored.** (6 need not be written as $2 \cdot 3$.)

■ **Powers of variables need not be represented as the product of several equal factors.** (a^2b need not be written as $a \cdot a \cdot b$.)

MODEL PROBLEMS

1. Express 700 as a product of prime factors.

    Solution:

    $$
    \begin{aligned}
    700 &= 2 \cdot 350 \\
    700 &= 2 \cdot 2 \cdot 175 \\
    700 &= 2 \cdot 2 \cdot 5 \cdot 35 \\
    700 &= 2 \cdot 2 \cdot 5 \cdot 5 \cdot 7 \text{ or } 2^2 \cdot 5^2 \cdot 7 \quad Ans.
    \end{aligned}
    $$

2. Find the greatest common factor of the monomials $60r^2s^4$ and $36rs^2t$.

    Solution:

    $60r^2s^4 = 2 \cdot 2 \cdot 3 \cdot 5 \cdot r \cdot r \cdot s \cdot s \cdot s \cdot s$ or $2^2 \cdot 3 \cdot 5 \cdot r^2 \cdot s^4$

    $36rs^2t = 2 \cdot 2 \cdot 3 \cdot 3 \cdot r \cdot s \cdot s \cdot t$ or $2^2 \cdot 3^2 \cdot r \cdot s^2 \cdot t$

    The greatest common factor is $2 \cdot 2 \cdot 3 \cdot r \cdot s \cdot s$ or $2^2 \cdot 3 \cdot r \cdot s^2$ or $12rs^2$. *Ans.*

| EXERCISES |

In 1–10, tell whether or not the integer is a prime.

1. 5 **2.** 8 **3.** 13 **4.** 18 **5.** 73
6. 36 **7.** 41 **8.** 49 **9.** 57 **10.** 1

In 11–14, write all the prime numbers between the given numbers.

11. 1 and 10 **12.** 10 and 20 **13.** 20 and 30 **14.** 30 and 40

In 15–24, express the integer as a product of prime numbers.

15. 35 **16.** 18 **17.** 144 **18.** 77 **19.** 128
20. 400 **21.** 202 **22.** 129 **23.** 590 **24.** 316

In 25–30, write all the positive integral factors of the number.

25. 26 **26.** 50 **27.** 36 **28.** 88 **29.** 100 **30.** 242

31. The product of two integers is 144. Find the second factor if the first factor is: **a.** 2 **b.** 8 **c.** 18 **d.** 36 **e.** 48
32. The product of two monomials is $36x^3y^4$. Find the second factor if the first factor is:
 a. $3x^2y^3$ **b.** $6x^3y^2$ **c.** $12xy^2$ **d.** $-9x^3y$ **e.** $18x^3y^2$

In 33–40, find the greatest common factor of the given integers.

33. 10; 15 **34.** 12; 28 **35.** 14; 35 **36.** 18; 24; 36
37. 75; 50 **38.** 72; 108 **39.** 144; 200 **40.** 96; 156; 175

In 41–49, find the greatest common factor of the given monomials.

41. $4x; 4y$ **42.** $6; 12a$ **43.** $4r; 6r^2$
44. $8xy; 6xz$ **45.** $10x^2; 15xy^2$ **46.** $7c^3d^3; -14c^2d$
47. $36xy^2z; -27xy^2z^2$ **48.** $50m^3n^2; 75m^3n$ **49.** $24ab^2c^3; 18ac^2$

2 FACTORING POLYNOMIALS WHOSE TERMS HAVE A COMMON MONOMIAL FACTOR

To *factor a polynomial* over a designated set of numbers means to express it as a product of polynomials whose coefficients are members of that set. The distributive property tells us that $2(x + y) = 2x + 2y$. Therefore, we can say that when $2x + 2y$ is expressed as a product of factors, the result is $2 \cdot (x + y)$. Notice that the monomial 2 is a factor of each term of the polynomial $2x + 2y$. Therefore, 2 is called a *common monomial factor* of the polynomial $2x + 2y$.

When we factor a polynomial, we look first for the ***greatest common monomial factor***, that is, the greatest monomial that is a factor of each term of the polynomial. For example:

1. Let us factor $4rs + 8st$. There are many common factors such as 2, 4, $2s$, and $4s$. The greatest common monomial factor is $4s$. Hence, we divide $4rs + 8st$ by $4s$ to obtain the quotient $(r + 2t)$, which is the second factor. Therefore, $4rs + 8st = 4s(r + 2t)$.

2. Let us factor $3x + 4y$. We notice that 1 is the only common factor. The second factor is $3x + 4y$. We say that $3x + 4y$ is a ***prime polynomial***. A polynomial with integers as coefficients is a prime polynomial if its only factors are 1 and the polynomial itself.

■ **PROCEDURE.** To factor a polynomial whose terms have a common monomial factor:

1. Find the greatest monomial that is a factor of each term of the polynomial.

2. Divide the polynomial by the monomial factor. The quotient is the other factor.

3. Express the polynomial as the indicated product of the two factors.

We can check by multiplying the factors to obtain the original polynomial.

| MODEL PROBLEMS |

1. Write in factored form: $5x - 5y$

Solution

(1) 5 is the greatest common factor of $5x$ and $5y$.

(2) To find the other factor, divide $5x - 5y$ by 5.
$(5x - 5y) \div 5 = x - y$

(3) $5x - 5y = 5(x - y)$ *Ans.*

2. Write in factored form: $6c^3d - 12c^2d^2 + 3cd$

Solution

(1) $3cd$ is the greatest common factor of $6c^3d$, $12c^2d^2$, and $3cd$.

(2) To find the other factor, divide $6c^3d - 12c^2d^2 + 3cd$ by $3cd$.

$(6c^3d - 12c^2d^2 + 3cd) \div 3cd = 2c^2 - 4cd + 1$

(3) $6c^3d - 12c^2d^2 + 3cd = 3cd(2c^2 - 4cd + 1)$ *Ans.*

EXERCISES

In 1–51, write the expression in factored form.

1. $2a + 2b$	2. $5c + 5d$	3. $8m + 8n$
4. $3x - 3y$	5. $7l - 7n$	6. $6R - 6r$
7. $bx + by$	8. $sr - st$	9. $xc - xd$
10. $4x + 8y$	11. $3m - 6n$	12. $12t - 6r$
13. $15c - 10d$	14. $12x - 18y$	15. $18c - 27d$
16. $8x + 16$	17. $6x - 18$	18. $8x - 12$
19. $7y - 7$	20. $8 - 4y$	21. $6 - 18c$
22. $y^2 - 3y$	23. $2x^2 + 5x$	24. $3x^2 - 6x$
25. $32x + x^2$	26. $rs^2 - 2r$	27. $ax - 5ab$
28. $3y^4 + 3y^2$	29. $10x - 15x^3$	30. $2x - 4x^3$
31. $p + prt$	32. $s - sr$	33. $hb + hc$
34. $\pi r^2 + \pi R^2$	35. $\pi r^2 + \pi rl$	36. $\pi r^2 + 2\pi rh$
37. $4x^2 + 4y^2$	38. $3a^2 - 9$	39. $5x^2 + 5$

40. $3ab^2 - 6a^2b$	41. $10xy - 15x^2y^2$
42. $21r^3s^2 - 14r^2s$	43. $2x^2 + 8x + 4$
44. $3x^2 - 6x - 30$	45. $ay - 4aw - 12a$
46. $c^3 - c^2 + 2c$	47. $2ma + 4mb + 2mc$
48. $9ab^2 - 6ab - 3a$	49. $15x^3y^3z^3 - 5xyz$
50. $8a^4b^2c^3 + 12a^2b^2c^2$	51. $28m^4n^3 - 70m^2n^4$

52. The perimeter of a rectangle is represented by $2L + 2W$. Express the perimeter as a product of two factors.

In 53–56, the expression represents the area of a rectangle. Write this expression as the product of two factors.

53. $5x + 5y$ **54.** $18x + 6$ **55.** $x^2 + 2x$ **56.** $4x^3 + 6x^2$

3 SQUARING A MONOMIAL

To square a monomial means to use that monomial as a factor two times. For example:

$(3x)^2 = (3x)(3x) = (3)(3)(x)(x) = (3)^2(x)^2$ or $9x^2$

$(5y^2)^2 = (5y^2)(5y^2) = (5)(5)(y^2)(y^2) = (5)^2(y^2)^2$ or $25y^4$

$(-6b^4)^2 = (-6b^4)(-6b^4) = (-6)(-6)(b^4)(b^4) = (-6)^2(b^4)^2$ or $36b^8$

$(4c^2d^3)^2 = (4c^2d^3)(4c^2d^3) = (4)(4)(c^2)(c^2)(d^3)(d^3) = (4)^2(c^2)^2(d^3)^2$
 or $16c^4d^6$

■ Notice that when a product that has several factors is squared, the operation of squaring is distributed over each factor of the product.

In general, when a and b are signed numbers and m and n are positive integers:

$$(a^m b^n)^2 = a^{2m} b^{2n}$$

Observe that in the case we are discussing, when a monomial is a square, its numerical coefficient is a square and the exponent of each variable is an even number. This is the case with each of the previous results: $9x^2$, $25y^4$, $36b^8$, $16c^4d^6$, $a^{2m}b^{2n}$.

| MODEL PROBLEMS |

In each of the following, square the monomial mentally.

	Think	*Write*	
1. $(4a^3)^2$	$= (4)^2 \cdot (a^3)^2$	$= 16a^6$	*Ans.*
2. $(\frac{2}{5}ab)^2$	$= (\frac{2}{5})^2 \cdot (a)^2(b)^2$	$= \frac{4}{25}a^2b^2$	*Ans.*
3. $(-7xy^2)^2$	$= (-7)^2 \cdot (x)^2 \cdot (y^2)^2 = 49x^2y^4$		*Ans.*

| EXERCISES |

In 1–20, square the monomial mentally.

1. $(a^2)^2$ 2. $(b^3)^2$ 3. $(-d^5)^2$ 4. $(rs)^2$

5. $(m^2n^2)^2$ 6. $(-x^3y^2)^2$ 7. $(3x^2)^2$ 8. $(-5y^4)^2$

9. $(9ab)^2$ 10. $(10x^2y^2)^2$ 11. $(-12cd^3)^2$ 12. $(\frac{3}{4}a)^2$

13. $\left(\frac{5}{7}xy\right)^2$ 14. $\left(-\frac{7}{8}a^2b^2\right)^2$ 15. $\left(\frac{x}{6}\right)^2$ 16. $\left(-\frac{4x^2}{5}\right)^2$

17. $(.8x)^2$ 18. $(.5y^2)^2$ 19. $(.1xy)^2$ 20. $(-.6a^2b)^2$

21. Represent the area of a square whose side is represented by:

    a. $4x$ **b.** $10y$ **c.** $\frac{2}{3}x$ **d.** $1.5x$ **e.** $3x^2$ **f.** $4x^2y^2$

4 MULTIPLYING THE SUM AND DIFFERENCE OF TWO TERMS

Let us multiply the sum of two terms by the difference of the same two terms. Study each of the following examples to see why the product contains two terms, not three:

$$
\begin{array}{l}
a\ +\ 4 \\
\underline{a\ -\ 4} \\
a^2 + 4a \\
\underline{\ -\ 4a\ -\ 16} \\
a^2\ -\ 16
\end{array}
\qquad
\begin{array}{l}
a\ +\ b \\
\underline{a\ -\ b} \\
a^2 + ab \\
\underline{\ -\ ab\ -\ b^2} \\
a^2\ -\ b^2
\end{array}
\qquad
\begin{array}{l}
3x^2 + 5y \\
\underline{3x^2 - 5y} \\
9x^4 + 15x^2y \\
\underline{\ -\ 15x^2y\ -\ 25y^2} \\
9x^4\ -\ 25y^2
\end{array}
$$

These examples illustrate the following procedure, which will enable us to find the products mentally:

■ **PROCEDURE.** To multiply the sum of two terms by the difference of the same two terms:

1. Square the first term.

2. From this result subtract the square of the second term.

┌─────────── **KEEP IN MIND** ───────────┐

$$(a + b)(a - b) = a^2 - b^2$$

└──┘

| MODEL PROBLEMS |

In 1 and 2, find the product mentally.

	Think	*Write*	
1. $(y + 7)(y - 7)$	$= (y)^2 - (7)^2$	$= y^2 - 49$	*Ans.*
2. $(3a + 4b)(3a - 4b)$	$= (3a)^2 - (4b)^2$	$= 9a^2 - 16b^2$	*Ans.*

| EXERCISES |

In 1–22, find the product mentally.

1. $(x + 8)(x - 8)$ 2. $(y + 10)(y - 10)$
3. $(m - 4)(m + 4)$ 4. $(n - 9)(n + 9)$
5. $(10 + a)(10 - a)$ 6. $(12 - b)(12 + b)$
7. $(c + d)(c - d)$ 8. $(r - s)(r + s)$
9. $(3x + 1)(3x - 1)$ 10. $(5c + 4)(5c - 4)$
11. $(8x + 3y)(8x - 3y)$ 12. $(5r - 7s)(5r + 7s)$
13. $(x^2 + 8)(x^2 - 8)$ 14. $(3 - 5y^2)(3 + 5y^2)$
15. $(a + \frac{1}{2})(a - \frac{1}{2})$ 16. $(r + .5)(r - .5)$
17. $(.3 + m)(.3 - m)$ 18. $(ab + 8)(ab - 8)$
19. $(r^3 - 2s^4)(r^3 + 2s^4)$ 20. $(a + 5)(a - 5)(a^2 + 25)$
21. $(x - 3)(x + 3)(x^2 + 9)$ 22. $(a + b)(a - b)(a^2 + b^2)$

In 23–26, express the area of the rectangle whose length L and width W are given.

23. $L = x + 7, W = x - 7$ 24. $L = 2x + 3, W = 2x - 3$
25. $L = c + d, W = c - d$ 26. $L = 2a + 3b, W = 2a - 3b$

5   FACTORING THE DIFFERENCE OF TWO SQUARES

An expression of the form $a^2 - b^2$ is called a *difference of two squares*. Factoring an expression that is the difference of two squares is the reverse of multiplying the sum of two terms by the difference of the same two terms. Since the product of $a + b$ and $a - b$ is $a^2 - b^2$, the factors of $a^2 - b^2$ are $a + b$ and $a - b$. Therefore:

$$a^2 - b^2 = (a + b)(a - b)$$

Remember that for a monomial to be a square (the case we have discussed), its numerical coefficient must be a square and the exponent of each of its variables must be an even number.

■ **PROCEDURE.** To factor a binomial that is a difference of two squares:

Express each of its terms as the square of a monomial; then apply the rule $a^2 - b^2 = (a + b)(a - b)$.

| MODEL PROBLEMS |

In 1–3, factor the polynomials mentally.

	Think	*Write*	
1. $r^2 - 9$	$= (r)^2 - (3)^2$	$= (r + 3)(r - 3)$	*Ans.*

2. $25x^2 - \frac{1}{49}y^2 = (5x)^2 - (\frac{1}{7}y)^2 = (5x + \frac{1}{7}y)(5x - \frac{1}{7}y)$ *Ans.*

3. $.04 - c^6d^4 = (.2)^2 - (c^3d^2)^2 = (.2 + c^3d^2)(.2 - c^3d^2)$ *Ans.*

4. Express $x^2 - 100$ as the product of two binomials.

   Solution: Since $x^2 - 100$ is a difference of two squares, we can factor $x^2 - 100$ and get $(x + 10)(x - 10)$ as the result.

   Answer: $(x + 10)(x - 10)$

| EXERCISES |

In 1–9: If possible, express the binomial as the difference of the squares of monomials; if not possible, tell why.

1. $y^2 - 64$ 2. $4r^2 - b^2$ 3. $r^2 + s^2$
4. $t^2 - 7$ 5. $9n^2 - 16m^2$ 6. $c^2 - .09d^2$
7. $p^2 - \frac{9}{25}q^2$ 8. $16a^4 - 25b^6$ 9. $-9 + m^2$

In 10–45, factor the binomial.

10. $a^2 - 4$ 11. $b^2 - 25$ 12. $c^2 - 100$
13. $r^2 - 16$ 14. $s^2 - 49$ 15. $t^2 - 81$

16. $9 - x^2$

17. $144 - c^2$

18. $121 - m^2$

19. $16a^2 - b^2$

20. $25m^2 - n^2$

21. $d^2 - 4c^2$

22. $r^4 - 9$

23. $x^4 - 64$

24. $25 - s^4$

25. $100x^2 - 81y^2$

26. $64e^2 - 9f^2$

27. $r^2s^2 - 144$

28. $w^2 - \frac{1}{64}$

29. $s^2 - \frac{1}{100}$

30. $\frac{1}{81} - t^2$

31. $49x^2 - \frac{1}{9}$

32. $\frac{4}{25} - \frac{49d^2}{81}$

33. $\frac{1}{9}r^2 - \frac{64s^2}{121}$

34. $x^2 - .64$

35. $y^2 - 1.44$

36. $.04 - 49r^2$

37. $.16m^2 - 9$

38. $81n^2 - .01$

39. $.81x^2 - y^2$

40. $64a^2b^2 - c^2d^2$

41. $25r^2s^2 - 9t^2u^2$

42. $81m^2n^2 - 49x^2y^2$

43. $49m^4 - 64n^4$

44. $25x^6 - 121y^{10}$

45. $x^4y^8 - 144a^6b^{10}$

In 46–50, the given polynomial represents the area of a rectangle. Express the area as the product of two binomials.

46. $x^2 - 4$ 47. $y^2 - 9$ 48. $t^2 - 49$ 49. $t^2 - 64$ 50. $4x^2 - y^2$

In 51–53, express the area of the shaded region as **(a)** the difference of the areas shown and **(b)** the product of two binomials.

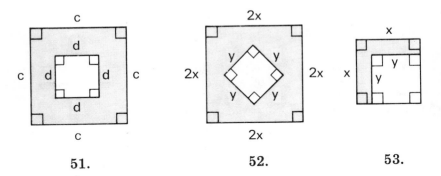

51.   **52.**   **53.**

In 54, express the area of the shaded region as the product of two binomials.

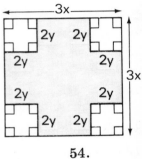

54.

6 FINDING THE PRODUCT OF TWO BINOMIALS

Let us learn how to find the product of two binomials of the form $ax + b$ and $cx + d$ mentally.

Study carefully the multiplication example at the right, which makes use of the distributive property.

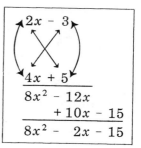

$(2x - 3)(4x + 5)$
$\quad = (2x - 3)(4x) + (2x - 3)(5)$
$\quad = (2x)(4x) + (-3)(4x) + (2x)(5) + (-3)(5)$
$\quad = (8x^2) + (-12x) + (10x) + (-15)$
$\quad = (8x^2) + (-2x) + (-15)$
$\quad = 8x^2 - 2x - 15$

Note the following:

1. $8x^2$, the first term in the product, is equal to the product of $2x$ and $4x$, the first terms in the binomials.

2. -15, the last term in the product, is equal to the product of -3 and $+5$, the last terms in the binomials.

3. $-2x$, the middle term, is obtained by multiplying the first term of each binomial by the second term of the other and adding these products: $(-12x) + (+10x) = -2x$.

If we arrange the two multipliers horizontally, we can find the middle term by adding the product of the two inner terms of the binomials and the product of the two outer terms of the binomials.

$$\overbrace{(2x - 3)(4x + 5)}^{-12x}_{+10x} \qquad \text{Think: } (-12x) + (+10x) = -2x$$

■ **PROCEDURE.** To find the product of two binomials of the form $ax + b$ and $cx + d$:

1. Multiply the first terms of the binomials.

2. Multiply the first term of each binomial by the last term of the other binomial and add these products.

3. Multiply the last terms of the binomials.

4. Add the results obtained in steps 1, 2, and 3.

MODEL PROBLEMS

1. Multiply: $(x - 5)(x - 7)$

   Solution:

   $$\overset{\overset{\displaystyle -5x}{\frown}}{(x - 5)(x - 7)}$$
   $$\underset{\underset{\displaystyle -7x}{\smile}}{}$$

   Think:
   1. $(x)(x) = x^2$
   2. $(-5x) + (-7x) = -12x$
   3. $(-5)(-7) = +35$

   Write: $(x - 5)(x - 7) = x^2 - 12x + 35$ *Ans.*

2. Multiply: $(3y - 8)(4y + 3)$

   Solution:

   $$\overset{\overset{\displaystyle -32y}{\frown}}{(3y - 8)(4y + 3)}$$
   $$\underset{\underset{\displaystyle +9y}{\smile}}{}$$

   Think:
   1. $(3y)(4y) = 12y^2$
   2. $(-32y) + (+9y) = -23y$
   3. $(-8)(+3) = -24$

   Write: $(3y - 8)(4y + 3) = 12y^2 - 23y - 24$ *Ans.*

EXERCISES

In 1–36, perform the indicated operation mentally.

1. $(x + 5)(x + 3)$
2. $(y + 9)(y + 2)$
3. $(6 + d)(3 + d)$
4. $(x - 10)(x - 5)$
5. $(y - 1)(y - 9)$
6. $(8 - c)(3 - c)$
7. $(x + 7)(x - 2)$
8. $(y + 11)(y - 4)$
9. $(m - 15)(m + 2)$
10. $(n - 20)(n + 3)$
11. $(5 - t)(9 + t)$
12. $(2x + 1)(x + 1)$
13. $(3x + 2)(x + 5)$
14. $(c - 5)(3c - 1)$
15. $(m - 6)(3m + 2)$
16. $(y + 8)^2$
17. $(Z - 4)^2$
18. $(y + 5)^2$
19. $(1 - t)^2$
20. $(2x + 1)^2$
21. $(3x - 2)^2$
22. $(7x + 3)(2x - 1)$
23. $(2y + 3)(3y + 2)$
24. $(5Z - 3)(2Z - 5)$
25. $(2y + 3)(2y + 3)$
26. $(3x + 4)^2$
27. $(2x - 5)^2$
28. $(3t - 2)(4t + 7)$
29. $(5y - 4)(5y - 4)$
30. $(2t + 3)(5t + 1)$
31. $(2c - 3d)(5c - 2d)$
32. $(4a - 3b)(3a + b)$
33. $(5a + 7b)(5a - 7b)$
34. $(5a + 7b)(5a + 7b)$
35. $(5a + 7b)(7a + 5b)$
36. $(5a + 7b)(7a - 5b)$

37. Represent the area of a rectangle whose length and width are:
    a. $(x + 5)$ and $(x + 4)$ b. $(2x + 3)$ and $(x - 1)$
38. Represent the area of a square each of whose sides is:
    a. $(x + 6)$ b. $(x - 2)$ c. $(2x + 1)$ d. $(3x - 2)$

7 FACTORING TRINOMIALS OF THE FORM
$ax^2 + bx + c$

We have learned that $(x + 3)(x + 5) = x^2 + 8x + 15$. Therefore, the factors of $x^2 + 8x + 15$ are $(x + 3)$ and $(x + 5)$. Factoring a trinomial of the form $ax^2 + bx + c$ is the reverse of multiplying binomials of the form $(dx + e)$ and $(fx + g)$. When we factor a trinomial of this form, we list the possible pairs of factors and test them out one by one until we find the correct result.

For example, let us factor $x^2 + 7x + 10$.

1. The product of the first terms of the binomials must be x^2. Therefore, each first term must be x. We write:

$$x^2 + 7x + 10 = (x\qquad)(x\qquad)$$

2. Since the product of the last terms of the binomials must be +10, these last terms must be either both positive or both negative.

   The pairs of integers whose product is +10 are (+10) and (+1); (+5) and (+2); (−10) and (−1); (−5) and (−2).

3. From the products obtained in steps 1 and 2, we see that the possible pairs of factors are:

   $(x + 10)(x + 1)$ $(x - 10)(x - 1)$
   $(x + 5)(x + 2)$ $(x - 5)(x - 2)$

4. Now, we test each pair of factors. For example,

$(x + 10)(x + 1)$ is not correct because the middle term, $(+10x) + (+1x)$, is $+11x$, not $+7x$.

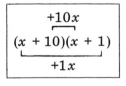

$(x + 5)(x + 2)$ is correct because the middle term, $(+5x) + (+2x)$, is $+7x$.

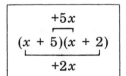

None of the remaining pairs of factors is correct.

5. $x^2 + 7x + 10 = (x + 5)(x + 2)$ *Ans.*

Observe that, in this trinomial, the first and last terms are both positive: x^2 and +10. Since the middle term of the trinomial is *positive*, the last terms of both binomial factors must be *positive*.

■ **PROCEDURE.** To factor a trinomial of the form $ax^2 + bx + c$, we must find two binomials which have the following characteristics:

1. The product of the first terms of both binomials must be equal to the first term in the trinomial (ax^2).

2. The product of the last terms of both binomials must be equal to the last term of the trinomial (c).

3. When the first term of each binomial is multiplied by the second term of the other and the sum of these products is found, this result must be equal to the middle term of the trinomial (bx).

MODEL PROBLEMS

1. Factor: $y^2 - 8y + 12$

   Solution:

   1. The product of the first terms of the binomials must be y^2. Therefore, each first term must be y. We write:

      $$y^2 - 8y + 12 = (y \quad)(y \quad)$$

   2. Since the product of the last terms of the binomials must be +12, these last terms must be either both positive or both negative. The pairs of integers whose product is +12 are (+1) and (+12); (+6) and (+2); (+4) and (+3); (−1) and (−12); (−6) and (−2); (−4) and (−3).

   3. The possible factors are:

      $$(y + 1)(y + 12) \qquad (y - 1)(y - 12)$$
      $$(y + 6)(y + 2) \qquad (y - 6)(y - 2)$$
      $$(y + 4)(y + 3) \qquad (y - 4)(y - 3)$$

   4. When we find the middle term in each of the trinomial products, we find that only $(y - 6)(y - 2)$ yields a middle term of $-8y$.

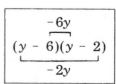

   5. $y^2 - 8y + 12 = (y - 6)(y - 2)$ *Ans.*

Observe that, in this trinomial, the first and last terms are both positive: y^2 and +12. Since the middle term of the trinomial is *negative*, the last terms of both binomial factors must be *negative*.

2. Factor: $c^2 + 5c - 6$

Solution:

1. The product of the first terms of the binomials must be c^2. Therefore, each first term must be c. We write:

$$c^2 + 5c - 6 = (c \quad)(c \quad)$$

2. Since the product of the last terms of the binomials must be -6, one of these last terms must be positive, the other negative. The pairs of integers whose product is -6 are $(+1)$ and (-6); (-1) and $(+6)$; $(+3)$ and (-2); (-3) and $(+2)$.

3. The possible factors are:

$$(c + 1)(c - 6) \qquad (c + 3)(c - 2)$$
$$(c - 1)(c + 6) \qquad (c - 3)(c + 2)$$

4. When we find the middle term of each of the trinomial products, we find that only $(c - 1)(c + 6)$ yields a middle term of $+5c$.

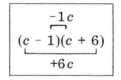

5. $c^2 + 5c - 6 = (c - 1)(c + 6)$ *Ans.*

3. Factor: $2x^2 - 7x - 15$

Solution:

1. Since the product of the first terms of the binomials must be $2x^2$, one of these terms must be $2x$, the other x. We write:

$$2x^2 - 7x - 15 = (2x \quad)(x \quad)$$

2. Since the product of the last terms of the binomials must be -15, one of these last terms must be positive, the other negative. The pairs of integers whose product is -15 are $(+1)$ and (-15); (-1) and $(+15)$; $(+3)$ and (-5); (-3) and $(+5)$.

Notice that these four pairs of integers will form eight pairs of binomial factors since the order in which the integers are written will produce different pairs of factors: $(2x + 1)(x - 15)$ is not the same product as $(2x - 15)(x + 1)$.

3. The possible pairs of factors are:

$$(2x + 1)(x - 15) \qquad (2x - 1)(x + 15)$$
$$(2x + 15)(x - 1) \qquad (2x - 15)(x + 1)$$
$$(2x + 3)(x - 5) \qquad (2x - 3)(x + 5)$$
$$(2x + 5)(x - 3) \qquad (2x - 5)(x + 3)$$

4. When we find the middle term of each of the trinomial products, we find that only $(2x + 3)(x - 5)$ yields a middle term of $-7x$.

$$+3x$$
$$(2x + 3)(x - 5)$$
$$-10x$$

5. $2x^2 - 7x - 15 = (2x + 3)(x - 5)$ *Ans.*

KEEP IN MIND

In factoring a trinomial of the form $ax^2 + bx + c$, when a is a positive integer $(a > 0)$:

1. If the last term, the constant c, is positive, the last terms of the binomial factors must be either both positive or both negative.

2. If the last term, the constant c, is negative, one of the last terms in the binomial factors must be positive, the other negative.

EXERCISES

In 1–45, factor.

1. $a^2 + 3a + 2$
2. $c^2 + 6c + 5$
3. $x^2 + 8x + 7$
4. $r^2 + 12r + 11$
5. $m^2 + 5m + 4$
6. $y^2 + 12y + 35$
7. $x^2 + 11x + 24$
8. $a^2 + 11a + 18$
9. $16 + 17c + c^2$
10. $x^2 + 2x + 1$
11. $z^2 + 10z + 25$
12. $a^2 - 8a + 7$
13. $a^2 - 6a + 5$
14. $x^2 - 5x + 6$
15. $x^2 - 11x + 10$
16. $y^2 - 6y + 8$
17. $15 - 8y + y^2$
18. $x^2 - 10x + 24$
19. $c^2 - 14c + 40$
20. $x^2 - 16x + 48$
21. $x^2 - 14x + 49$
22. $x^2 - x - 2$
23. $x^2 - 6x - 7$
24. $y^2 + 4y - 5$
25. $z^2 - 12z - 13$
26. $c^2 - 2c - 15$
27. $c^2 + 2c - 35$
28. $x^2 - 7x - 18$
29. $z^2 + 9z - 36$
30. $x^2 - 13x - 48$
31. $x^2 - 16x + 64$
32. $2x^2 + 5x + 2$
33. $2x^2 + 7x + 6$
34. $3x^2 + 10x + 8$
35. $16x^2 + 8x + 1$
36. $2x^2 + x - 3$
37. $3x^2 + 2x - 5$
38. $2x^2 + x - 6$
39. $4x^2 - 12x + 5$
40. $10a^2 - 9a + 2$
41. $18y^2 - 23y - 6$
42. $x^2 + 3xy + 2y^2$
43. $r^2 - 3rs - 10s^2$
44. $3a^2 - 7ab + 2b^2$
45. $4x^2 - 5xy - 6y^2$

In 46–48, express the polynomial as the product of two binomial factors.

46. $x^2 + 9x + 18$
47. $x^2 - 9x + 14$
48. $y^2 - 5y - 24$

In 49–51, the trinomial represents the area of a rectangle. Express the dimensions of the rectangle as binomials.

49. $x^2 + 8x + 7$ **50.** $x^2 + 9x + 18$ **51.** $3x^2 + 14x + 15$

In 52–54, the trinomial represents the area of a square. Express each side of the square as a binomial.

52. $x^2 + 10x + 25$ **53.** $81x^2 + 18x + 1$ **54.** $4x^2 + 12x + 9$

8 FACTORING COMPLETELY

The polynomials $x^2 + 4$ and $x^2 + x + 1$ cannot be factored over the set of polynomials with integral coefficients. We say that these polynomials are *prime over this set of polynomials.*

To factor a polynomial completely means to find the *prime factors* of the polynomial over a designated set of numbers. Therefore, whenever we factor a polynomial, we will continue the process of factoring until all factors other than monomial factors are prime factors over the designated set of numbers.

■ **PROCEDURE.** To factor a polynomial completely, use the following steps:

1. Look for the greatest common factor. If there is one, factor the given polynomial. Then examine each factor.
2. If one of these factors is a binomial, see if it is a difference of two squares. If it is, factor it as such.
3. If one of these factors is a trinomial, see if it can be factored. If it can, find its binomial factors.
4. Write the answer as the product of all the factors. Make certain that in the answer all factors other than monomial factors are prime factors.

MODEL PROBLEMS

1. Factor: $by^2 - 4b$

   How to Proceed   *Solution*

   1. Find the greatest common factor.

      $$by^2 - 4b = b(y^2 - 4)$$

   2. Factor the difference of 2 squares.

      $$by^2 - 4b = b(y + 2)(y - 2) \qquad Ans.$$

2. Factor: $3x^2 - 6x - 24$

How to Proceed	*Solution*
1. Find the greatest common factor.	$3x^2 - 6x - 24 = 3(x^2 - 2x - 8)$
2. Factor the trinomial.	$3x^2 - 6x - 24 = 3(x - 4)(x + 2)$ *Ans.*

3. Factor: $x^4 - 16$

How to Proceed	*Solution*
1. Factor $x^4 - 16$ as the difference of 2 squares.	$x^4 - 16 = (x^2 + 4)(x^2 - 4)$
2. Factor $x^2 - 4$ as the difference of 2 squares.	$x^4 - 16 = (x^2 + 4)(x + 2)(x - 2)$ *Ans.*

EXERCISES

In 1–39, factor completely.

1. $2a^2 - 2b^2$
2. $6x^2 - 6y^2$
3. $4x^2 - 4$
4. $ax^2 - ay^2$
5. $cm^2 - cn^2$
6. $st^2 - s$
7. $2x^2 - 18$
8. $2x^2 - 32$
9. $3x^2 - 27y^2$
10. $18m^2 - 8$
11. $12a^2 - 27b^2$
12. $63c^2 - 7$
13. $x^3 - 4x$
14. $y^3 - 25y$
15. $z^3 - z$
16. $4a^3 - ab^2$
17. $4c^3 - 49c$
18. $9db^2 - d$
19. $4a^2 - 36$
20. $x^4 - 1$
21. $y^4 - 81$
22. $\pi R^2 - \pi r^2$
23. $\pi c^2 - \pi d^2$
24. $100x^2 - 36y^2$
25. $ax^2 + 3ax + 2a$
26. $3x^2 + 6x + 3$
27. $4r^2 - 4r - 48$
28. $x^3 + 7x^2 + 10x$
29. $4x^2 - 6x - 4$
30. $2ax^2 - 2ax - 12a$
31. $abx^2 - ab$
32. $z^6 - z^2$
33. $16x^2 - x^2y^4$
34. $x^4 + x^2 - 2$
35. $a^4 - 10a^2 + 9$
36. $y^4 - 13y^2 + 36$
37. $2x^2 + 12x + 8$
38. $16x^2 - 16x + 4$
39. $25x^2 + 100xy + 100y^2$

chapter fifteen

Fractions and First-Degree Equations and Inequalities Involving Fractions

1 THE MEANING OF AN ALGEBRAIC FRACTION

A fraction is a symbol that indicates the quotient of any two numbers (remember that division by zero is not possible). For example, the arithmetic fraction $\frac{3}{4}$ indicates the quotient of 3 and 4.

An *algebraic fraction* is a quotient of polynomials. An algebraic fraction is sometimes called a *rational expression*.

Examples of algebraic fractions are: $\frac{2}{5}, \frac{x}{2}, \frac{2}{x}, \frac{a}{b}, \frac{4c}{3d}, \frac{x+5}{x-2}, \frac{x^2+4x+3}{x+1}$

The fraction $\frac{a}{b}$ means that the number represented by a, the numerator, is to be divided by the number represented by b, the denominator. Since division by zero is not possible, the value of the denominator, b, may not be zero. In all our work with fractions we will assume that the denominator is not zero.

MODEL PROBLEM

Find the value of x for which $\dfrac{12}{x-9}$ has no meaning.

Solution: $\dfrac{12}{x-9}$ is not defined when the denominator $x-9$ is equal to 0.

Let $x - 9 = 0$. Then $x = 9$.   *Answer:* 9

| EXERCISES |

In 1–9, find the value of the variable for which the fraction is not defined.

1. $\dfrac{2}{x}$ 2. $\dfrac{-5}{6x}$ 3. $\dfrac{12}{y^2}$ 4. $\dfrac{1}{x-5}$ 5. $\dfrac{x}{x-8}$

6. $\dfrac{7}{2-x}$ 7. $\dfrac{y+5}{y+2}$ 8. $\dfrac{10}{2x-1}$ 9. $\dfrac{2y+3}{4y+2}$

In 10–14, represent the answer to the problem as a fraction.

10. Represent the cost of 1 piece of candy if 5 pieces cost c cents.
11. Represent the cost of 1 meter of lumber if p meters cost 98 cents.
12. If a piece of lumber $10x + 20$ centimeters in length is cut into y pieces of equal length, represent the length of each of the pieces.
13. What fractional part of an hour is m minutes?
14. If the perimeter of a square is represented by $4x + 2y$, represent each side of the square.

2 REDUCING FRACTIONS TO LOWEST TERMS

A fraction is said to be *reduced to lowest terms* when its numerator and denominator have no common factor other than 1 or -1.

Each of the fractions $\dfrac{5}{10}$ and $\dfrac{1a}{2a}$ becomes the fraction $\dfrac{1}{2}$ when reduced to lowest terms. Let us use the multiplication property of 1 to show that $\dfrac{5}{10}$ names the same number as $\dfrac{1}{2}$ and that $\dfrac{1a}{2a}$ also names the same number as $\frac{1}{2}$. Remember that any nonzero number divided by itself equals 1.

$$\frac{5}{10} = \frac{1 \cdot 5}{2 \cdot 5} = \frac{1}{2} \cdot \frac{5}{5} = \frac{1}{2} \cdot 1 = \frac{1}{2} \quad \text{and} \quad \frac{1a}{2a} = \frac{1 \cdot a}{2 \cdot a} = \frac{1}{2} \cdot \frac{a}{a} = \frac{1}{2} \cdot 1 = \frac{1}{2}$$

These examples illustrate the *division property of a fraction:* If the numerator and denominator of a fraction are divided by the same non-zero number, the resulting fraction is equal to the original fraction.

In general, for any numbers x, y, and a, where $y \neq 0$ and $a \neq 0$:

$$\frac{x}{y} = \frac{x \div a}{y \div a}$$

Note the following examples of the division property of fractions:

$$\frac{4x}{5x} = \frac{4x \div x}{5x \div x} = \frac{4}{5} \qquad\qquad \frac{cy}{dy} = \frac{cy \div y}{dy \div y} = \frac{c}{d}$$

$$\frac{3(x + 5)}{18} = \frac{3(x + 5) \div 3}{18 \div 3} = \frac{x + 5}{6}$$

When reducing a fraction, the division of the numerator and the denominator by a common factor may be indicated by a *cancellation*. For example:

$$\frac{3(x + 5)}{18} = \frac{\overset{1}{\cancel{3}}(x + 5)}{\underset{6}{\cancel{18}}} = \frac{x + 5}{6}$$

■ **PROCEDURE.**   To reduce a fraction to its lowest terms:

Method 1

1. Factor both its numerator and its denominator.

2. Examine the factors and determine the greatest common factor of the numerator and the denominator.

3. Express the given fraction as the product of two fractions, one of which has as its numerator and its denominator the greatest common factor determined in step 2.

4. Use the multiplication property of 1.

Method 2

1. Factor both its numerator and its denominator.

2. Divide both the numerator and the denominator by their greatest common factor.

| MODEL PROBLEMS |

1. Reduce $\dfrac{15x^2}{35x^4}$ to lowest terms.

Solution

Method 1

$$\frac{15x^2}{35x^4} = \frac{3}{7x^2} \cdot \frac{5x^2}{5x^2}$$

$$= \frac{3}{7x^2} \cdot 1$$

$$= \frac{3}{7x^2} \quad Ans.$$

Method 2

$$\frac{15x^2}{35x^4} = \frac{3 \cdot 5x^2}{7x^2 \cdot 5x^2}$$

$$= \frac{3 \cdot 5x^2 \div 5x^2}{7x^2 \cdot 5x^2 \div 5x^2}$$

$$= \frac{3}{7x^2} \quad Ans.$$

2. Express $\dfrac{2x^2 - 6x}{10x}$ as an equivalent fraction in lowest terms.

Solution

Method 1

$$\frac{2x^2 - 6x}{10x} = \frac{2x(x - 3)}{2x \cdot 5}$$

$$= \frac{(x - 3)}{5} \cdot \frac{2x}{2x}$$

$$= \frac{(x - 3)}{5} \cdot 1$$

$$= \frac{x - 3}{5} \quad Ans.$$

Method 2

$$\frac{2x^2 - 6x}{10x} = \frac{2x(x - 3)}{10x}$$

$$= \frac{\overset{1}{\cancel{2x}}(x - 3)}{\underset{5}{\cancel{10x}}}$$

$$= \frac{x - 3}{5} \quad Ans.$$

| EXERCISES |

In 1–21, reduce the fraction to lowest terms.

1. $\dfrac{4}{12}$ 2. $\dfrac{27}{36}$ 3. $\dfrac{24c}{36d}$

4. $\dfrac{9r}{10r}$ 5. $\dfrac{ab}{cb}$ 6. $\dfrac{3ay^2}{6by^2}$

7. $\dfrac{5xy}{9xy}$ 8. $\dfrac{2abc}{4abc}$ 9. $\dfrac{15x^2}{5x}$

10. $\dfrac{5x^2}{25x^4}$ 11. $\dfrac{27a}{36a^2}$ 12. $\dfrac{8xy^2}{24x^2y}$

13. $\dfrac{+12a^2b}{-8ac}$ 14. $\dfrac{-20x^2y^2}{-90xy^2}$ 15. $\dfrac{-32a^3b^3}{+48a^3b^3}$

16. $\dfrac{+5xy}{+45x^2y^2}$ 17. $\dfrac{3x+6}{4}$ 18. $\dfrac{8y-12}{6}$

19. $\dfrac{5x-35}{5x}$ 20. $\dfrac{8m^2+40m}{8m}$ 21. $\dfrac{2ax+2bx}{6x^2}$

3   MULTIPLYING FRACTIONS

The product of two fractions is a fraction with the following properties:

1. The product's numerator is the product of the numerators of the given fractions.

2. The product's denominator is the product of the denominators of the given fractions.

In general, for any numbers a, b, x, and y, when $b \neq 0$ and $y \neq 0$:

$$\frac{a}{b} \cdot \frac{x}{y} = \frac{ax}{by}$$

We can find the product of $\frac{7}{27}$ and $\frac{9}{4}$ in lowest terms by using either one of the following two methods:

Method 1   *Method 2*

$$\frac{7}{27} \cdot \frac{9}{4} = \frac{7 \cdot 9}{27 \cdot 4} = \frac{63}{108} = \frac{7 \cdot \overset{1}{\cancel{9}}}{12 \cdot \underset{1}{\cancel{9}}} = \frac{7}{12} \qquad\qquad \frac{7}{27} \cdot \frac{9}{4} = \frac{7 \cdot \overset{1}{\cancel{9}}}{\underset{3}{\cancel{27}} \cdot 4} = \frac{7}{12}$$

Notice that method 2 requires less computation than method 1 since the reduced form of the product was obtained by dividing the numerator and the denominator by a common factor *before* the product was found. This method may be called the *cancellation method*.

When we multiply algebraic fractions, the product has the same properties as when we multiply arithmetic fractions.

Thus, to multiply $\dfrac{5x^2}{7y}$ by $\dfrac{14y^2}{15x^3}$, we may use either one of the following two methods:

Method 1

$$\frac{5x^2}{7y} \cdot \frac{14y^2}{15x^3} = \frac{5x^2 \cdot 14y^2}{7y \cdot 15x^3} = \frac{70x^2y^2}{105x^3y} = \frac{2y}{3x} \cdot \frac{35x^2y}{35x^2y} = \frac{2y}{3x} \cdot 1 = \frac{2y}{3x}$$

Method 2 (the cancellation method)

$$\frac{5x^2}{7y} \cdot \frac{14y^2}{15x^3} = \frac{\overset{1}{\cancel{5x^2}}}{\underset{1}{\cancel{7y}}} \cdot \frac{\overset{2y}{\cancel{14y^2}}}{\underset{3x}{\cancel{15x^3}}} = \frac{2y}{3x}$$

In some problems it is helpful to factor the numerator and the denominator before applying the cancellation method. For example:

$$\frac{3x + 15}{4y} \cdot \frac{2}{3} = \frac{\overset{1}{\cancel{3}(x + 5)}}{\cancel{4}y} \cdot \frac{\overset{1}{\cancel{2}}}{\underset{1}{\cancel{3}}} = \frac{x + 5}{2y}$$

| **MODEL PROBLEM** |

Multiply and express the product in reduced form: $\dfrac{5a^3}{9bx} \cdot \dfrac{6bx}{a^2}$

<table>
<tr><td> How to Proceed </td><td> Solution </td></tr>
<tr>
<td>(1) Divide the numerators and the denominators by the common factors $3bx$ and a^2.</td>
<td>$\dfrac{5a^3}{9bx} \cdot \dfrac{6bx}{a^2} = \dfrac{\overset{5a}{\cancel{5a^3}}}{\underset{3}{\cancel{9bx}}} \cdot \dfrac{\overset{2}{\cancel{6bx}}}{\underset{1}{\cancel{a^2}}}$</td>
</tr>
<tr>
<td>(2) Multiply the remaining numerators and then multiply the remaining denominators.</td>
<td>$= \dfrac{10a}{3}$ Ans.</td>
</tr>
</table>

EXERCISES

In 1–15, find the product in lowest terms.

1. $\frac{8}{12} \cdot \frac{30}{36}$

2. $36 \cdot \frac{5}{9}$

3. $\frac{1}{2} \cdot 20x$

4. $\frac{5}{d} \cdot d^2$

5. $\frac{x^2}{36} \cdot 20$

6. $mn \cdot \frac{8}{m^2 n^2}$

7. $\frac{24x}{35y} \cdot \frac{14y}{8x}$

8. $\frac{12x}{5y} \cdot \frac{15y^2}{36x^2}$

9. $\frac{m^2}{8} \cdot \frac{32}{3m}$

10. $\frac{6r^2}{5s^2} \cdot \frac{10rs}{6r^3}$

11. $\frac{30m^2}{18n} \cdot \frac{6n}{5m}$

12. $\frac{24a^3 b^2}{7c^3} \cdot \frac{21c^2}{12ab}$

13. $\frac{7}{8} \cdot \frac{2x+4}{21}$

14. $\frac{3a+9}{15a} \cdot \frac{a^3}{18}$

15. $\frac{5x-5y}{x^2 y} \cdot \frac{xy^2}{25}$

4 DIVIDING FRACTIONS

We know that the operation of division may be defined by means of the multiplicative inverse, the reciprocal. A quotient can be expressed as the product of the dividend and the reciprocal of the divisor. Thus,

$$8 \div 5 = \frac{8}{1} \cdot \frac{1}{5} = \frac{8 \cdot 1}{1 \cdot 5} = \frac{8}{5} \quad \text{and} \quad \frac{8}{7} \div \frac{5}{3} = \frac{8}{7} \cdot \frac{3}{5} = \frac{8 \cdot 3}{7 \cdot 5} = \frac{24}{35}$$

In general, for any numbers a, b, c, and d, when $b \neq 0$, $c \neq 0$, and $d \neq 0$:

$$\frac{a}{b} \div \frac{c}{d} = \frac{a}{b} \cdot \frac{d}{c} = \frac{ad}{bc}$$

■ **PROCEDURE.** To divide by an algebraic fraction, multiply the dividend by the reciprocal of the divisor.

MODEL PROBLEM

Divide: $\frac{16c^3}{21d^2} \div \frac{24c^4}{14d^3}$

How to Proceed

Multiply the dividend by the reciprocal of the divisor.

Solution

$$\frac{16c^3}{21d^2} \div \frac{24c^4}{14d^3} = \frac{\overset{2}{\cancel{16c^3}}}{\underset{3}{\cancel{21d^2}}} \cdot \frac{\overset{2d}{\cancel{14d^3}}}{\underset{3c}{\cancel{24c^4}}} = \frac{4d}{9c} \quad \textit{Ans.}$$

| EXERCISES |

In 1-11, divide and express the quotient in lowest terms.

1. $\dfrac{7}{10} \div \dfrac{21}{5}$ 2. $\dfrac{12}{35} \div \dfrac{4}{7}$ 3. $8 \div \dfrac{1}{2}$ 4. $\dfrac{x}{9} \div \dfrac{x}{3}$

5. $\dfrac{3x}{5y} \div \dfrac{21x}{2y}$ 6. $\dfrac{7ab^2}{10cd} \div \dfrac{14b^3}{5c^2d^2}$ 7. $\dfrac{xy^2}{x^2y} \div \dfrac{x}{y^3}$ 8. $\dfrac{6a^2b^2}{8c} \div 3ab$

9. $\dfrac{4x+4}{9} \div \dfrac{3}{8x}$ 10. $\dfrac{3y^2+9y}{18} \div \dfrac{5y^2}{27}$ 11. $\dfrac{a^3-a}{b} \div \dfrac{a^3}{4b^3}$

5 ADDING OR SUBTRACTING FRACTIONS THAT HAVE THE SAME DENOMINATOR

We know that the sum (or difference) of two arithmetic fractions that have the same denominator is a fraction whose numerator is the sum (or difference) of the numerators and whose denominator is the common denominator of the given fractions. We use the same rule to add algebraic fractions that have the same nonzero denominator. Thus:

<table>
<tr><td align="center">Arithmetic fractions</td><td align="center">Algebraic fractions</td></tr>
<tr><td align="center">$\dfrac{5}{7} + \dfrac{1}{7} = \dfrac{5+1}{7} = \dfrac{6}{7}$</td><td align="center">$\dfrac{a}{x} + \dfrac{b}{x} = \dfrac{a+b}{x}$</td></tr>
<tr><td align="center">$\dfrac{5}{7} - \dfrac{1}{7} = \dfrac{5-1}{7} = \dfrac{4}{7}$</td><td align="center">$\dfrac{a}{x} - \dfrac{b}{x} = \dfrac{a-b}{x}$</td></tr>
</table>

■ **PROCEDURE.** **To add (or subtract) fractions that have the same denominator:**

1. Write a fraction whose numerator is the sum (or difference) of the numerators and whose denominator is the common denominator of the given fractions.

2. Reduce the resulting fraction to lowest terms.

| MODEL PROBLEMS |

Add or subtract as indicated. Reduce answers to lowest terms.

1. $\dfrac{5}{4x} + \dfrac{9}{4x} - \dfrac{8}{4x}$

2. $\dfrac{4x + 7}{6x} - \dfrac{2x - 4}{6x}$

Solution

$\dfrac{5}{4x} + \dfrac{9}{4x} - \dfrac{8}{4x}$

$= \dfrac{5 + 9 - 8}{4x}$

$= \dfrac{6}{4x}$

$= \dfrac{3}{2x}$ *Ans.*

Solution

$\dfrac{4x + 7}{6x} - \dfrac{2x - 4}{6x}$

$= \dfrac{(4x + 7) - (2x - 4)}{6x}$

$= \dfrac{4x + 7 - 2x + 4}{6x}$

$= \dfrac{2x + 11}{6x}$ *Ans.*

Note: In model problem 2, since the fraction bar is a symbol of grouping, we place numerators that have more than one term in parentheses.

| EXERCISES |

In 1–20, add or subtract (combine) the fractions as indicated. Reduce answers to lowest terms.

1. $\dfrac{1}{8} + \dfrac{4}{8}$

2. $\dfrac{9}{15} - \dfrac{6}{15}$

3. $\dfrac{2}{x} + \dfrac{3}{x}$

4. $\dfrac{11}{4c} + \dfrac{5}{4c} - \dfrac{6}{4c}$

5. $\dfrac{3x}{4} + \dfrac{2x}{4}$

6. $\dfrac{12y}{5} - \dfrac{4y}{5}$

7. $\dfrac{2c}{5} - \dfrac{3d}{5}$

8. $\dfrac{x}{2} - \dfrac{y}{2} + \dfrac{z}{2}$

9. $\dfrac{x}{a} + \dfrac{y}{a}$

10. $\dfrac{5r}{t} - \dfrac{2s}{t}$

11. $\dfrac{9}{8x} + \dfrac{6}{8x}$

12. $\dfrac{8}{9y} + \dfrac{4}{9y} - \dfrac{3}{9y}$

13. $\dfrac{6a}{4x} + \dfrac{5a}{4x}$

14. $\dfrac{11b}{3y} - \dfrac{4b}{3y}$

15. $\dfrac{19c}{12d} + \dfrac{9c}{12d}$

16. $\dfrac{6}{10c} + \dfrac{9}{10c} - \dfrac{3}{10c}$

17. $\dfrac{2x + 1}{2} + \dfrac{3x + 6}{2}$

18. $\dfrac{4x + 12}{16x} + \dfrac{8x + 4}{16x}$

19. $\dfrac{5x - 4}{3} - \dfrac{2x + 1}{3}$

20. $\dfrac{12a - 15}{12a} - \dfrac{9a - 6}{12a}$

In 21–24, copy and complete the table, showing the results of adding, subtracting, multiplying, and dividing the expressions that represent A and B.

	A	B	$A + B$	$A - B$	$A \cdot B$	$A \div B \text{ or } \dfrac{A}{B}$
21.	$\dfrac{12}{y}$	$\dfrac{3}{y}$				
22.	$\dfrac{3x}{8}$	$\dfrac{x}{8}$				
23.	$\dfrac{r}{t}$	$\dfrac{p}{t}$				
24.	$\dfrac{7k}{2x}$	$\dfrac{5k}{2x}$				

6 ADDING OR SUBTRACTING FRACTIONS THAT HAVE DIFFERENT DENOMINATORS

Each of the fractions $\dfrac{2}{8}, \dfrac{3}{12},$ and $\dfrac{1a}{4a}$ is equivalent to the fraction $\dfrac{1}{4}$ since each one names the fraction $\tfrac{1}{4}$. Let us use the multiplication property of 1 to show that this statement is true $\left(\text{remember that } \dfrac{a}{a} = 1 \text{ when } a \neq 0\right)$:

$$\frac{1}{4} = \frac{1}{4} \cdot 1 = \frac{1}{4} \cdot \frac{2}{2} = \frac{2}{8} \quad \bigg| \quad \frac{1}{4} = \frac{1}{4} \cdot 1 = \frac{1}{4} \cdot \frac{3}{3} = \frac{3}{12} \quad \bigg| \quad \frac{1}{4} = \frac{1}{4} \cdot 1 = \frac{1}{4} \cdot \frac{a}{a} = \frac{1a}{4a}$$

These examples illustrate the *multiplication property of a fraction:* If the numerator and the denominator of a fraction are multiplied by the same nonzero number, the resulting fraction is equivalent to the original fraction.

To add $\tfrac{5}{4}$ and $\tfrac{7}{6}$, we first transform them to equivalent fractions that have a common denominator. Any integer that has both 4 and 6 as factors can become a common denominator. To simplify our work, we will use the *lowest common denominator* (L.C.D.). We have learned that, for 4 and 6, the L.C.D. is 12.

To find the integer by which to multiply the numerator and the denominator of $\frac{5}{4}$ to transform it into an equivalent fraction whose denominator is the L.C.D. 12, we divide 12 by the denominator 4. The result is 3. Then, $\dfrac{5}{4} = \dfrac{5 \cdot 3}{4 \cdot 3} = \dfrac{15}{12}$.

To find the integer by which to multiply the numerator and the denominator of $\frac{7}{6}$ to transform it into an equivalent fraction whose denominator is the L.C.D. 12, we divide 12 by 6. The result is 2. Then, $\dfrac{7}{6} = \dfrac{7 \cdot 2}{6 \cdot 2} = \dfrac{14}{12}$.

Now we add $\dfrac{15}{12}$ and $\dfrac{14}{12}$ and obtain $\dfrac{15 + 14}{12}$ or $\dfrac{29}{12}$ as the result.

The entire solution may be written as follows:

$$\frac{5}{4} + \frac{7}{6} = \frac{5 \cdot 3}{4 \cdot 3} + \frac{7 \cdot 2}{6 \cdot 2} = \frac{15}{12} + \frac{14}{12} = \frac{15 + 14}{12} = \frac{29}{12} \quad Ans.$$

Algebraic fractions are added in the same manner as arithmetic fractions.

■ **PROCEDURE.** To add (or subtract) fractions that have different denominators:

1. Factor each denominator in order to find the lowest common denominator, L.C.D.

2. Transform each fraction to an equivalent fraction by multiplying its numerator and denominator by the quotient that is obtained when the L.C.D. is divided by the denominator of the fraction.

3. Write a fraction whose numerator is the sum (or difference) of the numerators of the new fractions and whose denominator is the L.C.D.

4. Reduce the resulting fraction to lowest terms.

| MODEL PROBLEMS |

1. Add: $\dfrac{5}{a^2b} + \dfrac{2}{ab^2}$

   Solution

   $a^2b = a^2 \cdot b;\ ab^2 = a \cdot b^2$

   L.C.D. $= a^2 \cdot b^2 = a^2b^2$

   $\dfrac{5}{a^2b} + \dfrac{2}{ab^2}$

   $= \dfrac{5(b)}{a^2b(b)} + \dfrac{2(a)}{ab^2(a)}$

   $= \dfrac{5b}{a^2b^2} + \dfrac{2a}{a^2b^2}$

   $= \dfrac{5b + 2a}{a^2b^2}$ *Ans.*

2. Subtract: $\dfrac{2x + 5}{3} - \dfrac{x - 2}{4}$

   Solution

   $3 = 3 \cdot 1;\ 4 = 2 \cdot 2 = 2^2$

   L.C.D. $= 3 \cdot 2^2 = 12$

   $\dfrac{2x + 5}{3} - \dfrac{x - 2}{4}$

   $= \dfrac{4(2x + 5)}{4(3)} - \dfrac{3(x - 2)}{3(4)}$

   $= \dfrac{8x + 20}{12} - \dfrac{3x - 6}{12}$

   $= \dfrac{(8x + 20) - (3x - 6)}{12}$

   $= \dfrac{8x + 20 - 3x + 6}{12}$

   $= \dfrac{5x + 26}{12}$ *Ans.*

| EXERCISES |

In 1–10, find the lowest common denominator for two fractions whose denominators are:

1. $2; 3$ 2. $6; 5$ 3. $4; 12$ 4. $8; 12$ 5. $5; 10$

6. $x; 4x$ 7. $5x; 2x$ 8. $r; s$ 9. $xy; yz$ 10. $12x^2; 15y^2$

In 11–43, add or subtract (combine) the fractions as indicated. Reduce answers to lowest terms.

11. $\dfrac{5}{3} + \dfrac{3}{2}$ 12. $\dfrac{9}{5} - \dfrac{2}{3}$ 13. $\dfrac{7}{4} + \dfrac{10}{3}$ 14. $\dfrac{4}{10} - \dfrac{7}{100}$

15. $\dfrac{5}{6} + \dfrac{1}{12}$ 16. $\dfrac{7}{8} - \dfrac{1}{4}$ 17. $\dfrac{1}{3} - \dfrac{1}{6}$ 18. $\dfrac{5}{4} + \dfrac{3}{2} - \dfrac{1}{3}$

19. $\dfrac{x}{3} + \dfrac{x}{2}$ 20. $\dfrac{d}{3} - \dfrac{d}{5}$ 21. $\dfrac{5x}{6} - \dfrac{2x}{3}$ 22. $\dfrac{y}{6} + \dfrac{y}{5} - \dfrac{y}{2}$

23. $\dfrac{ab}{5} + \dfrac{ab}{4}$ 24. $\dfrac{8x}{5} - \dfrac{3x}{4} + \dfrac{7x}{10}$ 25. $\dfrac{5a}{6} - \dfrac{3a}{4}$ 26. $\dfrac{a}{7} + \dfrac{b}{14}$

27. $\dfrac{9}{4x} + \dfrac{3}{2x}$ 28. $\dfrac{1}{2x} - \dfrac{1}{x} + \dfrac{3}{8x}$ 29. $\dfrac{9a}{8b} - \dfrac{3a}{4b}$ 30. $\dfrac{1}{a} + \dfrac{1}{b}$

31. $\dfrac{2}{a^2} - \dfrac{5}{b}$ 32. $\dfrac{1}{xy} + \dfrac{1}{yz}$ 33. $\dfrac{5}{rs} + \dfrac{9}{st}$ 34. $\dfrac{x}{3ab} - \dfrac{y}{2bc}$

35. $\dfrac{9}{ab} + \dfrac{2}{bc} - \dfrac{3}{ac}$ 36. $\dfrac{1}{x^2} + \dfrac{3}{xy} - \dfrac{5}{y^2}$ 37. $\dfrac{a-3}{3} + \dfrac{a+1}{6}$

38. $\dfrac{x+7}{3} - \dfrac{2x-3}{5}$ 39. $\dfrac{3y-4}{5} - \dfrac{y-2}{4}$ 40. $\dfrac{a-b}{4} - \dfrac{a+b}{6}$

41. $\dfrac{x+5}{2x} + \dfrac{2x-1}{4x}$ 42. $\dfrac{d+6}{d} + \dfrac{d-3}{4d}$ 43. $6x - \dfrac{4x-9}{5}$

44. The sides of a triangle are represented by $\dfrac{x}{2}$, $\dfrac{3x}{5}$, and $\dfrac{7x}{10}$, respectively. Represent the perimeter of the triangle in simplest form.

7 SOLVING EQUATIONS CONTAINING FRACTIONAL COEFFICIENTS

Examples of equations that contain fractional coefficients are:

$$\tfrac{1}{2}x = 10 \quad or \quad \tfrac{x}{2} = 10 \qquad\qquad \tfrac{1}{3}x + 60 = \tfrac{5}{6}x \quad or \quad \tfrac{x}{3} + 60 = \tfrac{5x}{6}$$

Each of these equations can be solved by transforming it into an equivalent equation that does not contain fractional coefficients. This can be done by multiplying both members of the equation by a common denominator for all the fractions present in the equation. We usually multiply by the lowest common denominator, the L.C.D.

■ **PROCEDURE.** To solve an equation that contains fractional coefficients:

1. Find the L.C.D.

2. Multiply both members of the equation by the L.C.D.

3. Solve the resulting equation using the usual methods.

| MODEL PROBLEMS |

1. Solve and check: $\dfrac{x}{3} + \dfrac{x}{5} = 8$

How to Proceed	*Solution*	
(1) Write the equation.	$\dfrac{x}{3} + \dfrac{x}{5} = 8$	
(2) Find the L.C.D.	L.C.D. $= 3 \cdot 5 = 15$	
(3) Multiply both members of the equation by the L.C.D.	$15\left(\dfrac{x}{3} + \dfrac{x}{5}\right) = 15(8)$	*Check*
(4) Use the distributive property.	$15\left(\dfrac{x}{3}\right) + 15\left(\dfrac{x}{5}\right) = 15(8)$	$\dfrac{x}{3} + \dfrac{x}{5} = 8$
(5) Multiply.	$5x + 3x = 120$	$\dfrac{15}{3} + \dfrac{15}{5} \overset{?}{=} 8$
(6) Combine like terms.	$8x = 120$	$5 + 3 \overset{?}{=} 8$
(7) D_8 or $M_{\frac{1}{8}}$	$x = 15$	$8 = 8$ (True)

Answer: $x = 15$ *or* solution set is $\{15\}$

2. Solve: $\dfrac{3x}{4} = 20 + \dfrac{x}{4}$ **3.** Solve: $\dfrac{2x+7}{6} - \dfrac{2x-9}{10} = 3$

Solution

$\dfrac{3x}{4} = 20 + \dfrac{x}{4}$

L.C.D. $= 4$

$4\left(\dfrac{3x}{4}\right) = 4\left(20 + \dfrac{x}{4}\right)$

$4\left(\dfrac{3x}{4}\right) = 4(20) + 4\left(\dfrac{x}{4}\right)$

$3x = 80 + x$

$2x = 80$ S_x

$x = 40$

Answer: $x = 40$ *or* solution set is $\{40\}$

Solution

$\dfrac{2x+7}{6} - \dfrac{2x-9}{10} = 3$

L.C.D. $= 30$

$30\left(\dfrac{2x+7}{6} - \dfrac{2x-9}{10}\right) = 30(3)$

$30\left(\dfrac{2x+7}{6}\right) - 30\left(\dfrac{2x-9}{10}\right) = 30(3)$

$5(2x+7) - 3(2x-9) = 90$

$10x + 35 - 6x + 27 = 90$

$4x + 62 = 90$

$4x = 28$ S_{62}

$x = 7$

Answer: $x = 7$ *or* solution set is $\{7\}$

In problems 2 and 3, the check is left to the student.

EXERCISES

In 1–23, solve and check.

1. $\dfrac{x}{7} = 3$ **2.** $\dfrac{1}{6}t = 18$ **3.** $\dfrac{3x}{5} = 15$

4. $\dfrac{5}{7}n = 35$ **5.** $\dfrac{x+8}{4} = 6$ **6.** $\dfrac{m-2}{9} = 3$

7. $\dfrac{2r+6}{5} = -4$ **8.** $\dfrac{5y-30}{7} = 0$ **9.** $\dfrac{5x}{2} = \dfrac{15}{4}$

10. $\dfrac{m-5}{35} = \dfrac{5}{7}$ **11.** $\dfrac{2x+1}{3} = \dfrac{6x-9}{5}$ **12.** $\dfrac{3y+1}{4} = \dfrac{44-y}{5}$

13. $\dfrac{x}{5} + \dfrac{x}{3} = \dfrac{8}{15}$ **14.** $10 = \dfrac{x}{3} + \dfrac{x}{7}$ **15.** $\dfrac{r}{3} - \dfrac{r}{6} = 2$

16. $\dfrac{3t}{5} - \dfrac{t}{5} = 3$ **17.** $1 = \dfrac{7r}{8} - \dfrac{3r}{8}$

18. $\dfrac{3t}{4} - 6 = \dfrac{t}{12}$ **19.** $\dfrac{a}{2} + \dfrac{a}{3} + \dfrac{a}{4} = 26$

20. $\dfrac{7y}{12} - \dfrac{1}{4} = 2y - \dfrac{5}{3}$ **21.** $\dfrac{y+2}{4} - \dfrac{y-3}{3} = \dfrac{1}{2}$

22. $\dfrac{t-3}{6} - \dfrac{t-25}{5} = 4$ **23.** $\dfrac{3m+1}{4} = 2 - \dfrac{3-2m}{6}$

24. The sum of one-half of a number and one-third of that number is 25. Find the number.

25. The difference between one-fifth of a number and one-tenth of that number is 10. Find the number.

26. If one-half of a number is increased by 20, the result is 35. Find the number.

27. If two-thirds of a number is decreased by 30, the result is 10. Find the number.

28. If the sum of two consecutive integers is divided by 3, the quotient is 9. Find the integers.

29. If the sum of two consecutive odd integers is divided by 4, the quotient is 10. Find the integers.

30. In an isosceles triangle each of the congruent sides is two-thirds of the base. The perimeter of the triangle is 42. Find the length of each side of the triangle.

8 SOLVING FRACTIONAL EQUATIONS

An equation is called a *fractional equation* when a variable appears in the *denominator* of one, or more than one, of its terms. For example, $\frac{1}{3} + \frac{1}{x} = \frac{1}{2}$ and $\frac{2}{3d} + \frac{1}{3} = \frac{11}{6d} - \frac{1}{4}$ are called fractional equations. To solve such an equation, we can clear the equation of fractions by multiplying both of its members by the lowest common denominator (L.C.D.) for the denominators of the fractions present in the equation. If we multiply by an expression that involves the variable, we will obtain an equivalent equation only when the variable does not represent a number that makes the value of the multiplier zero. If the variable does represent a number that makes the value of the multiplier zero, we are multiplying both members of the equation by zero, and the resulting equation may not be equivalent to the original equation.

Remember: We may multiply both members of an equation only by a nonzero number in order to obtain an equivalent equation.

| MODEL PROBLEM |

Solve and check: $\frac{1}{3} + \frac{1}{x} = \frac{1}{2}$

Solution: Multiply both members of the equation by the L.C.D., $6x$.

$$\frac{1}{3} + \frac{1}{x} = \frac{1}{2}$$

$$6x\left(\frac{1}{3} + \frac{1}{x}\right) = 6x\left(\frac{1}{2}\right) \qquad M_{6x}$$

$$6x\left(\frac{1}{3}\right) + 6x\left(\frac{1}{x}\right) = 6x\left(\frac{1}{2}\right)$$

$$2x + 6 = 3x$$

$$6 = x$$

Answer: $x = 6$ *or* solution set is $\{6\}$

Check

$$\frac{1}{3} + \frac{1}{x} = \frac{1}{2}$$

$$\frac{1}{3} + \frac{1}{6} \overset{?}{=} \frac{1}{2}$$

$$\frac{2}{6} + \frac{1}{6} \overset{?}{=} \frac{1}{2}$$

$$\frac{3}{6} \overset{?}{=} \frac{1}{2}$$

$$\frac{1}{2} = \frac{1}{2} \quad \text{(True)}$$

| EXERCISES |

In 1–18, solve and check.

1. $\frac{10}{x} = 5$

2. $\frac{15}{y} = 3$

3. $\frac{6}{x} = 12$

4. $\frac{8}{b} = -2$

5. $\frac{3}{2x} = \frac{1}{2}$

6. $\frac{15}{4x} = \frac{1}{8}$

7. $\dfrac{7}{3y} = -\dfrac{1}{3}$
8. $\dfrac{4}{5y} = -\dfrac{1}{10}$
9. $\dfrac{10}{x} + \dfrac{8}{x} = 9$

10. $\dfrac{15}{y} - \dfrac{3}{y} = 4$
11. $\dfrac{7}{c} + \dfrac{1}{c} = 16$
12. $\dfrac{9}{2x} = \dfrac{7}{2x} + 2$

13. $\dfrac{30}{x} = 7 + \dfrac{18}{2x}$
14. $\dfrac{y-2}{2y} = \dfrac{3}{8}$
15. $\dfrac{5}{c} + 6 = \dfrac{17}{c}$

16. $\dfrac{y+9}{2y} + 3 = \dfrac{15}{y}$
17. $\dfrac{5+x}{2x} - 1 = \dfrac{x+1}{x}$
18. $\dfrac{2+x}{6x} = \dfrac{3}{5x} + \dfrac{1}{30}$

19. If 24 is divided by a number, the result is 6. Find the number.
20. When 10 is divided by a number, the result is 30. Find the number.
21. The sum of 20 divided by a number, and 7 divided by the same number, is 9. Find the number.
22. If 3 times a number is increased by one-third of that number, the result is 280. Find the number.
23. When the reciprocal of a number is decreased by 2, the result is 5. Find the number.
24. The numerator of a fraction is 8 less than the denominator of the fraction. The value of the fraction is $\frac{3}{5}$. Find the fraction.
25. If one-half of a number is 8 more than one-third of the number, find the number.

9 EQUATIONS AND FORMULAS INVOLVING SEVERAL VARIABLES

When we solve an equation involving several variables for one of those variables, we express this variable in terms of the other variables. We may "think" of the other variables as we "thought" of numbers in equations and follow the procedure we learned earlier for solving an equation. For example, to solve $\dfrac{3x}{2a} + b = 3b$ for the variable x, "think" of solving $\dfrac{3x}{2} + 1 = 3$; the same procedure is followed in both instances.

How to Proceed	*Solution*
(1) Clear the fraction by multiplying by the L.C.D. Here, the L.C.D. is $2a$.	$\dfrac{3x}{2a} + b = 3b$
	$2a\left(\dfrac{3x}{2a} + b\right) = 2a(3b)$
	$2a\left(\dfrac{3x}{2a}\right) + 2a(b) = 2a(3b)$

(2) Collect on one side of the equation all terms involving the variable for which we are solving. Collect all other terms on the other side.

$$3x + 2ab = 6ab$$
$$3x + 2ab + (-2ab) = 6ab + (-2ab)$$
$$3x = 4ab$$

(3) Divide both members of the equation by the coefficient of the variable.

$$x = \frac{4ab}{3} \quad Ans.$$

EXERCISES

In 1–12, solve for x and check.

1. $\frac{x}{5} = t$

2. $\frac{x}{c} = d$

3. $\frac{x}{3a} = b$

4. $\frac{x}{3} = \frac{b}{4}$

5. $\frac{x}{a} - \frac{b}{3} = 0$

6. $\frac{x}{3} + b = 4b$

7. $\frac{r}{x} = t$

8. $\frac{t}{x} - k = 0$

9. $\frac{x - 4b}{5} = 8b$

10. $\frac{a + b}{x} = c$

11. $\frac{mx}{r} + d = 2d$

12. $\frac{x}{3a} + \frac{x}{5a} = 8$

In 13–18, solve the formula for the indicated variable.

13. $C = \frac{360}{n}$ for n

14. $R = \frac{E}{I}$ for I

15. $v = \frac{s}{t}$ for t

16. $F = \frac{mv^2}{gr}$ for m

17. $V = \frac{L}{RA}$ for R

18. $F = 32 + \frac{9}{5}C$ for C

19. If $S = \frac{1}{2}at^2$, express a in terms of S and t.

20. If $A = p + prt$, express t in terms of $A, r,$ and p.

In 21 and 22, find the value of the variable indicated when the other variables have the stated values.

21. If $\frac{D}{R} = T$, find the value of R when $D = 120$ and $T = 4$.

22. If $A = \frac{1}{2}h(b + c)$, find the value of h when $A = 48$, $b = 12$, and $c = 4$.

chapter sixteen

Probability

1 EMPIRICAL PROBABILITY

A decision is sometimes reached by the toss of a coin. "Heads, we'll go to the movies; tails, we'll go bowling." When we toss a coin, we don't know whether the coin will land "heads" facing upwards, or "tails" up. However, we believe that "heads" and "tails" have an *equal chance* of happening whenever we toss a "fair coin." We can describe this situation by saying that the *probability* of heads is $\frac{1}{2}$ and the *probability* of tails is $\frac{1}{2}$, symbolized as:

$$P(\text{heads}) = \tfrac{1}{2} \quad or \quad P(H) = \tfrac{1}{2}$$

and

$$P(\text{tails}) = \tfrac{1}{2} \quad or \quad P(T) = \tfrac{1}{2}$$

Before we define probability, let us consider a few more situations.

1. Suppose a girl tosses a coin and it lands "heads" up. If she were to toss the coin a second time, will the coin now land "tails" up? We hope your answer is, "I don't know." We cannot say that the coin must now be "tails" because, in probability, *we cannot predict the next result with certainty* when we toss a coin.

2. Suppose we take a card made of stiff cardboard, such as an index card or a computer punch card, and fold it down the center. When we toss the card and let it fall, there will be only three possible results. The card may land

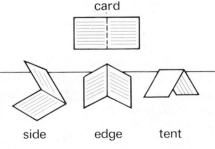

card

side   edge   tent

on its side, or it may land on its edge, or it may form a tent when it lands. Can we say that $P(\text{edge}) = \frac{1}{3}$, $P(\text{side}) = \frac{1}{3}$, and $P(\text{tent}) = \frac{1}{3}$?

We hope your answer is, "I don't know." *We cannot assign a number as a probability until we have some evidence to support our claim.* In fact, if we were to gather evidence by tossing this card, we would find that the probabilities are *not* $\frac{1}{3}$, $\frac{1}{3}$, and $\frac{1}{3}$.

An Empirical Study

Let us go back to the problem of tossing a coin. While we cannot predict the result of one toss of a coin, we can still say that the probability of heads is $\frac{1}{2}$, based on observations made in an empirical study. In an *empirical study* we perform an experiment many times, we keep records of the results, and we analyze these results. For example, ten students decided to take turns tossing a coin. Each student completed 20 tosses and the number of heads was recorded as shown.

	Number of Heads	Number of Tosses
Albert	8	20
Peter	13	20
Thomas	12	20
Maria	10	20
Elizabeth	6	20
Joanna	12	20
Kathy	11	20
Jeanne	7	20
Debbie	13	20
James	9	20

If we look at the results and try to think of probability as some "sort of fraction," then only Maria with 10 heads out of 20 tosses had results where the probability was $\frac{10}{20}$ or $\frac{1}{2}$. This fraction is called the *relative frequency*. Elizabeth had the lowest relative frequency of heads with $\frac{6}{20}$. Peter and Debbie tied for the highest relative frequency with $\frac{13}{20}$. This table does *not* mean that Maria had correct results while the other students were incorrect; the coins simply fell that way. The students decided to put their results together, by expanding the chart, to see what happened with 200 tosses of the coin. As shown on the facing page, in columns 3 and 4 the *cumulative* results are found by adding the results "to date." For example, in the second row, by adding the 8 heads that Albert tossed and the 13 heads that Peter tossed, we find that the total number of heads tossed by Albert and Peter together is 21; this total is called the cumulative number of heads. By adding the 20 tosses that Albert made and the 20 tosses that Peter made, we find the cumulative number of tosses is 40.

	(Col. 1) Number of Heads	(Col. 2) Number of Tosses	(Col. 3) Cumulative Number of Heads	(Col. 4) Cumulative Number of Tosses	(Col. 5) Cumulative Relative Frequency
Albert	8	20	8	20	8/20 = .400
Peter	13	20	21	40	21/40 = .525
Thomas	12	20	33	60	33/60 = .550
Maria	10	20	43	80	43/80 = .538
Elizabeth	6	20	49	100	49/100 = .490
Joanna	12	20	61	120	61/120 = .508
Kathy	11	20	72	140	72/140 = .514
Jeanne	7	20	79	160	79/160 = .494
Debbie	13	20	92	180	92/180 = .511
James	9	20	101	200	101/200 = .505

In column 5 the *cumulative relative frequency* is found by dividing the total number of heads "to date" by the total number of tosses "to date." Notice that the cumulative relative frequency is shown as a fraction and then, for easy comparison, as a decimal. The decimal is given to the nearest thousandth.

While the relative frequency for individual students varied greatly from $\frac{6}{20}$ to $\frac{13}{20}$, the cumulative relative frequency is $\frac{101}{200}$, a number very close to $\frac{1}{2}$.

A *graph* of the results of columns 4 and 5 in the previous chart will tell us even more. In the graph on the following page the horizontal axis is labeled "Number of Tosses" to show the cumulative results of column 4; the vertical axis is labeled "Cumulative relative frequency of heads" to show the results of column 5.

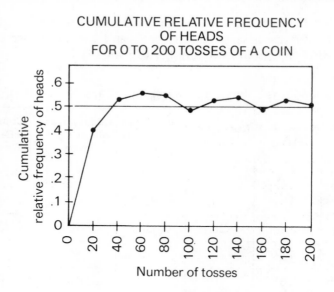

CUMULATIVE RELATIVE FREQUENCY
OF HEADS
FOR 0 TO 200 TOSSES OF A COIN

Number of tosses

In the graph we have plotted the points which represent the data in columns 4 and 5 in the previous chart and we have connected these points to form a line graph. Notice how the line moves back and forth around the relative frequency of .5 or $\frac{1}{2}$. The more times that the coin is tossed, the closer the relative frequency comes to $\frac{1}{2}$. The graph shows us that the line seems to "level out" at a relative frequency of $\frac{1}{2}$.

What would probably have happened if the students had tossed the coin 400 times? Or 1,000 times? Or 10,000 times? The line would appear to become a straight horizontal line, similar to the line whose equation is $y = .5$ or $y = \frac{1}{2}$. Hence, we can say that the cumulative relative frequency *converges* to the number $\frac{1}{2}$ and the coin will "probably" land heads up $\frac{1}{2}$ of the time.

When a line graph "levels out" or "converges" to a number, we call this the ***stabilization of a cumulative relative frequency***. Even though the cumulative relative frequency of $\frac{101}{200}$ is not exactly $\frac{1}{2}$, we "seem to sense" that the line will approach the number $\frac{1}{2}$. We use this carefully collected evidence to guess that the probability of "heads" is $\frac{1}{2}$ when tossing a fair coin.

■ **Empirical probability may be defined as the most accurate scientific "guess" of the cumulative relative frequency of an event happening.**

Experiments in Probability

A single "attempt" at doing something, such as tossing a coin only once, is called a *trial*. We perform *experiments* in probability by repeating the same trial many times. Experiments are aimed at finding the probabilities to be assigned to different events occurring, such as "heads" or "tails" on a coin. The objects used in an experiment may be classified into one of two categories:

1. *Fair and unbiased objects* have not been weighted or made unbalanced. An object is fair when the different results have an *equal chance* of happening. Objects such as coins, dice, cards, and spinners will always be treated in this book as fair objects, unless otherwise noted.

2. *Biased objects* are those that have been tampered with or are weighted to give one result a *better chance* of happening than another. The folded index card, described earlier in this chapter, is a biased

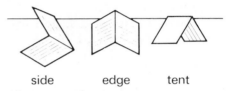

side   edge   tent

object because the probability of each of three results is not $\frac{1}{3}$. The card is weighted so that it will fall on its side more often than it will fall on its edge.

Uses of Probability

Mathematicians first studied probability by looking at situations involving games. Today probability is used in a wide variety of fields. In medicine it helps us to know the chances of catching an infection, of controlling an epidemic, and the rate of effectiveness of a drug in curing a disease. In industry probability tells us how long a manufactured product should last. We can predict when more tellers are needed at bank windows, when and where traffic jams usually occur, and the expected weather for the next few days. In biology the study of genes inherited from one's parents and grandparents is a direct application of probability. While this list is almost endless, all of these applications demand a strong knowledge of higher mathematics. Like the early mathematicians, we will begin our study of probability by looking at games and rather simple applications.

| MODEL PROBLEMS |

We have seen how to determine empirical probability by the charts and graphs previously shown in this chapter. Sometimes it is possible to "guess" the probability that should be assigned to the result described before we start an experiment.

In 1-5, use common sense to "guess" the probability that might be assigned to the result described. (The solutions are given without comment here. We will learn how to determine these probabilities in the next section.)

1. A *die* is a six-sided solid object. Each side (or face) is a square. The sides are numbered 1, 2, 3, 4, 5, 6. The plural of die is *dice*.

    In rolling a fair die, find the probability of getting a 4, or $P(4)$.

    Die   Faces of a die

    Solution: $P(4) = \frac{1}{6}$

2. A *standard deck of cards* contains 52 cards. There are 4 suits called hearts, diamonds, spades, and clubs. Each suit contains 13 cards: 2, 3, 4, 5, 6, 7, 8, 9, 10, jack, queen, king, ace. The diamonds and hearts are red; the spades and clubs are black.

    In selecting a card from the deck without looking, find the probability of drawing: **(a)** the seven of diamonds; **(b)** a seven; **(c)** a diamond.

    Solution: **(a)** $P(\text{seven of diamonds}) = \frac{1}{52}$

               (b) $P(\text{seven}) = \frac{4}{52}$ *or* $\frac{1}{13}$

               (c) $P(\text{diamond}) = \frac{13}{52}$ *or* $\frac{1}{4}$

3. There are 10 *digits* in our numeral system: 0, 1, 2, 3, 4, 5, 6, 7, 8, 9. After selecting a digit without looking, what is the probability it will be: **(a)** the 8; **(b)** an odd digit?

    Solution: **(a)** $P(8) = \frac{1}{10}$; **(b)** $P(\text{odd}) = \frac{5}{10}$ *or* $\frac{1}{2}$

4. An *urn* or a jar contains 8 marbles: 3 are white and the remaining 5 are blue. In selecting a marble without looking, what is the probability that it is blue? (All marbles are the same size.)

    Solution: $P(\text{blue}) = \frac{5}{8}$

5. The English alphabet contains 26 letters: There are 5 *vowels* (A, E, I, O, U) and the remaining 21 letters are *consonants*. If a person turns 26 tiles from a Scrabble game face down and each tile represents a different letter of the alphabet, what is the probability of turning over: **(a)** the A; **(b)** a vowel; **(c)** a consonant?

Solution: **(a)** $P(A) = \frac{1}{26}$; **(b)** $P(\text{vowel}) = \frac{5}{26}$; **(c)** $P(\text{consonant}) = \frac{21}{26}$

EXERCISES

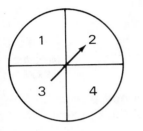

1. The figure at the left shows a disk, with an arrow that can be spun so that it has an equal chance of landing on one of four regions on the disk. The regions are equal in size and they are numbered 1, 2, 3, and 4.

  An experiment was conducted by five people to find the probability that the arrow will land on the 2. Each person spun the arrow 100 times. When the arrow landed on a line, it did not count and the arrow was spun again.

a. Before doing the experiment, what probability would you assign to the arrow landing on the 2? (In symbols, $P(2) = \underline{\ ?\ }$)

b. Copy and complete the chart to find the *cumulative* results of this experiment. In the last column record the cumulative relative frequencies as fractions and as decimals to the *nearest thousandths*.

	Number of Times "2" Appeared	Number of Spins	Cumulative Number of Times "2" Appeared	Cumulative Number of Spins	Cumulative Relative Frequency
Barbara	29	100	29	100	$\frac{29}{100} = .290$
Tom	31	100	60	200	
Ann	19	100			
Eddie	23	100			
Cathy	24	100			

c. Did the experiment provide evidence that the probability assigned in part **a** was correct?

In 2-7, a result is described for a *fair, unbiased object*. What probability should be assigned to the result described? These questions should be answered *without* conducting an experiment; take a "guess."

2. A six-sided die is rolled; the sides are numbered 1, 2, 3, 4, 5, 6. In rolling the die, find $P(5)$.

3. In drawing a card from a standard deck without looking, find P(any heart).

4. Each of ten pieces of paper contains a different number from the set $\{0, 1, 2, 3, 4, 5, 6, 7, 8, 9\}$. The pieces of paper are folded and placed into a paper bag. In selecting a piece of paper without looking, find $P(7)$.

5. An urn (jar) contains 5 marbles, all the same size. Two marbles are black and the other three are white. In selecting a marble without looking, find P(black).

Ex. 5

6. Using the lettered tiles from a Scrabble set, a boy places 26 tiles face down on a table, one tile for each letter of the alphabet. After mixing up the tiles, he takes one. What is the probability that the tile contains one of the letters in the word MATH?

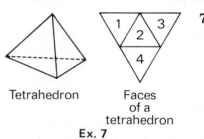

Tetrahedron   Faces
of a
tetrahedron

Ex. 7

7. A *tetrahedron* is a four-sided object. Each side, or face, is an equilateral triangle. The numerals 1, 2, 3, and 4 are used to number the different faces. A trial consists of rolling the tetrahedron and reading the number that is face down. Find $P(4)$.

8. By yourself, or with some classmates, conduct any of the experiments described in exercises 2-7 to verify that you have assigned the correct probability to the event or result described. A good experiment should contain at least 100 trials.

In 9-13, a *biased object* is described. A probability can be assigned to a result described only by conducting an experiment to determine the cumulative relative frequency of the event. While you may wish to "guess" at the probability of the event before starting the experiment, conduct at least 100 trials to determine the best probability to be assigned.

9. An index card is folded in half and tossed (as described earlier in this chapter). The card may land in one of three positions: on its

side, on its edge, or in the form of a tent. In tossing a folded card, find P(tent), the probability that the card will form a tent when it lands.

10. A paper cup is tossed. It can land in one of three positions: on its top, on its bottom, or on its side. In tossing the cup, find P(top), the probability of landing on its top.

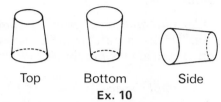

Top   Bottom   Side

Ex. 10

11. A nickel and a quarter are glued or taped together so that the two faces seen are the head of the quarter and the tail of the nickel. This is a very crude model of a weighted coin. In tossing the coin, find P(head).

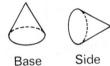

Base   Side

Ex. 12

12. A paper cup in the shape of a cone is tossed. It can land in one of two positions: on its base or on its side. In tossing this cup, find P(side), the probability of landing on its side.

13. A thumbtack is tossed. It may land either with the pin up or with the pin down (touching the table). In tossing a thumbtack, find P(pin is up).

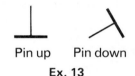

Pin up   Pin down

Ex. 13

2 THEORETICAL PROBABILITY

An empirical approach to probability is necessary whenever we deal with biased objects. However, common sense tells us that there is a simple way to define the probability of an event when we deal with fair, unbiased objects. For example:

Alma is playing a game in which each player must roll a die. To win, Alma must roll a number *greater than 4*. What is the probability that Alma will win on her next turn?

Common sense tells us:

(1) The die has an equal chance of falling *six* ways: **1, 2, 3, 4, 5, 6.**

(2) There are *two* ways for Alma to win: rolling a **5** or a **6.**

(3) Therefore, P(Alma wins) $= \dfrac{\text{number of ways to win}}{\text{number of possible results}} = \dfrac{2}{6} = \dfrac{1}{3}.$

Terms and Definitions

Let us examine the correct terminology to be used with the previous problem.

An *outcome* is a result of some activity or experiment. In rolling a die, "1" is an outcome, "2" is an outcome, "3" is an outcome, and so on. There are six outcomes here.

A *sample space* is a set of all possible outcomes for the activity or experiment. In rolling a die, there are six possible outcomes in the sample space: 1, 2, 3, 4, 5, and 6.

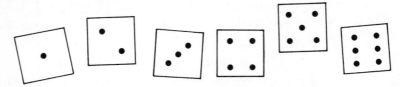

When we roll a die, we may define many different situations or results; each of these is called an *event*.

1. For Alma, the event of rolling a number *greater than 4* contains only two outcomes that are correct: 5 and 6.

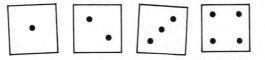

2. For Lee, a different event might be rolling a number *less than 5*. This event contains four outcomes that will be true: 1, 2, 3, and 4.

3. For Sandy, the event of rolling a 2 contains only one correct outcome: 2.

We can now define *theoretical probability* for fair, unbiased objects:

■ **The theoretical probability of an event is the number of ways that the event can occur, divided by the total number of possibilities.**

In symbolic form, we write:

$$P(E) = \frac{n(E)}{n(S)} \text{ where } \begin{cases} P(E) \text{ represents the probability of an event } E; \\\\ n(E) \text{ represents the number of ways that event } E \text{ can occur;} \\\\ n(S) \text{ represents the total number of possibilities, or the total number of possible outcomes in the sample space } S. \end{cases}$$

For Alma's problem there are 2 ways to roll a number greater than four, and there are 6 possible ways that the die may fall. We say:

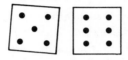

E = event of rolling a number greater than 4 = 5 and 6. Then $n(E)$ = 2.

S = sample space of 6 possible outcomes = 1, 2, 3, 4, 5, 6. So $n(S)$ = 6.

Therefore:

$$P(E) = \frac{n(E)}{n(S)} = \frac{\text{number of ways to roll a number greater than 4}}{\text{total number of outcomes for the die}} = \frac{2}{6} \text{ or } \frac{1}{3}$$

We can also say that the probability of rolling a number *less than five* is found by $P(E) = \dfrac{n(E)}{n(S)} = \dfrac{4}{6}$ or $\dfrac{2}{3}$. Likewise, the probability of rolling a "2" is $P(E) = \dfrac{n(E)}{n(S)} = \dfrac{1}{6}$.

Notice that the theoretical probability of an event is the ratio of the number of ways the event can occur to the total number of possibilities in the sample space.

Uniform Probability

A sample space is said to have *uniform probability*, or to contain *equally likely outcomes*, when each of the possible outcomes has an *equal chance* of occurring. In rolling a die there are six possible outcomes in the sample space; each is equally likely to occur. So, $P(1) = \frac{1}{6}$; $P(2) = \frac{1}{6}$; $P(3) = \frac{1}{6}$; $P(4) = \frac{1}{6}$; $P(5) = \frac{1}{6}$; $P(6) = \frac{1}{6}$; and we say that the die has uniform probability.

If a die is "weighted" to make it biased, then one or more sides will have a probability greater than $\frac{1}{6}$, while one or more sides will have a probability less than $\frac{1}{6}$. A weighted die does not have uniform probability. Remember that the rule for theoretical probability does not apply to weighted objects.

Random Selection

When we select an object "without looking," or with our eyes shut, we are making a *random selection*. Random selections are made when drawing a marble from a bag, when taking a card from a deck, or when picking a name out of a hat. In the same way we may use the word *random* to describe outcomes when tossing a coin or rolling a die; the outcomes happen without any special selection on our part.

■ **Procedure for finding the simple probability of an event:**

1. Count the total number of outcomes in the sample space: $n(S)$

2. Count all the possible ways that event E can occur: $n(E)$

3. Substitute these values in the formula for the probability of event E: $P(E) = \dfrac{n(E)}{n(S)}$

| MODEL PROBLEMS |

1. A standard deck of 52 cards is shuffled. Lillian draws a single card from the deck at random. What is the probability that the card is a jack?

Solution

S = sample space of all possible outcomes. There are 52 cards in the deck. Hence, $n(S) = 52$.

J = event of selecting a jack. There are 4 jacks in the deck: jack of hearts, jack of diamonds, jack of spades, and jack of clubs. So, $n(J) = 4$.

$$P(J) = \frac{n(J)}{n(S)} = \frac{\text{number of ways to draw a jack}}{\text{total number of possible cards}} = \frac{4}{52} \text{ or } \frac{1}{13} \quad Ans.$$

2. A spinner contains eight regions, numbered 1 through 8. The arrow has an equally likely chance of landing on any of the eight regions. If the arrow lands on a line, it is not counted and the arrow is spun again.

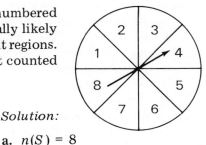

Solution:

a. How many possible outcomes are in the sample space S?

    a. $n(S) = 8$

b. What is the probability that the arrow lands on the 4? Simply, what is $P(4)$?

    b. Since there is only 1 way to land on the 4 out of 8 possible numbers, $P(4) = \frac{1}{8}$.

c. List the possible outcomes for the event O in which the arrow lands on an odd number.

    c. Event O = 1, 3, 5, 7

d. Find the probability that the arrow lands on an odd number.

    d. Since event O = 1, 3, 5, 7, then $n(O) = 4$.

$$P(O) = \frac{n(O)}{n(S)} = \frac{4}{8} \text{ or } \frac{1}{2}$$

EXERCISES

1. A fair coin is tossed. a. List the sample space. b. What is $P(\text{head})$, the probability that a head will appear? c. What is $P(\text{tail})$?
2. A fair die is tossed. For each part of this question, (1) list the outcomes for the event and (2) state the probability of the event.
    a. The number 3 appears.
    b. An even number appears.
    c. A number less than 3 appears.
    d. An odd number appears.
    e. A number greater than 3 appears.
    f. A number greater than or equal to 3 appears.

3. A spinner is divided into 5 equal regions, numbered 1 through 5. An arrow is spun and lands in one of the regions. For each part of this question, (1) list the outcomes for the event; (2) state the probability of the event.

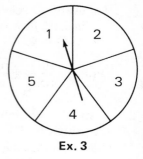

Ex. 3

   a. The number 3 appears.
   b. An even number appears.
   c. A number less than 3 appears.
   d. An odd number appears.
   e. A number greater than 3 appears.
   f. A number greater than or equal to 3 appears.

4. A standard deck of 52 cards is shuffled and one card is drawn. What is the probability that the card is:
   a. the queen of hearts?   b. a queen?   c. a heart?
   d. a red card?   e. the seven of clubs?   f. a club?
   g. an ace?   h. a red seven?   i. a black ten?
   j. a picture card (king, queen, jack)?

5. A person does not know the answer to a test question and takes a guess. Find the probability that the answer is correct if the question is: (a) a multiple-choice question with 4 choices; (b) a true-false question; (c) a question where the choices given are "sometimes, always, or never."

6. A marble is drawn at random from a bag. Find the probability that the marble is green when the bag contains marbles whose colors are:
   a. 3 blue, 2 green   b. 4 blue, 1 green
   c. 5 red, 2 green, 3 blue   d. 6 blue, 4 green
   e. 3 green, 9 blue   f. 5 red, 2 green, 93 blue

7. The digits of the number 1776 are written on disks and placed into a jar. What is the probability that the digit 7 will be chosen on a single draw?

8. A class contains 16 boys and 14 girls. The teacher calls students at random to the chalkboard. What is the probability that the first person called is: (a) a boy? (b) a girl?

9. There are 840 tickets sold in a raffle. Jay bought 5 tickets and Lynn bought 4 tickets. Express, as a fraction in lowest terms, the probability that (a) Jay has the winning ticket; (b) Lynn has the winning ticket.

10. A letter is chosen at random from a given word. Find the probability that the letter is a vowel {A, E, I, O, U} if the word is:
    a. APPLE   b. BANANA   c. GEOMETRY   d. MATHEMATICS

11. In the figure there are eight polygons shown: a square; a rectangle; a parallelogram (which is not a rectangle); a right triangle; an isosceles triangle (not containing a right angle); a trapezoid (not containing a right angle); an equilateral triangle; a regular hexagon.

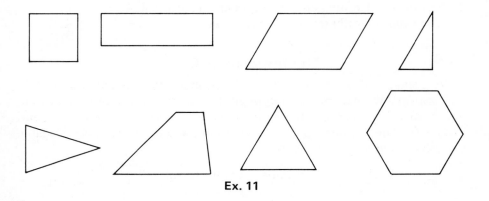

Ex. 11

One of the figures is selected at random. What is the probability that the polygon:

a. contains a right angle?   b. is a quadrilateral?
c. is a triangle?   d. has at least one acute angle?
e. has all sides congruent?   f. has at least two sides congruent?
g. has less than five sides?   h. has an odd number of sides?
i. has four or more sides?   j. has at least two obtuse angles?

12. Explain why each of the following statements is *incorrect*.
   a. There are 50 states in the United States so, for citizens born in our country, the probability of being born in New Jersey is $\frac{1}{50}$.
   b. Since there are 12 months in a year, the probability of being born in September is $\frac{1}{12}$.
   c. A pin containing a small head is tossed, as shown at the right. Since the pin can fall either point up or point down, the probability of falling point down is $\frac{1}{2}$.

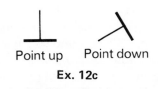

Point up   Point down

Ex. 12c

   d. Since there are 7 days in a week, the probability that a person attends religious services on a Wednesday is $\frac{1}{7}$.

3 EVALUATING SIMPLE PROBABILITIES

If there is only one way that an event can occur, we call this event a *singleton*. For example, in rolling a single die, there is only one way to roll the number "3."

However, when rolling a single die, there can be more than one way for an event to occur. For example:

1. The event of rolling an even number on a die = 2, 4, 6.
2. The event of rolling a number less than 6 on a die = 1, 2, 3, 4, 5.

The Impossible Case

On a single roll of a die, what is the probability that the number "7" will appear? We call this an *impossibility* because there are no ways in which this event can occur. In this example, event E = rolling a 7, and $n(E) = 0$. The sample space S for rolling a die contains six possible outcomes, and $n(S) = 6$. Therefore,

$$P(E) = \frac{n(E)}{n(S)} = \frac{\text{number of ways to roll a 7}}{\text{total number of outcomes for the die}} = \frac{0}{6} = 0$$

In general, for any sample space S containing k possible outcomes, we say $n(S) = k$. For any impossible event E in which there are no ways for the event E to occur, we say $n(E) = 0$. Thus, the probability of an impossible event is $P(E) = \frac{n(E)}{n(S)} = \frac{0}{k} = 0$.

In general, we say:

■ **The probability of an impossible event is zero.**

There are many other examples of impossibilities where the probability must equal zero. For example, the probability of selecting the letter E from the word PROBABILITY is zero.

Also, selecting a coin worth 9¢ from a bank containing a nickel, a dime, and a quarter is an impossible event.

The Certain Case

On a single roll of a die, what is the probability that a number "less than 7" will appear? We call this a *certainty* because every one of the possible outcomes in the sample space is also an outcome for this event. In this example, event E = rolling a number "less than 7," and $n(E) = 6$. The sample space S for rolling a die contains six possible outcomes, and $n(S) = 6$. Therefore,

$$P(E) = \frac{n(E)}{n(S)} = \frac{\text{number of ways to roll a number "less than 7"}}{\text{total number of outcomes on the die}} = \frac{6}{6} = 1$$

In general, for any sample space S containing k possible outcomes, we say $n(S) = k$. When the event E is certain, then every possible outcome for the sample space is also an outcome for the event E, or $n(E) = k$. Thus, the probability of a certainty is given as $P(E) = \dfrac{n(E)}{n(S)} = \dfrac{k}{k} = 1$. In general, we say:

■ **The probability of an event that is certain to occur is 1.**

There are many other examples of certainties where the probability must equal 1. Such examples include the probability of selecting a consonant from the letters JFK or selecting a red sweater from a drawer containing only red sweaters.

The Probability of Any Event

Let us consider a series of events for rolling a six-sided die:

Event A, a number less than 1, has no outcomes. $P(A) = \frac{0}{6} = 0$

Event B, a number less than 2, has one outcome:
$$1 \qquad\qquad P(B) = \tfrac{1}{6}$$

Event C, a number less than 3, has two outcomes:
$$1, 2 \qquad\qquad P(C) = \tfrac{2}{6}$$

Event D, a number less than 4, has three outcomes:
$$1, 2, 3 \qquad\qquad P(D) = \tfrac{3}{6}$$

Event F, a number less than 5, has four outcomes:
$$1, 2, 3, 4 \qquad\qquad P(F) = \tfrac{4}{6}$$

Event G, a number less than 6, has five outcomes:
$$1, 2, 3, 4, 5 \qquad\qquad P(G) = \tfrac{5}{6}$$

Event H, a number less than 7, has six outcomes:
$$1, 2, 3, 4, 5, 6 \qquad\qquad P(H) = \tfrac{6}{6} = 1$$

The smallest probability here is 0. The largest probability is 1. Each of the other events has a probability that falls between 0 and 1. This example illustrates the following:

■ **The probability of any event E must be equal to or greater than zero, and less than or equal to one. Or simply:**

$$0 \le P(E) \le 1$$

| MODEL PROBLEMS |

1. A bank contains a nickel, a dime, and a quarter. A person selects one of the coins. What is the probability that the coin is worth: (a) exactly 10 cents; (b) exactly 3 cents; (c) more than 3 cents?

Solution

a. There is only one coin worth exactly 10 cents: the dime. There are three coins in the bank.

Thus, $P(\text{coin is worth 10 cents}) = \dfrac{n(E)}{n(S)} = \dfrac{1}{3}$. *Ans.*

b. There are no coins worth exactly 3 cents. This is an impossible event. Thus, $P(\text{coin is worth 3 cents}) = \dfrac{n(E)}{n(S)} = \dfrac{0}{3} = 0$. *Ans.*

c. All three coins are worth more than 3 cents. This is a certain event. Thus, $P(\text{coin is more than 3 cents}) = \dfrac{n(E)}{n(S)} = \dfrac{3}{3} = 1$. *Ans.*

2. Express the probability of getting a head on a single toss of a coin as: (a) a fraction; (b) a decimal; (c) a percent.

Solution

a. A coin has two possible outcomes when tossed, so $n(S) = 2$. There is only one outcome for a head, so $n(H) = 1$.

Then $P(\text{head}) = \dfrac{n(H)}{n(S)} = \dfrac{1}{2}$. *Ans.*

b. Since $\frac{1}{2} = .5$, we can say $P(\text{head}) = \frac{1}{2} = .5$. *Ans.*

c. Since $\frac{1}{2} = 50\%$, we can say $P(\text{head}) = \frac{1}{2} = 50\%$. *Ans.*

| EXERCISES |

1. Ted has 2 quarters, 3 dimes, and 1 nickel in his pocket. He pulls out a coin at random. Find the probability that the coin is worth:
   a. exactly 5 cents   b. exactly 10 cents   c. exactly 25 cents
   d. exactly 50 cents   e. less than 25 cents   f. less than 50 cents
   g. more than 25 cents   h. more than 1 cent

2. A single fair die is rolled. Find the probability for each event described.
    a. the number 8 appears
    b. a whole number appears
    c. the number is less than 5
    d. the number is less than 1
    e. the number is less than 10
    f. the number is negative

3. A standard deck of 52 cards is shuffled and you pick a card at random. Find the probability that the card is:
    a. the jack of stars
    b. a jack
    c. a star
    d. a red club
    e. a card from the deck
    f. a club
    g. a seventeen
    h. a black club

4. A class contains 15 girls and 10 boys. The teacher calls on a student at random to answer a question. Express the probability in decimal form that the student called upon is: **(a)** a girl; **(b)** a boy; **(c)** a pupil in the class; **(d)** the teacher of the class.

5. The last digit of a telephone number can be any of the following: 0, 1, 2, 3, 4, 5, 6, 7, 8, or 9. Express the probability as a percent that the last digit is: **(a)** 7; **(b)** odd; **(c)** more than 5; **(d)** a whole number; **(e)** the letter R.

6. A girl is holding 5 cards in her hand. They are the 3 of hearts, 3 of diamonds, 3 of clubs, 4 of diamonds, 7 of clubs. A player to her left takes one of these cards at random. (If the player takes the 3 of hearts, we describe the probability of this event as $\frac{1}{5}$.) Find the probability that the card selected from the 5 cards in the girl's hand is:
    a. a three
    b. a diamond
    c. a four
    d. a black four
    e. a club
    f. 4 of hearts
    g. a five
    h. 7 of clubs
    i. a red card
    j. a number card
    k. a spade
    l. a number less than 8

7. The measures of three interior angles of a triangle are given as 40°, 60°, and 80°. The measures of the exterior angles of the triangle are 140°, 120°, and 100°, respectively. One of the six angles is chosen at random. Find the probability that the angle is:

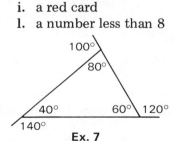

Ex. 7

    a. an interior angle
    b. a straight angle
    c. a right angle
    d. an acute angle
    e. a 60° angle
    f. an acute exterior angle
    g. an angle whose measure is less than 180°

8. List three situations where the probability of an event is 0.

9. List three situations where the probability of an event is 1.

10. Explain why the following sentence is *incorrect:* "I did so well on the test that the probability of my passing is greater than 1."

11. Explain why the following sentence is *incorrect:* "The probability that we'll go swimming in Maine next December is less than 0."
12. Explain why this sentence is *correct:* "The probability that Tuesday comes after Monday is 100%."

4   PROBABILITY AND SETS

Terms and definitions in theoretical probability may be stated in the language of sets. The ideas involved in counting the number of ways an event can happen and counting all possible outcomes in a sample space will still be true when using set terminology.

A **sample space** is a *set* of all possible outcomes for the activity or experiment. The sample space is sometimes called an **outcome set**. In rolling a die, the sample space is the set $\{1, 2, 3, 4, 5, 6\}$.

An *event* is any *subset* of the sample space. In rolling a die, the event of rolling an even number is the subset $\{2, 4, 6\}$. A **singleton** event is a subset containing only one outcome or element, as in the event of rolling a 3, namely $\{3\}$.

To describe an **impossible event**, we may use the *empty set* or *null set*, written as $\{\ \}$ or $\emptyset$. This is true because the empty set is a subset of every set; thus the empty set is a subset of the sample space. To list the outcomes for rolling a "9" on a single toss of a die, we show the subset $\{\ \}$ because there are no ways in which this can be done. Thus, we say $P(\{\ \}) = 0$, or $P(\emptyset) = 0$.

To describe an *event that is certain*, we may use the sample space itself. This is true because every set S is a subset of itself; thus the sample space is itself an event. To list the outcomes for rolling a number "less than 7" on a single toss of a die, we can show this event S as the subset $\{1, 2, 3, 4, 5, 6\}$. Thus, we say $P(S) = 1$.

Subscripts in Sample Spaces

A sample space may sometimes contain two or more objects that are exactly alike. To distinguish one object from another, we make use of a device called a *subscript*. A *subscript* is a number, usually written in smaller size, that always appears to the lower right of a term. For example:

A box contains six jellybeans: 2 red, 3 green, and 1 yellow. Using R, G, and Y to represent the colors red, green, and yellow, respectively, we can list this sample space in full, using subscripts:

$$\{R_1, R_2, G_1, G_2, G_3, Y_1\}$$

Since there is only one yellow jellybean, we could have listed the last element as Y instead of Y_1.

MODEL PROBLEM

An arrow is spun once and lands on one of three equally likely regions, numbered 1, 2, and 3.

a. List the sample space for this experiment.

b. List all 8 possible events for one spin of the arrow.

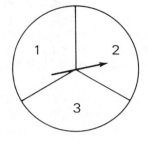

Solution

a. The sample space $S = \{1, 2, 3\}$.

b. Since events are subsets of the sample space S, the 8 possible events are the 8 subsets of S:

    $\{\ \}$ = the empty set, for *impossible* events.

    $\{1, 2, 3\}$ = the set itself, for events with *certainty*.

    $\{1\}, \{2\}, \{3\}$ = the *singleton* events.

    $\{1, 2\}, \{1, 3\}, \{2, 3\}$ = events with *two possible* outcomes. Although the arrow is spun only once, an event such as "getting an odd number" has two possible outcomes, that is, $\{1, 3\}$.

EXERCISES

1. A fair coin is tossed and its sample space $S = \{H, T\}$.
    a. List all 4 possible events for the toss of a coin.
    b. Find the probability of each event named in part a.

2. A spinner is divided into 7 equal regions, numbered 1 through 7. An arrow is spun to fall into one of the regions. For each part of this question:

    (1) List the elements of the event, shown as a subset of $\{1, 2, 3, 4, 5, 6, 7\}$.

    (2) Find the probability that the arrow lands on the number described.

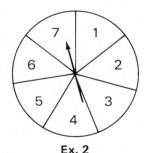

Ex. 2

  a. The number 5   b. An even number
  c. A number less than 5   d. An odd number
  e. A number greater than 5   f. A number greater than 1

3. A marble is drawn at random from a bag. Find the probability that the marble is black if the bag contains marbles whose colors are:
   a. 5 black, 2 green   b. 2 black, 1 green   c. 3 black, 4 green, 1 red
   d. 9 black   e. 3 green, 4 red   f. 3 black

4. A letter is chosen at random from a given word. For each part of this question: (1) List the elements of the event, using subscripts if needed. (2) Find the probability of the event.

   a. Selecting the letter E from the word EVENT
   b. Selecting the letter S from the word MISSISSIPPI
   c. Selecting a vowel from the word TRIANGLE
   d. Selecting a vowel from the word RECEIVE
   e. Selecting a consonant from the word SPRY

5 THE PROBABILITY OF "*A* AND *B*"

The connective "**and**" has been used in logic. As we will see, the connective "and" is sometimes used to describe events in probability.

For example, a fair die is rolled. What is the probability of obtaining an even number?

We may call this event A. Since there are three ways to obtain an even number, we say that

$$P(A) = \frac{n(A)}{n(S)} = \frac{3}{6}.$$

When a fair die is rolled, what is the probability of obtaining a number less than 3?

We may call this event B. Since there are two ways to obtain a number less than 3, we say that

$$P(B) = \frac{n(B)}{n(S)} = \frac{2}{6}.$$

Now, what is the probability of obtaining a number on the die that is even **and** less than 3? We may think of this as the event "*A* and *B*."

In logic we learned that a sentence "*p* and *q*," written $p \wedge q$, is true only when *p* is true *and* *q* is true.	In probability an outcome is in event "*A* and *B*" only when the outcome is in event *A* *and* the outcome is also in event *B*.

The only outcome in the event "*A* and *B*" is "2," because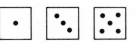
"2 is even" and "2 is less than 3." No other outcome on the die
is true for both events. Since $n(A$ and $B) = 1$ and there are 6
outcomes on the die, or $n(S) = 6$, we can say:

$$P(A \text{ and } B) = \frac{n(A \text{ and } B)}{n(S)} = \frac{1}{6}$$

Consider another example in which a fair die
is rolled.

Event C = the number is odd.

Here, $P(C) = \frac{n(C)}{n(S)} = \frac{3}{6}$.

Event D = the number is "4."

Here, $P(D) = \frac{n(D)}{n(S)} = \frac{1}{6}$.

Then, event "*C* and *D*" = the number is odd **and** the number is "4."

Since there are *no* outcomes common to both event C and event D,
we can say that there are *no* outcomes in the event "*C* and *D*," or

$n(C$ and $D) = 0$. Therefore, $P(C$ and $D) = \frac{n(C \text{ and } D)}{n(S)} = \frac{0}{6} = 0$.

Using Sets to Look at *P(A and B)*

We have seen that an outcome is in the event "*A* and *B*" only when
the outcome is in event A *and* in event B. A set diagram can help us to
understand the event "*A* and *B*."

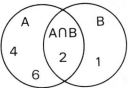

Event "*A* and *B*" = the number is even *and* less than 3. Since event
$A = \{2, 4, 6\}$ and event $B = \{1, 2\}$, we can see that the event "*A* and
B" = $\{2\}$, the ***intersection*** of the two sets, or $A \cap B$. By counting
the number of outcomes in this intersection, we say:

$$P(A \text{ and } B) = P(A \cap B) = \frac{n(A \cap B)}{n(S)} = \frac{1}{6}$$

Event "C and D" = the number is odd and the number is 4. Here, events C and D are disjoint sets, so their intersection is empty, or $C \cap D = \{\ \}$. Thus, we say $P(C$ and $D) = P(C \cap D) = \dfrac{n(C \cap D)}{n(S)} = \dfrac{0}{6} = 0$.

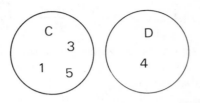

Observe that *there is no simple rule or formula that works for all problems* whereby we can use the values of $P(A)$ and $P(B)$ to find $P(A$ and $B)$. We must simply observe the intersection of the two sets and count the number of elements in that intersection. Or we count the number of outcomes that are common to both events.

KEEP IN MIND

The event "A and B" consists of outcomes that are true for event A and true for event B. Event "A and B" may be regarded as the intersection of sets, namely $(A \cap B)$.

MODEL PROBLEM

A fair die is rolled once. Find the probability of obtaining a number that is greater than 3 and less than 6.

Solution

Event A = the number is greater than 3 = $\{4, 5, 6\}$.

Event B = the number is less than 6 = $\{1, 2, 3, 4, 5\}$.

Event "A and B" = outcomes common to both events = $\{4, 5\}$, or $(A \cap B) = \{4, 5\}$.

Therefore:

$$P(A \text{ and } B) = \frac{n(A \text{ and } B)}{n(S)} = \frac{2}{6} \quad or \quad \frac{n(A \cap B)}{n(S)} = \frac{2}{6} \quad Ans.$$

| EXERCISES |

1. A fair die is rolled once. The sides are numbered 1, 2, 3, 4, 5, 6. Find the probability that the number rolled is:
   a. greater than 2 and odd.   b. less than 4 and even.
   c. greater than 2 and less than 4. d. less than 2 and even.
   e. less than 6 and odd.   f. less than 4 and greater than 3.

2. From a standard deck of cards one card is drawn. Find the probability that the card will be:
   a. the king of hearts   b. a red king   c. a club king
   d. a black jack   e. a diamond ten   f. a red club
   g. the two of spades   h. a black two   i. a red picture card

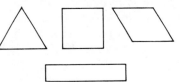

3. A set of polygons consists of an equilateral triangle, a square, a rhombus, and a rectangle as shown at the left. One of the polygons is selected at random. Find the probability that the polygon contains:

Ex. 3

   a. all sides congruent and all angles congruent.
   b. all sides congruent and all right angles.
   c. all sides congruent and two angles not congruent.
   d. at least 2 congruent sides and at least 2 congruent angles.
   e. at least 3 congruent sides and at least 2 congruent angles.

4. At a St. Patrick's Day party some of the younger people take turns singing songs. Of the 5 boys: Patrick and Terence are teenagers; younger boys include Brendan, Drew, and Kevin. Of the 7 girls: Heather and Claudia are teenagers; younger girls include Maureen, Elizabeth, Gwen, Caitlin, and Kelly. Find the probability that the first song is sung by:
   a. a girl   b. a boy   c. a teenager   d. someone under 13 years old
   e. a boy under 13   f. a girl whose initial is C   g. a teenage girl
   h. a girl under 13   i. a boy whose initial is C   j. a teenage boy

6 THE PROBABILITY OF "A OR B"

The connective "or" has been used in logic. As we will see, the connective "or" is sometimes used to describe events in probability.

For example, a fair die is rolled. What is the probability of obtaining an even number?

We call this event A and we have seen that

$$P(A) = \frac{n(A)}{n(S)} = \frac{3}{6}.$$

When a die is rolled, what is the probability of obtaining a number less than 2?

We call this event C. Since there is only one possible outcome for this event (the number 1), we say $P(C) = \dfrac{n(C)}{n(S)} = \dfrac{1}{6}$.

Now, what is the probability of obtaining a number on the die that is even **or** less than 2? We may think of this as the **event "A or C."**

In logic we learned that a sentence "p **or** q," written $p \lor q$, is true when p is true, or when q is true, or when both p and q are true.

In probability an outcome is in event "A **or** C" when the outcome is in event A, or the outcome is in event C, or when the outcome is in both event A and event C.

There are four outcomes that satisfy the event "A or C": 1, 2, 4, and 6. Each of these numbers is even or it is less than 2. Since $n(A \text{ or } C) = 4$, and there are 6 outcomes on the die, or $n(S) = 6$, we can say $P(A \text{ or } C) = \dfrac{n(A \text{ or } C)}{n(S)} = \dfrac{4}{6}$.

Observe that $P(A) = \frac{3}{6}$, $P(C) = \frac{1}{6}$, and $P(A \text{ or } C) = \frac{4}{6}$. In this case it appears that $P(A) + P(C) = P(A \text{ or } C)$. Will this simple addition rule be true for all problems?

Consider another example in which a fair die is rolled.

Event A = the number is even.

Here, $P(A) = \dfrac{n(A)}{n(S)} = \dfrac{3}{6}$.

Event B = the number is less than 3.

Here, $P(B) = \dfrac{n(B)}{n(S)} = \dfrac{2}{6}$.

Then, event "A **or** B" = the number is even **or** the number is less than 3.

There are still only four outcomes that satisfy this new event: 1, 2, 4, and 6. Each of these numbers is even or it is

less than 3. Therefore, we say $P(A \text{ or } B) = \dfrac{n(A \text{ or } B)}{n(S)} = \dfrac{4}{6}$.

Observe that $P(A) = \frac{3}{6}$, $P(B) = \frac{2}{6}$, and $P(A \text{ or } B) = \frac{4}{6}$. In this case, the simple rule of addition does not work. $P(A) + P(B) \neq P(A \text{ or } B)$. What made this example different from $P(A \text{ or } C)$, shown previously?

A Rule for the Probability of "A or B"

Probability is based upon counting the outcomes in the event. For the event "A or B," we observe that the outcome "2" is found in event A *and* in event B. Therefore, we may describe the outcome "2" as the event "A and B."

We realize that the simple addition rule does not work for the event "A or B" because we have counted the outcome "2" twice: first in event A, then again in event B. Since we counted this outcome twice, we must take it away, or subtract it, *once*.

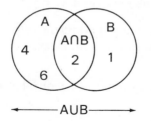

Hence, the rule becomes $n(A) + n(B) - n(A \text{ and } B) = n(A \text{ or } B)$. By counting, we see $3 + 2 - 1 = 5 - 1 = 4$, the correct number of outcomes for the event "A or B." We may divide every term in the "counting" rule by $n(S)$ to get an equivalent equation, $\dfrac{n(A \text{ or } B)}{n(S)} =$ $\dfrac{n(A)}{n(S)} + \dfrac{n(B)}{n(S)} - \dfrac{n(A \text{ and } B)}{n(S)}$, which becomes $\dfrac{n(A \text{ or } B)}{n(S)} = \dfrac{3}{6} + \dfrac{2}{6} - \dfrac{1}{6} = \dfrac{4}{6}$.

This is the rule for the probability of "A or B" since $P(A \text{ or } B) = \dfrac{n(A \text{ or } B)}{n(S)}$. In general, we say:

$$P(A \text{ or } B) = P(A) + P(B) - P(A \text{ and } B)$$

Using Sets to Look at P(A or B)

A set diagram can help us to understand the event "A or B" just discussed. Event "A or B" = the number is even *or* less than 3.

Since event "A or B" = {1, 2, 4, 6}, we recognize that "A or B" is shown as the *union* of the two sets, or $A \cup B$.

Recall that the event "A and B" = {2}, which is the intersection of the two sets, or $A \cap B$. We can again see how the counting procedure works:

1. Count the number of elements in one set.

2. Add the number of elements from the second set.

3. Subtract the number of elements in their intersection since they were counted twice.

4. This result is the number of elements in the union of the two sets, or $n(A \cup B)$.

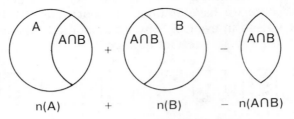

$$n(A) \qquad + \qquad n(B) \qquad - \quad n(A \cap B)$$

In set terminology, the rule for probability becomes:

$$P(A \cup B) = P(A) + P(B) - P(A \cap B)$$

Disjoint Sets

Event "A or C" = the number is even or less than 2.

Here, event A = {2, 4, 6} and event C = {1}, shown below by disjoint sets. Since A and C are disjoint, there are no elements in their intersection, or $(A \cap C) = \{ \ \}$.

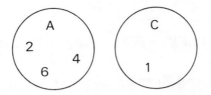

Recall that the probability of the empty set is zero. Thus, $P(A \cup C) = P(A) + P(C) - P(A \cap C)$ becomes $P(A \cup C) = P(A) + P(C) - 0$, or simply:

For disjoint sets, $P(A \cup C) = P(A) + P(C)$.

This tells us that the simple addition rule first observed will always be true for events that do not intersect, or that have no outcomes in common.

For disjoint events, $P(A \text{ or } C) = P(A) + P(C)$.

┌─────────────── KEEP IN MIND ───────────────┐

The event "*A* or *B*" consists of outcomes that are
true for event *A*, or true for event *B*, or true for both
event *A* and event *B*. Event "*A* or *B*" may be regarded as the *union* of sets, namely ($A \cup B$).

└──┘

| MODEL PROBLEMS |

1. A standard deck of 52 cards is shuffled. One card is drawn at random. Find the probability that the card is:
   a. a king or an ace   b. red or an ace

Solution

a. There are 4 kings in the deck, so $P(\text{king}) = \frac{4}{52}$.

   There are 4 aces in the deck, so $P(\text{ace}) = \frac{4}{52}$.

   Kings and aces are disjoint events, having no outcomes in common.

   So, $P(\text{king or ace}) = P(\text{king}) + P(\text{ace}) = \frac{4}{52} + \frac{4}{52} = \frac{8}{52}$. *Ans.*

b. There are 26 red cards in the deck, so $P(\text{red}) = \frac{26}{52}$.

   There are 4 aces in the deck, so $P(\text{ace}) = \frac{4}{52}$.

   Two cards in the deck are red aces, so $P(\text{red and ace}) = \frac{2}{52}$.

   Then: $P(\text{red or ace}) = P(\text{red}) + P(\text{ace}) - P(\text{red and ace})$

   $\qquad\qquad = \frac{26}{52} + \frac{4}{52} - \frac{2}{52} = \frac{28}{52}$ *or* $\frac{7}{13}$ *Ans.*

or

By a counting procedure there are 26 red cards and 2 more aces
not already counted (the ace of spades; the ace of clubs). Therefore, there are 26 + 2, or 28, cards, in this event.

   So, $P(\text{red or ace}) = \frac{28}{52}$, or $\frac{7}{13}$. *Ans.*

2. There are two events, *A* and *B*. Given that $P(A) = .3$, $P(B) = .5$, and
   $P(A \cap B) = .1$, find $P(A \cup B)$.

Solution: $P(A \cup B) = P(A) + P(B) - P(A \cap B)$
$\qquad\qquad\qquad = .3 + .5 - .1 = .8 - .1 = .7$ *Ans.*

| EXERCISES |

1. A spinner consists of 5 regions as shown, equally likely to occur when an arrow is spun. For a single spin of the arrow, find the probability of the given event.

   a. 4   b. 3 or 4
   c. an odd number   d. an odd number or 2
   e. less than 4   f. 4 or less
   g. 2 or 3 or 4   h. an odd number or 3

2. A fair die is rolled once. The sides are numbered 1, 2, 3, 4, 5, 6. Find the probability of the event described.

   a. 4   b. 3 or 4   c. an odd number
   d. an odd number or 2   e. less than 4   f. 4 or less
   g. 2 or 3 or 4   h. an odd number or 3
   i. less than 2 or more than 5   j. less than 5 or more than 2

3. From a standard deck of cards one card is drawn. Tell what the probability is that the card will be:

   a. a queen or an ace   b. a queen or a 7   c. a heart or a spade
   d. a queen or a spade   e. a queen or a red card
   f. jack or queen or king   g. a 7 or a diamond
   h. a club or a red card   i. an ace or a picture card

4. A bank contains 2 quarters, 6 dimes, 3 nickels, and 5 pennies. A coin is drawn at random. Find the probability that the coin is:

   a. a quarter   b. a quarter or a dime   c. a dime or a nickel
   d. worth 10 cents   e. worth more than 10 cents
   f. worth 10 cents or less   g. worth 1 cent or more
   h. worth more than 1 cent   i. a quarter, nickel, or penny

In 5–13, choose the correct numeral preceding the word or expression that best completes the statement or answers the question.

5. If a single card is drawn from a standard deck, what is the probability that it is a four or a nine?

   (1) $\frac{2}{52}$ (2) $\frac{8}{52}$ (3) $\frac{13}{52}$ (4) $\frac{26}{52}$

6. If a single card is drawn from a standard deck, what is the probability that it is a four or a diamond?

   (1) $\frac{8}{52}$ (2) $\frac{16}{52}$ (3) $\frac{17}{52}$ (4) $\frac{26}{52}$

7. A manufacturer of radios knows that the probability of a defect in any of his products is $\frac{1}{400}$. If 10,000 radios are manufactured in January, how many will probably be defective?

   (1) 20   (2) 25   (3) 40   (4) 400

8. Past records from the weather bureau indicate that it has rained 2 out of every 7 days in August at Cape Cod. If Joan goes to Cape Cod for two weeks in August, how many days will it probably rain if the records hold true?
    (1) 8   (2) 2   (3) 7   (4) 4
9. If $P(A) = .2, P(B) = .5$, and $P(A \cap B) = .1$, then $P(A \cup B) =$
    (1) .6   (2) .7   (3) .8   (4) .9
10. If $P(A) = .5, P(B) = .4$, and $P(A$ and $B) = .3$, then $P(A$ or $B) =$
    (1) .5   (2) .6   (3) .9   (4) 1.2
11. If $P(A) = \frac{1}{3}, P(B) = \frac{1}{2}$, and $P(A$ and $B) = \frac{1}{6}$, then $P(A$ or $B) =$
    (1) $\frac{2}{5}$ (2) $\frac{2}{3}$ (3) $\frac{5}{6}$ (4) 1
12. If $P(A) = \frac{1}{4}, P(B) = \frac{1}{2}$, and $P(A \cap B) = \frac{1}{8}$, then $P(A \cup B) =$
    (1) $\frac{1}{8}$ (2) $\frac{5}{8}$ (3) $\frac{3}{4}$ (4) $\frac{7}{8}$
13. If $P(A) = .3, P(B) = .35$, and $(A \cap B) = \emptyset$, then $P(A$ or $B) =$
    (1) .05   (2) .38   (3) .65   (4) 0

7   THE PROBABILITY OF "NOT A"; PROBABILITY AS A SUM

The Probability of "Not A"

In rolling a fair die, let event A = rolling the number "4." We know that $P(A) = P(4) = \frac{1}{6}$ since there is only one outcome for this event.

Since it is *certain* that we roll a 4 or do not roll a 4, we can say:

$$P(4) + P(\text{not getting } 4) = 1$$

Hence, by subtracting, $P(\text{not getting } 4) = 1 - P(4) = 1 - \frac{1}{6} = \frac{6}{6} - \frac{1}{6} = \frac{5}{6}.$

In terms of sets, the event "**not** A" is seen as the *complement* of set A, namely $\overline{A}$. Therefore, we may also say:

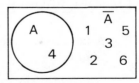

$P(\text{not } A) = P(\overline{A}) = 1 - P(A) = 1 - \frac{1}{6} = \frac{6}{6} - \frac{1}{6} = \frac{5}{6}$

A Rule for the Probability of "Not A"

In general, if $P(A)$ = the probability that an event will happen, and $P(\text{not } A)$ = the probability that an event will not happen, then we can say:

$P(A) + P(\text{not } A) = 1$ *or* $P(A) = 1 - P(\text{not } A)$ *or* $P(\text{not } A) = 1 - P(A)$

Probability as a Sum

When sets are disjoint, we have seen that the probability of a union can be found by the rule, $P(A \cup B) = P(A) + P(B)$. Since the possible outcomes that are singletons represent disjoint sets, we can say:

■ **The probability of any event is equal to the sum of the probabilities of the singleton outcomes in the event.**

For example, when you draw a card from a standard deck, there are 52 singleton outcomes, each with a probability of $\frac{1}{52}$. Since all singleton events are disjoint, we can say $P(\text{king}) = P(\text{king of hearts}) + P(\text{king of diamonds}) + P(\text{king of spades}) + P(\text{king of clubs})$, or $P(\text{king}) = \frac{1}{52} + \frac{1}{52} + \frac{1}{52} + \frac{1}{52} = \frac{4}{52}$, or $\frac{1}{13}$.

We also say:

■ **The sum of the probabilities of all possible singleton outcomes for any sample space must always equal 1.**

For example, in tossing a coin, $P(S) = P(\text{head}) + P(\text{tail}) = \frac{1}{2} + \frac{1}{2} = 1$.

Also, in rolling a die, $P(S) = P(1) + P(2) + P(3) + P(4) + P(5) + P(6) = \frac{1}{6} + \frac{1}{6} + \frac{1}{6} + \frac{1}{6} + \frac{1}{6} + \frac{1}{6} = 1$.

KEEP IN MIND

The event "not A" consists of outcomes that are not true for event A. Event "not A" may be regarded as the complement of set A, namely $\overline{A}$.

MODEL PROBLEMS

1. A fair die is tossed. Find the probability of not rolling a number less than 5.

   Solution: The event of rolling a number "less than 5" has four outcomes: 1, 2, 3, 4. Hence, $P(\text{less than 5}) = \frac{4}{6}$ and we can say:

   $P(\text{not less than 5}) = 1 - P(\text{less than 5}) = 1 - \frac{4}{6} = \frac{6}{6} - \frac{4}{6} = \frac{2}{6}$ or $\frac{1}{3}$ *Ans.*

2. A letter is drawn at random from the letters in the word ERROR.
   a. Find the probability of drawing each of the letters used in the word.
   b. Demonstrate that the sum of these probabilities is 1.

Solution:

a. $P(E) = \frac{1}{5}; P(R) = \frac{3}{5}; P(O) = \frac{1}{5}$ *Ans.*

b. $P(E) + P(R) + P(O) = \frac{1}{5} + \frac{3}{5} + \frac{1}{5} = \frac{5}{5} = 1$ *Ans.*

EXERCISES

1. A fair die is rolled once. Find the probability that the number is:
   a. 3   b. not 3   c. even
   d. not even   e. less than 3   f. not less than 3
   g. odd or even   h. not odd or even
2. The weather bureau predicted a 30% chance of rain. Express in fractional form: (a) the probability that it will rain; (b) the probability that it will not rain.
3. From a standard deck of cards one card is drawn. Find the probability that the card will be:
   a. a club   b. not a club   c. a picture card   d. not a picture card
   e. not an 8   f. not a red 6   g. not the queen of spades
4. A bank contains 3 quarters, 4 dimes, and 5 nickels. A coin is drawn at random.
   a. Find the probability of drawing: (1) a quarter; (2) a dime; (3) a nickel.
   b. Demonstrate that the sum of the three probabilities given as answers in part a is 1.
5. A letter is selected at random from the letters in the word PIC-NICKING.
   a. Find the probability of drawing each of the different letters used in the word.
   b. Demonstrate that the sum of these probabilities is 1.
6. If the probability of an event happening is $\frac{1}{7}$, what is the probability of that event not happening?
7. If the probability of an event happening is .093, what is the probability of that event not happening?

General Exercises

8. A jar contains 7 marbles, all the same size: 3 are red and 4 are green. If a marble is chosen at random, find the probability that it is:
   a. red   b. green   c. not red   d. red or green   e. red and green
9. A box contains three times as many black marbles as green, all the same size. If a marble is drawn at random, find the probability that it is:
   a. black   b. green   c. not black   d. black or green   e. not green

10. The morning mail contained 2 letters, 3 bills, and 5 ads. Mr. Jacobsen picked up the first piece of mail without looking at it. Express, in decimal form, the probability that this piece of mail is:

    a. a letter   b. a bill   c. an ad   d. a letter or an ad
    e. a bill or an ad   f. not a bill   g. not an ad   h. a bill and an ad

11. A letter is chosen from the word PROBABILITY. Find the probability that the letter chosen is:

    a. A   b. B   c. C
    d. A or B   e. A or I   f. a vowel
    g. not a vowel   h. A or B or L   i. A or not A

12. A single card is drawn from a well-shuffled deck of 52 cards. Find the probability that the card is:

    a. a six   b. a club   c. six of clubs
    d. a six or a club   e. not a club   f. not a six
    g. six or seven   h. not the six of clubs   i. a six and a seven
    j. a black six   k. a six or a black card

13. A telephone dial contains the ten digits: 0, 1, 2, 3, 4, 5, 6, 7, 8, 9. Mabel is dialing a friend. Find the probability that the last digit in the telephone number is:

    a. 6   b. 6 or more   c. less than 6   d. 6 or odd
    e. 6 or less   f. not 6   g. 6 and odd   h. not more than 6
    i. less than 2 and more than 6   j. less than 2 or more than 6
    k. less than 6 and more than 2   l. less than 6 or more than 2

8 THE COUNTING PRINCIPLE AND SAMPLE SPACES

So far we have looked at simple problems involving a *single* activity, such as the roll of one die or choosing one card. More realistic problems occur when there are *two or more* activities, such as rolling two dice or holding a hand of five cards. Before studying the probability of such events, let us study an easy way to count the number of elements in a sample space when two or more "activities" are involved. For example:

A store offers 5 flavors of ice cream: vanilla, chocolate, strawberry, peach, and raspberry. A sundae can be made with either a hot fudge topping or a marshmallow topping. If a sundae consists of one flavor of ice cream and one topping, how many elements are in the "sample space of sundaes"?

Let us use initials to represent the 5 flavors of ice cream {V, C, S, P, R} and the 2 toppings {F, M}. We can show the number of elements in the sample space in three ways:

(1) The *tree diagram* at the right first "branches out" to show the 5 flavors of ice cream. For each of these flavors the tree continues to "branch out" to show the 2 toppings. Looking from the far right, we see that there are 10 paths or "branches" to follow, each with one flavor of ice cream and one topping. These 10 branches show us that the sample space consists of 10 possible sundaes.

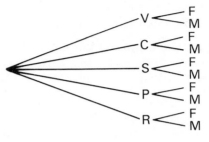

Tree diagram

(2) It is normal to order a sundae by telling the clerk the flavor of ice cream and the type of topping. This suggests a *listing of ordered pairs*. The

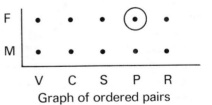

List of ordered pairs

first component of the ordered pair is the ice-cream flavor, and the second component is the type of topping. The set of pairs (ice cream, topping) is shown above.

These 10 ordered pairs show us that the sample space consists of 10 possible sundaes.

(3) Instead of listing ordered pairs, we may construct a *graph of the ordered pairs*. At the right the 5 flavors of ice cream appear on a horizontal scale or line, and the 2 toppings appear on a vertical line. Each point in the graph represents

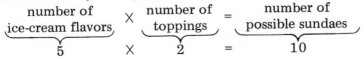

Graph of ordered pairs

an ordered pair. For example, the point circled shows the ordered pair (P, F) or (peach ice cream, fudge topping). This graph of 10 points, or 10 ordered pairs, shows us that the sample space consists of 10 possible sundaes.

Whether using a tree diagram, a list of ordered pairs, or a graph of ordered pairs, we see that the sample space consists of 10 sundaes. A "shortcut" method for counting the number of elements in the sample space can be found by multiplication:

$$\underbrace{\text{number of ice-cream flavors}}_{5} \times \underbrace{\text{number of toppings}}_{2} = \underbrace{\text{number of possible sundaes}}_{10}$$

Suppose the store offered 30 flavors of ice cream and 7 possible toppings. Rather than display the sample space, we may say 30 × 7 = 210 possible sundaes. This simple multiplication procedure is known as the *counting principle*, because it helps us to "count" the number of elements in a sample space.

■ **The Counting Principle:** If one activity can occur in any of "*m*" ways and, following this, a second activity can occur in any of "*n*" ways, then both activities can occur in the order given in "*m · n*" ways.

We can extend this rule to include three or more activities by extending the multiplication process. We can also display three or more activities by extending the branches on a tree diagram, or by listing ordered elements such as ordered triples and ordered quadruples.

For example, a coin is tossed three times in succession.

On the first toss the coin may fall in any of two ways: a head or a tail.
On the second toss the coin may fall in any of two ways: a head or a tail.
On the third toss the coin may fall in any of two ways: a head or a tail.

By the **counting principle**, the sample space must contain 2 · 2 · 2, or 8, possible outcomes.

By letting *H* represent a head and *T* represent a tail, we can illustrate the sample space by a tree diagram, or by a set or ordered "triples," both shown below. Observe that the list of triples corresponds to each of the branches in the tree diagram, in the order given.

Notice that we did *not* attempt to draw a graph of this sample space since we would need a horizontal scale, a vertical scale, and a third scale making the graph three-dimensional. Although such a graph can

THREE TOSSES OF A COIN

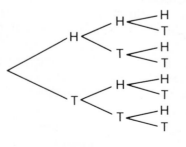

Tree diagram	List of ordered triples

be drawn, it is too difficult for us to do so at this time. We can conclude:

1. *Tree diagrams,* or *lists of ordered elements,* are effective ways to indicate any compound event of two or more activities.

2. *Graphs should be limited to ordered pairs,* or only to those events consisting of exactly two activities.

MODEL PROBLEMS

1. The school cafeteria offers 4 types of sandwiches, 3 types of beverages, and 5 types of desserts. If a lunch consists of 1 sandwich, 1 beverage, and 1 dessert, how many possible lunches can be chosen?

    Solution: By the counting principle, we multiply the number of ways that each "activity" can occur:

    $$4 \cdot 3 \cdot 5 = 12 \cdot 5 = 60$$

    This sample space consists of 60 possible lunches. *Ans.*

2. There are 12 staircases going from the first floor to the second in our school. Roger goes up one staircase and then comes down a different staircase. How many possible ways can this event occur?

    Solution: Roger can choose any of 12 staircases going up. Since he goes down a different staircase, he now has 11 choices left for going downstairs. By the counting principle, there are $12 \cdot 11 = 132$ ways. *Ans.*

EXERCISES

1. Tell how many possible outfits consisting of one shirt and one pair of pants Terry can choose if Terry owns:
    a. 5 shirts, 2 pair of pants   b. 10 shirts, 4 pair of pants
    c. 4 shirts, 1 pair of pants   d. 6 shirts, an equal number of pants
2. There are 10 doors into the school and 8 staircases from the first floor to the second. How many possible ways are there for a student to go from outside the school to a classroom on the second floor?

3. A tennis club has 15 members: 8 women and 7 men. How many different teams may be formed consisting of 1 woman and 1 man on each team?

4. A dinner menu lists 2 soups, 7 meats, and 3 desserts. How many different meals consisting of 1 soup, 1 meat, and 1 dessert are possible?

5. There are 3 ways to go from town A to town B. There are 4 ways to go from town B to town C. How many different ways are there to go from town A to town C, passing through town B?

6. The school cafeteria offers the menu shown at the right.

Main Course	Dessert	Drink
Pizza	Ice cream	Milk
Frankfurter	Cookies	Juice
Ham sandwich	Jello	
Tuna sandwich	Apple pie	
Jelly sandwich		

   a. How many meals consisting of one main course, one dessert, and one drink can be selected from this menu?

   b. Joe hates ham and jelly. How many meals (again one main course, one dessert, and one drink) can Joe select, not having ham and not having jelly?

   c. JoAnn is at the end of the lunch line. The pizza, frankfurters, ice cream, and cookies have been sold out. How many menus can JoAnn select?

7. A quarter and a penny are tossed simultaneously. Each coin may fall "heads" or "tails." The tree diagram at the left shows the sample space involved. a. List the sample space as a set of ordered pairs. b. Use the counting principle to demonstrate that there are four outcomes in the sample space. c. In how many outcomes do the coins fall both "heads" up? d. In how many outcomes do the coins land showing one "head" and one "tail"?

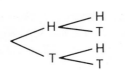

Quarter   Penny

8. A teacher gives a quiz consisting of two questions. Each question may be answered either "true" or "false." a. Using T and F, make a tree diagram to show all possible ways the questions can be answered. b. List this sample space as a set of ordered pairs. c. State the relationship that exists between this sample space and the table of truth values for two statements, p and q, developed in the study of logic.

9. A quiz consists of three "true-false" questions. a. How many possible ways are there to answer the questions on this test? b. List the ordered triples to show this sample space.

10. A test consists of multiple-choice questions. Each question has 4 choices. Tell how many possible ways there are to answer the questions on the test if the test consists of:
    a. 1 question   b. 2 questions   c. 3 questions
    d. 4 questions   e. *n* questions

11. Options on a bicycle include 2 types of handlebars, 2 types of seats, and a choice of 15 colors. The bike may also be ordered in ten-speeds, in three-speeds, or standard. How many possible versions of a bicycle can customers choose from, if they select the type of handlebars, seat, color, and speed?

12. Two six-sided dice are rolled simultaneously. Each die may land with one of six numbers face up. a. Use the counting principle to determine the number of outcomes in this sample space. b. Display the sample space by constructing a graph of the set of ordered pairs.

13. A state issues license plates consisting of letters and numbers. There are 26 letters and the letters may be repeated in a plate; there are 10 digits and the digits may be repeated. Tell how many possible license plates the state may issue when a license consists of:
    a. two letters, followed by three numbers
    b. three numbers, followed by three letters
    c. four numbers, followed by two letters
         (*Note:* The license 1-ID is actually 0001-ID.)

14. An ice-cream company offers 31 different flavors. Hilda orders a double-scoop cone. In how many different ways can the clerk put the ice cream on the cone if: (a) Hilda wanted two different flavors? (b) Hilda wanted the same flavor on both scoops? (c) Hilda could not make up her mind and told the clerk, "Anything at all"?

9 PROBABILITIES AND THE COUNTING PRINCIPLE

We know that the probability of rolling 1 on the single toss of a die is $\frac{1}{6}$, or $P(1) = \frac{1}{6}$. What is the probability of rolling a "pair of ones" when two dice are tossed?

When we roll two dice, the number obtained on one die is completely, absolutely, without question, *independent* of the result obtained on the second die. When two activities or events have nothing to do with each other, we call them *independent events*. In cases where two

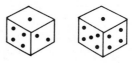

activities are independent, we may extend the counting principle to find the probability that both independent events occur at the same time. For example:

$P(1 \text{ on first die}) = \frac{1}{6}$

$P(1 \text{ on second die}) = \frac{1}{6}$

$P(1 \text{ on both dice}) = P(1 \text{ on first}) \cdot P(1 \text{ on second}) = \frac{1}{6} \cdot \frac{1}{6} = \frac{1}{36}$

When an event consists of two or more independent events or "activities," it is called a *compound event*. Compound events are illustrated when we are rolling 2 dice, or tossing 3 coins, or selecting 5 cards, or spinning an arrow 3 times in succession.

In general, we can extend the counting principle to help us find the probability of any compound event consisting of two or more independent events:

■ **When events E and F are not dependent upon each other, and when the probability of event E is given as m ($0 \leq m \leq 1$) and the probability of event F is given as n ($0 \leq n \leq 1$), then the probability of the compound event in which E and F occur jointly is given as the product $m \cdot n$.**

Note 1: The product $m \cdot n$ is within the range of values for a probability, namely ($0 \leq m \cdot n \leq 1$).

Note 2: Not all events are independent. Hence, this simple product rule cannot be used to find the probability of every compound event.

| MODEL PROBLEM |

Mr. Gillen may take any of three buses to get to the same train station. The buses are marked A or B or C. He may then take the 6th Avenue train or the 8th Avenue train to get to work. The buses and trains arrive at random. What is the probability that Mr. Gillen takes the B bus and the 6th Avenue train to get to work?

Solution

$P(B \text{ bus}) = \frac{1}{3}$ and $P(\text{6th Ave. train}) = \frac{1}{2}$. Since the train taken is not dependent on the bus taken, we can say:

$P(B \text{ bus and 6th Ave. train}) = P(B \text{ bus}) \cdot P(\text{6th Ave. train})$

$= \frac{1}{3} \cdot \frac{1}{2} = \frac{1}{6}$ *Ans.*

| EXERCISES |

(All the events described in Exercises 1–10 are independent events.)

1. A fair coin and a six-sided die are tossed simultaneously. What is the probability of obtaining: **a.** a head on the coin? **b.** a "4" on the die? **c.** a head on the coin and a "4" on the die jointly?

2. A fair coin and a six-sided die are tossed simultaneously. What is the probability of obtaining jointly: **a.** a head and a "3"? **b.** a head and an even number? **c.** a tail and a number less than "5"? **d.** a tail and a number more than "4"?

3. Two fair coins are tossed. What is the probability that both land "heads" up?

4. When I enter school, 3 out of 4 times I use the main door. When I leave school, I use the main door only 1 out of 3 times. On any given day, what is the probability that I both enter and leave by the main door?

5. In our school cafeteria the menu rotates so that P(hamburger) = $\frac{1}{4}$, P(apple pie) = $\frac{2}{3}$, and P(soup) = $\frac{4}{5}$. On any given day, what is the probability that the cafeteria offers hamburger, apple pie, and soup on the same menu?

6. A quiz consists of "true-false" questions only. Harry has not studied and guesses every answer. Find the probability that he will guess correctly to get a perfect paper if the test consists of: **a.** 1 question   **b.** 2 questions   **c.** 3 questions   **d.** 4 questions   **e.** 10 questions   **f.** n questions

7. The probability of the Tigers beating the Cougars is $\frac{2}{3}$. The probability of the Tigers beating the Mustangs is $\frac{1}{4}$. If the Tigers play one game with the Cougars and one game with the Mustangs, find the probability of the Tigers **(a)** winning both games and **(b)** losing both games.

8. Three fair coins are tossed. **a.** Find $P(H, H, H)$. **b.** Find $P(T, T, T)$.

9. A spinner contains 8 equally likely regions, numbered 1 through 8. If the arrow is spun twice, find the probability that: **(a)** it lands on "7" both times; **(b)** it does not land on "7" either time.

10. As shown in the diagram, 6th Avenue runs north and south. The lights are not "timed" to accommodate traffic traveling along 6th Avenue; they are independent of one another. At each of the intersections shown, P(red light) = .7 and P(green light) = .3 for cars traveling along 6th Avenue.

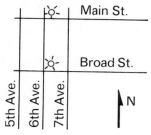

Find the probability that a car traveling north on 6th Avenue will be faced with the given conditions at the two traffic lights shown.

a. both lights are red
b. the first is red and the second is green
c. both lights are green
d. the first is green and the second is red
e. one of the two lights is red

10 EVALUATING PROBABILITIES WITH TWO OR MORE ACTIVITIES

The counting principle, involving simple probabilities, works for a limited number of problems. We will now examine a procedure that can be used to find the probability of any compound event.

For example, a family moves in next door. We have heard that they have three children, but we do not know how many are boys and how many are girls. The counting principle tells us that the sample space consists of $2 \cdot 2 \cdot 2$, or 8, possibilities for listing the sex of the three children in this family.

By letting G represent a girl and B represent a boy, we can illustrate the sample space by a tree diagram, or by a set of ordered "triples," both shown below.

FAMILY OF THREE CHILDREN

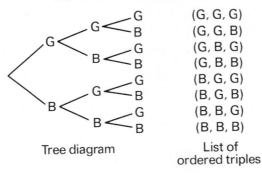

Tree diagram   List of
                      ordered triples

The Probability of Different Events

To find the probability of any event, we must know two values:

1. the number of ways in which event E can occur, or $n(E)$;
2. the total number of possible outcomes for the sample space S, or $n(S)$.

We have just seen that the sample space for a family of three children contains 8 ordered triples, or $n(S) = 8$. Let us consider some possible events for this sample space.

What is the probability that the family contains two girls and one boy?

By examining the 8 outcomes in the sample space listed earlier, we see that this event can happen in 3 possible ways: (G, G, B); (G, B, G); (B, G, G).

Therefore $n(E) = 3$, and $P(2 \text{ girls and 1 boy}) = \dfrac{n(E)}{n(S)} = \dfrac{3}{8}$.

What is the probability that the family contains at least one boy?

When we say "at least one," there may be 1 boy or 2 boys or 3 boys. By examining the sample space of 8 outcomes, we see that there are 7 possible ways for this event to happen: (G, G, B); (G, B, G); (G, B, B); (B, G, G); (B, G, B); (B, B, G); (B, B, B).

Therefore $n(E) = 7$, and $P(\text{at least one boy}) = \dfrac{n(E)}{n(S)} = \dfrac{7}{8}$.

Note: Since "at least one boy" has the same meaning as "not all girls," it is also correct to use this alternate approach to the problem: $P(\text{at least one boy}) = P(\text{not all girls}) = 1 - P(\text{all girls}) = 1 - \frac{1}{8} = \frac{8}{8} - \frac{1}{8} = \frac{7}{8}$.

■ **Procedure for Finding Probabilities of Compound Events:**

1. List the sample space by constructing a tree diagram or a set of ordered elements.

2. Count the number of elements in the sample space, $n(S)$.

3. For the event E being described, count the number of elements from the sample space that will be true for the event, $n(E)$.

4. Substitute these numbers in the rule for the probability of an event E, namely $P(E) = \dfrac{n(E)}{n(S)}$.

MODEL PROBLEMS	

1. A fair coin is tossed two times in succession.
   a. List the sample space by using (1) a tree diagram, (2) a set of ordered pairs, and (3) a graph of ordered pairs.
   b. Find the probability of each event: (1) Event A = the coin is heads both times; (2) Event B = 1 head and 1 tail are tossed.

Solution

a. (1) Tree diagram   (2) Set of ordered pairs   (3) Graph of
                                                        ordered pairs

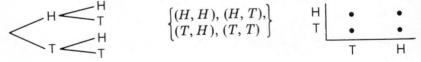

$$\left\{ \begin{array}{l} (H, H), (H, T), \\ (T, H), (T, T) \end{array} \right\}$$

b. (1) In event A, only one pair has heads on both tosses: (H, H).

Since $n(A) = 1$ and $n(S) = 4$, we say $P(A) = \dfrac{n(A)}{n(S)} = \dfrac{1}{4}$. *Ans.*

(2) In event B, there are two ways to toss 1 head and 1 tail: (H, T); (T, H).

Since $n(B) = 2$ and $n(S) = 4$, we say $P(B) = \dfrac{n(B)}{n(S)} = \dfrac{2}{4}$. *Ans.*

2. In an experiment the first step is to pick one number from the set $\{1, 2, 3\}$. The second step of the experiment is to pick one number from the set $\{3, 5\}$.
   a. Draw a tree diagram or list the sample space of all possible pairs that are outcomes.
   b. Determine the probability that: (1) both numbers are the same; (2) the sum of the numbers is even; (3) the first number is larger than the second.

Solution

a.   *or* $\left\{ \begin{array}{l} (1, 3), (2, 3), (3, 3), \\ (1, 5), (2, 5), (3, 5) \end{array} \right\}$

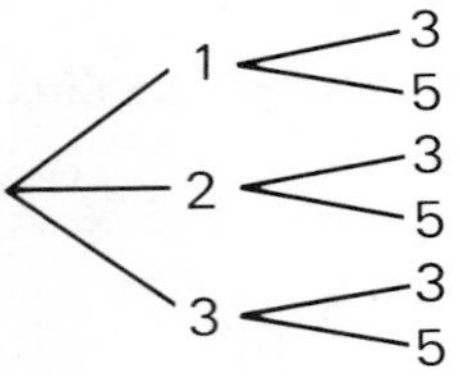

b. (1) In event A, only one pair has both numbers the same: $(3, 3)$.

Since $n(A) = 1$ and $n(S) = 6$, we say $P(A) = \dfrac{n(A)}{n(S)} = \dfrac{1}{6}$. *Ans.*

(2) In event B, four pairs have an even sum: $(1, 3), (1, 5), (3, 3), (3, 5)$.

Since $n(B) = 4$ and $n(S) = 6$, we say $P(B) = \dfrac{n(B)}{n(S)} = \dfrac{4}{6}$. *Ans.*

(3) In event C there are no pairs in which the first number is larger than the second. Since $n(C) = 0$, then $P(C) = \dfrac{n(C)}{n(S)} = \dfrac{0}{6} = 0$. *Ans.*

3. Two fair dice are rolled, each containing six sides. Find the probability that the sum of the numbers on the dice is 8.

Solution

The sample space consists of $6 \cdot 6$, or 36, outcomes, as shown by a graph of ordered pairs at the right.

For this event E there are 5 ordered pairs in which the sum of the numbers on the dice is 8. These 5 pairs, encircled on the graph, are: $(2, 6)$, $(3, 5)$, $(4, 4)$, $(5, 3)$, $(6, 2)$.

Since $n(S) = 36$ and $n(E) = 5$, we say:

$$P(E) = \frac{n(E)}{n(S)} = \frac{5}{36} \quad Ans.$$

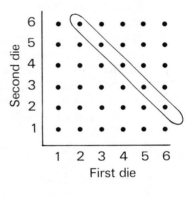

Second die

First die

EXERCISES

1. Two fair coins are tossed simultaneously. **a.** Draw a tree diagram or list the sample space of all possible pairs of outcomes. **b.** Find P(both coins are tails). **c.** Find P(no tails). **d.** Find P(at least one coin is a head).

2. In a family of two children determine the following probabilities:
   a. both are boys
   b. both are girls
   c. there is one boy and one girl
   d. both are of the same sex
   e. there is at least one girl
   f. the younger is a boy
   g. the older is a girl and the younger is a boy

3. In a family of three children determine the probability that:
   a. all are boys
   b. all are girls
   c. all are of the same sex
   d. exactly two are boys
   e. the youngest is a girl
   f. there is at least one boy
   g. the oldest and the youngest are both girls

4. Draw a tree diagram or list the ordered elements of the sample space to indicate the possible sexes of four children in a family. Then reanswer the questions in **3a** through **3g** for the sample space of *four* children.

5. Three fair coins are tossed simultaneously.
   a. Indicate the sample space as a tree diagram or as a set of ordered triples.
   b. Find P(all are tails).   c. Find P(there are exactly 2 tails).
   d. Find P(there are at least 2 tails).

6. In a certain game, darts are thrown at two boards so that *each board* will contain exactly *one dart*. If any darts miss or land on a line, they are not counted and the person tries again.

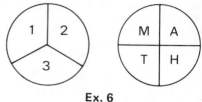

Ex. 6

   The first board contains three equally likely regions numbered {1, 2, 3} and the second board contains four equally likely regions lettered {M, A, T, H}.
   a. Draw a tree diagram or list the sample space of all possible pairs that are outcomes for placing one dart on each board.
   b. Find the probability of obtaining the result $(2, M)$, or simply $P(2, M)$.   c. Find $P(3, T)$.
   d. Find P(odd number, H).   e. Find P(even number, vowel).
   f. Find P(odd number, consonant)
   g. Find P(5, vowel).

7. Two standard dice are rolled, each with six faces numbered 1 through 6. When the numbers on the dice are added, the smallest possible sum is "2" from the pair (1, 1). The largest possible sum is "12" from the pair (6, 6). Find the probability of rolling two dice to get a sum of: a. 2   b. 3   c. 4   d. 5   e. 6   f. 7   g. 8   h. 9   i. 10   j. 11   k. 12

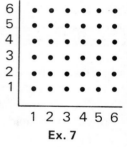

Ex. 7

8. What is the sum of all the probabilities obtained in exercise 7?

9. The faces on a standard die are numbered 1 through 6. The die is rolled twice, so that the sample space consists of 36 ordered pairs as shown in the diagram in exercise 7. Find the probability of getting, on *two* rolls of the die:
   a. the pair (3, 3)   b. the pair (5, 2)   c. the pair (7, 1)
   d. a pair of even numbers   e. a pair of odd numbers
   f. a pair whose sum is even   g. a pair whose sum is odd
   h. a sum less than "5"   i. a sum less than "15"

In 10–12, select the choice that best answers the question.

10. When a coin and a six-sided die are tossed simultaneously, the number of outcomes in the sample space is:
    (1) 8   (2) 2   (3) 12   (4) 36

11. A spinner shows three regions, numbered {1, 2, 3}, all equally likely to occur. When the arrow is spun twice, the number of pairs in the outcome set is:
    (1) 6   (2) 2   (3) 3   (4) 9
12. Two coins and a six-sided die are tossed simultaneously. The number of outcomes in the sample space is:
    (1) 10   (2) 24   (3) 3   (4) 8

11   PERMUTATIONS

Mrs. Hendrix, a teacher, has announced that she will call upon three students of her class to give oral reports today. The students are Al, Betty, and Chris. How many possible ways are there for Mrs. Hendrix to choose the order in which these students will give their reports?

Let us use a tree diagram to picture the possible orders. From the diagram at the right we see that there are 6 possible arrangements. For example, Al, Betty, Chris is one possible arrangement; Al, Chris, Betty is another possible ar-

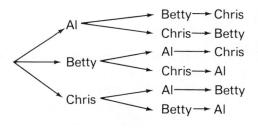

rangement. Each of these arrangements is called a ***permutation***. A permutation is an arrangement of objects in some specific order. By letting A represent Al, B represent Betty, and C represent Chris, we may show the 6 possible permutations as a set of ordered triples:

$$\{(A, B, C), (A, C, B), (B, A, C), (B, C, A), (C, A, B), (C, B, A)\}$$

Let us see, from another point of view, why there are 6 possible orders. We know that any one of 3 students can be called to give the first report. Once the first report is given, the teacher may call on any one of the 2 remaining students. After the second report is given, the teacher must call the 1 remaining student. Using the counting principle, we see that there are $3 \cdot 2 \cdot 1$, or 6 possible orders.

A chef is preparing a recipe with 10 ingredients. The chef puts all of one ingredient into a bowl, followed by all of another ingredient, and so on. How many possible orders are there for placing the 10 ingredients into a bowl using the stated procedure? By using the counting principle, we have:

$10 \cdot 9 \cdot 8 \cdot 7 \cdot 6 \cdot 5 \cdot 4 \cdot 3 \cdot 2 \cdot 1$, or 3,628,800 possible ways.

Factorials

If there are more than 3 million possible ways of placing 10 ingredients into a bowl, can you imagine in how many ways 300 people who want to buy tickets for a football game can be arranged in a straight line? Using the counting principle we would have $300 \cdot 299 \cdot 298 \cdot 297 \ldots 3 \cdot 2 \cdot 1$. To deal with such an example we make use of a *factorial symbol* (!). We represent the product of these 300 numbers by the symbol "300!," read "three hundred factorial" or "factorial 300." By using this symbol we can avoid performing the annoying multiplication process.

In general, for any natural number n, we define "n factorial" or "factorial n" as follows:

$$n! = n(n - 1)(n - 2)(n - 3) \ldots 3 \cdot 2 \cdot 1$$

Note that we define 1! as the natural number 1.

Permutations

We have said that permutations are arrangements of objects in different orders. For example, the number of different ways for 4 people to board a bus can be shown as 4!, or $4 \cdot 3 \cdot 2 \cdot 1$, or 24. This example tells us that there are 24 permutations, that is 24 different arrangements of these 4 people, in which all the 4 people get on the bus.

We may also represent this number of permutations by the symbol "$_4P_4$", read as "the permutation of four objects taken four at a time." In "$_4P_4$":

The letter "P" represents the word "permutation."

The small "$_4$" written to the lower left of P tells us there are 4 objects available to be used in an arrangement, as in 4 waiting for a bus.

The small "$_4$" written to the lower right of P tells us how many of these objects are to be used in each arrangement, as in all 4 getting on the bus.

Thus, $_4P_4 = 4! = 4 \cdot 3 \cdot 2 \cdot 1 = 24$.

Similarly, $_5P_5 = 5! = 5 \cdot 4 \cdot 3 \cdot 2 \cdot 1 = 120$.

In the next section we will study examples where all the objects are not used in the arrangement. For now, let us make the following observation.

■ In general, for any natural number n, "the permutation of n objects taken n at a time" can be represented as:

$$_nP_n = n! = n(n - 1)(n - 2) \ldots 3 \cdot 2 \cdot 1$$

| MODEL PROBLEMS |

In 1 and 2, compute the value of the expression.

1.   6!   *Solution:* $6! = 6 \cdot 5 \cdot 4 \cdot 3 \cdot 2 \cdot 1 = 720$ *Ans.*
2. $_2P_2$ *Solution:* $_2P_2 = 2! = 2 \cdot 1 = 2$ *Ans.*

3.   A word, even if it is a "nonsense" word, is described as an arrangement of letters. Consider the letters in {N, O, W}:
     a. How many three-letter words can be formed if each letter is used only once in the word? b. List the words.

   Solution: a. Because we are arranging letters in different orders, this is a permutation. Thus, $_3P_3 = 3! = 3 \cdot 2 \cdot 1 = 6$ possible words. *Ans.*

   b. NOW; NWO; ONW; OWN; WNO; WON. *Ans.*

   Note that even the "nonsense" arrangements are counted as words.

4.   Paul wishes to call Virginia but he has forgotten her unlisted telephone number. He knows that the exchange is 555 and he knows that the last four digits are 1, 4, 7, and 9, but he cannot remember their order. What is the maximum number of telephone calls that Paul may have to make in order to dial the correct number?

   Solution: The telephone number is 555-_ _ _ _. Since the last four digits will be an arrangement of 1, 4, 7, and 9, this is a permutation of "four numbers, taken four at a time."
   Thus, $_4P_4 = 4! = 4 \cdot 3 \cdot 2 \cdot 1 = 24$ possible orders.

   The maximum number of telephone calls that Paul may have to make is 24. *Ans.*

| EXERCISES |

In 1–12, compute the value of the expression.

1. 2!   2. 4!   3. 6!   4. 7!
5. 3! + 2!   6. (3 + 2)!   7. $_3P_3$ 8. $_8P_8$
9. $_5P_5$ 10. $\dfrac{8!}{5!}$ 11. $\dfrac{15!}{15!}$ 12. $(_3P_3) \cdot (_4P_4)$

13. Using the letters E, M, I, T: a. How many words of four letters can be found if each letter is used only once in the word? b. List these words.
14. In how many different ways can 5 students be arranged in a row?

15. How many possible three-letter arrangements of the letters X, Y, and Z can be made if each letter is used only once in each arrangement?

16. How many different 4-digit numbers can be made using the digits 2, 4, 6, and 8 if each digit appears only once in each number?

17. In a game of cards Gary held exactly one club, one diamond, one heart, and one spade. In how many different ways can Gary arrange these four cards in his hand?

18. There are nine players on a baseball team. The manager must establish a batting order for the players at each game. The pitcher will bat last. How many different batting orders are possible for the 8 remaining players on the team?

In 19–21, numerical answers may be left in factorial form.

19. In how many different ways may 60 people line up to buy tickets at a theater?

20. We learn the alphabet in an order, starting with A, B, C, and going down to Z. How many possible orders are there for saying the letters of the English alphabet?

21. In how many different ways can the librarian put 35 different novels on a shelf, with one book following another?

12   MORE ABOUT PERMUTATIONS

At times we deal with situations involving permutations in which we are given "n" objects, but we use "fewer than n" objects in each arrangement. For example:

Mr. Brown has announced that he will call students from the first row to explain homework problems at the board. The students in the first row are George, Helene, Jay, Karla, and Lou. If there are only two homework problems, and each problem is to be explained by a different student, in how many ways may Mr. Brown select students to go to the board?

We know that the first problem can be assigned to any of 5 students. Once this problem is explained, the second problem can be assigned to any of the 4 remaining students. By the *counting principle* we see that there are 5 · 4, or 20, possible selections.

There are 8 basketball players on a team. In how many ways can 3 of them be seated on a bench?

Seat	First	Second	Third
Players to choose from	8	7	6

By the counting principle we can see that the number of possible seating arrangements is $8 \cdot 7 \cdot 6 = 336$. Observe that the first factor 8 is the number of players on the team; once that player is chosen, the next factor is 7, and so on. Each factor is "one less than the previous factor."

The number of factors, 3, is the number of players in the seating arrangement or the number of seats available.

Using the language of permutations, we would say that "the number of permutations of 8 different things taken 3 at a time" is 336. In symbols we would write:

$$_8P_3 = 8 \cdot 7 \cdot 6 = 336$$

The Symbols for Permutations

In general, if we have a set of n different objects, and we make arrangements of r objects from this set, we would represent the number of arrangements by the symbol $_nP_r$. Notice that r, the number of factors being used, must be less than or equal to n, the total number of objects in the set. We can now say:

■ In general, for numbers n and r where $r \leq n$, the "permutation of n things, taken r at a time" is found by the formula:

$$_nP_r = \underbrace{n(n-1)(n-2)\ldots}_{r \text{ factors}}$$

| MODEL PROBLEMS |

1. Evaluate $_6P_2$.

    Solution: This is a permutation of "6 things, taken 2 at a time." We begin to write the factors of 6! but we stop upon reaching 2 factors:

    $$_6P_2 = \underbrace{6 \cdot 5}_{2 \text{ factors}} = 30 \qquad\qquad Answer: 30$$

2. There are 12 horses in a race. Winning horses are those crossing the finish line in first, second, and third place, commonly called "win, place, and show." How many possible winning orders are there for a race with 12 horses?

    Solution: This is a permutation of "12 things, taken 3 at a time," since there are 3 winning positions in a race. Thus:

    $$_{12}P_3 = \underbrace{12 \cdot 11 \cdot 10}_{3 \text{ factors}} = 1320 \text{ possible orders } Ans.$$

3. How many 3-letter words can be formed from the letters L, O, G, I, C if each letter is used only once in a word?

    Solution: Forming 3-letter words from a set of 5 letters is a "permutation of 5 things, taken 3 at a time." Thus:

    $$_5P_3 = \underbrace{5 \cdot 4 \cdot 3}_{\text{3 factors}} = 60 \qquad Answer:\ 60\ \text{words}$$

4. A lottery ticket contains a four-digit number. How many possible four-digit numbers are there when: **a.** a digit may appear only once in the number? **b.** digits may appear more than once in the number?

    Solution

    a. If a digit appears only once in a four-digit number, this is a "permutation of 10 digits, taken 4 at a time." Hence,

    $$_{10}P_4 = 10 \cdot 9 \cdot 8 \cdot 7 = 5040 \quad Ans.$$

    b. If a digit may appear more than once, we can choose any of 10 digits for the first position, then any of 10 digits for the second position, and so forth. By the counting principle we have:

    $$10 \cdot 10 \cdot 10 \cdot 10 = 10{,}000 \text{ possible four-digit numbers} \quad Ans.$$

EXERCISES

In 1–12, evaluate the expressions.

1. $_6P_3$ **2.** $_{10}P_2$ **3.** $_{25}P_2$ **4.** $_4P_3$ **5.** $_{20}P_2$ **6.** $_{11}P_4$
7. $_{22}P_3$ **8.** $_{10}P_4$ **9.** $_7P_6$ **10.** $_{101}P_3$ **11.** $_8P_5$ **12.** $_6P_6$

13. How many 3-letter words can be formed from the given letters, if each letter is used only once in a word?
     a. LION **b.** TIGER **c.** MONKEY **d.** LEOPARD **e.** MAN

14. There are 30 students in a class. Every day the teacher calls on different students to write homework problems on the board, with each problem done by only one student. In how many ways can the teacher call students to the board if the homework consists of:
     a. only 1 problem? **b.** 2 problems? **c.** 3 problems?

15. Tell how many possible winning orders there are for a horse race where 3 horses finish in winning positions and the race consists of:
     a. 7 horses **b.** 9 horses **c.** 11 horses **d.** n horses

16. A scalene triangle is shown at the right. How many different ways are there to label the 3 vertices of the triangle, using no letter more than once, when: **(a)** we use the letters R, S, T? **(b)** we use all the letters of the English alphabet?

17. A class has 31 students. They elect 4 people to office, namely the President, Vice-President, Secretary, and Treasurer. In how many possible ways can 4 people be elected from this class? (Answer may be left as a series of factors.)

18. How many possible ways are there to write 2 initials, using the letters of the English alphabet, if: **(a)** an initial may appear only once in each pair? **(b)** the same initial may be used twice?

13 PROBABILITY WITH REPLACEMENT; PROBABILITY WITHOUT REPLACEMENT

"Without Replacement"

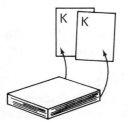

Two cards are drawn at random from an ordinary pack of 52 cards. In this situation we should understand that a single card is drawn from a deck of 52 cards and then a second card is drawn from the remaining 51 cards in the deck. What is the probability that both cards drawn are kings?

On the first draw there are 4 kings in a deck of 52 cards. Hence, P(first king) = $\frac{4}{52}$. If a second card is drawn without replacing the first king selected, there are now only 3 kings in the deck of 51 cards remaining. Hence, P(second king) = $\frac{3}{51}$.

By the counting principle:

P(both kings) = P(first king) · P(second king)

$$= \frac{4}{52} \quad \cdot \quad \frac{3}{51}$$

$$= \frac{1}{13} \quad \cdot \quad \frac{1}{17}$$

$$= \frac{1}{221}$$

This is called a problem "without replacement" because the first king drawn was not placed back into the deck. Typical problems "without replacement" include spending coins from your pocket, eating jelly beans from a jar, and choosing students to give reports.

"With Replacement"

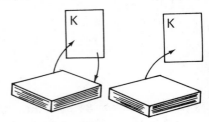

A card is drawn at random from an ordinary deck, placed back into the deck, and a second card is then drawn. In this situation we should understand that the deck contains 52 cards each time that a card is drawn. What is the probability that each time the card drawn is a king?

On the first draw there are 4 kings in a deck of 52 cards. Hence, $P(\text{first king}) = \frac{4}{52}$. If the first king drawn is now placed back into the deck, then on the second draw there are again 4 kings in a deck of 52 cards. Hence, $P(\text{second king}) = \frac{4}{52}$.

By the counting principle:

$$P(\text{both kings}) = P(\text{first king}) \cdot P(\text{second king})$$
$$= \frac{4}{52} \cdot \frac{4}{52}$$
$$= \frac{1}{13} \cdot \frac{1}{13}$$
$$= \frac{1}{169}$$

This is called a problem "with replacement" because the first card drawn was placed back into the deck. Since the card drawn is replaced, the number of cards in the deck remains constant.

Rolling two dice is similar to drawing two cards "with replacement" because the number of faces on each of the dice remains constant, as did the number of cards in the deck. Typical problems "with replacement" include rolling dice, tossing coins (each coin always has two sides), and spinning arrows.

KEEP IN MIND

1. If the problem does not specifically mention "with replacement" or "without replacement," ask yourself: "Is this problem with replacement?" or "Is this problem without replacement?"

2. Every probability problem can always be solved by: counting the number of elements in the sample space, $n(S)$; counting the number in the event, $n(E)$; and substituting in the formula for probability, $P(E) = \dfrac{n(E)}{n(S)}$.

| MODEL PROBLEMS |

1. A fair die is thrown three times. What is the probability that a "5" comes up each time?

Solution

This is a problem "with replacement." On the first toss there is only one way to obtain a "5" from the six possible outcomes of 1, 2, 3, 4, 5, 6. Thus $P(5 \text{ on } \textit{first} \text{ toss}) = \frac{1}{6}$.

On the second toss there is again one way to obtain a "5." So, $P(5 \text{ on second toss}) = \frac{1}{6}$.

On the third toss there is again one way to obtain a "5." So, $P(5 \text{ on third toss}) = \frac{1}{6}$.

By the counting principle:

$P(\text{rolling "5" each time}) = P(5 \text{ on first}) \cdot P(5 \text{ on second}) \cdot P(5 \text{ on third})$

$$= \frac{1}{6} \quad \cdot \quad \frac{1}{6} \quad \cdot \quad \frac{1}{6}$$

$$= \frac{1}{216} \quad \textit{Ans.}$$

2. If two cards are drawn from an ordinary deck without replacement, what is the probability that the cards form a pair?

Solution

On the first draw, any card at all may be chosen. So, $P(\text{any card}) = \frac{52}{52}$.

There are now 51 cards left in the deck. Of these 51, there are 3 that "match" the first card taken to form a pair. So, $P(\text{second card forms a pair}) = \frac{3}{51}$.

Then, $P(\text{pair}) = P(\text{any card}) \cdot P(\text{second card forms a pair})$

$$= \frac{52}{52} \quad \cdot \quad \frac{3}{51} \quad = \frac{1}{1} \cdot \frac{1}{17} = \frac{1}{17} \quad \textit{Ans.}$$

3. An urn contains 4 white marbles and 2 blue marbles, all the same size. A marble is drawn at random and not replaced. A second marble is then drawn from the urn. Find the probability that:
   a. both marbles are white
   b. both marbles are blue
   c. both marbles are the same color

Solution

a. On the first draw, $P(\text{white}) = \frac{4}{6}$. Since the white marble drawn is not replaced, there are now 5 marbles left in the urn of which 3 are white.

So, on the second draw, $P(\text{white}) = \frac{3}{5}$.

Then $P(\text{both white}) = \frac{4}{6} \cdot \frac{3}{5} = \frac{12}{30}$ or $\frac{2}{5}$. *Ans.*

b. When we start with a full urn of 6 marbles, on the first draw $P(\text{blue}) = \frac{2}{6}$.

Since the blue marble drawn is not replaced, there are now 5 marbles left in the urn of which only 1 is blue. So, on the second draw, $P(\text{blue}) = \frac{1}{5}$.

Then $P(\text{both blue}) = \frac{2}{6} \cdot \frac{1}{5} = \frac{2}{30}$ or $\frac{1}{15}$. *Ans.*

c. If both marbles are the same color, then both are white or both are blue. These are disjoint events. So, $P(A \text{ or } B) = P(A) + P(B)$. Therefore:

$P(\text{both white or both blue}) = P(\text{both white}) + P(\text{both blue})$

$$= \frac{4}{6} \cdot \frac{3}{5} \qquad\qquad + \frac{2}{6} \cdot \frac{1}{5}$$

$$= \frac{12}{30} \qquad\qquad\quad + \frac{2}{30}$$

$$= \frac{14}{30} \text{ or } \frac{7}{15} \quad Ans.$$

4. Fred has 2 quarters and 1 nickel in his pocket. The pocket has a hole in it and a coin drops out. Fred picks up the coin and puts it back into his pocket. A few minutes later a coin drops out of his pocket again.

a. Draw a tree diagram or list the sample space for all possible pairs that are outcomes to describe the coins that fell.

b. What is the probability that the same coin fell out of his pocket both times?

c. What is the probability that the two coins that fell have a total of 30 cents?

d. What is the probability that a quarter fell out at least once?

Solution

a. Because there are 2 quarters, use subscripts. The three coins are $\{Q_1, Q_2, N\}$ where Q represents a quarter and N represents a nickel. This is a problem "with replacement."

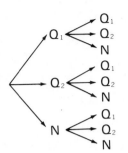

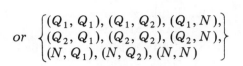

$$or \quad \begin{cases} (Q_1, Q_1), (Q_1, Q_2), (Q_1, N), \\ (Q_2, Q_1), (Q_2, Q_2), (Q_2, N), \\ (N, Q_1), (N, Q_2), (N, N) \end{cases}$$

b. Of the 9 outcomes, 3 name the same coin: (Q_1, Q_1); (Q_2, Q_2); (N, N). So, P(same coin) = $\frac{3}{9}$, or $\frac{1}{3}$. *Ans.*

c. Of the 9 outcomes, 4 consist of a quarter and a nickel, which have a total of 30 cents: (Q_1, N); (Q_2, N); (N, Q_1); (N, Q_2). So, P(coins total 30 cents) = $\frac{4}{9}$. *Ans.*

d. Of the 9 outcomes, 8 contain "one or more" quarters, the equivalent of "at least one" quarter. The only outcome not counted is (N, N). So, P(at least one quarter) = $\frac{8}{9}$. *Ans.*

| EXERCISES |

1. An urn contains 2 red and 5 yellow marbles. If one marble is drawn at random, what is the probability that it is: **(a)** red? **(b)** yellow?
2. An urn contains 2 red and 5 yellow marbles. A marble is drawn at random and then replaced. A second draw is made at random. Find the probability that:
   a. both marbles are red.
   b. both marbles are yellow.
   c. both marbles are the same color.
   d. the marbles are different in color. -
3. An urn contains 2 red and 5 yellow marbles. A marble is drawn at random. Without replacement, a second draw is made at random. Find the probability that:
   a. both marbles are red.
   b. both marbles are yellow.
   c. both marbles are the same color.
   d. the marbles are different in color.

4. In an experiment the arrow is spun twice on a wheel containing four equally likely regions, numbered 1 through 4.

   a. Indicate the sample space by drawing a tree diagram or writing a set of ordered pairs.
   b. Find the probability of spinning the digits 2 and 3 in that order.
   c. Find the probability that the digits are the same.
   d. What is the probability that the first digit is larger than the second?

5. Sal has a bag of hard candies: three are lemon and two are grape. He ate two of the candies while waiting for a bus, one after another.
   a. Draw a tree diagram or list the sample space of all possible outcomes showing which candies were eaten. (*Hint:* Use subscripts.)
   b. Find the probability that:
      (1) both candies were lemon.
      (2) neither candy was lemon.
      (3) the candies were the same flavor.
      (4) at least one candy was lemon.

6. Carol has five children: three girls and two boys. She had to correct one of her children at lunch. Later that day, Carol had to correct one of her children at supper.
   a. Indicate the sample space by a tree diagram or list of ordered pairs showing which children were corrected.
   b. Find the probability that:
      (1) both children corrected were girls.
      (2) both children corrected were boys.
      (3) the same child had to be corrected both times.
      (4) at least one of the children corrected was a boy.

7. Several players start playing a game with a full deck of 52 cards. Each player draws two cards at random, one at a time. Find the probability that:
   a. Flo drew two jacks.   b. Frances drew two hearts.
   c. Jerry drew two red cards.   d. Mary drew two picture cards.
   e. Carrie drew a 5 and a 10 in that order.
   f. Bill drew a heart and a club in that order.
   g. Ann did not draw a pair.
   h. Stephen drew two black nines.

8. Saverio has four coins: a half dollar, a quarter, a dime, and a nickel. He chooses one of the coins and puts it into a bank. He chooses another coin later on and also puts that into the bank.
   a. Indicate the sample space of coins saved.

    b. Find the probability that the coins saved:
      (1) were worth a total of 35¢.
      (2) added to an even amount.
      (3) included the half dollar.
      (4) were worth a total less than 30¢.

9. Farmer Brown must wake up before sunrise to start his chores. Dressing in the dark, he reaches into a drawer and pulls out 2 loose socks. There are 8 white socks and 6 red socks in the drawer.
    a. Find the probability that both socks are: (1) white; (2) red; (3) the same color.
    b. Find the maximum number of socks Farmer Brown must pull out of the drawer to guarantee that he will get a matching pair.

10. Tillie has 3 quarters and 4 dimes in her purse. She takes out a coin, but it slips from her hand and falls back into her purse. She reaches in and picks out a coin at random. Find the probability that:
    a. both coins were quarters.   **b.** both coins were dimes.
    c. the coins were a dime and a quarter, in any order.
    d. the same coin was picked both times.
    e. the coins picked totalled less than 40¢.
    f. the coins picked totalled exactly 30¢.
    g. at least one of the coins picked was a quarter.

11. An urn contains 9 orange disks and 3 blue disks. A girl chooses one at random and, without replacing it, chooses another. Letting "*o*" represent orange and "*b*" represent blue:
    a. Find the probability of each of the following outcomes:
      (1) (o, o) (2) (o, b) (3) (b, o) (4) (b, b)
    b. Now find the probability that, for the disks chosen:
      (1) neither was orange.   (2) only one was blue.
      (3) at least one was orange.   (4) they were the same color.
      (5) at most one was orange.   (6) they were the same disk.

chapter seventeen

Statistics

1 THE COLLECTION OF DATA

In our daily lives we often deal with problems that involve many related pieces of numerical information called *data*. For example, in the daily newspaper we can find "data" dealing with sports, with business, with politics, even with the weather.

Statistics is the study of numerical data. The typical steps in a statistical study are:

Step 1. The collection of data

Step 2. The organization of this data into tables, charts, and graphs

Step 3. The drawing of conclusions from an analysis of this data

These three steps, which describe and summarize a set of data, are often called *descriptive statistics*; we will study these steps in this first course. In some cases a fourth step is added in which the analyzed data is used to predict trends and future events. We will not study this type of statistics in this course.

Data can be collected in a number of ways, including:

1. a written *questionnaire* or list of questions in which a person can check one of several categories as an answer or fill in some written response;
2. an *interview*, either in person or by telephone, in which answers are given verbally and responses are recorded by the person asking the questions;
3. a *log* or a diary in which a person records information on a regular basis, such as a hospital chart or an hourly recording of the outdoor temperature.

The Census

Starting in 1790, and every ten years thereafter, the United States has conducted a *census* to count the number of people in the country and to determine the geographic regions in which they live. To collect this data, a "questionnaire" is mailed to every household in the country. For a portion of the citizens, more detailed questionnaires are mailed and, in some cases, workers from the Census Bureau visit homes to conduct "interviews." Important decisions are made on the basis of the data collected. For example, geographic regions with larger populations receive a greater share of the billions of dollars distributed in federal and state funds, and these regions are also entitled to more seats in the House of Representatives. Since there are more than 220,000,000 people living in the United States, the census is a major statistical study.

Sampling

Not all statistical studies are as large as the census. However, every statistical study demands that data be collected carefully and correctly if the study is to be useful. The following are some problems where a statistical study may be helpful:

1. A doctor wishes to know which medicine will be most effective in curing a disease.
2. A manufacturer wants to know the expected life span of a flashlight battery that his company makes.
3. A company advertising on television wishes to know the most frequently watched TV shows so that their ads will be seen by the greatest number of people.

Unlike the census, where every person is counted, these examples of statistical studies demand that only a *sample*, or a portion of the items to be counted, be actually considered. To find effective medicines, tests are usually conducted with a "sample," or portion, of patients having the same disease. Some patients receive one medicine and other patients receive different medicines.

The manufacturer of flashlight batteries cannot test the life span of every battery made because he would soon have a warehouse filled with dead batteries. He tests only a "sample" of the batteries to determine their average life span.

An advertiser cannot contact every person owning a TV set to see which shows are being watched. The advertiser will study TV ratings released by a firm that conducts polls based upon a small "sample" of TV viewers.

Techniques of Sampling

We must be careful when choosing samples:

1. The sample must be "fair," to reflect the entire population being studied.

To know what an apple pie tastes like, it is not necessary to eat the entire pie. A "sample," such as a piece of apple pie, would be a fair way of knowing how the pie tastes. However, eating only the crust or only the apples would be an "unfair sample"; these samples would not truly tell us what the entire pie tastes like.

2. The sample must contain a "reasonable" number of items being tested or counted.

If a medicine is generally effective, it must work for many people. The sample tested cannot include only one or two patients. Similarly, the manufacturer of flashlight batteries cannot make claims based on 5 or 10 batteries tested. A better sample might include 100 batteries.

3. "Patterns of sampling" or "random selection" should be employed in a study.

The manufacturer of flashlight batteries might set up a "pattern" to test every 1,000th battery to come off the assembly line. He may also select the batteries to be tested "at random."

These techniques will help to make the sample, or the small group, "representative" of the entire group of items being studied. From the study of the small group, reasonable conclusions are drawn about the entire group.

| MODEL PROBLEM |

To determine which television shows are the most popular in a large city, a poll is conducted by selecting people at random at a street corner and interviewing them. At which location would we find the "most fair" sample?
(1) outside a ball park   (2) outside a concert hall
(3) outside a supermarket

Solution

People outside a ball park may be going to a game or purchasing tickets for a game in the future; this sample might be "biased" in favor of sports shows. Similarly, those outside a concert hall may favor musical or cultural shows. The best sample or cross section of people for the three choices given would probably be found outside a supermarket.   *Answer:* (3)

| EXERCISES |

In 1–8, a sample of students is to be selected and the height of each student taken to determine the "average height of a student in high school." **a.** Tell if the sample is fair or unfair. **b.** If the sample is unfair, explain why.

1. The basketball team
2. The senior class
3. All 14-year-old students
4. All girls
5. Every tenth person selected from an alphabetical list of all students
6. Every fifth person selected from an alphabetical list of all boys
7. The first 3 students who report to the nurse on Monday
8. The first 3 students who enter each homeroom section on Tuesday

In 9–14, the Student Organization wishes to interview a sample of students to determine the general interests of the student body. Two questions will be asked: "Do you want more pep rallies for sports events? Do you want more dances?"

Tell whether the Student Organization would find a "fair" sample at the given location.

9. The gym, after a game
10. The library
11. The lunchroom
12. The cheerleaders' meeting
13. The next meeting of the Junior Prom committee
14. A homeroom section chosen at random

15. A statistical study is useful when reliable data is collected. At times people may exaggerate or lie when answering a question. Of the six questions that follow, find the *three* questions that will most probably produce the largest number of *unreliable* answers.
    a. What is your height?   **b.** What is your weight?
    c. What is your age?   **d.** In which state do you live?
    e. What is your income?   **f.** How many people are in your family?
16. List the three steps necessary to conduct a statistical study.

2 THE ORGANIZATION OF DATA INTO TABLES

Data is often collected in an unorganized and random manner. For example, as a teacher marked a set of 32 test papers, the grades or scores earned by the students were:

90, 85, 74, 86, 65, 62, 100, 95, 77, 82, 50, 83, 77, 93, 73, 72, 98,

66, 45, 100, 50, 89, 78, 70, 75, 95, 80, 78, 83, 81, 72, 75.

How many test scores are 60 or less? Are most of the scores "around 70" or "around 80"? These types of questions are difficult to answer, using ungrouped data. To answer such questions, we organize or *group* the data into a table.

The accompanying table contains six *intervals* of equal size: 41 to 50; 51 to 60; 61 to 70; 71 to 80; 81 to 90; 91 to 100. Each interval has a *length* of 10, found by subtracting the starting point of any interval from the starting point of the next higher interval. For example, 91 − 81 = 10; 81 − 71 = 10; and so on.

Interval	Tallies
91–100	卌 |
81–90	卌 |||
71–80	卌 卌 |
61–70	||||
51–60	
41–50	|||

For each test score, a *tally* or vertical mark (|) is placed in the interval containing that score. For example, since the first two test grades are 90 and 85, we place two tallies (||) in the interval 81–90. Since the third test score is 74, we place one tally (|) in the interval 71–80. We follow this process until all test scores are "grouped" into their proper intervals. To simplify counting, every fifth tally is written as a horizontal mark passing through four other tallies, as in 卌.

Once the data has been organized, we can convert the "tally marks" to "counting numbers." Each counting number tells us the *frequency* or the number of scores that will fall into each of the intervals. When no scores fall into one of the established intervals, as in 51–60, we say that the frequency for this interval is zero. The sum of all the frequencies is called the *total frequency*. Here, 6 + 8 + 11 + 4 + 0 + 3 = 32. Thus, the total frequency is 32. It is always wise to check the total frequency to see that a score was not overlooked in tallying. This table, containing a series of intervals and the

Interval	Frequency (*Number of Scores*)
91–100	6
81–90	8
71–80	11
61–70	4
51–60	0
41–50	3

corresponding frequency for each interval, is an example of *grouped data*.

From the table we now see that exactly 3 students scored 60 or less. Also, most test scores fell into the interval 71–80.

Rules for Grouping Data

When unorganized data is grouped into intervals, we must follow certain rules in setting up the intervals:

1. The intervals must be equal in size.
2. The number of intervals should be between 5 and 15. The use of too many intervals or too few intervals does not make for effective grouping of data. We usually use a large number of intervals, such as 15 intervals, only when we have a large set of data, such as hundreds of scores.
3. Every score to be tallied, from the highest to the lowest, must fall into one and only one interval. Thus, the intervals should not overlap each other. When an interval ends with a counting number, the following interval will begin with the next counting number.

These rules tell us that there are many ways to set up tables, all of them correct, for the same set of data. For example, here is another correct way to group the 32 unorganized test scores given at the beginning of this section. Note that the length of the interval is 8.

Interval	Tallies	Frequency (*Number*)
93–100	⊬⊬ I	6
85–92	IIII	4
77–84	⊬⊬ IIII	9
69–76	⊬⊬ II	7
61–68	III	3
53–60		0
45–52	III	3

MODEL PROBLEM

The following data consists of weights (in kilograms) of a group of 30 students:

70, 43, 48, 72, 53, 81, 76, 54, 58, 64, 51, 53, 75, 62, 84, 67, 72, 80, 88, 65, 60, 43, 53, 42, 57, 61, 55, 75, 82, 71.

a. Copy and complete the table to group this data.
b. Based on the grouped data, which interval contains the greatest number of students?
c. How many students weigh less than 70 kilograms?

Interval	Tallies	Frequency (*Number*)
80–89		
70–79		
60–69		
50–59		
40–49		

Solution: a.

Interval	Tallies	Frequency (Number)
80–89	卌	5
70–79	卌 ||	7
60–69	卌		6
50–59	卌 |||	8
40–49	||||	4

b. The interval 50–59 contains the greatest number of students, 8.

   Answer: (50–59)

c. The three lowest intervals, namely 40–49, 50–59, and 60–69, show weights less than 70 kilograms. Add the frequencies in these three intervals: 4 + 8 + 6 = 18.

   Answer: There are 18 students, each weighing less than 70 kg.

| EXERCISES |

1. a. Copy and complete the table to group the data, giving heights (in centimeters) of 36 students:

   162, 173, 178, 181,
   155, 162, 168, 147,
   180, 171, 168, 183,
   157, 158, 180, 164,
   160, 171, 183, 174,
   166, 175, 169, 180,
   149, 170, 150, 158,
   162, 175, 171, 163,
   158, 163, 164, 177.

Interval	Tallies	Frequency (Number)
180–189		
170–179		
160–169		
150–159		
140–149		

   b. Use the grouped data to answer the following questions:
      1. How many students are less than 160 centimeters in height?
      2. How many students are 160 centimeters or more in height?
      3. Which interval contains the greatest number of students?
      4. Which interval contains the least number of students?

2. **a.** Copy and complete the table to group the data that gives the life span in hours of 50 flashlight batteries:

73, 81, 92, 80, 108,

76, 84, 102, 58, 72,

82, 100, 70, 72, 95,

105, 75, 84, 101, 62,

63, 104, 97, 85, 106,

72, 57, 85, 82, 90, 54,

75, 80, 52, 87, 91, 85,

103, 78, 79, 91, 70, 88, 73,

67, 101, 96, 84, 53, 86.

Interval	Tallies	Frequency (*Number*)
100–109		
90–99		
80–89		
70–79		
60–69		
50–59		

b. Use the grouped data to answer the following questions:
  1. How many flashlight batteries lasted for 80 or more hours?
  2. How many flashlight batteries lasted less than 80 hours?
  3. Which interval contains the greatest number of batteries?
  4. Which interval contains the least number of batteries?

3. The following data shows test scores for 30 students:

  90, 83, 87, 71, 62, 46, 67, 72, 75, 100, 93, 81, 74, 75, 82,
  83, 83, 84, 92, 58, 95, 98, 81, 88, 72, 59, 95, 50, 73, 93.

a. Copy and complete the table, using these intervals of length 10.

Interval	Frequency
91–100	
81–90	
71–80	
61–70	
51–60	
41–50	

b. Copy and complete the table, using these intervals of length 12.

Interval	Frequency
89–100	
77–88	
65–76	
53–64	
41–52	

c. For the grouped data in part **a**, which interval contains the greatest number of students?

d. For the grouped data in part **b**, which interval contains the greatest number of students?

e. Do the answers for parts **c** and **d** indicate the same general region of test scores, such as "scores in the eighties"? Explain your answer.

4. The following data consists of the hours spent each week watching television, as reported by a group of 38 teenagers:

13, 20, 17, 36, 25, 21, 9, 32, 20, 17, 12, 19, 5, 8, 11, 28, 25, 18, 19, 22, 4, 6, 0, 10, 16, 3, 27, 31, 15, 18, 20, 17, 3, 6, 19, 25, 4, 7.

a. Construct a table to group this data, using intervals of 0–4; 5–9; 10–14; 15–19; 20–24; 25–29; 30–34; 35–39.

b. Construct a table to group this data, using intervals of 0–7; 8–15; 16–23; 24–31; 32–39.

5. For the "ungrouped" data from exercise 4, tell why each of the following sets of intervals is *not correct* for grouping the data.

a.

Interval
20–39
0–19

b.

Interval
30–36
20–29
11–19
0–10

c.

Interval
30–40
20–30
10–20
0–10

d.

Interval
31–40
21–30
11–20
1–10

3 USING GRAPHS TO PRESENT ORGANIZED DATA

We have seen that grouped data, or data organized into tables, is more useful than a set of unorganized data. If we go one step further, a *graph* or picture of organized data can often present the collected information in a way that is easier to understand than a table of numbers. We can find a variety of graphs in newspapers and magazines. Among these graphs are the bar graph, the picture graph, the line graph, and the circle graph. (The circle graph will be studied in chapter twenty-one).

Using Graphs to Compare Different Items

One of the uses of statistics is to compare *different* items, such as the sales records for different salesmen in a company; the heights of different buildings; the prices of different stocks; and so forth. The two most commonly used graphs to compare different items are the *bar graph* and the *picture graph*.

The Bar Graph

In a *bar graph*, the length of a bar is used to represent a numerical fact, that is, some piece of data. The length of the bar depends upon the size of the number that is to be represented. A *scale*, beginning with zero and consisting of equally spaced intervals, must accompany the bar graph so that the "approximate size" of a number may be read. The bars are drawn in the same direction, either all horizontally or all vertically.

The actual lengths of the world's six longest suspension bridges are not stated in the accompanying bar graph. However, the scale at the bottom of the graph allows us to compare the lengths of these six different bridges. We can observe many numerical facts, such as:

1. There are only 3 suspension bridges in the world longer than 1200 meters.

2. The bridge closest to 1300 meters in length is the Verrazano Narrows Bridge.

3. The largest suspension bridge in the world is the Humber Bridge, over 1400 meters in length.

4. Each of the world's six largest suspension bridges is longer than 1000 meters.

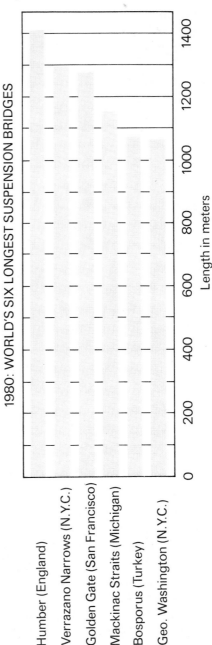

The Picture Graph

The *picture graph* is a graph in which a *symbol*, or picture, is used to represent a definite number. The symbol, its meaning, and the quantity that it represents must be stated.

1976: MOST POPULATED COUNTRIES

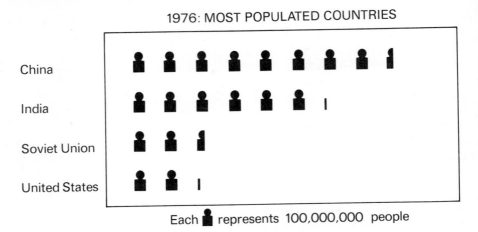

Each represents 100,000,000 people

In the picture graph just shown, each symbol " " represents one hundred million people. While the actual populations of these countries are not stated, we can observe many numerical facts, such as:

1. The $8\frac{1}{2}$ symbols, or pictures, shown for China tell us that its population is approximately $8\frac{1}{2} \times 100,000,000$, which is $850,000,000$ people.

2. India, with the second largest population, numbers approximately $6\frac{1}{10} \times 100,000,000$, or $610,000,000$ people.

3. Both the Soviet Union and the United States have a population slightly over $200,000,000$, with the Soviet Union closer to $250,000,000$.

Using a Line Graph to Compare Changes in the Same Item

To show how a particular item such as temperature, price of a stock, or population changes, we most often use the *line graph*, sometimes called a *broken line graph*. In making a line graph, a point is used to represent each numerical fact. Line segments are drawn connecting the consecutive points on the graph. A "rising" line segment shows that the item being studied is increasing. A "falling" line segment shows that the item being studied is decreasing.

The graph at the right shows the sales of Mr. Greenwald, a salesman, during the first five months of last year.

From the graph we can observe many numerical facts, such as:

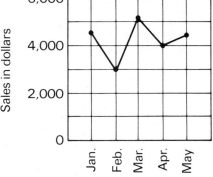

SALES RECORD: MR. GREENWALD

1. His highest sales occurred in March.
2. His lowest sales occurred in February.
3. The two months closest in sales were January and May.
4. The month closest to $4000 in sales was April.
5. The ratio of his sales in February to his sales in April is approximately $3000 to $4000, or 3 to 4.
6. The greatest decrease occurred from January to February. His sales dropped by approximately $1500 during that period.
7. The smallest increase occurred from April to May. His sales went up by less than $500 during that period.

Let us note that it is *not* appropriate to use a line graph to compare "different items" such as the lengths of the six suspension bridges that we previously studied.

EXERCISES

1. Of the six highest buildings in the world, three are in Chicago: the Sears Tower, the Standard Oil Building, and the John Hancock Building. The remaining three are in New York City: the Empire State Building, the World Trade Center, and the Chrysler Building. Use the information given in the graph to answer the following questions:

   HIGHEST BUILDINGS IN THE WORLD

   a. Find the height of each of the six buildings, to the nearest 50 feet.
   b. Name the tallest building.

    c. What is the approximate difference in height between the World Trade Center and the Empire State Building?

    d. What building is closest in height to the Standard Oil Building?

    e. What is the approximate difference between the height of the John Hancock Building and the height of the Sears Tower?

    f. Which buildings, if any, are less than 1000 feet tall?

2. Use the graph to answer the following questions:

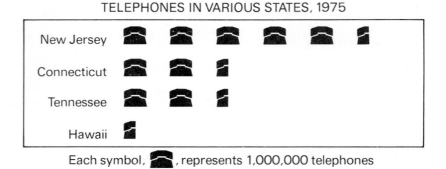

TELEPHONES IN VARIOUS STATES, 1975

Each symbol, , represents 1,000,000 telephones

    a. How many telephones were there in each of the states, to the nearest 500,000?

    b. Which two states had about the same number of telephones?

    c. Connecticut had how many times as many telephones as Hawaii?

    d. What was the ratio of the number of telephones in Tennessee to the number of telephones in Hawaii?

    e. How did the number of telephones in New Jersey compare to the total number of telephones in the other three states?

3. The bar graph shows the number of acres of different vegetables that a farmer planted during one season.

    a. How many acres of carrots were planted?

    b. Which vegetable had the least number of acres planted?

    c. What was the total number of acres planted?

    d. What percent of the total number of acres planted were reserved for carrots?

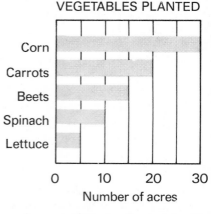

VEGETABLES PLANTED

    e. What is the ratio of the number of acres of beets planted to the number of acres of spinach planted?

4. In a bar graph, "1 centimeter represents 30 kilometers." Find the length of the bar needed to represent the given distance.
   a. 60 kilometers   b. 300 kilometers
   c. 15 kilometers   d. 75 kilometers

5. The scale on a bar graph is "$\frac{1}{4}$ inch represents 100 people." Find the length of the bar needed to represent the given number of people.
   a. 200 people   b. 400 people   c. 2000 people
   d. 500 people   e. 1500 people

6. The following graph shows the cash dividends per share that a large company paid to its stockholders during the years 1970 through 1980.

CASH DIVIDENDS PAID PER SHARE

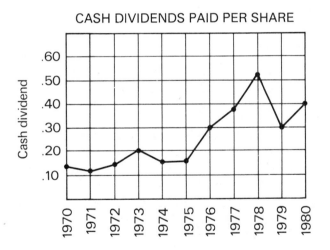

a. Approximately how much was the dividend per share during 1979?
b. In what year was the lowest dividend paid?
c. Between what two years did the dividend decrease most sharply?
d. Between what two years did the dividend remain constant?
e. For what two years was the dividend closest to $.40 per share?
f. What was the *range* of dividends over the period from 1970 through 1980, that is, the approximate difference between the highest and lowest dividends paid?

7. In the scale of the graph on the next page, a break appears between 0 and 61 to allow for a "closer look" at the increases in life expectancies for U.S. males, over the period from 1940 to 1980, inclusive. If this same scale were used "without a break," the graph would

LIFE EXPECTANCY IN YEARS
FOR U.S. MALES

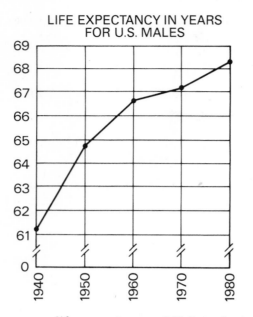

extend beyond the length of this page in the book. Answer the following questions related to the line graph, as shown:

a. In what decade (ten-year period) did the life expectancy increase the most?

b. In what decade did the life expectancy increase the least?

c. What was the life expectancy for U.S. males in 1940, to the nearest year?

d. What was the life expectancy for U.S. males in 1950, to the nearest year?

e. Which of the following ratios best compares the life expectancy of U.S. males in 1950 to that in 1940?

   (1) 3 to 1   (2) 5 to 1   (3) 61 to 65   (4) 65 to 61

f. It is true that females have a greater life expectancy than males. Which statement could be true for U.S. females?

   (1) In 1960 their life expectancy was 66 years.

   (2) In 1980 their life expectancy was greater than 68.3 years.

   (3) In 1970 their life expectancy was less than 67 years.

8. The heights of five dams are given as: Boulder, 730 ft.; Kensico, 310 ft.; Shasta, 600 ft.; Grand Coulee, 450 ft.; and Gatun, 120 ft.

   a. Make a bar graph to represent this data.

   b. Is it appropriate to display this data with a line graph? If no, explain why. If yes, construct the line graph.

9. The unemployment rate in the United States is given in five-year intervals for the years 1950–1975, as shown in the table at the right.

   a. Construct a bar graph to represent this data.

   b. Is it appropriate to display this data with a line graph? If no, explain why. If yes, construct the line graph.

U.S. Unemployment Rate (*per 100 workers*)	
1950	5.3
1955	4.4
1960	5.5
1965	4.5
1970	4.9
1975	8.5

4 THE HISTOGRAM

Back in section 2 of this chapter we learned how to organize data by "grouping" the data into intervals of equal length.

The table at the right consists of six intervals, each having a length of ten. This grouped data shows the distribution of test scores for 32 students in a class.

Test Scores (Intervals)	Frequency (Number of Scores)
91–100	6
81–90	8
71–80	11
61–70	4
51–60	0
41–50	3

The data can be displayed graphically by means of a *histogram*. A *histogram* is simply a bar graph in which the bars are placed next to each other. We bring these bars together to show that "as one interval ends, the next interval begins." Essentially the bars of the histogram show us *changes in the same item*, such as the distribution of scores for a single test.

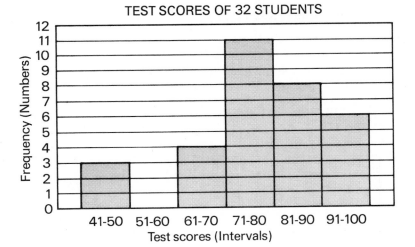

TEST SCORES OF 32 STUDENTS

In the above histogram the first bar shows us that 3 students had test scores in the interval 41–50. Since no students scored in the interval 51–60, we do not place a bar at this location. Then we can see that 4 students scored 61 to 70; 11 students had test scores between 71 and 80; 8 had scores between 81 and 90; and finally 6 students scored from 91 to 100. With the exception of an interval having a frequency of zero, as in 51–60, there are no gaps between the bars drawn in a histogram.

Since the histogram displays the frequency, or number, of scores falling into each interval, we sometimes call this graph a *frequency histogram*.

| MODEL PROBLEMS |

1. The table at the right represents the number of miles per gallon (mpg) of gasoline obtained by 40 drivers of compact cars in a large city.

    Construct a frequency histogram based on the data.

Interval	Number (*Frequency*)
40–43	1
36–39	3
32–35	7
28–31	5
24–27	8
20–23	11
16–19	5

    Solution

    Step 1. Draw and label a vertical scale to show frequencies. The scale starts at 0 and increases to include the highest frequency in any one interval (here, it is 11).

    Step 2. Draw and label intervals of equal length on a horizontal scale. Give a title to the horizontal scale, telling what the numbers represent.

    Step 3. Draw the bars vertically, leaving no gaps between the intervals.

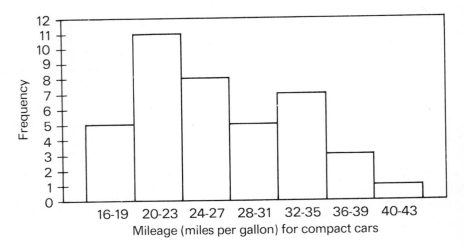

2. Use the histogram constructed in model problem 1 to answer the following questions:

a. In what interval is the greatest frequency found?

Answer: 20–23

b. What is the number (or frequency) of cars reporting mileage between 28 to 31 miles per gallon?

Answer: 5

c. In what interval are the fewest cars reported?

Answer: 40–43

d. How many of the cars reported mileages greater than 31 miles per gallon?

Solution: Add the frequencies for the three highest intervals. With 7 in (32–35), 3 in (36–39), and 1 in (40–43), we say 7 + 3 + 1 = 11. *Ans.*

e. What percent of the cars reported mileages from 24 to 27 mpg?

Solution: The interval 24–27 contains a frequency of 8. The total frequency for this survey is 40. Then, $\frac{8}{40} = \frac{1}{5} = 20\%$. *Ans.*

EXERCISES

In 1–3, construct a frequency histogram for the grouped data.

1.

Interval	Number (*Frequency*)
91–100	5
81–90	9
71–80	7
61–70	2
51–60	4

2.

Interval	Frequency
30–34	5
25–29	10
20–24	10
15–19	12
10–14	0
5–9	2

3.

Interval	Number
1–3	24
4–6	30
7–9	28
10–12	41
13–15	19
16–18	8

4. For the table of grouped data given in exercise 3, answer the following questions:

a. What is the total frequency, or the total number of pieces of data, in the table?

b. What interval contains the greatest frequency?

c. The number of scores reported for the interval 4–6 is what percent of the total number of scores?

d. How many scores were reported from 10 through 18?

5. Towering Ted McGurn is the star of the school's basketball team. The number of points scored by Ted in his last 20 games are:

36, 32, 28, 30, 33, 36, 24, 33, 29, 30,

30, 25, 34, 36, 34, 31, 36, 29, 30, 34.

a. Copy and complete the table to find the number (or frequency) in each interval.

b. Construct a frequency histogram based on the data found in part a.

Interval	Tallies	Number (*Frequency*)
35–37		
32–34		
29–31		
26–28		
23–25		

c. Answer the following questions for this set of data:
1. Which interval contains the greatest frequency?
2. In how many games did Ted score 32 or more points?
3. In what percent of these 20 games did Ted score fewer than 26 points?

6. Thirty students on the track team were timed when running a 200-meter dash. Each student's time was recorded to the nearest tenth of a second. The times were:

29.3, 31.2, 28.5, 37.6, 30.9, 26.0, 32.4, 31.8, 36.6, 35.0,

38.0, 37.0, 22.8, 35.2, 35.8, 37.7, 38.1, 34.0, 34.1, 28.8,

29.6, 26.9, 36.9, 39.6, 29.9, 30.0, 36.0, 36.1, 38.2, 37.8.

a. Copy and complete the table to find the number (or frequency) in each interval.

b. Construct a frequency histogram for the given data.

c. From the data determine the number of students who ran the 200-meter dash in under 29 seconds.

Interval	Tallies	Number (*Frequency*)
37.0–40.9		
33.0–36.9		
29.0–32.9		
25.0–28.9		
21.0–24.9		

5 THE MEAN, THE MEDIAN, AND THE MODE

In a statistical study, after we have collected the data, organized it, and presented it graphically, we then analyze the data and summarize our findings. When we do this, we frequently become involved with "average" scores.

Averages in Arithmetic

In your previous study of arithmetic you have no doubt solved problems in which you found the average of two or more numbers.

For example, find the average of 17, 25, and 30.

First we add these three numbers: $17 + 25 + 30 = 72$

Then we divide this sum by 3 since there are 3 numbers: $72 \div 3 = 24$

The average of the three numbers is 24. We can state the procedure in general terms.

■ **PROCEDURE.** To find the average of N numbers, add the numbers and divide the sum by N.

"Averages" in Statistics

The word "**average**" has many different meanings. For example, there is an *average* of our test scores; a batting *average*; the *average* television viewer; an *average* intelligence; the *average* size of a family; and so on. These measures, called "averages," are *not* necessarily found by the same rule or procedure. Because of this confusion, we avoid using the word "average" in statistics. Instead, we speak of the *measures of central tendency*. These measures are numbers, like an "average," that usually "tend" to fall somewhere in the "center" of a set of organized data.

We will study three measures of central tendency called the *mean*, the *median*, and the *mode*.

The Mean

In statistics the arithmetic average we previously studied is called the *mean* of a set of numbers. It is also called the "arithmetic mean" or the "numerical average." It is found in the same way as the arithmetic average is found. Hence, we can say the following:

■ **PROCEDURE.** To find the mean of a set of N numbers, add the numbers and divide the sum by N.

For example, if Ralph's grades on 5 tests in science during this marking period are 93, 80, 86, 72, and 94, he can find the mean (or mean average) of his test grades as follows:

Step 1. He adds the five pieces of data: $93 + 80 + 86 + 72 + 94 = 425$

Step 2. He divides this sum by 5, the number of tests: $425 \div 5 = 85$
Hence, the mean is 85.

Let us consider another example.

In a car wash there are seven employees whose ages are 17, 19, 20, 17, 46, 17, and 18. What is the mean (or mean average) of the ages of these employees?

Here we add the seven ages to get a sum of 154. Then $154 \div 7 = 22$. While the mean age of 22 is the correct answer, this measure does *not* truly represent the data. Notice that only one person is older than 22 while 6 of these people are under 22. For this reason, we will look at another measure of central tendency that will eliminate the extreme case (the employee at age 46) that is "distorting" the data.

The Median

The *median* is the "middle score" for a set of data, taken only when the data is arranged in numerical order. For example, the median of the ages 17, 19, 20, 17, 46, 17, and 18 can be found in the following manner:

Step 1. Arrange the ages in numerical order: 17, 17, 17, 18, 19, 20, 46

Step 2. Find the middle number: 17, 17, 17, 18, 19, 20, 46

The median is 18 because there are 3 ages below 18 and 3 ages above 18.

Notice that the median 18 is a better indication of the "average" age of the employees than the mean of 22 because there are so many younger people working at the car wash.

Let us find the median for the following scores: 6, 6, 21, 11, 8, 14.

Step 1. Arrange the scores in numerical order: 6, 6, 8, 11, 14, 21

Step 2. Find the "middle" number. In this case there are *two* "middle" numbers: 6, 6, 8, 11, 14, 21

Step 3. Find the mean (arithmetic average) of the two "middle" scores: $\dfrac{8 + 11}{2} = \dfrac{19}{2} = 9\dfrac{1}{2}$

Hence, the median is $9\dfrac{1}{2}$.

■ **PROCEDURE.** To find the median of N numbers:

1. Arrange the numbers in numerical order.

2. If N is odd, the median is the "middle" number.

3. If N is even, the median is the mean (arithmetic average) of the two middle numbers.

The Mode

The *mode* is the score that appears "most often" in a given set of data. It is usually best to arrange the data in numerical order before finding the mode.

Let us consider some examples of finding the mode:

1. The ages of employees in a car wash are 17, 17, 17, 18, 19, 20, 46. The mode, which is the number appearing most often, is 17.

2. The hours spent by six students in reading a book are 6, 6, 8, 11, 14, 21. The mode, or number appearing most frequently, is 6. Notice that, in this case, the mode is not a useful measure of central tendency. Better indications can be given by the mean or the median.

3. The number of photographs printed from Renee's last six rolls of film are 8, 8, 9, 11, 11, and 12. Since 8 appears twice and 11 appears twice, we say that there are two modes: 8 and 11. We do not take the average of these two numbers since the mode tells us where most of the scores appear; we simply report both numbers. When *two modes* appear within a set of data, we say that the data is *bimodal*.

4. The number of people living in houses on Meryl's street are 2, 2, 3, 3, 4, 5, 5, 6, 8. This data has *three* modes: 2, 3, and 5.

5. Ralph's test scores in science are 72, 80, 86, 93, and 94. Here, every number appears "an equal number of times." Since *no* number appears more often than others, we define such data as having *no mode*.

■ **PROCEDURE.** To find the mode for a set of data:

1. Select the score that appears "most often" in the data.

2. If two or more numbers appear the same number of times, and this is more than any other numbers, then each of these numbers is a mode.

3. If every number in the set of data appears an equal number of times, there is no mode.

┌─────────────────── KEEP IN MIND ───────────────────┐

Three measures of central tendency are:

1. the *mean*, or *mean average*, found by adding N pieces of data and then dividing the sum by N;

2. the *median*, or *middle* score, found only when data is arranged in numerical order;

3. the *mode*, or the score appearing *most often*.

└───┘

| MODEL PROBLEMS |

1. The weights of five players on the basketball team are 168 lb., 174 lb., 181 lb., 195 lb., and 182 lb. Find the average weight of a player on this team.

Solution

The word *average*, by itself, indicates the *mean*. Therefore:
(1) Add the five weights: $168 + 174 + 181 + 195 + 182 = 900$
(2) Divide the sum by 5, the number of players: $900 \div 5 = 180$

Answer: 180 lb.

2. Renaldo has marks of 75, 82, and 90 in three mathematics tests. What mark must he obtain on the next test to have an average of exactly 85 for the four math tests?

Solution

The word *average* by itself indicates the *mean* average.
Let x = Renaldo's mark on the fourth test.

The sum of the four
test marks divided by 4 is 85.

$$\frac{75 + 82 + 90 + x}{4} = 85$$

$$\frac{247 + x}{4} = 85$$

(Multiply by 4): $247 + x = 340$

(Subtract 247): $x = 93$

Check

$$\frac{75 + 82 + 90 + 93}{4} \stackrel{?}{=} 85$$

$$\frac{340}{4} \stackrel{?}{=} 85$$

$$85 = 85$$

(True)

Answer: Renaldo must obtain a mark of 93 on his fourth math test.

3. Find the median for each distribution.
   a. 3, 2, 5, 5, 1   b. 9, 8, 8, 7, 4, 3, 3, 2, 0, 0

Solution

a. Arrange the data in numerical order: 1, 2, 3, 5, 5.
   The median is the middle score.   1, 2, 3, 5, 5

   Answer: median = 3

b. Since there is an even number of
   scores, there are two middle   9, 8, 8, 7, 4, 3, 3, 2, 0, 0
   scores. Find the mean (average) $\dfrac{4 + 3}{2} = \dfrac{7}{2} = 3\dfrac{1}{2}$
   of the two middle scores.

   Answer: median = $3\dfrac{1}{2}$ *or* 3.5

4. Find the mode for each distribution.
   a. 2, 9, 3, 7, 3   b. 3, 4, 5, 4, 3   c. 1, 2, 3, 4, 5, 6, 7

Solution

a. Arrange the data in numerical order: 2, 3, 3, 7, 9. The mode, or
   "most frequent" score, is 3.   *Answer:* mode = 3

b. Arrange the data in numerical order: 3, 3, 4, 4, 5. Both 3 and 4
   appear twice. There are two modes.   *Answer:* modes = 3 and 4

c. No number appears "most often" in 1, 2, 3, 4, 5, 6, 7.
                                        Answer: no mode

| EXERCISES |
---

1. Sid received grades of 92, 84, and 70 on three tests. Find his test average.
2. Sarah received the mark 80 on two of her tests and 90 on each of three other tests. Find her test average.
3. Louise received the mark of x on two of her tests and y on each of three other tests. Represent her average for all the tests in terms of x and y.
4. Andy has grades of 84, 65, and 76 on three social studies tests. What grade must he obtain on the next test to have an average of exactly 80 for the four tests?
5. Rosemary has grades of 90, 90, 92, and 78 on four English tests. What grade must she obtain on the next test so that her average for the five tests will be 90?
6. The first three test scores are shown for each of four students. A fourth test will be given and averages taken for all four tests. Each student hopes to maintain an average of 85. Find the score needed

by each student on the fourth test to have an 85 average, or explain why such an average is not possible.

    a. Pat: 78, 80, 100   **b.** Bernice: 79, 80, 81

    c. Helen: 90, 92, 95   **d.** Al: 65, 80, 80

7. The smallest of three consecutive even integers is 32. Find the mean average of the three integers.

8. The average of the weights of Sue, Pam, and Nancy is 55 kilograms. How much does Agnes weigh if the mean weight of the four girls is 60 kilograms?

9. The average of three consecutive even integers is 20. Find the integers.

10. The mean average of three numbers is 31. The second is one more than twice the first. The third is four less than three times the first. Find the numbers.

11. Find the mean for each set of data.

    a. 7, 3, 9, 21, 10   **b.** 7, 3, 9, 21

    c. 7, 3, 9, 21, 0   **d.** 16, 16, 17, 19, 84

    e. $2\frac{1}{2}, 2\frac{1}{2}, 3\frac{1}{2}, 4, 7\frac{1}{2}$ **f.** 2, .2, 2.2, .02

12. If the heights of a group of students are 180 cm, 180 cm, 173 cm, 170 cm, and 167 cm, what is the mean height of these students?

13. Find the median for each set of data.

    a. 3, 4, 7, 8, 12   **b.** 2, 9, 10, 10, 12   **c.** 3.2, 4, 4.1, 5, 5

    d. 3, 4, 7, 8, 12, 13   **e.** 2, 9, 10, 10   **f.** 3.2, 4, 4.1, 5

14. Find the median for each set of data after placing the data into numerical order.

    a. 1, 2, 5, 3, 4   **b.** 2, 9, 2, 9, 7

    c. 3, 8, 12, 7, 1, 0, 4   **d.** 80, 83, 97, 79, 25

    e. 3.2, 8.7, 1.4   **f.** 2, .2, 2.2, .02, 2.02

    g. 21, 24, 23, 22, 20, 24, 23, 21, 22, 23   **h.** 5, 7, 9, 3, 8, 7, 5, 6

15. What is the median age of a family whose members are 42, 38, 14, 13, 10, and 8 years old?

16. What is the median age of a class where 14 students are 14 years old and 16 students are 15 years old?

17. In a charity collection ten people gave amounts of $1, $2, $1, $1, $3, $1, $2, $1, $1, and $1.50. What was the median donation?

18. The test results of an examination were 62, 67, 67, 70, 90, 93, and 98. What is the median test score?

19. What is the median for the digits 1, 2, 3, . . . , 9?

20. What is the median for the counting numbers from 1 through 100?

21. Find the mode for each distribution.

    a. 2, 2, 3, 4, 8   **b.** 2, 2, 3, 8, 8   **c.** 2, 2, 8, 8, 8

    d. 2, 3, 4, 7, 8   **e.** 2, 2, 3, 8, 8, 9, 9

    f. 1, 2, 1, 2, 1, 2, 1   **g.** 1, 2, 3, 2, 1, 2, 3, 2, 1

h. 3, 19, 21, 75, 0, 6   **i.** 3, 2, 7, 6, 2, 7, 3, 1, 4, 2, 7, 5
j. 19, 21, 18, 23, 19, 22, 18, 19, 20

22. Ellen's test scores are 65, 71, 73, 78, 90, 90, 92. What is the mode of her test scores?

23. A set of data consists of six numbers; 7, 8, 8, 9, 9, and x. Find the mode for these six numbers when:
    a. $x = 9$ **b.** $x = 8$ **c.** $x = 7$ **d.** $x = 6$

24. The set of data 2, 4, 5, x, 5, 4 is given. In each part find a possible value of x so that: **(a)** there is no mode because all scores appear an equal number of times; **(b)** there is only one mode; **(c)** there are two modes.

25. For the set of data 5, 5, 6, 7, 7, what statement is true?
    (1) mean = mode   (2) median = mode
    (3) mean = median   (4) mean < median

26. For the set of data 8, 8, 9, 10, 15, which statement is true?
    (1) mean < median   (2) mean > mode
    (3) median < mode   (4) mean = median

27. When the data consists of 3, 4, 5, 4, 3, 4, 5, which statement is true?
    (1) mean > median   (2) mean > mode
    (3) median < mode   (4) mean = median

28. For which set of data is there no mode?
    (1) 2, 1, 3, 1, 2   (2) 1, 2, 3, 3, 3
    (3) 1, 2, 4, 3, 5   (4) 2, 2, 3, 3, 3

29. For which set of data is there more than one mode?
    (1) 8, 7, 7, 8, 7   (2) 8, 7, 4, 5, 6
    (3) 8, 7, 5, 7, 6, 5   (4) 1, 2, 2, 3, 3, 3

30. For which set of data does the median equal the mode?
    (1) 3, 3, 4, 5, 6   (2) 3, 3, 4, 5
    (3) 3, 3, 4   (4) 3, 4

31. For which set of data will the mean, median, and mode all be equal?
    (1) 1, 2, 5, 5, 7   (2) 1, 2, 5, 5, 8, 9
    (3) 1, 1, 1, 2, 5   (4) 1, 1, 2

32. The weekly salaries of six employees in a small firm are $140, $145, $145, $150, $150, and $320.
    a. For these six salaries, find:
        1. the mean   2. the median   3. the mode
    b. If negotiations for new salaries are in session and you represent management, which measure of central tendency would you use as the "average" salary? Tell why.
    c. If negotiations are in session and you represent the labor union, which measure of central tendency would you use as an "average" salary? Tell why.

33. In a certain school, bus service is provided for students living more than $1\frac{1}{2}$ miles from school. The distances from school to home for ten students are $0, \frac{1}{2}, \frac{1}{2}, 1, 1, 1, 1, 1\frac{1}{2}, 3\frac{1}{2},$ and 10 miles.
   a. For this data, find: 1. the mean   2. the median   3. the mode
   b. How many of these ten students are entitled to bus service?
   c. Explain why the mean is not a good measure of central tendency to describe the "average" distance between home and school for these students.

34. Last month a carpenter used 12 boxes of nails each of which contained nails of only one size. The sizes marked on the boxes were $\frac{3}{4}'', \frac{3}{4}'', \frac{3}{4}'', \frac{3}{4}'', \frac{3}{4}'', \frac{3}{4}'', \frac{3}{4}'', \frac{3}{4}'', 1'', 1'', 2'',$ and $2''$.
   a. For this data, find: 1. the mean   2. the median   3. the mode
   b. Describe the "average" size nail used by the carpenter, using at least one of these measures of central tendency. Explain your answer.

6 MEASURES OF CENTRAL TENDENCY AND GROUPED DATA

Intervals of Length One

In a statistical study, when the range is small, we use intervals of length one to group data. For example, a class of 25 students reported on the number of books read during the first half of the school year. The data was given as:

5, 3, 5, 3, 1, 8, 2, 4, 2, 6, 3, 8, 8,
5, 3, 4, 5, 8, 5, 3, 3, 5, 6, 2, 3

Interval	Frequency (Number)
8	4
7	0
6	2
5	6
4	2
3	7
2	3
1	1

$N = 25$

This data was organized into a table as shown at the left. Since 25 students reported in this study, we indicate the total frequency by writing "$N = 25$" at the bottom of the Frequency column.

Let us now find the mode, median, and mean for this grouped data.

Mode

Since the greatest frequency, 7, appears in interval 3, the mode for this data is 3.

In general, the mode is the value of the interval that contains the greatest frequency.

Median

We have learned that the median for a set of data in numerical order is the middle score.

1, 2, 2, 2, 3, 3, 3, 3, 3, 3, 3, 3, 4, | 4, | 5, 5, 5, 5, 5, 5, 6, 6, 8, 8, 8, 8

Hence we know that for these 25 scores the median or middle score is 4. That is, there are 12 scores "above" the median 4, and 12 scores "below" the median 4.

When the data is grouped in the table that follows, a simple counting procedure can be used to find the median. Since the total frequency is 25, the median will be the 13th score, "above" which there are 12 scores and "below" which there are 12 scores.

Interval	Frequency
8	4
7	0
6	2
5	6
4	2
3	7
2	3
1	1

Counting the frequencies from the uppermost interval and moving down, we see that 4 + 0 + 2 + 6 = 12. Since these are the 12 scores "above" the median, the median must lie in the next lower interval, namely the interval "4."

Counting the frequencies from the lowermost interval and moving up, we see that 1 + 3 + 7 = 11. The next higher interval contains two scores, both the 12th number and the median or "middle" number. Again, this is the interval "4."

In general, the median is the value of the interval that contains the "middle" score for a set of grouped data.

Mean

In the table, the highest interval 8 has a frequency of 4. This tells us that "4 students read 8 books each." When we multiply these numbers, $(4)(8) = 32$, we see that these 4 students read a "*total* of 32 books." Notice that we can arrive at this same number by adding the four "8's" reported in the ungrouped data, that is, $8 + 8 + 8 + 8 = 32$. Let us apply this multiplication shortcut to each line of the table, obtaining column 3 of the following table:

Interval	Frequency	(Interval) · (Frequency)
8	4	8 · 4 = 32
7	0	7 · 0 = 0
6	2	6 · 2 = 12
5	6	5 · 6 = 30
4	2	4 · 2 = 8
3	7	3 · 7 = 21
2	3	2 · 3 = 6
1	1	1 · 1 = 1

$N = 25$ Total = 110

Then add the eight products obtained:

$$32 + 0 + 12 + 30 + 8 + 21 + 6 + 1 = 110$$

The **total (110)** represents **the sum of all 25 items of data.** We can check this by adding the 25 scores in the unorganized data.

Finally, to find the mean, we divide the total number, 110, by the number of scores, 25. Thus, $110 \div 25 = 4.4$, which is the mean.

■ **PROCEDURE.** To find the mean for a table of grouped data when the length of the interval is one:

1. For each of the intervals, multiply the interval value by its corresponding frequency.

2. Find the sum of these products.

3. Divide this sum by the number of scores.

Intervals Other Than Length One

While there are definite mathematical procedures to find the mean, median, and mode for grouped data with intervals other than length one, we will not study them at this time. Instead, we will simply identify the intervals that contain some of these measures of central tendency. Here is an example:

A small industrial plant surveyed 50 workers to find out the number of miles each person commuted to work. The commuting distances were reported to the nearest mile as:

0, 0, 1, 1, 2, 2, 2, 3, 3, 4, 4, 4, 5, 5, 6, 6, 6, 7, 7, 7, 9,

10, 10, 10, 10, 10, 10, 10, 10, 12, 12, 14, 15, 17, 17,

18, 22, 23, 25, 28, 30, 32, 32, 33, 34, 34, 36, 37, 37, 52.

This data was organized into a table with intervals of length ten, as follows:

Interval (Commuting Distance)	Frequency (Number of Workers)
50–59	1
40–49	0
30–39	9
20–29	4
10–19	15
0–9	21

$N = 50$

Modal Interval

In the table the interval 0-9 contains the greatest frequency, 21. We say that the interval 0-9 is the *group mode*, or *modal interval*, because this "group of numbers" has the greatest frequency.

Notice that the modal interval is *not* the same as the mode. The modal interval is a "group of numbers"; the mode is generally a single number. For this particular problem the original data (before being placed into the table) shows us that the number appearing "most often" is 10. Hence we say the mode is 10. The modal interval, which is 0-9, tells us that "of the six intervals in the table, the most popular commuting distance is 0 to 9 miles." We say that the modal interval = (0-9).

Both the mode and the modal interval depend upon the concept of greatest frequency. For the mode, we look for a single number that has the greatest frequency. For the modal interval, we look for the interval that has the greatest frequency.

Interval Containing the Median

To find the interval containing the median, we follow the same procedure described earlier in this section. For 50 scores the median or "middle" number will be at a point where 25 scores are "above" the median and 25 scores are "below" the median.

Interval	Frequency
50–59	1
40–49	0
30–39	9
20–29	4
10–19	15
0–9	21

$N = 50$

Counting the frequencies from the uppermost interval and moving downwards, we have $1 + 0 + 9 + 4 = 14$. Since there are 15 scores in the next lower interval, and $14 + 15 = 29$, we see that 25 scores will be reached somewhere in that interval, 10–19.

Counting from the bottom interval and moving up, we have 21 scores in the first interval. Since there are 15 scores in the next higher interval, and $21 + 15 = 36$, we see that 25 scores will be reached somewhere in that interval, 10–19. Notice that this is the same result that we previously obtained when we "moved downwards." We say that the interval containing the median = (10–19).

In this course we will not deal with problems in which the median is not found in any interval.

As a final note, there is no simple procedure to identify the interval that contains the mean when data is grouped using intervals other than length one. This problem will also be studied in higher-level courses.

MODEL PROBLEM

In the table, data is given to indicate the heights (in inches) of 17 basketball players. For this data find:

a. the mode   **b.** the median   **c.** the mean

Solution

a. The greatest frequency, 5, occurs for the interval where heights are 75 inches. The mode, or height appearing "most often," is 75.

Answer: mode = 75

Height (*Inches*)	Frequency (*Number*)
77	2
76	0
75	5
74	3
73	4
72	2
71	1

Height	Frequency
77	2
76	0
75	5
74	3
73	4
72	2
71	1

b. For 17 players, the median is the "middle" number (the 9th number) so that 8 scores are "above" the median and 8 scores are "below" the median.

Counting frequencies going down, 2 + 0 + 5 = 7 and 2 + 0 + 5 + 3 = 10. Thus, the middle number must lie in the interval 74.

Counting frequencies going up, 1 + 2 + 4 = 7 and 1 + 2 + 4 + 3 = 10. Thus, the middle number must lie in the interval 74.

Answer: median = 74

c. (1) Multiply each height given as an interval by the frequency for that interval.
(2) Find the total of these products. Here it is 1258.
(3) Divide this total of 1258 by the total frequency (here N = 17) to obtain the mean of 74.

Answer: mean = 74

$$
\begin{array}{rl}
77 \cdot 2 = & 154 \\
76 \cdot 0 = & 0 \\
75 \cdot 5 = & 375 \\
74 \cdot 3 = & 222 \\
73 \cdot 4 = & 292 \\
72 \cdot 2 = & 144 \\
71 \cdot 1 = & 71 \\
\hline
\text{Total} = & 1258
\end{array}
$$

$$
\begin{array}{r}
74 \\
17 \overline{\smash{\big)}\,1258} \\
119 \\
\hline
68 \\
68 \\
\hline
\end{array}
$$

EXERCISES

In 1–3, data is grouped in intervals of length one. Find (a) the total frequency, (b) the mean, (c) the median, and (d) the mode.

1.

Interval	Frequency
10	1
9	2
8	3
7	2
6	4
5	3

2.

Interval	Frequency
15	3
16	2
17	4
18	1
19	5
20	6

3.

Interval	Frequency
25	4
24	0
23	3
22	2
21	4
20	5
19	2

Grade	Frequency (*Number*)
20	
19	
18	
17	
16	
15	
14	
13	
12	

4. On a test consisting of 20 questions, fifteen students received the following scores:

   17, 14, 16, 18, 17, 19, 15, 15,

   16, 13, 17, 12, 18, 16, 17.

   a. On your answer paper, copy and complete the table shown at the right.

   b. Find the median score.

   c. Find the mode.

   d. Find the mean.

Interval (*Minutes*)	Number of People (*Frequency*)
6	12
5	20
4	36
3	20
2	12

5. A questionnaire was distributed to 100 people. The table at the left shows the time taken in minutes to complete the questionnaire.

   a. For this data, find:
      1. the mean
      2. the median
      3. the mode

   b. How are these three measures related for this data?

6. A store owner kept a tally of the sizes of suits purchased in his store, as shown in the table at the right.

   a. For this set of data find:
      1. the total frequency
      2. the mean
      3. the median
      4. the mode

   b. Which measure of central tendency should the store owner use to describe the "average" suit sold?

Size of Suit (*Interval*)	Number Sold (*Frequency*)
48	1
46	1
44	3
42	5
40	3
38	8
36	2
34	2

In 7–9, data is grouped in intervals other than length one. Find (a) the total frequency, (b) the interval which contains the median, and (c) the modal interval.

7.

Interval	Frequency
55–64	3
45–54	8
35–44	7
25–34	6
15–24	2

8.

Interval	Frequency
4–9	12
10–15	13
16–21	9
22–27	12
28–33	15
34–39	10

9.

Interval	Frequency
126–150	4
101–125	6
76–100	6
51–75	3
26–50	7
1–25	2

10. Test scores for a class of twenty students are given as:

93, 84, 97, 98, 100, 78, 86,

100, 85, 92, 72, 55, 91, 90,

75, 94, 83, 60, 81, 95.

Test Scores	Frequency (*Number*)
91–100	
81–90	
71–80	
61–70	
51–60	

a. On your answer paper, copy and complete the table shown at the right.
b. Find the modal interval.
c. Find the interval that contains the median.

11. The following data consists of weights in pounds of 35 adults:

176, 154, 161, 125, 138, 142,

108, 115, 187, 158, 168, 162,

135, 120, 134, 190, 195, 117,

142, 133, 138, 151, 150, 168,

172, 115, 148, 112, 123, 137,

186, 171, 166, 166, 179.

Interval	Frequency
180–199	
160–179	
140–159	
120–139	
100–119	

a. Copy and complete the table shown above.
b. Construct a frequency histogram based on the grouped data.
c. In what interval is the median for this grouped data?
d. What is the modal interval?

7 CUMULATIVE FREQUENCY HISTOGRAMS AND PERCENTILES

In a school a final examination was given to all students taking biology. The total number of students taking this examination was 240. The test grades of these students were grouped into a table as shown at the right. At the same time, a histogram of the results was constructed, shown below.

Interval (Test Scores)	Frequency (Number)
91–100	45
81–90	60
71–80	75
61–70	40
51–60	20

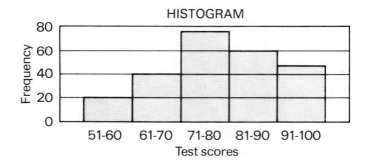

From the table and the histogram we can see that 20 students scored in the interval 51–60, 40 students scored in the interval 61–70, and so forth. We can use this data to construct a new type of histogram that answers the question:

"How many students scored below a certain grade?"

By answering the following questions we will gather some information before constructing the new histogram.

1. How many students scored "60 or less" on the test?
   From the bottom interval 51–60, we know the answer is 20 students.   *Answer:* 20

2. How many students scored "70 or less" on the test?
   By adding the frequencies in the two lowest intervals, 51–60 and 61–70, we see that 20 + 40, or 60, students scored "70 or less" on the test.   *Answer:* 60

3. How many students scored "80 or less" on the test?
   By adding the frequencies in the three lowest intervals, 51-60, 61-70, and 71-80, we see that 20 + 40 + 75, or 135, students scored "80 or less" on the test.   *Answer:* 135

4. How many students scored "90 or less" on the test?
   Here we add the frequencies in the four lowest intervals. Thus, 20 + 40 + 75 + 60, or 195, students scored "90 or less."   *Answer:* 195

5. How many students scored "100 or less" on the test?
   By adding the five lowest frequencies, 20 + 40 + 75 + 60 + 45, we see that 240 students scored "100 or less." This makes sense because 240 students took the test and all of them scored "100 or less."
                                                     Answer: 240

Constructing a Cumulative Frequency Histogram

The answers to the five questions we have just asked were found by adding or "accumulating" the "frequencies" from the intervals in the group data. The histogram that displays these "accumulated" figures is called a *cumulative frequency histogram*.

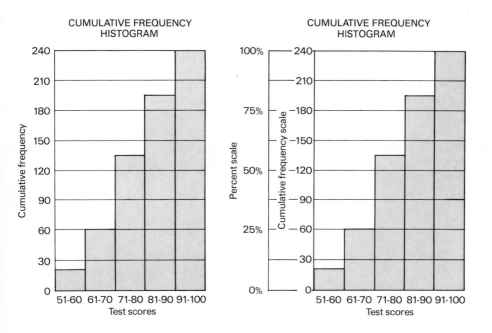

Notice that the frequency scale for this cumulative frequency histogram goes from 0 to 240 (the total frequency for this data).

It is also possible to place a different scale to the left of the cumulative frequency histogram, namely one involving *percents*. Since 240 students represent 100% of the population, we write 100% to correspond to 240 students. Since no students, or "zero" students, represent 0% of the population, we write 0% to correspond with 0 students.

On the percent scale we also label 25%, 50%, and 75%. From the graph we see that each cumulative frequency corresponds to a percent of the population. For example, 120 students (half of the population) will correspond to 50% of the population.

Let us examine the percent scale in relation to the question:

"What percent of students scored 70 or below on this test?"

In the interval 61–70 for the cumulative frequency histogram, the top of the bar shows **25%** scoring "70 or less." This makes sense because the top of the bar also shows **60 students** (out of a total population of 240) scoring "70 or less," and we know that $\frac{60}{240} = \frac{1}{4} = 25\%$.

Since the "bottom 25%" or the "lower 25%" of the population scored "70 or less," we say that the **test score of 70** represents the grade for the *bottom quartile*, also called the *lower quartile* or the *first quartile*.

Let us consider another question:

"What is the test score for the 'top quartile,' or what test grade is the cutoff point for the top quarter of the class?"

We can see that 75% falls somewhere into the interval 81–90 but we are not certain where this happens. To get a better approximation, let us construct one more graph by making use of the cumulative frequency histogram we have already drawn.

Constructing a Cumulative Frequency Polygon

A cumulative frequency polygon is simply a line graph connecting a series of points that answers the question that was given at the start of this section, namely, "How many students scored at or below a certain grade?"

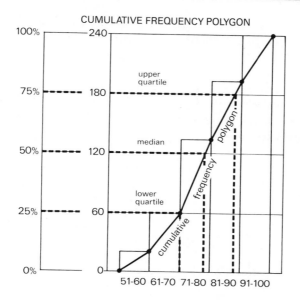

CUMULATIVE FREQUENCY POLYGON

For the interval 91–100, a point is placed at the upper right of the bar to show that "240 students scored 100 or less on the test."

For the interval 81–90, a point is placed at the upper right of this bar to show that "195 students scored 90 or less on the test."

We continue this process to plot six points as shown in the graph. Notice that the last point placed, at the bottom left of the interval 51–60, tells us that "0 students scored 50 or less on the test."

The cumulative frequency polygon is the line graph connecting these six points.

Percentiles, Quartiles, and the Median

Notice the three dashed lines drawn on the graph just shown. From 25% the first dashed line is drawn horizontally until it meets the cumulative frequency polygon. From this point of contact a vertical line is drawn to meet the horizontal scale. We can now see that the *lower quartile* has a test score of 70; that is, 25% of the students scored "70 or less on the test."

In a similar manner we can discover from the graph that 50% of the students scored approximately "77 or less on the test." This measure 77 is the *median*, or the middle score. This is the point at which 50% of the scores are "above" this score and 50% are "below" this score.

Likewise we can discover from the graph that 75% of the students scored approximately "86 or less on the test." This also tells us that 25% of the students scored above 86. The score 86 is called the *upper quartile*.

In general, **a percentile is a score or a measure that tells us what percent of the total population or the total frequency scored "at or below that measure."**

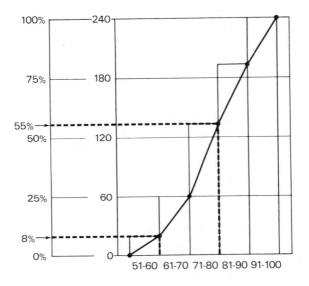

From the graph of the frequency polygon we can also discover the percentile that corresponds to a given score. For example, to find the percentile for a score of 60, we draw a vertical line at 60 on the score scale. At the point where this line meets the cumulative frequency polygon, we draw a horizontal line that meets the percent scale at approximately 8%. This tells us that approximately 8% of the students scored "60 or below 60." Hence *60 is the score for the 8th percentile*.

Similarly we can discover from the graph that 80 on the score scale corresponds approximately to 55% on the percent scale. This tells us that approximately 55% of the students scored "80 or less than 80." Hence *80 is the score for the 55th percentile*.

Notice that:

1. The upper quartile is the 75th percentile.

2. The median is the 50th percentile.

3. The lower quartile is the 25th percentile.

MODEL PROBLEM

For the given table of values at the right, in what interval is the lower quartile found?

Interval	Frequency
41–50	4
31–40	3
21–30	6
11–20	7
1–10	4

Solution

The total frequency = 4 + 3 + 6 + 7 + 4 = 24.

The lower quartile is the score below which 25% of the total frequency falls. Since 25% of $24 = \frac{1}{4} \times 24 = 6$, we have to find the interval (starting from the bottom) in which the 6th score falls.

In the lowest interval, 1–10, there are only 4 scores. Hence, the 6th score is found in the next interval, 11–20.

Answer: The lower quartile is in the interval 11–20.

EXERCISES

In 1–3, data is grouped into tables. For each group of data find: (a) the total frequency, (b) the interval in which the lower quartile lies, (c) the interval in which the median lies, and (d) the interval in which the upper quartile lies.

1.

Interval	Frequency
41–50	8
31–40	5
21–30	2
11–20	5
1–10	4

2.

Interval	Frequency
25–29	3
20–24	1
15–19	3
10–14	9
5–9	4

3.

Interval	Frequency
1–4	6
5–8	3
9–12	7
13–16	2
17–20	2

Interval	Frequency
21–25	5
16–20	4
11–15	6
6–10	3
1–5	2

4. a. For the data shown at the right, construct a cumulative frequency histogram.

    b. In what interval is the median found?

    c. Find the lower quartile.

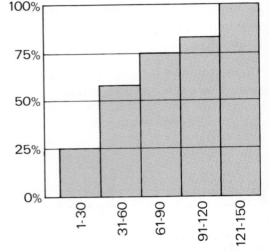

5. For the cumulative frequency histogram shown at the right:
    a. Copy the histogram and construct a cumulative frequency polygon.
    b. In what interval is the median found?
    c. What is the value of the 25th percentile?
    d. What is the value of the 75th percentile?
    e. Approximately what percent of scores are "60 or below"?
    f. What percent of scores are "150 or below"?

Interval	Frequency
33–37	4
28–32	3
23–27	7
18–22	12
13–17	8
8–12	5
3–7	1

6. For the data given in the table at the left:
    a. Construct a cumulative frequency histogram.
    b. Construct a cumulative frequency polygon.
    c. In what interval is the median found?
    d. In what interval is the upper quartile found?
    e. Approximately what percent of scores are "17 or less"?
    f. Approximate the value for the 25th percentile.
    g. What is the value of the 90th percentile?

chapter eighteen

Graphs of Linear Open Sentences in Two Variables

1 ORDERED NUMBER PAIRS AND POINTS IN A PLANE

Let us learn to describe points in a plane. We start with two signed number lines, called *coordinate axes*, drawn at right angles to each other. The horizontal line is called the *x*-axis. The vertical line is called the *y*-axis. In a *coordinate plane*, or *Cartesian plane*, the point *O* at which the two axes intersect is called the *origin*.

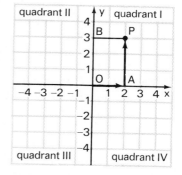

The Cartesian plane is named after the seventeenth-century mathematician René Descartes who, in 1637, made the wonderful discovery that algebraic relations between variables can be described by points and lines (straight or curved) in a plane.

The *x*-axis and the *y*-axis divide the set of points of the plane not on the axes into four regions called *quadrants*. These quadrants are numbered I, II, III, and IV in a counterclockwise order as shown in the drawing.

Point *P* in the plane can be located by starting at the origin, moving 2 units to the right along the *x*-axis, then moving 3 units upward in a direction parallel to the *y*-axis.

Distances measured to the *right* of the *y*-axis, along the *x*-axis or along a line parallel to the *x*-axis, are considered to be *positive*; distances measured to the *left* of the *y*-axis are considered to be *negative*.

Distances measured *upward* from the *x*-axis, along the *y*-axis or along a line parallel to the *y*-axis, are considered to be *positive*; distances measured *downward* from the *x*-axis are considered to be *negative*.

The distance of a point from the *y*-axis, measured either along the *x*-axis or along a line parallel to it, is called the *x-coordinate*, or *abscissa*. The distance of a point from the *x*-axis, measured either along the *y*-axis or along a line parallel to it, is called the *y-coordinate*, or *ordinate*. For example, consider point *P* previously discussed (page 531). The abscissa, *BP*, the distance from *B* to *P*, which can be read along the *x*-axis as *OA*, is +2, or 2; the ordinate, *AP*, the distance from *A* to *P*, which can be read along the *y*-axis as *OB*, is +3, or 3.

The two numbers that are associated with any particular point, the abscissa and ordinate of the point, are called the **coordinates** of the point. The coordinates of a point may be written as an ordered number pair in which the first number is always the abscissa and the second number is always the ordinate. Thus, the coordinates of point *P* in the graph' at the right may be written (2, 3).

The point *P* is called the **graph of the ordered number pair** (2, 3). In general, the coordinates of a point may be represented as (*x*, *y*).

We must be careful not to interchange the numbers 2 and 3 in the number pair (2, 3) because the resulting number pair (3, 2) would be associated with a point different from point *P*. In fact, it is impossible to find a point other than *P* whose coordinates are (2, 3). It is also impossible to find an ordered number pair other than (2, 3) to represent point *P*.

In the preceding graph, point *R* in quadrant II is 2 units to the left of the *y*-axis; thus, the abscissa of point *R* is -2. Since point *R* is 4 units above the *x*-axis, its ordinate is 4. The coordinates of point *R* may be written (-2, 4). Point *R* is the graph of the number pair (-2, 4).

Similarly, the point described by (-4, -3) is point *S* in quadrant III, and the point described by (4, -2) is point *T* in quadrant IV. When we graph the point described by an ordered number pair, we are *plotting the point*.

| EXERCISES |

1. Write as ordered number pairs the coordinates of points A, B, C, D, E, F, G, H, and O in the graph.

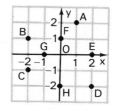

In 2–21, draw a pair of coordinate axes on a sheet of graph paper and graph the point associated with the ordered number pair.

2. (5, 4)	**3.** (-3, 2)	**4.** (2, -6)	**5.** (-4, -5)
6. (1, 6)	**7.** (-8, 5)	**8.** (4, -4)	**9.** (-2, -7)
10. (-1.5, -2.5)	**11.** (5, 0)	**12.** (-3, 0)	**13.** (8, 0)
14. (-10, 0)	**15.** (0, 4)	**16.** (0, -6)	**17.** (0, 1)
18. (0, -4)	**19.** (0, 0)	**20.** (|2|, |4|)	**21.** (|-5|, |3|)

In 22–26, name the quadrant in which the graph of the point described appears.

22. (5, 7)   **23.** (-3, -2)   **24.** (-7, 4)   **25.** (1, -3)   **26.** (|-2|, |-3|)

27. Graph the following points: $A(5, 3)$, $B(-5, 3)$, $C(-5, -3)$, $D(5, -3)$. Connect these points with straight lines in the order given. What kind of quadrilateral is $ABCD$?

28. Graph several points on the x-axis. What is the value of the ordinate for every point in the set of points on the x-axis?

29. Graph several points on the y-axis. What is the value of the abscissa for every point in the set of points on the y-axis?

30. What are the coordinates of the origin in the coordinate plane?

31. Name the quadrant in which the graph of point $P(x, y)$ lies when:
   a. $x > 0$ and $y > 0$
   b. $x > 0$ and $y < 0$
   c. $x < 0$ and $y > 0$
   d. $x < 0$ and $y < 0$

32. Name the quadrant in which the graph of the point $P(|x|, |y|)$ lies when:
   a. $x > 0$ and $y > 0$
   b. $x > 0$ and $y < 0$
   c. $x < 0$ and $y > 0$
   d. $x < 0$ and $y < 0$

2 FINDING SOLUTION SETS OF OPEN SENTENCES IN TWO VARIABLES

Open sentences such as $y = 3x$, $y - 2x = 4$, and $y > 2x + 4$ are called open sentences in two variables.

There are some replacements for x and y that cause $y = 3x$ to become a true sentence. For example, if x is replaced by 1 and y by 3, the resulting sentence $3 = 3 \cdot 1$ is a true sentence. Therefore, the pair of numbers $x = 1$, $y = 3$ is said to *satisfy* the open sentence in two variables, $y = 3x$. Such a pair of numbers is called a *root*, or *solution*, of $y = 3x$. We can write the solution $x = 1$, $y = 3$ as an ordered pair $(1, 3)$ if we agree that the first value in the pair always represents a value of the variable x and the second value always represents a value of the variable y.

On the other hand, there are some replacements for x and y that cause $y = 3x$ to become a false sentence. For example, when x is replaced by 3 and y is replaced by 1, $y = 3x$ becomes $1 = 3 \cdot 3$, which is a false sentence. Therefore, the pair of numbers $x = 3$, $y = 1$, which may be written as the ordered pair $(3, 1)$, is not a solution of the sentence $y = 3x$.

The solutions of $y = 3x$, when the replacement set for x and for y is $\{1, 2, 3, 4, 5, 6, 7, 8, 9\}$, are the ordered pairs $(1, 3)$, $(2, 6)$, and $(3, 9)$. We call this set of ordered pairs $\{(1, 3), (2, 6), (3, 9)\}$ the *solution set* of the sentence $y = 3x$. The solution set of a sentence involving two variables is the set whose members are all the ordered pairs that are solutions of the sentence. If there are no ordered pairs which are solutions of the sentence, we say the solution set is the empty set, $\emptyset$.

If the replacement set is the set of positive numbers, negative numbers, and zero, there are many more members in the solution set of $y = 3x$ than when the replacement set was $\{1, 2, 3, \ldots, 9\}$. Some members of this new solution set are $(-2, -6)$, $(-1, -3)$, $(\frac{1}{3}, 1)$, $(\frac{2}{3}, 2)$, $(10, 30)$. It is impossible to list all the members of the solution set because there is an infinite number of them. In such a case, we can describe the solution set as $\{(x, y) | y = 3x\}$, which is read "the set of all ordered pairs (x, y) such that $y = 3x$."

The solution set of $y > 3x$, when the replacement set for x and for y is $\{1, 2, 3, 4, 5, 6, 7, 8, 9\}$, is the set of ordered pairs $\{(1, 4), (1, 5), (1, 6), (1, 7), (1, 8), (1, 9), (2, 7), (2, 8), (2, 9)\}$.

To verify that $(1, 9)$ is a solution of $y > 3x$, we replace x by 1 and y by 9. We obtain $9 > 3 \cdot 1$, which is a true sentence. All the other ordered pairs of the solution set can be verified in the same way.

If the replacement set is the set of positive numbers, negative numbers, and zero, there are many more members in the solution set of $y > 3x$ than when the replacement set was $\{1, 2, 3, \ldots, 9\}$. Some members of this new solution set are $(-2, -4)$, $(-1, -2)$, $(-1, 2)$, $(-\frac{1}{3}, 1)$, $(\frac{2}{3}, 3)$, $(5, 16)$. It is impossible to list all the members of the solution set because there is an infinite number of them. In such a case, we can describe the solution set as $\{(x, y)|y > 3x\}$, which is read "the set of all ordered pairs (x, y) such that $y > 3x$."

MODEL PROBLEMS

1. Find the solution set of $y - 2x = 4$ when the replacement set for x is $R = \{1, 2, 3, 4, 5\}$ and the replacement set for y is $S = \{6, 7, 8, 9, 10\}$.

    How to Proceed   *Solution*

    (1) Transform the sentence into an equivalent sentence which has y alone as one member.

$$y - 2x = 4$$
$$y - 2x + 2x = 4 + 2x$$
$$y = 2x + 4$$

    (2) Replace x by each member of R, the replacement set for x. Then compute each of the corresponding y-values.

    (3) Determine whether or not each y-value computed in step 2 is a member of S, the replacement set for y. If the y-value belongs to S, then the ordered pair consisting of an x-value and its corresponding y-value is a solution of the sentence.

x	$2x + 4$	y
1	$2(1) + 4$	6 is a member of S
2	$2(2) + 4$	8 is a member of S
3	$2(3) + 4$	10 is a member of S
4	$2(4) + 4$	12 is not a member of S
5	$2(5) + 4$	14 is not a member of S

Answer: Solution set is $\{(1, 6), (2, 8), (3, 10)\}$.

2. Find the solution set of $y - 2x > 4$ when the replacement set for x is $R = \{1, 2, 3, 4, 5\}$ and the replacement set for y is $S = \{6, 7, 8, 9, 10\}$.

How to Proceed

(1) Transform the sentence into an equivalent sentence that has y alone as one member.

(2) Replace x by each member of R, the replacement set for x. Then compute the corresponding y-values.

(3) If any y-values computed in step 2 are members of S (S is the replacement set for y), then each ordered pair consisting of an x-value and its corresponding y-value is a solution of the sentence.

Solution

$$y - 2x > 4$$
$$y - 2x + 2x > 4 + 2x$$
$$y > 2x + 4$$

x	$2x + 4$	$y > 2x + 4$	y
1	2(1) + 4	$y > 6$	7, 8, 9, 10
2	2(2) + 4	$y > 8$	9, 10
3	2(3) + 4	$y > 10$	no values in S
4	2(4) + 4	$y > 12$	no values in S
5	2(5) + 4	$y > 14$	no values in S

Answer: Solution set is $\{(1, 7), (1, 8), (1, 9), (1, 10), (2, 9), (2, 10)\}$.

EXERCISES

In 1–5, find the missing member in each ordered pair if the second member of the pair is twice the first member.

1. (3, ?)   **2.** (0, ?)   **3.** (-2, ?)   **4.** (?, 11)   **5.** (?, -8)

In 6–10, find the missing member in each ordered pair if the first member of the pair is 4 more than the second member.

6. (?, 5)   **7.** $(?, \frac{1}{2})$ **8.** (?, 0)   **9.** $(9\frac{1}{4}, ?)$ **10.** (-8, ?)

In 11–18, state whether or not the given ordered pair of numbers is a solution of the sentence. The replacement set for x and for y is the set of whole numbers.

11. $y = 5x$; (3, 15)

12. $y = 4x$; (16, 4)

13. $y = 3x + 1$; (7, 22)

14. $3x - 2y = 0$; (3, 2)

15. $y > 4x$; $(2, 10)$

16. $y < 2x + 3$; $(0, 2)$

17. $3y > 2x + 1$; $(4, 3)$

18. $2x + 3y \leq 9$; $(0, 3)$

In 19-26, state whether or not the given ordered pair of numbers is a solution of the sentence. The replacement set for x and for y is the set of positive numbers, negative numbers, and zero.

19. $x + y = 8$; $(4, 5)$

20. $4x + 3y = 2$; $(\frac{1}{4}, \frac{1}{3})$

21. $3x = y + 4$; $(-7, -1)$

22. $x - 2y = 15$; $(1, -7)$

23. $y > 6x$; $(-1, -2)$

24. $3x < 4y$; $(5, 2)$

25. $y \geq 3 - 2x$; $(-1, 6)$

26. $5x - 2y \leq 19$; $(3, -2)$

27. Which of the ordered pairs of numbers $(8, -2)$, $(2, -6)$, $(7, 13)$, $(3, 9)$ is a member of the solution set of $x + y = 6$?

28. Which of the ordered number pairs $(5, 3)$, $(7, 2)$, $(1, -1)$, $(-2, -\frac{1}{4})$ is a member of the solution set of $y > 4x$?

29. Which of the ordered number pairs $(1, 8)$, $(5, 2)$, $(3, -1)$, $(0, -4)$ is not a member of the solution set of $y < 2x + 1$?

In 30-33, find the solution set of the sentence.

30. $x + y = 4$ when the replacement set for x is $\{5, 7\}$ and the replacement set for y is $\{$natural numbers$\}$.

31. $y = 3x - 1$ when the replacement set for x is $\{-3, -1, 2\}$ and the replacement set for y is $\{$positive numbers, negative numbers, zero$\}$.

32. $y < 2x - 1$ when the replacement set for x is $\{5, 6\}$ and the replacement set for y is $\{8, 9, 10, 11\}$.

33. $x + y \geq 12$ when the replacement set for x is $\{-7, 10, 12\}$ and the replacement set for y is $\{-2, 2, 6, 10\}$.

In 34-39, use set notation to describe the solution set when the replacement set for x and for y is the set of positive numbers, negative numbers, and zero.

34. $y = 6x$

35. $y = x + 9$

36. $3x + y = 11$

37. $y > 10x$

38. $y < 3x - 1$

39. $y - x \geq 4$

3. GRAPHING A LINEAR EQUATION IN TWO VARIABLES BY MEANS OF ITS SOLUTIONS

If we wish to find number pairs that satisfy the equation $x + y = 6$, we can replace one variable, for example x, by a convenient value. Then we can solve the resulting equation for the value of the other variable, y. If we let $x = 1$, then $1 + y = 6$ and $y = 5$. Thus, the ordered pair $(1, 5)$ is a solution of $x + y = 6$.

We can also transform the equation $x + y = 6$ into an equivalent equation in which y stands alone on one side of the equation, that is, y is expressed in terms of x. Then we can assign a value to x and find the corresponding value of y. For example:

$$x + y = 6$$
$$y = 6 - x \qquad S_x$$
Let $x = 1$: $\qquad y = 6 - 1$
$$y = 5$$

Thus, a solution of $x + y = 6$ is $(1, 5)$, the same result as before.

If the replacement set for both x and y is {signed numbers}, we can find an infinite number of ordered pairs that are solutions of $x + y = 6$. Some of these solutions are shown in the table that follows.

x	7	6	5	4	3	$2\frac{1}{2}$	2	1	$\frac{1}{2}$	0	-1
y	-1	0	1	2	3	$3\frac{1}{2}$	4	5	$5\frac{1}{2}$	6	7

Let us plot the points associated with the ordered number pairs that are shown in the table. Notice that these points seem to lie on a straight line. In fact, if {signed numbers} is the replacement set for both x and y, then the following is true:

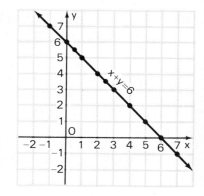

The graphs of all ordered pairs (x, y) that are solutions of $x + y = 6$ lie on this same line; the graphs of all ordered pairs that are not solutions of $x + y = 6$ do not lie on this line.

This line, which is the set of all those points and only those points whose coordinates satisfy the equation $x + y = 6$, is called the *graph* of $x + y = 6$. In other words, this line is the graph of $\{(x, y) | x + y = 6\}$.

A first-degree equation in two variables, such as $x + y = 6$, may be written in the form $Ax + By + C = 0$, where A, B, and C are signed numbers, with A and B not both zero. It can be proved that the graph of such an equation is a straight line. We therefore call such an equation a *linear equation*.

When we graph a linear equation, we may determine the straight line by plotting two points whose coordinates satisfy that equation because two points determine a line in a plane. However, we always plot a third point as a check on the first two. If the third point lies on the line determined by the first two points, we have probably made no error.

When two or more points lie on the same straight line, we say that the points are *collinear*. Points that do not lie on the same straight line are called *non-collinear* points.

■ **PROCEDURE.** To graph a linear equation by means of its solutions:
1. Transform the equation into an equivalent equation which is solved for y in terms of x.

2. Find 3 solutions of the equation by assuming values for x and computing corresponding values for y.

3. Graph in the coordinate plane the 3 ordered pairs of numbers found in step 2.

4. Draw the straight line that passes through the 3 points graphed in step 3.

Note: When we graph a linear equation involving the variables x and y, the replacement set of both variables is {signed numbers} unless otherwise indicated.

```
┌──────────────── KEEP IN MIND ────────────────┐
│                                               │
│   1. Every ordered pair of numbers that       │
│      satisfies an equation represents the     │
│      coordinates of a point on the graph of   │
│      the equation.                            │
│                                               │
│   2. Every point on the graph of an equation  │
│      has as its coordinates an ordered pair    │
│      of numbers that satisfies the equation.   │
│                                               │
└───────────────────────────────────────────────┘
```

MODEL PROBLEMS

1. Does the point $(2, -3)$ lie on the graph of $x - 2y = -4$?

    Solution:

    If the point $(2, -3)$ is to lie on the graph of $x - 2y = -4$, when we substitute 2 for x and -3 for y, the resulting equation must be true.

$$x - 2y = -4 \quad [\text{Let } x = 2 \text{ and } y = -3.]$$
$$(2) - 2(-3) \overset{?}{=} -4$$
$$2 + 6 \overset{?}{=} -4$$
$$8 \neq -4$$

Since $8 = -4$ is not true, the point $(2, -3)$ does not lie on the line $x - 2y = -4$. *Answer:* No

2. What must be the value of d if $(d, 4)$ lies on the line $3x + y = 10$?

Solution: The coordinate $(d, 4)$ must satisfy $3x + y = 10$.
Hence: $3d + 4 = 10$
$$3d = 6$$
$$d = 2 \quad Ans.$$

3. a. Write the following verbal sentence as an equation: "The sum of twice the abscissa of a point and the ordinate of that point is 4."
   b. Graph the equation written in part a.

a. *Solution:* Let x = the abscissa of the point.
Let y = the ordinate of the point.
Then $2x + y = 4$ *Ans.*

b.

How to Proceed	*Solution*

(1) Transform the equation into an equivalent equation which has y alone as one member.

$2x + y = 4$
$y = -2x + 4$

x	$-2x + 4 = y$
0	$-2(0) + 4 = 4$
1	$-2(1) + 4 = 2$
2	$-2(2) + 4 = 0$

(2) Determine 3 solutions of the equation by assuming values for x and computing the corresponding values for y.

(3) Plot the points that are associated with the 3 solutions found previously.

(4) Draw a straight line through the points that were plotted.

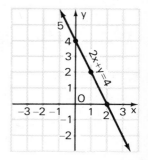

| EXERCISES |

1. In each part, state whether the pair of values for x and y satisfies the equation $2x - y = 6$.
   a. $x = 4, y = 2$ b. $x = 0, y = 6$ c. $x = 4, y = -2$

In 2–5, state whether the point whose coordinates are given is on the graph of the given equation.

2. $x + y = 7$; $(4, 3)$ 3. $2y + x = 7$; $(1, 3)$
4. $3x - 2y = 8$; $(2, 1)$ 5. $2y = 3x - 5$; $(-1, -4)$

In 6–8, find the number that can replace k so that the resulting ordered number pair will be on the graph of the given equation.

6. $x + 2y = 5$; $(k, 2)$ 7. $3x + 2y = 22$; $(k, 5)$
8. $x + 3y = 10$; $(13, k)$

In 9–11, find a value that can replace k so that the graph of the resulting equation will pass through the point whose coordinates are given.

9. $x + y = k$; $(2, 5)$ 10. $x - y = k$; $(5, -3)$
11. $5y - 2x = k$; $(-2, -1)$

In 12–17, solve the equation for y in terms of x.

12. $3x + y = -1$ 13. $4x - y = 6$ 14. $2y = 6x$
15. $12x = \frac{3}{2}y$ 16. $4x + 2y = 8$ 17. $6x - 3y = 5$

In 18–20, find the missing values of the variable needed to complete the table. Plot the points described by the pairs of values in the completed table; then draw the line on which they seem to lie.

18. $y = 4x$ 19. $y = 3x + 1$ 20. $x + 2y = 3$

x	y
0	?
1	?
2	?

x	y
-1	?
0	?
1	?

x	y
-1	?
2	?
5	?

In 21–38, graph the equation.

21. $y = 2x$ 22. $y = 5x$ 23. $y = -3x$
24. $y = -x$ 25. $x = 2y$ 26. $x = \frac{1}{2}y$

27. $y = x + 3$ 28. $y = 2x - 1$ 29. $y = 3x + 1$
30. $y = -2x + 4$ 31. $x + y = 8$ 32. $x - y = 5$
33. $y - x = 0$ 34. $x + 3y = 12$ 35. $x - 2y = 0$
36. $y - 3x = -5$ 37. $2x + 3y = 6$ 38. $3x - 2y = -6$

In 39 and 40, graph the indicated set of points.

39. $\{(x, y)\,|\,y = 3x\}$

40. $\{(x, y)\,|\,x - y = 6\}$

In 41–44: **a.** Write the verbal sentence as an equation. **b.** Graph the equation.

41. The ordinate of a point is twice the abscissa.
42. The ordinate of a point is 2 more than the abscissa.
43. The sum of the ordinate and abscissa of a point is 6.
44. Twice the ordinate of a point decreased by 3 times the abscissa is 6.

In 45–48: **a.** Graph the given points. **b.** Do the points appear to be collinear or non-collinear?

45. $(1, 3); (2, 5); (3, 7)$ 46. $(-1, 5); (0, 2); (1, -1)$
47. $(2, 5); (4, 9); (6, 15)$ 48. $(-4, -1); (0, 3); (2, 5)$

4   GRAPHING LINES PARALLEL TO THE X-AXIS OR Y-AXIS

Lines Parallel to the X-Axis

The *y-intercept* of a line is the y-coordinate of the point at which the line intersects the y-axis. In the figure at the right, $\overleftrightarrow{AB}$ intersects the y-axis at the point $(0, 2)$. Hence, the y-intercept of $\overleftrightarrow{AB}$ is 2.

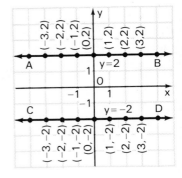

Likewise, the y-intercept of $\overleftrightarrow{CD}$ is -2.

Notice that the value of x at the point where the line intersects the y-axis is 0.

Study the graph. The line, $\overleftrightarrow{AB}$, whose y-intercept is 2, is parallel to the x-axis. Notice that the y-value of each ordered pair that is associated with a point on $\overleftrightarrow{AB}$ equals 2. This is true no matter what the value of x is. Therefore, an equation of the line, $\overleftrightarrow{AB}$, is written simply $y = 2$. Similarly, $y = -2$ represents an equation of a line $(\overleftrightarrow{CD})$ whose graph is parallel to the x-axis and whose y-intercept is -2.

■ An equation for a line parallel to the x-axis, when its y-intercept is b, is $y = b$.

> *Note:* $\overleftrightarrow{AB}$ is the graph of $\{(x, y)|y = 2\}$.
>
> $\overleftrightarrow{CD}$ is the graph of $\{(x, y)|y = -2\}$.
>
> Neither line has an x-intercept.

Lines Parallel to the Y-Axis

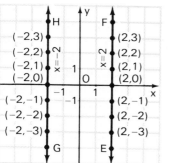

The *x-intercept* of a line is the x-coordinate of the point at which the line intersects the x-axis. In the figure at the left, $\overleftrightarrow{EF}$ intersects the x-axis at the point (2, 0). Hence, the x-intercept of $\overleftrightarrow{EF}$ is 2.

Likewise, the x-intercept of $\overleftrightarrow{GH}$ is -2.

Notice that the value of y at the point where the line intersects the x-axis is 0.

Study the graph. The line, $\overleftrightarrow{EF}$, whose x-intercept is 2, is parallel to the y-axis. Notice that the x-value of each ordered pair that is associated with a point of $\overleftrightarrow{EF}$ equals 2. This is true no matter what the value of y is. Therefore, an equation of the line, $\overleftrightarrow{EF}$, is written simply $x = 2$. Similarly, $x = -2$ represents an equation of a line ($\overleftrightarrow{GH}$) whose graph is parallel to the y-axis and whose x-intercept is -2.

■ An equation for a line parallel to the y-axis, when its x-intercept is a, is $x = a$.

> *Note:* $\overleftrightarrow{EF}$ is the graph of $\{(x, y)|x = 2\}$.
>
> $\overleftrightarrow{GH}$ is the graph of $\{(x, y)|x = -2\}$.
>
> Neither line has a y-intercept.

EXERCISES

In 1–10, draw the graph of the equation.

1. $x = 6$ 2. $x = \frac{2}{3}$ 3. $x = 0$ 4. $x = -3$ 5. $x = -5$
6. $y = 4$ 7. $y = 2\frac{1}{4}$ 8. $y = 0$ 9. $y = -4$ 10. $y = -7$

In 11–14, graph the indicated set of points.

11. $\{(x, y)|x = 4\}$ 12. $\{(x, y)|x = -1.5\}$

13. $\{(x, y)|y = -5\}$ 14. $\{(x, y)|y = 2\frac{1}{2}\}$

15. Write an equation of a line that is parallel to the x-axis and whose y-intercept is:

   a. 1   b. 5   c. -4 d. -8 e. -2.5

16. Write an equation of a line that is parallel to the y-axis and whose x-intercept is:

   a. 3   b. 10   c. $4\frac{1}{2}$ d. -6 e. -10

17. Which statement is true about the graph of the equation $y = 6$?
   (1) It is parallel to the y-axis.   (2) It is parallel to the x-axis.
   (3) It passes through the origin.   (4) It has an x-intercept.

18. Which statement is true about the graph of the equation $x = 5$?
   (1) It passes through the origin.   (2) It is parallel to the x-axis.
   (3) It is parallel to the y-axis.   (4) It has a y-intercept.

19. Which statement is true about the equation $y = x$?
   (1) It is parallel to the x-axis.   (2) It is parallel to the y-axis.
   (3) It passes through the point $(2, -2)$.
   (4) It passes through the origin.

5 THE SLOPE OF A LINE
Meaning of the Slope of a Line

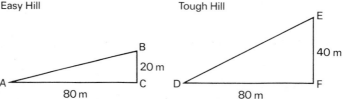

It is more difficult to hike up Tough Hill than it is to hike up Easy Hill. Tough Hill rises 40 m vertically over a horizontal distance of 80 m, whereas Easy Hill rises only 20 m vertically over the same horizontal distance of 80 m. Therefore, Tough Hill is steeper than Easy Hill. To compare the steepness of roads $\overline{AB}$ and $\overline{DE}$, roads that lead up the two hills, we compare their *slopes*.

The slope of road $\overline{AB}$ is the ratio of the change in vertical distance, CB, to the change in horizontal distance, AC:

$$\text{slope of road } \overline{AB} = \frac{\text{change in vertical distance, } CB}{\text{change in horizontal distance, } AC} = \frac{20 \text{ m}}{80 \text{ m}} = \frac{1}{4}$$

Also:

$$\text{slope of road } \overline{DE} = \frac{\text{change in vertical distance, } FE}{\text{change in horizontal distance, } DF} = \frac{40 \text{ m}}{80 \text{ m}} = \frac{1}{2}$$

Since road $\overline{DE}$ rises $\frac{1}{2}$ m vertically for each 1 m of horizontal distance, whereas road $\overline{AB}$ rises only $\frac{1}{4}$ m vertically for each 1 m of horizontal distance, road $\overline{DE}$ is steeper than road $\overline{AB}$.

Finding the Slope of a Line

To find the slope of the line deter- mined by the two points (2, 3) and (5, 8): (1) We graph the two points. (2) We find the vertical change, the difference in y-values. (3) We find the horizontal change, the difference in x-values. (4) We divide the difference in y-values by the difference in x-values as follows:

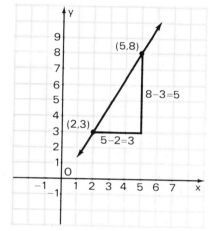

$$\text{slope} = \frac{\text{difference in } y\text{-values}}{\text{difference in } x\text{-values}}$$

$$= \frac{8 - 3}{5 - 2} = \frac{5}{3}$$

Suppose we change the order of the points in performing the compu- tation. We would then have:

$$\text{slope} = \frac{\text{difference in } y\text{-values}}{\text{difference in } x\text{-values}} = \frac{3 - 8}{2 - 5} = \frac{-5}{-3} = \frac{5}{3}$$

Observe that the result in both computations is the same. When we compute the slope of a line that is determined by two points, it does not matter which point is considered as the first point and which the second.

Also, when we find the slope of a line using two points on the line, it does not matter which two points on the line we use because all seg- ments of a line have the same slope as the line.

■ **PROCEDURE.** To find the slope of a line:
1. Select any two points on the line.
2. Find the horizontal change, the change in x-values, in going from the point on the left to the point on the right.
3. Find the vertical change, the change in y-values, in going from the point on the left to the point on the right.
4. Divide the vertical change by the horizontal change.

For example, in the figure:

slope of $\overleftrightarrow{LM}$ = $\dfrac{\text{vertical change}}{\text{horizontal change}}$

$= \dfrac{4}{2} = 2$

slope of $\overleftrightarrow{RS}$ = $\dfrac{\text{vertical change}}{\text{horizontal change}}$

$= \dfrac{-2}{3} = -\dfrac{2}{3}$

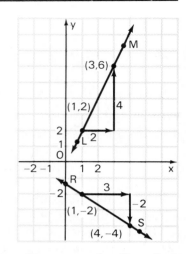

In general, the slope, m, of a line that passes through two points $P_1(x_1, y_1)$ and $P_2(x_2, y_2)$ when $x_1 \neq x_2$ is the ratio of the difference of the y-values of these points to the difference of the corresponding x-values. Thus:

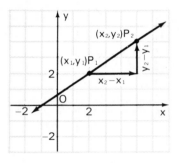

$$\text{slope of line} = \dfrac{\text{difference in } y\text{-values}}{\text{difference in } x\text{-values}}$$

$$\text{slope of } \overleftrightarrow{P_1 P_2} = m = \dfrac{y_2 - y_1}{x_2 - x_1}$$

The expression "difference in x-values," $x_2 - x_1$, can be represented by Δx, read "delta x." Similarly, the "difference in y-values," $y_2 - y_1$, can be represented by Δy, read "delta y." Therefore, we write:

$$\text{slope of line} = m = \dfrac{\Delta y}{\Delta x}$$

We have said that when we find the slope of a line passing through two points, it does not matter which point is considered as the first point (x_1, y_1) and which point is considered as the second point (x_2, y_2). This is so because

$$\dfrac{y_2 - y_1}{x_2 - x_1} = \dfrac{-1}{-1} \cdot \dfrac{(y_2 - y_1)}{(x_2 - x_1)} = \dfrac{-y_2 + y_1}{-x_2 + x_1} = \dfrac{y_1 - y_2}{x_1 - x_2}$$

Therefore we may also say: slope of $\overleftrightarrow{P_1 P_2} = m = \dfrac{y_1 - y_2}{x_1 - x_2}$

Positive Slopes

As a point moves along $\overleftrightarrow{AB}$ from left to right, for example, from C to D, the line is rising. As the x-values increase, the y-values also increase. Between point C and point D, the change in y is 1 (or $\Delta y = 1$); the change in x is 2 (or $\Delta x = 2$). Since both Δy and Δx are positive, the slope of $\overleftrightarrow{AB}$ must be positive.

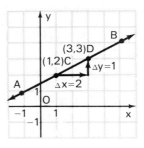

$$\text{slope} = m = \frac{\Delta y}{\Delta x} = \frac{1}{2}$$

This example illustrates:

■ **PRINCIPLE 1.** As a point moves from left to right along a line that is rising, y increases as x increases and the slope of the line is positive.

Negative Slopes

As a point moves along $\overleftrightarrow{EF}$ from left to right, for example, from C to D, the line is "falling." As the x-values increase, the y-values decrease. Between point C and point D, the change in y is -2 (or $\Delta y = -2$); the change in x is 3 (or $\Delta x = 3$). Since Δy is negative and Δx is positive, the slope of $\overleftrightarrow{EF}$ must be negative.

$$\text{slope} = m = \frac{\Delta y}{\Delta x} = \frac{-2}{3} = -\frac{2}{3}$$

This example illustrates:

■ **PRINCIPLE 2.** As a point moves from left to right along a line that is falling, y decreases as x increases and the slope of the line is negative.

Zero Slope

$\overleftrightarrow{GH}$ is parallel to the x-axis. Consider a point moving along $\overleftrightarrow{GH}$ from left to right, for example, from C to D: As the x-values increase, the y-values are unchanged. Between point C and point D, the change in y is 0 (or $\Delta y = 0$), and the change in x is 3 (or $\Delta x = 3$). Since Δy is 0 and Δx is 3, the slope of $\overleftrightarrow{GH}$ must be 0.

$$\text{slope} = m = \frac{\Delta y}{\Delta x} = \frac{0}{3} = 0$$

This example illustrates:

■ **PRINCIPLE 3.** If a line is parallel to the x-axis, its slope is 0.

[*Note:* The slope of the x-axis itself is also 0.]

No Slope

$\overleftrightarrow{LM}$ is parallel to the y-axis. Consider a point moving upward along $\overleftrightarrow{LM}$, for example, from C to D: The x-values are unchanged, but the y-values increase. Between point C and point D, the change in y is 3 (or $\Delta y = 3$), and the change in x is 0 (or $\Delta x = 0$). Since

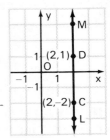

the slope of $\overleftrightarrow{LM} = \dfrac{\Delta y}{\Delta x} = \dfrac{3}{0}$, and a nonzero number cannot be divided by 0, line $\overleftrightarrow{LM}$ has no defined slope.

This example illustrates:

■ **PRINCIPLE 4.** If a line is parallel to the y-axis, it has no defined slope.

[*Note:* The y-axis itself has no defined slope.]

| **MODEL PROBLEMS** |

1. Find the slope of the straight line that is determined by the points $(-2, 4)$ and $(4, 2)$.

Solution: Plot the points $(-2, 4)$ and $(4, 2)$. Let the point $(-2, 4)$ be $P_1(x_1, y_1)$, and let the point $(4, 2)$ be $P_2(x_2, y_2)$. Then $x_1 = -2$, $y_1 = 4$; $x_2 = 4, y_2 = 2$.

$$\text{slope of } \overleftrightarrow{P_1 P_2} = \frac{\Delta y}{\Delta x} = \frac{y_2 - y_1}{x_2 - x_1}$$

$$= \frac{(2) - (4)}{(4) - (-2)}$$

$$= \frac{2 - 4}{4 + 2} = \frac{-2}{6} = -\frac{1}{3} \quad Ans.$$

2. Through the point $(2, -1)$ draw a line whose slope is $\frac{3}{2}$.

How to Proceed   *Solution*

(1) Graph the point $A(2, -1)$.

(2) Since slope $= \dfrac{\Delta y}{\Delta x} = \dfrac{\to 3}{\to 2}$, when x

     changes 2, then y changes 3.

(3) Start at point $A(2, -1)$ and move 2 units to the right and 3 units upward to locate point B. Start at B and repeat these movements to locate point C.

(4) Draw a straight line which passes through points A, B, and C.

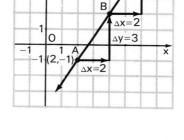

KEEP IN MIND

A fundamental property of a straight line is that its slope is constant. Therefore, any two points on a line may be used to compute the slope of the line.

EXERCISES

In 1-6: **a.** Tell whether the line has a positive slope, a negative slope, a slope of zero, or no slope. **b.** Find the slope of the line. If the line has no slope, indicate that fact.

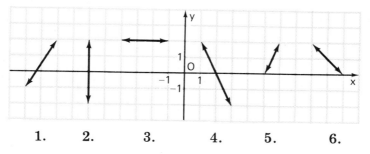

1.   2.   3.   4.   5.   6.

In 7-15, plot both points, draw the straight line that they determine, and find the slope of this line.

7. (0, 0) and (4, 4)   8. (0, 0) and (4, 8)   9. (0, 0) and (3, -6)
10. (1, 5) and (3, 9)   11. (7, 3) and (1, -1)   12. (-2, 4) and (0, 2)
13. (5, -2) and (7, -8)   14. (4, 2) and (8, 2)   15. (-1, 3) and (2, 3)

In 16-24, draw a line with the given slope, m, through the given point.

16. (0, 0); $m = 2$ 17. (1, 3); $m = 3$ 18. (2, -5); $m = 4$
19. (4, 6); $m = \frac{2}{3}$ 20. (-4, 5); $m = \frac{1}{2}$ 21. (-3, -4); $m = -2$
22. (1, -5); $m = -1$ 23. (2, 4); $m = -\frac{3}{2}$ 24. (-2, 3); $m = -\frac{1}{3}$

25. The points $A(2, 4)$, $B(8, 4)$, and $C(5, 1)$ are the vertices of triangle ABC. Find the slope of each side of triangle ABC.
26. The points $A(3, -2)$, $B(9, -2)$, $C(7, 4)$, and $D(1, 4)$ are the vertices of a quadrilateral.
   a. Graph the points and draw quadrilateral $ABCD$.
   b. What type of quadrilateral does $ABCD$ appear to be?
   c. Compute the slope of $\overline{BC}$ and the slope of $\overline{AD}$.
   d. What is true of the slope of $\overline{BC}$ and the slope of $\overline{AD}$?
   e. If two segments such as $\overline{AD}$ and $\overline{BC}$, or two lines such as $\overleftrightarrow{AD}$ and $\overleftrightarrow{BC}$, are parallel, what appears to be true of their slopes?
   f. Since $\overline{AB}$ and $\overline{CD}$ are parallel, what might be true of their slopes?
   g. Compute the slope of $\overline{AB}$ and the slope of $\overline{DC}$.
   h. Is the slope of $\overline{AB}$ equal to the slope of $\overline{DC}$?

6 THE SLOPE AND Y-INTERCEPT OF A LINE

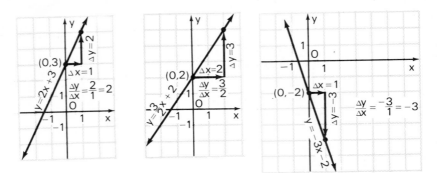

Figure 1   Figure 2   Figure 3

Each of the preceding figures shows the line that is the graph of the indicated equation. We can see that the slope of each line is the coefficient of the x-term in the equation and that the y-intercept of each line is the *constant* that follows the x-term in the equation.

	Equation	Slope $\left(\dfrac{\Delta y}{\Delta x}\right)$	y-intercept
In Fig. 1:	$y = 2x + 3$	2	3
In Fig. 2:	$y = \frac{3}{2}x + 2$	$\frac{3}{2}$	2
In Fig. 3:	$y = -3x - 2$	-3	-2

These examples illustrate the following general principle:

■ If a linear equation is expressed in the form $y = mx + b$, then the slope of the line is m, the coefficient of x; the y-intercept is b, the constant term.

The following general principle is also true:

■ The equation of the straight line whose slope is m and whose y-intercept is b can be written in the form $y = mx + b$.

Since the slope of a line describes the "slant" of a line, it is reasonable to believe that the following statements (which can be proved) are true:

1. If two lines are parallel, their slopes are equal.

2. If the slopes of two lines are equal, the lines are parallel.

What is the relationship between statement 1 and statement 2? If you said one statement is the converse of the other, you are right.

| MODEL PROBLEMS |

1. Find the slope and y-intercept of the line which is the graph of $4x + 2y = 10$.

How to Proceed	*Solution*
(1) Transform the equation into an equivalent equation of the form $y = mx + b$ by solving for y in terms of x.	$4x + 2y = 10$ $2y = -4x + 10$ $y = -2x + 5$
(2) m (the coefficient of x) is the slope.	slope $= -2$
(3) b (the constant term) is the y-intercept.	y-intercept $= 5$

Answer: slope $= -2$, y-intercept $= 5$

2. Write an equation of a line whose slope is $\frac{1}{2}$ and whose y-intercept is -4.

How to Proceed	*Solution*
(1) Write the equation $y = mx + b$.	$y = mx + b$
(2) Replace m by the numerical value of the slope; replace b by the numerical value of the y-intercept.	$m = $ slope $= \frac{1}{2}$ $b = y$-intercept $= -4$ $y = \frac{1}{2}x + (-4)$ *or* $y = \frac{1}{2}x - 4$

| EXERCISES |

In 1–15, find the slope and y-intercept of the line that is the graph of the equation.

1. $y = 3x + 1$
2. $y = x - 3$
3. $y = 2x$
4. $y = x$
5. $y = \frac{1}{2}x + 5$
6. $y = -2x + 3$
7. $y = -3x$
8. $y = -2$
9. $y = -\frac{2}{3}x + 4$
10. $y - 3x = 7$
11. $2x + y = 5$
12. $3y = 6x + 9$
13. $2y = 5x - 4$
14. $\frac{1}{2}x + \frac{3}{4} = \frac{1}{3}y$
15. $4x - 3y = 0$

In 16–23, write an equation of the line whose slope and y-intercept are respectively:

16. 2 and 7   **17.** 3 and -5 **18.** -1 and -3 **19.** -3 and 0

20. $\frac{2}{3}$ and 1   **21.** $\frac{1}{2}$ and 0   **22.** $-\frac{1}{3}$ and 2   **23.** $-\frac{3}{2}$ and 0

24. Write equations for three lines so that the slope of each line is 2.

25. Write equations for three lines so that the y-intercept of each line is -4.

26. What do the graphs of the lines described by the equations $y = 4x$, $y = 4x + 2$, and $y = 4x - 2$ all have in common?

27. How are the graphs of $y = mx + b$ affected when m is always replaced by the same number and b is replaced by different numbers?

28. What do the lines that are the graphs of the equations $y = 2x + 1$, $y = 3x + 1$, and $y = -4x + 1$ all have in common?

29. How are the graphs of $y = mx + b$ affected when b is always replaced by the same number and m is replaced by different numbers?

30. If two lines are parallel, what is the relation of their slopes?

31. What will be true of two lines whose slopes are equal?

In 32–35, state whether or not the lines are parallel.

32. $y = 3x + 2$, $y = 3x - 5$ **33.** $y = -2x - 6$, $y = 2x + 6$

34. $y = 4x - 8$, $y - 4x = 3$ **35.** $y = 2x$, $2y - 4x = 9$

36. Which of the following statements is true of the graph of the equation $y = -3x$?
(1) It is parallel to the x-axis.   (2) It is parallel to the y-axis.
(3) Its slope is -3.   (4) It does not have a y-intercept.

37. Which of the following statements is true of the graph of the equation $y = 8$?
(1) It is parallel to the x-axis.   (2) It is parallel to the y-axis.
(3) It has no slope.   (4) It passes through the origin.

7 GRAPHING A LINEAR EQUATION IN TWO VARIABLES BY THE SLOPE-INTERCEPT METHOD

The slope and y-intercept of a line can be used to draw the graph of a linear equation.

MODEL PROBLEM

Draw the graph of $2x + 3y = 9$ using the slope-intercept method.

How to Proceed	*Solution*
(1) Transform the equation into the form $y = mx + b$.	$2x + 3y = 9$ $3y = -2x + 9$ $y = \dfrac{-2}{3}x + 3$
(2) Find the slope of the line (the coefficient of x).	slope $= \dfrac{-2}{3}$
(3) Find the y-intercept of the line (the constant).	y-intercept $= 3$

(4) Graph a point A on the y-axis whose ordinate is the y-intercept.

(5) Use the slope to find two more points on the line. Since slope $= \dfrac{\Delta y}{\Delta x} = \dfrac{-2}{3}$,

when x changes 3, y changes -2. Start at point A and move 3 units to the right and 2 units down to locate point B. Start at point B and repeat this procedure to locate point C.

(6) Draw the line that passes through the three points.

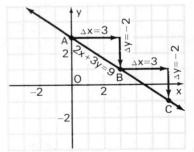

Note that this straight line is also the graph of $\{(x, y) | 2x + 3y = 9\}$.

EXERCISES

In 1–24, graph the equation using the slope and the y-intercept of each line (the slope-intercept method).

1. $y = 2x + 3$
2. $y = 2x - 5$
3. $y = 2x$
4. $y = x - 2$
5. $y = 2x - 2$
6. $y = 3x - 2$
7. $y = 3x$
8. $y = 5x$
9. $y = -2x$
10. $y = \frac{2}{3}x + 2$
11. $y = \frac{1}{2}x - 1$
12. $y = \frac{3}{2}x$

13. $y = \frac{1}{3}x$

14. $y = -\frac{4}{3}x + 5$

15. $y = -\frac{3}{4}x$

16. $y - 2x = 8$

17. $3x + y = 4$

18. $2y = 4x + 6$

19. $3y = 4x + 9$

20. $4x - y = 3$

21. $3x + 4y = 12$

22. $2x = 3y + 6$

23. $4x + 3y = 0$

24. $2x - 3y - 6 = 0$

8 WRITING AN EQUATION FOR A LINE

■ **PROCEDURE.** To write an equation for a line, determine its slope and y-intercept. Then use the slope-intercept formula: $y = mx + b$.

MODEL PROBLEMS

1. Write an equation of a line whose slope is 4 and which passes through the point $(3, 5)$.

How to Proceed	*Solution*
(1) In the equation of a line $y = mx + b$, replace m by the given slope, 4.	$y = mx + b$ $y = 4x + b$
(2) Since the given point $(3, 5)$ is on the line, its coordinates satisfy the equation $y = 4x + b$. Replace x by 3 and y by 5. Solve the resulting equation to find the value of b, the y-intercept.	$(5) = 4(3) + b$ $5 = 12 + b$ $-7 = b$
(3) In $y = 4x + b$, replace b by -7.	$y = 4x - 7$

Answer: $y = 4x - 7$

2. Write an equation of a line that passes through the points $(2, 5)$ and $(4, 11)$.

How to Proceed	*Solution*
(1) Find the slope of the line that passes through the two given points, $(2, 5)$ and $(4, 11)$.	Let P_1 be $(2, 5)$. $[x_1 = 2, y_1 = 5]$ Let P_2 be $(4, 11)$. $[x_2 = 4, y_2 = 11]$ $m = \dfrac{y_2 - y_1}{x_2 - x_1}$ $m = \dfrac{11 - 5}{4 - 2} = \dfrac{6}{2} = 3$

(2) In $y = mx + b$, replace m by the slope, 3.

$y = mx + b$
$y = 3x + b$

(3) Select one point that is on the line, for example $(2, 5)$. Its coordinates must satisfy the equation $y = 3x + b$. Replace x by 2 and y by 5. Solve the resulting equation to find the value of b, the y-intercept.

$(5) = 3(2) + b$
$5 = 6 + b$
$-1 = b$

(4) In $y = 3x + b$, replace b by -1.

$y = 3x - 1$

(5) Check whether the coordinates of the second point $(4, 11)$ satisfy the equation $y = 3x - 1$.

$11 \overset{?}{=} 3(4) - 1$
$11 = 11$ (True)

Answer: $y = 3x - 1$

EXERCISES

In 1–6, write an equation of the line that has the given slope, m, and which passes through the given point.

1. $m = 2$; $(1, 4)$ 2. $m = 2$; $(-3, 4)$ 3. $m = -3$; $(-2, -1)$

4. $m = \dfrac{1}{2}$; $(4, 2)$ 5. $m = \dfrac{-3}{4}$; $(0, 0)$ 6. $m = \dfrac{-5}{3}$; $(-3, 0)$

In 7–12, write an equation of the line that passes through the given points.

7. $(1, 4)$; $(3, 8)$ 8. $(3, 1)$; $(9, 7)$ 9. $(1, 2)$; $(10, 14)$
10. $(0, -1)$; $(6, 8)$ 11. $(-2, -5)$; $(-1, -2)$ 12. $(0, 0)$; $(-3, 5)$

13. Write an equation of the line that is:
    a. parallel to the line $y = 2x - 4$ and whose y-intercept is 7
    b. parallel to the line $y - 3x = 6$ and whose y-intercept is -2
    c. parallel to the line $2x + 3y = 12$ and which passes through the origin

14. Write an equation of the line that is:
    a. parallel to the line $y = 4x + 1$ and which passes through the point (2, 3)
    b. parallel to the line $2y - 6x = 9$ and which passes through the point (-2, 1)
    c. parallel to the line $y = 4x + 3$ and which has the same y-intercept as the line $y = 5x - 3$
    d. parallel to the line $y = -\frac{1}{2}x$ and which has the same y-intercept as the line $2y = 7x + 6$

15. A triangle is determined by three non-collinear points: $A(3, 5)$, $B(6, 4)$, and $C(1, -1)$. Write the equation of each line: (a) $\overleftrightarrow{AB}$; (b) $\overleftrightarrow{BC}$; (c) $\overleftrightarrow{CA}$.

9   GRAPHING A LINEAR INEQUALITY IN TWO VARIABLES

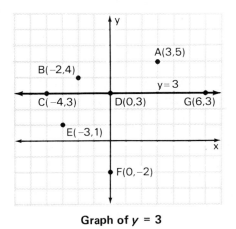

Graph of $y = 3$

We have learned that the graph of $y = 3$ is a line parallel to the x-axis. The y-coordinate of every point on this line is 3, that is, $y = 3$.

The line $y = 3$ is called a *plane divider* because it "divides" or "separates" the plane into two different regions called *half-planes*. One is a half-plane "above" the line; the other is a half-plane "below" the line. Notice that the set of points on the line is not a part of either region.

The Three Sets of Points Determined by the Line y = 3

The line $y = 3$ and the two half-planes that it forms determine three sets of points:

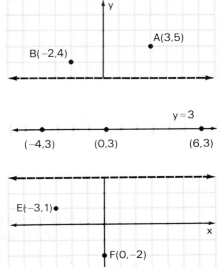

1. In the **half-plane "above"** the line $y = 3$, there is the set of all points whose y-coordinate is greater than 3, that is, $y > 3$. For example, at point A, $y = 5$; at point B, $y = 4$.

2. In the **line** itself, $y = 3$, there is the set of all points whose y-coordinate is equal to 3. For example, $y = 3$ at each of the points $(-4, 3)$, $(0, 3)$, $(6, 3)$.

3. In the **half-plane "below"** the line $y = 3$, there is the set of all points whose y-coordinate is less than 3, that is, $y < 3$. For example, at point E, $y = 1$; at point F, $y = -2$.

Notice that the three sets of points that we have just discussed can be "put together" to form the entire plane.

To graph an inequality in the coordinate plane, we can use the following procedure:

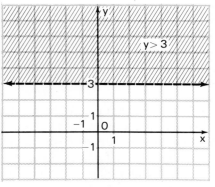

Graph of y > 3

1. On the plane, represent the plane divider, such as $y = 3$, by a *dashed line* to show that this divider does not belong to the graph of the half-plane.

2. *Shade the region* of the half-plane whose points satisfy the inequality. In the graph of $y > 3$, we shade the region above the plane divider. In the graph of $y < 3$, we shade the region below the plane divider.

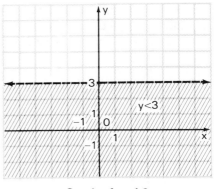

Graph of $y < 3$

Every straight line can be regarded as a plane divider, creating two half-planes. One of the half-planes will involve the inequality "greater than," while the other half-plane will involve the inequality "less than."

The line $y = 2x$ is the set of points in which each y-coordinate is equal to twice its x-coordinate. For example, $(1, 2)$, $(2, 4)$, $(3, 6)$, $(-2, -4)$, and so on are such points. Each of these points is on the line $y = 2x$.

Let us consider the following three situations:

1. When $x = 1$ and $y = 2$, we name a point $A(1, 2)$, which is on the line $y = 2x$, as is shown in the graph. Observe that the line $y = 2x$ can be considered as a plane divider that forms two half-planes, one "above" the line and one "below" the line.

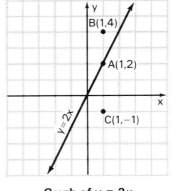

Graph of $y = 2x$

2. When $x = 1$ and y is any number "greater than" 2, we name a point in the half-plane $y > 2x$, which is above the plane divider. For example, point $B(1, 4)$ is such a point as is shown in the graph. Notice that at point $B(1, 4)$, $y > 2x$ because $(4) > 2(1)$.

3. When $x = 1$ and y is any number "less than" 2, we name a point in the half-plane $y < 2x$, which is below the plane divider. For example, point $C(1, -1)$ is such a point as is shown in the graph. Notice that at point $C(1, -1)$, $y < 2x$ because $(-1) < 2(1)$.

In graphing the inequality $y > 2x$ or $y < 2x$, we use a dashed line to indicate that the line $y = 2x$ is not a part of the graph. This dashed line acts as a "boundary line" for the half-plane being graphed.

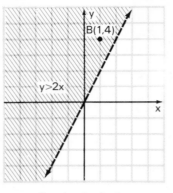

Graph of $y > 2x$

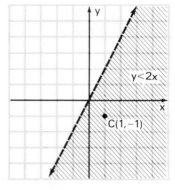

Graph of $y < 2x$

The graph of $y > 2x$ is the shaded half-plane "above" the line $y = 2x$. It is the set of all points in which the y-coordinate is *greater than* twice the x-coordinate.

The graph of $y < 2x$ is the shaded half-plane "below" the line $y = 2x$. It is the set of all points in which the y-coordinate is *less than* twice the x-coordinate.

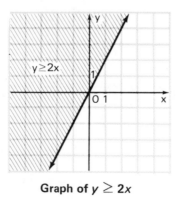

Graph of $y \geq 2x$

It is possible to graph a condition involving both inequality and equality, such as $y \geq 2x$. Since $y \geq 2x$ means $y > 2x$ or $y = 2x$, we can combine both sets of points into one graph by a *union* of the two disjoint sets of points. Notice that the line is now drawn as a "solid" line to indicate that $y = 2x$ is part of the graph of $y \geq 2x$. The region above $y = 2x$ is shaded to indicate that $y > 2x$ is part of the graph of $y \geq 2x$.

In general, the graph of $y = mx + b$ is a line that divides the coordinate plane into *three sets of points:*

1. The set of points on the line. Each ordered pair that describes a member of this set of points is a solution of $y = mx + b$. The line is the graph of the equation $y = mx + b$.

2. The set of points in the half-plane "above" the line. Each ordered pair that describes a member of this set of points is a solution of $y > mx + b$. The half-plane is the graph of the inequality $y > mx + b$.

3. The set of points in the half-plane "below" the line. Each ordered pair that describes a member of this set of points is a solution of $y < mx + b$. The half-plane is the graph of the inequality $y < mx + b$.

To check whether the correct half-plane has been chosen as the graph of a linear inequality, we select any point in that half-plane and find out whether it satisfies that inequality. If it does, we have chosen the correct half-plane. This is so because it is true that if one point in a half-plane satisfies an inequality, every point in that half-plane satisfies the inequality. On the other hand, if the point chosen does not satisfy the inequality, then the other half-plane is the graph of the inequality.

KEEP IN MIND

To graph $Ax + By + C > 0$ or $Ax + By + C < 0$, transform the inequality so that the left member is y alone: $y > rx + s$ or $y < rx + s$. This enables us first to graph the plane divider $y = rx + s$.

| MODEL PROBLEMS |

1. Graph the inequality $y - 2x \geq 2$.

How to Proceed	*Solution*
(1) Transform the sentence into one having y as the left member.	$y - 2x \geq 2$ $y \geq 2x + 2$
(2) Graph the resulting inequality by first graphing the plane divider, $y = 2x + 2$.	$y = 2x + 2$

$y = 2x + 2$

x	-1	0	1
y	0	2	4

(3) Shade the half-plane above the line. This region and the line are the required graph; the half-plane is the graph of $y - 2x > 2$; the line is the graph of $y - 2x = 2$. Note that the line is drawn solid to show that it is part of the graph.

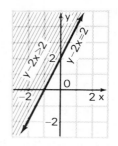

(4) Check the solution. Choose any point in the half-plane selected as the solution to see whether it satisfies the original inequality $y - 2x \geq 2$.

Select the point $(0, 5)$ that is in the shaded region.

$$y - 2x \geq 2$$
$$(5) - 2(0) \geq 2 \quad (?)$$
$$5 \geq 2 \quad (\text{True})$$

Note: The above graph is also the graph of $\{(x, y) | y - 2x \geq 2\}$.

2. Graph each of the following sentences in the coordinate plane:
   a. $x > 1$ b. $x \leq 1$ c. $y \geq 1$ d. $y < 1$

Solution

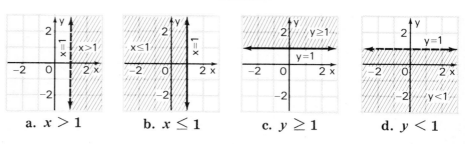

a. $x > 1$ b. $x \leq 1$ c. $y \geq 1$ d. $y < 1$

EXERCISES

In 1–6, transform the sentence into one whose left member is y.

1. $y - 2x > 0$ 2. $5x > 2y$ 3. $y - x \geq 3$
4. $2x + y \leq 0$ 5. $3x - y \geq 4$ 6. $4y - 3x \leq 12$

In 7–27, graph the sentence in the coordinate plane.

7. $x > 4$ 8. $x \leq -2$ 9. $y > 5$
10. $y \leq -3$ 11. $x \geq 6$ 12. $y \leq 0$

13. $y > 4x$ 14. $y \leq 3x$ 15. $y < x - 2$

16. $y \geq \frac{1}{2}x + 3$ 17. $x + y < 4$ 18. $x + y \geq 4$

19. $x + y \leq -3$ 20. $y - x \geq 5$ 21. $x - y \leq -1$

22. $x - 2y \leq 4$ 23. $2x + y - 4 \leq 0$ 24. $y - x + 6 > 0$

25. $2y - 6x > 0$ 26. $3x + 4y \leq 0$ 27. $2x - 3y \geq 6$

In 28–30, graph the indicated set.

28. $\{(x, y) | y \leq 3x\}$

29. $\{(x, y) | x + y \geq 4\}$

30. $\{(x, y) | x - 2y \leq 4\}$

In 31–33: **a.** Write the verbal sentence as an open sentence. **b.** Graph the open sentence in the coordinate plane.

31. The ordinate of a point is equal to or greater than 3 more than the abscissa.

32. The sum of the abscissa and ordinate of a point is less than or equal to 5.

33. The ordinate of a point decreased by three times the abscissa is greater than or equal to 2.

chapter nineteen

Systems of Linear Open Sentences in Two Variables

1 GRAPHIC SOLUTION OF A SYSTEM OF LINEAR EQUATIONS IN TWO VARIABLES

Consistent Equations

Consider the problem of finding two numbers whose sum is 4 and whose difference is 2. Let us see whether we have enough information to find the numbers.

Let x = the larger number. Let y = the smaller number.

Since the sum of the numbers is 4, we have the equation $x + y = 4$. Since the difference of the numbers is 2, we have the equation $x - y = 2$. Here, the two equations impose two conditions on the variables at the same time. We call the two equations a *system of simultaneous equations*.

A *solution* of a system of simultaneous equations in two variables is an ordered pair of numbers that satisfies both equations. The set of all solutions of the system is called the *solution set* of the system.

We have learned that the graph of a linear equation in two variables is a straight line. Let us graph both equations $x + y = 4$ and $x - y = 2$ in a coordinate plane, using the same set of axes. See the figure at the right. The coordinates of the point of intersection $(3, 1)$ satisfy the equations of both lines.

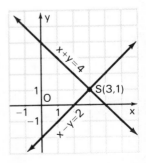

$x + y = 4$ [Let $x = 3$, $y = 1$.] $x - y = 2$ [Let $x = 3$, $y = 1$.]
$3 + 1 \overset{?}{=} 4$ $3 - 1 \overset{?}{=} 2$
$\quad\quad 4 = 4$ (True) $\quad\quad 2 = 2$ (True)

There is no other ordered pair that satisfies both equations because there is no point other than the point $(3, 1)$ that lies on both graphs. Hence, the ordered pair $(3, 1)$ is the solution of the system. We write $\{(3, 1)\}$ as the solution set of the system.

Therefore, the larger number is 3 and the smaller number is 1.

When a pair of straight lines is graphed in the same coordinate plane on the same set of axes, one and only one of the following three possibilities can occur. The pair of lines will:

1. intersect in one point and will have one ordered number pair in common;

2. be parallel and will have no ordered number pairs in common;

3. coincide, that is they will turn out to be the same line with an infinite number of ordered number pairs in common.

If a system of linear equations such as $x + y = 4$ and $x - y = 2$ has one common solution, it is called a *system of consistent equations*.

Inconsistent Equations

Sometimes, when two linear equations are graphed in a coordinate plane using the same set of axes, the lines are parallel and fail to intersect. This happens in the case of $x + y = 2$ and $x + y = 4$. There is no common solution for the system of equations $x + y = 2$ and $x + y = 4$. It is obvious that there can be no ordered number pair (x, y) such that the sum of those numbers, $x + y$, is both 2 and 4. Since the solution set of the system has no members, it is the empty set $\emptyset$.

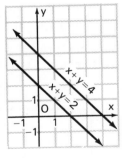

If a system of linear equations such as $x + y = 2$ and $x + y = 4$ has no common solution, it is called a *system of inconsistent equations*. The graphs of two inconsistent linear equations are straight lines that have equal slopes or straight lines that have no slopes. Such straight lines will be parallel.

Dependent Equations

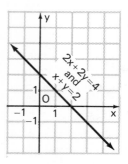

Sometimes, when two linear equations are graphed in a coordinate plane using the same set of axes, they turn out to be the same line; that is, they coincide. This happens in the case of $x + y = 2$ and $2x + 2y = 4$. Every one of the infinite number of solutions of $x + y = 2$ is also a solution of $2x + 2y = 4$. We see that $2x + 2y = 4$ and $x + y = 2$ are equivalent equations with identical solutions. Note that when both members of the equation $2x + 2y = 4$ are divided by 2, the result is $x + y = 2$.

If a system of two linear equations, for example $x + y = 2$ and $2x + 2y = 4$, is such that every solution of either one of the equations is also a solution of the other, it is called a *system of dependent equations*. The graphs of two dependent linear equations are the very same straight line.

■ **PROCEDURE.**   To solve a pair of linear equations graphically:

1. Graph one equation in a coordinate plane.

2. Graph the other equation in the same coordinate plane using the same set of coordinate axes.

3. Find the common solution that is the ordered number pair associated with the point of intersection of the two graphs.

4. Check the apparent solution by verifying that the ordered pair satisfies both equations.

KEEP IN MIND

The solution set of a system of two linear equations is the intersection of the solution sets of the individual equations.

| MODEL PROBLEM |

Solve graphically and check: $2x + y = 8$
$$y - x = 2$$

Solution:

(1) Graph $2x + y = 8$, or $y = -2x + 8$.

x	$-2x + 8 = y$
1	$-2(1) + 8 = 6$
3	$-2(3) + 8 = 2$
4	$-2(4) + 8 = 0$

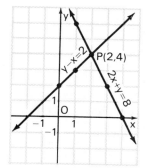

(2) Graph $y - x = 2$, or $y = x + 2$.

x	$x + 2 = y$
0	$0 + 2 = 2$
1	$1 + 2 = 3$
2	$2 + 2 = 4$

(3) Read the coordinates of the point of intersection $P(2, 4)$.

(4) *Check:* $(x = 2, y = 4)$

$$2x + y = 8 \qquad\qquad y - x = 2$$
$$2(2) + 4 \overset{?}{=} 8 \qquad\qquad 4 - 2 \overset{?}{=} 2$$
$$8 = 8 \quad \text{(True)} \qquad\qquad 2 = 2 \quad \text{(True)}$$

Answer: The common solution is $(2, 4)$. The solution set is $\{(2, 4)\}$.

| EXERCISES |

In 1–30, solve the systems of equations graphically. Check.

1. $y = 2x$
   $y = 3x - 3$

2. $y = x + 4$
   $y = 2x + 5$

3. $y = -2x + 3$
   $y = \frac{1}{2}x + 3$

4. $x + y = 7$
   $x - y = 1$

5. $x + y = 4$
   $x - y = 0$

6. $x + y = -4$
   $x - y = 6$

7. $x + y = 1$
   $x + 3y = 9$

8. $y = 2x + 1$
   $x + 2y = 7$

9. $x - y = 4$
   $x + 2y = 10$

10. $x + 2y = 17$
    $y = 2x + 1$

11. $y = 3x$
    $2x + y = 10$

12. $x + 3y = 9$
    $x = 3$

13. $y - x = -2$
    $x - 2y = 4$

14. $3x + y = 6$
    $y = 3$

15. $4x - y = 9$
    $2x + y = 12$

16. $y = 2x + 4$
    $x = y - 5$

17. $x + y = 3$
    $2x - y = -9$

18. $y - 3x = 12$
    $y = -3$

19. $2x - y = -1$
    $x = y + 1$

20. $3x + y = -9$
    $x + 3y = -11$

21. $x = 3$
    $y = 4$

22. $y = \frac{1}{3}x - 3$
    $2x - y = 8$

23. $3x + y = 13$
    $x + 6y = -7$

24. $x = 0$
    $y = -5$

25. $2x = y + 9$
    $6x + 3y = 15$

26. $5x - 3y = 9$
    $5y = 13 - x$

27. $x = 0$
    $y = 0$

28. $x + y + 2 = 0$
    $x = y - 8$

29. $y + 2x + 6 = 0$
    $y = 2x$

30. $7x - 4y + 7 = 0$
    $3x - 5y + 3 = 0$

In 31–36, graph both equations. Determine whether the system is consistent, inconsistent, or dependent.

31. $x + y = 1$
    $x + y = 3$

32. $x + y = 5$
    $2x + 2y = 10$

33. $y = 2x + 1$
    $y = 3x + 3$

34. $2x - y = 1$
    $2y = 4x - 2$

35. $y - 3x = 2$
    $y = 3x - 2$

36. $x + 4y = 6$
    $x = 2$

37. Are there any ordered number pairs that satisfy both equations $2x + y = 7$ and $2x = 5 - y$?

38. Are there any ordered number pairs that satisfy the equation $y - x = 4$ but which do not satisfy the equation $2y = 8 + 2x$?

In 39–42: a. Write a system of two first-degree equations involving the two variables x and y that represent the conditions stated in the problem. b. Solve the system graphically.

39. The sum of two numbers is 8. Their difference is 2. Find the numbers.

40. The sum of two numbers is 3. The larger number is 5 more than the smaller number. Find the numbers.

41. The perimeter of a rectangle is 12 meters. Its length is twice its width. Find the dimensions of the rectangle.

42. The perimeter of a rectangle is 14 centimeters. Its length is 3 centimeters more than its width. Find the dimensions of the rectangle.

2 ALGEBRAIC SOLUTION OF A SYSTEM OF SIMULTANEOUS LINEAR EQUATIONS BY USING ADDITION OR SUBTRACTION

We will now learn algebraic methods for solving a system of linear equations in two variables. Solutions by these methods usually take less time and lead to more accurate results than the graphic method previously used.

Systems of equations that have the same solution set are called *equivalent systems*. For example, the following two systems are equivalent systems since they have the same solution set $\{(3, 1)\}$.

<table>
<tr><td>*System A*</td><td>*System B*</td></tr>
<tr><td>$x + y = 4$</td><td>$x = 3$</td></tr>
<tr><td>$x - y = 2$</td><td>$y = 1$</td></tr>
</table>

To solve a system of linear equations such as system A, whose solution set is not obvious, we transform it into an equivalent system such as system B, whose solution set is obvious. To do this we make use of the properties of equality.

| MODEL PROBLEMS |

1. Solve the system of equations and check: $x + 3y = 13$
$$x + y = 5$$

How to Proceed	*Solution*
(1) The coefficients of the variable x are the same in both equations. Therefore, subtracting the members of equation $[B]$ from the corresponding members of equation $[A]$ will eliminate the variable x and will result in an equation that involves one variable, y.	$\begin{aligned} x + 3y &= 13 \ [A] \\ \underline{x + \ y = \ 5} \ [B] \\ 2y &= \ 8 \end{aligned}$
(2) Solve the resulting equation for the variable, y.	$y = 4$
(3) Replace y by its value in any equation involving both variables.	$\begin{aligned} x + y &= 5 \ [B] \\ x + 4 &= 5 \end{aligned}$
(4) Solve the resulting equation for the remaining variable, x.	$x = 1$

(5) *Check:* Substitute 1 for x and 4 for y in each of the given equations to verify that the resulting sentences are true.

$$x + 3y = 13 \qquad\qquad x + y = 5$$
$$1 + 3(4) \overset{?}{=} 13 \qquad\qquad 1 + 4 \overset{?}{=} 5$$
$$13 = 13 \quad \text{(True)} \qquad\qquad 5 = 5 \quad \text{(True)}$$

Answer: Since $x = 1$ and $y = 4$, the solution is $(1, 4)$, or solution set is $\{(1, 4)\}$.

2. Solve the system of equations and check: $5a + b = 13$
$$4a - 3b = 18$$

How to Proceed	*Solution*
(1) Multiply both members of equation [A] by 3. This yields an equivalent equation [C] in which the coefficient of b has the same absolute value as the coefficient of b in equation [B].	$5a + b = 13$ [A] $4a - 3b = 18$ [B] $\underline{15a + 3b = 39}$ [C]
(2) Add the corresponding members of equations [B] and [C] to eliminate the variable b.	$19a = 57$
(3) Solve the resulting equation for the variable a.	$a = 3$
(4) Replace a by its value in any equation involving both variables.	$5a + b = 13$ [A] $5(3) + b = 13$
(5) Solve the resulting equation for the remaining variable, b.	$15 + b = 13$ $b = -2$

(6) *Check:* Substitute 3 for a and -2 for b in each of the given equations to verify that the resulting sentences are true. This is left to the student.

Answer: $a = 3$ and $b = -2$, or $(a, b) = (3, -2)$.

3. Solve the system of equations and check: $7x = 5 - 2y$
$$3y = 16 - 2x$$

How to Proceed	*Solution*
(1) Transform each of the given equations [A] and [B] into equivalent equations [C] and [D] in which the terms contain-	$7x = 5 - 2y$ [A] $3y = 16 - 2x$ [B] $7x + 2y = 5$ [C] $2x + 3y = 16$ [D]

ing the variables appear on one side and the constant appears on the other side.

(2) To eliminate y, multiply both members of equation $[C]$ by 3; multiply both members of equation $[D]$ by 2. In the resulting equivalent equations $[E]$ and $[F]$, the absolute values of the coefficients of y are equal.

$$21x + 6y = 15 \qquad [E]$$
$$\underline{4x + 6y = 32} \qquad [F]$$

(3) Subtract the members of equation $[F]$ from the corresponding members of equation $[E]$ to eliminate the variable y.

$$17x \qquad = -17$$

(4) Solve the resulting equation for the variable x.

$$x = -1$$

(5) Replace x by its value in any equation containing both variables.

$$3y = 16 - 2x \quad [B]$$
$$3y = 16 - 2(-1)$$

(6) Solve the resulting equation for the remaining variable y.

$$3y = 16 + 2$$
$$3y = 18$$
$$y = 6$$

(7) *Check:* Substitute -1 for x and 6 for y in each of the given equations to verify that the resulting sentences are true. This is left to the student.

Answer: Since $x = -1$ and $y = 6$, the solution is $(-1, 6)$, or solution set is $\{(-1, 6)\}$.

EXERCISES

In 1 and 2, state which of the given ordered pairs is the solution of the system of equations.

1. $x + y = 5$
   $x - y = -1$

   $(2, 3)$ $(2, -3)$ $(3, -2)$ $(3, 2)$

2. $6x + 2y = 14$
   $3x + 2y = 8$

   $(1, 2)$ $(1, 4)$ $(2, 1)$ $(4, -2)$

In 3–47, solve each system of equations by eliminating one of the variables, using addition or subtraction. Check.

3. $x + y = 12$
    $x - y = 4$

4. $a + b = 13$
    $a - b = 5$

5. $r + s = -6$
    $r - s = -10$

6. $3x + y = 16$
    $2x + y = 11$

7. $c - 2d = 14$
    $c + 3d = 9$

8. $x + y = 10$
    $x - y = 0$

9. $a - 4b = -8$
    $a - 2b = 0$

10. $x + 2y = 8$
    $x - 2y = 4$

11. $8a + 5b = 9$
    $2a - 5b = -4$

12. $4x + 5y = 23$
    $4x - y = 5$

13. $-2m + 4n = 13$
    $6m + 4n = 9$

14. $3a - b = 3$
    $a + 3b = 11$

15. $3r + s = 6$
    $r + 3s = 10$

16. $4x - y = 10$
    $2x + 3y = 12$

17. $5m + 3n = 14$
    $2m + n = 6$

18. $2c - d = -1$
    $c + 3d = 17$

19. $2m + n = 12$
    $m + 2n = 9$

20. $r - 3s = -11$
    $3r + s = 17$

21. $a + 3b = 4$
    $2a - b = 1$

22. $3x + 4y = 26$
    $x - 3y = 0$

23. $5x + 8y = 1$
    $3x + 4y = -1$

24. $x - y = -1$
    $3x - 2y = 3$

25. $5a - 2b = 3$
    $2a - b = 0$

26. $5x - 2y = 20$
    $2x + 3y = 27$

27. $2x - y = 26$
    $3x - 2y = 42$

28. $2x + 3y = 6$
    $3x + 5y = 15$

29. $5r - 2s = 8$
    $3r - 7s = -1$

30. $3x + 7y = -2$
    $2x + 3y = -3$

31. $4x + 3y = -1$
    $5x + 4y = 1$

32. $4a - 6b = 15$
    $6a - 4b = 10$

33. $5y + x = -8$
    $x = 7$

34. $x + y = 4$
    $y = x$

35. $2x + y = 17$
    $5x = 25 + y$

36. $5r + 3s = 30$
    $2r = 12 - 3s$

37. $6r = s$
    $5r = 2s - 14$

38. $3a - 7 = 7b$
    $4a = 3b + 22$

39. $3x - 4y = 2$
    $x = 2(7 - y)$

40. $3x + 5(y + 2) = 1$
    $8y = -3x$

41. $\frac{1}{3}x + \frac{1}{4}y = 10$
    $\frac{1}{3}x - \frac{1}{2}y = 4$

42. $\frac{1}{2}a + \frac{1}{3}b = 8$
    $\frac{3}{2}a - \frac{4}{3}b = -4$

43. $c - 2d = 1$
    $\frac{2}{3}c + 5d = 26$

44. $2a = 3b$
    $\frac{2}{3}a - \frac{1}{2}b = 2$

45. $.04x + .06y = 26$
    $x + y = 500$

46. $.03x + .05y = 17$
    $x + y = 400$

47. $.03x = .06y + 9$
    $x + y = 600$

3 ALGEBRAIC SOLUTION OF A SYSTEM OF SIMULTANEOUS LINEAR EQUATIONS BY USING SUBSTITUTION

Another algebraic method, called the *substitution method*, can be used to eliminate one of the variables when solving a system of equations. When we use this method, we apply the substitution principle to transform one of the equations of the system into an equivalent equation that involves only one variable.

MODEL PROBLEMS

1. Solve the system of equations and check: $4x + 3y = 27$
   $$y = 2x - 1$$

How to Proceed	*Solution*

(1) In equation [B], both y and $2x - 1$ name the same number when the values of the common solution replace x and y. Therefore, eliminate y in equation [A] by replacing y with $2x - 1$.

$$4x + 3y = 27 \quad [A]$$
$$y = 2x - 1 \quad [B]$$
$$4x + 3(2x - 1) = 27$$

(2) Solve the resulting equation for x.

$$4x + 6x - 3 = 27$$
$$10x - 3 = 27$$
$$10x = 30$$
$$x = 3$$

(3) Replace x with its value in any equation involving both variables.

$$y = 2x - 1 \quad [B]$$
$$y = 2(3) - 1$$

(4) Solve the resulting equation for y.

$$y = 6 - 1$$
$$y = 5$$

(5) *Check:* Substitute 3 for x and 5 for y in each of the given equations to verify that the resulting sentences are true.

$$4x + 3y = 27$$
$$4(3) + 3(5) \stackrel{?}{=} 27$$
$$12 + 15 \stackrel{?}{=} 27$$
$$27 = 27 \quad \text{(True)}$$

$$y = 2x - 1$$
$$5 \stackrel{?}{=} 2(3) - 1$$
$$5 \stackrel{?}{=} 6 - 1$$
$$5 = 5 \quad \text{(True)}$$

Answer: Since $x = 3$ and $y = 5$, the solution is $(3, 5)$, or solution set is $\{(3, 5)\}$.

2. Solve the system of equations and check: $3x - 4y = 26$
   $x + 2y = 2$

How to Proceed	*Solution*
(1) Transform one of the equations [B] into an equivalent equation [C] in which one of the variables is expressed in terms of the other. In equation [B], solve for x in terms of y.	$3x - 4y = 26$ [A] $x + 2y = 2$ [B] $x = 2 - 2y$ [C]
(2) Eliminate x in equation [A] by replacing it with $2 - 2y$, the expression for x in equation [C].	$3(2 - 2y) - 4y = 26$
(3) Solve the resulting equation for y.	$6 - 6y - 4y = 26$ $6 - 10y = 26$ $-10y = 20$ $y = -2$
(4) Replace y by its value in any equation involving both variables.	$x = 2 - 2y$ [C] $x = 2 - 2(-2)$
(5) Solve the resulting equation for x.	$x = 2 + 4$ $x = 6$

(6) *Check:* Substitute 6 for x and -2 for y in each of the given equations to verify that the resulting sentences are true. This is left to the student.

Answer: Since $x = 6$ and $y = -2$, the solution is $(6, -2)$, or solution set is $\{(6, -2)\}$.

| EXERCISES |

In 1–18, solve each system of equations by eliminating one of the variables by the substitution method. Check.

1. $y = x$
   $x + y = 14$

2. $x = y$
   $5x - 4y = -2$

3. $y = 2x$
   $x + y = 21$

4. $x = 4y$
   $2x + 3y = 22$

5. $a = -2b$
   $5a - 3b = 13$

6. $r = -3s$
   $3r + 4s = -10$

7. $y = x + 1$
   $x + y = 9$

8. $x = y - 2$
   $x + y = 18$

9. $y = x + 3$
   $3x + 2y = 26$

10. $y = 2x + 1$
    $x + y = 7$

11. $a = 3b + 1$
    $5b - 2a = 1$

12. $a + b = 11$
    $3a - 2b = 8$

13. $3m - 2n = 11$
    $m + 2n = 9$

14. $a - 2b = -2$
    $2a - b = 5$

15. $7x - 3y = 23$
    $x + 2y = 13$

16. $2x = 3y$
    $4x - 3y = 12$

17. $4y = -3x$
    $5x + 8y = 4$

18. $2x + 3y = 7$
    $4x - 5y = 25$

4 SOLVING VERBAL PROBLEMS BY USING TWO VARIABLES

We have previously learned how to solve word problems using one variable. Frequently a problem can be solved more easily by using two variables rather than one variable. See how this is done in the solutions of the problems that follow.

■ **PROCEDURE.** To solve word problems by using a system of two equations involving two variables:

1. Use two different variables to represent the different unknown quantities in the problem.

2. Translate two given relationships in the problem into a system of two equations.

3. Solve the system of equations to determine the answer(s) to the problem.

4. Check the answer(s) in the original word problem.

Number Problems

The sum of two numbers is 10. Three times the larger decreased by twice the smaller is 15. Find the numbers.

How to Proceed   *Solution*

(1) Represent the two different unknown quantities by two different variables.

Let x = the larger number.
Let y = the smaller number.

(2) Translate two given relationships in the problem into a system of two equations.

The sum of two numbers is 10.
$$x + y = 10 \quad [A]$$

Three times the larger decreased by twice the smaller is 15.
$$3x - 2y = 15 \quad [B]$$

(3) Solve the system of equations. In equation [A], multiply both members by 2. Then add the members of the resulting equation to the corresponding members of equation [B].

$$x + y = 10 \ [A]$$
$$3x - 2y = 15 \ [B]$$
$$\underline{2x + 2y = 20}$$
$$5x \qquad = 35$$

(4) Solve the resulting equation for x.

$$x = 7$$

(5) Replace x with its value in any equation involving both variables.

$$x + y = 10 \ [A]$$
$$7 + y = 10$$

(6) Solve the resulting equation for y.

$$y = 3$$

Check: The sum of the larger number 7 and the smaller number 3 is 10. Three times the larger decreased by twice the smaller, $(3 \cdot 7) - (2 \cdot 3)$, equals $21 - 6$, or 15.

Answer: The larger number is 7; the smaller number is 3.

| EXERCISES |

In 1–7, solve the problem algebraically, using two variables.

1. The sum of two numbers is 36. Their difference is 24. Find the numbers.
2. The sum of two numbers is 77. The larger number is 3 more than the smaller number. Find the numbers.
3. The sum of two numbers is 104. The larger number is 1 less than twice the smaller number. Find the numbers.
4. The difference between two numbers is 34. The larger exceeds 3 times the smaller by 4. Find the numbers.
5. If 5 times the smaller of two numbers is subtracted from twice the larger, the result is 16. If the larger is increased by 3 times the smaller, the result is 63. Find the numbers.
6. One number is 15 larger than another. The sum of twice the larger and three times the smaller is 180. Find the numbers.
7. The sum of two numbers is 900. When 4% of the larger is added to 7% of the smaller, the sum is 48. Find the numbers.

Business Problems

The owner of a men's clothing store bought 6 shirts and 8 hats for $140. A week later, at the same prices, he bought 9 shirts and 6 hats for $132. Find the price of a shirt and the price of a hat.

Solution: Let s = the price of a shirt in dollars.
Let h = the price of a hat in dollars.

6 shirts and 8 hats   cost $140.

$$6s + 8h = 140 \quad [A]$$

9 shirts and 6 hats   cost $132.

$$9s + 6h = 132 \quad [B]$$

(1) In order to eliminate h, multiply both members of equation $[B]$ by 4 and both members of equation $[A]$ by 3. Then subtract the equations and solve for s.

$$
\begin{aligned}
36s + 24h &= 528 \\
\underline{18s + 24h} &= \underline{420} \\
18s &= 108 \\
s &= 6
\end{aligned}
$$

(2) In equation $[A]$ substitute 6 for s.

$$
\begin{aligned}
36 + 8h &= 140 \\
8h &= 104 \\
h &= 13
\end{aligned}
$$

Check: 6 shirts and 8 hats cost 6($6) + 8($13) = $36 + $104 = $140.
        9 shirts and 6 hats cost 9($6) + 6($13) = $54 + $78 = $132.

Answer: A shirt costs $6; a hat costs $13.

EXERCISES

In 1–5, solve the problem algebraically, using two variables.

1. At a quick-lunch counter 3 hot dogs and 1 can of soda cost $2.75. Two hot dogs and 1 can of soda cost $2.00. Find the cost of a hot dog and the cost of a can of soda.
2. On one day 4 plumbers and 4 helpers earned $360. On another day, working the same number of hours and at the same rate of pay, 5 plumbers and 6 helpers earned $480. How much does a plumber and how much does a helper earn each day?

3. A baseball manager bought 4 bats and 9 balls for $76.50. On another day he bought 3 bats and 1 dozen balls at the same prices and paid $81.00. How much did he pay for each bat and each ball?
4. Mrs. Black bought 2 pounds of salmon and 3 pounds of cod in a fish market for which she paid $20.00. Mrs. Cook, paying the same prices, paid $11.25 for 1 pound of salmon and 2 pounds of cod. Find the price of a pound of salmon and the price of a pound of cod.
5. One day Mrs. Rubero paid $18.70 for 4 kilograms of walnuts and 3 kilograms of pecans. On another day Mrs. Rubero paid $13.30 for 3 kilograms of walnuts and 2 kilograms of pecans. If the prices were the same on each day, find the price per kilogram for each type of nut.

Geometry Problems

To solve the following geometric problems, you should make use of the facts and relationships that we have studied previously.

In 1-7, solve the problem algebraically, using two variables.

1. The perimeter of a rectangle is 50 cm. The length is 9 cm more than the width. Find the length and the width of the rectangle.
2. A rectangle has a perimeter of 38 ft. The length is 1 ft. less than 3 times the width. Find the dimensions of the rectangle.
3. Two angles are supplementary. The larger angle measures 120° more than the smaller angle. Find the measure of each angle.
4. Two angles are supplementary. The larger angle measures 15° less than twice the smaller angle. Find the measure of each angle.
5. Two angles are complementary. The measure of the larger angle is 30° more than the measure of the smaller angle. Find the measure of each angle.
6. The larger of two complementary angles measures 6° less than twice the smaller angle. Find the measure of each angle.
7. In an isosceles triangle each base angle measures 30° more than the vertex angle. Find the measures of the angles of the triangle.

Miscellaneous Problems

In 1-10, solve the problem algebraically, using two variables.

1. Tickets for a high school dance cost $1.00 each if purchased in advance of the dance, but $1.50 each if bought at the door. If 100 tickets were sold and $120 was collected, how many tickets were sold in advance and how many were sold at the door?

2. A dealer sold 200 tennis racquets. Some were sold at $18 each and the rest were sold at $33 each. The total receipts from these sales were $4800. How many racquets did he sell at $18 each?

3. Mrs. Rinaldo changed a $100 bill in a bank. She received $20 bills and $10 bills. The number of $20 bills was two more than the number of $10 bills. How many bills of each kind did she receive?

4. Linda spent $1.80 for stamps. Some were 15-cent stamps and the rest were 10-cent stamps. The number of 10-cent stamps was 2 less than the number of 15-cent stamps. How many stamps of each kind did Linda buy?

5. A dealer has some hard candy worth $2.00 a kilogram and some worth $3.00 a kilogram. He wishes to make a mixture of 80 kilograms that he can sell for $2.20 a kilogram. How many kilograms of each kind should he use?

6. At the Savemore Supermarket 3 pounds of apples and 2 pounds of grapes cost $2.85. The cost of 4 pounds of apples and 5 pounds of grapes is $5.41. What is the cost of 1 pound of apples and what is the cost of 1 pound of grapes.

7. One year Roger Jackson and his wife Wilma together earned $47,000. If Roger earned $4000 more than Wilma earned that year, how much did each earn?

8. Mrs. Moto invested $1400, part at 5% and part at 8%. Her total annual income from both investments was $100. Find the amount she invested at each rate.

9. Mr. Stein invested a sum of money in bonds yielding 4% a year and another sum in bonds yielding 6% a year. In all he invested $4000. If his total annual income from the two investments was $188, how much did he invest at each rate?

10. Mr. May invested $21,000, part at 8% and the rest at 6%. If the annual incomes from both investments were equal, find the amount invested at each rate.

5 GRAPHING SOLUTION SETS OF SYSTEMS OF INEQUALITIES

In order to find the solution set of a system of inequalities, we must find the ordered pairs that satisfy all the open sentences of the system. We do this by a graphic method that is similar to the method used in finding the solution set of a system of equations.

MODEL PROBLEMS

1. Graph the solution set of the system: $x > 2$
                                            $y < -2$

   Solution:

   (1) Graph $x > 2$ by first graphing the plane divider $x = 2$. (In the figure, see the dashed line labeled l.) The half-plane to the right of this line is the graph of the solution set of $x > 2$.

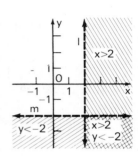

   (2) Using the same set of axes, graph $y < -2$ by first graphing the plane divider $y = -2$. (In the figure, see the dashed line labeled m.) The half-plane below this line is the graph of the solution set of $y < -2$.

   (3) The solution set of the system $x > 2$ and $y < -2$ consists of the intersection of the solution sets of $x > 2$ and $y < -2$. Therefore, the crosshatched region, which is the intersection of both graphs made in steps 1 and 2, is the graph of the solution set of the system $x > 2$ and $y < -2$. All points in this region, and no others, satisfy both sentences of the system. For example, the point $(4, -3)$, which lies in the region, satisfies both sentences of the system because its x-value $4 > 2$, and its y-value $-3 < -2$.

2. Graph the solution set of $3 < x < 5$ in a Cartesian coordinate plane.

   Solution:

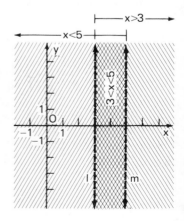

   (1) The sentence $3 < x < 5$ means $3 < x$ and $x < 5$. This may be written $x > 3$ and $x < 5$. Therefore, graph $x > 3$ by first graphing the plane divider $x = 3$. (In the figure, see the dashed line labeled l.) The half-plane to the right of the line $x = 3$ is the graph of the solution set of $x > 3$.

(2) Using the same set of axes, graph $x < 5$ by first graphing the plane divider $x = 5$. (In the figure, see the dashed line labeled m.) The half-plane to the left of the line $x = 5$ is the graph of the solution set of $x < 5$.

(3) The crosshatched region, which is the intersection of the graphs made in steps 1 and 2, is the graph of the solution set of $x > 3$ and $x < 5$, or $3 < x < 5$. All points in this region, and no others, satisfy $3 < x < 5$. For example, the point $(4, 3)$, which lies in the region and whose x-value is 4, satisfies $3 < x < 5$ because $3 < 4 < 5$ is a true statement.

3. Graph the following system of inequalities and label the solution set T.

$$x + y \geq 4$$
$$y \leq 2x - 3$$

Solution:

(1) Graph $x + y \geq 4$ by first graphing the plane divider $x + y = 4$. (In the figure, see the solid line labeled l.) The line $x + y = 4$ and the half-plane above this line together form the graph of the solution set of $x + y \geq 4$.

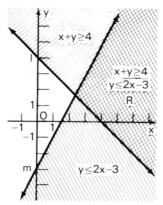

(2) Using the same set of axes, graph $y \leq 2x - 3$ by first graphing the plane divider $y = 2x - 3$. (In the figure, see the solid line labeled m.) The line $y = 2x - 3$ and the half-plane below this line together form the graph of the solution set of $y \leq 2x - 3$.

(3) The crosshatched region labeled R, the intersection of both graphs made in steps 1 and 2, is the graph of the solution set of the system $x + y \geq 4$ and $y \leq 2x - 3$. Any point in the region R such as $(5, 2)$ will satisfy $x + y \geq 4$ because $5 + 2 \geq 4$, or $7 \geq 4$, is true, and will also satisfy $y \leq 2x - 3$ because $2 \leq 2(5) - 3$, or $2 \leq 7$ is true.

| EXERCISES |

In 1–24, graph the system of inequalities and label the solution set S.

1. $x \geq 1$
   $y > -2$

2. $x < 2$
   $y \geq 3$

3. $x > 0$
   $y > 0$

4. $x < 0$
   $y > 0$

5. $y \geq x$
   $x < 2$

6. $y \leq x$
   $x \geq -1$

7. $y \geq 1$
   $y < x - 1$

8. $y \leq 5$
   $y < x + 3$

9. $y > x$
   $y < 2x + 3$

10. $y \geq 2x$
    $y > x + 3$

11. $y \leq 2x + 3$
    $y \geq -x$

12. $y - x \geq 5$
    $y - 2x \leq 7$

13. $y > x - 3$
    $y > -x + 5$

14. $y \geq -2x + 4$
    $y < x - 5$

15. $y < -x + 7$
    $y \geq 2x + 1$

16. $y < x - 1$
    $x + y \geq 2$

17. $x + y \leq 8$
    $y > x - 4$

18. $y + 3x \geq 6$
    $y < 2x - 4$

19. $x + y > 3$
    $x - y < 6$

20. $x - y \leq -2$
    $x + y \geq 2$

21. $2x + y \leq 6$
    $x + y - 2 > 0$

22. $2x + 3y \geq 6$
    $x + y - 4 \leq 0$

23. $y \geq x$
    $x = 0$

24. $x + y \leq 3$
    $y - 2x = 0$

In 25–28, graph the solution set in a coordinate plane.

25. $1 < x < 4$

26. $-5 \leq x \leq -1$

27. $2 < y \leq 6$

28. $-2 \leq y \leq 3$

chapter twenty

The Real Numbers

1 THE SET OF RATIONAL NUMBERS

The numbers with which you are familiar consist of positive and negative integers, fractions, and zero. Examples of these numbers are 5, -3, $\frac{7}{4}$, $\frac{-5}{4}$, and 0. Each of these numbers can be expressed in the form $y = \frac{a}{b}$ where a and b are integers and $b \neq 0$. Numbers which can be expressed in this form are called *rational numbers*.

Remember that 5 may be expressed as $\frac{5}{1}$, -3 as $\frac{-3}{1}$, and 0 as $\frac{0}{1}$. In fact, every integer n is a rational number because $n = \frac{n}{1}$, which is a quotient of two integers.

Properties of the Set of Rational Numbers

The set of rational numbers has all the addition and multiplication properties of the set of integers. This set also has additional properties.

■ **PROPERTY 1.** The set of rational numbers is closed under division by nonzero rational numbers as well as under addition, multiplication, and subtraction. When we divide one rational number by another nonzero rational number, we always get a unique rational number as the result.

For example, -3 divided by 2 is $\frac{-3}{2}$; 5 divided by -4 is $\frac{5}{-4}$; and $\frac{5}{2}$ divided by $\frac{-4}{3} = \frac{5}{2} \cdot \frac{3}{-4} = \frac{15}{-8}$, which is a rational number. That is to say, in the set of rational numbers division is a binary operation (with the exception of division by zero).

■ **PROPERTY 2.** For every nonzero rational number, there is a unique corresponding number such that the product of these numbers is 1, the identity element of multiplication.

For example, for the given number $\frac{2}{3}$, there is the unique corresponding number $\frac{3}{2}$ such that $\frac{2}{3} \times \frac{3}{2} = 1$. Recall that the number $\frac{3}{2}$ is called the *reciprocal*, or *multiplicative inverse*, of $\frac{2}{3}$.

The set of rational numbers shares the following two properties with the set of integers:

■ **PROPERTY 3.** The set of rational numbers can be associated with points on a number line.

■ **PROPERTY 4.** The set of rational numbers is an ordered set. Given any two unequal rational numbers, we can tell which is the greater.

Study the following model problems to see how different methods may be used to order rational numbers:

MODEL PROBLEMS

1. Which is the greater of the numbers $\frac{1}{2}$ and -1?

   How to Proceed: Graph the numbers on a standard real number line. Then determine which number is at the right. The number at the right is the greater number.

   Solution:

   We see that the number $\frac{1}{2}$ is to the right of the number -1.

   Answer: $\frac{1}{2} > -1$

2. Which is the greater of the numbers $\frac{7}{9}$ and $\frac{8}{11}$?

   How to Proceed: Express the numbers as decimals and then compare the decimals. [See pages 585 and 586 for examples of expressing rational numbers as decimals.]

   Solution: By performing the indicated divisions:

   $$\frac{7}{9} = .7777 \ldots \text{ and } \frac{8}{11} = .7272 \ldots .$$
   Since $.7777 \ldots > .7272 \ldots$, then $\frac{7}{9} > \frac{8}{11}$. $\frac{7}{9} > \frac{8}{11}$ *Ans.*

The next property of the set of rational numbers is not shared by the set of integers.

■ **PROPERTY 5.** The set of rational numbers is everywhere dense. That is, given any two unequal rational numbers, it is always possible to find a rational number between them. A number midway between them, which is their average, is such a rational number.

For example, a rational number between 1 and 2 is the average of 1 and 2; that is $\frac{1+2}{2} = \frac{3}{2}$, or $1\frac{1}{2}$. In fact, there is an infinite number of rational numbers between two rational numbers.

Likewise a rational number between $\frac{1}{4}$ and $\frac{3}{4}$ can be computed by finding their average: $(\frac{1}{4} + \frac{3}{4}) \div 2 = (1) \div 2 = \frac{1}{2}$.

Expressing a Rational Number as a Decimal

To express as a decimal a rational number named as a fraction, we simply perform the indicated division.

MODEL PROBLEM

Express as a decimal: **a.** $\frac{1}{2}$ **b.** $\frac{3}{4}$ **c.** $\frac{1}{16}$

Solution

a. $\frac{1}{2} = 2\overline{)1.000000}$ $.500000$

b. $\frac{3}{4} = 4\overline{)3.000000}$ $.750000$

c. $\frac{1}{16} = 16\overline{)1.000000}$ $.062500$

In each of the examples $\frac{1}{2}$, $\frac{3}{4}$, and $\frac{1}{16}$, when we perform the division, we reach a point after which we continually obtain only zeros in the quotient. Decimals which result from such divisions, for example, .5, .75, and .0625, are called *terminating decimals*.

Not all rational numbers can be expressed as terminating decimals, as we see in the following model problem.

| MODEL PROBLEM |

Express as a decimal: a. $\frac{1}{3}$ b. $\frac{2}{11}$ c. $\frac{1}{6}$

Solution

a. $\frac{1}{3} = 3\overline{)1.000000}$ → .333333 ...

b. $\frac{2}{11} = 11\overline{)2.000000}$ → .181818 ...

c. $\frac{1}{6} = 6\overline{)1.000000}$ → .166666 ...

In each of the examples, $\frac{1}{3}$, $\frac{2}{11}$, and $\frac{1}{6}$, when we perform the division, we find, in the quotient, that the same group of digits is continually repeated in the same order. Decimals that keep repeating endlessly, such as .333333 ... , .181818 ... , and .166666 ... , are non-terminating decimals. They are also called *repeating decimals*, or *periodic decimals*.

A repeating decimal may be written in an abbreviated form by placing a bar (¯) over the group of digits that is to be continually repeated. For example:

.333333 ... = $.\overline{3}$ .181818 ... = $.\overline{18}$ .166666 ... = $.1\overline{6}$

The six examples in the two preceding model problems illustrate the truth of the following statement:

■ Every rational number can be expressed as either a terminating decimal or a repeating decimal.

Note that the equalities .5 = $.5\overline{0}$ and .75 = $.75\overline{0}$ illustrate the fact that every terminating decimal can be expressed as a repeating decimal which, after a point, repeats with all zeros. Therefore, we may say:

■ Every rational number can be expressed as a repeating decimal.

Since every terminating decimal can be expressed as a repeating decimal, we will henceforth regard terminating decimals as repeating decimals.

Expressing a Decimal as a Rational Number

When we studied arithmetic, we learned how to express some terminating decimals as rational numbers.

| MODEL PROBLEM |

Express as a rational number:　**a.** .3　**b.** .37　**c.** .139　**d.** .0777

Solution

a. $.3 = \dfrac{3}{10}$　**b.** $.37 = \dfrac{37}{100}$　**c.** $.139 = \dfrac{139}{1000}$　**d.** $.0777 = \dfrac{777}{10,000}$

Study the following model problem to learn how to express any repeating decimal as a rational number.

| MODEL PROBLEM |

Find a fraction that names the same rational number as:
a. .6666 . . .　　　**b.** .4141 . . .

Solution

a. Let $N = .6666 \ldots$ [A]
Multiply both members
of [A] by 10.
Then $10N = 6.6666 \ldots$ [B]
Subtract [A] from [B].
$$10N = 6.6666 \ldots \text{ [B]}$$
$$\underline{N = \quad .6666 \ldots \text{ [A]}}$$
$$9N = 6$$
$$N = \tfrac{6}{9} = \tfrac{2}{3}$$

Answer: $.6666 \ldots = \tfrac{2}{3}$

b. Let $N = .4141 \ldots$ [A]
Multiply both members
of [A] by 100.
Then $100N = 41.4141 \ldots$ [B]
Subtract [A] from [B].
$$100N = 41.4141 \ldots \text{ [B]}$$
$$\underline{N = \quad .4141 \ldots \text{ [A]}}$$
$$99N = 41$$
$$N = \tfrac{41}{99}$$

Answer: $.4141 \ldots = \tfrac{41}{99}$

The six examples in the two preceding model problems illustrate the truth of the following statement:

■ **Every repeating decimal represents a rational number.**

Notice that this statement is the converse of:

■ **Every rational number can be expressed as a repeating decimal.**

Since both the statement and its converse are true, we know from our study of logic that we can say:

■ **A number is a rational number if and only if it can be represented by a repeating decimal.**

| EXERCISES |

In 1–12, state which of the given numbers is the greater.

1. $\dfrac{5}{2}, \dfrac{7}{2}$ 2. $\dfrac{-9}{3}, \dfrac{-11}{3}$ 3. $\dfrac{5}{6}, -\dfrac{13}{6}$ 4. $-\dfrac{1}{5}, -5$

5. $\dfrac{5}{2}, \dfrac{7}{4}$ 6. $\dfrac{-10}{3}, \dfrac{-13}{6}$ 7. $\dfrac{13}{6}, \dfrac{15}{10}$ 8. $\dfrac{-5}{8}, \dfrac{-5}{12}$

9. $1.4, 1\dfrac{3}{5}$ 10. $-3.4, -3\dfrac{1}{3}$ 11. $.06, \dfrac{1}{6}$ 12. $\dfrac{-15}{11}, \dfrac{-11}{15}$

In 13–22, find a rational number midway between the given numbers.

13. $5, 6$ 14. $-4, -3$ 15. $-1, 0$ 16. $\dfrac{1}{4}, \dfrac{1}{2}$

17. $\dfrac{1}{2}, \dfrac{7}{8}$ 18. $\dfrac{-3}{4}, \dfrac{-2}{3}$ 19. $-2.1, -2.2$

20. $2\dfrac{1}{2}, 2\dfrac{5}{8}$ 21. $-1\dfrac{1}{3}, -1\dfrac{1}{4}$ 22. $3.05, 3\dfrac{1}{10}$

In 23–29, write the rational number as a repeating decimal.

23. $\dfrac{5}{8}$ 24. $\dfrac{9}{4}$ 25. $-5\dfrac{1}{2}$ 26. $\dfrac{13}{8}$ 27. $-\dfrac{7}{12}$ 28. $\dfrac{5}{3}$ 29. $\dfrac{7}{9}$

In 30–35, find a fraction that names the same rational number as the decimal.

30. $.5$ 31. $.555\ldots$ 32. $-.\overline{2}$ 33. $.125\overline{0}$ 34. $.2525\ldots$ 35. $.0\overline{7}$

2 THE SET OF IRRATIONAL NUMBERS

There are infinitely many decimals that are nonrepeating. An example of such a decimal is:

$$.03003000300003\ldots$$

Observe that, in this numeral, only the digits 0 and 3 appear. First we have a 3 preceded by one 0, then a 3 preceded by two 0's, then a 3 preceded by three 0's, and so on. Since it can be shown that this numeral does not represent a repeating decimal, it cannot represent a rational number.

A number represented by a non-repeating (and hence non-terminating) decimal is called an *irrational number*. An irrational number cannot be expressed in the form $\frac{a}{b}$ where a and b are integers ($b \neq 0$).

When we use three dots, ". . .", after a series of digits to represent a number, the three dots indicate that the number is non-terminating. In an *irrational number*, we are not always certain what the next digit will be when ". . ." is used. For example, the irrational number .3824 . . . may be .38240 . . . , or .38241 . . . , or .38242 . . . , and so on. In a *rational number*, we can identify a pattern. For example, the rational number .8333 . . . means .83333333 . . . or simply $.8\overline{3}$.

Irrational numbers may be positive or negative. For example, .030030003 . . . represents a positive irrational number; - .030030003 . . . represents a negative irrational number.

The set of irrational numbers is not closed under addition. For example, the numbers a = .030030003 . . . and $-a$ = - .030030003 . . . are both irrational but their sum, $a + (-a) = 0$, is rational.

Also, the set of irrational numbers is not closed under multiplication because it can be shown that the reciprocal of an irrational number is irrational; and the product of a number and its reciprocal is 1, which is rational.

There are infinitely many irrational numbers. Among them is the number π = 3.14159 . . . , a number that you have met in previous mathematics courses and that you will meet again when we study the geometry of the circle. Another irrational number is the number that represents the length of a diagonal of a square whose side is 1. As we will later learn, this irrational number is symbolized by $\sqrt{2}$.

It is interesting to note that the sum (also the difference) of a rational number and an irrational number is an irrational number. For example, $10 + \pi$ is an irrational number; also, $10 - \pi$ is an irrational number.

EXERCISES

In 1–16, tell whether the number is rational or irrational.

1. .36
2. .363636 . . .
3. .363363336 . . .
4. $.3\overline{6}$
5. $-.9\overline{45}$
6. .989889888 . . .
7. $.363363336\overline{3}$
8. π
9. $.8\overline{3}$
10. .6789101112 . . .
11. .9856473512 . . .
12. $\sqrt{2}$
13. 5.08
14. .125612561256 . . .
15. .125125127 . . .
16. $3 + \pi$

In 17–20, find a rational number between the given numbers.

17. .7777 . . . and .868686 . . .
18. .151551555 . . . and .161661666 . . .
19. 3.6464 . . . and $3.\overline{125}$
20. 2.343343334 . . . and 2.414114111 . . .

3 THE SET OF REAL NUMBERS

The set that consists of all rational numbers and all irrational numbers is called the *set of real numbers*.

This definition can be stated in a more formal manner.

■ The union of the set of all rational numbers and the set of all irrational numbers is called the *set of real numbers*.

{real numbers} = {rational numbers} ∪ {irrational numbers}

We have seen that there is an infinite number of rational numbers. For each rational number there is a corresponding point on the number line. There is also an infinite number of irrational numbers. For each irrational number there is a corresponding point on the number line. Interestingly enough, it can be shown that all the points that are the graphs of the rational numbers and the irrational numbers, that is, the graphs of the real numbers, "fill" the number line. We say that the set of real numbers is complete. The *completeness property of real numbers* may be stated as follows:

■ Every point on the real number line corresponds to a real number, and every real number corresponds to a point on the real number line.

Ordering Real Numbers

We can order real numbers in the same way that we ordered rational numbers.

1. We can use a number line. The graph of the greater of two unequal numbers is always to the right of the graph of the smaller number on a standard real number line.

2. We can make use of decimals. Given any two unequal real numbers, we can determine which is the larger by first expressing each number as a decimal. Then we compare the resulting decimals.

EXERCISES

In 1–6, determine which is the greater number.

1. 2 or 2.5   2. -5.7 or -5.9 3. .5353 or .535353
4. .7 or $.\overline{7}$ 5. $-.53$ or $-.\overline{531}$ 6. .2121 . . . or .212112111 . . .

Properties of Real Numbers

The following properties are assumed for the set of real numbers under the operations of addition and multiplication. They are used in operations with real numbers.

In the following eleven statements, a, b, and c represent any numbers that are members of the set of real numbers.

Property	*Symbolization*
1. Addition is closed (or addition is a binary operation).	1. $a + b = c$ (c is a unique number in the set.)
2. Addition is commutative.	2. $a + b = b + a$
3. Addition is associative.	3. $(a + b) + c = a + (b + c)$
4. Zero is the additive identity.	4. $a + 0 = a$ and $0 + a = a$
5. Every number a has an additive inverse $-a$.	5. $a + (-a) = 0$
6. Multiplication is closed (or multiplication is a binary operation).	6. $ab = c$ (c is a unique number in the set.)
7. Multiplication is commutative.	7. $ab = ba$
8. Multiplication is associative.	8. $(ab)c = a(bc)$
9. The number 1 is the multiplicative identity.	9. $a \cdot 1 = a$ and $1 \cdot a = a$
10. Every nonzero number a has a unique multiplicative inverse $\frac{1}{a}$.	10. $a \cdot \frac{1}{a} = 1$ $(a \neq 0)$
11. Multiplication is distributive over addition.	11. $a(b + c) = ab + ac$

[*Note.* Subtraction can be performed by means of addition. We assume that $a - b = a + (-b)$. Division can be performed by means of multiplication. We assume that $a \div b = a \cdot \frac{1}{b}$ $(b \neq 0)$.]

| EXERCISES |

In 1–10, state whether the statement is true or false.

1. Every real number is a rational number.
2. Every rational number is a real number.
3. Every irrational number is a real number.
4. Every real number is an irrational number.
5. Every rational number corresponds to a point on the real number line.
6. Every point on the real number line corresponds to a rational number.
7. Every irrational number corresponds to a point on the real number line.
8. Every point on the real number line corresponds to an irrational number.
9. There are some numbers that are both rational and irrational.
10. Every repeating decimal corresponds to a point on the real number line.

11. Which is an illustration of the commutative property of addition?
    (1) $ab = ba$ (2) $a + 0 = a$
    (3) $a + b = b + a$ (4) $(a + b) + c = a + (b + c)$
12. Which is an illustration of the associative property of multiplication?
    (1) $ab = ba$ (2) $a(0) = 0$
    (3) $a(1) = a$ (4) $(ab)c = a(bc)$
13. Which is an illustration of the distributive property of multiplication over addition?
    (1) $a + b = b + a$ (2) $a(b + c) = ab + ac$
    (3) $(a + b) + c = a + (b + c)$ (4) $a(b + c) = ab + c$
14. What is the additive inverse of the real number represented by n?
15. What is the multiplicative inverse of the real number represented by n?
16. What is the additive identity for the set of real numbers?
17. What is the multiplicative identity for the set of real numbers?

4 FINDING A RATIONAL ROOT OF A NUMBER

We have learned that the area of a square whose side is 3 units is equal to 3 · 3 or 9 square units. Notice that we used 3 as a factor twice, that is, we squared 3, written as 3^2, to find the area.

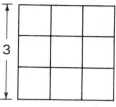

area=9

If we wish to find the length of a side of a square whose area is 16 square units, we have to find a number that, when squared (that is, used two times as a factor), would equal 16. Obviously, such a number is 4 because 4 · 4 = 16. We call this number 4 a *square root* of 16.

area=16

We see, therefore, that to find a *square root* of a number is to find one of its two equal factors. For example, "a square root of 25," written $\sqrt{25}$, is 5 because 5 · 5 = 25, or 5^2 = 25. In general, a number x is a square root of the number b, if and only if $x^2 = b$. Finding a square root of a number is the inverse operation of squaring the number.

To indicate a square root of a number, a *radical sign*, $\sqrt{}$, is used. The symbol $\sqrt{25}$ is called a *radical*; 25, the number under the radical sign, is called the *radicand*.

Since a square root of 25 is a number whose square is 25, we can write $(\sqrt{25})^2 = 25$.

In general, for every real non-negative number n:

$$(\sqrt{n})^2 = n$$

Since $(+5)(+5) = 25$ and $(-5)(-5) = 25$, both +5 and -5 are square roots of 25. This example illustrates the truth of the following statement:

■ Every positive number has two square roots that have the same absolute value, one root being a positive number, the other root being a negative number.

593

The positive square root of a number is called the *principal square root*. To indicate that the principal square root of a number is to be found, a radical sign, $\sqrt{}$, is placed over the number. For example:

$$\sqrt{25} = 5 \qquad \sqrt{\tfrac{9}{16}} = \tfrac{3}{4} \qquad \sqrt{.49} = .7$$

To indicate that the negative square root of a number is to be found, we place a minus sign in front of the radical sign. For example:

$$-\sqrt{25} = -5 \qquad -\sqrt{\tfrac{9}{16}} = -\tfrac{3}{4} \qquad -\sqrt{.49} = -.7$$

To indicate that both square roots are to be found, we place a plus sign and a minus sign in front of the radical. For example:

$$\pm\sqrt{25} = \pm 5 \qquad \pm\sqrt{\tfrac{9}{16}} = \pm\tfrac{3}{4} \qquad \pm\sqrt{.49} = \pm.7$$

Observe that 0 is the only number whose square is 0. Thus, $\sqrt{0} = 0$.

Since the square of any real number is never negative, no negative number has a square root in the set of real numbers. For example, $\sqrt{-25}$ does not exist in the set of real numbers; there is no real number whose square is -25.

Finding a cube root of a number is to find one of its three equal factors. For example, "a cube root of 8," written $\sqrt[3]{8}$, is 2 because $2 \cdot 2 \cdot 2 = 8$, or $2^3 = 8$. In general, a number x is a cube root of the number b, if and only if $x^3 = b$. Finding a cube root of a number is the inverse operation of cubing a number.

Likewise, for any positive integer n: If $x^n = b$, then x is an nth root of b, written $\sqrt[n]{b}$.

In the symbol $\sqrt[n]{b}$, n, the integer that indicates the root to be taken, is called the *index* of the radical. In $\sqrt[3]{8}$, the index is 3; in $\sqrt[4]{16}$, the index is 4. When no index appears, a square root is indicated. For example, $\sqrt{25}$ means a square root of 25.

We have said that $\sqrt{-25}$ does not exist in the set of real numbers. However, $\sqrt[3]{-8}$ does exist in the set of real numbers. Since $(-2)^3 = -8$, then $\sqrt[3]{-8} = -2$. These are examples of the truth of the following statement:

■ An even integral root of a negative real number does not exist in the set of real numbers; an odd integral root of a negative real number does exist.

For example, $\sqrt{-4}$ and $\sqrt[4]{-16}$ do not exist in the set of real numbers. But $\sqrt[3]{-1} = -1$ because $(-1)^3 = -1$ and $\sqrt[5]{-32} = -2$ because $(-2)^5 = -32$.

MODEL PROBLEMS

1. Find the principal square root of 64.

    Solution: Since $8 \cdot 8 = 64$, then $\sqrt{64} = 8$.   8 *Ans.*

2. Find the value of $\sqrt[3]{27}$.

    Solution: Since $3 \cdot 3 \cdot 3 = 27$, then $\sqrt[3]{27} = 3$.   3 *Ans.*

3. Find the value of $(\sqrt{13})^2$.

    Solution: Since $(\sqrt{n})^2 = n$, then $(\sqrt{13})^2 = 13$.   13 *Ans.*

4. Solve for x: $x^2 = 36$.

    Solution: If $x^2 = a$, then $x = \pm\sqrt{a}$ when a is a positive number.

$x^2 = 36$	*Check:* $x^2 = 36$	$x^2 = 36$
$x = \pm\sqrt{36}$	$(+6)^2 \overset{?}{=} 36$	$(-6)^2 \overset{?}{=} 36$
$x = \pm 6$	$36 = 36$ (True)	$36 = 36$ (True)

Answer: $x = +6$ or $x = -6$; solution set is $\{+6, -6\}$.

EXERCISES

In 1–5, state the index and the radicand of the radical.

1. $\sqrt{36}$ 2. $\sqrt[3]{125}$ 3. $\sqrt[4]{81}$ 4. $\sqrt[5]{32}$ 5. $\sqrt[n]{1}$

In 6–15, find the principal square root of the number.

6. 81   7. 1   8. 121   9. 225   10. 900

11. $\frac{1}{9}$ 12. $\frac{4}{25}$ 13. .49   14. 1.44   15. .04

In 16–40, express the radical as integer(s), fraction(s), or decimal(s).

16. $\sqrt{16}$ 17. $\sqrt{81}$ 18. $\sqrt{121}$ 19. $-\sqrt{64}$ 20. $-\sqrt{144}$

21. $\sqrt{0}$ 22. $\pm\sqrt{100}$ 23. $\pm\sqrt{169}$ 24. $\sqrt{400}$ 25. $-\sqrt{625}$

26. $\sqrt{\frac{1}{4}}$ 27. $-\sqrt{\frac{9}{16}}$ 28. $\pm\sqrt{\frac{25}{81}}$ 29. $\sqrt{\frac{49}{100}}$ 30. $\pm\sqrt{\frac{144}{169}}$

31. $\sqrt{.64}$ 32. $-\sqrt{1.44}$ 33. $\pm\sqrt{.09}$ 34. $-\sqrt{.01}$ 35. $\pm\sqrt{.0004}$

36. $\sqrt[3]{1}$ 37. $\sqrt[4]{81}$ 38. $\sqrt[5]{32}$ 39. $\sqrt[3]{-8}$ 40. $-\sqrt[3]{-125}$

In 41–54, find the value of the expression.

41. $\sqrt{(8)^2}$ 42. $\sqrt{(\frac{1}{2})^2}$ 43. $\sqrt{(.7)^2}$ 44. $\sqrt{(\frac{9}{3})^2}$

45. $\sqrt{(\frac{9}{5})^2}$ 46. $(\sqrt{4})^2$ 47. $(\sqrt{36})^2$ 48. $(\sqrt{11})^2$

49. $(\sqrt{39})^2$ 50. $(\sqrt{97})(\sqrt{97})$

51. $\sqrt{36} + \sqrt{49}$ 52. $\sqrt{100} - \sqrt{25}$

53. $(\sqrt{17})^2 + (\sqrt{7})(\sqrt{7})$ 54. $\sqrt{(-9)^2} - (\sqrt{83})^2$

55. In each part compare the positive real number with its square, using one of the symbols $>$, $<$, or $=$.

   a. $\frac{1}{2}$ b. $\frac{3}{4}$ c. 1   d. $\frac{3}{2}$ e. 4   f. 100

56. Compare the positive real number, n, with its square, n^2, when:

   a. $n < 1$ b. $n = 1$ c. $n > 1$

57. In each part compare the principal square root of the positive real number with the number.

   a. $\frac{1}{9}$ b. $\frac{4}{25}$ c. 1   d. $\frac{49}{25}$ e. 4   f. 9

58. Compare $\sqrt{m}$, when m is a positive real number with the number, m, when:

   a. $m < 1$ b. $m = 1$ c. $m > 1$

In 59–70, solve for the variable when the replacement set is the set of real numbers.

59. $x^2 = 4$ 60. $y^2 = 100$ 61. $z^2 = \frac{4}{81}$ 62. $x^2 = .49$

63. $x^2 - 16 = 0$ 64. $y^2 - 36 = 0$ 65. $2x^2 = 50$ 66. $3y^2 - 27 = 0$

67. $x^3 = 8$ 68. $y^3 = 1$ 69. $y^4 = 81$ 70. $z^5 = 32$

In 71–74, (a) find the length of each side of a square that has the given area, and (b) find the perimeter of the square.

71. 36 sq. ft.   72. 196 sq. yd.   73. 121 cm^2 74. 225 m^2

75. Express in terms of x the perimeter of a square whose area is represented by x^2.

5 SQUARE ROOTS THAT ARE IRRATIONAL NUMBERS

Positive rational numbers such as 9 and $\frac{4}{49}$ (also the number 0) are called **perfect squares** because they are squares of rational numbers. For example, $\sqrt{9} = 3$, and 3 is a rational number; $\sqrt{\frac{4}{49}} = \frac{2}{7}$, and $\frac{2}{7}$ is a rational number; $\sqrt{0} = 0$, and 0 is a rational number. Similarly, if any non-negative rational number n is a perfect square, then $\sqrt{n}$ is a non-negative rational number.

Suppose n is a non-negative rational number that is not a perfect square, for example, 2. What kind of number is $\sqrt{n}$? What is the value of $\sqrt{2}$?

Since $1 \times 1 = 1$ and $2 \times 2 = 4$, then $\sqrt{2}$ must be a number between 1 and 2: $1 < \sqrt{2} < 2$.

Since $1.4 \times 1.4 = 1.96$ and $1.5 \times 1.5 = 2.25$, then $\sqrt{2}$ must be a number between 1.4 and 1.5: $1.4 < \sqrt{2} < 1.5$.

Since $1.41 \times 1.41 = 1.9881$ and $1.42 \times 1.42 = 2.0164$, then $\sqrt{2}$ must be a number between 1.41 and 1.42: $1.41 < \sqrt{2} < 1.42$.

Regardless of how far we continue this work, we will never reach a point where the number $\sqrt{2}$ is expressed as a terminating or a repeating decimal. Therefore, we call $\sqrt{2}$ an **irrational number**. We have been finding only approximations of $\sqrt{2}$; the value of $\sqrt{2}$ cannot be expressed as a rational number.

If a number cannot be expressed in the form $\frac{a}{b}$, where a and b are integers ($b \neq 0$), it is an irrational number.

It can be proved that if n is a positive number that is not a perfect square, then $\sqrt{n}$ is an irrational number. It can also be shown that if n is a positive integer that is not the square of an integer, then $\sqrt{n}$ is irrational. Examples of irrational numbers are $\sqrt{2}, \sqrt{3}, \sqrt{5}, \sqrt{7}$, and $\sqrt{8}$.

Even though the value of an irrational number can be only approximated, every square root that is an irrational number can be associated with a point on the real number line.

Although we cannot do so here, it can be shown that there are infinitely many irrational numbers that cannot be expressed as a root of a rational number. π is such a number.

| MODEL PROBLEMS |

1. Between which consecutive integers is $\sqrt{42}$?

   Solution: Since 6 X 6 = 36 and 7 X 7 = 49, then $\sqrt{42}$ is between 6 and 7.

   Answer: $\sqrt{42}$ is between 6 and 7, or $6 < \sqrt{42} < 7$.

2. State whether $\sqrt{56}$ is a rational or an irrational number.

   Solution: Since 56 is a positive integer that is not the square of an integer, $\sqrt{56}$ is an irrational number.

   Answer: $\sqrt{56}$ is an irrational number.

| EXERCISES |

In 1–10, between which consecutive integers is each given number?

1. $\sqrt{5}$ 2. $\sqrt{13}$ 3. $\sqrt{40}$ 4. $-\sqrt{2}$ 5. $-\sqrt{14}$
6. $\sqrt{52}$ 7. $\sqrt{73}$ 8. $-\sqrt{125}$ 9. $\sqrt{143}$ 10. $-\sqrt{150}$

In 11–16, order the given numbers, starting with the smallest.

11. $2, \sqrt{3}, -1$ 12. $4, \sqrt{17}, 3$ 13. $-\sqrt{15}, -3, -4$
14. $0, \sqrt{7}, -\sqrt{7}$ 15. $5, \sqrt{21}, \sqrt{30}$ 16. $-\sqrt{11}, -\sqrt{23}, -\sqrt{19}$

In 17–26, state whether the number is rational or irrational.

17. $\sqrt{25}$ 18. $\sqrt{40}$ 19. $-\sqrt{36}$ 20. $-\sqrt{54}$ 21. $-\sqrt{150}$
22. $\sqrt{400}$ 23. $\sqrt{\frac{1}{2}}$ 24. $-\sqrt{\frac{4}{9}}$ 25. $\sqrt{.36}$ 26. $\sqrt{.1}$

6 USING A TABLE TO FIND SQUARES AND SQUARE ROOTS

When computing the square or the square root of a number, much time can be saved by using a table of squares and square roots such as the one that appears on page 670.

MODEL PROBLEMS

1. Find the square of 58.

    Solution: In the table on page 670, in the column headed "No.," we find 58. We look to the right of 58 in the column headed "Square" and find 3,364.

    Answer: $(58)^2 = 3,364$

2. Approximate $\sqrt{48}$ (a) to the *nearest tenth* and (b) to the *nearest hundredth*.

    Solution: In the table on page 670, in the column headed "No.," we find 48. We look to the right of 48 in the column headed "Square Root" and find 6.928. Then we round off the decimal.

    Answer: a. $\sqrt{48} \approx 6.9$ to the nearest tenth

    b. $\sqrt{48} \approx 6.93$ to the nearest hundredth

[*Note:* The symbol "$\approx$" means "is approximately equal to."]

EXERCISES

In 1–6, use the table on page 670 to find the square of the number.

1. 27   2. 68   3. 94   4. 119   5. 132   6. 147

In 7–21, use the table on page 670 to approximate the expression (a) to the *nearest tenth* and (b) to the *nearest hundredth*.

7. $\sqrt{13}$ 8. $\sqrt{53}$ 9. $-\sqrt{63}$ 10. $\sqrt{135}$
11. $-\sqrt{87}$ 12. $\sqrt{5}$ 13. $\sqrt{91}$ 14. $\sqrt{85}$
15. $-\sqrt{111}$ 16. $\sqrt{141}$ 17. $2+\sqrt{3}$ 18. $9-\sqrt{17}$
19. $\sqrt{55}+7$ 20. $\sqrt{120}-4$ 21. $-2-\sqrt{13}$

In 22–25, find c if $c = \sqrt{a^2 + b^2}$ and a and b have the given values. Use the table on page 670.

22. $a = 6, b = 8$ 23. $a = 5, b = 12$
24. $a = 15, b = 20$ 25. $a = 15, b = 36$

In 26–29, compute the perimeter of the figure by using the table on page 670 to find approximations to two decimal places before rounding off to the *nearest tenth*.

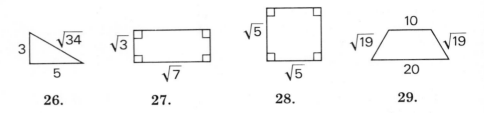

26.   27.   28.   29.

7 USING DIVISION TO FIND APPROXIMATE SQUARE ROOTS

Consider 144 and its square root, 12. $144 \div 12 = 12$ illustrates:

■ **PRINCIPLE 1.** When a divisor of a number and the quotient are equal, the square root of the number is either the divisor or the quotient.

From $144 \div 12 = 12$ we see that $\sqrt{144} = 12$, which is either the divisor or the quotient.

$144 \div 9 = 16$ and $144 \div 18 = 8$ illustrate:

■ **PRINCIPLE 2.** When a divisor of a number and the quotient are unequal, the square root of the number lies between the divisor and the quotient.

For example, from $144 \div 9 = 16$ we see that $\sqrt{144}$, which equals 12, lies between the divisor 9 and the quotient 16.

Also, from $144 \div 18 = 8$ we see that $\sqrt{144}$, which is 12, lies between the divisor 18 and the quotient 8.

The square root of a number may be approximated to any number of decimal places by applying the two preceding principles and using estimates, divisions, and averages.

| MODEL PROBLEM |

Approximate $\sqrt{14}$ to the nearest **(a)** integer, **(b)** tenth, and **(c)** hundredth.

How to Proceed   *Solution*

1. Approximate the square root of the number 14 by estimation.   Since $3^2 = 9$ and $4^2 = 16$, then $\sqrt{14}$ lies between 3 and 4, closer to 4. Estimate $\sqrt{14} \approx 3.8$.

2. Divide the number 14 by the estimate, 3.8, finding the quotient to one more decimal place than there is in the divisor.

$$3.8_\wedge\overline{)14.0_\wedge00}\qquad\frac{3.68}{}$$

$$\begin{array}{r} 3.68 \\ 3.8_\wedge\overline{)14.0_\wedge00} \\ \underline{11\ 4} \\ 2\ 6\ 0 \\ \underline{2\ 2\ 8} \\ 3\ 20 \\ \underline{3\ 04} \\ 16 \end{array}$$

[*Note:* The quotient is 3.68, not 3.8. This tells us that $\sqrt{14}$ is not 3.8, but lies between 3.68 and 3.8. Therefore, $3.68 < \sqrt{14} < 3.8$.]

3. Find the average of the divisor, 3.8, and the quotient, 3.68 (found in step 2).

$$\frac{3.8 + 3.68}{2} = \frac{7.48}{2} = 3.74$$

4. Divide the number 14 by the average, 3.74 (see step 3), finding the quotient to one more decimal place than there is in the divisor. Since $14 \div 3.74 \approx 3.743$, then $3.74 < \sqrt{14} < 3.743$.

$3.74\overline{)14.} \approx 3.743$

(The division is left to the student.)

5. Find the average of the divisor, 3.74, and the quotient, 3.743 (found in step 4).

$$\frac{3.74 + 3.743}{2} = \frac{7.483}{2} = 3.7415$$

[*Note:* This process may be continued to obtain as close an approximation as is desired.]

Since $\sqrt{14} \approx 3.7415$, we obtain the following approximations when we round off:

Answer: **a.** $\sqrt{14} \approx 4$ (nearest integer)

b. $\sqrt{14} \approx 3.7$ (nearest tenth)

c. $\sqrt{14} \approx 3.74$ (nearest hundredth)

EXERCISES

In 1–15, approximate the expression **(a)** to the nearest integer, **(b)** to the nearest tenth, and **(c)** to the nearest hundredth.

1. $\sqrt{2}$ 2. $\sqrt{3}$ 3. $\sqrt{21}$ 4. $\sqrt{39}$ 5. $\sqrt{80}$
6. $\sqrt{90}$ 7. $\sqrt{108}$ 8. $\sqrt{23.5}$ 9. $\sqrt{88.2}$ 10. $-\sqrt{115.2}$
11. $\sqrt{28.56}$ 12. $\sqrt{67.24}$ 13. $\sqrt{4389}$ 14. $\sqrt{123.7}$ 15. $\sqrt{134.53}$

In 16–20, find to the *nearest tenth* of a centimeter the length of a side of a square whose area is the given measure.

16. 8 cm^2 17. 29 cm^2 18. 96 cm^2 19. 140 cm^2 **20.** 200 cm^2

8 FINDING THE PRINCIPAL SQUARE ROOT OF A MONOMIAL

Since $(6a^2)(6a^2) = 36a^4$, then $\sqrt{36a^4} = 6a^2$. Observe that $6a^2$ is the product of two factors. The first factor 6 is $\sqrt{36}$ and the second factor a^2 is $\sqrt{a^4}$.

■ **PROCEDURE.** To find the square root of a monomial that has more than one factor, write the indicated product of the square roots of its factors.

Note: In our work we limit the domain of the variables that appear under a radical sign to non-negative numbers only.

MODEL PROBLEMS

In 1–3, find the principal square root.

1. $\sqrt{25y^2}$ 2. $\sqrt{16m^6}$ 3. $\sqrt{.81y^8}$

Solution

1. $\sqrt{25y^2} = (\sqrt{25})(\sqrt{y^2}) = 5y$ *Ans.*
2. $\sqrt{16m^6} = (\sqrt{16})(\sqrt{m^6}) = 4m^3$ *Ans.*
3. $\sqrt{.81y^8} = (\sqrt{.81})(\sqrt{y^8}) = .9y^4$ *Ans.*

| EXERCISES |

In 1–18, find the indicated root.

1. $\sqrt{4a^2}$ 2. $\sqrt{16d^2}$ 3. $\sqrt{49z^2}$ 4. $\sqrt{\frac{16}{25}r^2}$ 5. $\sqrt{.81w^2}$

6. $\sqrt{9c^2}$ 7. $\sqrt{36y^4}$ 8. $\sqrt{c^2d^2}$ 9. $\sqrt{x^4y^2}$ 10. $\sqrt{r^8s^6}$

11. $\sqrt{4x^2y^2}$ 12. $\sqrt{36a^6b^4}$ 13. $\sqrt{144a^4b^2}$ 14. $\sqrt{169x^4y^2}$

15. $\sqrt{.36m^2}$ 16. $\sqrt{.49a^2b^2}$ 17. $\sqrt{.04y^2}$ 18. $\sqrt{.01x^4y^2}$

In 19–22, (a) represent each side of the square whose area is given and (b) represent the perimeter of that square.

19. $49c^2$ 20. $64x^2$ 21. $100x^2y^2$ 22. $144a^2b^2$

9 SIMPLIFYING A SQUARE-ROOT RADICAL WHOSE RADICAND HAS A PERFECT SQUARE FACTOR

Since $\sqrt{4 \cdot 9} = \sqrt{36} = 6$, and $\sqrt{4} \cdot \sqrt{9} = 2 \cdot 3 = 6$, then $\sqrt{4 \cdot 9} = \sqrt{4} \cdot \sqrt{9}$.

Since $\sqrt{16 \cdot 25} = \sqrt{400} = 20$, and $\sqrt{16} \cdot \sqrt{25} = 4 \cdot 5 = 20$, then $\sqrt{16 \cdot 25} = \sqrt{16} \cdot \sqrt{25}$.

These examples illustrate the following property of square-root radicals:

■ **The square root of a product of non-negative numbers is equal to the product of the square roots of the numbers.**

In general, if a and b are non-negative numbers:

$$\sqrt{a \cdot b} = \sqrt{a} \cdot \sqrt{b} \quad and \quad \sqrt{a} \cdot \sqrt{b} = \sqrt{a \cdot b}$$

This rule can be used to transform a square-root radical into an equivalent radical. For example:

$$\sqrt{50} = \sqrt{25 \cdot 2} = \sqrt{25} \cdot \sqrt{2} = 5\sqrt{2}$$

Notice that we expressed 50 as the product of 25 (the greatest perfect square factor of 50) and 2. Then we expressed $\sqrt{25}$ as 5.

When we expressed $\sqrt{50}$ as $5\sqrt{2}$, we simplified $\sqrt{50}$.

A square-root radical is said to be in simplest form when:

1. the radicand has no perfect square factor other than 1, and
2. there is no fraction under the radical sign.

■ **PROCEDURE.**   To simplify the square root of a product:

1. Find two factors of the radicand, one of which is the largest perfect square factor of the radicand.

2. Express the square root of the product as the product of the square roots of the factors.

3. Find the square root of the factor that is a perfect square.

If we wish to find $\sqrt{200}$, correct to the nearest hundredth, by the use of the table on page 670, we can first simplify the radical as follows:

$$\sqrt{200} = \sqrt{100 \cdot 2} = \sqrt{100} \cdot \sqrt{2} = 10\sqrt{2} \approx 10(1.414) \approx 14.14$$

Note that 100 is the largest perfect square factor of 200.

| MODEL PROBLEM |

In each part, simplify the expression.

a. $\sqrt{18}$ **b.** $4\sqrt{50}$ **c.** $\frac{1}{2}\sqrt{48}$ **d.** $\sqrt{4y^3}$

Solution:

a. $\sqrt{18} = \sqrt{9 \cdot 2} = \sqrt{9} \cdot \sqrt{2} = 3\sqrt{2}$ *Ans.*

b. $4\sqrt{50} = 4\sqrt{25 \cdot 2} = 4\sqrt{25} \cdot \sqrt{2} = 4 \cdot 5\sqrt{2} = 20\sqrt{2}$ *Ans.*

c. $\frac{1}{2}\sqrt{48} = \frac{1}{2}\sqrt{16 \cdot 3} = \frac{1}{2}\sqrt{16} \cdot \sqrt{3} = \frac{1}{2} \cdot 4\sqrt{3} = 2\sqrt{3}$ *Ans.*

d. $\sqrt{4y^3} = \sqrt{4y^2 \cdot y} = \sqrt{4y^2} \cdot \sqrt{y} = 2y\sqrt{y}$ *Ans.*

| EXERCISES |

In 1–32, simplify the expression.

1. $\sqrt{8}$	**2.** $\sqrt{12}$	**3.** $\sqrt{20}$	**4.** $\sqrt{28}$
5. $\sqrt{40}$	**6.** $\sqrt{27}$	**7.** $\sqrt{54}$	**8.** $\sqrt{63}$
9. $\sqrt{90}$	**10.** $\sqrt{98}$	**11.** $\sqrt{99}$	**12.** $\sqrt{108}$
13. $\sqrt{162}$	**14.** $\sqrt{175}$	**15.** $\sqrt{300}$	**16.** $3\sqrt{8}$
17. $4\sqrt{12}$	**18.** $2\sqrt{20}$	**19.** $4\sqrt{90}$	**20.** $2\sqrt{45}$

21. $3\sqrt{200}$ 22. $\frac{1}{2}\sqrt{72}$ 23. $\frac{1}{4}\sqrt{48}$ 24. $\frac{3}{4}\sqrt{96}$
25. $\frac{2}{3}\sqrt{63}$ 26. $\sqrt{a^3}$ 27. $2\sqrt{b^5}$ 28. $\sqrt{r^2 s}$
29. $\sqrt{x^2 y^3}$ 30. $\sqrt{3x^3 y}$ 31. $\sqrt{49a}$ 32. $\sqrt{36r^2 s}$

33. Which of the expressions $2\sqrt{3}$, $4\sqrt{12}$, $4\sqrt{3}$, $16\sqrt{3}$ is equivalent to $\sqrt{48}$?

34. Which of the expressions $\sqrt{8}$, $\sqrt{42}$, $\sqrt{32}$, $\sqrt{64}$ is equivalent to $4\sqrt{2}$?

35. Which of the expressions $\sqrt{54}$, $3\sqrt{2}$, $9\sqrt{2}$, $3\sqrt{6}$ is equivalent to $3\sqrt{18}$?

36. Which of the expressions $\sqrt{9}$, $\sqrt{6}$, $\sqrt{12}$, $\sqrt{27}$ is equivalent to $3\sqrt{3}$?

In 37–40, use the table on page 670 to find the approximate value of the expression, correct to the nearest tenth.

37. $\sqrt{300}$ 38. $\sqrt{180}$ 39. $2\sqrt{288}$ 40. $\frac{1}{3}\sqrt{252}$

41. a. Does $\sqrt{9 + 16} = \sqrt{9} + \sqrt{16}$? Why?
    b. Is finding a square root always distributive over addition?

42. a. Does $\sqrt{25 - 9} = \sqrt{25} - \sqrt{9}$? Why?
    b. Is finding a square root always distributive over subtraction?

10 ADDING AND SUBTRACTING RADICALS

Adding and Subtracting Like Square-Root Radicals

Like radicals are radicals that have the same index and the same radicand. For example, $7\sqrt{3}$ and $5\sqrt{3}$ are like radicals, as are $4\sqrt[3]{7}$ and $9\sqrt[3]{7}$. However, $3\sqrt{5}$ and $5\sqrt{2}$ are unlike radicals because the radicands are different. Also, $\sqrt[3]{2}$ and $\sqrt{2}$ are unlike radicals because the index in one radical is 3 and the index in the second radical is 2.

To find the sum of the length and the width of the rectangle pictured at the right, we would add $7\sqrt{2}$ and $3\sqrt{2}$. We would obtain $7\sqrt{2} + 3\sqrt{2}$.

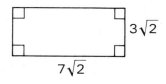

We can express this sum of two like radicals as a single term by using the distributive property as follows:

$$7\sqrt{2} + 3\sqrt{2} = (7 + 3)\sqrt{2} = 10\sqrt{2}$$

Similarly, $5\sqrt{3} - \sqrt{3} = 5\sqrt{3} - 1\sqrt{3} = (5 - 1)\sqrt{3} = 4\sqrt{3}$.

■ **PROCEDURE.**   To add or subtract like square-root radicals:

1. Add or subtract the coefficients of the radicals.

2. Multiply the sum or difference obtained by the common radical.

Adding and Subtracting Unlike Square-Root Radicals

The sum of the unlike radicals $\sqrt{5}$ and $\sqrt{2}$ is indicated as $\sqrt{5} + \sqrt{2}$, which cannot be expressed as a single term. Similarly, the difference of $\sqrt{5}$ and $\sqrt{2}$ is indicated as $\sqrt{5} - \sqrt{2}$.

However, when it is possible to transform unlike radicals into equivalent radicals that are like radicals, the resulting like radicals can be added or subtracted. For example, it would appear that the sum of $2\sqrt{3}$ and $\sqrt{27}$ can be indicated only as $2\sqrt{3} + \sqrt{27}$ since $2\sqrt{3}$ and $\sqrt{27}$ are unlike radicals. However, since $\sqrt{27} = \sqrt{9 \cdot 3} = \sqrt{9} \cdot \sqrt{3} = 3\sqrt{3}$, we can express $2\sqrt{3} + \sqrt{27}$ as $2\sqrt{3} + 3\sqrt{3}$ and then add the like radicals:

$$2\sqrt{3} + \sqrt{27} = 2\sqrt{3} + 3\sqrt{3} = (2 + 3)\sqrt{3} = 5\sqrt{3}$$

■ **PROCEDURE.**   To combine unlike square-root radicals:

1. Simplify each radical.

2. Combine like radicals by using the distributive property.

3. Indicate the sum or difference of the unlike radicals.

| MODEL PROBLEMS |

1. Combine: $8\sqrt{5} + 3\sqrt{5} - 2\sqrt{5}$

   Solution: $8\sqrt{5} + 3\sqrt{5} - 2\sqrt{5} = (8 + 3 - 2)\sqrt{5} = 9\sqrt{5}$ *Ans.*

2. Combine: $5\sqrt{3} + 4\sqrt{12}$

Solution: $5\sqrt{3} + 4\sqrt{12} = 5\sqrt{3} + 4\sqrt{4 \cdot 3}$

$$= 5\sqrt{3} + 4\sqrt{4} \cdot \sqrt{3}$$
$$= 5\sqrt{3} + 4 \cdot 2 \cdot \sqrt{3}$$
$$= 5\sqrt{3} + 8\sqrt{3}$$
$$= (5 + 8)\sqrt{3}$$
$$= 13\sqrt{3} \quad Ans.$$

EXERCISES

In 1–28, combine the radicals.

1. $8\sqrt{2} + 7\sqrt{2}$

2. $8\sqrt{5} + \sqrt{5}$

3. $5\sqrt{3} + 2\sqrt{3} + 8\sqrt{3}$

4. $14\sqrt{6} - 2\sqrt{6}$

5. $7\sqrt{2} - \sqrt{2}$

6. $4\sqrt{3} + 2\sqrt{3} - 6\sqrt{3}$

7. $5\sqrt{3} + \sqrt{3} - 2\sqrt{3}$

8. $4\sqrt{7} - \sqrt{7} - 5\sqrt{7}$

9. $3\sqrt{5} + 6\sqrt{2} - 3\sqrt{2} + \sqrt{5}$

10. $9\sqrt{x} + 3\sqrt{x}$

11. $15\sqrt{y} - 7\sqrt{y}$

12. $\sqrt{2} + \sqrt{50}$

13. $\sqrt{27} + \sqrt{75}$

14. $\sqrt{80} - \sqrt{5}$

15. $\sqrt{72} - \sqrt{50}$

16. $\sqrt{12} - \sqrt{48} + \sqrt{3}$

17. $3\sqrt{32} - 6\sqrt{8}$

18. $5\sqrt{27} - \sqrt{108} + 2\sqrt{75}$

19. $3\sqrt{8} - \sqrt{2}$

20. $5\sqrt{8} - 3\sqrt{18} + \sqrt{3}$

21. $3\sqrt{50} - 5\sqrt{18}$

22. $\sqrt{98} - 4\sqrt{8} + 3\sqrt{128}$

23. $\frac{2}{3}\sqrt{18} - \sqrt{72}$

24. $\sqrt{7a} + \sqrt{28a}$

25. $\sqrt{81x} + \sqrt{25x}$

26. $\sqrt{100b} - \sqrt{64b} + \sqrt{9b}$

27. $3\sqrt{3x} - \sqrt{12x}$

28. $\sqrt{3a^2} + \sqrt{12a^2}$

29. Express in simplest radical form the sum of:
    a. $3\sqrt{2}$ and $\sqrt{98}$ b. $5\sqrt{3}$ and $\sqrt{27}$ c. $2\sqrt{12}$ and $4\sqrt{75}$

30. Express in simplest radical form the difference between:
    a. $4\sqrt{2}$ and $\sqrt{18}$ b. $\sqrt{75}$ and $\sqrt{12}$ c. $4\sqrt{48}$ and $8\sqrt{12}$

31. Which of the numbers $\sqrt{2}$, $9\sqrt{2}$, $-11\sqrt{2}$, $18\sqrt{2}$ is equivalent to $5\sqrt{2} - \sqrt{32}$?

32. Which of the numbers $9\sqrt{10}$, $\sqrt{72}$, $18\sqrt{10}$, $12\sqrt{2}$ is equivalent to the sum of $3\sqrt{8} + 6\sqrt{2}$?

33. Which of the radicals $\sqrt{39}$, $5\sqrt{6}$, $13\sqrt{3}$, $5\sqrt{3}$ is equivalent to the sum of $\sqrt{12}$ and $\sqrt{27}$?

In 34 and 35: **a.** Express the perimeter of the figure in simplest radical form. **b.** Using the table on page 670, approximate the expression obtained in part **a** correct to the nearest tenth.

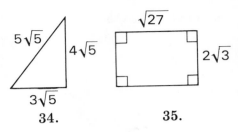

34. **35.**

11 MULTIPLYING SQUARE-ROOT RADICALS

Multiplying Monomials Containing Square-Root Radicals

To find the area of the rectangle pictured at the right, we multiply $5\sqrt{3}$ by $4\sqrt{2}$.

We have learned that $\sqrt{a} \cdot \sqrt{b} = \sqrt{ab}$ when a and b are non-negative numbers. For example, $\sqrt{3} \cdot \sqrt{7} = \sqrt{3 \cdot 7} = \sqrt{21}$.

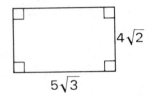

To multiply $4\sqrt{2}$ by $5\sqrt{3}$, we use the commutative and associative laws of multiplication as follows:

$$(4\sqrt{2})(5\sqrt{3}) = (4)(5)(\sqrt{2})(\sqrt{3}) = (4 \cdot 5)(\sqrt{2 \cdot 3}) = 20\sqrt{6}$$

In general, if a and b are non-negative numbers:

$$x\sqrt{a} \cdot y\sqrt{b} = xy\sqrt{ab}$$

■ **PROCEDURE.** To multiply two monomial square roots:

1. Multiply the coefficients to find the coefficient of the product.

2. Multiply the radicands to find the radicand of the product.

3. If possible, simplify the result.

| MODEL PROBLEMS |

1. Multiply: $3\sqrt{6} \cdot 5\sqrt{2}$

Solution: $3\sqrt{6} \cdot 5\sqrt{2} = 3 \cdot 5\sqrt{6 \cdot 2} = 15\sqrt{12} = 15\sqrt{4} \cdot \sqrt{3}$
$$= 15 \cdot 2 \cdot \sqrt{3}$$
$$= 30\sqrt{3} \quad Ans.$$

2. Find the value of $(2\sqrt{3})^2$.

Solution: $(2\sqrt{3})^2 = 2\sqrt{3} \cdot 2\sqrt{3}$

$$= 2 \cdot 2\sqrt{3 \cdot 3} = 4\sqrt{9} = 4 \cdot 3 = 12 \quad Ans.$$

3. Find the indicated product: $\sqrt{3x} \cdot \sqrt{6x}$

Solution: $\sqrt{3x} \cdot \sqrt{6x} = \sqrt{3x \cdot 6x}$

$$= \sqrt{18x^2}$$

$$= \sqrt{9x^2 \cdot 2} = \sqrt{9x^2} \cdot \sqrt{2} = 3x\sqrt{2} \quad Ans.$$

| EXERCISES |

In 1–24: Multiply, or raise to the power, as indicated. Then simplify the result.

1. $\sqrt{3} \cdot \sqrt{3}$ **2.** $\sqrt{7} \cdot \sqrt{7}$ **3.** $\sqrt{a} \cdot \sqrt{a}$

4. $\sqrt{2x} \cdot \sqrt{2x}$ **5.** $\sqrt{12} \cdot \sqrt{3}$ **6.** $2\sqrt{18} \cdot 3\sqrt{8}$

7. $\sqrt{14} \cdot \sqrt{2}$ **8.** $\sqrt{60} \cdot \sqrt{5}$ **9.** $3\sqrt{6} \cdot \sqrt{3}$

10. $5\sqrt{8} \cdot 7\sqrt{3}$ **11.** $\frac{2}{3}\sqrt{24} \cdot 9\sqrt{3}$ **12.** $5\sqrt{6} \cdot \frac{2}{3}\sqrt{15}$

13. $(-4\sqrt{a})(3\sqrt{a})$ **14.** $(-\frac{1}{2}\sqrt{y})(-6\sqrt{y})$ **15.** $(\sqrt{2})^2$

16. $(\sqrt{y})^2$ **17.** $(\sqrt{t})^2$ **18.** $(3\sqrt{6})^2$

19. $\sqrt{25x} \cdot \sqrt{4x}$ **20.** $\sqrt{27a} \cdot \sqrt{3a}$ **21.** $\sqrt{15x} \cdot \sqrt{3x}$

22. $\sqrt{9a} \cdot \sqrt{ab}$ **23.** $(\sqrt{5x})^2$ **24.** $(2\sqrt{t})^2$

In 25–30, **(a)** perform the indicated operation and **(b)** state whether the product is an irrational number or a rational number.

25. $(5\sqrt{12})(4\sqrt{3})$ **26.** $(3\sqrt{2})(2\sqrt{32})$ **27.** $(4\sqrt{6})(9\sqrt{3})$

28. $(8\sqrt{5})(\frac{1}{2}\sqrt{10})$ **29.** $(\frac{2}{3}\sqrt{5})^2$ **30.** $(\frac{1}{6}\sqrt{8})(\frac{1}{2}\sqrt{18})$

In 31–34, find the area of the square in which the length of each side is the given number.

31. $\sqrt{2}$ **32.** $2\sqrt{3}$ **33.** $6\sqrt{2}$ **34.** $5\sqrt{3}$

In 35 and 36: **a.** Express the area of the figure in simplest radical form. **b.** Using the table on page 670, approximate the expression obtained in part **a**, correct to the nearest tenth, if necessary.

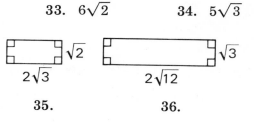

35.   **36.**

12 DIVIDING SQUARE-ROOT RADICALS

Since $\sqrt{\dfrac{4}{9}} = \dfrac{2}{3}$ and $\dfrac{\sqrt{4}}{\sqrt{9}} = \dfrac{2}{3}$, then $\sqrt{\dfrac{4}{9}} = \dfrac{\sqrt{4}}{\sqrt{9}}$.

Since $\sqrt{\dfrac{16}{25}} = \dfrac{4}{5}$ and $\dfrac{\sqrt{16}}{\sqrt{25}} = \dfrac{4}{5}$, then $\sqrt{\dfrac{16}{25}} = \dfrac{\sqrt{16}}{\sqrt{25}}$.

These examples illustrate the following property of square-root radicals:

■ The square root of a fraction that is the quotient of a non-negative number and a positive number is equal to the square root of its numerator divided by the square root of its denominator.

In general, if a is non-negative and b is positive:

$$\sqrt{\dfrac{a}{b}} = \dfrac{\sqrt{a}}{\sqrt{b}} \quad \text{and} \quad \dfrac{\sqrt{a}}{\sqrt{b}} = \sqrt{\dfrac{a}{b}}$$

See how we use this principle when we divide $\sqrt{72}$ by $\sqrt{8}$:

$$\dfrac{\sqrt{72}}{\sqrt{8}} = \sqrt{\dfrac{72}{8}} = \sqrt{9} = 3$$

To divide $6\sqrt{10}$ by $3\sqrt{2}$, we use the property of fractions, $\dfrac{ac}{bd} = \dfrac{a}{b} \cdot \dfrac{c}{d}$.

See how the division is performed:

$$\dfrac{6\sqrt{10}}{3\sqrt{2}} = \dfrac{6}{3} \cdot \dfrac{\sqrt{10}}{\sqrt{2}} = \dfrac{6}{3} \cdot \sqrt{\dfrac{10}{2}} = 2\sqrt{5}$$

In general, if a is non-negative, b is positive, and $y \neq 0$:

$$\dfrac{x\sqrt{a}}{y\sqrt{b}} = \dfrac{x}{y}\sqrt{\dfrac{a}{b}}$$

■ PROCEDURE. To divide two monomial square roots:

1. Divide the coefficients to find the coefficient of the quotient.

2. Divide the radicands to find the radicand of the quotient.

3. If possible, simplify the result.

| MODEL PROBLEM |

Divide: $8\sqrt{48} \div 4\sqrt{2}$

Solution: $8\sqrt{48} \div 4\sqrt{2} = \frac{8}{4}\sqrt{\frac{48}{2}} = 2\sqrt{24} = 2\sqrt{4 \cdot 6} = 2 \cdot \sqrt{4} \cdot \sqrt{6}$

$= 2 \cdot 2 \cdot \sqrt{6} = 4\sqrt{6}$ *Ans.*

| EXERCISES |

In 1–16, divide. Then simplify the quotient.

1. $\sqrt{72} \div \sqrt{2}$ 2. $\sqrt{75} \div \sqrt{3}$ 3. $\sqrt{70} \div \sqrt{10}$ 4. $\sqrt{14} \div \sqrt{2}$

5. $8\sqrt{48} \div 2\sqrt{3}$ 6. $\sqrt{24} \div \sqrt{2}$ 7. $\sqrt{150} \div \sqrt{3}$

8. $21\sqrt{40} \div \sqrt{5}$ 9. $9\sqrt{6} \div 3\sqrt{6}$ 10. $7\sqrt{3} \div 3\sqrt{3}$

11. $2\sqrt{2} \div 8\sqrt{2}$ 12. $\sqrt{9y} \div \sqrt{y}$ 13. $\dfrac{12\sqrt{20}}{3\sqrt{5}}$

14. $\dfrac{20\sqrt{50}}{4\sqrt{2}}$ 15. $\dfrac{25\sqrt{24}}{5\sqrt{2}}$ 16. $\dfrac{3\sqrt{54}}{6\sqrt{3}}$

In 17–22, state whether the quotient is a rational number or an irrational number.

17. $\dfrac{\sqrt{7}}{5}$ 18. $\dfrac{\sqrt{50}}{\sqrt{2}}$ 19. $\dfrac{\sqrt{18}}{\sqrt{3}}$ 20. $\dfrac{\sqrt{49}}{\sqrt{7}}$ 21. $\dfrac{\sqrt{9}}{\sqrt{16}}$ 22. $\dfrac{\sqrt{18}}{\sqrt{25}}$

In 23–28, simplify the given expression.

23. $\sqrt{\frac{36}{49}}$ 24. $\sqrt{\frac{3}{4}}$ 25. $4\sqrt{\frac{5}{16}}$

26. $\sqrt{\frac{8}{49}}$ 27. $10\sqrt{\frac{8}{25}}$ 28. $\frac{2}{3}\sqrt{\frac{144}{64}}$

29. Each of five real numbers is written on a separate piece of paper. The numbers are:

$$\sqrt{\tfrac{1}{4}} \qquad \sqrt{3} \qquad \sqrt{.4} \qquad \sqrt{.64} \qquad \sqrt{\tfrac{2}{9}}$$

These five pieces of paper are placed into a bag and one is chosen at random. Find the probability that the paper chosen contains:

a. a rational number   b. an irrational number   c. the number $\frac{1}{2}$

d. the number .2   e. .8 or $\frac{1}{2}$ f. a real number

chapter twenty-one

The Geometry of the Circle

1 DEFINITIONS AND FUNDAMENTAL RELATIONSHIPS

In Chapter 12 we worked with compasses. Imagine placing the point of a compass on a piece of paper and swinging the pencil portion of the compass around in a full rotation to form a closed figure. The figure drawn by the pencil is a circle.

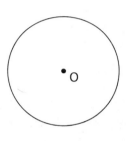

A *circle* is a set of points that lie in a plane so that each of these points is the same distance from a fixed point called the *center* of the circle. When the center is named by the capital letter O, we identify this circle as "circle O".

Segments and Circles

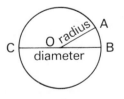

A *radius* of a circle (plural, *radii*) is a *line segment* drawn from the center of the circle to any point on the circle. At the left we see that the segment, $\overline{OA}$, is a radius of circle O. Note that $\overline{OB}$ and $\overline{OC}$ are also radii.

A *diameter* of a circle is a *line segment* that passes through the center of a circle and whose endpoints are on the circle. In the diagram just shown, $\overline{BC}$ is a diameter of circle O.

We will define radius and diameter to mean both the line segments and the lengths of these line segments. Thus, we may say "the length of a radius is 5," or we may simply say "the radius is 5."

A *chord* is a *line segment* whose endpoints are on the circle, such as the segment, $\overline{RS}$, in the diagram to the right.

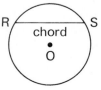

A study of the figure at the right will help us to accept the truth of the following relationships:

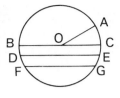

1. A circle has an infinite number of radii, all equal in length, as in $OA = OB = OC$. We may also say that all radii in a circle are congruent, as in $\overline{OA} \cong \overline{OB}$; $\overline{OB} \cong \overline{OC}$; $\overline{OA} \cong \overline{OC}$.

2. A circle has an infinite number of diameters, all equal in length. Also, all diameters in a circle are congruent.

3. A diameter of a circle is twice as large as any one of its radii. For example, the length BC is twice the length OB, written as $BC = 2(OB)$.

4. A circle has an infinite number of chords, which may be of various lengths, such as chords $\overline{BC}$, $\overline{DE}$, and $\overline{FG}$.

5. The largest chord that may be drawn in a circle will be a diameter of that circle. For example, the diameter $\overline{BC}$ is the largest chord in circle O.

Regions and the Circle

A circle separates a plane into three sets of points: the circle itself; a region inside the circle called the *interior region*; and a region outside the circle called the *exterior region*. We observe:

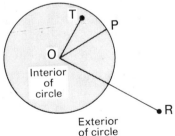

1. A point P is *on the circle* if the distance from the center of the circle to the point P is *equal to* the length of a radius. As shown in the diagram, $\overline{OP}$ is a radius in circle O, and the circle is said to *contain* point P.

2. A point T of the plane is *in the interior region* of the circle if the distance from the center of the circle to the point T is *less than* the length of a radius. As shown in the diagram, $\overline{OT}$ has a length that is less than the length of the radius $\overline{OP}$, written $OT < OP$.

3. A point R of the plane is *in the exterior region* of the circle if the distance from the center of the circle to the point R is *greater than* the length of a radius. As shown in the diagram, $\overline{OR}$ has a length that is greater than the length of the radius $\overline{OP}$, written $OR > OP$.

Relationships Between Circles

Congruent circles are circles whose radii are congruent, or equal in length. In the figure, circle O is congruent to circle O', written circle $O \cong$ circle O', because radius $\overline{OA}$ is congruent to radius $\overline{O'A'}$, written $\overline{OA} \cong \overline{O'A'}$. We may also observe that the diameters of congruent circles will be congruent, or equal in length.

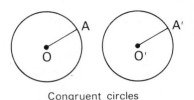

Congruent circles

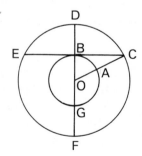

Concentric circles

Concentric circles are circles that lie in the same plane, that have the same center, and that have unequal radii. In the figure the two circles are concentric because they have the same center O but they have radii of different lengths.

MODEL PROBLEMS

1. In the diagram two concentric circles are shown with center O. Points A, B, and G are on the smaller circle; points C, D, E, and F are on the larger circle. $\overline{DF}$ is a line segment containing points B, O, and G; $\overline{OC}$ is a line segment containing point A; $\overline{EC}$ is a line segment containing point B.

   Name the points or segments that describe each condition.

Answers

a. The radii of the smaller circle

b. The radii of the larger circle

c. The chords shown for the larger circle

d. The diameter of the larger circle

e. The points in the exterior of the smaller circle

f. The points in the interior of the larger circle

a. $\overline{OA}$; $\overline{OB}$; $\overline{OG}$

b. $\overline{OC}$; $\overline{OD}$; $\overline{OF}$

c. $\overline{EC}$; $\overline{DF}$

d. $\overline{DF}$

e. C, D, E, F

f. O, A, B, G

2. Use the diagram found in model problem 1 to find the ratio of:
   a. *OD* to *DF*
                                                              b. *OG* to *OA*

   Solution

   a. In the larger circle, $\overline{OD}$ is a radius and $\overline{DF}$ is a diameter. If the radius $\overline{OD}$ measures 1 unit, then the diameter $\overline{DF}$ of the same circle measures 2 units. Hence, the ratio of *OD* to *DF* is 1 to 2, or $1:2$.
                                                              Answer: 1 to 2

   b. In the smaller circle, $\overline{OG}$ and $\overline{OA}$ are both radii. Since all radii of the same circle are equal in length, the ratio *OG* to *OA* is 1 to 1, or $1:1$.
                                                              Answer: 1 to 1

EXERCISES

1. Find the diameter of a circle whose radius measures:
   a. 2 inches   b. 13 feet   c. $2\frac{1}{8}$ inches
   d. 3.5 meters   e. 2.75 centimeters

2. Find the radius of a circle whose diameter measures:
   a. 4 feet   b. 7 inches   c. $3\frac{1}{2}$ inches
   d. 1.4 meters   e. 3.9 centimeters

3. What is the ratio of the radius of a circle to its diameter?
4. What is the ratio of the diameter of a circle to its radius?
5. What is the ratio of the radius of a circle to the radius of a congruent circle?
6. In a circle, what percent of the diameter is the radius?
7. In a circle, what percent of the radius is the diameter?

8. In the figure at the right, points *A*, *B*, and *C* are points on circle *O*. Segments $\overline{AB}$, $\overline{BC}$, $\overline{OB}$, and $\overline{AC}$ are drawn. $\overline{AC}$ contains point *O*. Name the segments that are (a) radii, (b) diameters, and (c) chords.

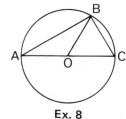

Ex. 8

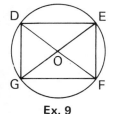

Ex. 9

9. In the figure at the left, points *D*, *E*, *F*, and *G* are points on circle *O*. The segments $\overline{DF}$ and $\overline{EG}$ intersect at *O*. Other segments are drawn connecting points wherever possible. Name all possible segments observed for circle *O* that are (a) radii, (b) diameters, and (c) chords.

In 10–14, circle O contains points A and B.

10. If the length of radius $\overline{OA}$ is 10, find the length of radius $\overline{OB}$.

11. If the length of radius $\overline{OA}$ is 8, find the length of a diameter of the circle.

12. If $OA = 2x + 10$ and $OB = 24$, find the value of x.

13. If $OA = 2x + 10$ and $OB = x + 15$, find the length of radius $\overline{OA}$.

14. If $OA = x + 20$ and $OB = 2x + 6$, find the length of a diameter of the circle.

Ex. 10–14

15. In a circle with diameter 6, a chord $\overline{AB}$ is drawn. What is the maximum length of $\overline{AB}$?

16. In a circle with radius 4, a chord $\overline{CD}$ is drawn. What is the maximum length of $\overline{CD}$?

17. Use compasses to construct:
    a. two congruent circles that do not intersect.
    b. two congruent circles that intersect at two points.
    c. two congruent circles that intersect at only one point.
    d. two concentric circles with a common center O.

18. Use compasses to construct two circles O and O' whose radii are not congruent and that intersect at points R and S. Draw $\overline{OR}$, $\overline{OS}$, $\overline{O'R}$, and $\overline{O'S}$. Answer *true* or *false:*
    a. $OR = OS$ b. $O'R = O'S$ c. $OR = O'R$ d. $O'S = OS$
    e. $\overline{RS}$ is a chord in circle O and circle O'.

2 THE CIRCUMFERENCE OF A CIRCLE

The distance around a circle, or the perimeter of the circle, is called its *circumference*, symbolized by the capital letter C. If we take measurements of different circles, no matter how large or small a circle, we will discover that the circumference of a circle will always be slightly more than 3 times the diameter of that circle. Mathematicians have shown that, for any circle, the ratio of its circumference C to the length of its diameter d will al-

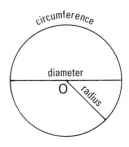

ways be a *constant* value represented by the Greek letter π (read as "pi"). Therefore, we have:

$$\frac{circumference}{diameter} = a\ constant \qquad or \qquad \frac{C}{d} = \pi$$

The Value of π

The number π is an irrational number. Hence, π cannot be represented exactly as a terminating or repeating decimal. Computers have calculated the value of π to more than a quarter million decimal places. Rounded to only ten decimal places, π is 3.1415926536. Most people accept less demanding "approximate" values for π, such as 3.14, $3\frac{1}{7}$, and $\frac{22}{7}$. When we use such numbers in place of π, our answers will be approximations. It is common practice simply to express answers in terms of π, as we shall see later. For now, remember that π is an irrational number found somewhere between 3.14 and $\frac{22}{7}$ on the real number line, that is:

$$3.14 < \pi < \tfrac{22}{7}$$

Finding the Circumference of a Circle

Since $\frac{C}{d} = \pi$, when we multiply both members of the equation by d, we have $\frac{C}{d} \cdot d = \pi \cdot d$. Hence, we obtain the formula:

$$C = \pi d$$

Since d, the length of a diameter of a circle, is equal to twice r, the length of a radius of the circle, that is $d = 2r$, we have $C = \pi d$ or $C = \pi \cdot 2r$. Hence, we obtain the formula:

$$C = 2\pi r$$

The circumference of a circle can be found by:

1. multiplying the length of its diameter by the constant value π, or

2. multiplying twice the length of its radius by the constant value π.

For example, the diameter of a circle is 7 feet. Its circumference is found by the formula $C = \pi d$. Thus, $C = \pi \cdot 7$, or $C = 7\pi$.

Answer: Circumference = 7π feet

Here, the circumference has been given in terms of π. Note that 7π is the *exact* numerical solution. Also, note that circumference is a linear measure, here given in feet, to show that we are measuring the length of the "curved" line.

If we had used an "approximate" value for π, perhaps letting $\pi = 3.14$, then we would say the circumference is "approximately" equal to $(7)(3.14)$, or 21.98 feet. By letting $\pi = \frac{22}{7}$, we would say the circumference is "approximately" equal to $(7)(\frac{22}{7})$, or 22 feet. These rational approximations produce approximate answers.

Approximate Answer: 21.98 feet *or* 22 feet

The Length of an Arc

An *arc* of a circle is any part of the circle. In the diagram at the right, the curved line FG is called arc FG, written in symbols as $\overset{\frown}{FG}$. The arc, $\overset{\frown}{FG}$, contains point F, point G, and all points of the circle between F and G.

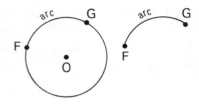

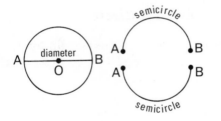

A diameter divides a circle into two parts, each of which is called a *semicircle*. In the diagram at the left, each arc, $\overset{\frown}{AB}$, is a semicircle. Notice that each of the two semicircles formed contains the endpoints A and B. We observe that:

The length of a semicircle is equal to one-half the circumference of the circle.

KEEP IN MIND

Circumference is a measure of length or distance, such as feet, meters, and centimeters.

$$C = \pi d \quad and \quad C = 2\pi r$$

MODEL PROBLEMS

1. Find the circumference of a circle whose radius is 14:
    a. expressed in terms of π b. using $\pi = \frac{22}{7}$ c. using $\pi = 3.14$

Solution

Method 1	Method 2
a. Substitute radius $r = 14$ in the formula $C = 2\pi r$: $$C = 2\pi \cdot 14$$ $$C = 28\pi$$	If the radius $r = 14$, then the diameter $d = 28$. Substitute $d = 28$ in the formula $C = \pi d$: $$C = \pi \cdot 28$$ $$C = 28\pi$$

Answer: $C = 28\pi$

b. Using the approximation $\pi = \frac{22}{7}$, substitute and multiply:

$$C = 28\pi = 28 \cdot \frac{22}{7} = \frac{\overset{4}{\cancel{28}}}{1} \cdot \frac{22}{\cancel{7}_1} = 88 \quad Ans.$$

c. Using the approximation $\pi = 3.14$, substitute and multiply:
$$C = 28\pi = 28(3.14) = 87.92 \quad Ans.$$

2. If the circumference of a circle is 80π, find the length of a radius of this circle.

Solution

(1) Write the formula for the circumference that involves the radius:

$$C = 2\pi r$$

(2) Substitute 80π for the circumference C:

$$80\pi = 2\pi r$$

(3) Solve for radius r by dividing both members of the equation by 2π:

$$\frac{\overset{40}{\cancel{80\pi}}}{\underset{1}{\cancel{2\pi}}} = \frac{\overset{1}{\cancel{2\pi r}}}{\underset{1}{\cancel{2\pi}}}$$

$$40 = r$$

Answer: $r = 40$

3. If the radius of a circle is tripled, what change takes place in the circumference?

Solution

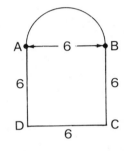

In the original circle, $C = 2\pi r$.
In the new circle, $C' = 2\pi r'$. Let $r' = 3r$ to show that the radius is triple that of the original circle. Then, $C' = 2\pi(3r) = 6\pi r$.

Compare the circumferences: $\dfrac{C'}{C} = \dfrac{6\pi r}{2\pi r}$.

Simplifying, $\dfrac{6\pi r}{2\pi r} = \dfrac{6}{2} = \dfrac{3}{1}$.

Answer: The new circumference is 3 times the original circumference, or the circumference is tripled.

4. In the figure at the right, $\overset{\frown}{AB}$ is a semicircle and $ABCD$ is a square each of whose sides measures 6. Find the perimeter of the geometric figure.

Solution

The perimeter, or distance "around the figure," consists of three sides of the square and the length of the semicircle.

(1) Add the lengths of the three segments which are sides of the square: $6 + 6 + 6 = 18$

(2) The length of semicircle AB is one-half the circumference of a circle whose diameter is 6. Since $C = \pi d = 6\pi$, the length of the semicircle is $\frac{1}{2}(6\pi) = 3\pi$.

(3) Add the lengths of the segments and the semicircle: $18 + 3\pi$

Answer: The perimeter is $18 + 3\pi$, or $3\pi + 18$.

EXERCISES

1. Find the circumference of a circle, expressed in terms of π, when its diameter is:

    a. 10   b. 16   c. 4.7   d. $\frac{1}{3}$ e. .08   f. $1\frac{3}{8}$

2. Find the circumference of a circle, expressed in terms of π, when its radius is:

    a. 4   b. 9   c. 3.8   d. $\frac{1}{5}$ e. .06   f. $1\frac{3}{4}$

3. Find the circumference of a circle, expressed in terms of π, for the given radius r or diameter d.
   a. $r = 5$ cm   b. $d = 9$ ft.   c. $r = 2.4$ mm   d. $d = \frac{1}{3}$ in.
4. Using $\pi = 3.14$, find the approximate length of the circumference of a circle when:
   a. $r = 8$ cm   b. $d = 8$ in.   c. $r = 2.5$ mm   d. $d = 3\frac{1}{2}$ in.
5. Using $\pi = \frac{22}{7}$, find the approximate length of the circumference of a circle when:
   a. $r = 14$ cm   b. $d = 7$ ft.   c. $r = 3.5$ mm   d. $d = 10\frac{1}{2}$ in.
6. How many inches does Joan's bicycle go in one turn of the wheels if the diameter of each wheel is 28 inches? Express your answer to the nearest inch.
7. A circular flower bed has a diameter of 4.2 meters. How many meters of fencing will be needed to enclose this garden? Express your answer to the nearest tenth of a meter.

In 8–12, for the circle whose circumference is given, **(a)** find the length of the diameter of the circle and **(b)** find the length of the radius of the circle.

8. $C = 30\pi$ 9. $C = 25\pi$ 10. $C = \pi$ 11. $C = 4.2\pi$ 12. $C = \frac{1}{3}\pi$

13. The distance around a circular track is 440 yards. Using $\pi = \frac{22}{7}$, find the diameter of the circular track.

In 14–18, select the best answer from the four choices given.

14. If the diameter of a circle is 7, the circumference of the circle is:
    (1) exactly 21.98   (2) exactly 22
    (3) between 21 and 22   (4) exactly 44
15. If the radius of a circle is 14, the circumference of the circle is:
    (1) between 43 and 44   (2) exactly 43.96
    (3) between 87 and 88   (4) exactly 88
16. If the circumference of a circle is exactly 10, then its diameter is:
    (1) $\dfrac{10}{\pi}$ (2) $\dfrac{5}{\pi}$ (3) 10π (4) 5π

17. If the circumference of a circle is exactly 12, then its radius is:
    (1) $\dfrac{12}{\pi}$ (2) $\dfrac{6}{\pi}$ (3) 12π (4) 6π

18. If the diameter of a circle is tripled, then its circumference is multiplied by:
    (1) π (2) 9   (3) 3   (4) 6

19. If the radius of a circle is doubled, what change takes place in its diameter?

20. If the radius of a circle is multiplied by 4, by what number is its circumference multiplied?

21. If the radius of a circle is divided by 2, what change takes place in its circumference?

22. Find the number of inches in the circumference of a circle in which the length of the longest chord that can be drawn is 5 inches. Answer may be expressed in terms of π.

23. Solve for r in terms of C and π: $C = 2\pi r$

24. Solve for d in terms of C and π: $C = \pi d$

25. Solve for π in terms of C and d: $C = \pi d$

26. Find, in terms of π, the length of a semicircle for a circle in which the radius or the diameter is the given measure.
    a. diameter = 8   b. diameter = 5   c. radius = 2   d. radius = 1

In 27–29, find the perimeter of the closed figure whose description is given. Answers should be expressed in terms of π.

27. Two semicircles are placed on opposite sides of a square with a side of length 8.

28. Four semicircles are placed on the sides of a square whose side has a length of 2.

29. Two semicircles, each with a diameter of 5, are removed from a 5 by 12 rectangle.

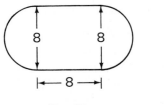

Ex. 27

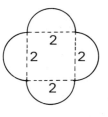

Ex. 28

Ex. 29

3 THE AREA OF A CIRCLE

To find the area of a circle, we must actually find the area of a "circular region." A *circular region* is the union of a circle and all points in the interior of the circle. For convenience, when we discuss the area of a circular region, we will simply refer to this as the *area of a circle*.

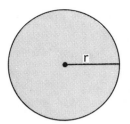

Mathematicians have discovered that the area, A, of a circle is equal to π multiplied by the square of its radius, r. In symbols, we write:

$$A = \pi r^2$$

Recall that area is a square measure. For example, if the radius $r = 3$ feet: $A = \pi r^2 = \pi \cdot (3)^2 = \pi \cdot 9 = 9\pi$. We say that the area is 9π square feet.

While 9π is an irrational number that tells us the exact area of the circle, we can find rational numbers to "approximate" the area. We have seen that $3.14 < \pi < \frac{22}{7}$. By letting $\pi = 3.14$, we approximate the area of 9π as $9(3.14)$, or 28.26 square feet. By letting $\pi = \frac{22}{7}$, we approximate the area of 9π as $9(\frac{22}{7}) = \frac{198}{7}$, or $28\frac{2}{7}$ square feet.

In the region shown at the right, $\overset{\frown}{AB}$ is a semicircle and $\overline{AB}$ is a diameter of circle O whose radius is r. The area of this region equals one-half the area of the circle.

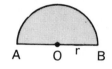

Circle Inscribed in a Polygon

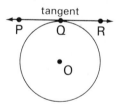

A *tangent* is a line in the plane of a circle that intersects the circle at one and only one point, called the "point of tangency." In the figure at the left, $\overleftrightarrow{PR}$ is a tangent line to circle O, and Q is the point of tangency.

A *circle is inscribed in a polygon* when each of the sides of the polygon is tangent to the circle. At the right, the circle is inscribed in triangle ABC because each of the three sides of the triangle is tangent to the circle. $\overline{AB}$ is tangent to the circle at point D; $\overline{BC}$ is tangent to the circle at point E; $\overline{AC}$ is tangent to the circle at point F.

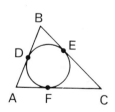

When a circle is inscribed in a polygon, we may also say that the *polygon is circumscribed about the circle.*

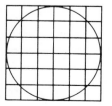

At the left, a circle is inscribed in a square whose side is 6 units in length. Notice the four points of tangency. Whenever a circle is inscribed in a square, we can easily find the length of the diameter of the circle. The diameter is the distance between two points of tangency found on opposite sides of the square. Thus, the diameter is the same length as a side of the square. Here, the diameter is 6 units and the radius is $\frac{1}{2}(6)$ or 3 units. Now we are ready to find the area of the inscribed circle.

We know that the radius of the circle is 3 units. Hence, $A = \pi r^2 = \pi \cdot (3)^2 = \pi \cdot 9 = 9\pi$. We say that the area is 9π square units.

Polygon Inscribed in a Circle

A *polygon is inscribed in a circle* when each of the vertices of the polygon is a point on the circle. At the right, quadrilateral *ABCD* is inscribed in the circle because the vertices *A*, *B*, *C*, and *D* are all points on the circle. Also, triangle *EFG* is inscribed in the circle because the circle passes through *E*, *F*, and *G*, that is, the three vertices of the triangle.

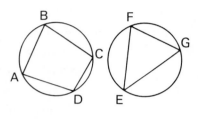

When a polygon is inscribed in a circle, we may also say that the *circle is circumscribed about the polygon.*

In the figure at the left, triangle *RST* is inscribed in circle *O* so that $\overline{RS}$ passes through the center of the circle *O*, and $RS = 12$.

Here we can say that $\overline{RS}$ is a diameter of the circle. Since $RS = 12$, we know that a radius of this circle is 6, and we can then find the area of the circle:

$$A = \pi r^2 = \pi \cdot (6)^2 = \pi \cdot 36 = 36\pi \text{ square units}$$

KEEP IN MIND

Area is a measure of square units, such as square inches (sq. in.) and square centimeters (cm^2).

In a circle, $A = \pi r^2$.

MODEL PROBLEMS

1. Find the area of a circle whose radius is 14:

   a. expressed in terms of π b. using $\pi = 3.14$ c. using $\pi = \frac{22}{7}$

Solution

a. $A = \pi r^2$

$A = \pi \cdot (14)^2$

$A = \pi \cdot 14 \cdot 14$

$A = \pi \cdot 196$

$A = 196\pi$ *Ans.*

b. $A = \pi r^2$

$A = (3.14) \cdot (14)^2$

$A = (3.14) \cdot (196)$

$A = 615.44$ *Ans.*

c. $A = \pi r^2$

$A = \frac{22}{7} \cdot (14)^2$

$A = \frac{22}{\cancel{7}\,1} \cdot \overset{2}{\cancel{14}} \cdot 14$

$A = 616$ *Ans.*

2. If the radius of a circle is tripled, what change takes place in the area of the circle?

   Solution:

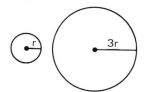

In the original circle, area $A = \pi r^2$.

In the new circle, let the radius $r' = 3r$ to show that the radius is tripled. Then:

$A' = \pi(3r)^2 = \pi \cdot (3r)(3r)$
$\qquad = \pi \cdot (9r^2) = 9\pi r^2$

Compare the areas: $\dfrac{A'}{A} = \dfrac{9\pi r^2}{\pi r^2} = \dfrac{9}{1}$.

   Answer: The new area is 9 times the original area, or the area is multiplied by 9.

3. In the figure at the right, square $ABCD$ is circumscribed about circle O. The radius of circle O is 5. The region between the square and the circle is shaded. Find: **(a)** the diameter of the circle; **(b)** the length of a side of the square; **(c)** the area of the square; **(d)** the area of the circle; **(e)** the area of the shaded region.

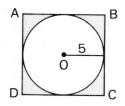

Solution

(a) The length of the diameter d is twice the length of the radius 5. Hence, $d = 2(5) = 10$.   *Ans.*

(b) The length of the side of the square s is equal to the length of the diameter of the inscribed circle. Hence, $s = 10$.   *Ans.*

(c) The area of a square is found by the formula $A = s^2$. Thus, $A = 10^2 = 100$.   *Ans.*

(d) The area of a circle is found by the formula $A = \pi r^2$. Here, $A = \pi r^2 = \pi \cdot (5)^2 = \pi \cdot 25 = 25\pi$.   *Ans.*

(e) The area of the shaded region is the difference between the area of the square and the area of the circle, namely, $100 - 25\pi$. Notice that the smaller area must be subtracted from the larger area.   *Answer:* $100 - 25\pi$

EXERCISES

1. Find the area of a circle, expressed in terms of π, when its radius is:
   a. 4   b. 9   c. .8   d. .3   e. $\frac{1}{3}$ f. $1\frac{1}{2}$

2. Find the area of a circle, expressed in terms of π, when its diameter is:
   a. 12   b. 2   c. 2.4   d. .4   e. $\frac{2}{5}$ f. $2\frac{1}{2}$

3. Find the area of a circle, expressed in terms of π, for the given radius r or diameter d:
   a. $r = 8$ in.   b. $d = 18$ cm   c. $r = \frac{1}{4}$ in.
   d. $d = 0.6$ mm   e. $r = 1.5$ m

4. Using $\pi = 3.14$, find the approximate area of a circle when:
   a. $r = 10$ cm   b. $d = 20$ ft.   c. $r = .4$ mm
   d. $d = 3$ in.   e. $r = .1$ m

5. Using $\pi = \frac{22}{7}$, find the approximate area of a circle when:
   a. $r = 7$ ft.   b. $d = 140$ mm   c. $r = 21$ cm
   d. $d = 7$ in.   e. $r = \frac{1}{2}$ in.

6. What is the length of the radius of a circle when its area is:
   a. 16π b. 81π c. 225π d. $\frac{1}{64}\pi$ e. 1.96π

7. If the area of a circle is 100π, find its (a) radius, (b) diameter, and (c) circumference.

8. If the radius of a circle is 12, find its (a) diameter, (b) circumference, and (c) area.

9. If the diameter of a circle is 2, find its (a) radius, (b) circumference, and (c) area.

10. If the circumference of a circle is 16π, find its (a) diameter, (b) radius, and (c) area.

11. The radius of a circular flower bed is 3.5 meters. a. Express its area in terms of π. b. Use $\pi = \frac{22}{7}$ to find its approximate area.

12. A circular mirror has a diameter of 18 inches. Use $\pi = 3.14$ to find its approximate area.

In 13–16, select the best answer from the four choices given.

13. If the radius of a circle is 7, then the area of the circle is:
    (1) exactly 44   (2) exactly 153.86
    (3) between 153.86 and 154   (4) exactly 154

14. If the diameter of a circle is 20, then the area of the circle is:
    (1) exactly 314   (2) exactly $314\frac{2}{7}$
    (3) between 314 and 315   (4) between 1256 and 1257

15. If the radius of a circle is tripled, then its area is multiplied by:
    (1) 27   (2) 9   (3) 3   (4) 6
16. If the radius of a circle is doubled, then its area is:
    (1) doubled   (2) multiplied by 2
    (3) squared   (4) multiplied by 4

17. If the diameter of a circle is tripled, state the change that takes place in: **a.** its area   **b.** its circumference
18. State the number by which the area of a circle is multiplied when its radius is multiplied by: **a.** 4   **b.** 5   **c.** n
19. If the length of the largest chord that can be drawn in a circle is 10, express the area of the circle in terms of π.
20. In the figure at the right, a circle is inscribed in a square whose side has a length of 12.
    a. Find the diameter of the circle.
    b. Find the radius of the circle.
    c. Find the area of the square.
    d. Find the area of the circle in terms of π.
    e. Using the results of **c** and **d**, express the area of the shaded portion of the diagram in terms of π.

Ex. 20

21. In the diagram at the left, rectangle $ABCD$ is inscribed in circle O. $AB = 6$, $BC = 8$, and $AC = 10$. The diagonal of the rectangle, $\overline{AC}$, is also the diameter of the circle. [Wherever possible, answers may be left in terms of π.]
    a. Find OC.
    b. Find the circumference of circle O.
    c. Find the perimeter of the rectangle.
    d. Find the area of circle O.
    e. Find the area of the rectangle.
    f. Find the area of the shaded region.

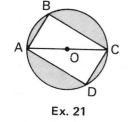

Ex. 21

22. In a metal shop three congruent circles are cut out from a rectangular piece of metal. Each circle has a radius of 4 mm, and the rectangular piece of metal is 12 mm by 30 mm. [Answers may be given in terms of π, where applicable.]

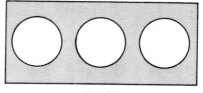

Ex. 22

    a. Find the circumference of any one circle.
    b. Find the perimeter of the rectangle.
    c. Find the area of the rectangular piece before the circles were cut out.

d. Find the area of any one circle.
e. Find the area of the piece of metal after the three circles were cut out.

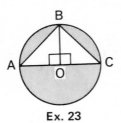

Ex. 23

23. In the figure at the left, triangle ABC is inscribed in circle O, $\overline{AC}$ is a diameter of the circle. The radius, $\overline{OB}$, is an altitude of triangle ABC. OB = 8. [Where possible, express answers in terms of π.]
   a. Find AC.   b. Find the area of circle O.
   c. Find the area of $\triangle ABC$.
   d. Find the area of the shaded region.

24. The diagram at the right shows two circles with the same center. The radii of these concentric circles are 3 and 6, respectively. [Answers may be left in terms of π.]
   a. Find the area of the larger circle.
   b. Find the area of the smaller circle.
   c. Find the area of the shaded region.
   d. Find the circumference of the smaller circle.
   e. Find the circumference of the larger circle.
   f. Complete the statement: If the radius of a circle is doubled, then its circumference is multiplied by ___ .
   g. Complete the statement: If the radius of a circle is doubled, then its area is multiplied by ___ .

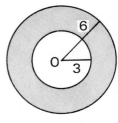

Ex. 24

In 25–27, find the area of the closed figure whose description is given. Express answers in terms of π.

25. Two semicircles are placed on opposite sides of a square with a side of length 8.

26. Four semicircles are placed on the sides of a square whose side has a length of 2.

27. Two semicircles, each with a diameter of 6, are removed from a 6 by 12 rectangle.

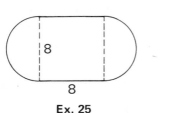

Ex. 25

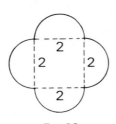

Ex. 26

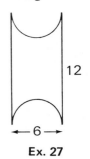

Ex. 27

28. An 8-inch pizza has a diameter of 8 inches; a 12-inch pizza has a diameter of 12 inches. Two boys purchased an 8-inch pizza for $3.20 and shared the pie equally. Four girls purchased a 12-inch pizza for $5.40 and shared the pie equally. Assume that both pies are of the same thickness.

    a. Who got a larger piece of pizza, a boy or a girl? Explain why. [*Hint:* Relate the problem to the area of a circle.]

    b. How much did each boy pay for his share of the pie?

    c. How much did each girl pay for her share of the pie?

    d. Which size pie is the better buy? Explain why.

4 CIRCLES, CENTRAL ANGLES, AND ARCS

In Chapter 11 we learned about angles and their measures. We will now study angles related to the circle.

Central Angle

A *central angle* of a circle is an angle whose vertex is at the center of the circle. In the figure at the right, $\angle AOB$ is a central angle of circle O. If we rotate radius $\overline{OA}$ $\frac{45}{360}$ of a complete rotation to become radius $\overline{OB}$, we say that "the measure of angle AOB is 45 degrees," symbolized as $m\angle AOB = 45°$. We also say that the central angle, $\angle AOB$, *intercepts* or "cuts off" the arc, $\widehat{AB}$.

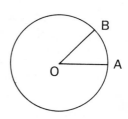

Types of Arcs

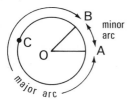

When two distinct points on a circle, such as points A and B, are selected, two arcs are created.

1. The arc that is "smaller" than a semicircle is called a *minor arc*. A minor arc is named by its endpoints, such as $\widehat{AB}$.

2. The arc that is "greater" than a semicircle is called a *major arc*. A major arc is named by three points: the two endpoints and any other point on the major arc. In the figure the major arc is arc ACB, symbolized as $\widehat{ACB}$.

The Degree Measure of an Arc

Before we can say that one arc is greater than another arc or smaller than another arc, we must have some way of measuring an arc. In order to do this, we will make use of the following statement:

■ **The measure of a minor arc is the measure of the central angle that intercepts the arc.**

For example, in circle O, if $m\angle AOB = 35°$, the measure of arc $\overarc{AB}$ is $35°$, symbolized $m\overarc{AB} = 35°$.
Also, if $m\angle COD = 120°$, then $m\overarc{CD} = 120°$.

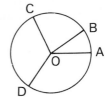

Caution: Do not confuse the *degree measure* of an arc with the *linear measure* of the arc.

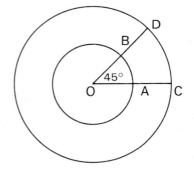

In the figure at the right, $m\overarc{AB} = 45°$ and $m\overarc{CD} = 45°$. The arcs are equal in degree measure.

Suppose the circumferences of the two circles are 8 cm and 16 cm. Since $m\overarc{AB} = 45°$, the length of $\overarc{AB}$ is $\frac{45}{360}$, or $\frac{1}{8}$, of the circumference of the small circle, that is, $\frac{1}{8}$ (8 cm) = 1 cm. Likewise, the length of $\overarc{DC}$ is $\frac{1}{8}$ (16 cm) = 2 cm. Hence, although these arcs are equal in degree measure, they are not equal in linear measure.

In terms of *degree measure:* $\qquad m\overarc{AB} = 45°$
$\qquad\qquad\qquad\qquad\qquad\qquad\quad m\overarc{CD} = 45°$

In terms of *linear measure:* length of $\overarc{AB}$ = 1 cm
$\qquad\qquad\qquad\qquad\qquad\qquad$ length of $\overarc{CD}$ = 2 cm

In our work we will make use of the following relationships:

1. The measure of a circle is 360°.

2. The measure of a semicircle is 180°.
    This is so because a diameter of a circle deter-
mines two semicircles that are equal in measure.
In the figure at the right, $\overline{FE}$ is a diameter.
Hence, $m\overset{\frown}{FGE} = 180°$ and $m\overset{\frown}{FHE} = 180°$.

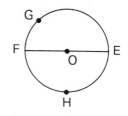

3. The measure of a major arc is equal to 360° minus the measure of
the minor arc named by the same endpoints.

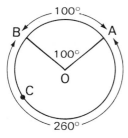

In circle O at the left, $m\angle AOB = 100°$ and
$m\overset{\frown}{AB} = 100°$. Since the minor arc, $\overset{\frown}{AB}$, and the
major arc, $\overset{\frown}{BCA}$, are both named by the same
endpoints, we can say $m\overset{\frown}{BCA} = 360° - m\overset{\frown}{AB} =$
$360° - 100° = 260°$. In general terms, if $m\overset{\frown}{AB} = x°$,
then $m\overset{\frown}{BCA} = (360 - x)°$.

Congruent Arcs

Congruent arcs are arcs that have the *same degree measure* and the
same *linear measure*, or length.

In circle O, $m\overset{\frown}{AB} = 70°$ and $m\overset{\frown}{CD} =$
70°. Since these arcs are found on
the same circle, we know that the
length of $\overset{\frown}{AB}$ equals the length of
$\overset{\frown}{CD}$; that is, each arc has a length of
$\frac{70}{360}$ of the circumference of circle O.
Hence, we can say that "arc AB is
congruent to arc CD," written $\overset{\frown}{AB} \cong \overset{\frown}{CD}$.

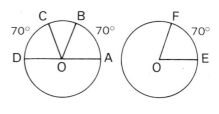

When circle O and circle O' have the same radii, then we know that
circle O is congruent to circle O'. Since the arc, $\overset{\frown}{EF}$, has a degree measure of 70°, we know that its length is $\frac{70}{360}$ of the same length circum-
ference as circle O. Thus we can say that $\overset{\frown}{EF} \cong \overset{\frown}{AB}$ and $\overset{\frown}{EF} \cong \overset{\frown}{CD}$.

**In the same circle, or in congruent circles, arcs that have equal degree
measures will have equal lengths. Such arcs are called congruent arcs.**

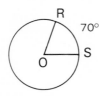

Notice that the arc, $\overset{\frown}{SR}$, has a degree measure of 70° in the circle at the left. Since this circle is *not* congruent to circle O' shown above, $\overset{\frown}{SR}$ and $\overset{\frown}{EF}$ are *not* congruent arcs. While both arcs have the same degree measures, they have different lengths.

We should now be able to prove informally the following statement:

■ **In a circle, or in congruent circles, congruent arcs have congruent chords.**

In circle O we are given congruent arcs $\overset{\frown}{AB}$ and $\overset{\frown}{CD}$. We wish to prove that they have congruent chords, that is, $\overline{AB} \cong \overline{CD}$.

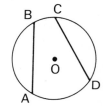

1. From the center O of the circle, we draw radii $\overline{OA}$, $\overline{OB}$, $\overline{OC}$, and $\overline{OD}$. Thus, two triangles are formed: $\triangle AOB$ and $\triangle DOC$.

2. Since $\overset{\frown}{AB}$ and $\overset{\frown}{CD}$ are given to us as congruent arcs, we know that these arcs have the same measure, that is, $m\overset{\frown}{AB} = m\overset{\frown}{CD}$.

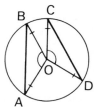

3. If $m\overset{\frown}{AB} = x°$, then $m\overset{\frown}{CD} = x°$. Since a central angle is equal in measure to its intercepted arc, $m\angle AOB = x°$ and $m\angle COD = x°$. Hence, $m\angle AOB = m\angle COD$ and $\angle AOB \cong \angle COD$.

4. All radii of the same circle are congruent. So, $\overline{OA} \cong \overline{OD}$ and $\overline{OB} \cong \overline{OC}$.

5. From steps 3 and 4 we see that $\triangle AOB \cong \triangle DOC$ [s.a.s.].

6. Therefore, $\overline{AB} \cong \overline{DC}$, because corresponding sides of congruent triangles are congruent.

MODEL PROBLEMS

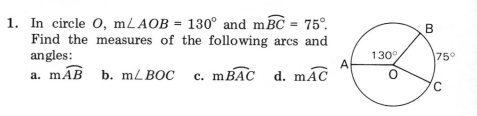

1. In circle O, $m\angle AOB = 130°$ and $m\overset{\frown}{BC} = 75°$. Find the measures of the following arcs and angles:

    a. $m\overset{\frown}{AB}$ b. $m\angle BOC$ c. $m\overset{\frown}{BAC}$ d. $m\overset{\frown}{AC}$

Solution

a. The measure of a minor arc is equal to the measure of the central angle that intercepts the arc. Hence, $m\overarc{AB} = m\angle AOB = 130°$. *Ans.*

b. The measure of a central angle is equal to the measure of the minor arc it intercepts. Hence, $m\angle BOC = m\overarc{BC} = 75°$. *Ans.*

c. The arc $\overarc{BAC}$ is a major arc associated with the minor arc $\overarc{BC}$. The measure of a major arc is $360°$ minus the measure of its associated minor arc. Thus, $m\overarc{BAC} = 360° - m\overarc{BC} = 360° - 75° = 285°$. *Ans.*

d. From part a we know $m\overarc{AB} = 130°$, and we are given $m\overarc{BC} = 75°$. The sum of the measures of all the minor arcs on the circle (which have only endpoints in common) is equal to the measure of the circle itself:

$$m\overarc{AB} + m\overarc{BC} + m\overarc{CA} = 360°$$

Substitute the values: $130° + 75° + m\overarc{CA} = 360°$

Hence, $m\overarc{CA} = 360° - (130° + 75°) = 360° - 205° = 155°$. *Ans.*

2. In circle O, $m\overarc{CD} = 100°$ and chord $\overline{CD}$ is drawn. Find $m\angle ODC$.

Solution

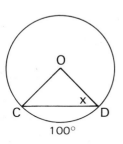

Since $\overline{OC}$ and $\overline{OD}$ are radii in the same circle, they are congruent: $\overline{OC} \cong \overline{OD}$.

Thus, $\triangle COD$ is isosceles. The measure of vertex $\angle COD = m\overarc{CD} = 100°$. Then, $\angle ODC$ is a base angle. So, $m\angle ODC = \frac{1}{2}(180° - 100°) = \frac{1}{2}(80°) = 40°$. *Ans.*

EXERCISES

1. Find the measure of a central angle that intercepts an arc whose measure is:
   a. $70°$ b. $140°$ c. $23°$ d. r e. $4x$
2. Find the measure of the arc intercepted by a central angle whose measure is:
   a. $30°$ b. $60°$ c. $117°$ d. r e. $180 - x$

In 3–7, O is the center of each circle. Find the value of x.

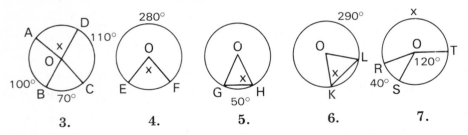

3.   4.   5.   6.   7.

In 8–11, complete each sentence with a word or a number to make the sentence true.

8. In a circle, $\overline{RS}$ is a diameter and T is a point on the circle. Then $m\widehat{RTS}$ = _____.

9. Arcs with the same degree measure and the same linear measure are called _____ arcs.

10. Points A, B, and C are on circle O. If $m\widehat{ABC} = 260°$, then $m\widehat{AC}$ = _____ degrees.

11. Points A, B, and C are on circle O. If $\overline{AB}$ is a diameter and $m\widehat{AC} = 45°$, then $m\widehat{CB}$ = _____ degrees.

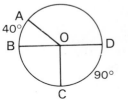

In 12–16, use circle O at the left. Here $\overline{BD}$ is a diameter, $m\widehat{CD} = 90°$, and $m\widehat{AB} = 40°$.

12. In each part find the measure of the central angle that is named.
   a. $\angle AOB$ b. $\angle DOC$ c. $\angle COB$
   d. $\angle AOD$ e. $\angle AOC$

13. In each part find the measure of the arc of circle O that is named.
   a. $\widehat{AD}$ b. $\widehat{DC}$ c. $\widehat{CB}$ d. $\widehat{AC}$ e. $\widehat{ADC}$ f. $\widehat{DAC}$

14. Name the semicircles found in circle O.

15. Name an arc of circle O congruent to $\widehat{CD}$.

16. Give one name for the major arc of circle O that is associated with the minor arc, $\widehat{CB}$.

17. In circle O at the right, $m\widehat{ST} = 130°$, $m\angle ROU = 50°$, and $\widehat{TU} \cong \widehat{RS}$. In each part find the measure named.
   a. $m\widehat{RU}$ b. $m\angle TOS$ c. $m\widehat{TU}$
   d. $m\angle SOR$ e. $m\angle SOU$ f. $m\widehat{RT}$

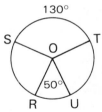

18. Angle AOB is a central angle in circle O, and chord $\overline{AB}$ is drawn. If the length of chord $\overline{AB}$ is equal to the length of a radius, find $m\angle AOB$.

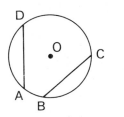

19. In the circle at the left, $m\widehat{AB} = 30°$, $m\widehat{DC} = 130°$, and $m\widehat{AD} = m\widehat{BC}$.
   a. Find $m\widehat{AD}$. b. Find $m\widehat{BC}$. c. Find $m\widehat{ABC}$.
   d. If $AD = 3x + 5$ and $BC = x + 17$, find the length of the chord $\overline{AD}$.

20. A square $ABCD$ is inscribed in circle O.
   a. Find $m\angle AOB$.   b. If $AB = 5$, find BC.

21. A regular pentagon $ABCDE$ is inscribed in circle O.
   a. Find $m\angle DOE$.
   b. If $AB = 3x - 2$ and $CD = 5x - 14$, find the length of $\overline{AB}$.

22. In circle O, $m\widehat{RST} = 220°$ and $\widehat{RS} \cong \widehat{ST}$. Find the measures named.   a. $m\widehat{RS}$ b. $m\widehat{ST}$ c. $m\widehat{RT}$ d. $m\widehat{RTS}$

23. In circle O, $m\widehat{ABC} = 300°$ and $m\widehat{AB} = 90°$. Find the measures named.   a. $m\widehat{AC}$ b. $m\widehat{ACB}$ c. $m\widehat{BC}$

5   THE CIRCLE GRAPH

A direct application of central angles can be found in a *circle graph*. Here a circle is used to represent a whole quantity, such as a budget or the total number of people interviewed in a statistical study. To show how this whole quantity is divided into parts, we divide the circle into sectors.

A *sector* is a part of a circle whose boundaries are the two radii of a central angle and the arc intercepted by that angle.

In every circle graph the ratio of the sector to the whole circle must be equal to the ratio of the quantity that the sector represents to the whole quantity. Thus, the size of the sector is determined by the number of degrees in its central angle. As we will see in the following examples, the measure of the central angle divided by 360° will equal the fractional part of the whole quantity represented by a sector.

| MODEL PROBLEM |

The distribution by ages of the 60 students who are enrolled in computer courses in a high school is shown by the following circle graph. Use this graph to answer questions 1–6.

1. What percent of the students are 14 years of age?
   Answer: 15%

2. Which age group has 25% of the enrolled students?
   Answer: 16 years of age

3. What is the largest age group in the class?
   Answer: 15 years of age

4. What is the smallest age group in the class?
   Answer: 17 years of age

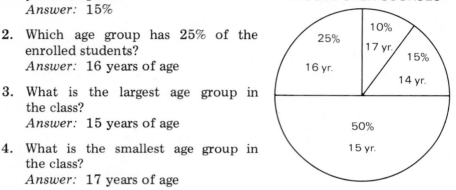

AGES OF STUDENTS
IN COMPUTER COURSES

5. What is the ratio of the number of students who are 15 years old to the number of those that are 16 years old?

   Solution: The ratio of the 15-year-olds to that of the 16-year-olds is 50% to 25%, or 2 to 1.   *Answer:* 2 to 1

6. Find the number of students in each age group that are enrolled in the computer courses.

Solution

Age Group	Percent	Part of Total	Number of Students
14 yr.	15%	$\frac{15}{100} = \frac{3}{20}$	$\frac{3}{20} \times 60 = 9$
15 yr.	50%	$\frac{50}{100} = \frac{1}{2}$	$\frac{1}{2} \times 60 = 30$
16 yr.	25%	$\frac{25}{100} = \frac{1}{4}$	$\frac{1}{4} \times 60 = 15$
17 yr.	10%	$\frac{10}{100} = \frac{1}{10}$	$\frac{1}{10} \times 60 = 6$
Total	100%	$\frac{100}{100} = 1$	60

Answer: 9 are 14 years old; 30 are 15 years old; 15 are 16 years old; and 6 are 17 years old.

| EXERCISES |

1. The graph at the right shows the uses to which a merchant put each sales dollar in his business. During the year, his total sales were $120,000.

a. How much out of every dollar was devoted to expenses?

b. What percent of profit did the merchant realize?

c. What percent of his sales was spent on the cost of goods?

d. How much out of every dollar was not profit?

e. Using total sales of $120,000 for the year, find the dollar amount of (1) his expenses for the year, (2) his profit for the year, and (3) the cost of goods for the year.

f. Find the number of degrees in each of the three central angles shown on the circle graph.

THE SALES DOLLAR

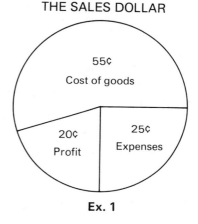

Ex. 1

MARGARET'S BUDGET

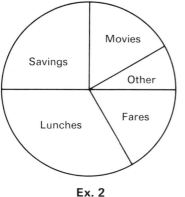

Ex. 2

2. The circle graph at the left shows how Margaret planned to spend her $6 weekly allowance: $33\frac{1}{3}\%$ lunches; 25% savings; $16\frac{2}{3}\%$ fares; $16\frac{2}{3}\%$ movies; $8\frac{1}{3}\%$ other.

a. What fractional part of her weekly allowance did she plan to spend on each item in her budget?

b. How much did she plan to spend on each item in her budget?

c. What are the measures of the central angles depicted for the five categories of Margaret's budget?

3. A circle is to be divided into three sectors that are to be $\frac{1}{4}$, $\frac{1}{3}$, and $\frac{5}{12}$ of the circle. Find the number of degrees in the central angle of each sector.

4. In a circle graph four sectors are shown representing $36°$, $60°$, $90°$, and $174°$. Express each sector as a fraction of the circle, reduced to lowest terms.

5. The senior class of Highview High School posted the graph pictured at the right, showing what the seniors planned to do after graduation. The measures of the central angles are given for each sector.

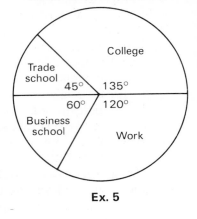

WHAT WE PLAN TO DO

Ex. 5

a. What fractional part of the graduating class plans to go to (1) college? (2) work? (3) business school? (4) trade school?
b. How many times as many seniors plan to go to work as those who plan to go to business school?
c. If there are 240 seniors in the graduating class, how many plan to go to (1) college? (2) work? (3) business school? (4) trade school?

6. Mr. Cummings has planned a budget of his income: 20% for rent; 30% for food; 40% for expenses; 10% for savings. If this budget were shown on a circle graph, how many degrees would there be in the central angle of each sector?

6 ANGLES FORMED BY CHORDS

Let us recall a principle involving a triangle that we have previously studied, namely:

The measure of an exterior angle of a triangle is equal to the sum of the measures of the two remote interior angles.

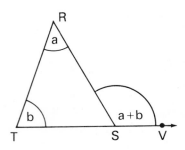

In the figure at the right, $m\angle RSV = m\angle SRT + m\angle STR$. If $m\angle SRT = a$ and $m\angle STR = b$, then $m\angle RSV = a + b$.

We will use this principle to prove statements about angles formed by chords in a circle.

Inscribed Angle

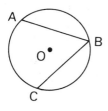

An *inscribed angle* of a circle is an angle whose vertex lies on the circle and whose sides are chords of the circle. In circle O at the left, $\angle ABC$ is called an inscribed angle. The sides of the angle, $\overline{AB}$ and $\overline{BC}$, are chords of the circle, and the vertex of the angle, B, is a point on the circle.

Notice that the inscribed angle, $\angle ABC$, *intercepts* or "cuts off" the arc, $\overset{\frown}{AC}$. Let us study a relationship that exists between the measure of an inscribed angle of a circle and the measure of its intercepted arc.

In figure 1, with the use of a protractor, we find that $m\angle ABC = 75°$ and $m\overset{\frown}{AC} = 150°$. Hence, $m\angle ABC = \frac{1}{2}m\overset{\frown}{AC}$. In figure 2, with the use of a protractor, we find that $m\angle DEF = 40°$ and $m\overset{\frown}{DF} = 80°$. Hence, $m\angle DEF = \frac{1}{2}m\overset{\frown}{DF}$.

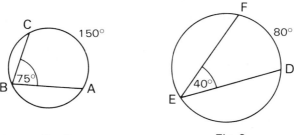

Fig. 1   Fig. 2

These examples illustrate the following relationship, which is always true.

■ **The measure of an angle inscribed in a circle is equal to one-half the measure of its intercepted arc.**

Let us informally prove the truth of this statement.

■ **Case I:** *The center of the circle is on one side of the angle.*

In circle O, $\angle ABC$ is an inscribed angle and $\overline{AB}$ is a diameter.

(1) Draw radius $\overline{OC}$.

(2) Suppose $m\angle ABC = x$.

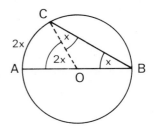

(3) In $\triangle BOC$, $\overline{OB}$ and $\overline{OC}$ are congruent because they are radii of the same circle. Hence, $\triangle BOC$ is an isosceles triangle in which $m\angle OBC = m\angle OCB = x$.

(4) Since diameter $\overline{AB}$ is a straight line, $\angle AOC$ is an exterior angle to $\triangle BOC$. Hence, $m\angle AOC = m\angle OBC + m\angle OCB$, or $m\angle AOC = x + x$, that is, $m\angle AOC = 2x$.

(5) Since $\overline{OA}$ and $\overline{OC}$ are radii of circle O, $\angle AOC$ is a central angle whose measure is equal to the measure of its intercepted arc, $\overset{\frown}{AC}$. Thus, $m\overset{\frown}{AC} = 2x$.

(6) Since $m\angle ABC = x$ and $m\overset{\frown}{AC} = 2x$, it follows that $m\angle ABC = \frac{1}{2}m\overset{\frown}{AC}$.

Now let us consider what happens when the center of the circle does not lie on one side of the angle.

■ **Case II:** *The center of the circle is in the interior of the angle.*

(1) From vertex B of the inscribed angle ABC, draw diameter $\overline{BD}$ through O.

(2) $m\angle ABD = \frac{1}{2}m\overset{\frown}{AD}$, and $m\angle DBC = \frac{1}{2}m\overset{\frown}{DC}$.

(3) Hence, $m\angle ABD + m\angle DBC = \frac{1}{2}m\overset{\frown}{AD} + \frac{1}{2}m\overset{\frown}{DC}$ because when equal quantities are added to equal quantities, the results will be equal.

(4) By the addition of angles, $m\angle ABC = \frac{1}{2}m\overset{\frown}{AD} + \frac{1}{2}m\overset{\frown}{DC}$, or $m\angle ABC = \frac{1}{2}(m\overset{\frown}{AD} + m\overset{\frown}{DC})$.

(5) Hence, $m\angle ABC = \frac{1}{2}m\overset{\frown}{AC}$.

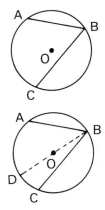

■ **Case III:** *The center of the circle is in the exterior of the angle.*

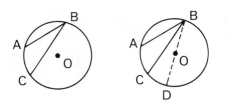

The proof of this case, which is similar to the proof of Case II, is left as an exercise for the student.

[*Hint:* Draw diameter $\overline{BD}$. Show that because $m\angle ABC + m\angle CBD = m\angle ABD$, it follows that $m\angle ABC = m\angle ABD - m\angle CBD$.]

Hence, we can see that for all cases:

The measure of an angle inscribed in a circle is equal to one-half the measure of its intercepted arc.

In circle O, $m\angle ABC = \frac{1}{2}m\widehat{AC}$.

MODEL PROBLEMS

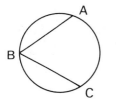

1. In the accompanying circle, arc AC measures $130°$. Find the number of degrees in inscribed angle ABC.

   Solution: $m\angle ABC = \frac{1}{2}m\widehat{AC} = \frac{1}{2}(130) = 65$.

   Answer: $65°$

2. Triangle DEF is inscribed in circle O, $\overline{DF}$ is a diameter, $m\angle EFD = 25°$. Find:
   a. $m\widehat{DE}$ b. $m\angle DEF$

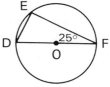

   Solution

   a. The measure of an inscribed angle is half the measure of its intercepted arc. Therefore, the intercepted arc has a measure that is twice the measure of the inscribed angle. Hence, $m\widehat{DE} = 2 \cdot m\angle EFD = 2 \cdot 25 = 50$.   *Answer:* $50°$

   b. $\angle DEF$ is an inscribed angle that intercepts the arc, $\widehat{DF}$. Since $\overline{DF}$ is a diameter, the intercepted arc is a semicircle that measures $180°$. Thus, $m\angle DEF = \frac{1}{2} \cdot 180 = 90$.   *Answer:* $90°$

EXERCISES

1. Find the measure of an inscribed angle that intercepts an arc whose measure is:
   a. 80   b. 140   c. 102   d. 95   e. $2b$ f. x
2. Find the measure of the arc intercepted by an inscribed angle whose measure is:
   a. 60   b. 160   c. 84   d. 105   e. $4k$ f. y
3. Inscribed angle ABC of circle O measures $75°$. Find $m\widehat{AC}$.

In 4–13, O is the center of each circle. Find the value of both x and y, where indicated.

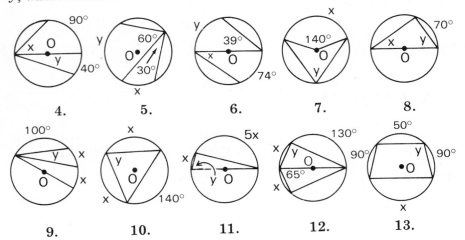

4.   5.   6.   7.   8.

9.   10.   11.   12.   13.

14. Equilateral triangle ABC is inscribed in circle O. Find the measures named.   a. $m\angle A$ b. $m\overarc{BC}$ c. $m\overarc{BAC}$

15. $\overline{AB}$ is a diameter of a circle, $\overline{AC}$ is a chord, and $m\overarc{AC} = 100°$. Find $m\angle CAB$.

16. Inscribed angle RST of circle O measures $80°$. Radii $\overline{RO}$ and $\overline{TO}$ are drawn. Find $m\angle ROT$.

17. Square $ABCD$ is inscribed in circle O. Find: a. $m\overarc{ABC}$ b. $m\overarc{ABD}$

Angles Formed by Two Chords

In circle O at the right, chords $\overline{AB}$ and $\overline{CD}$ intersect at point E. Let us consider one of the angles formed, for example $\angle AED$ (which has the same measure as $\angle CEB$). We say that this angle intercepts two arcs on the circle, namely, $\overarc{AD}$ and $\overarc{CB}$.

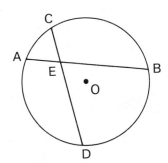

Using a protractor, we find that $m\overarc{AD} = 130°$, $m\overarc{CB} = 90°$, and $m\angle AED = 110°$. Notice that $m\angle AED = \frac{1}{2}(m\overarc{AD} + m\overarc{CB})$ because $110° = \frac{1}{2}(130° + 90°)$.

This example illustrates the truth of the following statement, which we will prove informally:

■ In a circle the measure of an angle formed by two chords intersecting within the circle is equal to one-half the sum of the measures of the intercepted arcs.

Let us consider a general case in which $m\widehat{AD} = x$ and $m\widehat{CB} = y$. In the figure, $\overline{AB}$ and $\overline{CD}$ intersect at point E.

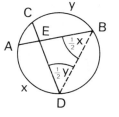

(1) Draw $\overline{BD}$, creating $\triangle BED$.

(2) $\angle ABD$ is an inscribed angle. Its measure must equal one-half the measure of its intercepted arc, $\widehat{AD}$. Thus, $m\angle ABD = \frac{1}{2} m\widehat{AD} = \frac{1}{2} x$.

(3) $\angle CDB$ is an inscribed angle whose intercepted arc is $\widehat{CB}$. Thus, $m\angle CDB = \frac{1}{2} m\widehat{CB} = \frac{1}{2} y$.

(4) Since chord $\overline{AB}$ is a straight line, at vertex E, $\angle AED$ is an exterior angle to $\triangle BED$. Also, $\angle ABD$ and $\angle CDB$ are the two remote interior angles. Thus,

$$m\angle AED = m\angle ABD + m\angle CDB$$
$$m\angle AED = \frac{1}{2} x + \frac{1}{2} y = \frac{1}{2} (x + y)$$

(5) Since we were given $m\widehat{AD} = x$ and $m\widehat{CB} = y$, we can substitute to say

$$m\angle AED = \frac{1}{2} (m\widehat{AD} + m\widehat{CB}).$$

In a similar manner we can prove that:

$$m\angle CEB = \frac{1}{2} (m\widehat{AD} + m\widehat{CB}) \qquad m\angle AEC = \frac{1}{2} (m\widehat{AC} + m\widehat{BD})$$
$$m\angle BED = \frac{1}{2} (m\widehat{AC} + m\widehat{BD})$$

MODEL PROBLEMS

1. In circle O, chords $\overline{AC}$ and $\overline{BD}$ intersect at E; $m\widehat{BC} = 90°$; $m\widehat{CD} = 50°$; $m\widehat{AD} = 120°$. Find $m\angle BEA$.

Solution

The measure of $\angle BEA$ is half the sum of the measures of its intercepted arcs, $\widehat{AB}$ and $\widehat{CD}$. Since the degree measure of a circle is $360°$, $m\widehat{AB} = 360 - (90 + 50 + 120) = 360 - 260 = 100$. Then $m\angle BEA = \frac{1}{2} (m\widehat{AB} + m\widehat{CD}) = \frac{1}{2} (100 + 50) = \frac{1}{2} (150) = 75$.

Answer: $75°$

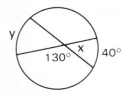

2. In the circle shown at the left, two chords intersect to form an angle whose measure is x. This angle intercepts arcs of $40°$ and y degrees. The chords also form an angle of $130°$.

a. Find x.   b. Find y.

Solution

a. The angles with measures of x and 130 form a linear pair.
Thus, $x + 130 = 180$, or $x = 50$.

Answer: $50°$

b. Since $x = 50$, we can say:
$$50 = \tfrac{1}{2}(y + 40)$$
Multiplying by 2, we get:
$$100 = y + 40$$
$$60 = y$$

Answer: $60°$

| EXERCISES |

1. Find the measure of the angle formed by two chords intersecting within a circle if the opposite arcs they intersect measure:
   a. 30 and 70   b. 20 and 110   c. 72 and 116   d. $4x$ and $14x$

In 2-6, two chords intersect within a circle. Find the measure of the angle or the arc marked as x.

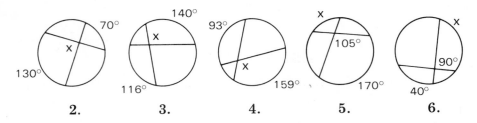

2.   **3.**   **4.**   **5.**   **6.**

7. Two chords intersect within a circle to form an angle whose measure is 60. One of the intercepted arcs measures 80. What is the measure of the other intercepted arc?

In 8–12, O is the center of the circle. Chords $\overline{AB}$ and $\overline{CD}$ intersect within the circle. Find the value of x and y, as indicated.

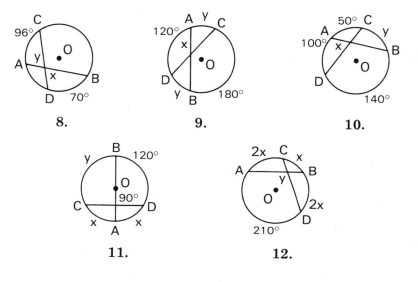

8.   9.   10.

11.   12.

7 MORE ABOUT VOLUMES OF SOLID FIGURES

There are three solid figures that are related to the circle in some way. Let us see how.

The Right Circular Cylinder

The upper and lower bases of a *right circular cylinder* are parallel, congruent circles. The perpendicular distance between the two bases is the height of the right circular cylinder.

The rule for finding the volume of a right circular cylinder is: "The volume, V, of a right circular cylinder is equal to the area of the base, B, multiplied by the height, h."

This rule gives us the following formula:

$$V = Bh$$

Since the base is a circle whose area is πr^2, another formula for the volume of a right circular cylinder is:

$$V = \pi r^2 h$$

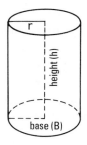

Right Circular Cylinder

The Cone

In the *cone* and the *right circular cylinder* pictured at the left, the bases are congruent circles and the heights are also congruent. If we were to fill the cone with water three times and each time pour the water into the cylinder, we would find that the cylinder would be full. This means that the volume, or capacity, of the cone is $\frac{1}{3}$ of the volume of the right circular cylinder.

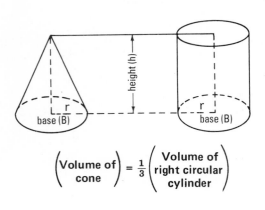

$$\left(\begin{array}{c}\textbf{Volume of}\\\textbf{cone}\end{array}\right) = \frac{1}{3}\left(\begin{array}{c}\textbf{Volume of}\\\textbf{right circular}\\\textbf{cylinder}\end{array}\right)$$

Since the formula for the volume of a right circular cylinder is $V = Bh$, or $V = \pi r^2 h$, the formula for the volume of the cone is:

$$V = \tfrac{1}{3} Bh \quad or \quad V = \tfrac{1}{3}\pi r^2 h$$

The Sphere

A circle has been described as a set of points on a *plane* that are equally distant from one fixed point called the center.

A *sphere* is the set of all points in *space* that are equally distant from one fixed point called the center. A line segment, such as $\overline{OC}$, which joins the center O to any point on the sphere, is called a *radius* of the sphere. A line segment, such as $\overline{AB}$, which joins two points of the sphere and passes through its center, is called a *diameter* of the sphere.

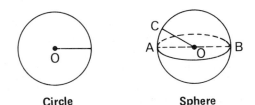

Circle   Sphere

The volume of a sphere is found by multiplying $\frac{4}{3}\pi$ by the cube of the radius:

$$V = \tfrac{4}{3}\pi r^3$$

MODEL PROBLEM

A cylindrical can has a radius of $3\frac{1}{2}$ inches and a height 8 inches. Express the volume:

     a. in terms of π **b.** as a rational approximation, using $\pi = \frac{22}{7}$

Solution

  a. $V = \pi r^2 h = \pi \cdot \frac{7}{2} \cdot \frac{7}{2} \cdot \frac{8}{1} = 98\pi$ *Answer:* 98π cu. in.

  b. $V = \pi r^2 h = \frac{22}{7} \cdot \frac{7}{2} \cdot \frac{7}{2} \cdot \frac{8}{1} = 308$ *Answer:* 308 cu. in.

EXERCISES

In 1-4, find the volume of a right circular cylinder that has the given dimensions: **a.** in terms of π **b.** using $\pi = \frac{22}{7}$

1. $r = 21$ in., $h = 10$ in.   **2.** $r = 28$ ft., $h = \frac{3}{4}$ ft.

3. $r = 10$ cm, $h = 4.2$ cm   **4.** $r = 1.4$ m, $h = 6$ m

In 5-8, find the volume of a cone that has the given dimensions:

a. in terms of π **b.** using $\pi = 3.14$

5. $r = 10$ in., $h = 12$ in.   **6.** $r = 6$ ft., $h = \frac{1}{3}$ ft.

7. $r = 1$ mm, $h = 3$ mm   **8.** $r = .2$ cm, $h = 2.4$ cm

9. Find the volume of a sphere with radius 10:
     a. in terms of π **b.** using $\pi = 3.14$

10. Find the volume of a sphere with radius $3\frac{1}{2}$:
     a. in terms of π **b.** using $\pi = \frac{22}{7}$

11. A tank in the form of a right circular cylinder is used for storing water. It has a diameter of 12 feet and a height of 14 feet. How many gallons of water will it hold? Use $\pi = \frac{22}{7}$. [1 cubic foot contains 7.5 gallons.]

12. Two right circular cylinders have equal bases. The height of one cylinder is twice the height of the other. How do their volumes compare?

13. Two right circular cylinders have equal heights. The radius of the first cylinder is twice the radius of the other. How do their volumes compare?

In 14–18, select the numeral indicating the true answer.

14. The formula for the volume of a sphere is $\frac{4}{3}\pi r^3$. If its radius is doubled, the volume is:
(1) doubled   (2) squared   (3) cubed   (4) multiplied by 8

15. The formula for the volume of a cone is $\frac{1}{3}\pi r^2 h$. If its radius is doubled and the height is unchanged, the volume is:
(1) doubled   (2) squared
(3) multiplied by 4   (4) increased by 4

16. The radius of a cone is tripled while its height is held constant. Then its volume is:
(1) tripled   (2) cubed
(3) multiplied by 6   (4) multiplied by 9

17. The radius and height of a right circular cylinder are each doubled. Its volume is then multiplied by:
(1) 8   (2) 2   (3) 6   (4) 4

18. If the height of a right circular cylinder is divided by 4 while its radius is doubled, the new cylinder will have a volume that is:
(1) half the original volume   (2) twice the original volume
(3) the same as the original   (4) 4 times the original volume

chapter twenty-two

Quadratic Equations

1 THE STANDARD FORM OF A QUADRATIC EQUATION

A *polynomial equation* is an equation that involves polynomials.

For example, $x^2 - 3x - 10 = 0$ is a polynomial equation in one variable. We say that this equation is of degree two, or second degree, because the greatest exponent of the variable x is 2. The equation is in *standard form* because all terms of the equation are collected in one member and the other member is 0.

An equation of the second degree, such as $x^2 - 3x - 10 = 0$, is called a *quadratic equation*.

In general, the standard form of a quadratic equation in one variable is:

$$ax^2 + bx + c = 0$$

where a, b, and c are real numbers and $a \neq 0$.

MODEL PROBLEM

Transform the equation $x(x - 4) = 5$ into an equivalent quadratic equation that is in the standard form $ax^2 + bx + c = 0$.

Solution

$$x(x - 4) = 5$$
$$x^2 - 4x = 5$$
$$x^2 - 4x - 5 = 0 \quad Ans.$$

| EXERCISES |

In 1-9, transform the equation into an equivalent equation in the standard form $ax^2 + bx + c = 0$.

1. $x^2 + 9x = 10$

2. $2x^2 + 7x = 3x$

3. $x^2 = 3x - 8$

4. $4x + 3 = x^2$

5. $3x^2 = 27x$

6. $x(x - 3) = 10$

7. $x^2 = 5(x + 4)$

8. $\dfrac{x^2}{2} + 3 = \dfrac{x}{4}$

9. $x^2 = 6 - \dfrac{x}{2}$

2   USING FACTORING TO SOLVE A QUADRATIC EQUATION

There are many problems whose solution depends on knowing how to solve a quadratic equation. For example, to find two consecutive integers whose product is 20, we would have to solve the equation $x(x + 1) = 20$, that is, $x^2 + x = 20$, where x represents the smaller integer. Now we will learn how to solve such a quadratic equation.

Consider the following products:

$$5 \times 0 = 0 \qquad \tfrac{1}{2} \times 0 = 0 \qquad (-2) \times 0 = 0$$
$$0 \times 7 = 0 \qquad 0 \times \tfrac{1}{3} = 0 \qquad 0 \times (-3) = 0$$

These examples illustrate the following principle, which is called the *multiplication property of zero:*

■ **The product of 0 and any other real number is 0.**

Consider the equation $ab = 0$: If $a = 5$, then $b = 0$; if $a = -4$, then $b = 0$; if $b = 3$, then $a = 0$; if $b = -\tfrac{1}{2}$, then $a = 0$.

These examples illustrate the following principle:

■ **If the product of two real numbers is 0, then at least one of the numbers is 0.**

In general, if a and b are real numbers, then:

$$ab = 0 \text{ if and only if } a = 0 \text{ or } b = 0$$

This principle will now be applied to solving quadratic equations.

Let us first solve the equation $(x - 2)(x - 1) = 0$. Since $(x - 2)(x - 1) = 0$, then either $x - 2$ must be 0 or $x - 1$ must be 0. If $x - 2 = 0$, then $x = 2$. If $x - 1 = 0$, then $x = 1$.

Check

$$(x - 2)(x - 1) = 0$$
If $x = 2$, $(2 - 2)(2 - 1) \overset{?}{=} 0$
$$(0)(1) \overset{?}{=} 0$$
$$0 = 0 \quad \text{(True)}$$

$$(x - 2)(x - 1) = 0$$
If $x = 1$, $(1 - 2)(1 - 1) \overset{?}{=} 0$
$$(-1)(0) \overset{?}{=} 0$$
$$0 = 0 \quad \text{(True)}$$

Since both 2 and 1 satisfy the equation $(x - 2)(x - 1) = 0$, the solution set of this equation is $\{2, 1\}$. We may also say that the roots of the equation are 2 or 1.

Let us now solve the equation $x^2 - 3x + 2 = 0$. If we factor the left member of the equation, we get an equivalent equation $(x - 2)(x - 1) = 0$. The solution set of this equation, as we have just seen, is $\{2, 1\}$. Therefore, the solution set of the given equation $x^2 - 3x + 2 = 0$ is also $\{2, 1\}$.

The two roots of a quadratic equation are not always different numbers. Sometimes the roots are the same number, as in the case of $x^2 - 2x + 1 = 0$, which can be written $(x - 1)(x - 1) = 0$. Both roots are 1. Such a root is called a ***double root*** and is written only once in the solution set.

■ **PROCEDURE.** To solve a quadratic equation by using factoring:

1. If necessary, transform the equation into standard form. Do this by removing parentheses, clearing fractions and combining like terms in the left member, and making the right member zero.

2. Factor the left member of the equation.

3. Set each factor containing the variable equal to zero.

4. Solve each of the resulting equations.

5. Check by substituting each value of the variable in the original equation.

| MODEL PROBLEMS |

1. Solve and check: $x^2 - 7x = -10$

<table>
<tr><td align="center">How to Proceed</td><td align="center">Solution</td></tr>
</table>

$$x^2 - 7x = -10$$

(1) Transform into standard form.　　　　$x^2 - 7x + 10 = 0$

(2) Factor the left member.　　　　$(x - 2)(x - 5) = 0$

(3) Let each factor = 0.　　　　$x - 2 = 0 \mid x - 5 = 0$

(4) Solve each equation.　　　　$x = 2 \mid x = 5$

(5) Check both values in the original equation.

<table>
<tr><td align="center">Check for x = 2</td><td align="center">Check for x = 5</td></tr>
</table>

$$x^2 - 7x = -10$$
$$(2)^2 - 7(2) \overset{?}{=} -10$$
$$4 - 14 \overset{?}{=} -10$$
$$-10 = -10 \quad \text{(True)}$$

$$x^2 - 7x = -10$$
$$(5)^2 - 7(5) \overset{?}{=} -10$$
$$25 - 35 \overset{?}{=} -10$$
$$-10 = -10 \quad \text{(True)}$$

Answer: $x = 2$ or $x = 5$; solution set is $\{2, 5\}$.

2. Solve and check: $x^2 = 9$

<table>
<tr><td align="center">How to Proceed</td><td align="center">Solution</td></tr>
</table>

$$x^2 = 9$$

(1) Transform into standard form.　　　　$x^2 - 9 = 0$

(2) Factor the left member.　　　　$(x - 3)(x + 3) = 0$

(3) Let each factor = 0.　　　　$x - 3 = 0 \mid x + 3 = 0$

(4) Solve each equation.　　　　$x = 3 \mid x = -3$

(5) Check both values in the original equation.

<table>
<tr><td align="center">Check</td></tr>
</table>

$$x^2 = 9$$
$$\text{If } x = 3, (3)^2 \overset{?}{=} 9$$
$$9 = 9 \quad \text{(True)}$$

$$x^2 = 9$$
$$\text{If } x = -3, (-3)^2 \overset{?}{=} 9$$
$$9 = 9 \quad \text{(True)}$$

Answer: $x = 3$ or $x = -3$; solution set is $\{3, -3\}$.

3. List the members of the set $\{x \mid 2x^2 = 3x\}$.

How to Proceed	*Solution*
	$2x^2 = 3x$
(1) Transform into standard form.	$2x^2 - 3x = 0$
(2) Factor the left member.	$x(2x - 3) = 0$
(3) Let each factor = 0.	$x = 0 \mid 2x - 3 = 0$
(4) Solve each equation.	$2x = 3$
	$x = \frac{3}{2}$

The check is left to the student.

Answer: $\{0, \frac{3}{2}\}$

Caution: Never transform an equation by dividing both members of the equation by an expression involving the variable. If we had divided both members of the equation $2x^2 = 3x$ by x, we would have obtained the equation $2x = 3$ whose solution is $x = \frac{3}{2}$. We would have lost the solution $x = 0$.

4. Solve and check: $x(x + 2) = 24$

How to Proceed	*Solution*
	$x(x + 2) = 24$
(1) Use the distributive property.	$x^2 + 2x = 24$
(2) Transform into standard form.	$x^2 + 2x - 24 = 0$
(3) Factor the left member.	$(x - 4)(x + 6) = 0$
(4) Let each factor = 0.	$x - 4 = 0 \mid x + 6 = 0$
(5) Solve each equation.	$x = 4 \mid x = -6$

The check is left to the student.

Answer: $x = 4$ or $x = -6$; solution set is $\{4, -6\}$.

KEEP IN MIND

To solve a quadratic equation by using factoring, one member of the equation must be zero.

EXERCISES

In 1–48, solve and check the equation.

1. $x^2 - 3x + 2 = 0$ 2. $z^2 - 5z + 4 = 0$ 3. $x^2 - 8x + 16 = 0$
4. $r^2 - 12r + 35 = 0$ 5. $c^2 + 6c + 5 = 0$ 6. $m^2 + 10m + 9 = 0$
7. $x^2 + 2x + 1 = 0$ 8. $y^2 + 11y + 24 = 0$ 9. $x^2 - 4x - 5 = 0$
10. $x^2 - 5x - 6 = 0$ 11. $x^2 + x - 6 = 0$ 12. $x^2 + 2x - 15 = 0$
13. $r^2 - r - 72 = 0$ 14. $x^2 - x - 12 = 0$ 15. $x^2 - 49 = 0$
16. $z^2 - 4 = 0$ 17. $m^2 - 64 = 0$ 18. $3x^2 - 12 = 0$
19. $d^2 - 2d = 0$ 20. $s^2 - s = 0$ 21. $x^2 + 3x = 0$
22. $z^2 + 8z = 0$ 23. $2x^2 - 5x + 2 = 0$ 24. $3x^2 - 10x + 3 = 0$
25. $3x^2 - 8x + 4 = 0$ 26. $5x^2 + 11x + 2 = 0$ 27. $x^2 - x = 6$
28. $y^2 - 3y = 28$ 29. $c^2 - 8c = -15$ 30. $2m^2 + 7m = -6$
31. $r^2 = 4$ 32. $3x^2 = 12$ 33. $y^2 = 6y$
34. $s^2 = -4s$ 35. $y^2 = 8y + 20$ 36. $2x^2 - x = 15$
37. $x^2 = 9x - 20$ 38. $30 + x = x^2$ 39. $x^2 + 3x - 4 = 50$
40. $2x^2 + 7 = 5 - 5x$ 41. $\frac{1}{3}x^2 + \frac{4}{3}x + 1 = 0$ 42. $\frac{1}{2}x^2 - \frac{7}{6}x = 1$
43. $x(x - 2) = 35$ 44. $y(y - 3) = 4$ 45. $x(x + 3) = 40$
46. $\dfrac{x + 2}{2} = \dfrac{12}{x}$ 47. $\dfrac{y + 3}{3} = \dfrac{6}{y}$ 48. $\dfrac{x}{3} = \dfrac{12}{x}$

3 SOLVING INCOMPLETE QUADRATIC EQUATIONS

A quadratic equation in which the first-degree term is missing is called an *incomplete quadratic equation*, or a *pure quadratic equation*. For example, $x^2 - 36 = 0$ (in general, $ax^2 + c = 0$ when $a \neq 0$) is an incomplete quadratic equation.

One method of solving $x^2 - 36 = 0$ is to factor the left member. We obtain $(x + 6)(x - 6) = 0$, from which we find that the solution set is $\{-6, 6\}$.

Another method which we may use to solve $x^2 - 36 = 0$ makes use of the following principle:

■ **Every positive real number has two real square roots, one of which is the opposite of the other.**

Solution

$$x^2 - 36 = 0$$
$$x^2 = 36$$
$$x = \sqrt{36} \text{ or } x = -\sqrt{36}$$
$$x = 6 \text{ or } x = -6$$

Check

$x^2 - 36 = 0$	$x^2 - 36 = 0$
If $x = 6$, $(6)^2 - 36 \overset{?}{=} 0$	If $x = -6$, $(-6)^2 - 36 \overset{?}{=} 0$
$36 - 36 \overset{?}{=} 0$	$36 - 36 \overset{?}{=} 0$
$0 = 0$ (True)	$0 = 0$ (True)

Answer: $x = 6$ or $x = -6$, which may be written $x = \pm 6$; solution set is $\{6, -6\}$.

■ **PROCEDURE.** To solve an incomplete quadratic equation:

1. Transform the equation into the form $x^2 = n$, where n is a non-negative real number.

2. Let $x = \sqrt{n}$ and let $x = -\sqrt{n}$.

3. Check the resulting values for x in the original equation.

MODEL PROBLEMS

1. Find the solution set:
   $7y^2 = 3y^2 + 36$

   Solution

   $$7y^2 = 3y^2 + 36$$
   $$7y^2 - 3y^2 = 36$$
   $$4y^2 = 36$$
   $$y^2 = 9$$
   $$y = \sqrt{9} = 3 \text{ or}$$
   $$y = -\sqrt{9} = -3$$

   Answer: Solution set is $\{3, -3\}$.

   (Roots are rational numbers.)

2. Solve: $4x^2 - 14 = 2x^2$

   Solution

   $$4x^2 - 14 = 2x^2$$
   $$4x^2 - 2x^2 - 14 = 0$$
   $$2x^2 - 14 = 0$$
   $$2x^2 = 14$$
   $$x^2 = 7$$
   $$x = \sqrt{7} \text{ or}$$
   $$x = -\sqrt{7}$$

   Answer: $x = \pm\sqrt{7}$

   (Roots are irrational numbers.)

The checks in model problems 1 and 2 are left to the student.

EXERCISES

In 1–15, solve and check the equation.

1. $x^2 = 4$
2. $a^2 - 25 = 0$
3. $\frac{1}{2}x^2 = 50$
4. $5y^2 = 45$
5. $3k^2 = 147$
6. $2x^2 - 8 = 0$
7. $r^2 - 11 = 70$
8. $4x^2 + 5 = 21$
9. $2x^2 - 11 = 39$
10. $2x^2 + 3x^2 = 45$
11. $6x^2 - 4x^2 = 98$
12. $4y^2 - 13 = y^2 + 14$
13. $\frac{y^2}{3} = 12$
14. $\frac{x}{9} = \frac{4}{x}$
15. $\frac{4x}{25} = \frac{4}{x}$

In 16–24, solve for x in simplest radical form.

16. $x^2 = 10$
17. $x^2 = 27$
18. $3x^2 = 6$
19. $2x^2 - 16 = 0$
20. $x^2 + 25 = 100$
21. $x^2 - 4 = 4$
22. $8x^2 - 6x^2 = 54$
23. $3x^2 - 28 = 2x^2 + 33$
24. $\frac{2x}{9} = \frac{6}{x}$

In 25–27, find the positive value of x, correct to the *nearest tenth*. Use the table on page 670.

25. $x^2 = 24$
26. $4x^2 - 160 = 0$
27. $7x^2 = x^2 + 198$

In 28–33, solve for x in terms of the other variable(s).

28. $x^2 = b^2$
29. $x^2 = 25a^2$
30. $9x^2 = r^2$
31. $4x^2 - a^2 = 0$
32. $x^2 + a^2 = c^2$
33. $x^2 + b^2 = c^2$

In 34–39, solve for the indicated variable in terms of the other variable(s).

34. Solve for S: $S^2 = A$
35. Solve for r: $A = \pi r^2$
36. Solve for r: $S = 4\pi r^2$
37. Solve for r: $V = \pi r^2 h$
38. Solve for t: $s = \frac{1}{2}gt^2$
39. Solve for v: $F = \dfrac{mv^2}{gr}$

4 USING THE THEOREM OF PYTHAGORAS

We are now ready to study, understand, and apply a most useful relationship that exists among the sides of a right triangle.

The figure at the right represents a *right triangle*. Recall that such a triangle contains one and only one right angle. In right triangle ABC, side $\overline{AB}$, which is opposite the right angle, is called the *hypotenuse*. The hypotenuse is the longest side of the triangle. The other two sides of the triangle, $\overline{BC}$ and $\overline{AC}$, form the right angle. They are called the *legs* of the right triangle.

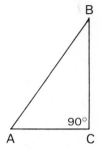

More than 2000 years ago the Greek mathematician Pythagoras demonstrated the following property of the right triangle, which is called the *Pythagorean Theorem:*

■ **In a right triangle the square of the length of the hypotenuse is equal to the sum of the squares of the lengths of the other two sides.**

If we represent the length of the hypotenuse of right triangle ABC by c and the lengths of the other two sides by a and b, the Theorem of Pythagoras may be written as the following formula:

$$c^2 = a^2 + b^2$$

We can use our knowledge of geometry to help us understand the Pythagorean Theorem.

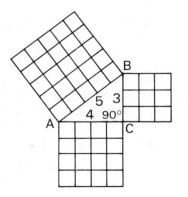

Triangle ABC represents a right triangle in which the length of side $\overline{AC}$ = 4 cm, the length of side $\overline{BC}$ = 3 cm, and the length of the hypotenuse $\overline{AB}$ = 5 cm.

On side $\overline{BC}$ we make a square, each of whose sides measures 3 cm. On side $\overline{AC}$ we make a square, each of whose sides measures 4 cm. On hypotenuse $\overline{AB}$ we make a square, each of whose sides measures 5 cm.

The area of the square on side $\overline{BC}$ is $3 \times 3 = 3^2 = 9$ cm^2.

The area of the square on side $\overline{AC}$ is $4 \times 4 = 4^2 = 16$ cm^2.

The area of the square on hypotenuse $\overline{AB}$ is $5 \times 5 = 5^2 = 25$ cm^2.

Since 25 cm$^2 = 9$ cm$^2 + 16$ cm^2, we have $5^2 = 3^2 + 4^2$.

In general, we see once again that when the length of the hypotenuse of a right triangle is represented by c and the lengths of the other two sides by a and b, we will have:

$$c^2 = a^2 + b^2$$

Three logical statements can be made for any right triangle where c represents the length of the hypotenuse, and a and b represent the lengths of the other two sides. All of these statements are true.

1. The *conditional* form of the Pythagorean Theorem:
   If a triangle is a right triangle, then the square of the length of the hypotenuse is equal to the sum of the squares of the lengths of the other two sides. (If a triangle is a right triangle, then $c^2 = a^2 + b^2$.)

2. The *converse* of the Pythagorean Theorem:
   If the square of the length of the largest side of a triangle is equal to the sum of the squares of the lengths of the other two sides, then the triangle is a right triangle. (If $c^2 = a^2 + b^2$ in a triangle, then the triangle is a right triangle.)

3. The *biconditional* form:
   A triangle is a right triangle if and only if $c^2 = a^2 + b^2$.

| MODEL PROBLEMS |

1. A ladder is placed 5 ft. from the foot of a wall. The top of the ladder reaches a point 12 ft. above the ground. Find the length of the ladder.

   Solution: Let the length of the hypotenuse $= c$, the length of side $a = 5$, the length of side $b = 12$.

$c^2 = a^2 + b^2$ [Theorem of Pythagoras]

$c^2 = 5^2 + 12^2$

$c^2 = 25 + 144$

$c^2 = 169$

$c = \sqrt{169} = 13$ or

$c = -\sqrt{169} = -13$ [Reject the negative value because the length of the hypotenuse cannot be a negative number.]

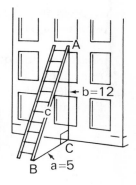

Answer: 13 feet

2. The hypotenuse of a right triangle is 20 centimeters long and one leg is 16 centimeters long. **a.** Find the length of the other leg. **b.** Find the area of the triangle.

Solution

a. Let the length of the unknown leg = a, the length of the hypotenuse c = 20, the length of side b = 16.

$c^2 = a^2 + b^2$ [Theorem of Pythagoras]

$20^2 = a^2 + 16^2$

$400 = a^2 + 256$

$144 = a^2$

$12 = a$ or

$-12 = a$ [Reject the negative number.]

Answer: 12 centimeters

b. Area of $\triangle ABC = \frac{1}{2}bh$ [b = base = 16; h = height = 12]

$= \frac{1}{2}(16)(12)$

$= 96$

Answer: Area of $\triangle ABC$ = 96 cm^2.

3. Express in simplest radical form the length of a side of a square whose diagonal is 10.

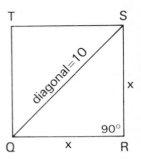

Solution: In square $QRST$, angle QRS is a right angle. Therefore, triangle QRS is a right triangle. Let x = the length of each side of the square.

$a^2 + b^2 = c^2$ $[a = x, b = x, c = 10]$

$x^2 + x^2 = 10^2$

$2x^2 = 100$

$x^2 = 50$

$x = \pm\sqrt{50}$

$x = \pm\sqrt{25 \cdot 2}$ [Reject the negative number.]

$x = 5\sqrt{2}$

Answer: The side of the square is $5\sqrt{2}$.

4. Is a triangle whose sides measure 10 centimeters, 7 centimeters, and 4 centimeters a right triangle?

Solution: The square of 10, the length of the longest side, = 10^2 = 100. The sum of the squares of the lengths of the other two sides = $7^2 + 4^2 = 49 + 16 = 65$.

Answer: Since 100 does not equal 65, the triangle is not a right triangle.

| EXERCISES |

In 1–9, let c represent the length of the hypotenuse in a right triangle, and let a and b represent the lengths of the other two sides. Find the length of the side of the right triangle whose measure is not given.

1. $a = 3, b = 4$ 2. $a = 8, b = 15$ 3. $c = 10, a = 6$

4. $c = 13, a = 12$ 5. $c = 17, b = 15$ 6. $c = 25, b = 20$

7. $a = \sqrt{2}, b = \sqrt{2}$ 8. $a = 4, b = 4\sqrt{3}$ 9. $a = 5\sqrt{3}, c = 10$

In 10–15: a. Express in simplest radical form the length of the third side of the right triangle the length of whose hypotenuse is represented by c and the lengths of whose other sides are represented by a and b.

b. Approximate the length of this third side correct to the *nearest tenth*.

10. $a = 2, b = 3$ **11.** $a = 3, b = 3$ **12.** $a = 4, c = 8$

13. $a = 7, b = 1$ **14.** $b = \sqrt{3}, c = \sqrt{15}$ **15.** $a = 4\sqrt{2}, c = 8$

In 16-19, find x and express irrational results in simplest radical form.

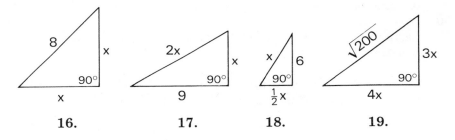

16.   **17.**   **18.**   **19.**

20. A ladder 39 feet long leans against a building and reaches the ledge of a window. If the foot of the ladder is 15 feet from the foot of the building, how high is the window ledge above the ground?

21. What must be the length of a ladder that Mr. Rizzo can use if he wishes to place the bottom of the ladder 5 feet from a wall and he wishes to reach a window that is 15 feet above the ground? Give the answer, correct to the *nearest tenth* of a foot.

22. Miss Murray traveled 24 kilometers north and then 10 kilometers east. How far was she from her starting point?

23. One day Ronnie walked from his home at A to his school at C by walking along $\overline{AB}$ and $\overline{BC}$, the sides of a rectangular open field that was muddy. When he returned home, the field was dry and Ronnie decided to take a short cut by walking diagonally across the field along $\overline{CA}$. How much shorter was the trip home than the trip to school?

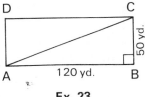

Ex. 23

In 24–27, find the length of a diagonal of a rectangle whose sides are the given measurements.

24. 8 inches and 15 inches
25. 15 centimeters and 20 centimeters
26. 10 feet and 24 feet
27. 30 meters and 40 meters

28. The diagonal of a rectangle measures 13 centimeters. One side is 12 centimeters long. **a.** Find the length of the other side. **b.** Find the area of the rectangle.

29. Find the area of a rectangle in which the diagonal measures 26 and one side measures 10.

30. Approximate, to the *nearest inch*, the measure of the base of a rectangle whose diagonal measures 25 inches and whose altitude measures 18 inches.

In 31–35, approximate, to the *nearest tenth of a meter*, the length of a diagonal of a square whose side has the given measurement.

31. 2 meters
32. 4 meters
33. 5 meters
34. 6 meters
35. 7 meters

36. A baseball diamond has the shape of a square 90 feet on each side. Approximate, to the *nearest tenth of a foot*, the distance from home plate to second base.

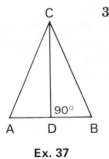

Ex. 37

37. In the figure, ABC is an isosceles triangle in which sides $\overline{AC}$ and $\overline{CB}$ are of equal length, $AC = CB$. $\overline{CD}$, which is drawn so that angle CDB is a right angle, is called the altitude drawn to the base of the triangle. When altitude $\overline{CD}$ is drawn, it divides the base $\overline{AB}$ into two segments of equal measure, $AD = DB$. Each of the sides $\overline{AC}$ and $\overline{CB}$ measures 26 centimeters and the base of the triangle measures 20 centimeters. **a.** Find the length of the altitude drawn to the base. **b.** Find the area of triangle ABC.

38. In an isosceles triangle each of the equal sides measures 25 in. and the altitude drawn to the base measures 15 in.
     a. Find the length of the base.   **b.** Find the area of the triangle.

In 39–43, find the length of the altitude of equilateral triangle ABC when each of its sides has the given measure. (Express the answer in simplest radical form.)

39. 4 cm
40. 6 cm
41. 8 cm
42. 10 cm
43. 5 cm

44. **a.** On coordinate graph paper draw the triangle whose vertices are $A(0, 5)$, $B(4, 5)$, $C(4, 9)$.
    b. Find the length of each side of $\triangle ABC$.
    c. Find the area of $\triangle ABC$.
45. The length of a side of a square is represented by s and the length of a diagonal by d. Show that $d = s\sqrt{2}$.

In 46–49, tell whether or not the measurements can be the lengths of the sides of a right triangle.

46. 6 yards, 10 yards, 8 yards
47. 7 m, 4 m, 5 m
48. 12 cm, 16 cm, 20 cm
49. 10 feet, 15 feet, 20 feet

5 SOLVING VERBAL PROBLEMS BY USING QUADRATIC EQUATIONS

The solutions of some verbal problems involve the solution of a quadratic equation. The most convenient method of solving the quadratic equation should be used.

Number Problems

1. The square of a number decreased by 4 times the number equals 21. Find the number.

Solution: Let x = the number.

The square of the number decreased by 4 times the number equals 21.

$$x^2 - 4x = 21$$
$$x^2 - 4x - 21 = 0$$
$$(x - 7)(x + 3) = 0$$
$$x - 7 = 0 \quad | \quad x + 3 = 0$$
$$x = 7 \quad | \quad x = -3$$

Check for the number 7:
$(7)^2 - 4(7) \stackrel{?}{=} 21$
$49 - 28 \stackrel{?}{=} 21$
$21 = 21$ (True)

Check for the number -3:
$(-3)^2 - 4(-3) \stackrel{?}{=} 21$
$9 + 12 \stackrel{?}{=} 21$
$21 = 21$ (True)

Answer: The number is 7 or -3.

2. The product of two positive consecutive even integers is 80. Find the integers.

Solution:

Let x = the first positive even integer.
Then $x + 2$ = the next consecutive positive even integer.

The product of two positive consecutive even integers is 80.

$$x(x + 2) = 80$$
$$x^2 + 2x = 80$$
$$x^2 + 2x - 80 = 0$$
$$(x - 8)(x + 10) = 0$$

$x - 8 = 0$	$x + 10 = 0$
$x = 8$	$x = -10$ [Reject because the integer
$x + 2 = 10$	must be positive.]

Check: The product of the two positive consecutive even integers 8 and 10 is $(8)(10)$, or 80.

Answer: The integers are 8 and 10.

| EXERCISES |

1. The square of a number increased by 3 times the number is 28. Find the number.
2. When the square of a certain number is diminished by 9 times the number, the result is 36. Find the number.
3. A certain number added to its square is 30. Find the number.
4. The square of a number exceeds the number by 72. Find the number.
5. Find a positive number that is 20 less than its square.
6. If the square of a positive number is added to 5 times the number, the result is 36. Find the number.
7. The square of a number decreased by 15 is equal to twice the number. Find the number.
8. Find two positive numbers whose ratio is 2:3 and whose product is 600.

9. The larger of two positive numbers is 5 more than the smaller. The product of the numbers is 66. Find the numbers.

10. One number is 5 more than another. Their product is 14. Find the numbers.

11. One number is 6 less than another. The sum of the squares of these numbers is 20. Find the numbers.

12. One number is 7 more than another. The sum of the squares of these numbers is 29. Find the numbers.

13. The product of two consecutive integers is 56. Find the integers.

14. The product of two consecutive odd integers is 99. Find the integers.

15. Find two consecutive positive integers such that the square of the smaller increased by 4 times the larger is 64.

16. Find two consecutive positive integers such that the square of the first decreased by 17 equals 4 times the second.

17. Find three consecutive positive integers such that the product of the second integer and the third integer is 20.

18. Find three consecutive odd integers such that the square of the first increased by the product of the other two is 224.

19. Find two consecutive integers such that the sum of their squares is 61.

20. Find the smallest of three consecutive positive integers such that the product of the two smaller integers is 38 more than twice the largest.

21. Nine times a certain number is 5 less than twice the square of the number. Find the number.

22. The sum of two numbers is 10. The sum of their squares is 52. Find the numbers.

23. The sum of a number and its reciprocal is $\frac{5}{2}$. Find the number.

24. If a positive number is decreased by its reciprocal, the result is $\frac{8}{3}$. Find the number.

25. The sum of a number and the square of its additive inverse is 42. Find the number.

Geometric Problems

The base of a parallelogram measures 7 centimeters more than its altitude (height). If the area of the parallelogram is 30 square centimeters, find the measure of its base and the measure of its altitude (height).

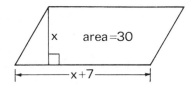

Solution

Let x = the number of centimeters in the altitude (height) of the parallelogram.

Then $x + 7$ = the number of centimeters in the base of the parallelogram.

The area of the parallelogram is 30.

$$x(x + 7) = 30 \quad \text{[Area = base} \cdot \text{altitude]}$$
$$x^2 + 7x = 30$$
$$x^2 + 7x - 30 = 0$$
$$(x - 3)(x + 10) = 0$$

$$x - 3 = 0 \quad \bigg| \quad x + 10 = 0$$
$$x = 3 \quad \bigg| \qquad x = -10 \quad \text{[Reject because the altitude cannot be a}$$
$$x + 7 = 10 \quad \bigg| \qquad\qquad\qquad \text{negative number.]}$$

Check: When the base of a parallelogram measures 10 and its altitude measures 3, the area is $10 \cdot 3$, or 30. Also, the measure of the base, 10, is 7 more than the measure of the altitude, 3.

Answer: The altitude (height) measures 3 centimeters; the base measures 10 centimeters.

| EXERCISES |

1. The length of a rectangle is 2 times its width. The area of the rectangle is 72 square centimeters. Find the dimensions of the rectangle.
2. The ratio of the measures of the base and altitude of a parallelogram is $3:4$. The area of the parallelogram is 1200 square centimeters. Find the measure of the base and of the altitude (height) of the parallelogram.
3. The length of a rectangular garden is 4 meters more than its width. The area of the garden is 60 square meters. Find the dimensions of the garden.
4. The altitude of a parallelogram measures 11 cm less than its base. The area of the parallelogram is 80 cm². Find the measure of its base and the measure of its altitude.
5. The perimeter of a rectangle is 20 inches and its area is 16 square inches. Find the dimensions of the rectangle.
6. If the measure of one side of a square is increased by 2 centimeters and the measure of an adjacent side is decreased by 2 centimeters, the area of the resulting rectangle is 32 square centimeters. Find the measure of one side of the square.

7. The length of a rectangle is 3 times its width. If the width is diminished by 1 meter and the length is increased by 3 meters, the area of the rectangle that is formed is 72 square meters. Find the dimensions of the original rectangle.

8. A rectangle is 6 feet long and 4 feet wide. If each dimension is increased by the same number of feet, a new rectangle is formed whose area is 39 square feet more than the area of the original rectangle. By how many feet was each dimension increased?

9. Joan's rectangular garden is 6 meters long and 4 meters wide. She wishes to double the area of her garden by increasing its length and width by the same amount. Find the number of meters by which each dimension must be increased.

10. The length of the base of a parallelogram is twice the length of its altitude. The area of the parallelogram is 50 square centimeters. Find the length of its base and altitude.

11. The altitude of a triangle measures 5 centimeters less than its base. The area of the triangle is 42 square centimeters. Find the lengths of its base and altitude.

12. A baseball diamond has the shape of a square 90 feet on each side. The pitcher's mound is 60.5 feet from home plate on the segment joining home plate and second base. Find the distance from the pitcher's mound to second base to the nearest tenth of a foot.

13. One leg of a right triangle is 1 cm longer than the other leg. The hypotenuse measures 5 cm. Find the measure of each leg of the triangle.

14. The measure of one leg of a right triangle exceeds the measure of the other leg by 7 meters. The hypotenuse of the triangle is 13 meters long. Find the measurements of the legs of the triangle.

15. The hypotenuse of a right triangle is 2 centimeters longer than one leg and 4 centimeters longer than the other leg. Find the length of each side of the triangle.

16. The length of the hypotenuse of a right triangle is 25 centimeters. One of the legs is 5 centimeters longer than the other. a. Find the length of each leg. b. Find the area of the triangle.

17. The ratio of the lengths of the two legs of a right triangle is 3:4. a. Find the length of each leg when the length of the hypotenuse is the given measure. b. Find the area of the triangle.
    a. 10 cm   b. 20 cm   c. 25 cm   d. 100 cm

18. The perimeter of a right triangle is 30 centimeters. If the hypotenuse measures 13 centimeters, (a) find the length of each leg and (b) find the area of the triangle.

19. Denise and Dawn start from the same point and travel at the rates of 30 mph and 40 mph along straight roads that are at right angles to each other. In how many hours will they be 100 miles apart?

6 GRAPHING A QUADRATIC EQUATION IN TWO VARIABLES OF THE FORM $y = ax^2 + bx + c$

We have learned that the graph of every first-degree equation in two variables is a straight line. For example, the graph of $x + y = 6$ is a straight line. Now we will learn how to graph a quadratic equation of the form $y = ax^2 + bx + c$.

| MODEL PROBLEMS |

1. Graph the quadratic equation $y = 2x^2$ using integral values for x from $x = -3$ to $x = 3$ inclusive, that is, $-3 \leq x \leq 3$.

    Solution

    (1) Develop the following table of values:

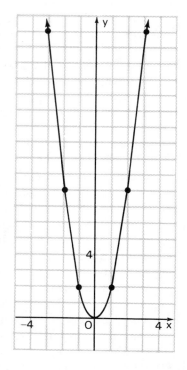

x	$2x^2$	$= y$
-3	$2(-3)^2$	18
-2	$2(-2)^2$	8
-1	$2(-1)^2$	2
0	$2(0)^2$	0
1	$2(1)^2$	2
2	$2(2)^2$	8
3	$2(3)^2$	18

    (2) Plot the point associated with each ordered number pair (x, y): $(-3, 18)$, $(-2, 8)$, $(-1, 2)$, and so on.

    (3) Draw a smooth curve through the points. Notice that the graph of $y = 2x^2$ is a curve; it is not a straight line. This curve is called a *parabola*.

The graph of every quadratic equation of the form $y = ax^2 + bx + c$ (where a, b, and c are real numbers and $a \neq 0$) is a parabola.

2. Graph the quadratic equation $y = x^2 - 2x - 8$ using integral values of x from $x = -3$ to $x = 5$ inclusive, that is, $-3 \leq x \leq 5$.

Solution

(1) Develop the following table of values:

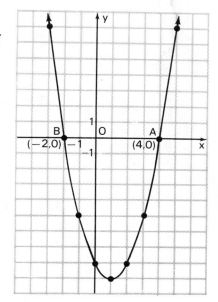

x	$x^2 - 2x - 8 = y$	
-3	$9 + 6 - 8$	7
-2	$4 + 4 - 8$	0
-1	$1 + 2 - 8$	-5
0	$0 - 0 - 8$	-8
1	$1 - 2 - 8$	-9
2	$4 - 4 - 8$	-8
3	$9 - 6 - 8$	-5
4	$16 - 8 - 8$	0
5	$25 - 10 - 8$	7

(2) Plot the point associated with each ordered number pair (x, y): $(5, 7)$, $(4, 0)$, etc. Draw a smooth curve through the points. The curve is a parabola.

EXERCISES

In 1–20, graph the quadratic equation. Use the integral values for x indicated in parentheses to prepare the necessary table of values.

1. $y = x^2$ $(-3 \leq x \leq 3)$ 2. $y = 3x^2$ $(-2 \leq x \leq 2)$
3. $4x^2 = y$ $(-2 \leq x \leq 2)$ 4. $5x^2 = y$ $(-2 \leq x \leq 2)$
5. $y = -x^2$ $(-3 \leq x \leq 3)$ 6. $y = -2x^2$ $(-2 \leq x \leq 2)$
7. $y = \frac{1}{2}x^2$ $(-4 \leq x \leq 4)$ 8. $-\frac{1}{2}x^2 = y$ $(-2 \leq x \leq 2)$
9. $y = x^2 + 1$ $(-3 \leq x \leq 3)$ 10. $x^2 - 1 = y$ $(-3 \leq x \leq 3)$
11. $y = x^2 - 4$ $(-3 \leq x \leq 3)$ 12. $-x^2 + 4 = y$ $(-3 \leq x \leq 3)$
13. $y = x^2 - 2x$ $(-1 \leq x \leq 3)$ 14. $x^2 + 2x = y$ $(-3 \leq x \leq 1)$
15. $y = -x^2 + 2x$ $(-1 \leq x \leq 3)$ 16. $y = x^2 - 6x + 8$ $(0 \leq x \leq 6)$
17. $y = x^2 - 4x + 3$ $(-1 \leq x \leq 5)$ 18. $x^2 - 2x - 3 = y$ $(-2 \leq x \leq 4)$
19. $x^2 - 2x + 1 = y$ $(-2 \leq x \leq 4)$ 20. $y = x^2 - 3x + 2$ $(-1 \leq x \leq 4)$

Squares and Square Roots

No.	Square	Square Root	No.	Square	Square Root	No.	Square	Square Root
1	1	1.000	51	2,601	7.141	101	10,201	10.050
2	4	1.414	52	2,704	7.211	102	10,404	10.100
3	9	1.732	53	2,809	7.280	103	10,609	10.149
4	16	2.000	54	2,916	7.348	104	10,816	10.198
5	25	2.236	55	3,025	7.416	105	11,025	10.247
6	36	2.449	56	3,136	7.483	106	11,236	10.296
7	49	2.646	57	3,249	7.550	107	11,449	10.344
8	64	2.828	58	3,364	7.616	108	11,664	10.392
9	81	3.000	59	3,481	7.681	109	11,881	10.440
10	100	3.162	60	3,600	7.746	110	12,100	10.488
11	121	3.317	61	3,721	7.810	111	12,321	10.536
12	144	3.464	62	3,844	7.874	112	12,544	10.583
13	169	3.606	63	3,969	7.937	113	12,769	10.630
14	196	3.742	64	4,096	8.000	114	12,996	10.677
15	225	3.873	65	4,225	8.062	115	13,225	10.724
16	256	4.000	66	4,356	8.124	116	13,456	10.770
17	289	4.123	67	4,489	8.185	117	13,689	10.817
18	324	4.243	68	4,624	8.246	118	13,924	10.863
19	361	4.359	69	4,761	8.307	119	14,161	10.909
20	400	4.472	70	4,900	8.367	120	14,400	10.954
21	441	4.583	71	5,041	8.426	121	14,641	11.000
22	484	4.690	72	5,184	8.485	122	14,884	11.045
23	529	4.796	73	5,329	8.544	123	15,129	11.091
24	576	4.899	74	5,476	8.602	124	15,376	11.136
25	625	5.000	75	5,625	8.660	125	15,625	11.180
26	676	5.099	76	5,776	8.718	126	15,876	11.225
27	729	5.196	77	5,929	8.775	127	16,129	11.269
28	784	5.292	78	6,084	8.832	128	16,384	11.314
29	841	5.385	79	6,241	8.888	129	16,641	11.358
30	900	5.477	80	6,400	8.944	130	16,900	11.402
31	961	5.568	81	6,561	9.000	131	17,161	11.446
32	1,024	5.657	82	6,724	9.055	132	17,424	11.489
33	1,089	5.745	83	6,889	9.110	133	17,689	11.533
34	1,156	5.831	84	7,056	9.165	134	17,956	11.576
35	1,225	5.916	85	7,225	9.220	135	18,225	11.619
36	1,296	6.000	86	7,396	9.274	136	18,496	11.662
37	1,369	6.083	87	7,569	9.327	137	18,769	11.705
38	1,444	6.164	88	7,744	9.381	138	19,044	11.747
39	1,521	6.245	89	7,921	9.434	139	19,321	11.790
40	1,600	6.325	90	8,100	9.487	140	19,600	11.832
41	1,681	6.403	91	8,281	9.539	141	19,881	11.874
42	1,764	6.481	92	8,464	9.592	142	20,164	11.916
43	1,849	6.557	93	8,649	9.644	143	20,449	11.958
44	1,936	6.633	94	8,836	9.695	144	20,736	12.000
45	2,025	6.708	95	9,025	9.747	145	21,025	12.042
46	2,116	6.782	96	9,216	9.798	146	21,316	12.083
47	2,209	6.856	97	9,409	9.849	147	21,609	12.124
48	2,304	6.928	98	9,604	9.899	148	21,904	12.166
49	2,401	7.000	99	9,801	9.950	149	22,201	12.207
50	2,500	7.071	100	10,000	10.000	150	22,500	12.247

index

O

P